Exposing Feminism

The Thirty Years' War Against Men

Swayne O'Pie

The Men's Press

Exposing Feminism: The Thirty Years' War Against Men

The Men's Press

First published in Britain in 2011 by
The Men's Press PO Box 2220 Bath

Bibliography: Men's Studies – Equality –
Gender Studies – Women's Studies –
Feminist Studies – Sociology – Politics –
Philosophy – Sexual Harassment – Employment

A CIP record for this book is available from the British Library

Typesetting: Matt Swann 21stBookDesign.blogspot.com

Cover Design: Matt McArdle

Cover photograph: Peter Canning

Printed and bound worldwide by Lightning Source Inc.

ISBN: 978 – 0 – 9568219 – 1 – 1

Foreword

This book is of international relevance. It was first published in Britain only, in October 2011, with the title Why Britain Hates Men: Exposing Feminism. A British readership was anticipated, but to the author's surprise (and delight) orders for the book also arrived from readers in other developed countries, most notably the United States, Canada and Australia. Many of these buyers reported parallels in their own countries, especially with respect to the strategies used by feminists to justify their continued existence and to perpetuate their cultural and political power, now that equal rights and equal opportunities for women have been achieved. Swayne O'Pie refers to the feminist strategies of deliberately creating 'women's issues', 'inequalities' and 'discriminations' as the 'Feminist Fraud', leading to 'Forever Feminism' – a phenomenon found in many developed countries. He concludes that for feminists success will never be enough, they can *never* allow themselves to be satisfied.

O'Pie, often referred to in Britain as 'The Feminists' Nemesis', is a well-known and highly regarded speaker on feminism and sexual politics. Exposing Feminism explores in forensic detail and with examples the deceit that feminism has become. There is no war between men and women... but there has been a thirty years' war waged by feminists against men; and the majority of men haven't realised that they are *in* a war.

Exposing Feminism identifies feminism as the root cause of all the discriminations and disadvantages that men experience in western societies. Its analysis of the feminist agenda is applicable to the condition of men and women in all developed countries. The book is confrontational and O'Pie makes no apology for that. He's a brave man, addressing issues which other writers have feared to confront – the deliberate exaggeration of rape statistics, the widespread influence of lesbian feminism, the deliberate cheating and lying of feminist 'research', the feminists' psychological make-up and their *need* for anger. His honesty and integrity have made him a figure of hate and a target for the animosity of feminists; his motor home has already been attacked and seriously damaged three times by lesbian feminists (and *signed* by them).

Feminism has become a malign and highly influential ideology in contemporary western societies, and it's astonishing that it hasn't been seriously questioned and challenged... until now. Exposing Feminism is a powerful examination of how and why misandry (the hatred of men) spread so easily across the developed world; it shows why men are universally blamed, demonised, and whenever possible, punished. The book's evidence and research exposes the deceits of modern feminism – issue by issue.

For all its serious content Exposing Feminism is extremely readable and inspiring, a 'must read' for men and women who've become disillusioned with the feminist movement and the ravages it has caused for thirty years in contemporary western societies. The book is a timely and valuable contribution to the critique of feminism in the modern world. Its eye-opening content is making waves; it deserves to become a bestseller.

Mike Buchanan May 2012

***

Author's Note

Exposing Feminism is in four Parts:

1. Part One looks at the spread of cultural man-hating in modern Britain: Spreading Misandry

2. Part Two exposes the Movement that has men-hating at its core: Feminism

3. Part Three exposes the mentality, the psychological make-up, of the women who hate men: Feminists

4. Part Four exposes every major Feminist issue, showing how each is a deceit, and how each is deliberately constructed to benefit Feminists and to blame, demonise and punish men: the Feminist Fraud

The Parts may be read independently, and in any order. In addition, each chapter within each Part addresses a separate issue and stands as a premise, an argument, in its own right. Collectively the Parts and chapters represent a devastating exposé of the fraud that Feminism has become. The reader will be made aware of how and why men in Britain are seriously disliked, how this is expressed and who is responsible.

Some of the chapters may not seem to be of interest to men; for example, 'Women Choose to Marry and be the Primary Parent' and 'Women Choose to Study the Arts and Humanities'. But they *will* be of interest; not only are they informative but they offer insights into the Feminist mentality, into the way governments favour and preference Feminists and their Ideology; they show the political influence that these people enjoy.

I should also like to record my appreciation for a fellow British writer on sexual politics, Mike Buchanan, for his input into this edition. He has to date written three books about feminism, which show notable insights into the ideology and its impact in the modern world. He runs a blog http://fightingfeminism.wordpress.com which I would recommend to anyone with an interest in feminism. We are jointly interested in publishing books on the subject through The Men's Press. Feel free to contact me if you have a book-related project you wish us to bring to fruition: info@exposingfeminism.com.

Swayne O'Pie May 2012

***

Preface

For the past thirty years men have been under siege by a culture and State that too often has embraced the ideas that men are to blame for all society's ills, that men are 'bad people' by virtue of their DNA...whilst women have been cast as victims worthy of preferential treatment and special privileges. Feminism is responsible for this siege, for this mindset.

***

This is an angry book. I have no personal axe to grind, no chip on my shoulder. But I'm angry at the continual deceit of Feminism, I'm angry at its relentless claims and demands, I'm angry at the way these claims and demands are believed and taken seriously, I'm angry at Feminism's continual manufacture of inequalities and discriminations, I'm angry at the way it blames and demonises men, and I'm angry at men for not confronting Feminism.

Feminism is not a fringe Movement from the 1970s. It is assumed that we are in a 'post-Feminist' society. Not so. Feminism is not only alive and well, it has entered the mainstream; our culture, society and State have all been affected by its power. Men, especially, have been negatively affected. Women, but mainly Feminists themselves, are the beneficiaries of this influential Movement; men are its target.

***

Since 2000 there has sprung up a revitalised Feminism. Equality between the sexes has been achieved, most of it during the 1980s, but today's Feminists are *still* demanding 'liberation', *still* 'striving to advance women's rights'. These politically-driven women are constantly seeking out inequalities, constantly creating discriminations, constantly fabricating oppressions in order to justify their existence. Two active members of this latest breed of Feminists state:

> *'Since the start of this millennium a staggering number of feminist organisations and campaigning groups have formed in the UK. A name has even been coined for this new activity: "third-wave feminism".'* [1]

And having no opposition they are confident people:

> *'The majority of feminists we surveyed were optimistic about feminism's future – with good reason. Feminism is a vibrant, living movement with an inspirational past and present...'* [2]

***

A microcosm of this modern forceful Feminism can be seen in higher education. The Professional Feminists Catherine Redfern and Kristin Aune are ecstatic at the success Feminism has had in our universities:

'Feminism still holds a vibrant place in UK universities…Gender studies remains popular at M.A. and Ph.D. level, and feminist modules are available as options on most undergraduate degree courses in the arts, social sciences and humanities. The National Union of Students (NUS) Women's Campaign has been going for twenty years, and NUS women's officers are promoting women's rights in most universities. Student women's groups and feminist societies are also active in at least a dozen universities many of them having been set up in the last few years.'[3]

***

In 2009 male students at two universities, the Universities of Manchester and Oxford, attempted to set up a society for male students - Ben Wild at Manchester (the MENS Society) and Alex Linsley at Oxford (the Man Collective).[4] Feminists were livid that male students should want equality. Both groups and founders faced aggressive opposition from strident student Feminists and *their* long-standing established and officially sanctioned (and funded) officers and groups; promotional posters were defaced and torn down and personal attacks ensued. Feminist students attempted to justify their undemocratic behavior. Olivia Bailey, NUS national women's officer, claimed:

'Discrimination against men on the basis of gender is so unusual as to be non-existent, so what exactly will a men's society do…To suggest that men need a specific space to be "men" is ludicrous, when everywhere you turn you will find male-dominated spaces.'[5]

So outraged was Vicky Thompson, a Feminist student at Manchester, at men wanting to have equal rights with women, that she set up a Facebook group specifically to oppose the MENS Society:

'Men's societies, groups and organisations represent nothing more than a backlash against the fragile gains made by the women's liberation movement.'[6]

Thompson again,

'There is no Women's Society at the University of Manchester Students' Union. There is a Women's Rights Collective who campaign exclusively for women's liberation. We live in a patriarchal society, women form an oppressed group and men do not. Therefore, not only does it create a huge imbalance to have a Men's Society and not a Women's Society, it actually makes a mockery out of the fight for women's rights…There's no men's liberation campaign because men don't need liberating!'[7]

- It is aggressive, anti-male women such as these, the young Feminist gender-warriors, who will be entering the professions and carrying their bigotry with them, influencing decisions and policy. Their older university-educated Sisters have been doing so since the late 1970s

The above prejudice and inequality against male students is reflected throughout our society, culture and State. For example, there is a Minister for Women but no Minister for Men.

***

Left-wing Feminist fascism is just as repugnant as Right-wing fascism; worse, in fact, because the Left claims to be the upholder of equality, liberty and freedom of speech; because of this, the intolerance and bigotry of Feminists is that much more repulsive. It is because this situation is widespread in Britain today, and has been for three decades with no one questioning or challenging it, that this book needed to be written. The Feminist confidence trick, the Feminist Fraud, its manufactured and synthetic 'issues', and particularly its man-hating, needs to be exposed.

In many areas of culture and policy-making today there is contempt for men. Men should set up specific political groups to promote their problems and issues, and to protect the erosion of their rights by an aggressive Feminism. I'm angry that they are not doing this. Ben's and Alex's milder work is a start; but the viciousness that they encountered shows that those with power will not give it up easily, and that the road ahead for men to gain respect and equal representation for their own specific issues and rights is going to be difficult. We have tended to forget that men are people too.

CONTENTS

Introduction

Exposing Feminism: A Brief Against Feminism

Feminism has become a huge confidence trick, a 21ˢᵗ century deceit and fraud. We have become slaves to received opinions. Feminism is the modern political equivalent of the Emperor's New Clothes, it is devoid of any rational credibility, it is morally and rationally naked and we are all being conned. Feminism is the reason why the developed world hates men.

Feminism has been presented, and has been widely received by our conventional wisdom, as a liberating force, a view of the relations between the sexes that emphasises openness, 'gender equality', freedom from oppression, discriminations, inequalities, sexism and stereotyping. This presentation is a masquerade. The burden of this book is to show in a broad theoretical perspective and in practical detail that our conventional wisdom and State have been wrong to embrace this malign and dangerous Ideological Movement.

Modern British women are among the most cosseted, privileged groups of people in the world. Yet Feminism still promotes them as oppressed victims requiring preferential treatment and policy-favouritism. And where there are victims there have to be victimisers.

At the same time, although many women do not always approve of everything said by Feminists, or even identify themselves as Feminists, most have consciously or subconsciously absorbed the rhetoric, dogma, cant, and sound-bites of Feminism. Many men, the Male Feminists, have also consciously or subconsciously absorbed Feminist myths, accepting them as truths.

This book is not anti-women, but it *is* anti-Feminist and it *is* pro-justice. In Britain today we have a female elite that is more fiercely committed to the banner of Feminism and male-bashing than it is to the welfare and well-being of traditional women – except where the genuine interests of the latter happen to coincide with Feminism's own political and Ideological agenda. Feminism is taken to be the voice of women. It isn't.

- Critiquing Feminism is *not* attacking women. The battle of the sexes is not women versus men but *Feminists* versus men. And Feminists have been continually winning

There is no point in gently critiquing Feminism; it is a hard-nosed, thick-skinned Movement, with its adherents similarly mentally and emotionally endowed.

***

People might see an example of Feminism 'having gone too far' here and there; or of men being discriminated against 'here and there...occasionally'. What they do not see is the *deliberate strategy* behind these observations, they do not see the *political pattern*, they are unable to join up the dots to reveal a concerted Ideological agenda, the progressing of a Quiet Revolution. The vast majority of us have been blind to this pattern, all examples of which 'coincidentally' benefit Feminists and Feminism and 'coincidentally' discriminate against men. There *are* no 'coincidences'. There has been a very clever, incremental, unnoticed Quiet Revolution to radically transform British society, culture and State.

- Feminism has carefully crafted cultural, economic and political strategies to manufacture problems and grievances 'suffered' by women, labelling these 'gender inequalities' or 'women's issues' in order to justify and legitimise its continuing existence, and thereby its misandrous agenda

Modern Feminism has an emotional, professional, egotistical, Ideological and financial investment in women's 'victimhood'. Furthermore, political correctness, introduced from the United States by Feminism as a device to be used as a 'gagging' mechanism, prevents us from investigating this fraud. Feminism has sunk into our national consciousness and is thereby given a free ride as a Movement advocating 'gender equality' and spreading misandry.

But any criticism, questioning of, or challenge to Feminism is taken as an attack on women. So it is hardly surprising that there is a universal reluctance and fear preventing Feminism's claims and demands from being subjected to an audit to assess just how relevant they are to changing realities. Political correctness and the deliberate creation of sexist sensitivities have done their job. Any serious critic or criticism is maligned – dismissed as a 'backlash', 'misogynist', 'Right-wing', 'sexist', 'reactionary', 'anti-progressive', or an attempt 'to take back women's fragile gains': so we all keep quiet - Feminism's desired response. It is noticeable that Feminism's reaction to even a *slight* questioning, even a slightly raised eyebrow at some of its absurd claims and demands, never includes addressing the *content* of the questioning (which it is morally and rationally incapable of defending) but focuses on a personal attack upon the critic.

- There must be something suspicious about a political Movement that does not allow itself to be questioned, challenged and analysed. Feminism has become an intellectual tyranny

This book dismantles Feminism, exposing it as a deceit, identifying and dismissing its issues, one by one – the pay gap, the glass ceiling, sexual harassment, domestic violence, rape, men treating women as sex objects, and so on. It shows how men are blamed for causing inequalities, discriminations and oppressions that have been deliberately fabricated to demonise and where possible, punish men. It identifies and analyses the mechanisms and strategies that Feminists use to produce these issues. It exposes as myths all Feminist claims that women in modern Britain suffer from 'gender inequalities'. Essentially, it offers compelling evidence that Feminism has caused modern Britain to hate men.

***

The new emphasis on preferencing women, giving special privileges and protection to women and policy-favouring women, has dangerously eroded men's rights. There is an unspoken assumption that women's needs are more important than men's needs. More insidiously, Feminism's seeking out, creating and exaggerating inequalities, discriminations and oppressions, has necessarily been accompanied by a preoccupation with men's supposed mistreatment of women.

Blaming and demonising men is an integral part of the engine driving modern Feminism: there can be no discriminations without having discriminators, there can be no victims without having victimisers, there can be no inequalities and oppressions without something (the patriarchy) or someone (individual men) causing these.

- It is a vital point of this book that Feminism cannot exist *without* blaming and demonising men. It needs to spread misandry as a necessary device to justify its existence. Misandry is the fuel that drives the Feminist Ideology and agenda, and keeps its Grievance Gravy-Train Industries in business

***

Since the 1970s the doctrines of Feminism have been introduced into our culture, conventional wisdom and political zeitgeist so quickly, so cleverly, and so subtly that most people have not recognised what has been happening; we can truthfully speak of a Quiet Revolution – advantaging women, where this coincides with the Feminist agenda, whilst promoting a systematic and systemic institutional discrimination against men, spreading misandry.

This book's purpose is to expose Feminism for what it has become – a selfish, self-serving Movement that needs to condemn men in order for it to continue enjoying its power and its individual and collective privileges. As long as Feminists can get moderate men and women to believe that they are fighting for 'gender equality', for 'women's rights' then they have a winning formula. I think that we need to inform men and women just what Feminism has become and what Feminists are now really like, not just for the sake of contemporary men's well-being but also for that of our sons and grandsons (and, indeed, our daughters and granddaughters).

- Privileging and preferencing one half of the population whilst demonising the other cannot result in a wholesome and healthy society
- Men have had to become the sacrificial victims of society because of Britain's neurotic and obsessive pandering to Feminist demands

Feminism has focused on the dark side of men and on the light side of women, resulting in a 'good women'/'bad men' script - a script that has become the sole narrative for sexual politics and gendered social policy in modern Britain. And we have all bought into this script.

- The book will show that Feminism has not gone away. Feminism is more powerful today than it has ever been. A great many of its most radical principles have been internalised into the 'mainstream'.

EQUALITY LAW GIVES WOMEN
JOB PRIORITY OVER MEN

(The Daily Telegraph: Friday, 3 December 2010)

'Employers will be able to reject male job applicants in favour of women who are not better qualified under new laws to promote equality at work.

Lynne Featherstone, the Liberal Democrat equalities minister, said yesterday companies that failed to promote a fairer deal for women could be named and shamed. She said sexism was present in too many workplaces.

Leading companies must promote more women to board level. They could be forced to disclose how much they pay male staff if they refused to do so voluntarily, she said.'

***

This book is an indictment of the Feminist establishment, which includes Male Feminists. To those readers who will be affronted and outraged by this book then I say 'good'. By exposing your erroneous statistics, your totalitarian tactics and your male-bashing falsehoods I will have succeeded. In addition, it is one of my goals to seriously disturb the views of the general public with regard to their unquestioned acceptance of Feminism.

Feminism has become a lucrative and powerful Movement. Many think that it went away and that modern Britain is a post-Feminist society. Not so. Feminist angst and self-righteousness manifests itself in every aspect of modern British life, our culture, the education system, the trade union movement, academia, the law, the media and the political system. It is driven by a self-serving desire to demonstrate that it is still needed, and it is animated by a spirit of resentment, the tactic of blame and the desire to triumph over men that is founded on a dogmatic assumption that women are the innocent victims of individual men, or of a male conspiracy. If you believe this to be a paranoid rant then read on, join up the dots; the hard evidence, the facts and examples, cannot be so easily dismissed. You are holding onto your beliefs tenaciously because the truth is so much less comfortable – we continue to show our gullibility (our bigotry?) by continuing to believe what can be shown to be a fallacy, a confidence trick, a fraud. We believe in Feminism because we *want* (and *need*?) to believe in Feminism. I hope to shake your belief. To do this it is necessary to expose Feminism for what it has become.

***

Modern Feminism is an artificial construction with no rational or moral base and it has become a cultural and political taboo to criticise it. On the fortieth anniversary of the publication of Germaine Greer's 'The Female Eunuch' perhaps this is now the time. After four decades of craven passivity the time has come to stand up and confront Feminism's self-perpetuating strategies that cause cultural and institutional discrimination against men. Perhaps now is the time to break through the barrier of political correctness, and the fear of Feminism, that have closed the minds of the great majority of academics, politicians, media people, lawyers, the chattering classes, the policy-making fraternity – the Feminist-friendly coterie that makes the laws, passes the legislation, forms public, cultural and political opinions, and informs and teaches our young people.

'There is nothing so powerful as an idea whose time has come'

(Victor Hugo)

We claim that we want our rulers to be honest and genuine but in reality there are certain areas of our culture and politics that are too sensitive to encroach upon, they are honesty 'no-go areas'. We 'Know Things' but 'Are Not Allowed to Say'. Feminism and its dislike of men is a major player in this 'no-go' area. Political correctness and fear of Feminism are powerful censorship weapons, they draw cultural and political lines across which we dare not go, that we cross at our peril because if we did the pack of truth-deniers will spring at our throats. Read this book and let's cross that line together.

***

'If we are to be a truly healthy democracy we must exorcise the cultural and political taboo that prevents our questioning and challenging Feminism's issues and Ideology, and its claim to gender righteousness'

(Swayne O'Pie)

***

Part One

Spreading Misandry

Chapter 1

Cultural Misandry: The Widespread Disrespect for Men

Misandry: *'Hatred of or hostility towards men; man hating'*.[1] The opposite of misogyny.

Hate: *'To feel hatred towards, loathe, detest. To find deeply distasteful or disagreeable, dislike, odious.'*[2]
The reader may wish to keep this definition in mind whilst reading the book. The word 'hate' is a hard word and it needs to be used appropriately. I use the word to range from 'constant universal disrespect' through to a 'very serious dislike' to 'punish'.

Part One demonstrates the prevalence of misandry, the hatred of men, in modern Britain. It looks at some of its most objectionable cultural facets: how men are disrespected, insulted, ridiculed, belittled, disposable. It identifies misandry as a Feminist's sexual political weapon, showing how it influences social policy and how the hatred of men has a negative effect upon society as a whole.

It shows how cultural and institutional misandry are symbiotic, how they support and feed from each other. A society and culture that has no respect for men, whilst constantly focusing on women's issues, has led to a State that has no qualms about discriminating against men, about implementing institutional misandry.

The widespread cultural and institutional misandry in modern Britain is due to Feminism. Feminism expresses misandry wherever possible. Hating men is an integral ingredient of Feminism, and in Britain's post-1970s Left-wing/liberal/progressive political climate this aspect of Feminism has blossomed. Creating and spreading misandry greatly assists Feminism in implementing its agenda and achieving its aims.

> *'Misandry has not unified all feminists, to be sure, but it has certainly unified enough of them – explicitly or implicitly, directly or indirectly, consciously or subconsciously – to create a powerful movement.'*[3]

In many areas of culture and policy-making in Britain today there is a widespread and accepted contempt for men.

It was a rainy November morning in 2003, and I was wet and weary. The library, my destination, was a dry haven. I quietly arranged my books on the table.

A young woman was studying two tables away. A few minutes after my arrival a black guy seated himself at the table directly between us. The librarian walked over to the girl and spoke to her quietly, "Are you comfortable with this black man sitting near you?"

I should think that almost everyone reading this would be shocked and disgusted that such a thing can happen in 21st century Britain.

The above story is true except in one respect: there was no black guy in the library – the librarian actually asked the young woman, who had the good grace to be embarrassed, "Are you comfortable with a man sitting near you"? You see, in my haste to get out of the rain and get myself settled I had inadvertently sat in the 'women-only' section of this particular library.

- I am an innocuous, white, heterosexual, able-bodied, male. And I refuse to apologise for that

Public libraries are publicly funded: yet as a male member of the public I'm treated like a leper. I suspect that this particular librarian was expressing a personal anger/hate toward men, and found relief, and perhaps pleasure, in being able to express this prejudice publicly, and legally, in a library system that supported and encouraged discrimination against men. So here we have an example of *personal, cultural* and *institutional* misandry.

Not only do we have special designated 'women-only' spaces in libraries, but public swimming pools have designated 'women-only' swimming times. There are 'women-only' car parks. As far as I am aware there are no designated 'men-only' spaces or swimming sessions. Why? Why are there special places and times designated solely for women but there are none for men? One thinks of apartheid in South Africa, or segregation in the American South.

• Having 'special spaces' and 'special times' for women-only is actually saying that 'men are bad people'. This is misandrous

• A serious dislike of men is just as abhorrent as racism, or anti-Semitism – or misogyny

BUSINESSMAN SUES BA FOR 'TREATING ALL MEN LIKE PERVERTS'

(Daily Mail, Saturday, 16 January, 2010)

'A businessmen is suing British Airways over a policy that bans male passengers from sitting next to children they don't know even if the child's parents are on the same flight.

Mirko Fischer has accused the airline of branding all men as potential sex offenders and says innocent travellers are being publicly humiliated.

Mr. Fischer, who lives in Luxembourg with his wife and their daughter Sophia, said: "This policy is branding all men as perverts for no reason. The policy and the treatment of male passengers is absolutely outrageous. A plane is a public place – cabin crew regularly walk down the aisles and passengers are sat so close to each other...I was made to feel like a criminal in front of other passengers".'

• Mr. Fischer is a tad naive with regard to sexual politics (as are most people, except Feminists). 'The policy of branding all men perverts' serves Feminism well; it is a deliberate policy. Spreading misandry is, in fact, a political strategy crafted and cultivated by Feminism

But the Feminist strategy of cultivating misandry is damaging society. For example:

'The repercussions of society's ill will toward men won't long be limited to individual embarrassment. Increasingly, innocent men are afraid to participate fully in society – whether leading Scouts or teaching school – for fear of being scrutinised as possible perverts, kidnappers, and murderers. Eventually, they'll simply stop showing up.'[4]

• Discouraging males from participating in the voluntary sector, very few male teachers, one in five children living in a fatherless home...Is Britain telling us that it doesn't really like men?

***

Sugar and spice and all things nice

That's what little girls are made from.

Frogs and snails and puppy dog's tails

That's what little boys are made from.

In modern Britain this 18th century children's rhyme is taken literally, expressed culturally, expressed in courts of law and expressed in anti-male policies and legislation. 'Men are bad people' has become part of Britain's conventional wisdom.

In the early 1970s Erin Pizzey opened and ran the first refuge for battered women. She genuinely cared about the women who entered her refuge. In the mid-1970s Pizzey attended a Feminist meeting. She was appalled at what she found:

> *'What I saw were groups of left-leaning, white, middle-class women gathering together to hate men. Their slogan was "make the personal political".'*[5]

Hating men, as we shall see in Part Two, is a central element of Feminism. And to a greater or lesser extent, as we shall see in Part Three, it is a personality characteristic of individual Feminists.

***

Misandry can be expressed in numerous ways, and in varying degrees:

- In the way women talk about men

- By claiming that women are 'superior' to men (more caring, co-operative, less aggressive, more empathetic, more sympathetic, more nurturing, more insightful...)

- By using negative stereotypes to ridicule men in popular culture (television programmes, advertisements, films, books and plays)

- By labelling men, as a group, as 'bad people', the cause of all wrongs in society (blaming, condemning and demonising men; for example, the unquestioning acceptance of the Feminist perspective on domestic violence)

- By making men feel 'guilty' about the 'wrongs' they have done, and are supposedly continuing to do

- By promoting women's issues and rights in policy-making - often at the direct expense of men's. In a dualist scenario, where there are only two groups, then if one is preferred and advantaged then the other, logically, is being disadvantaged. Disadvantaging a group is an expression of seriously disliking that group; in this case an expression of misandry

- By deliberately ignoring men's problems, issues and rights the State is further expressing a serious dislike for men. There has been no specifically male-friendly piece of legislation in living memory. The current policy of increasing paternity leave is not male specific; it is intentionally linked to the mother's return to full-time employment and is therefore a Feminist-friendly policy

- Misandry is a distinctive and *deliberate* sexual political phenomenon

There is a cultural transmission of dislike and disrespect for men: there is a process. Cultural misandry morphs into legal, educational and political misandry; in other words, into institutional misandry. Cultural misandry 'softens up' the public, the policy-making fraternity, the politicians, to accept and implement institutional misandry, allowing it to go unquestioned. And then, in turn, institutional misandry encourages cultural disrespect for men.

Pizzey noticed this link:

> 'It was bad enough that this relatively small group of women was influencing social workers and police. But I became aware of a far more insidious development in the form of public policy-making by powerful women, which was creating a poisonous attitude towards men'.[6]

• Both cultural and institutional misandry have become systemic in modern Britain, and both have become acceptable

> 'Like misogyny (misandry) is often expressed as negative stereotypes of the opposite sex. But unlike misogyny, misandry is not closely monitored, because, from a gynocentric perspective, it is considered morally and legally acceptable. Even though misandry is clearly visible to anyone with eyes to see and ears to hear, it is not visible to many people as a problem. On the contrary, most people ignore it.[7]

Misandry, in whatever form it takes, or however trite it may seem, is a deliberate attack on men.

Misandry and Popular Culture

Men are systematically depicted as fools in popular culture; they are ridiculed and belittled; examples include the anti-male messages presented on merchandise and the way men are negatively portrayed in situation comedies and in advertisements. This depiction has become widespread and acceptable. Insulting and ridiculing men is fun. It has also become big business. Until recently, W.H. Smith, the High Street stationers, sold a New Year Diary entitled 'All Men Are Bastards'.

These diaries were not placed on the top shelf, which contain the pornographic magazines that Feminists are so anxious to complain about, but were stacked along with other diaries at a very visible height. Child's viewing height. Imagine a young boy seeing this diary; would he ask if his dad was a bastard? Would he think that he might grow up to be a bastard? Would he know what a bastard was? Would he find out from his pals...and how would he then feel? When Feminists denigrate men they also hurt male children.

Substitute the word 'Pakistanis', or 'Jews', or even 'women' for the word 'men' and it becomes obvious that these diaries are insulting and would not be permitted. They would, in fact, now be classified as expressing a 'hate crime'. Yet it is permissible to say this about men. Why is this so?

When this nasty anti-male publication was brought to the attention of Macmillan (who published this diary) their senior editor, a woman, replied:

'We regret that you find it offensive. It is, of course, intended to be a light-hearted look at the "war between the sexes" and we've found over the years that this is how most people take it. Please may I assure you that no personal offence is intended.'[8]

- So really, then, it's my *own* fault for not having a sense of humour and laughing at my being insulted. There was no statement to say that the diary would be discontinued; there was no apology – only a 'regret' that I don't like being insulted and that the diary isn't targeted at me personally (but at all men)

- Sexism against men is 'fun', and 'light-hearted'...whilst sexism against women is condemned for being politically incorrect, and possibly illegal

- If the 'top shelf' magazines are offensive to women then being called a bastard is offensive to men. An example of Feminist hypocrisy and double standards

***

Greetings cards that carry the 'Men Are Stupid' type of message are ubiquitous. Yet one does not see greetings cards, anywhere, that denigrate women. Fridge magnets and 'T' shirts that carry slogans that insult men are now commonplace.

'Boys are STUPID; throw rocks at them'

The makers and sellers of these cards and shirts defend them as harmless fun – playful products that one shouldn't take too seriously. Do a gender-switch. Imagine if someone had tried to sell the same shirts, but this time saying 'girls' rather than 'boys'. The reaction would be intense and immediate.

***

The Moral Maze is a Radio 4 programme. On Saturday, 22 July, 2006, the moral question was 'Are Men Necessary'? Replace the word 'men' with 'black people', 'Jews', 'gays', or 'women'- would the reader find that offensive? Do you see how misandry has entered our cultural bloodstream to such an extent that we don't notice it even when men are so flagrantly insulted?

Would the BBC broadcast a programme entitled: 'Are Women Necessary?' The media would be in uproar, a documentary would be produced proving just how prevalent misogyny is, Academic Feminists would be frantically writing 'papers' denouncing men and the BBC, otherwise strong and aggressive women would faint, Jenni Murray, on the BBC's Woman's Hour, would declare a 'crisis' and an 'epidemic', a Parliamentary Commission would be set up...the Prime Minister would agree to be interviewed, and to apologise, on Mumsnet...

- Caring about *men's* feeling and rights is a step too far for the BBC's Equality and Diversity Mission Statement

***

Feminists used to complain about the way women were depicted in the media. Feminism still complains about this:

> 'If women are ever to be treated as equal members of society something must be done to change the way they are portrayed in the media. The media shapes our perceptions of each other. It influences our expectations and self-image. It helps create a climate where women are treated as inferior beings and where our needs and desires...come second-place to men's. It implicitly supports discrimination against women.'[9]

- I agree with the argument made here – but it is not *women* who are the victims of negative media portrayal in today's Britain but *men*. The reader might want to keep the above, cogent, arguments in mind whilst reading the following examples of cultural misandry

***

It is fashionable, and perfectly acceptable, for comediennes like Jo Brand and Kathy Lette to tell stories and jokes that ridicule and demean men. But male comedians are not permitted to make jokes where women are the butt. In the 1980s the national holiday camps Pontins and Butlins banned their entertainers from telling 'mother-in-law' jokes.

Benny Hill had his world-wide popular television shows banned on British television because Feminists deemed them to be too sexist and misogynistic. The comedian Les Dawson was similarly censored. Yet everywhere it is acceptable for *men* to be the target of sexist humour.

On Monday, 15 June, 2009, Kathy Lette, the misandrous comedienne, was interviewed on Radio 4's Today programme. The subject was erotic literature. Lette commented that 'men will have sex with anything living in the garden' (presumably any animal). She was not challenged about this obnoxious insult by the male interviewer, whose only response was an obsequious giggle.

***

In modern-day sit-coms it's man's lot to be the butt of jokes and to be made to look ridiculous. Where women can be negatively portrayed as a bit crazy, or ditzy, or indecisive, men are made to look just plain dense. If their characters are not entirely stupid then they are at least incompetent – especially in undertaking housework, picking out clothes, or dealing with women. In contrast, their wives and girlfriends are always jazzy, witty and bright, and highly competent.

The popular cartoon The Simpsons portrays, in every episode, Homer and Bart doing stupid things and being embarrassingly dim, whilst Marge and Lisa are the balanced, sensible, characters, holding the family together and having a social conscience. There isn't *one* normal male character in The Simpsons. Every one of the male characters is dysfunctional.

- How many have noticed this anti-male prejudice in The Simpsons (or elsewhere in our culture)? We have become so conditioned to accepting misandry as 'normal' that we *don't* notice it. Yet, we have seen that even a Feminist admits that the media: 'shapes our perceptions...influences our expectations and self-image...it helps create a climate where women (now boys and men) are inferior beings...it supports discrimination against women (now boys and men)'

- Children and young adults, both male and female, being subjected to such a regular barrage of negativity about men, must subliminally take on board that, somehow, men actually *are* ridiculous and stupid...and inferior – and they will take this 'knowledge' with them into adulthood

***

Current advertising may be even worse than sit-coms, if that is possible, when it comes to the negative portrayal of men:

> '"Men (in advertising) are typically defined as useless fools, sexual predators or extreme action junkies", laments an article in the Australian Financial Review. Mike Morrison, the chief strategy officer of the American advertising agency Young and Rubicon, voices his protest in the same article: "As a marketer and a male, I see more ads that are offensive and demeaning to men than I ever did... Does every pay-off have to be at the expense of men?"'[10]

- In Britain we have similar television advertisements – the idiot husband who doesn't know how to wash his own clothes: the dishwasher that is so simple to use that even a man can use it: men who get themselves into silly situations and have to telephone for help...

- Do a gender-switch, showing women as bumbling incompetents, say, with a computer, or driving a car (which always used to be the typical 'cheap shot' at women) and all hell would break loose

TV ADS ARE TURNING DRAGON-SLAYERS INTO 'CASTRATED DWEEBS'

(The Times, Friday, 30 June, 2006)

'Every man has noticed it: we hunky males are slowly being emasculated by too much oestrogen in television commercials...

Virtual castration of the male is the topic of a bullish debate in 'Campaign', the advertising industry's weekly bible.

'Campaign' this week accuses the advertising industry of portraying men as "castrated dweebs" who appeal to neither men nor women.

By portraying men as wimps, nerds and idiots, the advertising industry claims that it is trying to be more realistic.'

- Well thanks a lot, Advertising Industry! Bastards

Portraying men as inferior to women in advertisements has now been officially sanctioned (whilst portraying women in a negative role is politically incorrect and unacceptable):

IT'S OFFICIAL: YOU'RE ALLOWED TO MOCK MEN IN ADVERTS. JUST DON'T TRY DOING IT TO WOMEN

(Daily Mail, Wednesday, 20 May, 2009)

'A television advert that lampoons men as incapable of performing simple domestic tasks has been cleared by advertising watchdogs....

Industry observers said the prevailing view now appeared to be that it is fine to treat men as sex objects or fools, as this represents turning a stereotype on its head and is therefore ironic and funny.

In the Oven Pride advert, a man is shown throwing a tantrum at the thought of having to clean an oven.

A voice-over says "so easy, even a man can do it" as he is shown using the product with exaggerated delight while being watched by a disapproving pregnant woman.

A study from the Chartered Institute of Marketing in 2001 found two thirds of people believe women are now portrayed in adverts as intelligent, assertive and caring, while men are shown as pathetic and silly. Only 14 per cent said men came across as intelligent.'

Amanda Platell, a Daily Mail columnist, notes this widespread disrespect for men, this cultural and institutional misandry:

'Talk about double standards!...As a society, we have become so institutionally sexist against men that it is now accepted practice to treat them as second-class citizens. Think of the huge number of TV comedies in which the men are portrayed as under-performing dolts who are vastly inferior to the female characters...

Think of all those women's magazines that routinely reinforce the stereotype of men as being helpless inadequates who think only with their lower organs.

On a more serious note, think of the raft of legislation that has been put in place to benefit women, and indeed positively discriminate in favour of them, often at the expense of male interests.

In the supposed attempt to impose equality across the board there is – often quite literally – one rule for women and another for men. What's equal about that?'[11]

- Note the comment: 'think of the raft of legislation...'. Part Four will extensively address this institutional privileging of women and discrimination against men

***

22

We see the same misandrous prejudice with plots and characterisation in dramas and films:

MEN PORTRAYED BADLY

(The Sunday Times, 1 March, 1998, AA Gill and Nicholas Hellen)

'Just as it is standard casting on American cop series that the police captain will always be black, so in English drama the interesting, rounded, sympathetic characters are now nearly always women...

...certain types of male role have effectively ceased to exist. The respectable male hero can now appear only in costume drama..

And as John Mortimer, the creator of Rumpole, recently revealed, programmes that might mock female figures in the manner that has now become common for male figures do not get far...on screen men are now just risible Mr. Punch glove puppets.

It is now unthinkable for people to ridicule women. But it appears to be *de rigueur* to ridicule and verbally attack men. John Webster, who has created several of Britain's best-loved commercials, confirms that it is always best to laugh at men while... "It's pretty dangerous to poke fun at women".'

- Under the excuse-label of 'humour', men are ridiculed and made to be the target for contemptuous laughter

***

However, when it suits our conscience there will be occasional exceptions; firemen, for example:

'First responders don't count (in man-hating) as it's accepted wisdom post 9/11 that rescue-men are good, but only in a severe pinch and as long as they disappear after the flames are doused. Nice job, boys, now go home and shut up, and no pin-ups in the firehouse. Otherwise, in film and music, men are variously portrayed as dolts, bullies, brutes, deadbeats, rapists, sexual predators and wife beaters. Even otherwise easygoing family men in sitcoms are invariably cast as, at best, bumbling, dim-witted fools. One would assume from most depictions that the smart, decent man who cares about his family and who pets the neighbours dog is the exception rather than the rule.'[12]

Misandry and Belittling Men

A further aspect of misandry, akin to ridiculing, is the disparaging and belittling of men – making them look small and unimportant. Society, especially the media, now has a cultural licence to do this. It is a form of bullying, as are other forms of misandry.

WOMEN'S KILLER INSTINCT

(The Sunday Times, 18 September, 2005: India Knight)

'A survey by JWT, the advertising agency, found that...Many men interviewed said they were tired of feeling belittled, especially in advertising. One in two men felt less sure of himself than he used to...'

It is worth repeating that children and young adults, both male and female, being subjected to such a regular barrage of negativity about men, must subliminally take on board that, somehow, men actually *are* ridiculous and stupid – and they will act upon this 'knowledge', taking it with them into adulthood, where it may well warp not only young men's self-esteem but also their personal relationships with the opposite sex. Misandry in Britain has been prevalent since the early 1980s. Ask five women what they think of men and the majority will give a negative or ambiguous answer, especially if they have attended university. Try it.

***

'Bring Your Husband to Heel' was a series of six television programmes broadcast on BBC2, that began on Monday, 22 August, 2005. Annie Clayton, a former actress and now a professional dog trainer, showed wives how to 'train' their husbands like she trains dogs. Here is one female commentator's view of this disgraceful programme:

THE TV TIDE AGAINST MEN

(Radio Times, Saturday, 20 August, 2005: Alison Graham)

'Imagine a programme called "Bringing Your Wife to Heel". Imagine that programme being transmitted during a prime evening slot on BBC2. Imagine the content of that programme – husbands being encouraged to use dog-training techniques to bring their lazy or untidy wives into line. They'd be given experience first on making dogs do their bidding, before being let loose on their partners. Their beloveds would have no idea that they were being subjected to this kind of subtle training – their reactions would be filmed by hidden cameras dotted around their home. All would eventually be revealed when the wife was shown the footage and realised that she was being trained as if she were a dog.

There'd be an outcry, don't you think? Quite right, too, marches by furious women on BBC Television Centre, angry letters and emails, newspaper editorials – the lot. "Bring Your Wife to Heel" would be a programme beyond the pale, something that might have been given airtime in, say, 1955, but in these enlightened, post-feminist times, not a chance.

But what's this on BBC2 on Monday evening? "Bring Your Husband to Heel"...

...It is just one more example of TV's insistence on presenting men as saps.

We've discussed such portrayals on this page before, but "Bring Your Husband to Heel" also coincides with the start of a new series of polemics on Five, "Don't Get Me Started". In the first, Michael Buerk argues that men are increasingly being rendered obsolete. Naturally, he takes issue with his sex's representation by television as "ineffectual, clueless and idiotic". Gentlemen, he's right.'

- Men are being portrayed as the inferior sex, a lesser version of the species that couldn't cope unless handed directly from the care of their mother to the care of their wife

Why do men tolerate such programmes? A partial answer is that we don't have a choice. Almost all forms of the media are now heavily influenced by Feminism, pursuing a Feminist agenda.

Many senior posts in the media are now filled by women. Nothing wrong with that – in itself. But the majority of these women will have been politicised into Feminism during their time at university; they will be gender-warriors. They carry into their profession the Feminist Ideology, a central tenet of which is the hatred of men (held to a greater or lesser degree) and will express this in the choice and commissioning of programmes, and in their general decision-making. So women in senior positions in the media (as in other professions, especially academia, the law and politics) will not simple be *females* in positions of power – but *misandrous Feminists* in positions of power. This has been a very unwholesome development over the past three decades and is one of the main causes of cultural and institutional misandry.

- British males, now in their 20s and 30s, have never experienced a culture in which men are respected

***

The problem of misandry extends much further than the age-old battle of the sexes. It reaches into every area of public life in which a supposedly weaker group is entitled to mock or denigrate anyone or anything male...but must never, ever, be ridiculed or criticised in return.

How can this be right? Surely equality should be a two-way street in which the jokes, the criticisms and the views are allowed to flow freely in both directions without minority (but powerful) lobby groups dictating what is, and what is not, acceptable; without these groups dictating who should, and who should not, be targeted for ridicule, belittling and blaming?

People may notice examples of misandry, but they are unaware of its extent and how it has become a national cultural pattern; they are unaware of how it is employed as a major sexual political weapon in the Feminist armoury a) to be used to condemn and demonise men (punishing men), and b) to be used to facilitate the implementation of the Feminist agenda.

- People have not been joining up the dots in this concerted pattern

If what is routinely thrown at men were directed at any of our 'minority' victim groups – women, black people, ethnic minorities, gays – British society would be condemned for its prejudice and bigotry, discrimination and even persecution. In modern Britain there is a war against men, a war that has been quietly waged for three decades; few people realise that it's in progress. And fewer still realise that it is deliberate, orchestrated and Ideological.

- This war is not *women* versus men...it is *Feminists* versus men and it is unilateral; Feminists have no opposition...hence their power in today's Britain

Misandry and Children's Literature

Even children's reading books, which ought to be innocent of politics and Ideology, carry misandrous messages. William Leith gives a long list of children's books that he has read to his son and realises that they all depict men negatively:

WHY DO MY SON'S BOOKS TELL HIM ALL MEN ARE USELESS?

(Daily Mail, Tuesday, 2 June, 2009)

'As the penny dropped, I looked at all the other books I've been reading to my son.... And something else began to strike me as I looked at these stories – the stories I use to introduce my son to the ways of the world. Not only were they full of bad male stereotypes – deadbeat dads, absent fathers, idiots, wimps and fools – but I have been totally colluding with them. It didn't bother me at all. Until I started to think about it, it had seemed normal to me.

What are men like? Dumb. I just accepted it.

And it never mattered to me that the one thing that defines Tinky Winky, the only definable male in the Teletubbies, is his general ineffectuality.

And it's also never bothered me that Iggle Piggle, in another children's TV programme In The Night Garden seems like a drunk, and that most of the Mr. Men are deeply inadequate.

Why has this never bothered me? Because it's all around us, everywhere we look. For years, men in our stories – not just for children, but adults, too – have been losing their authority. Not just years – decades. It's crept up on us and now it's everywhere.

And wherever you look, things seem to be getting worse for guys. In a survey of 1,000 TV adverts, made by writer Frederic Hayward, he points out that "100 per cent of the jerks singled out in male-female relationships were male."'

- To William Leith Britain's culture of hating men appeared *normal* until there was a 'click' effect, until he started to join up the dots...' it's crept up on us and now it's everywhere'; this is the relentless progression of Feminism towards what I term its Quiet Revolution

***

Others are also noticing the misandry in children's literature:

WHERE ARE ALL THE NICE, NORMAL DADDIES?

Fathers in children's books are often stupid, wicked or absent. But with dads doing more childcare, isn't it time publishers took note, asks hands-on dad Damon Syson

(The Times, Tuesday, 26 May, 2009)

'The result was a shock. Not only did I find precious few role-model dads, I found hardly any dads at all. In all the picture books piled up around our house – more than 100 of them, in unsightly towers – mothers appeared in just under half and were invariably portrayed in a positive light. Fathers cropped up in nine, of which only five took a positive role in parenting.

Of course, I shouldn't base my judgment on our collection of books alone. But academic studies confirm that men are underrepresented in children's books. When they do appear they are often withdrawn and ineffectual.'

***

Women have a very high profile, and therefore power, in the publishing industry. Even Helen Kennedy's husband (Kennedy is a Feminist lawyer) was verbally abused at a Women in Publishing conference[13] and Doris Lessing remembers a striking scene from her past:

'A building in London that houses a feminist publishing house has in it other offices, one of which is regularly visited by a friend of mine from the Middle East, as it happens an exemplary husband and father. It took him a long time, he said, to understand why it was that every time he passed the door of the (Feminist) publishing house, one of the females came out and deliberately stamped on his feet, as hard as she could...Not least depressing was that this kind of thing was thought of...as a political action.'[14]

- Children's literature has become politicised, gender-politicised, by a culture that is driven by Feminist Ideology.

- And children will internalise these anti-male messages, taking this deliberately taught perception of 'good women'/ 'bad and stupid men' with them into their student and then adult lives

***

To sum up: 'All Men are Bastards' diaries, T-shirts, fridge stickers, greetings cards, radio programmes, comediennes, sit-coms, advertisements, television programmes, drama casting, children's literature...

For children and young people popular culture is an essential ingredient in their learning. The above areas of popular culture don't just get them to laugh at men, they teach them to view all aspects of men and maleness negatively. Culture is part of the process of how they learn about gender. In modern Britain this message is 'bad boys/men': 'good girls/women'.

And this sexual political cultural script is formally taught to children and young people in our education system.

27

Misandry and Education

We teach young children to be kind to one another, to be thoughtful and caring to other people. And then, when they reach a certain age, the Feminist Fairy comes along and sprinkles boys and all things male with poo dust.

'Somehow, its always men who are to blame. Even in the school yard, little boys suffer from puzzlement, pain, and ostracism as little girls make comments and express expectations they cannot quite grasp or respond to. Thus boys are trained into a lifelong awareness of inferiority.'[15]

Education, in addition to the media, culture and children's literature, is also a major vehicle by which Feminism spreads misandry. Male-bashing has been introduced into the education system and cross-seeded back into mainstream culture.

***

A BAD TIME TO BE A BOY

(The Sunday Times, 24 November, 2002: Minette Marrin)

'Illogical people…think that all men are awful and the root of all evil. Many more are doing so, and increasingly…

Even little children sense this prevailing orthodoxy in the playground. I will never forget the moment my nine-year-old daughter told my four-year-old son that men do all the bad and cruel things in the world and are wicked. But not girls. The poor little fellow looked at her in shame and horror. Since then he has been growing up in a climate of increasing misandry, the opposite of misogyny.'

Since the 1980s school teachers, and lecturers in higher education, have become misandrous in their teaching and in their promotion of the Feminist Ideology and agenda. This proselytising is a serious mental conditioning of the nation's pupils and students – something that would not be permitted if it were of a macro-political nature. For example, if the education system presented and taught *only* a Labour perspective, or *only* a Conservative perspective in our schools and universities.

The author, Doris Lessing, is an Equality Feminist:

LAY OFF MEN, LESSING TELLS FEMINISTS

(The Guardian, 14 August, 2001: Fiachra Gibbons)

'Doris Lessing, who became a feminist icon with the books, The Grass is Singing and The Golden Notebook, said a "lazy and insidious" culture had taken hold within feminism that revelled in flailing men.

Young boys were being weighed down with guilt about the crimes of their sex, she told the Edinburgh book festival.

"I find myself increasingly shocked at the unthinking and automatic rubbishing of men which is now so part of our culture that it is hardly even noticed", the 81-year-old Zimbabwean-born writer said yesterday.

"I was in a class of nine- and ten-year-olds, girls and boys, and this young woman was telling these kids that the reason for wars was the innately violent nature of men. You could see the little girls, fat with complacency and conceit while the little boys sat there crumpled, apologising for their existence, thinking this was going to be the pattern of their lives".

Lessing said that the teacher tried to "catch my eye, thinking that I would approve of this rubbish".

She added: "This kind of thing is happening in schools all over the place and no one says a thing".

It is time we began to ask who are these women who continually rubbish men. The most stupid, ill-educated and nasty woman can rubbish the nicest, kindest and most intelligent man and no one protests.

Men seem to be so cowed that they cannot fight back. And it is time they did.'

- Universities have a great deal to answer for by producing Ideologically-driven teachers who prejudice the minds of children against their fathers and their brothers, against the male half of the population. Totalitarian States, fascist and communist, also used the education system to create an Ideologically-complicit populace, to create a compliant conventional wisdom. We don't expect it to be so used in Britain

- I find it embarrassing that men need an 81-year-old woman to tell them to summon up the courage to 'fight back' against Feminism

***

Pathologising Males in Education

Boys are considered to be 'problematic' in school. The junior school is a world where mostly female teachers treat the playground boisterousness of young male pupils as deviant rather than healthy and normal.

Christina Hoff Sommers, in the preface to her book, 'The War Against Boys: How Misguided Feminism is Harming Young Men', comments:

'This book tells the story of how it has become fashionable to attribute pathology to millions of healthy male children. It is a story of how we are turning against boys and forgetting a simple truth; that the energy, competitiveness, and corporal daring of normal, decent males is responsible for much of what is right in the world.'[16]

Feminism has also succeeded in classifying adult males as 'problematic'. The following is taken from 'Fatherhood: Contemporary Theory, Research, and Social Policy'.[17] It describes the rationale behind the whole series of SAGE books on men and masculinities:

'Contemporary research on men and masculinity, informed by recent feminist thought and intellectual breakthroughs of women's studies and the women's movement, treats masculinity not as a normative referent but as a problematic gender.'

- Here it is clearly seen who and what is responsible for driving educational and institutional misandry in Britain – 'feminist thought', 'feminist breakthroughs', 'women's studies', and the 'women's movement'

- The books in this particular series of SAGE are set titles on many Sociology and Social Policy courses, and used to train social workers...teaching and training young people that men are 'problematic' – simply because they have been born male

- So it is being widely taught that men are 'not normal'

By having men classified as 'problematic' Feminism has made it easier for itself to manipulate the State, governments and the professions into producing pro-female/anti-male policy and legislation. For example:

'A study by Newcastle-based Children North East in 2004 found that institutional sexism is damaging the educational prospects and social development of young people, and that unconscious practices disregard the needs of men and fail to recognise the role of fathers, in other cases, conscious discrimination labels men as "dangerous oppressors", or "perpetrators".'[18]

- Such an observation of misandry is almost unique

Misandry, man-hating, has reached such a level in Britain that Feminists and Male Feminists can openly refer to men as being 'the problem sex'. This truly bigoted attitude is reminiscent of the way men, prior to the late 20th century, thought about women being 'problematic' – their 'frailty', their 'incapacity to benefit from education', their 'menstrual problems'. It is also reminiscent of the way black people were once thought to be 'problematic' in the American South.

- Our decision-makers have found it morally acceptable to use 'hate legislation' as a way of protecting women and minorities from negative stereotyping, but not as a way of protecting men from equally negative stereotyping

Labelling men 'problematic' also makes it easier for Feminism to introduce seriously anti-male policy in such gender areas as domestic violence, prostitution, sexual harassment, rape, child custody and post-divorce father contact with his children.

Misandry and Social Policy

Establishing a misandrous culture and conventional wisdom has aided (as it was meant to) the generally held perception that compared with women men are 'bad people'. This perception, in turn, facilitates the implementation of many pro-Feminist/anti-male policies.

- In Part Two we see how Feminism has created the perception of men being 'bad people'

Creating and spreading cultural misandry is a Feminist aim in itself, but it needs to be noted that cultural misandry is a device used to 'soften up' the public and decision-makers to facilitate the introduction of *institutional* misandry. This 'softening up' process goes some way to explain the phenomenon of Male Feminists. For example, it explains why male MPs, judges and other male influentials consider it 'morally' easier to discriminate against men, the 'bad people', than it is to be gender-neutral or to discriminate against women; and it explains why Male Feminists engage in institutional misandry.

Cultural misandry has made these men feel 'guilty' about being male; Male Feminists assuage their self-imposed 'guilt' by identifying and sympathising with Feminism and its aims and policies. Pro-Feminist decisions, and being prejudiced against your own group, are a kind of penance for these men, a pay-back, a form of compensation for all the supposed wrongs done by men to women. In addition, Feminists tap into and manipulates men's traditional chivalry, conditioning them to believe that women need protection from 'bad men', making preferential treatment, special privileges and policy-favouritism for women that much easier to secure.

And so we have institutional misandry:

WHY DOES MODERN BRITAIN HATE MEN?
(Daily Mail, 10 June, 2000: Melanie Phillips)

'The Government assumes that all men accused of rape are guilty.

Anti-male prejudice, in fact, runs through Government thinking. Baroness Jay and her Women's Unit constantly bring out the old chestnut that one woman in four is assaulted by her partner.

In fact, most British domestic violence studies on which the Government relies for such claims are effectively rigged, they ask only women, not men, for their domestic violence experiences, mainly from self-selecting samples of abused women.

Yet reputable international research shows overwhelmingly that acts of domestic violence are initiated by women upon men as least as frequently as vice versa.

The courts are institutionally biased against husbands, ousting them from their homes on the slightest pretext, stripping the man of his children and his assets – even if the wife has gone off with a lover and his own behaviour has been exemplary.

The judges also accept a wife's claims that the man is violent on the basis of no evidence...

The majority of men are divorced against their will...

Most violence against children is perpetrated by mothers or boyfriends. A child's natural father is least likely to be violent towards it.

Many judges think mothers are intrinsically vulnerable and must be protected, as they are generally to be the parent with care of the children.

Yet why should this be? If a mother has gone off with her lover, jeopardising the well-being of her children and demonstrating infidelity to their father, promise-breaking, deceit and selfishness, why should she be automatically regarded as the fitter parent to bring up the children?'

- Here we see a litany of institutional discriminations against men. Widespread and deep cultural misandry has created a mindset that 'men are wrong' and that 'women are right', that 'men are bad people' and 'women are good people'. I don't claim this as a simplistic polemical sound-bite, Part Two explains why this is and Part Four offers extensive examples of this phenomenon. In modern Britain institutional misandry, like cultural misandry, is *political* and *deliberate*

***

Widespread cultural misandry has resulted in systemic institutional discrimination against men. Discrimination against men is not merely an odd, isolated, occasional incident occurring haphazardly here and there. Anyone who wishes to look will see a concerted pattern of privileging women and disadvantaging men. These are not 'coincidences'.

For example, positive discrimination for female prospective parliamentary candidates; equal pay policies, worse health-care for men than for women, harsher treatment for male than female criminals who commit a similar offence, maternal custody, child maintenance payments, sexual harassment, domestic violence. And rape – changing the court process in order to secure more (male) convictions, innocent or guilty, publicising the name of the accused (male) in rape trials whilst giving anonymity to the (female) accuser. In all cases women are preferenced while men are identified as 'the bad people' deserving of lesser consideration, deserving not to have *their* perspective addressed, deserving to be disadvantaged. Men's rights (individual, human or natural) are never considered. This disrespect for men is Feminist-inspired man-hating.

'Feminist ideologues have found ways of embedding misandry in culture, ultimately in the form of law, without calling it that. Even men find it hard to see systemic discrimination against themselves, although that situation is changing, just as women once found it hard to see systemic discrimination against themselves.'[19]

'Men have become the pariah sex; and cultural misandry gives the State a mandate to institutionally treat men badly'

(Swayne O'Pie)

Misandry and Men's Lesser Worth

The stereotyping of a group as 'bad people' makes us callous to the death of its members.

IT'S SO HARD BEING A MAN

(The Sunday Telegraph, 7 November, 1993)

'Last week the chief executive of the Samaritans drew attention to the growing number of young men committing suicide. There was little reaction...

Men are the last group that can be freely prejudicially denounced. It is perfectly acceptable to make general slurs about men that could never be made about an ethnic group and certainly not about women'.

- That was written in 1993. Nothing has changed since – the male suicide rate is *still* four times greater than the rate of female suicide. Do a gender-switch...and imagine the media and political outcry that would ensue

- Suicide is overwhelmingly a male issue; deliberately ignoring it is a misandrous 'policy' (as is the neglect of other male issues)

On Monday, 22 March, 1999, the Bath Chronicle carried a small article (only about 8cm long by one column in width) entitled: 'Three bodies found in Bath over weekend'. During the course of one weekend three bodies – all male – had been found in different locations in Bath, all having died of ill-health and exposure.

- If it were three *women's* bodies that had been found in similar circumstances, in *one* city, over *one* weekend, it would have been a national news feature, questions would be asked in the House, Feminist MPs would be masochistically delighted at finding yet one further example of misogyny, a Commission would be set up. But these were only *male* corpses... so only 8cm in a local paper

- Widespread misandry dehumanises men. In numerous ways, men in modern Britain have become disposable, have become of lesser worth than women

A female columnist writes:

A HYMN TO HIM: MEN ARE SEXY, SMART, AND GOOD FOR WOMEN

(The Sunday Times, 12 July, 2009: Minette Marrin)

'Are men really necessary? That was the question that raised its ugly head following reports that scientists had created human sperm from embryonic stem cells. A team from Newcastle University claims to have produced fully mature, mobile sperm in the laboratory, which may soon be able to create a living child. If men are no longer needed for producing sperm, perhaps they are no longer needed at all – that was the suggestion humming in the media and the blogosphere last week, often rather nastily disguised as humour, with lists of ways in which men are worse than useless. Misandry – the dislike of men – is a powerful force.

With the feminisation of the media and of education and with decades of so-called positive discrimination favouring women, we have seen a growing female triumphalism; it has been accompanied by a growing bewilderment and displacement of men. There is an increasing sense that women can do well enough without them, and more and more women are embarking on a life to which men are only incidental.'

***

Misandry, demonising and dehumanising men, has devalued men's worth compared to that of women's; it has made society blasé about the disposability of men. It is responsible, for example, for the shocking bias in the lack of attention to men's health in general. It is responsible for our blindness towards domestic violence against men. Britain today cares more about saving whales than about saving males, more interested in the rights of foxes than in the natural right of divorced fathers to see their children.

- Almost anything can be said about men or done to men, without the expectation of a public outcry

The Public are Unaware of Misandry

Both men and women fail to see misandry as a problem. This is because 'sexism' has been defined exclusively in terms of misogyny. So nobody is looking for 'sexism' against men, for misandry, and people don't find what they are not looking for (have they even heard of the word or concept?). Everyone would admit to noticing examples of men 'perhaps losing out', now and again, here or there, occasionally. But because Feminism has never been exposed to public debate, to questioning and analysis, people have failed to see the pattern, they fail to see the intended political strategy...because of this heavy censorship people have been *deliberately* denied the knowledge and the political insight to see Feminism for what it has become. After decades of society's and the State's relentless searching and probing, exploring in every nook and cranny of society, culture, education, the law, the media, employment, politics, to seek out misogyny and sexism against women, it can be very difficult for individuals, steeped in this conventional wisdom, conditioned in this monopolistic, blinkered search, to see the dangers of widespread man-hating.

- Here is one reason why this book needed to be written. Part Four offers the reader the knowledge, the insights, to see the pro-Feminist/anti-male pattern in sexual politics, to see how modern Britain expresses institutional misandry; to expose the Feminist fraud

- In the Preface we saw how Feminist students (already well entrenched in their *own* political groups) aggressively attempted to prevent male students at the Universities of Manchester and Oxford from forming even non-political, innocuous, Men's Societies

People have, so far, been unaware of how misandry has been employed as a major sexual political weapon in the Feminist armoury:

- in condemning and demonising men (and thereby legitimising the institutional 'punishment' of men via laws, policies and by ignoring male-specific problems and issues)

- how it is used to ease and facilitate the implementation of the Feminist agenda

- And neither are they aware of how Feminism's Quiet Revolution is being cleverly orchestrated

***

Or they may have purposely chosen *not* to be aware of these aspects of misandry. Male Feminists are particularly deserving of opprobrium for their lack of concern for men, their obsequious refusal to address misandry, and their obdurate refusal to even acknowledge its existence. Male politicians, male trade union officials and male academics should be particularly singled out for condemnation.

CAMERON: ABSENT DADS
AS BAD AS DRINK DRIVERS

(The Sunday Telegraph, 19 June, 2011)

'David Cameron today launches a full-scale attack on fathers who abandon their families, calling for them to be "stigmatised" by society in the same way as drink-drivers.

The Prime Minister's intervention – in an article for The Sunday Telegraph to mark Father's Day – is one of the most outspoken he has made in defence of traditional family life... He says: "It's high time runaway dads were stigmatised, and the full force of shame was heaped upon them. They should be looked at like drink-drivers, people who are beyond the pale. They need the message rammed home to them, from every part of our culture, that what they're doing is wrong, that leaving single mothers, who do a heroic job against all odds, to fend for themselves simply isn't acceptable.

He says fathers must make the decision to support "financially and emotionally" their children even if they have separated from their mothers, spending time with them at weekends, attending nativity plays and "taking an interest in their education".'

This is an attack on men, not just fathers. Cameron chose Father's Day to make his words especially painful for those divorced men who are desperate to see their children but have been prevented from doing so, sometimes for many years, by vindictive ex-wives.

- 4 out of 5 divorces are petitioned for by wives;[20] it is *fathers* who are ditched and required to leave the family home. How can this fact possibly be construed as 'runaway dads'? Such dishonesty could only be alchemised in the warped perspective of the Feminist and the Male Feminist. It isn't *fathers* who are breaking up traditional families but wives and mothers...but this dare not be openly admitted in our politically correct culture. So men are used as the scapegoats; in a misandrous culture it is easier to demonise men than to face the wrath of Feminists by being truthful

Or is Ms. Cameron thinking of young men who irresponsibly impregnate girls and then refuse to commit? Well hang on, there are two sides to this story. Young women *are just as culpable* as young men with their sexual behaviour. For every male youth who impregnates a girl and then disappears from the scene there is an equal number of (if not more) young women who have had children by *numerous fathers* and who refuse to live with any of them because this would reduce their State single-parent benefits, including jeopardising their State-provided free flat or house. In addition, there is extensive and compelling evidence to show that young women actually *choose* to become single-parent mothers.[21] For example:

Senior research fellow Patricia Morgan:

'Most unwed mothers conceive and deliver their babies deliberately, not accidentally.'[22]

Again,

Geoff Dench, senior research fellow:

'The existence of state benefits as a source of economic security seems to be encouraging young mothers not to bother with male resident partners.'[23]

And Cameron's *own* research team, a body specifically set up to investigate the breakdown of the traditional family, reached the same conclusion. Iain Duncan Smith speaks for his Social Justice Policy group, Breakthrough Britain:

> *'However, over the lifetime of this working group we have been concerned by the extent to which it appears that the current benefits system incentivises lone parenthood and acts as a driver towards family breakdown.'*[24]

- So young men *don't* leave single mothers to fend for themselves. Today, single-parent motherhood is mostly driven by young women, it is not caused by 'runaway dads'. By disregarding all the evidence, all the research, including his own, we can see that Cameron is bloody-minded in his determination to blame men, fathers, for the supposed 'victimhood', and the huge public cost, of the single-parent mother phenomenon

Cameron goes on to say that divorced fathers should be involved with their children and have an emotional input. He suggests 'spending time with the kids at weekends, taking them to football matches, going to the nativity play, taking an interest in their education'.

The man's an idiot. He has no idea just how difficult it is for the majority of divorced fathers to even *see* their children, let alone be permitted to participate in their emotional care (this ostracism is also experienced by many *unmarried* fathers). These loving fathers spend £1000s desperately trying to have some sort of meaningful contact – against the combined might of their vindictive ex-wives (free legal-aided to keep the fathers away from 'her' children), the Feminist-friendly Family Courts and successive Feminist-sympathetic governments (both the latter supporting and encouraging the cruelty of the ex-wife). Cameron offers not a word of comfort, in the form of father-friendly policy, for these seriously distressed and desperate men.

Cameron's statement is virulently anti-male. It is not *accidentally* insensitive; he deliberately chose Father's Day to inflict his cruelty on already-hurting divorced fathers. So not only is his attack on men delusional; it is despicable. And it encapsulates (and proves) the thesis of this book – that modern Britain hates men; and that this systemic misandry is not only *cultural* but *institutional*. Here we see man-hating from the very top.

Why did Cameron perpetrate this deliberate hurt, this planned misandry? Two reasons: by blaming and demonising men, by further hurting and tormenting divorced fathers, he appeased and pleased the Feminists. It is dangerous for a politician today to incur the wrath of the powerful Feminist lobby, sycophancy is a much easier policy to keep these influential Ideologues 'on side'. Secondly, by cuddling up to and flattering single-parent mothers he hopes to glean and secure the 'women's vote'. Cameron's motives were political, dishonest, devoid of integrity, insensitive and lacking in compassion.

- Cameron did it because he could. Today anything can be said about men, or done to men, and nobody protests. Men are the whipping boys, they are an easy target. Modern Britain hates men

- With regard to sexual politics Britain is no longer a democracy. It would be unwise for me to propose actions that I would dearly love to propose...but when men are constantly maligned and demonised, when they have been abandoned by the political and legal process, where else is there for them to turn...?

The Social Consequences of Misandry

What is happening to men as a result of this massive assault on their identity? How do men feel about being depicted as bumbling fools to be ridiculed and laughed at? How do young men feel about being constantly portrayed as psychotics, wife-batterers, rapists and thugs? How do they feel about being classified as 'problematic people', as a group of victimisers and oppressors, as 'feckless fathers' or 'runaway, deadbeat dads'? How do young men feel about having their problems, issues and rights ignored whilst they see preferential treatment, special privileges and policy-favouritism widely given to girls and women?

Those who promote misandry, in all its manifestations, need to be aware of the consequences of what they are doing. Misogyny has been studied and taken seriously for decades; political pressure and political correctness have eliminated a great deal of it. Yet no pressure has been used to eliminate misandry; in fact, this phenomenon is State-encouraged and State-implemented. As a result Britain has become neurotically and pathologically focused on the needs and problems of women and the disrespecting and wickedness of men. Consistently maligning and attacking a major group in a population is an extremely dangerous thing to do.

***

I suggest that the cultural and institutional misandry that has been experienced by men for three decades has been a driving force behind much of Britain's present social ills.

An observation from someone with first-hand experience of the problem, June 2010:

> 'As a writer-in-residence at Huntercombe Young Offenders institution, best-selling crime writer Martyn Waites saw at first hand how boys would seek role models when none was available at home. It was one reason they were in trouble, he says. "There was such a lack of positive male role models in their lives, they would get what they could from TV, violent films and games," Waite recalls.
>
> The boys he met needed examples to live up to, not ones to dumb down to. No wonder the father-of-two rages: "To men, promoting the image of men as juvenile, mean and stupid is cynical and exploitative".'
>
> Which makes the tide of inverse sexism that has swamped out screens more appalling.'[25]

In modern Britain boys and young men have a dire lack of good role models; especially if they are raised in a single-parent mother home (as one in five children now are). Teachers are overwhelmingly female. Dr. Jim Macnamara, an Australian professor of public communication who analysed *two thousand* mass media portrayals of men and male identities, found that men were depicted mostly as villains, aggressors, perverts, and philanderers. He wonders how boys will navigate their search for a good male identity:

> 'Highly negative views of men and male identity provide little by way of positive role models for boys to find out what it means to be a man and gives boys little basis for self-esteem...In the current environment where there is an identified lack of positive male role models in the physical world through absentee fathers in many families, and a shortage of male teachers, the lack of positive role models in the media and presence of overwhelmingly negative images should be of concern...Ultimately such portrayals could lead to negative social and even financial costs for society in areas such as male health, rising suicide rates and family disintegration.'[26]

- It is impossible to teach young people effectively that hatred and revenge are wrong, when they are learning directly and indirectly that this is apparently acceptable – when they are targeted at men

***

If men are told over and over again that they are society's 'bad people' they are likely to say, 'so be it'; ignoring men's issues will inevitably lead to resentment – you lose your child after a divorce and *you have nothing else to lose*. Our governments should consider the danger of a self-fulfilling prophecy. Psychologists tell us that if we treat people badly, with contempt and disdain, then they will react in kind. Social order in Britain is not in good condition right now. Perhaps we have identified just one reason for this. If boys and men continue to be discriminated against, held in contempt, treated with disrespect, demonised and told, and shown, that they have little value or worth, disposable as husbands, as fathers and as people, then it might be understandable if they react by treating society in the same manner. They who sow the wind reap the whirlwind.

Observe the many dysfunctional socially behavioural trends in contemporary society and you will see that the whirlwind is gathering force. I put to you that a major causal factor is that Britain is now a misandrous society and State.

'The symptoms of the male malaise are already showing as men of all ages become increasingly angry, suspicious, reactionary, and isolated. Men are opting out, coming apart, and falling behind. They are losing their sense of place in society and their direction as individuals. Trapped between unattainable ideals and a downsized reality, they risk morphing into muscle-bound weaklings who seek solace in the hypermasculine rituals of violence and aggression with an ugly undercurrent of homophobia, misogyny, and masochism.'[27]

- What is not realised by these commentators is that this treatment of boys, juveniles and men is an intended Feminist *Ideological aim*, deliberately subscribed to and advanced, for three decades, by successive Feminist-friendly governments...especially Labour governments

By disrespecting men, treating men as having no worth, condemning and demonising men, modern Feminist Britain is encouraging a stroppy male slouch towards Gomorrah. Enjoy.

NEWSFLASH: Britain, August 2011. Riots

***

Misandry and Girls

The spread of misandry tells boys and men that they are stupid, inferior, and of little worth. This Feminist-cultivated view of maleness gives girls and women the legitimacy to think of themselves as superior, cleverer and more worthy of privileges, than boys and men. Here we see the origins of the sanctimonious righteousness that is an observable characteristic in young Feminists today. If we are to be a truly healthy democracy we must have the courage to face up to Feminism and exorcise the cultural and political taboos that prevent our questioning its claim to gender-righteousness.

Cultural male-bashing has been treated as a kind of retributive justice by women who have been disappointed and hurt by men. And some of that woundedness has been passed on to their daughters, who have absorbed the message that men are 'bad people', resulting in young women turning against their male peers.

In this particular context the use of misandry as a sexual political weapon has also resulted in young men and women having a distorted perspective of each other. Daughters have been especially wounded by the 'bad men/father' narrative they've heard from their mothers, the wider culture, the media and from politicians. How does a little girl reconcile her love of her first 'hero' with the anti-male messages all around her? This will play out negatively in her later personal relationships, as we can now see happening in dysfunctional courtships, marriages, co-habitee relationships, and the relentless and rapid increase in the number of single-parent mothers.

- Four out of five divorces are applied for by wives...and one in five children now live in a single-mother, fatherless, home

- Young women's hostility towards men is validated by an applauding misandrous culture

Feminism's creation of widespread misandry is rebounding against ordinary women. This is ironic, but not surprising. For all its cant and rhetoric Feminism doesn't represent women; it uses a facade of 'gender equality' to justify its existence and to sweeten and cleanse its public (and political) image. Its Ideology and agenda are of paramount importance, not women; only where women's genuine issues happen to coincide with Feminism's agenda and aims can Feminism accurately, but accidentally and by default, claim to 'represent women'.

> *'Rendering women either unwilling or unable to see men as fully human beings, as people who can indeed be hurt both individually and collectively, might well be the single most serious flaw in feminism.'*[28]

It is my hope that we can destroy man-hating before it overwhelms and destroys our son's and daughter's relationships.

***

And the Feminist's response to the disastrous social consequences of their spreading misandry?

> *'We have come a long way, but we still have a long way to go'*
>
> (Feminist mantra)

Misandry and Feminists

In the late summer of 2005 the Feminist Marian Salzman published her book, The Future of Men. On 4 September Jasper Gerard interviewed her for The Sunday Times:

> *'The good news is that since writing the book Salzman has subtly changed her mind.*
>
> *"I started as a feminist and came out much more realistic. Men should rise up. We have pushed men too far. They are going to have to shove back."*
>
> *Since being in Britain she has been horrified by a television show that teaches wives to make husbands walk on a lead: "How is this allowed? The straight white male is the only one that doesn't have a royal society protecting his rights. If this programme showed maids rather than men it would be called slavery."*
>
> *During her research she actually came to feel sorry for men. The trendsetter says it starts going wrong for us round about nursery time: "Schools are now populated almost entirely by women and boys are falling behind. If this were happening to girls something would have been done".'*

- If an American Feminist is appalled by how much disrespect and negativity men in Britain experience and is calling upon men to 'rise up and shove back' (as did another former Feminist, Doris Lessing) – then something, surely, 'must be rotten in the State of Britain'.

***

I'll leave Part One by offering the reader the following comments:

- 'Looking how easy it is to treat men badly is oddly liberating' (the influential Feminist, Naomi Wolf)[29]

- 'How did we get to this point? Like misogyny, misandry is about hatred, not anger. And hatred is seldom, if ever, a grassroots movement. It is a culturally propagated movement.'[30]

- 'I watched the feminist movement build its bastions of hatred against men, fortresses where women were to be taught that all men were rapists and bastards, and I witnessed the damage done to the children in the refuges who were taught that men were not to be trusted.'(Erin Pizzey)[31]

- Marilyn French was a hard-line misandrous Feminist; she died in May, 2009. The columnist, Libby Purves, celebrated French's pathological dislike of men:

  'The human side of a man-hating feminist...Marilyn French was angry – and scary. But sometimes we need people to kick against the traces...she aimed a blowtorch straight at the collective groin of Man the Master...Salute her.'[32]

- Salute a nasty, man-hating Feminist? Here we see a prime example of modern British Feminism's true colours; an instruction from a mainstream Feminist to recognise and respect a woman who spent her life hating men. It is indicative of modern Feminism's aggression towards men...note the violent imagery attacking manhood and masculinity

***

'Misandry has not unified all feminists, to be sure, but it has certainly unified enough of them – explicitly or implicitly, directly or indirectly, consciously or subconsciously – to create a powerful movement.'[33]

What *is* this aggressive anti-male 'Movement'? Who *are* these unpleasant women who are determined to make the world worse for men? We will now turn to exposing this Feminist Movement, its ideas, aims and agenda: and exposing the mentality and psychological make-up of its adherents, the Feminists. Welcome to Part Two and Part Three.

Part Two

What *is* Feminism?

Chapter 2

Why Would Anyone Want to Disagree with Feminism?

Essentially, there are two kinds of Feminism. This chapter identifies the principles of Equality Feminism and shows why it was needed. Ideological Feminism is introduced, its elements identified and briefly discussed. It is shown that the Feminism we have in Britain today is a belief system that is ideologically-based, whereas Equality Feminism was firmly grounded within a moral and philosophical base of principles – justice, liberty, individualism and equality.

Equality Feminism

Equality Feminism (often referred to as first-wave Feminism) began with Mary Wollstone-craft, who wrote 'A Vindication of the Rights of Women' in 1792. It continued, with tracts and low-key, middle-class meetings (including men as well as women) throughout the nineteenth century. The key words for first-wave Feminism were 'liberation' and 'emancipation' – freedom and release from the oppressions and constraints imposed on women by social, cultural and economic conventions. Such freedom was unquestionably necessary if women were to be treated as equal citizens to men. The centrality of 'liberation' and 'equality' in first-wave Feminism have led to some referring to it as Liberal Feminism. Essentially, its aims were equal rights and equality of opportunity for women.

There can be no doubt that women needed liberation, emancipation and equality. For example, a father had been, until recent years, the sole guardian of a child, deciding on its education, religion and residence; he was the only one who could consent to an operation for the child; he could take the child abroad without permission but the mother could not. Wives had to reveal their income and tax forms to their husbands (whereas husbands did not have to reciprocate). A woman had to get her husband's permission for a number of actions, for example, using an inter-uterine device to prevent pregnancy.

A woman couldn't buy a house without her husband's signature. She couldn't sit on a jury because a juror had to be a householder and few women were. Women were kept out of medical school, law school and business school. There were moral double standards, especially in sexual behaviour and adultery. Wives didn't have equal access to divorce: men could obtain a divorce if their wives merely committed adultery; women could only obtain a divorce if their husbands had committed incest or adultery combined with desertion, cruelty or unnatural offences. Some inequalities and discriminations persisted until the early 1970s.

- So there were many disadvantages and discriminations that women experienced and ought not to have experienced in a liberal society. Without doubt, there was justification for a women's equality movement

The original mid-19th century concept of 'liberalism' incorporated the principle of individualism; that is, the belief that all individuals are of equal importance regardless of sex, race or religion. So Equality Feminism naturally sprung from this liberal philosophy – pronouncing that women should have the same opportunities, respect, treatment and rights as men. Indeed, the 'father' of political liberalism, John Stuart Mill, strongly supported Liberal (Equality) Feminism. The liberal concept of 'individualism' is of importance to this book's narrative because modern-day Feminism is the opposite - it is a 'collectivist' political movement, as opposed to the 'individualism' of Equality Feminism. Conceptually, as well as in their tactics and aims, the two Feminisms are very different. For example, Equality Feminists assume that the sexes have different natures and inclinations; an example being that women 'naturally' lean towards the family more than do men.

***

Equality Feminism has five basic principles:

1. Equal opportunities for women
2. Equal rights for women
3. Equal respect for women
4. Equal treatment for women
5. Equal choices for women

The above human rights are, or ought to be, fundamental to all citizens in a liberal democracy. However, before the 1970s these five concepts really did need to be addressed and fought for. I actively supported Equality Feminism and still believe in its principles, all of which have now been achieved.

Feminism Today

During the1950s and 1960s Equality Feminism gave way to a second wave of Feminism, which spawned numerous schools - Socialist Feminism, Marxist Feminism, Radical Feminism, Revolutionary Feminism, Postmodern Feminism, Lesbian Feminism, Separatist Feminism and even Psychoanalytic Feminism.[1] Unlike Equality Feminism which had a moral and philosophical base, second-wave Feminism, including all its schools, is based upon an Ideology, the central elements of which are:

- Men have all the power in society
- Men and women are basically 'the same', apart from their sex organs
- Socialist Marxism
- Lesbianism
- A belief system with ideological and political aims, and an agenda
- A desire to radically change society

- Ideological Feminism is the Feminism that we have in Britain today

Please note that henceforth, unless otherwise stated, it is Ideological Feminism to which I refer when I use the word 'Feminism'. This is the Feminism to which I was referring in Part One. In addition, any word or concept specifically related to this Feminism will begin with an upper-case letter in order to emphasise the connection; for example, Feminist Ideology and Male Feminist. Feminism itself I consider to be a political Movement, almost a 'Party' in its own right.

***

Unlike Equality Feminism, which was based upon an individual's rights and opportunities, modern British Feminism is a *belief system*, it has a dogma of tenets, it is doctrinal. These are core criteria of any ideology, as has been shown by Claire Fulenwider. Following standard social scientific usage, she defines 'ideology':

> '...an ideology is a system of beliefs (as opposed to a set of attitudes) "which describe present reality... explain present reality – that is, show how it has developed historically (and prescribe in what ways it is good or bad and posit a plan for changing present reality)".'[2]

- It will be shown conclusively throughout the book that modern Feminism has a dogma of tenets, it is doctrinal and 'plans to change reality'; that it is Ideologically revolutionary in nature and wishes to radically change British society, culture and State

It has been widely assumed that modern Feminism is a continuation of Equality Feminism. This is not so. Equality for women is not a central element of today's Feminism, in spite of its rhetoric regarding 'gender equality'.

Two Equality Feminists confirm that Ideological Feminism has little concern with equality for women and that it has man-hating at its core, as an essential ingredient of its belief system. Feminism is:

> '...not merely about equal rights for women...Feminism aspires to be much more than this. It bids to be a totalising scheme resting on a grand theory...Feminist theory provides a doctrine of original sin: the world's evils originate in male supremacy.'[3]

- So modern Feminism is Ideological – it has a 'totalising theory', is 'doctrinal' and is misandrous

Melanie Phillips, the social commentator, also notes that at the heart of modern Feminism and its driving force is the blaming of men:

> 'The unifying factor has always been the belief that men oppress women. As Coote and Campbell observed, all feminists agreed the fight was against men...'[4]

Others have also noted that Feminism is now Ideological, with its central tenet being the condemnation of men; for example:

> 'This phenomenon (misandry) did not originate spontaneously at the grass-roots level but was initiated and is still promoted by a segment of the academic elite that is affiliated with one branch of feminism. We called that branch "ideological feminism"...'[5]

- Notice that 'ideological feminism' was initiated by the 'academic elite' in the universities

Feminism's Ideological all-embracing grand theory and doctrine is that men are all-powerful and use this power to advantage themselves and to disadvantage women. This is the Feminist concept of 'patriarchy'. It is Feminism's firm doctrinal belief in the patriarchy that is at the root of present day, widespread man-hating.

Fulenwider notes the centrality of the patriarchal Ideology to Feminism:

> *'...women are unjustly treated, that they are maintained in subordinate roles and positions, and that they are consistently removed from most vital decision-making opportunities of society. Furthermore, this discrimination against and exploitation and oppression of women are seen by feminists as rationally justified by a dominant sexist ideology...'[6]*

- The 'dominant sexist ideology' is the 'patriarchy'. Feminists claim that (all) men subjugate, exploit and discriminate against (all) women

These theorists conclude that 'equality' is not the central aim of modern Feminism, even though it regularly and hypocritically uses the term 'gender equality'. It has a quite different agenda:

> *'What they want, and what they are in the process of achieving with the support of their allies and under the protection of post-modernism, is either utopian or dystopian, depending on your point of view: a radical reorganisation of society, one that requires either writing new constitutions or reinterpreting current ones.[7]*

- Like all other 20th century ideologies, Marxism, communism, Nazism and fascism, modern Feminism is radical and revolutionary. *Unlike* all other 20th century ideologies Feminism has never been questioned, challenged, analysed or critiqued by academia, the media or politicians
- This is why I refer to present-day Feminism progressing towards a Quiet Revolution

Feminism, then, seeks revolution rather than equal rights for women, equal opportunities for women, 'gender equality' for women. So on this measure, all those marching under the banner of Feminism today cannot be counted as true friends of women, or speak on their behalf. It has its own Ideological agenda, and only when that agenda accidentally coincides with ordinary women's interests can it be said that today's Feminism speaks for, and represents, the interests of the majority of women. An example of this is the following in which Cristina Odone considers the Labour Government's plans to get all women into paid employment (an aim of Feminism, making women independent of men) referring to Feminism as 'the cosy careerists' club':

GIVE WORKING MOTHERS
WHAT THEY REALLY NEED

(The Daily Telegraph, Friday, 12 March, 2010: Cristina Odone)

'If Labour had paid attention to its own national 1997-8 consultation, "Listening to Women", it would have seen that getting mothers into full-time work, and their children parked in state-run care centres, was never a vote winner.

So if Labour was not "Listening to Women", to whom was it listening? The cosy careerists' club that for too long has monopolised the public debate on what women want. This tiny elite, devoted to their high-flying, remunerative careers, are totally unrepresentative of the ordinary woman.

They are work-centred, while the overwhelming majority of women want part-time work to support their family...Because of their status, these women wield immense influence, and have been able to shape the Government's agenda. So we see Labour pumping billions of pounds of taxpayer's money into a childcare system that is unpopular with ordinary mothers; and setting up a tax system that penalises the stay-at-home mum – despite evidence that the majority of mothers of children under five want to stay at home.

They rate career above caring and believe that self-realisation comes only through professional success.'

- Feminists do not represent women
- Modern Feminism is powerful and influential
- Ideological Feminism has been the monopolistic form of Feminism in Britain since the mid-1970s

What ordinary women in Britain today stand in most need of is not liberation from male oppression but from the intellectual and political tyranny that modern Feminism has become.

***

To sum up: what we have in Britain today is *Ideological* Feminism, not Equality Feminism. There are five elements that constitute and define modern Feminism; these elements will be constantly confirmed throughout the book:

1. A belief system at the centre of which is the Ideology of patriarchy and the hatred of men
2. A belief system which claims that men and women are 'the same'
3. A belief system that embraces Marxist Socialism
4. A belief system that declares heterosexual relations undermine Feminism (the influential element of Lesbian Feminism)
5. A belief system that is radical and revolutionary

In 'Feminisms: A Reader' Maggie Humm gives a glossary of terms. Humm is Co-ordinator of Women's Studies at the University of East London:

'Feminism: the definition incorporates both a doctrine of equal rights for women (the organised movement to attain women's rights) and an ideology of social transformation aiming to create a world for women beyond simple social equality.'[8]

- What might constitute *'beyond* simple social equality...'?

These elements of modern Feminism will now be addressed in detail. The creation and widespread use of cultural misandry was observed in Part One.

Chapter 3
Feminism's Devil Weapon

This chapter explains why modern Britain hates men, and looks at the Ideology that drives this phenomenon. It also places into context all Feminist claims, demands and created issues.

The paramount idea upon which all modern Feminism's issues are based is the Ideology of 'patriarchy'. Patriarchy, according to Feminist rhetoric, actively discriminates against women and in favour of men – that is, men collectively (the patriarchy) *intentionally* discriminate against women. For tactical reasons front-line Feminists (Feminist politicians, for example) do not use the term 'patriarchy' as it sounds too dated, too revolutionary and too Ideological. For public relations reasons, these Feminists focus on the supposed *outcomes* of Britain's patriarchal system (their claims of inequalities and discriminations). Nevertheless, patriarchy is still the predominant Ideology that drives Feminism and it is used as the rationale for Feminism's agenda and social policies. For example, patriarchy is used to explain why men are paid more than women (the pay gap), and why women are under-represented in higher status positions (the glass ceiling); it is used to explain the phenomena of domestic violence, sexual harassment, pornography, prostitution and rape.

Yes, men *are* over-represented in positions of influence and power – but this numerical imbalance is not patriarchy. The *essence* of the Feminist interpretation of patriarchy is that men *intentionally* abuse their over-representation as a power to advantage themselves and to disadvantage women.

It is sometimes claimed that Feminism isn't about man-hating. This is untrue; this chapter will show that the very *essence* of Feminism is man-hating. Every Feminist issue inherently blames men, directly or indirectly, and mostly the former.

'Damn you, The Patriarchy!'

(Caitlin Moran: anti-racist, anti-homophobe, misandrist)

We have seen that today's Feminism is an Ideology. This Ideology is defined by the concept of 'patriarchy'. Patriarchy has been the sexual political Hiroshima experience for quelling men in positions of power and influence into doing Feminism's bidding. Mixing metaphors, patriarchy is the bedrock Ideology upon which Feminism is based. Patriarchy is at the heart of today's Feminism, it is its life-blood, it is the origin of its dogma, its issues and its agenda, and ultimately, its policy recommendations. So what exactly *is* a 'patriarchy'? The dictionary informs us:

Patriarchy: *'A society or social system founded by men and serving their interests alone, so they retain and inherit power, wealth, privileges and opportunities that women do not.'*[1]

And the Encyclopaedia of Feminism:

'Patriarchy is the universal political structure which privileges men at the expense of women.'

And a Feminist explains:

'(Patriarchy)...is used as shorthand for a social system based on male domination and female subordination and has become standard among feminists.'[2]

Feminists declare that:

'The goal of feminism is the overthrow of patriarchy and the ending of sexist oppression.'[3]

A Feminist lecturer, Lynne Segal, admits:

'In radical feminist theory all relations between women and men are, and always have been, determined by men's collective effort to assert and maintain power over women. This is the nature of patriarchy – the first and most fundamental power relation in all societies.'[4]

'Proving' that Britain is a patriarchy is simple for Feminists, they only have to point to the fact that there are many more men in positions of power and influence than there are women. And we have all accepted this as 'proof' that a patriarchy exists. Yet the essence of the concept of patriarchy is the *abuse* of power by men – men using their 'power' to intentionally advantage themselves and to disadvantage women. This cannot be proved because it simply isn't true. It is in fact men, not women, who experience discrimination and who are disadvantaged in modern Britain.

- If Britain really were a patriarchy would men permit the widespread cultural and institutional misandry that was identified in Part One?

***

The concept of patriarchy was first used in the second-wave of Feminism by the influential Ideological Feminist Kate Millett in 'Sexual Politics' (1969). Millett gave nine aspects of patriarchy, all of which condense to 'rule by men, for men.'[5]

Feminism sees the patriarchy not just as a few men in positions of power, but *all* men; it is *all* men, in every socioeconomic class and in all capacities who, apparently, oppress *all* women. Marilyn French states:

'The entire system of female oppression rests on ordinary men, who maintain it with a fervour and dedication to duty that any secret police force might envy. What other system can depend on almost half of the population to enforce a policy daily, publicly and privately, with utter reliability?'[6]

- 'Ordinary men' includes *you* (male reader), or *your* husband, *your* father, *your* sons and *your* grandsons...*all* the males in your family are demonised, condemned as oppressors of women. And if you think French's view is extreme, then think again; British social policy and sexual politics is based upon the Feminist Ideology of patriarchy, extensive evidence to substantiate this claim is given in Part Four

The influential Feminist Andrea Dworkin explains:

'No personal accommodation with the system of patriarchy will stop this relentless gynocide (men harming women). Under patriarchy no woman is safe to live her life, or to love, or to mother children. Under patriarchy, every woman is a victim, past and present, and future. Under patriarchy, every woman's daughter is a victim, past, present and future. Under patriarchy every woman's son is her potential betrayer and also the inevitable rapist or exploiter of another woman...That means we will have to attack and destroy every institution, law, philosophy, religion, custom and habit of this patriarchy.'[7]

- So yes, reader, Feminists *do* include *your* family's menfolk – the males in your family are the oppressors, the victimisers, the exploiters, the rapers of women

- 'We will have to attack and destroy every institution'? Here we see once again the radical and revolutionary nature of Feminism, its dedication to its Quiet Revolution

- The man-hating is self-evident

And Gloria Steinem, another doyenne of Feminism:

> 'The patriarchy requires violence or the subliminal threat of violence in order to maintain itself...The most dangerous situation for a woman is not an unknown man in the street, or even the enemy in wartime, but a husband or lover in the isolation of their own home.'[8]

- In other words, every married woman is oppressed by her patriarchal husband (we can't dismiss this as extreme – domestic violence policy is built around the Feminist claim that 'a husband is more dangerous than an enemy in wartime'). What an absurd claim: what an absurd policy; what an absurd State that embraces Feminism and implements its policies

- Feminism is very anti- the traditional two-parent family, in which, we are told, a woman's husband, partner, father, son is more dangerous than a raping, pillaging soldier. Feminism has created a thriving domestic violence Industry based upon this belief, and upon the gullibility of Male Feminists who have cravenly succumbed to its pressure. Part Four addresses the fraud of domestic violence

***

Men have become stereotyped as the 'bad people', the 'oppressors'. In discourse Feminists prefer to use the word 'male' instead of 'man' because it is more abstract and impersonal; its use allows Feminists to male-bash impersonally. They speak of '*male* aggression', '*male* dominance', '*male* violence', '*male* insensitivity', '*male* chauvinism'. When they are reviling and ridiculing the 'male sex' they can disassociate the men in their own lives from what they are saying – their *own* fathers, their *own* brothers, their *own* lovers and their *own* sons.

- Individual Feminists are constantly surprised that the particular man they love doesn't fit their repellent caricatured image

- By claiming that men are 'all the same' they are doing to men exactly what they are accusing men of doing to women – 'stereotyping' them

***

Misandry in Britain, misandry in all its forms – cultural, social, institutional – is the end-product of Feminism's success in having its Ideology of patriarchy accepted throughout all areas of society and the State. The following has been the process:

- Feminism states that Britain is a patriarchal society (a society run by men, for the benefit of men, to the disadvantage of women) and....

- In a patriarchal society men have all the power, which...

- Men use to discriminate, dominate, oppress, victimise and abuse all women, so...

- Men must be regarded as 'the bad people' (this is how we arrive at widespread misandry), which means...

- Women, who have suffered at the hands of individual men and the patriarchy (that is, *all* women) must be compensated with preferential treatment, special privileges and policy-favouritism (which, as we will see in Part Four, is what has been occurring in Britain since the late 1970s)

- The above has been the Ideological template used to determine Britain's sexual politics and social policy since the early 1980s. So in practice, in terms of the Feminist patriarchal Ideology being expressed in everyday culture and social policy, this means that:

- *Men are society's official scapegoats and are to be held responsible for all evil.* This even extends to the evil committed by *women* – because, it is claimed, these women have been deluded or 'abused' or intimidated by men and this experience is responsible for their doing bad things

- *Women are to be viewed and treated as society's official 'victims'* and are responsible for all good (for example, it must never be admitted that women are frequent perpetrators of domestic violence, mothers must be awarded custody of the children in a divorce; people find it difficult to believe that a woman would make a false allegation of rape)

- Men must be punished, even as innocent individuals, for the collective guilt of *contemporary men* and for *the actions of men throughout history*. 'Punished'? Punished via social, cultural and institutional misandry; for example, by being ridiculed, belittled, treated as disposable, blamed, condemned, made to feel guilty, and demonised; and 'punished' by having their problems, issues and rights ignored (this is one reason why there isn't a Minister for Men). Punished, also, by numerous anti-male policies

- Women must be compensated, even as undeserving individuals, for their collective *contemporary victimisation* and *for their suffering throughout history* (for example, compensated in the form of positive discrimination, quotas, the 'right' to enjoy the presumption of innocence and be believed in court in domestic violence, sexual harassment and rape cases)

So modern Feminism, interpreting British society through the perspective of the patriarchal Ideology, is predicated upon two essentials:

1. Women's 'oppression' and 'victimhood' and concomitant compensation (preferential treatment)
2. Men's blameworthiness, demonisation and punishment (misandry)

- These are the two essential dynamics (wrapped in the patriarchal Ideology) that are driving sexual politics in Britain today

To retain all these benefits, and to ensure that they *continue*, Feminists must continue convincing society and males in positions of power that Britain is a 'patriarchal' society, run by men, for the benefit of men, and at the expense of women. Feminists have been strikingly successful in this aim.

***

The wonder is not so much that otherwise sensible women have come to believe this nonsense, but astonishingly, the majority of *men themselves* believe it; and even more astonishingly (and frighteningly), actually *act* upon it. Daphne Patai, an Equality Feminist, has called such men 'honorary women' and 'grovelling men'. I use the term Male Feminist.

• By focusing on women's personal grievances, Feminism creates a kind of collective female narcissism, connecting with the myth of female moral superiority and the demonisation of men

   'Let me therefore be clear that what I am mainly criticising here is an important – and to me profoundly disturbing – aspect of feminism: its predilection for turning complex human relations into occasions for mobilising the feminist troops against men.'[9]

The belief that men as a group (the patriarchy) are bent on attacking and oppressing women as a group has become a fixed part of our conventional wisdom, even being held by those within professions and organisations that make up the British Establishment. It has become a primal obsession, a 'given' so entrenched that it is unquestioningly accepted. This universal, unchallenged orthodoxy greatly facilitates the implementation of Feminist policies.

The patriarchal Ideology is a fearsome weapon employed by Feminism. By viewing and presenting all sexual political issues through the perspective of 'the patriarchy', Feminism has been able to manipulate every dimension of the British State – politics, academia, law, the media and its culture.

***

Why has the claim that 'Britain is a patriarchy' become so widely accepted? To achieve the acceptance of its patriarchal view of society Feminism has been required to create a constant flow of horror stories showing male perfidy and female humiliation, victimisation and oppression. And so we have regular media regurgitation of 'epidemics' (timetabled to appear throughout the year...timetabled to run consecutively rather than concurrently in order to maximise the publicity value) - domestic violence against women, rape, sexual harassment; the pay gap is caused by male discrimination against women, the glass ceiling is caused by male prejudice, it is men who 'force' women to 'sacrifice their careers' by making them stay at home and care for the children. These views are always acted upon in the form of policy and legislation in a positive way for women and in a disadvantageous way for men.

***

It may be thought that the concept of 'the patriarchy' is only a product of the 1970s and 1980s and that it has no contemporary relevance. This is not so. For example, the following is a quote from The London Feminist Network's website, 2009:

   'We work closely with other groups in London, supporting various feminist campaigns in order that we can broaden our movement and work together for women's rights and against patriarchy in all its forms.'

The term 'patriarchy' is still used in contemporary Feminism, but less so than it was. This is because the more acceptable terms 'gender equality' and 'equality and diversity' (both assume that there *is* a patriarchal system) are felt to be less politically divisive, less confrontational and revolutionary, and therefore more conducive to Ideological gains in easing the implementation of agenda aims. For example, a judge might jib at being compelled to attend an 'Anti-Patriarchy Course' (to be taught that women are always 'victims' of all men and why they should receive preferential treatment in the courts), but such a judge would not jib if the course were cosily entitled (as it is) an 'Equality and Diversity Course' (the Feminist content remaining the same).

- Unsurprisingly, it has now been made compulsory for all judges to attend Equality and Diversity Courses (written by Feminists and presented by Feminists)
- Social policy is formed, and legal decisions made, in the belief that modern Britain is a patriarchy ('men are bad'/ 'women are victims and are good')

***

A further function of the patriarchal model of society is that *it releases women from any personal responsibility for their behaviour or actions* - women being the 'good' and 'oppressed' people, and men the 'bad' and 'oppressors'. This makes it acceptable for a Feminist-sympathetic State to excuse women's bad behaviour, to release them from personal responsibility.

In a society and State where it has been universally accepted that a patriarchy exists, as is so in modern Britain, men are the universal scapegoats, even for women's bad behaviour. If a woman commits a serious criminal offence her behaviour will be excused by attempting to place the blame on men – 'her father sexually abused her as a child', 'her partner has physically abused her', 'her husband/boyfriend made her do it.' If the crime was committed jointly then 'she was forced to co-operate with her male colleague.'

By stripping women of any personal responsibility for their behaviour and actions Feminism actually infantilises them, it views them as people who are too immature to know their own mind, too immature to make their own choices and, therefore, as with children, women are immune from serious punishment or condemnation. By infantilising women in this way Feminism actually disrespects women. This is not a criticism of women, it is a criticism of Feminism's *presentation* of women in sexual politics. The following is a real scenario described by a student who attended a Women's Studies course:

> *'A lot of people got triggered by "men, men, men, men, men". I remember somebody just going off and saying, "Can't you blame anything else but men?" Yeah, sometimes people got furious. In one class this girl said, "All you do is blame men. I happen to like men". And she was completely at a disadvantage, because here she was sitting in full make-up, a skirt, heels, well-done hair. Guns were drawn. She was attacked. There were mainly three people who jumped in, and they just completely cut her to pieces.'[10]*

- Feminists do not easily take criticism

The acceptance of Britain being a patriarchy permits Feminism to absolve women from blame and to shift it onto men; this process is frequently expressed in social policy (a woman choosing to become a prostitute is not *her* fault, it is the fault of men, the male sex drive or women being paid less than men). Women have been given an escape route from personal responsibility ('I didn't get the promotion because I am a woman - it was sex discrimination').

It needs to be said that not all women will use Feminist Ideology, the patriarchy, to absolve themselves from personal responsibility; such women must be respected and celebrated. However, the *option is available* for all women if they ever do choose to use it. It is to many women's credit that they choose not to.

***

Feminism now focuses not on *women's rights,* as did Equality Feminism, but upon *men's wrongs,* how women throughout history have been 'wronged' by men (and continue to be) – insisting on, and capitalising on its self-created women's 'victimhood and oppressed status'.

Ann Widdecombe is a female politician whose integrity and honesty is widely respected:

> 'I've no time for 1990s feminism. I have a lot of time for 1970s feminism which said, "Give us the equal opportunities, we'll show you that we're just as good as you, if not better than you".'[11]

• Widdecombe neatly makes the distinction between Equality Feminism and today's Feminism

Every topic that I discuss in this book is founded on the Feminist premise that women are innocent victims who must use legal and legislative measures to curb the oppressive and overwhelming power of men, and to secure 'compensatory' privileges. Feminism today has nothing to do with 'equality of opportunity' or with the ubiquitous contemporary Feminist mantra 'gender equality'.

In 'Fire in the Belly' Sam Keen notes:

> 'Ideological feminism...is animated by a spirit of a resentment, the tactic of blame, and the desire for vindictive triumph over men that comes out of the dogmatic assumption that women are the innocent victims of a male conspiracy.'[12]

• And we see this message of male sinfulness broadcast constantly

An Equality Feminist admits:

> 'But it is plain and irrefutable that much contemporary feminism is indeed marred by hostility toward men. The virulence of it varies from group to group. But the antagonism is pervasive.'[13]

What should have been a Movement to bring genuine equality between women and men, for the betterment of both, became bogged down in a sewer swamp of dogma, cant and intolerance that is today's Feminism.

***

A reader sceptical of my analysis may wish to compare the above discussion of Feminism's Ideology of patriarchy and its use as a gender-weapon with the following definition of Feminism taken from a contemporary Dictionary of Sociology:

'Feminism: 1. A holistic theory concerned with the nature of women's global oppression and subordination to men. 2. A socio-political theory and practice which aims to free all women from male supremacy and exploitation. 3. A social movement encompassing strategic confrontations with the sex-class system. 4. An ideology which stands in dialectical opposition to all misogynous ideologies and practices.'[14]

- Believing in 'men's badness' is critical to the belief in 'women's goodness' and, importantly, in her status as 'victim'; these have practical, professional and Ideological benefits for Feminists

- Logically, then, Feminism cannot *exist* without it expressing hatred for men (to a greater or lesser extent)

***

A variant of the patriarchal model of society that Feminists use to retain their privileges and condemn men is Catherine MacKinnon's 'dominance model' – a similar sexual political device to patriarchy. The dominance model was purposely fabricated to encompass and 'explain' all inequalities, discriminations and oppressions from which ordinary women are supposedly suffering. Like patriarchy, it is a catch-all concept:

'Catherine MacKinnon has offered a different understanding of discrimination, one which she calls the dominance model. This approach focuses not just on discrimination as traditionally understood, but more generally on the distribution of power in society, and on ways in which this power distribution is maintained...the dominance approach allows one to examine the structure of society and its differential effects on men and women. That structure may well be one in which women can be said to be "dominated" even if no discrimination, as commonly understood, is taking place.'[15]

The dominance model is used by Feminists to 'explain' women's supposed 'inferior position' in society and all the inequalities, discriminations and oppressions are supposed to follow from this. It is also used to deny men equality and the democratic right to have *their* problems, issues and rights represented. We saw examples of this in the Preface, with the fascistic Feminists at the University of Manchester and Oxford preventing male students from setting up a Men's Society. The dominance model, like the patriarchal model, is used to prevent the establishing of Men's Officers, Men's Units, Men's Committees, Men's Sections, a Minister for Men. I quote the Feminists at the University of Manchester:

'There is no Women's Society at the University of Manchester Student's Union. There is a Women's Rights Collective who campaign exclusively for women's liberation. We live in a patriarchal society; women form an oppressed group and men do not. Therefore, not only does it create a huge imbalance to have a Men's Society and not a Women's Society, it actually makes a mockery out of the fight for women's rights.'[16]

Men should *never* accept the Feminist claim that there is male dominance and patriarchal power in Britain. The patriarchy and dominance model are Feminist frauds, deliberate constructions to prevent men from claiming their democratic right to have their male-specific problems, issues and rights politically represented and addressed. And these fraudulent claims have been very successful; nowhere in Britain are male-specific issues represented.

Are British Women 'Oppressed'?

Many supposedly intelligent people believe that women in Britain today are 'oppressed' people who need 'liberating' from the male patriarchy. For example, we have seen that Feminist *students* at the University of Manchester declared in 2009:

> 'There is a Women's Rights Collective who campaign exclusively for women's liberation. We live in a patriarchal society, women form an oppressed group and men do not.'[17]

• And these people, these gender-warriors, will be entering professions from where they will be spreading their Ideology, their misandry

***

Oppression: 'Subjugation or persecution by tyrannical use of force or authority.'[18]

Women's 'oppression' is a central plank in Feminism's claim that Britain is a patriarchy. Melanie Phillips notes:

> 'The unifying factor (of the different forms of Feminism), however, has always been the belief that men oppress women. As Coote and Campbell observed, all feminists agreed the fight was against men... the consistent line throughout was that men oppressed women through the patriarchal traditional family.'[19]

And,

> 'Fundamentally, feminism is a political movement organised for the purpose of getting women out from under subordination.'[20]

Carol Iannone became a student on a Feminist course in the mid-1970s:

> 'I enjoyed, revelled, in the utterly systematic property feminism takes on when used as a tool of analysis, especially when to the exclusion of all others. Like Marxism, feminism can explain everything from advertising to religion by following its single thread, the oppression of women.'[21]

A Feminist declares:

> 'Systematic oppression of women isn't going to just go away. But we can change our own worlds – and others, by proxy.'[22]

The 'oppression of women' is a given. The Feminist claim that women are 'oppressed' is completely and naively accepted by the policy-making community. It is a mindset, an orthodoxy that drives gender-related social policy – in favour of women and against men:

> 'The idea that men oppress women, who therefore have every interest in avoiding the marriage trap and must achieve independence from men at all costs, may strike many as extreme and having little to do with everyday life. Yet it is now the galvanic principle behind social, economic, and legal policy-making.'[23]

• We need to ask why the Feminist message of women as victims of oppression continues to have such a gullible audience, and why does it remain the basis for a large part of our social policy? Why are policy-makers and Male Feminists so utterly credulous?

Do women in Britain *look* as if they are 'oppressed'? In answering this question we ought not to allow our belief that Feminism is a 'good thing' to paralyse our reasoning and common sense.

However often Feminists declare that Britain is a patriarchal society it doesn't make it true. This claim is a nonsense. On the one hand men are maligned, denigrated, suffer cultural misandry, experience institutional misandry, and have their problems, issues and rights ignored. On the other hand, women are *demonstrably* given greater attention and advantages in the form of preferential treatment, special privileges and policy-favouritism. How can this be construed as 'oppression'?

One sure way of determining which group is the most powerful group in a society is to compare its level of health with other groups. In *every* area of health women score over men, including suicide and death – for young men the suicide rate is four times greater than that for same-age young women. Men die, on average, six to seven years earlier than women. It is ridiculous and irrational for Feminism to claim that Britain is a patriarchy in which women are oppressed...in which men have all the power and use it to advantage themselves at the expense of women.

To assert that women in modern Britain are an 'oppressed' group which needs 'liberating' is preposterous. Look around you...are the women driving their 4 by 4s (no doubt paid for by their hardworking husbands) – 'oppressed'? Go into any of the trendy coffee shops mid-morning and see the mothers who have dropped their children off at nursery/school leisurely socialising with friends – 'oppressed'? Country clubs during the day will be peopled overwhelmingly by women – 'oppressed'? Women's fashion shops are packed with customers – 'oppressed'? More female students than male students in our universities... having achieved higher 'A' level passes – 'oppressed'?

- If we are to use the word 'oppressed' to describe the condition of women in today's Britain then what word are we to use to describe the condition of slaves during the height of the slave trade? Or the people of Malaysia today?

- To describe all women in Britain as 'oppressed' just because they are female is doing a great injustice to the genuinely oppressed people around the world

And who, then, is the more 'oppressed' – the wife of a wealthy businessman/celebrity/ footballer, or the man living rough in a cardboard box? To collectivise people into groups and to say that *all* individuals in one group are guilty (men), and *all* individuals in the other group (women) are deserving of special privileges, is a Feminist theme that will be exposed in later chapters.

- Women oppressed? 9 out of 10 people living rough are men (non-oppressors I would suggest). This is why the problem of homelessness, an overwhelmingly male issue, is never to be seen on the political agenda

Feminists use the evocative word 'oppressed' in order to continually squeeze out of politicians a better deal for themselves, and women, than for men. Take the following Feminist demand as an example:

> *'Jails must be made more woman-friendly – cleaner, safer, and more conducive to seeing one's children, and with therapy, job training and other services. But improving prisons is just treating the symptom, not the disease, of women's oppression.'*[24]

- This suggests that punishing women by imprisoning them for committing a serious crime is, according to Feminism, an 'oppression'

Feminism uses the terms: 'discrimination against women', 'oppression' and 'victimisation' in order to demand preferential treatment for women and policy-favouritism. This has been a successful strategy for thirty-five years. Health comparisons between men and women have already been noted, but need to be reiterated:

> *'There is one certain mark of oppression. Oppressors have greater access to comfort and health care, and thus live longer than their victims. In technologically developed nations since early in the twentieth century, women have outlived men by an average of eight years...It is an insult to the oppressed of the world to have rich and powerful women included within the congregation of the downtrodden merely because they are female.'[25]*

***

Britain today, for all Feminism's dogmatic and self-righteous platitudes regarding 'gender equality', is certainly *not* a patriarchy. It is difficult to see how anyone, except Feminists, can believe this nonsense. Yet we know that politicians and the policy-making fraternity do, and actually act upon this myth. Have they all been deceived by Feminism's confidence trick, the Feminist Fraud...or are they complicit in pursuing this Ideology?

Antonia Senior asks in The Times, referring her question to Harriet Harman, the Minister for Women:

> *'Enough. No more laws, no more quangos, or panels, or equality drives. We are not victims, Harriet. This is not the 1970s. How can we possibly term ourselves victims any more...Only when it suits us to keep playing the victim.'[26]*

***

To re-cap: the patriarchal Ideology, upon which today's Feminism is based, is a four-fold weapon:

- It is used to blame and condemn men and all things male (the source of misandry)

- It justifies 'punishing' men (for being 'bad people')

- It justifies preferential treatment, special privileges and policy-favouritism for women by labelling them, collectively, as being discriminated against, oppressed, subjugated, victimised and abused

- It absolves women from personal responsibility for any negative consequences of their choices, actions and behaviour a) allowing women to escape censure or punishment b) legitimising women's abusive behaviour towards men; for example, vindictive ex-wives banning divorced fathers from contact with their children

- Patriarchy is an extremely valuable weapon for Feminism, one that is used unremittingly; a valued and treasured weapon, a weapon that must be preserved at all costs. Part Four identifies the numerous strategies Feminism has devised to preserve this valued and treasured devil-weapon

I leave the last word on patriarchy, the Ideological driving force behind Feminism, to Sam Keen, who neatly sums up Feminism's manufacture, use and abuse of the Ideology of 'patriarchy':

> *'Perhaps the best rule of thumb to use in detecting ideological feminism is to pay close attention to the ideas, moral sentiments, arguments, and mythic history that cluster around the notion of "patriarchy". "Patriarchy" is the devil term, the code word for the evil empire of men, the masculine conspiracy that has dominated human history since the time of the fall. All of the great agonies of our time are attributed to the great Satan of Patriarchy. The rule of men is solely responsible for poverty, injustice, violence, warfare, technomania, pollution, and the exploitation of the Third World.'*[27]

- Feminism has ensured that men are universally blamed, condemned, demonised for all society's wrongs and ills. Modern Britain truly is a man-hating society and State

Chapter 4

Jack and Jill are the Same: Except Where Jill's Better

Something that Feminism has always argued is that there is no inborn masculinity in boys or inborn femininity in girls. Feminists argue that if we treat little boys and little girls in exactly the some way as they grow up, then their behaviour and choices will be the same. They disregard the fact that evolution has been working against this genderless idea for more than a million years. But for Ideological reasons Feminists stick to their guns and declare that essentially, boys and girls are the same.

So a major element in modern Feminism is 'sameness' – the idea that both sexes are born the same but that it is our culture, the way that boys and girls are raised (socialised) that determines how they behave and function when they become adults. This chapter explores this belief and shows how and why Feminism blames this supposed difference in socialisation for many of the inequalities that women are supposed to experience. Important to this belief is its misandrous element; Feminism blames the patriarchy (the devil weapon, again) for *deliberately* socialising girls into what it considers to be an 'inferior status'. Here we have a further reason why Feminists hate men.

This chapter looks at Feminism's 'sameness' belief system as an essential tenet in its Ideology; it has been, and continues to be, an important and influential doctrine, influencing social policy in Britain.

The Feminist Kate Millett pronounced:

> *'The sexes are inherently in everything alike, save reproductive systems, secondary sexual characteristics, orgasmic capacity, and genetic and morphological structure.'*[1]

Essentially, the Feminist argument is that men and women are born the same but are socialised to act and behave in different ways: In Feminist jargon 'sex' is biological whereas 'gender' (the way men and women operate in their everyday lives) is cultural. Feminism declares that women are socialised (by a male-dominated society and culture) into what they consider to be subordinate roles. This introduces us to two social science terms - how do we become what we are?:

- *Biological Determinism*: Our behaviour is innate, determined by natural male or female sex characteristics, so *cannot* be changed to any significant extent. Some would say, for example, that motherhood is biologically determined and that women naturally want to have children

- *Cultural Determinism*: our behaviour is not determined by our sex but by cultural forces, social conditioning and socialisation, and so *can* be changed. Feminists say that it is not natural for women to want to bear children and to care for them, and that this is simply a result of our culture which 'tells' women this

Anna van Heeswijk is the grass-roots co-ordinator for Object, a Feminist organisation, set up in 2003 to object to the 'sex objectification of women'. She declares:

> *'From birth women are conditioned to be passive and focused on fitting into ingrained sexist culture.'*[2]

Here we see the origins of one of Feminism's pet hates – stereotyping women. Women are 'stereotyped', it is said, into being mothers, carers, housewives, sex objects; and apparently, women are *made* to look and be 'feminine'. All these discriminations (Feminist-defined) it is argued, are due to women being socialised into female roles and behaviours.

- And stereotyping leads to sexism

***

The process of the Feminist belief system regarding socialising girls, which supposedly leads to sexism and inequalities against women, is complex:

- Girls are socialised into having a false consciousness that deprives them of the opportunity to make a genuine free choice. The term 'false consciousness' is a 1970s doctrine; modern Feminists still utilise the concept but now tend to call it 'learned roles' (girls are socialised into 'learned roles'). I'll use both terms

- A learned role, depriving young women of the opportunity to make a free choice, leads to young women *making* choices that disadvantage them but advantage men (as defined by Feminism, not the women themselves). Girls are taught roles, they are socialised by the patriarchal, male-dominated, culture

- Because the majority of young women are making 'female' choices then other young woman (it is claimed) feel that they, too, *ought* to make similar choices

- So because *many* women make these choices, and feel that they ought to make these choices, then, the belief system goes, they are *expected* to make these choices

- These feelings and expectations (held by both sexes) lead to women being 'sex stereotyped'

- The sex stereotyping of women leads to sexism *against* women...by men

- Bingo! Feminism has a powerful gender-weapon

This bizarre Feminist belief system has been extremely influential in policy-making, as numerous examples in this and following chapters show. For thirty years it has been deemed 'sexist' to stereotype women (in practice the term 'sexist' only applies to women – I was told on a Feminist Course that the concept of 'sexist/sexism' could not, *by definition,* apply to men).

Stereotyping women has not only become seriously politically incorrect but in some cases actually illegal. For example, the majority of women wish to have children and choose to be the primary carer. Yet it has been illegal for employers interviewing female potential employees, to inquire about their plans for having a family and their arrangements for child care. Such a question is basic business sense, even *female* employers wish to ask this fundamental question, but are forbidden to do so by politically correct laws that, under Feminist pressure, have deemed this important question sexist and illegal (because it is 'stereotyping' women as mothers and primary carers). In our Feminist-dominated society and State the Feminist Ideology trumps common sense and business efficiency.

Feminism's gender sameness/socialisation/sex stereotyping belief system, used to explain many assumed inequalities between the sexes, is misguided. It encourages women to see sexism where none exists. Worst of all it encourages Feminists and Male Feminists in the policy-making community to pursue a policy of social engineering (such as artificial quotas to advantage women). Not only is this unequal, undemocratic and discriminatory against men, but it is also dangerous. For example, the fire service has diluted its fitness and training standards for female applicants in order to allow and encourage more women to enter the service; in a rescue training/simulation exercise the women have to carry a lesser weight 'body' over a much shorter distance. Who would you prefer to rescue you/your husband/ wife/mother/father/son/daughter from a dangerous conflagration – a Feminist-installed token-woman or a fully and efficiently trained fireman? (But in a politically correct and seriously censored society we are not permitted to ask such a question...in public).

***

The sameness/socialisation/sex stereotyping belief system necessarily leads to a further bizarre element of Feminism; heterosexuality is, apparently, no more 'natural' or desirable than homosexuality and we only 'fancy' the opposite sex because we have been 'taught', socialised, to do so by the male patriarchy (I'm not making this up, this is a serious Feminist theory expressed in social policy). It is not surprising, then, to note that one of the most active and misandrous types of Feminism is Lesbian Feminism.

Changes in the social and cultural environment (the revolutionary social reorganisation and restructuring of society) to make the roles of men and women identical is a Feminist objective. Feminism has been successfully advancing an agenda that demands radical social engineering to eliminate any differences between the sexes. One of the mechanisms it uses to do this is the education system. The publisher Pergamon printed a series of works on Feminism, entitled the Athene Series. It called this series 'An International Collection of Feminist Books'. The following has been distilled from this series of books (the observant reader will note that much of Feminism's belief systems is encapsulated in these short extracts):

> *'As it emerges from these sources, feminism in its contemporary form has four central tenets:*
>
> 1. *Anatomical differences apart, men and women are the same. Infant boys and girls are born with virtually the same capacities to acquire skills and motives, and if raised identically would develop identically.*
>
> 2. *Men unfairly occupy positions of dominance because the myth that men are more aggressive than women has been perpetuated by the practice of raising boys to be oriented toward mastery and girls to be oriented toward people. If this stereotyping ceased, leadership would be equally divided between the sexes.*
>
> 3. *Traditional femininity is a suffocating and pathological response to women's heretofore restricted lives, and will have to be abandoned.*
>
> 4. *These desirable changes will require the complete transformation of society.'*[3]

Here we see the Ideological origin of many Feminist claims, grievances, resentments and issues – girls are born the same as boys but...they are *deliberately* socialised by our society to ensure that they become inferior in status to men (for example, by choosing to enter part-time jobs). It is declared that femininity is suffocating and bad for women (note that this resonates powerfully with lesbian sexuality) leading to women being treated as sex objects. A revolution is necessary to bring about a 'transformation' of society and culture

(Feminism's Quiet Revolution) to ensure that boys and girls will be socialised identically. I suggest that the reader keeps in mind these claims, distilled from a large body of Feminism's own literature, whilst reading this book; each claim can be identified within the context of contemporary Feminism's interpretation of 'women's issues'.

- Many of Feminism's 'sameness' issues are addressed (and dismissed) in Part Four

  'The gender perspective of radical feminism is easy to ridicule but it must be taken seriously. It attacks not only men but the institution of the family, it is hostile to traditional religion, it demands quotas in every field for women, and it engages in serious misrepresentation of facts. Worst of all, it inflicts great damage on persons and essential institutions in a reckless attempt to remake human beings and create a world that can never exist.'[4]

- Feminism is a serious radical and revolutionary Ideology, and yet it has been embraced by the British State, the Establishment and all political parties

So according to Feminist dogma, the statistical imbalances and disparities between men and women in senior jobs (the glass ceiling) are artificial, not due to individual abilities, talents or choices but to the different ways boys and girls are socialised.

The 'sameness' element in Feminism is essential to its revolutionary objective of removing all differences between men and women in the roles they play in society. If it can be shown that certain abilities and preferences are predominantly male and other talents are predominantly female *by nature*, then the Feminist objective is defeated. Hence, Feminists insist that the differing roles of the sexes have nothing at all to do with biology but are almost entirely due to socialisation...and, they say, what can be socialised *in* can also be socialised *out*. Once this revolutionary objective has been achieved women will appear in every profession and occupation in proportion to their representation in the population at large, that is, 50 per cent.

- It is a central objective of the Feminist agenda to re-train/re-socialise/re-construct boys and girls in order to bring about 'gender equality'
- In the meantime they demand that sympathetic (Labour/Liberal Democrat) and appeasing (Conservative) governments implement positive discrimination and quota schemes for women

***

It will be clear to the reader that Feminism's revolutionary objective of socialising boys and girls to be 'the same' is frighteningly Ideological, with overtones of eugenics and totalitarian regimes (frightening because it has been taken seriously in Britain for three decades). The Soviet Union tried to create the New Soviet Man with gulags, psychiatric hospitals and firing squads for seventy years and failed. Feminists are having a similarly corrupting effect on our culture with their weapon of moral intimidation, particularly the use of political correctness, positive discrimination and quotas for women.

- The idea that men and women are 'culturally socialised' to be 'men' and to be 'women' and that by changing the culture we can make them identical is completely absurd to anyone who is not driven by an Ideological fantasy. However, it is easy to ridicule but as a reality in British politics we need to be concerned about it

Experiments in social engineering and manipulating human nature not only failed in the Soviet Union. Those who established the phenomenon of Israeli kibbutzim had the same Ideological objective as Feminists – sexual *equality* meant sexual *identity*, and a sexual *difference* was a sexual *inequality*. For a short period the kibbutzim Ideologues attempted to raise children apart from their families and to raise boys and girls in ways that would destroy sex roles. The programme was as extreme as the most Ideological Feminist could want. But it collapsed within a few years. Boys and girls returned to their natural sex roles. An American Sociologist studied the kibbutzim, writing that he wanted:

> '..to observe the influence of culture on human nature or, more accurately, to discover how a new culture produces a new human nature...I found (against my own intentions) that I was observing the influence of human nature on culture.'[5]

We've all seen or heard (or experienced personally) tales about Feminist-sympathetic mothers who think that there are no innate differences between boys and girls...until they have children of their own. However 'Feminist' or politically correct these mothers try to be to discourage stereotyping somehow they always end up with daughters in frilly dresses and boys who are rowdy and make a lot of noise with their toy guns ('I would *never* buy my son a toy gun!' No? He improvises, using his fingers and thumb, or a suitable stick).

- Such mothers are reluctantly tempted (but never to their peer group) to explain their children's behaviour in terms of biological sex, rather than their own failure to socialise them out of stereotypical roles

One would have to be very unobservant, or very stubborn, or very much an Ideologue, to deny that some traits are more common in one sex or the other, and that these traits are innate and natural.

THE REASON BOYS LOVE TOY CARS? EVOLUTION

(The Daily Telegraph, Friday, 16 April, 2010)

'Baby boys actively choose to pay with cars, and baby girls with dolls, as soon as they are physical able to make a decision, a new study claims.

Researchers found that children favour "gender specific" toys as soon as they are able to crawl and pick them up and long before they will have been exposed to major male-female stereotypes.

Dr. Brenda Todd, a psychologist at City University London, who supervised the research, said: "Due to evolution, boys have adapted to prefer toys associated with hunting, and girls with nurturing".'

- Other researchers have reached similar conclusive results[6]

***

64

Feminism uses its sameness/socialisation/sex stereotyping belief system to explain perceived inequalities between the sexes; in doing so, it infantilises and disrespects women. For example, it declares that femininity is a 'bad thing' because it is socially constructed:

'Traditional femininity is a suffocating and pathological response to women's heretofore restricted lives, and will have to be abandoned.'[7]

- 'Will have to be abandoned' when the Feminist Quiet Revolution is completed, presumably? When this Revolution has been accomplished will there be serious repercussions for those women who *still* wish to be 'feminine'? Will they be punished by their Ideologue Sisters? Will they be sent to psychiatric hospitals to be 're-educated' if they don't comply? Yes, they will...

Jessie Bernard is a notorious anti-family iconic and influential Lesbian Feminist:

'The standards of femininity, however suitable they may have been in the past, may now be dysfunctional. They are not standards of good mental health.'[8]

- So we have a leading Feminist theorist declaring that any woman who is a non-Feminist and who wishes to celebrate her femininity has mental health problems
- How do ordinary decent women who freely choose to use make-up, and dress in feminine clothes, feel about being classified as mentally deficient? How do *they* now feel about Feminism?

The Feminist issues surrounding femininity and straight sex are examined in Part Four.

***

Feminism's socialisation argument is hypocritical. We have seen that Feminists dislike women being stereotyped – but they have no qualms about stereotyping men. Feminism abhors women being stereotyped – yet at the same time, it uses the concept of patriarchy as we have seen, to universally and consistently *stereotype men* in multiple negative ways – stereotyping them into being 'bad people', rapists, wife-batterers, sexual harassers, scoundrels – simply because they are male.

So Feminists argue that there are no natural sex differences between Jack and Jill – except where there are. We are told in one breath that 'men and women are the same' and in the next breath we are told that 'women are superior to men', or that women are innocents and essentially 'good people' whilst men are beasts and 'bad people'.

A common claim of Feminists is that women are less belligerent than men and that the world would be a better place if many more women were leaders. Again, we are constantly told that women make better managers because they have a more 'co-operative' approach than men, that they are 'less confrontational', 'less competitive', that 'women are better at relationships than men', that women are more 'sensitive' than men. These arguments are used, for example, to quota more women onto boards of directors. Yet these claims would seem to involve a strong commitment to innate natural and biological sex differences. Let's explore this hypocritical stance.

Is the supposed greater co-operativeness of women natural, or is it caused by socialisation? The claim faces difficulty on either interpretation. If female co-operativeness is natural, how are women to reach positions of leadership (which Feminism desires) the attainment of which requires competitiveness? On the other hand, if female co-operativeness is the result of socialisation, how did *patriarchal oppression* produce women's moral superiority? And if oppression *does* produce morally superior beings, then using female co-operativeness to ensure world peace, or better management, would require the *continued use* of patriarchal oppression. Yet patriarchy is a particular hate of Feminists...

- Feminism is an irrational and illogical (as well as a hypocritical) Ideology. It possesses many irreconcilable contradictions (none of which are ever challenged)

Feminism's Machiavellian machinations to engineer social change result in many hypocrisies and illogicalities. But Feminism is unconcerned about this. In modern Britain, in which it is continuing to progress its Quiet Revolution, it could demand that black should now be white or that the 'man in the moon' is, in fact, a 'Guardian-reading Feminist vegan' - and our Feminist-sympathetic governments would declare it to be so.

It should be unnecessary to say (but one can never be too careful with Feminists listening) that natural *male-female differences do not in any way suggest inequalities, positions of superiority or inferiority.* Whenever and wherever they want to women can, and do, compete very successfully with men, almost everywhere. *Equality* should not be confused with *sex identity*, as Feminism tries to do (and has been successful in doing). There will continue to be statistical disparities in men's and women's presence in many professions and in many areas and levels of society. But these disparities will be due to the freely made choices of individual men and women, as they are now. Not to the misogynistic patriarchy which, it is claimed, socialises boys to be superior and socialises girls to be inferior.

***

So the sameness/socialisation/sex stereotype belief system, a key element running through Feminism, has many cultural, economic and political facets, and affects Britain in numerous negative ways. And what has been done to restrain this bizarre but influential element of Feminism?

> *'From one angle, the attempt to create a gender-neutral society, never before recorded in human history, has been an amazing success. It has aroused virtually no open opposition...'*[9]

- We are all too fearful of Feminism, of the personal and professional repercussions if we stand up and question and challenge it; any honest analysis and critique has been closed down, censored. Political correctness is efficiently doing the job that it was introduced into Britain, by Feminists, to do. So Feminists will continue to personally benefit...and men, in the form of the patriarchal culture, will continue to be blamed and demonised.

Chapter 5

Ms. Marx and Her Brothers

So far we have seen that Feminism's aims include spreading misandry; blaming, demonising and punishing men, and privileging and policy-favouring women (where this coincides with its own agenda). This chapter looks at a darker aim of Feminism – its wish to bring about a fundamental and radical change in our society.

This revolutionary change is based upon the Marxist-Socialist ideology. Feminism and Socialism share a similar ideology. This chapter offers evidence of this. I go on to claim that so close are the two ideologies that Feminism is being used as Socialism's Trojan Horse, introducing a far-Left revolution unobserved; the Quiet Revolution.

The concept of 'collectivism' is also common to Marxist-Socialism and Feminism and acts as a further bond between the two movements. We also see how the concept of 'collectivism' benefits modern Feminism in numerous ways.

The chapter concludes with some disturbing thoughts on identity politics, and men's present inability to participate in this modern political phenomenon.

The Quiet Revolution

An Equality Feminist declares:

> *'Feminism, today, is the most utopian project around. That is, it demands the most radical and truly revolutionary transformation of society, and it is going on in an extraordinary variety of ways.'*[1]

The central theme of Socialist Feminism is that patriarchy can only be understood in the light of social and economic factors. Socialist Feminism argues that the relationship between the sexes is an essential part of the social and economic structure, and that nothing but a profound change, a social revolution, can offer women genuine 'liberation'. This is argued in Friedrich Engels's 'The Origins of the Family, Private Property and the State'. Like many subsequent Socialist Feminists, Engels believed that women's 'oppression' originates in the family:

> *'The first class oppression that appears in history coincides with the development of the antagonism between men and women in monogamous marriage, the first class oppression coincides with that of the female sex by the male.'*[2]

- Here we see a significant Ideological connection between Feminism and one of the founders of Marxism

Andrea Dworkin:

> *'Only women now remain on the left. "Far to the left, off the mainstream continuum...are women whose politics are animated by commitment to listening to those who have been hurt and finding remedies that are fair".*[3] *All men belong, moreover, to the culture of "dead white males".'*[4]

Beatrix Campbell, Feminist, university lecturer, author, social commentator:

'The development of socialist feminism as a distinct political current within women's liberation began as a response to the challenge of radical feminism. For the most part, it was made up of women who were determined not to abandon their associations with left-wing politics. They belonged, variously, to the Labour Party, the Communist Party, the International Socialists (later the Socialist Workers Party) and the International Marxist Group...'[5]

Lynne Segal, Feminist, university lecturer and author:

'Women are central to the struggle against capitalist social relations...a Marxism which does not base itself on feminism, which does not recognise the division within the working class and society as a whole necessitates a strong and autonomous women's movement, is not what we call "socialist". It will not liberate women.'[6]

Germaine Greer, Feminist, university lecturer, social commentator and author:

'Women's revolution is necessarily situationist: we cannot argue that all will be well when the socialists have succeeded in abolishing private property and restoring public ownership of the means of production. We cannot wait that long. Women's liberation, if it abolishes the patriarchal family, will abolish a necessary substructure of the authoritarian state, and once that withers away Marx will have come true, willy nilly, so let's get on with it.'[7]

Valerie Bryson, Feminist, university lecturer and author:

'The struggle for sex equality is integrally connected to the economic class struggle, full freedom for women requires the replacement of capitalism by communism.'[8]

Joan Bakewell, influential Feminist social commentator and broadcaster:

'Feminists changed the world. They came from the Left in politics and the trade union movement.'[9]

***

Feminism is much more than just being of the Left; it is *revolutionary*:

'Feminism is not concerned with Band-Aids but with a radical restructuring of society.'[10]

And the influential Gloria Steinem:

'We're talking about a revolution, not just reform. It's the deepest possible change there is.'[11]

Shulamith Firestone:

'If there were another word more all-embracing than revolution, then I would embrace it.'[12]

Sheila Rowbotham, active Socialist and Professional Feminist:

'There have been two decades of interaction between feminists and trade unionists in Britain. This has shaped its history as much as the inheritance of political assumptions from the American New Left and from European Marxist traditions.'[13]

So many influential Feminists, whose thoughts and works have directed the Movement - including de Beauvoir, Millett, Firestone, Mitchell, Chodorow, MacKinnon, Steinem, Sheila Rowbotham, Barbara Ehrenreich - identify themselves as Socialists or Marxists of some sort and advocate an all-encompassing revolution. It will have been noticed that many are employed in the universities. According to Germaine Greer:

'The forcing-house of most of the younger women's liberation groups was the university left wing.'[14]

- We see again that universities are implicated as hot-houses for Feminism, and Feminism's desire for a transforming revolution

***

Sheila Rowbotham, Lynne Segal and Hilary Wainwright wrote 'Beyond the Fragments: Feminism and the Making of Socialism'.[15] Even within the first few pages it is acknowledged that Feminism has an Ideological, philosophical, conceptual and political affinity with other Left-wing, revolutionary groups: these include Trotskyism, the New Left, Leninism, the Communist Party, International Socialism, The Socialist Labour League, the Workers Revolutionary Party, the Socialist Workers Party. These Feminists continue:

'We do realise that only a revolutionary transformation of capitalist society can overcome women's oppression, class exploitation, and all forms of social domination...the Communist party argues that it wishes to make broad alliances with an autonomous women's movement.'[16]

And,

'The International Marxist Group (the British section of the Trotskyist Fourth International), does appear to have a more consistent theory and practice in support of the need for an autonomous women's movement.'[17]

- One can see why the Labour Party (and the trade union movement) is the natural home for Feminism

However, one really needs to ask why senior members of today's Conservative Party, including David Cameron, have declared themselves to be Feminists. Are Conservative back-benchers, the constituency workers, the rank-and-file of the Conservative Party, happy with the re-alignment of Brother Dave's, and his senior Comrades', marxist-lite political views? The question requires a serious answer because these politicians now form the core of a Coalition Government.

However, Natasha Walter, Professional Feminist, appears to have no concerns about her Movement's future success:

'Feminism in the twentieth century has already achieved half a revolution. Now, as we approach the twenty-first century, it is time to look to the next half.'[18]

Feminism's declared objective is to revolutionise all aspects of British society, culture and State. This Quiet Revolution has been progressing since the late 1970s. Because of this declared objective, and its continuing success, it is legitimate to ask any woman who is standing for political office, *whichever political party she represents*, whether she is, or is not, a Feminist. Unless, of course, we actually *want* Britain to become a Marxist-Socialist Feminist State.

> 'The far-Left and Feminism are so Ideologically close that Socialism could be said to be an essential criterion, a defining element, of Feminism. The influential Feminist Simone de Beauvoir greatly admired the Soviet Union because it promised that "women would be trained and raised exactly like men".'[19]

> 'De Beauvoir is so far from alone among feminists in admiring Marxist-Leninism that this admiration, together with hostility to "capitalism", can be considered virtually a further distinguishing mark of feminism.'[20]

Feminism: Socialism's Trojan Horse

We are not just talking 'soft' Socialism with today's Feminism; its agenda is clear – it is distinctly revolutionary. This deeper, darker agenda has been cleverly disguised in order to gull the public and traditional chivalrous male politicians into believing that Feminism is a Movement 'for the betterment of women' whose aim is 'gender equality'.

I suggest that those on the Left of politics are using the 'cover' of modern Feminism, its supposedly 'just and moral cause', to promote the Socialist Revolution that eluded them in the 1960s; I refer specifically to the Labour Party, the Liberal Democratic Party, the majority of university lecturers and the trade union movement. The majority of people, including politicians and the policy-making fraternity, think that Feminism is a 'good thing' and that its aims are just and moral. We have seen that they are not. Feminism's deceit has been extremely successful. We now have a Feminism wallowing in sanctimonious self-righteousness, selling itself as a just cause concerned with, and fighting for, 'women's equality'; a Feminism whose power is therefore given a free political ride – unquestioned and unchallenged.

> '"The women's revolution is the final revolution of them all". Brownmiller wasn't interested in tweaking the system already in place. "The goals of liberation go beyond a simple concept of equality", she wrote. What Brownmiller and her radical sisters really wanted was a total transfiguration of society – politics, business, child-rearing, sex, romance, housework, entertainment, academics.'[21]

- Operating comfortably within Britain's Left-wing/liberal/progressive consensus Feminism is being relentlessly successful, achieving its 'total transfiguration of society', incrementally and inexorably progressing its Quiet Revolution
- 'The goals of liberation (the Feminism revolution) go beyond a simple concept of equality'. And so the presence of the genuine and morally-based Equality Feminism has been air-brushed from British culture and politics

Feminism is Socialism's Trojan Horse. This explains why it has been embraced so enthusiastically by the Labour Party, the Liberal Democratic Party, the trade union leadership and by academics. It is being courted by the Conservative Party because a) many are closet Feminists (influenced/conditioned by their time at university); or b) it is a cynical strategy to glean the 'women's vote'; or c) Conservatives are unaware of, or naive about, sexual politics (unlike Labour MPs, who are frighteningly bigoted on the subject).

Feminism is devious. It uses the concept of 'equality' as an innocuous, righteous 'front', a deception, a disguise for implementing its Socialist/Marxist Ideological agenda. An example of this is the behaviour of Betty Friedan, one of the disaffected women who launched modern Feminism:

'In order to attract as wide a base as possible, the sixties Leftists hid their socialist sympathies and, in some cases, actual Communist party membership. Betty Friedan is a classic case. In the book that launched the modern feminist movement – The Feminine Mystique, published in 1963 – she portrayed herself as a politically inactive housewife who simply had had enough of sexism...Forty years later, Friedan told the real story. In Life So Far, published in 2000, she recounts, "I would come into New York on my days off from the hospital and would go to Communist Front meetings and rallies...I looked up the address of the Communist Party headquarters in New York and... went into their dark and dingy building on 13th Street and announced I wanted to become a member..." Friedan's revelation that, while she may have been a bored and frustrated housewife, she had also been a member of the Communist Party, sheds some much-needed light on how left-wing politics has been masquerading as authentic feminism.'[22]

- '...how left-wing politics has been masquerading as authentic feminism': Feminism is Socialism's Trojan Horse. Feminism is not what it seems

'Socialist feminists, who represented a strong current within the Women's Liberation Movement, argued (convincingly, in our view) that there was in fact no conflict between the goals of feminism and the goals of socialism. After all, wasn't socialism about the redistribution of power and resources... Women's liberation was the rock on which socialism had to be built.'[23]

I pose the question again, are the Conservative rank-and-file, the hardworking constituency people, aware that their leaders are Feminist sympathisers; Feminist appeasers whose support for this Movement is helping to progress Feminism's Marxist-Socialist agenda, its Quiet Revolution? And now that they *are* aware of this will they, together with the back-benchers and the Party's financial backers, rein in their Feminist sycophantic marxist-lite leaders?

'We have come a long way, but we still have a long way to go'

(Feminism's revolutionary mantra)

Feminism's 'Us' and 'Them' Mentality

The Marxist-Socialist ideology is a 'collectivist' ideology; that is, it sees society as a duality, an 'us and them' *confrontation* – a 'class war', the working class versus the bourgeoisie, each looked upon as a group, a 'collection' of similar types of people. Feminism is also a 'collectivist' Ideology. The two complement each other – 'women versus men', with men (the bourgeoisie) dominating women (the working class) giving rise to the patriarchal Ideology ('men are bad people'/'women are good people': 'the bourgeoisie are bad people'/ 'the working-class are the good people'). The following comments give an indication of the Feminist 'us and them' Ideology.

'Ideological feminism is a collectivist movement, which is why adherents make claims about women or men as a class. They must explain away individual women who disagree with this or that claim – and there are many in some cases – as the victims of "false consciousness" and thus the dupes of men.'[24]

71

- In other words, the many women who don't believe in Feminism have been 'socially conditioned' by men to accept having a stereotypical female role in society. I have already addressed Feminism's claim that 'men and women are the same' and that it is 'socialisation' and conditioning ('false consciousness') by the patriarchy that makes women accept, and be happy in, 'inferior' roles and jobs than men. How Feminism uses and abuses (literally) these non-Ideological women will be addressed in Part Four

Erin Pizzey, the Equality Feminist who opened the first refuge for battered women, attended a meeting run by Ideological Feminists in the late 1970s; she noted:

'We were told that we were to call ourselves a collective, to refer to each other as "comrades" and pay three pounds ten shillings to join the Women's Liberation Movement. There were posters of fierce women waving guns over their heads and a very large portrait of Chairman Mao on the wall. The violence of the posters upset me because I was a child born in 1939 – a child born into a terrible war.'[25]

***

Ideological Feminism seriously dislikes Equality Feminism because of its political 'liberal' element. We have seen that central to liberalism is the belief in the principle of 'individualism', the belief that all individuals are of equal importance regardless of sex, race or religion. This stress on individualism makes it impossible for Ideological Feminists to get women to act *collectively* (as a group) against men, or to act *collectively* to demand and benefit from special privileges (as a group). With the individualism of Equality Feminism the common bond of Sisterhood (as Feminists see it) is lost. 'Sisters Against Patriarchy', 'Women Against Rape', 'Women Against Violence', and so on. As we will see in Part Three, political bonding is an integral part of today's Feminism. Feminist organisations, Feminist Interest Groups, Feminist university departments, are all built on the Socialist and Feminist Ideology of 'collectivism'. As well as seeing women as a 'collective' group Feminists also see men as a 'collective' group – the patriarchy, the enemy.

Because Feminism is a 'collectivist' Ideology it is a mystery why the *Liberal* Democratic Party is so sympathetic to it: maybe it's been gulled like everyone else, or just don't understand the essential nature of Feminism...or perhaps it isn't concerned about Feminism's deeper, darker and revolutionary agenda (perhaps even supporting this). Or perhaps Liberal Democrats have simply become disorientated and befuddled in the idiotic race to become Britain's most 'progressive' political party?

A 'collectivist' Ideology is a dangerous Ideology. It focuses on group rights rather than on individuals' rights. In this way modern Feminism is far removed from the original Liberal/Equality Feminism that focused on the equality of individuals, as in the 'equality of opportunity', on an individual's skills, talents and abilities. With 'collectivist' Feminism the rights and responsibilities of the individual are lost – to be replaced by 'group rights' (as expressed in quotas for women in certain professions), and 'group protection'. To make the point again, according to Feminism no *individual* woman can have 'personal responsibility' because she is a member of a *group* that is being discriminated against, oppressed and victimised; whatever negative experience she has, it is never her fault but is due to the fact that she is a member of 'womankind':

'The spiral down and away from individual liberty can be traced directly to the rejection of the rights of each person in favour of the rights of the many. This group-rights mentality is nothing new; it derives from the "progressive" concept that the individual must submit to what is best for everyone

else. This concept, however, stems not from the ideal of civil rights but from the well of socialism, the foundational model of the Far Left. Once we accept group theory, it becomes not only easier to reject individual rights (such as freedom of expression) but also actually essential that we do so.'[26]

- In addition to absolving women from personal responsibility 'collectivism' insulates the members of the 'victim group' from any kind of criticism which might well apply in any other situation. It does this by claiming that anyone who questions or challenges the status quo (that women are victims and oppressed) is himself or herself an oppressor (by the very fact of questioning and challenging). Clever stuff.

With the widespread and unquestioning acceptance of Feminism in modern Britain the concept of 'collectivism' has produced a society and State that believes that one group (men) is always in the wrong – they are the 'oppressors' (the 'bad people'), whilst the other group (women) is always in the right – as they are the 'oppressed' (the 'good people'). And so we have a situation where a woman's word becomes law – it is *she* who must be automatically believed in any gender conflict, not the man (domestic violence, rape, sexual harassment). The man's word is of no value, of no worth. And so we see how social, cultural and institutional misandry is sown and spread. A 'collectivist' society is a society in which reverse-discrimination is morally right, a society that has jettisoned 'equality of opportunity' for 'equality of outcome'; a society that has abandoned the concepts of fairness and justice in sexual politics and gender issues. A society that hates men.

- 'Collectivism' therefore makes it easier (morally and with public acceptance) to blame, demonise and punish the group which is supposedly doing the oppressing and the victimising

Feminist 'collectivism' is responsible for the labyrinth of positive discrimination programmes for women allowing them widespread preference and policy-favouritism. Modern Britain has lost sight of the concept of the individual responsibility of women. If women fail in an endeavour Feminism has *taught* them to believe that this is because of their sex, not because of the inadequacy of their abilities or experience. For example, anti-discrimination laws have been gradually revolutionised so that they are no longer confined to simply prohibiting discrimination against individuals because of their group membership – they now call for *proactive* preferential treatment for people defined by their group identity. And so we now have a situation where it is legal (and encouraged) to give preference to women over men in job interviews.

- And British Sex Discrimination laws have been designed to accommodate and encourage this Feminist sexual political teaching

Feminism's 'collectivist Ideology' is a valuable asset, and as such is carefully nurtured and promoted into the public and political consciousness; for example, women are always referred to by Feminists as being a single entity...'women...'. We never hear a Feminist refer to '*some* women...'

The Austrian philosopher F. A. Hayek noted (1944):

'Collectivism has no room for the wide humanitarianism of liberalism but only for the narrow particularism of the totalitarian.'[27]

***

73

And what of the future?

The 'collectivist' dimension of Feminist Ideology has become entrenched since the late 1970s. It will ultimately result in the polarisation of the sexes, culminating in group-identity politics; men on the one side (if they ever manage to summon up any sexual political nous) and women on the other side (who have benefited from the sexual political nous of Feminists for three decades). This phenomenon is already seen in the political behaviour of many Feminist-sympathetic women. For example, women voters will vote for a female candidate because she is a woman (a member of their own group; we saw this in the U.S. when Hillary Clinton ran for the Presidency) but today men wouldn't think of voting for a man simply because he was a man (they might, in the past, preferred not to have voted for a *woman*, but that is a different, and dated, phenomenon). Men are not conscious of themselves as a 'political collective group'. Feminists have been benefiting from group-identity politics for many years. Sadly, with regard to sexual politics men are gormless Neanderthals, fighting a 21st century sex war with a stone-age mentality and with stone-age weapons.

- So here we see an interesting phenomenon of Feminism's 'collectivist identity' politics – the fact that a) men are unaware of women's 'political collectivist group identity', and b) men are unaware that *they themselves* are devoid of such a powerful political weapon

Feminists see women as a collectivist sexual political group to be advantaged; they see men as a collectivist sexual political group to be blamed and punished. But on the other hand, men do not see *themselves* as a collectivist sexual political group, nor do they see women as a collectivist sexual political group. This means that men cannot, and certainly do not, individually bond as a sexual political group in order to protect themselves and their rights against an influential, powerful and longstanding and well organised Feminist political and Ideological Movement.

Because of this male phenomenon, this weakness, men in modern Britain are politically unprotected and politically unrepresented. In this way men are at the mercy of Feminism with this being one of the main reasons why Feminism has been allowed for so long to abuse its power – men's political innocence in failing to coalesce into a political collectivist grouping. Here we have a major reason why modern Britain has been permitted to hate men, a misandry expressed in every dimension of society, culture and policy-making.

- Men are not yet mentally or ideologically equipped to participate in sex identity-politics, and so they will continue to experience misandry and institutional discrimination. Yes, some men may get angry at their individual treatment (with a messy divorce, for example) – but this has never developed and formed into a strong *political* 'collectivist' men's movement. It would be good to know if young men, particularly students, became motivated enough to form such a movement using the knowledge, facts and research with which this book arms them

***

A revisit to a definition of Feminism, given by Maggie Humm, Co-ordinator of Women's Studies at the University of East London:

'Feminism: The definition incorporates both a doctrine of equal rights for women (the organised movement to attain women's rights) and an ideology of social transformation aiming to create a world for women beyond simple social equality.'[28]

- 'a social transformation beyond simple social equality...'. This refers to Feminism's Quiet Revolution
- The reader won't need me to point out that we again see the complicity of our universities in cultivating and disseminating Feminist (revolutionary) Ideology. Why is this permitted in a democracy? Answer: because with regard to sexual politics Britain is *not* a democracy but a totalitarian State with a one-party system – the Feminist 'Party' (and as in all one-party States, it abuses its power)

The Labour Party is the natural political home for Feminism; post-1997 Labour governments relished implementing the Feminist agenda. But it is ironic, and worrying, that David ('insult fathers, they have no voter-value') Cameron, the present leader of the Conservative Party, has declared himself to be a Feminist. In this sense he has become the first Marxist-leaning leader of Toryism. Baffling. A number of his senior team are also closet Feminists, including George ('families don't need fathers') Osborne and Michael ('always blame men, because they never fight back') Gove.

- And no political party has ever considered introducing a Minister for Men. Some equality, some democracy

***

The successful, unchallenged progression of the Socialist-Feminist Quiet Revolution impacts negatively on men. The more cultural, legal and political power Feminism continues to gain the more our compliant State will be manipulated into implementing the Feminist agenda. The cultural and institutional spread of misandry will continue.

- Considering the evidence in this chapter I would like male readers to understand that a vote for the Labour Party is a vote for the Feminist 'Party'; in this sense it would be a masochistic vote. But what do we do about the Conservatives? More to the point, what will *Conservatives* do about the 'Conservatives'...?

Chapter 6

The Power of Lesbian Feminism

A Feminist belief system that is held by a number of Feminists and is politically powerful is Lesbian Feminism. This chapter is not an attack on lesbianism. I have no personal difficulty with lesbians or lesbianism as a sexual orientation. But if I am to be consistently honest in my analysis and show how and why the developed world hates men by exposing Feminism then I cannot avoid the political lesbian dimension. So to put it in context, although I have no issue with lesbianism itself I *do* have an issue with politically driven man-hating Lesbian Feminism. This faction has an inordinate amount of cultural, political and policy-making power, and as we will see, approximately one-third of Feminists are lesbians. The post-1997 Labour governments were particularly active in promoting Lesbian Feminists into positions of policy-making power.

This chapter explores Lesbian Feminism; its influence within the Feminist Movement and its misandry. Some would say that my analysis is not politically correct. I would argue that it is legitimate to identify those who regard men as their enemy. If I were a black guy I would want to know what kind of person joins a racist organisation or gang; if I were a Jew I would want to know what kind of person is involved in anti-Semitism and from where they derive. Peter Tatchell, the leading gay rights advocate, has a right to identify members of any group that *particularly* and actively hates gay people. And as it is with racism, anti-Semitism and homophobia, so with misandry.

'Men are the enemy. Heterosexual women are collaborators with the enemy.'[1]

Many Lesbian Feminists are also Socialist Feminists. Erin Pizzey, accompanied by some of the women from her refuges, attended a number of meetings run by Ideological Feminists. She notes:

> *'We were astonished and frightened that many of the radical lesbian and feminist activists that I had seen in the collectives attended. They began to vote themselves into a national movement across the country.'*[2]

Sheila Jeffreys, author, lecturer and Lesbian Feminist, comments:

> *'Every woman who lives with or fucks a man helps to maintain the oppression of her sisters and hinders our struggle.'*[3]

Adrienne Rich, lecturer, author and Feminist:

> *'Woman-identification is a source of energy, a potential spring-board of female power, violently curtailed and wasted under the institution of heterosexuality.'*[4]

The influential Lesbian Feminists Beatrix Campbell and Anna Coote are quoted:

> *'They (British Radical Feminists) insisted that women's personal and political autonomy could be safeguarded only if women's relationships with men were severely curtailed: "As long as women's sights are fixed on closeness to men, the ideology of male supremacy is safe". As for sex, they concluded that "liberation for women is not possible as long as vaginal sex is accepted as the norm rather than as a possible variation".'*[5]

- Anna Coote was employed as a Feminist adviser to the Labour Party's Minister for Women immediately it gained power in 1997

- Coote's partner, Beatrix Campbell, is a Professor at Newcastle University, and has been for many years. She has the opportunity to influence generations of students (who generally believe what their lecturers tell them) into the Feminist Ideology – including, one supposes, that part of it which advocates hating men. There are literally thousands of Feminists teaching in British universities. I have spoken to very many students over the years asking them about their university experience; the vast majority agreed that their university was 'Feminist'

HOW I WENT FROM COMMITTED LESBIAN TO A HAPPILY MARRIED MUM OF FOUR

(Daily Mail, Saturday, 26 June, 2010)

'Tim was incredibly bright and extremely good looking. He was my first love and we had a passionate physical relationship.

But as I reached 22 I realised that the people I liked best were all women and in truth always had been, if only on a friendship basis.

I had studied feminist literature at university and it opened my eyes to the possibility of sexuality as a life choice.'

- One wonders exactly what is being 'taught' on these Feminist courses

Lesbian Feminism has a great deal of cultural, academic and political power. One Equality Feminist admits:

'Small though they are in number, the convert lesbians, with what seemed a holier-than-thou brand of feminism, exerted a powerful influence.'[6]

Campbell and Coote again:

'A precept which unites all radical feminists is that the fight for women's liberation is primarily against men: they see it as overriding all other struggles and are deeply suspicious of any attempt to link it to a wider political strategy. The question then is whether one is fighting in order to destroy masculinity as a social construct, and so transform men as human beings, with a view to developing a harmonious relationship in which they wield no power over women; or whether one seeks to end the necessity of the biological distinction by establishing ways of living and reproduction which are entirely independent of men.'[7]

- Here we encounter again the Feminist belief in 'sameness'. These Feminists are suggesting that 'maleness' could be 'socialised out' of men, that 'masculinity could be destroyed' by a social and cultural revolution

- An unpleasant and condescending view of half the population: 'problematic men need to be "transformed as human beings"'. Again we see Feminists flirting with eugenics and the social engineering usually only associated with communist and fascist regimes. These malicious Feminists wouldn't dare make such a vile comment about any other group in society, for example, the disabled, black people or Jews. And would they advocate that 'gayness' (their own brand of sexuality) should be 'destroyed' or 'transformed', as some far-Right Christians have done? Again we notice Feminist irrationality, hypocrisy and double standards

Sheila Jeffreys again:

> 'Our definition of a political lesbian is a woman-identified woman who does not fuck men...Men are the enemy.'[8]

So for the Lesbian Feminist, 'straight' sex is political; a man and woman making love is an Ideological act, with the woman betraying her sex.

As Rosemarie Tong, in 'Feminist Thought', confirms:

> 'For the Lesbian-Feminist, it (sex) is not private; it is a political matter of oppression, domination, and power.'[9]

- So Lesbian Feminists, especially, hate men

***

Most of the seminal Ideological Feminist authors are lesbian. Their texts are noted for their anti-male virulence. As an exercise, I invite the reader to check the truth of this. It is an important point when considering why contemporary western societies hate men, because their misandrous message carries into policy-making in the form of advantaging women (mainly Feminists themselves) whilst demonising and blatantly discriminating against men.

I'm not suggesting that *all* lesbians are Feminists, they certainly are not. But what I am suggesting, on the evidence of my reading and personal experience, is that those Feminists who *are* lesbian appear to be the most *aggressively misandrous*, and tend to hold leading roles in women's groups and organisations.

I need to emphasise again that I have no problem with lesbianism as a sexual orientation. But I do have a problem with a Lesbian Feminist Ideology whose aim is to discriminate against, to condemn and to demonise me and all my fellow men: like the BNP...I have no problem, being a democrat, with its having a *political presence*, but I do have a problem with its members insulting or harming black, ethnic and gay people.

***

It is very much a part of the Feminist agenda to encourage lesbian involvement in their Movement. In their thirteen-point agenda for Feminism, Jennifer Baumgardner and Amy Richards urge Feminists...

> 'To support and increase the visibility and power of lesbians and bisexual women in the feminist movement, in high schools, colleges, and the workplace. To recognise that queer women have always been at the forefront of the feminist movement.'[10]

***

In the 1970s and 1980s many towns and cities had 'consciousness raising groups', whose aim was to teach women how they were being subconsciously socialised by a male-dominated society into being oppressed (the belief system of 'sameness' and 'false consciousness'). The groups were used to indoctrinate women into the Feminist Ideology. I have researched these groups, speaking to women who attended them. Many were run by Lesbian Feminists. I was told by a number of women (from different areas) that one of the 'training exercises' they had to engage in was for each member to take a mirror to the group so that they could inspect their own vaginas...and then those of other members. One can imagine why these groups were extremely popular with lesbians; stories of same-sex partnerships developing were commonplace.

- I'm not making this up. If any reader disbelieves me let him or her do their own research on these 'consciousness raising groups'

On this subject Kathleen Parker observes:

'All across the nation, women were getting a gander of what only their doctors had seen before...For those women not quite able to grasp the concept, Vulva Sherpas were invented...a young woman is lying on the floor sans britches and with her speculum properly situated. Another woman is perched in the bird's-eye view seat, holding a mirror so that her supine sister can view Her Very Own Self.'[11]

- One very attractive woman I know, a Julie Christie look-alike, was pestered to death by Feminists in the late 1970s to join a 'consciousness raising group' in a country house near Bath

Kathleen Parker continues:

'From sister helpin' sister came the vagina mirror party in Fried Green Tomatoes, in which Kathy Bates joins a gathering of other culturally oppressed women to admire their vulvas. Their bottoms unsheathed beneath skirts, the gals gamely perch over mirrors as the group leader guides them through one of the most memorable scenes in movie history: "And tonight, we're gonna begin to explore our own femaleness by examining the source of our strength and our separateness. Our vaginas. So if y'all just slip off your panties and straddle your mirrors".'[12]

- Promoting your sexual politics whilst sexually pleasuring. A really neat combination:

'So what do you call a group of women displaying their sex organs, massaging one another, and having group orgasms? Bingo! A lesbian orgy!

But because they're women scuttling male oppression through self-expression, we're supposed to pretend that it's, oh, I dunno, feminist liberation sexology. Throw in an ism and an ology and you can justify nearly any narcissistic perversion.'[13]

***

Lesbian women have always been at the forefront of the Feminist movement, driving misandry side by side with their Socialist Sisters, and both belief systems denounce marriage. The Leeds Revolutionary Feminist Group in a paper entitled: 'Political Lesbianism; The Case Against Heterosexuality' states, with regard to heterosexual intercourse:

'Only in the system of oppression that is male supremacy does the oppressor actually invade and colonise the interior of the body of the oppressed...Penetration is an act of great symbolic significance in which the oppressor enters the body of the oppressed...its function and effect is the punishment and control of women...every act of penetration for a woman is an invasion which undermines her confidence and saps her strength.'[14]

Lesbian Feminists hate the idea of heterosexuality, and by extension, the institution of marriage. Valerie Bryson, lecturer, author and Ideological Feminist:

'Many modern radical feminists share this hostility to heterosexual intercourse, which they see as inherently oppressive to women; lesbianism rather than chastity is however now the more commonly preferred solution.'[15]

And,

'...liberation for women is not possible as long as vaginal sex is accepted as the norm rather than as a possible variation.'[16]

Apparently, men make women marry them so that they can then subjugate and enslave them:

'(Marriage is) imposed upon women for the benefit of men, as a means of dividing and controlling women and ensuring that they serve men domestically and emotionally as well as sexually...the rejection of heterosexuality is therefore...a political act that strikes at the very heart of patriarchy.'[17]

Lesbian Feminism seriously dislikes the institution of marriage; so much so that it advocates women living apart from men – the Feminist belief system of 'separatism'. In 1998 Janet Dixon's 'Radical Records: Perspectives on Thirty Years of Lesbian and Gay History', was published. Dixon states:

'It is my belief that without us, feminism would never have been more than a caucus of the broad Left. Separatism was right there in the middle, influencing all women...What we separatists did was to reduce the very complex set of circumstances which combine to oppress women, to a single uncluttered issue. That is the stark injustice of the total humiliation of women on all levels by men.'[18]

And the Lesbian Feminists Campbell and Coote declare (after wondering whether maleness should be eradicated):

'...whether one (Feminism) seeks to end the necessity of the biological distinction by establishing ways of living and reproduction which are entirely independent of men.'[19]

- Feminists wish to see artificial ways to reproduce, rather than sexual intercourse between men and women. And scientists are now seeking such methods

***

Lesbian Feminists, then, are a powerful driving force in modern Feminism, directing much of its agenda and policy-making. In 2010 we read in the Women's Resource Centre Winter Newsletter:

'Lesbian and bisexual women have traditionally been almost invisible in the history books. However, these women have been heavily involved in both the Women's Liberation Movement and the lesbian, gay, bisexual and trans (LGBT) movement as campaigners and activists.'[20]

- So Feminism's Quiet Revolution also includes a revolution in sexual orientation, reproduction and 'families'. Readers might have noticed evidence of this in successive Labour Government's policies since 1997 (for example, offering IVF treatment on the NHS to lesbian couples – 'no father required'...men are disposable)

***

Lesbian Feminists seriously dislike marriage. Lesbian Feminists seriously dislike heterosexual relations. Lesbian Feminists seriously dislike men. It is the powerful influence of Lesbian Feminism that accounts for Feminists seriously disliking men looking at, and appreciating, attractive women ('objectifying women', in misandrous Feminist-speak). Lesbian Feminism goes further, it seriously dislikes women being feminine and wearing make-up and clothes that make them look attractive; the caricature of Feminists wearing Doc Martin boots and dungarees is a cliché – but has a strong kernel of truth which holds a heavily doctrinal message. The Lesbian Feminist Jessie Bernard again:

'The standards of femininity, however suitable they may have been in the past, may now be dysfunctional. They are not standards of good mental health.'[21]

- So women who wish to look attractive and feminine, according to Lesbian Feminism, are suffering from mental health issues
- The Lesbian Feminist issues of femininity, sex objectification, and the sex industries are explored in Part Four

In fact, Lesbian Feminists seem to dislike heterosexual women, full stop. We saw this in the politics of the Greenham Common Women's Peace Camp during the 1980s:

'According to some women who spent time there, Greenham was "taken over" by a powerful lesbian contingency which managed to intimidate heterosexual women and which used the camp to dwell on political ideas which were nothing to do with peace.'[22]

Ann Pettit, one of the earliest Greenham campers, gave an interview in 1986 for a tabloid paper, in which she spoke of how *'...it became a haven for nutcases and women trying to escape from hideous realities. This was not what we had come for. The camp became increasingly separatist and husbands couldn't come to visit with children'.*[22]

- Under the disguise of a 'peace movement', Lesbian Feminists expressed their dislike of heterosexual women by bullying them (ironic, in a 'peace' camp); they expressed their dislike of men by bullying them also – by denying fathers access to their children; having a captive audience, these 'nutcases' propagated their Feminist Ideology 'which had nothing to do with peace' (very much like the unethical behaviour of Feminists lecturing in our universities, to their captive audiences of young, impressionable students)
- Lesbian Feminists punishing men by not allowing them to see their children? Who is oppressing who here?

So Lesbian Feminists seriously dislike 'straight' women who exhibit femininity. They seriously dislike the institution of marriage. They hate men. Correction. They hate *maleness*, that is, 'straight' men. Gay men are accepted into the Feminist fold as allies, as 'Complementary Feminists'. It is *masculinity* and *male characteristics* that are seriously disliked. This dimension of misandry is an interesting phenomenon that needs to be further explored (but won't be as it is too politically incorrect).

'The question then is whether one is fighting in order to destroy masculinity as a social construct, and so transform men as human beings...'[23]

- Apart from the fascist-like eugenics, notice the reference to 'socialisation' here – masculinity is 'socially constructed', according to Feminism (as is femininity)

***

Lesbian Feminist power is universal. Erin Pizzey, having done so much for battered women, was treated despicably by Lesbian Feminists:

'I was asked to visit New Zealand in 1978 and I had hoped to be invited to speak to groups involved with refuges in Australia. At that time New Zealand had not yet fallen into the arms of the totalitarian women's movement (it has now), but I was denied a visit to Australia because the militant lesbian movement there had control of most of the refuges. Since, as in many other countries, the lesbian movement was in control of most of the financing, they merely instructed the Australian refuges to withdraw their invitations.'[24]

Ideologically driven Lesbian Feminists have immense cultural, academic, political and institutional power that is used wherever possible not just to grab government 'minority group' handouts (including national lottery money), cultural advantages and policy-favouritism for Feminists, but is also used to humiliate, demonise, hurt and harm men – for the driven Lesbian Feminist 'men are the enemy'.

***

Before leaving this chapter I would like to make two further observations. It was seen in the Preface that in 2010 a male student at the University of Manchester attempted to set up a Men's Society. The NUS and Feminist groups strongly opposed men having this equality (there were already Feminist Groups). A powerful group that opposed the Men's Society was the Lesbian, Gay, Bi and Trangender (LGBT) group:

'Just wanted to say well done on starting the No group to UMSU Men's Society...I was shocked and appalled to hear about this...There is no place or need for a Men's Society or officer in Student Unions anywhere in the UK and people need to stand up and make their voice heard regarding this issue. Tara Hewitt: NUS LGBT Committee Trans Rep; NUS LGBT National Campaigner of the Year; Liverpool Guild of Students LGBT Officer.' (Women's Place)[25]

• The hatred of the male is palpable. It is 'shocking and appalling' that men should want space to discuss their male-specific problems, issues and rights; 'there is no place in the UK for men to have equality'. And this attitude pervades, and is given expression, throughout our culture and political system

• LGBT man-hating groups are supported and funded by the NUS and by their host universities

The authors of 'Reclaiming the F Word: The New Feminist Movement', undertook a survey of over 1000 Feminists. One of their findings was that 37 percent were lesbian, bisexual or other.[26] This is a large percentage and explains, together with a seriously misandrous attitude, why Lesbian Feminism is so powerful a force in the Feminist Movement; it is one explanation why this Movement has man-hating at its core.

Chapter 7

So What Happened to Equality Feminism?

This chapter is a lesson in Feminist skulduggery. Equality Feminism was hijacked, stolen, thieved, robbed – usurped by Ideological Feminists. Here we observe the true nature of today's Feminists. We get a flavour of their strategies and their ruthlessness. The chapter also shows how modern Feminism has disguised its essential character, using the moral base of Equality Feminism to give it a veneer of respectability; it shows how its rhetoric of 'gender equality' has disguised its revolutionary and misandrous agenda. It is seen how this deception has been successfully achieved, and how it has allowed today's Feminists to enjoy special privileges, whilst spreading misandry.

I wish the reader to note that the remarks made in this chapter regarding modern-day Feminists are not made by misogynistic or sexist males but by *women*, by Equality Feminists and female commentators.

Equality Feminism was Hijacked

There is a widespread belief that modern Feminism is a Movement to better the condition of women. This is not so:

> *'Contemporary feminism is also a literary movement, a movement of lesbian advocacy, and, above all, a vast effort of cultural propaganda directed against what are usually viewed as the positive bases of the human condition: family, motherhood, gender, and the love between the sexes...Feminism took a wrong turn at the very beginning, with Betty Friedan's anti-feminine complaint in The Feminine Mystique, and went completely off course just as it emerged from sixties radicalism as a national movement. What should have been a movement to uplift women, and men, bogged down in a fever swamp of dogma and intolerance.'*[1]

Erin Pizzey opened Britain's first refuge for battered women in the early 1970s. Pizzey was the first second-wave Feminist in Britain to *actively* work, hands-on, for women's rights. She visualised that her brand of Feminism, Equality Feminism, would encompass the needs of women who required help, but her work was stolen, hijacked, by Ideological Feminists. In Pizzey's own words:

> *'I believe that vision was hijacked by vengeful women who have ghetto-ised the refuge movement and used it to persecute men. Surely the time has come to challenge this evil ideology...'*[2]

- Note the character and mentality of modern Feminists – 'vengeful women' (Part Three exposes the Feminist's mentality and psychological make-up)

After running refuges for battered women for a number of years Pizzey could see that Ideological Feminism (what she calls the women's movement) was becoming ever more powerful:

> 'By this time I had attracted the two things that the women's movement wanted: a just cause to clothe their political agenda and money to fund this agenda...I could see that the feminist movement everywhere had hijacked the whole issue of domestic violence to fulfil their political ambitions and to fill their pockets.'[3]

- For 'a just cause to clothe their agenda' read 'a moral base with which to disguise their true aims'. A social, cultural and political Trojan Horse...accepted in good faith by public and politicians alike, was drawn into the State and offered special privileges and policy-favouritism...opportunities to progress its Quiet Revolution...offered cultural and institutional means to spread misandry...A successful and hugely beneficial deception

Because she refused to accept the aims and agenda of Ideological Feminists, Pizzey was excluded from every part of the women's Movement and her work was sidelined. She was ostracised (worldwide) by women's organisations:

> 'I was denied a visit to Australia because the militant lesbian movement there had control of most of the refuges. Since, as in many other countries, the lesbian movement was in control of most of the financing, they merely instructed the Australian refuges to withdraw their invitations.'[4]

Wherever she did manage to get a speaking engagement she was spat on and harassed. Pizzey, the woman who opened the first women's refuge and tirelessly worked for, and with, abused women, concludes:

> 'However, the ideology of feminism today goes far beyond the original and widely supported goal of equal treatment for both sexes.'[5]

It may be claimed that Pizzey has a chip on her shoulder, an axe to grind. Not so. Two Ideological Feminists confirm Pizzey's analysis of what happened. It has already been noted that Anna Coote was an adviser to the Minister for Women in the post-1997 Labour governments, helping to formulate social policy; and that Beatrix Campbell is a senior lecturer at Newcastle University. Both are obviously in influential and powerful cultural and political positions:

> 'The Women's Aid Federation, to which almost all groups who run refuges belong, operates quite separately from Erin Pizzey's Chiswick outfit. It has its own headquarters, its own non-hierarchical structure and explicitly feminist objectives. Its aims include the demands of the women's liberation movement.'[6]

- So Erin Pizzey's version is corroborated – those who hijacked her funding and moral base *did* have 'explicit feminist objectives...and demands' of their own to pursue

It is legitimate, then, to ask whether the primary aim of today's Feminists in the Women's Aid Federation (the leading organisation in Feminism's domestic violence Industry) is *to care for women* or *to promote their own personal agenda*, their 'explicitly feminist objectives and demands'...their Ideology. Feminism's domestic violence Industry will be exposed as a fraud in a later chapter.

***

Others noted the hijacking of Equality Feminism:

'Kathleen Parker argues that the feminist movement veered off course from its original aim of helping women achieve equality and ended up making enemies of men.'[7]

And,

'As Joan Kennedy Taylor has recently observed, "originally, in the early nineteenth century, the Women's Movement was a classical liberal, individualist movement". Even when, in the nineteen sixties, this movement underwent a dramatic revival, it still retained for a considerable time much of its original individualist character. It has only been in its most recent guise that feminism has acquired its totalitarian and collectivist features.'[8]

- Today's Feminism cleverly disguises its 'totalitarian' and 'collectivist' aims and agenda

The Equality Feminist Christina Hoff Sommers, author of the book 'Who Stole Feminism?', comments:

'The women's movement has been hijacked by a small group of chronically offended gender feminists who believe that women are from Venus and men are from hell....I do not believe that women are oppressed; or are members of a subordinate class. It is no longer reasonable to say that as a group, women are worse off than men.'[9]

And Melanie Phillips, social commentator, columnist, panellist, comments:

'Post-war feminism took hold in the universities on the back of the New Left, the political radicalism that swept the campuses in the 1960s and 1970s taking politics into new areas of culture and personal life. This new "gender feminism"...was different from the "equity feminism"...Gender feminism owed much to Marxism, from which in time it became an acceptable substitute by providing a new narrative of oppression as socialism progressively collapsed.'[10]

- The use of universities to nurture and promote Feminist Ideology was identified in earlier chapters. Universities are key institutions for creating generations of Feminists, and for propagating Feminist Ideology. We have already seen how Feminism embraced Marxism

Again,

'The feminist battle has evolved from a fight for legal and social equality to a fight for special treatment and affirmative action.'[11]

And,

'Although the current wave of feminism began as a political movement with the limited goal of integrating women into the workplace and other areas of public life, some feminists have turned it into an ideological movement with a global mandate.'[12]

85

There can be no question that Equality Feminism, that type of Feminism with which one could say almost everyone agrees, was commandeered by Ideological Feminists, whose aims in doing so were a) to preference and policy-favour women (but mainly to benefit Feminists themselves), b) to spread misandry, and c) to progress their Quiet Revolution.

Feminism in modern Britain has nothing to do with 'gender equality' or 'equal opportunities for women'. It hijacked Equality Feminism long ago, and substituted its own, malign, agenda. Yet it is still widely believed that Feminism is a Movement concerned with 'women's issues'. An astonishing belief, when there is so much evidence to the contrary.

- Stealing Equality Feminism's moral and legitimate base was necessary because modern Feminism has no moral or rational base of its own: as we have seen, it is an Ideology, with its own specific dogma, doctrines and political, sexual, cultural and economic belief systems

Feminism's Machiavellian Deceit and its Benefits

It has been shown that Equality Feminism's equality and liberal principles are being used (and abused) by modern Feminists as a public face, as a deception to facilitate their Trojan Horse strategy. This deception is not only used to surreptitiously introduce a Socialist and sexual revolution, but also to glean public and political sympathy for its supposed 'moral' aims thereby attracting funding, resources, preferential treatment and policy-favouritism, and to facilitate the implementation of its agenda. In addition, by attracting public and political sympathy it automatically justifies its existence (knowing that in the 21st century a 'women's movement' is no longer necessary):

> 'Two different forms of feminism, therefore, need to be clearly distinguished, one classical, the other modern. The former is feminism's original form, classically liberal in both inspiration and aspiration. The latter is a more recent and far more insidious movement. Unfortunately, of late it is this latter form of feminism which has captured the headlines and made the running in setting the policy agenda. Arguably, since women now enjoy the same civil and political rights as men, there is no longer any need today for a distinctly feminist perspective. Modern feminism is something from which today's women need liberation if both sexes are fully to enjoy their common humanity.'[13]

Stealing and using Equality Feminism's fundamental principles of equality, morality, justice and liberalism to inveigle themselves into the public's and politicians' sympathy (and thereby into the tax-payers' fund-box) is an essential part of the Ideological Feminists' strategy. They wish, and need, to be seen and thought of as a righteous people. And undoubtedly, the public's and politicians' perception of Feminism *is* that it is a benign and moral Movement dedicated to 'gender equality', addressing 'women's issues' and 'equal rights for women'. Feminism's public relations have deliberately and successfully created this perception, this persona:

> 'By this time I had attracted the two things that the women's movement wanted: a just cause to clothe their political agenda...'[14]

Gaining widespread approval led to gaining benefits.

> *'By this time I had attracted the two things that the women's movement wanted... (a just cause) and money to fund (its) agenda.'[15]*

- We will see in Part Four just how focused and aggressive Feminism is about attracting money, funding, grants, salaries...to its members and its numerous Industries

***

The success of Feminism's deceit has also brought *policy* advantages.

Melanie Phillips noted how Feminists fooled and deceived civil servants and politicians in the 1980s and 1990s:

> *'Anti-man ideas were slipped into the political agenda under a softer guise to gain support from the majority who would be unaware they were subscribing to a gender war. Who, after all, could possibly object to the promotion of female equality?'[16]*

- Male politicians are particularly naive (or spineless? or complicit?) when it comes to sexual politics

So Feminist policies are presented in ways that appear to represent justice and equality. And many women, and men, identify with these ideals (spurious as they are, in the hands of Feminists). On the other hand there are repercussions for those who are reluctant to be fooled:

> *'...feminist groups always present themselves as representatives of women voters in general, warning legislatures and political parties that rejection of their demands demonstrates contempt for women's needs.'[17]*

- Feminist politics inevitably involves threats of electoral thuggery, a kind of protection racket: 'submit to our demands or we'll ensure that the "women's vote" goes against you'. And, of course, craven male politicians always *do* submit

Ann Carlton worked as a political adviser to both Anthony Crosland and John Silkin and was a former senior national officer of the Labour Party. As such, her views on Feminists carry experience and validity:

> *'Politicians on all sides have caved in, issuing worthless charters to show they care...Like so many who want to subvert natural justice, the Feminist Thought Police start from the need to correct an obvious injustice, then proceed by a series of illogical steps to create another injustice which just happens to benefit their careers.'[18]*

***

The Feminist racket of offering the public and politicians an iron fist in a velvet glove has won Feminists huge cultural, financial, employment and political benefits.

In Part One we saw many examples of cultural misandry. Reading some of the anti-male comments of Feminists like Andrea Dworkin it might be easy to dismiss them as extreme or irrelevant. They are not; such people participated in the hijacking of Equality Feminism:

> 'The women's movement, in a way, was starting to be co-opted. I think the MacKinnonites and the Dworkinites definitely moved in at that point. And remember, Dworkin is the one who said intercourse is an act of rape, inherently an act of rape.'[19]

- Since the 1980s hard-line Feminists have been 'co-opted' into government departments, 'co-opted' onto advisory bodies, 'co-opted' into non-governmental organisations. They have been 'moving in' to the policy-making process. Their Trojan Horse has been disgorging its gender-warriors into academia, into the legal profession, into the media, into the civil service and the trade unions...and into local and central government

> 'Many people suppose that feminism today is a continuation of the reform movement of the past. They occasionally notice a ranting Bella Abzurg or an icy Gloria Steinem, but imagine them to be merely the froth of extremism, on an otherwise sensible movement. That is not the case; the extremists are the movement.'[20]

- Modern Feminists, by their nature, by definition, *are* the extremists

Melanie Phillips again notes the success, and the effects, of Ideological Feminism's deception:

> 'The extent to which feminism in its most extreme form has embedded itself within the institutions and thinking of Britain has simply not been grasped. Feminism now dominates moral discourse. Its fundamental tenets have been absorbed into the national bloodstream. It has become the unchallengeable orthodoxy in even the most apparently conservative institutions and drives forward the whole programme of domestic social policy. Yet this orthodoxy is not based on the concept of fairness or justice or social solidarity. It is based on hostility towards men.'[21]

And so with the successful use and abuse of Equality Feminism's moral base today's Feminism has established a wide range of benefits and advantages:

- Feminism has embedded itself in our institutions and culture; and its righteousness has been so much accepted that it has become part of our conventional wisdom
- Feminism, being successful in its deceit, now monopolises, and therefore dominates, moral discourse on sexual politics and gender issues
- Feminism has become unchallengeable
- Feminism has become the oracle of gendered social policy; if a policy isn't approved by Feminists then it is rejected (one reason why there has been no specifically male-friendly piece of legislation in living memory; as far as I can determine)
- Feminism has been accepted even in conservative institutions (including the Conservative Party and the Church of England)

The hijacking of Equality Feminism and the accompanying shift from *women's rights* to *men's wrongs* has had far-reaching implications on British sexual politics. Women's 'victimhood' has become central to Britain's social policy. In domestic violence and rape, for example, believing accusations by one person (the woman) has become an issue of *sexual politics* rather than an issue of *fact* and *justice*. A man accused of violence toward a woman now faces a virtual presumption of guilt. Marital conflict, involving *both* parties, is interpreted as 'male abuse'. A clumsy and gauche sexual approach to a woman, perhaps for a date, becomes 'sexual harassment'. Male prejudice is the cause of the glass ceiling. Male discrimination the cause of the pay gap.

***

Men themselves have been gulled by the Feminist racket, the Feminist deception. Ironically, many of these men have become its victims:

> 'The feminist movement is one of the most powerful political forces in the United States today. Unfortunately, the public including the middle-class professional men most affected by custody litigation, still tends to perceive feminists as the near powerless victims they portray themselves to be.'[22]

The same phenomenon has occurred in Britain. Even men who have been treated abominably by Feminist policies, those 'affected by custody litigation', for example, *still continue* to perceive Feminists as the powerless victims they portray themselves to be. How sad that even these middle-class fathers still persist in viewing Feminism as an innocuous, benign Movement... even after experiencing great personal difficulty achieving equality and justice in the Family Courts.

- For Feminism not to incur the wrath of such fathers (who direct their anger solely at the Family Courts and governments) is clever Machiavellian politics; the disguise of its stolen moral base provides excellent cover...making Feminism invisible as the true culprit, invisible from blame

***

Stealing Equality Feminism's moral and legitimate base was a political public relations master-stroke that has permitted modern Feminists to continue pursuing their Quiet Revolution and to incrementally implement their agenda.

An Equality Feminist confirms the success of this deceptive Quiet Revolution:

> 'The evolution underway in women's roles was overtaken by a radical revolution that scored victories beyond feminists' wildest fantasies of thirty years ago. The changes they couldn't impose by constitutional amendment they have imposed through the schools, college faculties, and the culture, by judicial fiat and advocacy dressed up as legislation.'[23]

***

One of the major reasons that I was moved to write this book was because I am an Equality Feminist who is disgusted at what Feminism has become.

> 'If equality had remained the chief goal of feminists, it would have continued and enhanced the liberal revolution that began, falteringly, more than two hundred years ago. But equality has not remained the goal of all feminists. Some of them, fewer in number than egalitarian feminists but greater in influence by the later twentieth century, have moved considerably beyond political equality in connection with "life, liberty and the pursuit of happiness...".'[24]

***

Contemporary Feminism is badly in need of scrutiny; only an honest appraisal – openly questioning, analysing and challenging Feminism – can diminish the inordinate power that it now possesses. If others question their own naivety about Feminism and join in an honest and frank critique then Feminism may have its power curtailed. But it will not give up its power easily.

Today's Feminism is:

> 'Not merely about equal rights for women...Feminism aspires to be much more than this. It bids to be a totalising scheme resting on a grand theory, one that is as all-inclusive as Marxism.'[25]

And,

> 'Feminists' calls for equality, or even equity, sound at first like nothing other than calls for justice. Lurking just below the surface, though, is often the call for gynocentrism...equality is not only the legitimate expression of egalitarian feminism, therefore, but also the ideal front for ideological feminism.'[26]

It is this disguise, *deliberately* adopted by today's Feminists, that has allowed them to gain so much cultural and political power – to benefit themselves and to spread misandry, to widen their opportunities to blame and demonise men. I hope this book goes some way to expose this deceit.

> 'What should have been a movement to uplift women, and men,
> bogged down in a fever swamp of dogma and intolerance.'[27]

Chapter 8

The Suffragettes: Early Man-Hating Feminists

Man-hating has 'form' in Feminism. Much of today's misandry can also be seen in the late-Victorian and Edwardian Suffragette Movement. Therefore misandry is not new. All modern Feminism's views, aims, claims and tenets can be found in the Suffragette Movement; including:

Man-hating * the idea that women are morally superior to men * Lesbian Feminism * separatism * the belief that men are responsible for all society's ills * the serious dislike of 'straight' sex * the claim that men are responsible for prostitution * the belief that men treat women only as sex objects * the patriarchy * Male Feminists * anti-marriage * the belief that men are 'bad people' and women are 'good people' * Socialist Feminism

This chapter discusses these similarities. The Suffragette Movement was not a wholesome Movement; its misandrous element has been air-brushed, censored out of our school curriculum by a politically correct education system.

A Feminist Myth to Justify Man-Hating

The Victorian and Edwardian Feminists based their assault on men on an anthropological interpretation of history, a pseudo-science during this period. The proponents of this interpretation were men (then, as now, Male Feminists possessed a masochistic streak in their psychological make-up). Friedrich Engels, Johann Bachofen and Lewis Morgan are three examples.

In 1884 Engels's 'Origin of the Family, Private Property and the State' was published. Engels claimed that early human history communities were ruled by women but were then usurped by men who established a patriarchal system. Men then held women in slavery through marriage:

> 'The overthrow of the mother-right as the world historical defeat of the female sex. The man took command in the home also; the woman was degraded and reduced to servitude; she became the slave of his lust and a mere instrument for the production of children.'[1]

• Engels's claim, for which he could offer no evidence, became extremely influential in the Victorian and Edwardian Feminist Movement, and remains so today – even though there is *still* no evidence to substantiate this outrageous claim

Bachofen and Morgan held similar pro-female/anti-male views. Originally, they asserted, men and women lived in groups that were savage and primitive but women created a matriarchal system and were responsible for bringing civilisation and culture to mankind:

> 'At the darkest stage of human existence, they said, mother-child love was the only light in the moral darkness. Women were more altruistic than men because of their maternal instincts and more virtuous because of their weaker sex drives.'[2]

• Like Engels, Bachofen and Morgan provided absolutely no evidence for these claims. Yet Feminists in the Suffragette Movement eagerly adopted these baseless statements and politicised them into a 'patriarchal' Ideology that suited their misandrous agenda

Because the views of women's superiority appeared to be 'scientific' these claims were very persuasive. Feminists of both sexes unquestioningly accepted these mythical ideas of human development as, indeed, do modern Feminists of both sexes. It is upon such spurious views that Victorian and Edwardian Feminism built its assertion that 'women were morally superior to men'.

In the Westminster Review (in 1888 and 1894) Mona Caird wrote that her aim was to prove that the evils of society had their origins thousands of years ago:

> '...in the dominant abuse of patriarchal life: the custom of women purchase.'[3]

- And so we have a Movement focusing on patriarchy as the universal evil, Feminism's 'devil weapon', a social and political system in which men, supposedly, have sole power and abuse this power to advantage themselves and to disadvantage women

These 'scientific' pronouncements provided ammunition for an extreme, man-hating agenda to develop within the nineteenth-century women's Movement.

***

Resonating with modern Feminism, the Suffragettes proclaimed:

> 'We are now reaping the consequences of the wrong that has been done to our mothers and grandmothers, and the more closely one studies sociology and observes life, the more obvious it becomes that man is called upon to suffer, inch by inch and pang by pang, for that which he has inflicted.'[4]

- And today's Quiet Revolution is, 'inch by inch', succeeding in making men 'suffer', 'pang by pang', for being 'bad people'

Suffragettes and Lesbianism

The strongly held Feminist view that men were inherently 'bad people' and a danger to women resulted in the Suffragette claim that men were best avoided; this conclusion provided a justification for many women to avoid marriage. 'Spinsterhood' became an Ideology – the physical separation from men. We have seen that a modern school of Lesbian Feminism advocates the concept of 'separatism' (in practice, women living in communes together, physically apart from men). It is also expressed in gender-cleansing families of adult males, via Feminist policies of promoting unmarried motherhood and in easy and rewarded divorce for wives.

- So 'separation' from men is a long-standing Feminist aim

***

Suffragettes, like their present-day Sisters, were anti-marriage:

> 'There was much talk of new forms of marriage: communes, trial marriage and, from Cicely Hamilton, about bargaining within marriage and wages for housework...Mrs Caird, however, was vindictive in her dislike of marriage and her desire to undermine it. For her, even happy marriages were wholly destructive and joyless.'[5]

- Caird's views sound frighteningly contemporary; we will hear similar comments from numerous second-wave Feminists

Again,

> 'Whatever the contradictions and impossible burdens of economic independence for women, feminists believed that women had to be liberated from men who were perceived as akin to slave owners.'[6]

Not only were the Suffragette Feminists anti-marriage but, again like modern Feminists, felt that the result of marriage, child-bearing and motherhood, were additional burdens for women:

> 'The maternal role, said Dora Marsden, was the cause of women's oppression: to the door of the "legitimate mother" and the "protection" accorded to her by popular sentiment is to be traced the responsibility for most of the social ills from which we suffer.'[7]

***

So many Suffragettes turned to lesbianism.

> 'In the nineteenth century, same-sex relationships between women were thought normal. Many leading feminists had close emotional ties with other women, including passionate declarations, explicit pronouncements of love in letters and diaries, and maybe kissing and fondling and sharing a bed.'[8]

And in the Suffragette Movement the anti-marriage, anti-family and anti-male faction were numerically and politically dominant:

> 'Spinsters were the backbone of the turn-of-the-century women's movement. By 1913 sixty-three per cent of the Women's Social and Political Union were spinsters...Many spinsters were what we would consider today to be lesbians.'[9]

- 63 per cent of Suffragettes were likely to be Lesbian Feminists. This faction, then, had a huge amount of power to influence and direct the Suffragettes' political aims and Ideology

Lesbianism became increasingly politicised in the Suffragette Movement; with a central theme being the hatred of men:

> 'Among the great army of sex, the regiment of aggressively man-hating women is full of strength, and signs of the times that it is steadily being recruited. On its banner is emblazoned "Woe to Man" and its call to arms is shrill and loud. These are the women who are "independent of men".'[10]

- This sounds very 21st century

For Victorian Feminists 'spinsterhood' became a political statement (as it still is for today's Lesbian Feminists). Consider the following:

Nearly two-thirds of Suffragettes were Ideologically-driven Lesbian Feminists; Suffragettes were very aggressive (their violent behavior, property damage and demonstrations have been recorded); Suffragettes were man-hating, anti-marriage, anti-family...

This cocktail is replicated in present-day Feminism (the percentage of ingredients will vary slightly, with more added). This is a chilling thought when we realise just how much cultural and political power today's Feminists hold, with approximately 37 per cent being lesbian or bisexual.

***

The social and political commentators Nathanson and Young point out, with regard to modern Feminism:

> 'One message to girls and women is that they should strive for complete autonomy. That means liberation, freedom, or even separation from men. And that reveals a profoundly gynocentric worldview. But it reveals a profoundly misandric one, too, because it implies that all men should be kept under permanent suspicion.'[11]

- Everywhere in Britain today men are 'under suspicion' – simply because they are male. This is a form of misandry, of man-hating. In periods of our history people have (universally) been suspicious of black people. This is racism, no different in concept to misandry

Bestial Men

In or out of marriage, men's sexual desire was condemned and demonised:

> 'The proof of men's primitive savagery, the issue that had to be challenged and tamed and indeed transfigured by female control to which the vote was the key, was male sexuality. It was through sexual relations that men held women in their power both in and out of marriage, wounding and abusing them and keeping them enslaved.'[12]

- We have seen similar man-hating claims made by modern Feminists

Men were confirmed, and demonised, as 'morally inferior people':

> '...feminists then made the leap to the proposition that sexual relations should not be practiced by men. Sexuality was an expression of the bestial and lowering side of human nature which had to be suppressed for the benefit of all. This meant that men had to restrain themselves since it was male sexuality that was animalistic and dehumanising; even worse, that it threatened the very existence of the nation and the race.'[13]

- Men's behavior was deemed to be 'animalistic' and 'dehumanising'. So by extension, men themselves were thought of as animalistic and sub-human. We have seen modern Feminists refer to men as the 'problematic sex', with others wanting to 'transform masculinity'

Apparently, not only was men's sex drive bad for women it was also bad for the nation; the underlying script being that not only Feminists but *everyone* should blame men. And many did, including many men. This Feminist aim has came to pass; as we saw in Part One misandry in Britain is now widespread, it's in our cultural bloodstream, it is taught in schools and in the universities and constantly and blatantly culturally expressed in all areas of the media.

***

Men were held responsible for the phenomenon of prostitution. Once thought to be the purveyors of vice, prostitutes now came to be seen as the victims of men:

> *'Women were still the fount of domestic virtue; but if they "fell" into prostitution, it was because they had been corrupted by men. It was men who were responsible for prostitution, by creating the demand that resulted in the supply. Women were the active promoters of sexual virtue; but men were the active promoters of sexual vice.'*[14]

* Modern Feminists, of both sexes, *still* blame men for 'driving women into prostitution'. The fact that these professional ladies actually *freely choose* this lifestyle (discounting the tiny minority who are trafficked) cuts no ice with these bigots – their Ideology and the Feminist 'Party'-line brooks no contradiction or deviation

* The Feminist issues of pornography and prostitution, and their blaming and demonising men, will be discussed in Part Four

Suffragettes made the ridiculous claim that 'straight' sex is damaging to women and to the nation. Men who wanted sex with women were the enemy; so in this sense, women were taught to view *all* men as the enemy:

> *'Sexual continence, in the form of both chastity and celibacy, was now a dominant motif of the women's crusade.'*[15]

By these devious and moral machinations, the Suffragettes' justification for its man-hating became accepted by an ever-widening audience in cultural and learned circles, and its misandrous 'blame men' mantra became ever more entrenched, continuing into the 21st century.

> *'And as the suffrage struggle intensified, male sexuality came to the fore as the dominant problem to be resolved.'*[16]

Suffragettes Declare: 'Women are Superior to Men'

Carnality belonged to the animal kingdom; men were carnal; women were spiritual. If society was to be improved then men had to move from being bestial creatures to being spiritual; and it was women's job, the Suffragettes proclaimed, to bring about this conversion:

> 'It was women who would raise men from the savage to the spiritual. Women were to be the redeemers of mankind... (there was) not only the deep iniquity of men but the mission of women to rescue both them and the world from base animalistic masculinity.'[17]

- Feminism, then, was to be the saviour of the human race (or at least, the British race), saving it from 'masculinity'

- This view is mirrored in present-day Feminism's patronising, sanctimonious attitude toward men and maleness

In her book, 'The Power of Womanhood', the Suffragette Ellice Hopkins declared that if women *had* to marry, then it was the wife's duty to:

> '...purge all that was dark in him (her husband) into purity; all that is failing in him she must strengthen into truth; from her, through all the world's clamour, he must win his praise; in her, through all the world's warfare, he must find his peace.'[18]

***

It's generally thought (and taught to schoolchildren) that the Suffragette Movement was an innocent one-dimensional fight for women's equality, a just and virtuous campaign to extend the franchise to women. Not so; it also had a far deeper and darker agenda. It was a self-righteous precursor of modern Britain's misandrous Feminism, which is purporting to be fighting for 'gender equality'. Our education system does not allow the truth about the Suffragette Movement to be taught in schools.

The Suffragettes' assertion that men are 'inferior' to women was adopted as a weapon with which to attack men, maleness and masculinity in general, and is still used effectively as such. Melanie Phillips comments on this new Feminist weapon:

> 'This (the inferiority of men) provided incendiary ammunition for an extreme, man-hating agenda to develop within the nineteenth-century women's movement.'[19]

- This misandrous device is still employed by Feminism today. It is a belief held by Feminists of both sexes, used to justify the adoption of Feminism's anti-male agenda

And as today, there was to be no compromise:

> 'The militant suffragettes took this assumption of moral superiority much further. Instead of arguing for female values to share the public platform with male virtues, the militants attacked men, masculinity and marriage as the fount of society's ills and declared that only women could raise humankind from the degradation to which men had brought it....the antidote was sexual separatism; celibacy, chastity and lesbianism.'[20]

Male Suffragettes

Like today's Male Feminists, the men who supported the Suffragette Movement were naïve with regard to sexual politics. And in common with contemporary Male Feminists it appears that they possessed a pathological character trait that included: self-disgust for being male, a sense of 'guilt' for being male, a masochistic tendency, a fashionable desire to appease Feminism, and a lack of conscience in betraying their own sex (fathers, brothers and sons). Their support for Feminism had nothing at all to do with the concepts of equality and justice...although they were gulled into thinking it had. Today's Male Feminists, and Feminist supporters, are just as delusional...but far more dangerous to the male populace because of their ubiquity and their power within all professions and elements of our culture, media, legal system, academia and State.

An example of a Suffragette Male Feminist was Fred Pethick-Lawrence. Emmeline and Fred Pethick-Lawrence were the organisational geniuses who had been instrumental in creating the Suffragette Movement. Then they had the temerity to question the rise of Suffragette violence. They were given short shrift by the Pankhursts:

'If you do not accept Christabel's policy (of violence) we shall smash you!'[21]

And they *were* smashed. Mrs. Pankhurst packed them off to Canada supposedly on a 'fact-finding' trip. When they returned they found that she had thrown them out of the Movement. They were shocked, and couldn't believe that Christabel, whom they had treated as part of their family, had agreed with her mother that they should be so ignominiously dismissed from the Movement that they had done so much to support and finance. But she had. Even Annie Kenney, Christabel's sycophantic sidekick, was astonished at the brutality.

'His (Fred Pethick-Lawrence's) departure powerfully symbolised a further change that had come over the organisation for which he had done so much. For the WSPU had become explicitly anti-male. Yet as Annie Kenney pointed out, men had supported militancy; they had helped in the processions, sacrificed their own businesses or professions and some had even been force-fed.'[22]

- Feminism continues to be a malign totalitarian, Stalinesque Movement, with man-hating at its core...and yet there are Male Feminists who continue to support it. This is a bizarre phenomenon; perhaps a perverse personality trait?

Fred Pethick-Lawrence was pursued for costs that he had incurred in supporting the Suffragette Movement. He had undergone many sacrifices for 'the cause of freedom for women' – imprisonment, hunger strike, forcible feeding, loss of financial substance – even going into bankruptcy, yet he was still shat on by the Suffragettes.[23] They don't teach our children *that* kind of male selfless sacrifice (or Male Feminist masochism/stupidity?) and Suffragette betrayal in school history lessons; to a Feminist a man is a man...and therefore disposable...the enemy.

- And how about our own Male Feminists? I suggest that their support for today's misandrous, male-blaming, male-condemning Feminism involves a similarly complex psychological and political personality dysfunction. What else would explain their passive, active, or enthusiastic support for an Ideology that theoretically and practically hates them and maleness in general? Masochism;... a cultural and political Ms Whiplash?

Is God a Feminist?

As with modern Feminism, the Suffragette Movement used a facade of justice and moral righteousness to disguise its darker and deeper doctrines and agenda – progressing a social and political revolution, the preferencing of women and the hatred of men.

Because of their 'inherent badness' men were blamed for the world's ills, and especially condemned for their treatment of women. And so we reach the 1914 – 1918 War:

> 'Christabel (Pankhurst) immediately decided that the war was a judgment on the iniquity of men. She wrote in The Suffragette on 7 August 1914: "A man-made civilisation, hideous and cruel enough in time of peace, is to be destroyed...This great war...is nature's vengeance – is God's vengeance upon the people who held women in subjection...that which has made men for generations past sacrifice women and the race to their lusts, is now making them fly at each other's throats and bring ruin upon the world".'[24]

- This is a particularly repugnant misandrous remark, considering the human carnage, and the agonies millions of men suffered in the trenches

- So even God, apparently, is on the side of Feminists, wishing to punish men. Modern Feminism has declared for decades that God could be female. Perhaps the Devil could also be female?

***

This chapter ends with a contemporary (male) issue to ponder, and with a request that the reader ask female colleagues a vital and fundamental question.

I believe that women should not have had to fight for the vote; the progress towards universal franchise should have been concurrent for women and men. But having said that, I would like the reader to seriously consider the following question: 'Which was the more important – the Suffragette Movement or Fathers 4 Justice, (divorced fathers who wish to see their children)?'

The issue of divorced fathers being denied contact with their children by vindictive ex-wives, (with this cruelty being sanctioned by the Family Courts and by successive governments) has never personally affected me because I was granted custody of my children. However, I was an active member of Fathers 4 Justice, the pressure group for divorced fathers, in the early to mid- 2000s, when F4J undertook many peaceful demonstrations, climbing public buildings. One activist even climbing onto Buckingham Palace. But unlike the violent and aggressive Suffragette movement no damage was ever done to property (even accidentally), and no one was ever hurt or accidentally injured. Yet F4J was condemned outright by Feminist organisations, with Labour Government politicians even refusing to *speak* to its representatives in any meaningful way.

In the Autumn of 2003 David Chick demonstrated by climbing onto a mobile crane overhanging busy London Streets. Mr. Chick had repeatedly been denied access to his children; he had appealed to the Family Courts on ten occasions, to no avail; he had spent many thousands of pounds in a desperate attempt to see his children, a natural and human right repeatedly denied to him by his ex-wife. The following is a response to Mr. Chick's desperate action from an Ideological Male Feminist Left-wing politician:

> 'Ken Livingstone, the Mayor of London, said Mr. Chick "amply demonstrated" why some men should not have access to their children. "The idea that an individual can hold London to ransom is completely unacceptable," he said: "We would not put up with it if it were Osama bin Laden, I do not see why anyone would expect we would put up with it from this man".'[25]

- Here we have a Left-wing senior politician comparing a desperate and loving father to Osama bin Laden. Livingstone's comments are obnoxious. Do a gender-switch. Would Livingstone have said of the violent, rampaging Suffragettes, having seriously damaged and fire-bombed property, that they 'amply demonstrated why women should not be given the right to vote'? The man is an irrational misandrist (despite being a father himself)

- In 2012 there is to be an election for the next Mayor of London. Ken Livingstone has said that he will stand. Will fathers, in London, particularly divorced fathers, remember how he despises them? Will they actively organise a campaign to keep this odious Male Feminist out of office?

***

But, I hear the Feminist reader say: 'The Suffrage campaign to gain women the vote was *much more important* than "a few" divorced fathers not seeing their children'. No, it was *not*. I ask the reader to try the following 'research' exercise:

Ask any group of mothers, of any age and in any situation, the following question:

'Which would you rather have *taken away* from you:-

a) Your children, or

b) Your right to vote in future General Elections?'

Never once have I encountered a mother who was prepared to have her children taken away from her in order retain the right to vote. Try it, it's an important question to pose. So the F4J pressure group *is* more important than the Suffragette Movement. The issue of divorced men seeing their children *is* more important than women (or men) having the right to vote.

Part Three

What *is* a Feminist?

Chapter 9

Who *Are* These Women Who Make the World Worse for Men?

A main aim of this book is to expose Feminism – its lies, its myths, its Ideology, its claims of inequalities, discriminations and oppressions that women suffer; these will be addressed in Part Four. Part Three exposes the mind, the emotional and psychological make-up of the Feminist.

It is possible to tell something of a cause from the people it attracts. Likewise, it is possible to tell something about a person from the cause they believe in. My objective in Part Three is to show that the Feminist is a certain 'type' of person.

My building a psychological profile of 'a Feminist' was triggered by something that Bob Geldof said during a short conversation a few years ago. He had been meeting Feminists in London, researching for a television programme he was producing on fathers and marriage. He related his encounter with Feminists, which resonated with numerous similar encounters of my own. The similarity in our experiences made me wonder whether there was a specific Feminist psychological/personality/mental/emotional profile.

'Who is she that looks forth as the dawn,

Fair as the moon,

Clear as the sun,

Terrible as an army with banners?'

(The Song of Songs 6:10)

Those involved with an Ideology in which there is a collectivist group-identity and where a targeted enemy is central to their cause always appear to have more aggressive personalities than the rest of the population. They are single-minded, determined and driven by their Ideology. Witness the behaviour of the communists and fascists in Europe during the inter-war years. Such people have ingrained attitudes in which intolerance, rage and anger predominate. Many people, women as well as men, who have dealt with Feminists will recognise these emotions as being common elements in a Feminist's make-up. Some would say that there is a common 'pathology'.

As far as I can ascertain no research has been carried out on the Feminist 'personality', presumably because such a study would be too politically incorrect. I contacted Psychology Departments in various universities for references to research and books on the subject, but no one wanted to get involved, even though I had only requested innocuous literature and had promised anonymity.

So I have had to rely on personal observations, encounters and experiences, and those of others, and the empirical and anecdotal research that I managed to find. I conclude that there *is* a psychological make-up that is specific to a Feminist. If the reader recognises any of the characteristics mentioned then this is a bonus proof.

***

It may be thought impolite to investigate the psychological make-up of a particular group of individuals and classify them as a 'type'. However, these are the people, the female Ideologues, and their followers and sympathisers, who are not only responsible for spreading misandry, but who have formed, directed, and implemented pro-women/anti-men sexual politics and gendered social policy for the last three decades. Looking at their psychological make-up is not, therefore, patronising, it is an overdue necessity. Any group that has a collective dualist 'us and them' Ideology, especially where a moral dimension is involved ('we are better than them', 'we are victims of them'), and where the emotion of 'hate' is very much part of the Ideology (as with racism, white supremacy, homophobia, misogyny, anti-Semitism...and misandry) needs to have the psychological make-up of its members addressed and exposed.

Is there a certain 'type' of woman who enjoys disliking men; who freely voices her disdain of men; who wishes to preference and defend women under *any* circumstances, justified or not; who carries anger and rage against men within her; who is continually dissatisfied with political gains; who will instigate and implement anti-male policy? Yes, there is. There is a spectrum, of course, but *all* Feminists, to a greater or lesser extent, will exhibit what this Part of the book identifies as a Feminist personality, mentality, psychological make-up.

The spectrum ranges from the fascistic young Feminist students at the University of Manchester (and other universities) who wish to stop their fellow male students from having equality of expression and representation, to the Minister for Women and her Sisters in government (especially Labour governments) who are hell-bent on pursuing legislation that will either preference women or discriminate against men (or both). It includes those women who would not label themselves Feminists but nevertheless still embrace Feminist myths and lies. For example, it includes those women who believe that *all* divorced men who have been denied contact with their children by a vindictive ex-wife and a Feminist-dominated Family Court system, are wife-batterers or paedophiles (labelling these fathers as 'paedophiles' is a Feminist political strategy intentionally designed to prevent them receiving any public sympathy for their plight...a simple strategy - just *demonise* them). Many women are Feminists by proxy.

- There is a certain 'type' of woman who buys into an artificially created set of sexual political sensibilities in order that she can satisfy her emotional need for being perpetually 'offended'

In addition, it takes a certain type of person to constantly, and *deliberately*, seek out situations and incidents that, with a little bit of conjuring and linguistic skulduggery, can be construed as 'sexist', 'misogynist' or a 'discrimination against women'.

***

So yes, it *is* possible to tell something of a person from the cause they believe in. It is in the context of the present chapter that I again refer to the Dictionary of Sociology for the definition of Feminism:

> *'Feminism: 1. A holistic theory concerned with the nature of women's global oppression and subordination to men. 2. A socio-political theory and practice which aims to free all women from male supremacy and exploitation. 3. A social movement encompassing strategic confrontations with the sex-class system. 4. An ideology which stands in dialectical opposition to all misogynous ideology and practices.'[1]*

- This is the Feminist cause

- The reader will know that a dictionary is supposed to be a value-free, politically neutral resource. This is not the case with this dictionary; a very strong sexual political bias is evident. Sociology is a subject dominated by Feminism, from GCSE to postgraduate level

- Note the confrontational language, the expression of *anger* – 'women suffer oppression and subordination by men', 'women are not free, they are enslaved by male supremacy', 'in this condition of slavery women are exploited by men'. The whole definition represents an Ideology that is confrontational, aggressive, angry, man-hating, which *intentionally* uses pejorative and emotive language; Feminism is defined as an oppositional Ideology, a group ('collective') enemy has been appointed (men)...which must be blamed and attacked

We see a similar type of confrontational aggression and emotion in an individual Feminist's hyperbolic vocabulary: 'subjugation' (of women), 'subordination', 'domination', 'oppression', 'victim', 'abused'. Only a certain kind of person, a certain kind of *mind*, would seek to use such words, words which are so obviously inaccurate and inappropriate to describe women's everyday lives in today's Britain.

***

The above is the political cause. The following definitions provide reference points, a framework, a focus, by which the psychological make-up of those attracted to this cause can be identified and assessed:[2]

Psychology: *'The scientific study of the human mind and its functions, especially those affecting behaviour in a given context. Capable of influencing the mind or emotions.'*

Personality: *'The distinctive character or qualities of a person, often distinct from others. The pattern of collective behavioural, temperamental, emotional and mental traits of an individual. The psyche that animates the individual person.'*

Mentality: *'Mental character or disposition: Cast or turn of mind; mental make-up or inclination.'*

***

The following is taken from a Feminist website:

> *'Third Wave feminism encourages personal empowerment and action. Third Wave feminists like to think of themselves as survivors, not victims.'*[3]

- 'Feminists like to think of themselves as survivors'? To be a 'survivor' one must obviously have had a traumatic experience (as in being a victim of a serious crime, for example, or having escaped a serious car accident). So Third Wave Feminists are 'survivors' of what, exactly? They are 'survivors' of being 'female' – and therefore, by definition (the Feminist definition), being a 'victim'. So today's Feminists are 'women who have survived female victimhood.' I ask the reader, what kind of mentality is it that would wish to classify oneself as a 'survivor' simple because one is born with a vagina. It's pathetic, paranoid and neurotic...and the reason that this Part Three needed to be written

- Feminists bemoan the fact of being women. We will see later that Feminists abhor women being 'feminine'

***

If I were a Jew I would want to know what drives anti-Semites, as a black person I would want to know what type of mentality motivates the racist, as a gay I would want to know what gives rise to homophobic behaviour. As a man I want to know what mental process leads a woman to be a misandrist (a misandrist who locates at any point on the 'hating men – ambiguity towards men' spectrum).

***

In Part Four we will see that Feminists have a political and Ideological need to find and create artificial inequalities and discriminations. In Part Three we will see that they also have a deep *psychological need* for this behaviour. Consequently, for the Feminist, there is a perpetual search for things to be 'offended' by.

I look at three areas of a Feminist's psychological make-up – personality (her behaviour, temperament and emotions), emotional expression (her anger, rage and dissatisfaction) and mentality (her disposition and mindset). I invite the reader to factor in their own empirical evidence of Feminists and assess whether my analysis rings true for them.

> *'Left-wing fascism, including Feminism, is just as*
> *intolerant and pathological as Right-wing fascism'*
>
> (Swayne O'Pie)

Chapter 10

Is There a Feminist 'Personality'?

This chapter offers my own observations of the Feminist 'personality', and the experiences of other men, as well as incorporating research findings. It identifies a common characteristic in many Feminists – a dysfunctional relationship with their father. This phenomenon is observed in a number of leading Feminist icons and Lesbian Feminists. However, many of the observations also apply to *non*-Lesbian Feminists.

The Equality Feminist, Doris Lessing, expressed an interest in the Feminist 'personality':

> *'It is time we began to ask who are these women who continually rubbish men. The most stupid, ill-educated, and nasty woman can rubbish the nicest, kindest and most intelligent man and no one protests.'*[1]

• The above speaks for itself

***

In the early 1990s I was living in Cornwall and had just experienced a divorce. I was awarded custody of my three children so I had no axe to grind. But as I spoke to divorced husbands, who had been denied access to their children, it became clear that something was 'not quite right' with the divorce system...the fairness and justice that one naturally assumes exist in the legal system just weren't there for divorced fathers. I came to realise that men experiencing divorce were being systematically shat on. So I set up a counselling 'service' to offer advice to these fathers (it sounds grander than it actually was). This was before mobile phones and the internet, so it relied on the Royal Mail and land-line telephones.

• It needs to be said that I was a Socialist and Feminist at the time, and had been for many years

Collecting, hearing and reading the personal experiences and stories of the men who contacted me was fascinating. A pattern emerged, and became so striking as a phenomenon that at the time I was surprised (naively) that it had not been researched and sociologically studied (although I now know that male-friendly and therefore politically incorrect issues do not attract funding or research kudos for universities). The pattern showed...

...That many of these divorced men were approximately ten years older than their wives... the men fell into the category of what people would generally label as being 'nice, quiet, gentle'...their marriage had lasted for between 3 to 7 years...there were usually no (or only one) children...the wife had been an 'only child'...the wife had had, in some way, a dysfunctional relationship with her father...(many of the men suggested, with hindsight, that their wives had probably married them as an 'escape' into a stable, adult male relationship and perhaps saw them as a substitute father)...a few months prior to the divorce the wife's behaviour had regressed into 'early twenties single female' behaviour such as dressing provocatively to go out socialising 'with friends', wearing heavy make-up, returning home late...the request for a divorce always came from the wives...the divorce soon became acrimonious, with post-divorce father-child contact being used as a 'weapon' against the former husband...during the divorce, and after, a distinctive, 'anti-male' attitude (their words, not mine) became very evident in the ex-wives...

The pattern became so clear and common that whilst these men were relating their experience I would interrupt them and tell them 'their' story. They would always be astonished at its accuracy, or near accuracy. However, the fact that other men had had a very similar experience, and had been in a similar predicament, seemed to offer them a small amount of consolation and comfort.

• The point is, that in some women there is a very definite 'pattern' of 'using' a man and showing animosity towards men in general

In every aspect of divorce the wife is supported by the divorce laws (or the Family Court Judge's interpretation of the divorce laws), and the institutional backing of governments. Assess the truth of this claim by questioning *any* divorced father. They can't *all* be wrong.

In short, my counselling 'research' suggested that there was a certain type of woman (a certain type of 'personality') who was attracted to Feminism. However, my observation exposed only *one* type of Feminist personality; there are others.

***

Some of the most influential leaders of second-wave Feminism were Betty Friedan, Kate Millett, Germaine Greer, Gloria Steinmen, and Simone de Beauvoir. Of these five only Betty Friedan married and had children.

Friedan compared her married home to 'a comfortable concentration camp', characterising her marriage as one 'not based on love but on dependent hate.'[2] Friedan's mother had a 'complete inability to nurture'; and she blamed her father for this.[3] Friedan had violent fits of temper, and physically abused her husband, once throwing a glass ashtray at him and breaking his hand. They divorced and Friedan subsequently spent some time in an institution.

The other four were unacquainted with motherhood and the marriage experience. Kate Millett was a lesbian and Simone de Beauvoir bisexual. Simone de Beauvoir allowed herself to be debased and humiliated by Jean-Paul Sartre, her long-term lover. She taught in the *lycées* at Marseilles, Rouen, and later in Paris. De Beauvoir seduced numerous female students and after charges were brought by the parents of one of them, she was barred from the university and lost her licence to teach anywhere in France.

Gloria Steinem's father abandoned the family, and she was left as a young girl to care for her mentally ill mother. Steinem's dysfunctional childhood persuaded her that 'you become a non-person when you get married' and 'a woman needs a man like a fish needs a bicycle'. Thousands of her acolytes adopted her slogans, born of misery and abandonment. She refused to marry and have children. Then, when she was sixty-six Steinem *did* get married (to a Male Feminist) – abandoning her followers and leaving them to grow old without the love of a husband or children.

Germaine Greer described her childhood as filled with pain and humiliation, with an abusive mother, and a father she later said she never really knew. She has written:

> '...during the years and years that we lived in the same small house, daddy never once hugged me. If I put my arms around him he would grimace and pretend to shudder and put me from him...I clung to the faith that he was not genuinely indifferent to me and did not really find me repulsive, although I never quite succeeded in banishing the fear of such a thing...I thought him weak and craven...I could not respect him.'[4]

- Other influential Feminists share similar backgrounds and experiences

These are the women whose views on men, marriage and the traditional two-parent family (to which Feminism is very much opposed) inform today's Feminist Movement, which in turn informs British social policy.

***

The following finding is pertinent to the question: 'Is there a Feminist 'personality-type'?

> 'There is anthropological evidence suggesting that low father availability in early childhood is associated with later sex-role conflicts for girls as well as for boys...many women who had been father-absent as young children complained of difficulties in achieving satisfactory sexual relationships with their husbands...Case studies of father-absent girls are often filled with details of problems concerning interactions with males, particularly sexual relationships...Other investigations have also found a high incidence of delinquent behaviour among father absent girls...Such acting-out behaviour may be a manifestation of frustration associated with the girl's unsuccessful attempts to find a meaningful relationship with an adult male.'[5]

So we have a father dysfunction relationship that may lead to: i) 'delinquent behaviour', and ii) 'unsatisfactory sexual relationships'. I suggest that for a number of women father dysfunction takes a different form, instead of manifesting anti-social behaviour ('delinquent behaviour') it manifests into *anti-male behaviour*, that is, Feminism.

- '...difficulties in achieving satisfactory sexual relationships with their husbands'. A sexual orientation issue?

Further research on this subject shows that:

> 'Inappropriate and/or inadequate fathering is a major factor in the development of homosexuality in females as well as in males.'[6]

And again:

> 'Feminism is capable of providing an explanatory system to women who are marked by difficult relationships with their fathers. This is not the whole story of feminism – but it is an important part of it. It is my personal observation that every feminist I know has two predictable elements in her life history, the first of which is an unusually strained relationship with her father. The feminist perspective has often given such women an easy way out. Their personal traumas and tragedies become intelligible as part of the great tragedy which, according to the feminist perspective, men have imposed on women throughout history. Feminism has often given such "wounded women" a way to strike back at the oppressor – superficially a less demanding route than to confront the reality of their frayed personal lives.'[7]

So we see a personality-forming trauma developing that is likely to produce:

- A lesbian woman (we have seen that over a third of Feminists are lesbian)
- Politicised 'delinquent behaviour' aimed at men
- An 'explanatory belief system' (Ideology) that is easy to understand and easy to put into practice - Feminism

If the Feminist trait of taking the personal (an individual) and extending it to the general (collectivist/group) is factored in then we have a powerful type of Feminism that hates men. A personal difficulty with a father (or husband) is extended to *all* men.

Combining these outcomes we arrive at the single-minded, politically-driven misandrous (possibly lesbian) Feminist Ideologue...a strong and identifiable personality-type that has inordinate influence within the Feminist Movement.

- It can be argued that being a member of the Feminist Movement *legitimises* the hurt and anger that women who have experienced difficulties with their fathers possess. It also *legitimises* (from their own perspective) the expression of their contempt (to a greater or lesser degree) for *all* men

Although a dysfunctional relationship with one's father is a common element in many Feminists, drawing them into the Movement, it is far from being an *absolute* criterion. Since the early 1980s young women have been introduced to the Feminist Ideology in school, directly or indirectly by Feminist teaching staff (as we saw in Part One). In addition, many young women will have been seduced by Feminism, directly or indirectly, during their years at university. Media presentations, news, articles, documentaries, will also have reinforced their bias towards the Ideology (biased because it will never have been questioned or challenged, or an opposing male view presented to give balance). However, by whichever route a woman finds Feminism, whether she seeks it out or has been indoctrinated, the fundamental elements of a Feminist personality and mentality are present.

***

As well as having characteristics of totalitarianism Feminism also has characteristics of a pseudo-religion. Common to all Feminists is the *psychological* dimension of the 'cult' and 'sect'.

Cult: 'Obsessive devotion or veneration for a person, principle or ideal; the object of such devotion; An exclusive group of persons sharing an esoteric interest.'[8]

Sect: 'A breakaway religious body, especially one regarded as extreme, intolerant; Any faction united by common interests and beliefs.'[9]

- For 'principle or ideal...an esoteric interest' and 'Common interests and beliefs' read 'Feminist Ideology, aims and agenda'
- It will be observed that the Feminist's psychological dimension closely resembles that of a cult member

And like all cults and sects Feminism is a very tight-knit Movement. Feminism provides an Ideological 'social club', a 'home', a bonding of similarly-minded individuals, either with similar father-dysfunctional backgrounds or similar specific political beliefs, or both. A 'home and family' for women with similar life-stories and personalities; the commonality of their experience with their father acts as a personal and political bond (but which may not be expressed or even understood), a bond that energises their Feminist behaviour.

However, the common bond within the Feminist Movement extends not just to the Lesbian element but to all participants and sympathisers. It is worthwhile thinking of the Movement as a close-knit network of people with a similar attitude, with similar sexual political aims. We can think of modern Feminism as a 'community', a 'collective of like-minded women' bound by their sexual politics. There is a close sense of clan, of helping one another, of common aims and beliefs. Think of modern Feminism as a close-knit family. Think of Feminists as being the female equivalent of the 'old boy network', but stronger and much more political and Ideological.

- Think of inclusiveness and exclusiveness, think Sisterhood. Above all, think political coterie, think Ideological caucus; *that* is today's Feminism

'Feminism' is their life, it provides community, very often a workplace, family, friends and lovers. It represents a social and political structure and quite often a reason for being. For all these reasons many Feminists are *driven* people.

- There is a *collective*, as well as an *individual*, psychological make-up of Feminists

Feminism offers its members a psychologically safe and mutually supportive political home for what Doris Lessing terms 'stupid, ill-educated (but many are well-educated), and nasty women who continually rubbish men'. And 'collectivism', as we have seen, provides cover to avoid *individual* responsibility, which can be shifted onto the group: 'we' are the oppressed, victimised minority group fighting for gender equality against 'them'. So fraudulent political behaviour and political demands are thus excused by a Feminist-friendly society and State. Avoiding personal responsibility is very much a part of a Feminist's psychological make-up.

- Feminism provides meaning and a life-framework for its members
- Feminists have seized power through political collectivism, expressed through collective rhetoric, dogma and doctrine
- Being a Feminist gives a woman an individual political power (empowerment) that she would not otherwise have had, and a legitimacy to express that power

- The reader will note that there is no such thing as a 'lone' Feminist; even non-activists are bound and connected by the commonality of aims, dogma and myth

These cult, group, community, collective characteristics go a long way to explain why the Feminist Movement has been, and remains, so powerful and successful – a tight, mutually supportive, 'army unit' type of club with common, easily understood, political aims. An individual personality, mentality, psychological make-up coalesces into a united whole, giving greater cultural and political power than the sum of individuals would otherwise produce.

> *'The radical feminist movement not only explains that any dissatisfaction she may experience is the fault of others, namely men, but comforts her with a sense of solidarity and common purpose in the way that some men find the battalion a welcome relief from the freedom of civilian life. There is probably more to it than that, however. Radical feminism is not merely a way of discovering that a woman is not free. It is also a cause that creates an orientation and a meaning in her life...'* [10]

We have seen the virulent prejudice of Feminism against men; this is expressed by individual Feminists in various offensive ways. Do all Feminists express extreme views? No, obviously not (although they may hold them). But there are common personality traits that bind these 'moderate' Feminists to their more Ideologically motivated misandrous Sisters. In this sense they are part of the Feminist Political Community Club and Family.

The Austrian philosopher F. A. Hayek noted (1944) the place of the subsumed 'personality' of the individual in the 'community' of a fascist or communist (totalitarian) State. His observation neatly summarises the condition of today's Feminist:

> *'If the "community" of the state is prior to the individual, if they have ends of their own independent of and superior to those of the individuals, only those individuals who work for the same ends can be regarded as members of the community. It is a necessary consequence of this view that a person is respected only as a member of the group, that is, only if and in so far as he (she) works for the recognised common ends, and that he (she) derives his (her) whole dignity only from this membership and not merely from being a man (woman).'* [11]

Feminists *Emotionally* Need 'Inequalities and Discriminations'

Whilst following a Masters degree in Gender and Social Policy it was noticeable that a large proportion of my fellow students (mostly mature students and all female), and the lecturers (all female) showed evidence of actually *wanting* women, as a group, to be discriminated against, oppressed, victimised and abused. This phenomenon was so bizarre that I really had to be very careful in coming to this conclusion. They would go to a great deal of trouble to *seek out* 'discriminations' and 'oppressions', and notching them up as 'successes', or 'trophies' when they were 'discovered' (or managed to interpret a situation as one). In addition, there seemed to be an *emotional need* to belong to a group that could officially be classified as a 'victim group'; and a further need to find a target, an enemy to blame, condemn, demonise and punish, toward which they could direct their anger.

- These women *needed* 'discriminations' and 'oppressions' to justify their Ideological stance and their anger. I concluded that there was a definite Feminist 'personality' that exhibited Feminist characteristics. The political and Ideological significance of this escaped me at the time, with my thinking that these were simply 'odd' women, as many men probably still do when they have encountered a Feminist – not realising how this collective 'oddness' has been institutionalised (in the political sense) and transformed into an Ideological dynamic that culturally and politically impacts negatively upon every aspect of their, and all men's, daily lives

Feminists not only have a *political need* to seek out and/or create issues but also an *emotional need* to do so. Here we have two strong forces that are driving modern Feminism. This double-dynamic to 'seek out' (or create) misogynies, discriminations, victimisations, inequalities and oppressions has been transferred into a number of Feminist political strategies which have become necessary in order to justify the Movement's continuing existence (because all Equality Feminism's aims have long since been achieved). These strategies, applied to present-day 'issues', will be explored and exposed in Part Four.

***

At the initial interview for acceptance on the course, I was warned by the (female) Director that, I 'should expect to meet a number of "damaged" women.' And I certainly did. This type of woman being attracted to Women's/Gender/Feminist Studies is confirmed by a lecturer who taught on such a course, but left because she became so disillusioned:

'I hate to reduce things to the psychological dimension zone. It's not my usual mode of interpretation, but in this case I think there just are some temperaments that are really troubled. I think we acted like a dysfunctional family.'[12]

- Many of these 'damaged' 'troubled' and 'dysfunctional' Feminists, from this and from many other university Gender/Women's/Feminist Courses over the last twenty years, are now in positions of power – politicians, lawyers, academics, the civil service, the media, trade unions, local government...pushing their agenda, their Ideology, their Quiet Revolution. I find this very disturbing; it accounts for the widespread cultural and institutional man-hating in today's Britain

***

Like all those who pursue an ideological cause the Feminist personality exhibits a single-mindedness and a sanctimonious self-righteousness. The public, legislators and the policy-making fraternity need to be aware of the psychological make-up of these self-appointed representatives and promoters of 'women's issues'...

'It is time we began to ask who are these women who continually rubbish men'.

(Doris Lessing)

If we are to identify the answer to the question of why contemporary western societies hate men, we, as well as Doris Lessing, need to know that these women are Feminists, whose nature it is to be 'vengeful women'[13] whose personality makes them constantly 'chronically offended', [14] and who are always 'chronically dissatisfied'.[15]

Chapter 11

Anger and Rage:
A Feminist Neurosis or Strategy?
Or Both?

Among the numerous characteristics of a Feminist's psychological make-up are dissatisfaction (with their lot in life), intolerance (with those who disagree with them), anger and rage (directed at men). In this chapter I shall address 'anger' and 'rage' (as one item). Dissatisfaction and intolerance will not be addressed separately, not because they are not important but because they are evident throughout the book. The Feminist's perpetual dissatisfaction is addressed in later chapters, in different contexts, whilst Feminist intolerance is the other side of the coin to anger and rage; the latter presupposes the presence of the former.

Many people have noticed that Feminists are 'angry people'. I suggest in this chapter that 'anger', or a potential for 'sexual political anger', is a prerequisite for a Feminist. It is an emotion that is actually cultivated in Feminist women, to be used as a weapon in the sexual political war against men. It has numerous uses. For example, in an inter-face encounter with a Feminist (discussion, public debate, media interview – none of which are common occurrences) a male will back off if the encounter becomes a confrontation with an angry Ideologue. Men avoid a fierce public argument with a woman for chivalrous reasons, but when attacked fiercely by an enraged Feminist they will always concede, always appease, always surrender. This is one of the reasons why Feminism has gone unquestioned and unchallenged for so long, and why public and media debate with Feminists is such a rare occurrence.

A Feminist-sympathetic woman reading this chapter will say: 'This isn't me, I'm not like this'. But yes, it *is* you and you *are* like this if you admit to being a Feminist, or even a Feminist-sympathiser. The following will apply to you, to a greater or lesser extent, even if you are uncomfortable with it.

'Feminists delight in creating opportunities to express their outrage'

(Swayne O'Pie)

Anger directed against men is, to a greater or lesser extent, a common characteristic of all Feminists. Most people who have conversed with Feminists will know this.

Anger: *'A feeling of extreme displeasure; hostility; indignation, enraged.'*[1]

- Here we have a definition that identifies the emotions of 'hostility', and 'rage'. We know that Feminism is based upon the Ideology of patriarchy – that 'men are bad people to be blamed, demonised and punished' (blaming and demonising are, in fact, punishments in themselves). If the characteristics of the patriarchal Ideology express 'extreme displeasure', 'hostility', 'indignation' and 'rage' towards men then so will the personal characteristics of its followers. We have already encountered many examples of these emotions directed at men by individual Feminists

***

There are two aspects with regard to a Feminist's 'anger':

1. Angry women are *attracted* to Feminism
2. Feminism creates and *cultivates* anger in its followers as a political strategy

Firstly, women who are prone to anger against men (a dysfunctional relationship with their father, or a difficult divorce, for example) are likely to be drawn to Feminism.

In this context I'll revisit Erin Pizzey:

> *'What I saw were groups of left-leaning, white, middle-class women gathering together to hate men. Their slogan was "make the personal political". I saw that the most vociferous and the most violent of the women took their own personal damage, their anger against their fathers, and expanded their rage to include all men.'[2]*

- Pizzey noticed the characteristics of a Feminist pathology – 'the most vociferous and violent', their 'hate', their 'anger', their 'rage' – all directed 'at men'. Pizzey found these character traits to be common in the Feminists she encountered

The phenomenon of father-dysfunction and how and why women are attracted to Feminism (how potential Feminists *already possess* a misandrous anger) have already been addressed so this chapter will discuss the second aspect of Feminist anger – the *deliberate* creation and cultivation of anger as a political strategy.

***

Women's/Feminist/Gender Courses in universities specialise in creating and cultivating anger. One student commented:

> *'I was not a person who invited confrontation or felt comfortable with it. But anger was absolutely a measure of one's feminist commitment. It was taken as a sign of one's authenticity, one's radical credentials. I remember sounding angry a lot, and I remember hearing myself and thinking, "this has become sort of a way that I talk". It was very strange.'[3]*

- As the only male on a Feminist Masters degree course I too noticed the Feminist commitment to anger. And I, too, found it bizarre (not realising at the time that it was being cultivated to be used as a gender-weapon)

Some Feminist writers even speak of 'tending' their anger, of periodically stoking the flames to use it as an energy source for political action.[4] The experiences of Erin Pizzey, expressed above, would certainly confirm this.

It would not be an exaggeration to say that there is a kind of *fetish* of anger within Feminism – what might be called an 'Anger Cult'. Again, anyone who has been involved with Feminists or Feminist activism will have noticed this. The 'Anger Cult' is kept fired up by the regular (intentionally regular) media presentations of Feminist issues – rape, domestic violence, sexual harassment, forced prostitution, and other issues. It is no accident that these are also topics-of-choice for university Women's Studies courses and Social Science Feminist modules. Two disillusioned Equality Feminists who taught on (and who subsequently left) Women's Courses modules note:

'Women's Studies seems to need angry students in order to "keep the momentum going," as one feminist professor put it... From a feminist viewpoint cultivating anger not only increases the likelihood that students will turn to activism but also serves as a precondition for equipping them with an authentic feminist conceptual framework. Those who are not full of rage "just don't get it".'[5]

- It needs to be remembered that almost every university in Britain offers at least one module on Feminism, even if not a full-blown course; such modules are likely to be found in Sociology (especially) and Social Policy courses, but are also present in History, Political Science, Religion and Law (I analysed the prospectuses of over 30 universities, with follow-up enquiries)

- 'Cultivating anger increases the likelihood that students will turn to activism.' Female students are *deliberately* being made angry. Are they aware of this? British universities are producing regular waves of gender-warriors (gender-chiefs if they undertake Feminist postgraduate studies). The implications are not good for society, for the legal and political system, or for democracy (these fired-up, angry, misandrous women enter all professions); and especially not good for men, the target of Feminist anger

- Here we see one of the dynamics that drives Britain to hate men

***

Even if they don't attend a specific Women's/Feminist/Gender Course young women are 'taught' misandrous anger elsewhere during their time at university, directly and indirectly: '1 in 4 women suffer domestic violence'; '1 in 2 women have experienced rape or attempted rape', 'women receive less pay than men for doing the same job'...and so on – complete distortions or untruths. Young women, naturally, believe and become politically energised with what they are told by their lecturers; they are unaware that they are being 'used', are being spoon-fed a misandrous Ideology – it permeates every aspect of university life. In this way young women can become Feminists by osmosis. If the reader thinks that I am paranoid then I advise speaking to any student who has attended university since the early 1980s and seriously question them on the issue. Perhaps many of you will recognise the truth of my claim from your *own* student days? I would like to hear of any pro-Feminist or anti-male experiences you encountered during your university years.[6] We have seen that the National Union of Students is a Feminist organisation (they have Women's Officers at every level – but no Men's Officers, at *any* level).

- Being told that 'men are doing bad things to women', with there being no opportunity to question or challenge this Ideological claim, will obviously create 'anger' in young women – an excellent recruiting technique for the Feminist Movement (it is also used as a strategy to create Male Feminists)

- Being told that 'men are doing bad things to women' belittles and denigrates male students; the universal acceptance and promotion of the Feminist perspective in universities is so strong that any objection by a male student is dismissed as misogynistic. Many that I have spoken to have been angry at the way that men are depicted, and just as angry at their impotence to do anything about this institutional bigotry (we know that there are no Men's Courses or modules, addressing men's specific problems, issues and rights, in *any* of our universities. Not *one* Course; not *one* module)

114

The reader may wish to consider the implications of a university system that indoctrinates young men and women with the idea that 'men are bad people/men are the enemy'. For example, the effect on interpersonal relationships; with this misandrous idea fixed in their minds how will young women view marriage, or see a husband as a decent person; what will be the effect on the divorce rate? How will a young man, informed that because he is male and therefore a 'bad person' towards women, feel about entering a marriage and caring for a wife? By professing the Feminist perspective universities are perverting and corrupting young people's personal relationships. The personal, social, cultural and economic ramifications of this institutional misandry are huge.

- And a complicit State has done nothing about this mass perversion of young people's minds and attitudes, during a Quiet Revolution that has progressed for three decades

In earlier chapters in the book I presented the reader with numerous examples of angry Feminist pronouncements against men; more will be encountered. These are not one-offs, occurring here and there, they are not innocuous sleights; they are malicious and offensive; for example, men being referred to as 'the problematic sex', and the Feminist aim 'to transform men as human beings'. Where anger is not expressed in sexual political issues it is expressed culturally, as we saw in Part One.

- '...to transform men as human beings.'[7] It is difficult to believe that such anger and hate can be freely expressed by a university lecturer and a Labour Government adviser. Yet they are. Men's complacency in the face of this expression of hate is difficult to comprehend

Feminists have succeeded in classifying adult males as 'problematic'. The following is taken from Fatherhood: Contemporary Theory, Research, and Social Policy. It describes the rationale behind the whole series of SAGE books on men and masculinities; it is a textbook used on Sociology, Social Policy and Social Services courses:

'Contemporary research on men and masculinity, informed by recent feminist thought and intellectual breakthroughs of women's studies and the women's movement, treats masculinity not as a normative referent but as a problematic gender.'[8]

- So men have been classified as 'not normal'; they are the 'problematic sex'. This is culturally and legally acceptable. This is being taught in colleges and universities. But to say that Jewish people are 'not normal' and are the 'problematic race' is illegal and designated as a 'hate crime' (quite rightly). You see how Britain hates men?

***

But what of non-university Feminists, from where is *their* anger created and cultivated? Feminism uses the media (and Feminists in the media, both male and female) to whip up anger. Sexual political topics are cleverly chosen to be presented at regular timetabled intervals throughout the year, to ensure a continual 'bad men'/'good women' (patriarchal) script. The truth, the facts, are never pursued, media/press releases from Feminists and Feminist organisations and Interest Groups are accepted at face value, never to be questioned; and the male perspective on any sexual political issue is never offered, there is no gender balance. All aspects of the media – print, audio and visual – participate in this orchestrated Feminist misandrous symphony for sympathy. If there *is* any questioning of this exercise in mass indoctrination it is dismissed, condemned as 'misogynistic', 'part of a backlash', 'part of the New Right', 'trying to roll back women's gains...'.

- Political correctness has done its job; men in the media just shut up, or giggle syco-phantically when interviewing an angry Feminist

    'When it comes to gender issues, journalists generally have suspended all their usual scepticism. We accept at face value whatever women's groups say. Why? Because women have sold themselves to us as an oppressed group and any oppressed group gets a free ride in the press...I can't blame feminists for telling us half-truths and sometimes even complete fabrications. I do blame my colleagues in the press for forgetting their scepticism.'[9]

- What Goldberg has failed to understand is that media people have not 'forgotten their scepticism'. The majority, male and female, are actually *part of* the 'Feminist Community'. And people never criticise or seriously question their own

- The timetabled presentation of Feminist issues in the media, like the use of universities, is an excellent anger-producing vehicle and recruiting forum

***

An example of the rage and anger directed at men can be seen in the mouthings of certain Feminist comediennes, columnists and commentators who possess a misandrous anger that they disguise and express as 'humour' or 'social comment'. They appear to be in denial regarding their man-hating, refusing to see it as a personality dysfunction. It was noted in an earlier chapter, for example, that one such comedienne declared on national prime-time radio that 'men will have sex with anything they find moving in the garden'. Such comments are supposed to be humorous and light-hearted fun.

Such Feminist comediennes, columnists and commentators are the kind of natural bullies who, in an earlier age, would have directed their vindictive, fish-wife rage and anger, culturally sanctioned, at some other target group – Jews, lepers, foreigners, the disabled. Every age and culture has a scapegoat group for which there is social and political legitimacy to denigrate, ridicule and bully. In modern Britain this officially approved scapegoat group, towards which anger and rage is acceptable, is men.

***

Anger is a central element of a Feminist's psychological make-up. It is a common denominator that stimulates Feminists to coalesce into a political Movement with like-minded people. 'Anger against men' (the hatred of men, to a greater or lesser degree) is the bonding glue that forms Feminist Networks, Feminist Organisations, Feminist Interest Groups, Feminist Industries; in short, the Feminist Political and Ideological Community Club, the Feminist Family.

Sure, men get angry too, at the (genuine) injustices they experience with Britain's sexual politics and institutional misandry. The difference is that Feminist anger has been *deliberately* created and cultivated as a political strategy and has been translated into misandrous and women-friendly policy and legislation; whilst men's anger is ignored, or dismissed as 'misogynistic', or part of the 'backlash', or simply as 'whining men'.

- Men have not collectivised their anger, or given their *individual* anger at 'the anti-male system' a political thrust. And so they remain, as a group, politically impotent, politically ignored and politically unrepresented. And so they continue to be institutionally discriminated against

***

Anger is so much part of a Feminist's personality, of her psychological make-up, and so necessary as a political stratagem, that even well-placed, well salaried, influential Feminists are 'angry'. Natasha Walter, a Professional Feminist (one of legions), notes that:

'Yet no one can deny that there is still a great dragging weight of inequality on the backs of even powerful women; a knowledge of injustice; and anger'[10]

- The reader will note the irrationality of Walter's claim: how on earth can 'powerful women' claim to suffer from 'inequality' and 'injustice'? As successful and powerful women how on earth can 'a great weight be dragging them down'? It's a complete contradiction. Feminists are more interested in irrational cant and dogma and in creating 'issues' to fuel their anger, than they are in honesty, logic, or truth. But no doubt Walter, using Feminist-speak, and linguistic skulduggery, can explain how successful and powerful women can *still* be 'oppressed', can still be 'victims', how they still have a 'right' to be angry at men. This irrationality is, itself, an expression of the Feminist's mentality

Others have noticed the same phenomenon; that Feminists in senior positions still hold a personalised anger. For example:

'Christina Hoff Sommers tells of attending a feminist conference at which the speakers, female professors tenured at good universities, were each introduced as "enraged". Nothing in their professional situations would seem to explain why women so fortunately placed are furious, but that is a requirement for membership in the radical sisterhood. It is precisely the disconnection between reality and feminist claims that requires constant rage and hatred to keep the movement viable. And rage must be stoked with falsehoods and irrationality.'[11]

Feminists *need* to be angry, it fuels and drives the implementation of their aims and agenda. It helps to create issues and have these fabricated issues politically accepted as *genuine* ('If women are *so* outraged and angry about this, then it must be a *genuine* issue...it must be addressed'). Anger for a Feminist is not just a 'requirement for the Sisterhood', it is a political necessity that has to be cultivated and honed. The Feminist Harriet Harman was the Labour Government's Minister for Women.

- In this way a Feminist's personal anger (even for those in senior positions) stokes the engine that helps keep the Feminist Grievance Gravy-Train in perpetual motion, and ensures the spread of misandry

***

Feminism is the most dangerous force-field of anger directed at men. Like racists, misogynists, homophobics and anti-Semites I suggest with Feminists – to a greater or lesser extent - there is a personality impairment involved. And in today's Britain this impairment appears 'normal', it is embedded in our conventional wisdom and therefore goes unquestioned and unchallenged. Hence, anything can be said about men, and done to men, without anyone feeling uncomfortable, without any form of censorship, with no one protesting. Feminist anger and rage at men is not bound by any cultural sense of decency or sense of what is acceptable.

- Racism was 'normal' for white supremacists in apartheid South Africa. Racism was 'normal' for whites in America's Deep South. Misandry, in various degrees and forms, is 'normal' in today's Britain

Anger and rage are essential to a Feminist:

- They are an integral part of her psychological make-up that attracts her to Feminism in the first place
- They are deliberately cultivated and nurtured
- They are worn as her credentials: 'angry, outraged and offended' - these are a Feminist's badges of honour, her *esprit de corps*
- They are her membership card to the universal Feminist Community Club and Family
- They are a necessary and effective political strategy and gender-weapon

- A Feminist's anger and outrage must be kept well honed, and regularly displayed, if it is to be effective as a gender-weapon. Sceptical? Part Four is devoted to showing how Feminists *do* intentionally seek out opportunities to express their anger and outrage, how they *deliberately* create and exaggerate 'issues'

In Britain today the Feminist has an on-going licence to disrespect men, to treat men badly, to blame men, and she has the 'right' to feel enraged about anything that she would like to be enraged about. The reader will notice this in the regular features written by Feminist columnists in national newspapers. And *every* national daily newspaper has its Resident Feminist.

***

'Feminists need inequalities, discriminations and oppressions to justify, validate and stoke their anger; their anger at the world, and particularly their anger at men'

(Swayne O'Pie)

Anger and rage: a Feminist neurosis or strategy? Or both? The Feminist Sue Bruley writes in 'No Turning Back: Writings from the Women's Liberation Movement':

'The only possible response to the full realisation of what it means to be female in our society is anger. The challenge is to use our anger in the cause of women's liberation. Firstly, this means learning to express our anger by showing intolerance to continue our lives in the same way and, secondly, learning to channel our anger into a women's movement so that it can become a force for social change.'[12]

With anger towards men being an integral ingredient in the Feminist's temperament and with Feminism being such a widespread and influential Movement in all aspects of British society, culture and the State, at every level and in all professions, it is legitimate to ask any woman who is applying for a senior post, or standing for public office, especially *political* office, whether she is, or is not, a Feminist.

- In fact, such a question should be compulsory

Listen to one Feminist who researched this subject:

> *'To express man-hating, which itself comprises anger along with other emotions, is an angry act. And just as anger often disguises itself, so does hatred of men. And as guilt, sorrow, and fear cannot quite suffocate anger, the pulse of man-hating, though denied, keeps pounding in the temples. Internally, prohibitive emotions mix with prohibited emotions to yield nothing more comforting than ambivalence. But externally, dissembling is often effective. In my researches I was struck by how self-evident the idea of man-hating was to women – "Wow, of course," "yes" were the usual responses – whereas men were frequently surprised to be informed about it. One male editor who read my proposal said he felt he was being let in on a secret.'[13]*

- Women standing for high office really *ought* to be assessed for their commitment to Feminism and for their Feminist sympathies. Consider the consequences of having a great many man-haters in powerful positions in politics, the universities, the legal system, the media, the trade unions, the civil service.... In fact, this is a phenomenon that has already occurred - and the consequence is that modern Britain hates men

We are reminded of the angry Feminist fascists at the Universities of Manchester and Oxford, noted in the Preface, who, in 2009/10, went to extraordinary lengths to prevent two male students from setting up Men's Societies to discuss male-specific problems, issues and rights. It is angry and disturbed Feminists such as these who have entered our professions for more than two decades, at every level, and who now have immense influence in Britain, spreading misandry.

- Why men passively accept this misandrous phenomenon is a mystery. The very *least* we need is a Minister for Men, committed to representing and defending male-specific problems, issues and rights

> *'Men seem to be so cowed they can't fight back, and it is time they did'*
>
> (Doris Lessing)[14]

***

The following is from 'Reclaiming the F Word: The New Feminist Movement', published in 2010 and co-written by two Professional Feminists, Catherine Redfern and Kristin Aune. In 2003 Redfern was named by the Guardian as one of the fifty (Feminist) 'women to watch'. Aune is senior lecturer in Sociology at the University of Derby, where she teaches courses in Feminism. The quote neatly captures the Feminist Community's mentality and anger:

'Feminism assures you that you're not alone, that the problems you experience are shared by others, and that, as a woman or a gender non-conforming person, your concerns are important:

"Thank fuck for feminism, then. You can either go on feeling like the freak, insecure because you just can't be like them, even though you are told you are supposed to be like them. Or you can say 'fuck it' and just be who you are, because that's what makes you happy. And feminism kind of helps you foster that attitude...(feminism) is about ending sexism and liberating everyone from centuries of oppression (by men) based on gender."

...feminism provides you with a support network for your interests and campaigns. It enables us to band together on issues we agree on.'[15]

***

Feminists are dangerous people, aggressively seeking out and creating discriminations, oppressions, causes and issues to justify the continued existence of their Movement; and in the process targeting, blaming, demonising and, whenever possible punishing, men. Thirty years of passively tolerating and *appeasing* these people, allowing them to gain more and more cultural, legal, academic, media and political power, is why modern Britain now hates men.

- Modern British culture and policy shows more respect and consideration for foxes than it does for men: too much of 'Save the Whales' and not enough 'Respect the Males'

Chapter 12

Is There a Feminist 'Pathology'?

We have seen that part of a Feminist's psychological make-up is a certain type of anti-male personality and mentality. We have also seen the Feminist's need to possess, and to cultivate, 'anger'. This chapter looks at the misandrous *expression* of these characteristics. Does holding and expressing them represent a man-hating pathology?

Many Feminists with these characteristics are married...to men. They justify this by saying: 'Well, my husband/son is different, he's OK...but it's the *rest* of them'. This is the same rationale used by the racist: 'Well, that black guy I play dominoes with down the pub, old George, he's OK...but the *rest* are crap'. Fay Weldon, the novelist, lost her misandry after raising four sons. Such converts need to be celebrated; it takes courage.

It is sometimes claimed that Feminism isn't about man-hating. This chapter gives the lie to this claim. Every Feminist issue inherently blames men, directly or indirectly, and mostly the former.

Someone once said that 'political creeds are often rationalisations of emotional problems'. And so it appears to be with many Feminists. In this respect I would like to introduce the reader to a number of psychological concepts against which Feminists' pronouncements may be assessed.[1]

Monomania – '*A pathological obsession with one idea...exaggerated enthusiasm for a subject or idea.*' (Feminist enthusiasm for searching out 'issues', blaming men and privileging women. The 'one idea' being the patriarchy).

Mythomania – '*A compulsion to embroider the truth, exaggerate or tell lies*'. These 'compulsions' are fundamental characteristics of Feminism. Some of these have been observed, and Section 7 is dedicated to these phenomena.

Persecution Complex – '*A psychological delusion that other people feel hostility towards one or are attempting to victimise one*' (Feminists believe that men collectively, the patriarchy, wish to disadvantage women whilst advantaging themselves; Feminists insist that all women are victims of discriminations, inequalities, oppressions and abuses).

Fanatic – '*A person possessed by an excessive and irrational zeal, especially for a religious or political cause...extreme or unscrupulous dedication, monomania*' (fanatics are always present when an ideology is to be spread and imposed – the 'one true' ideology – Communist Russia, Nazi Germany...Feminist Britain).

Psychosis – '*Severe mental derangement, especially when resulting in delusions and loss of contact with external reality*'.

- I would like the reader to carry with him or her throughout the book the word 'psychosis' and bring its definition to mind immediately prior to reading each chapter. Applying the definition of 'psychosis' ('delusional' and 'loss of contact with reality') to Feminist statements, claims and demands will be an eye-opening experience. For example, Feminists claim that women in 2011 Britain are 'oppressed' and 'need to be "liberated" from male subjugation and the patriarchy'. Measuring Feminism and Feminists against the 'psychotic' definition will explain much of why this book needed to be written

***

Feminists and Feminism tick all the above boxes. I suggest that the reader uses the above terms to assess the mentality of *individual* Feminists.

With regard to a Feminist pathology we also have to factor in the Feminists' emotional need for 'anger'. Is it 'normal' to have a perpetual need for anger and to seek out opportunities to both cultivate and express it? And what are we to make of someone who seriously believes that, in 2011 Britain, women are 'oppressed people', who need to be 'liberated' from the subjugation of men? Or what are we to think of a person who has a 'need' to have inequalities and discriminations in her life? Together with the above medical definitions the ingredients are all present for there being a Feminist misandrous pathology.

***

A number of the following anti-male comments have been offered before; but I would like the reader to reconsider them here in the context of an *individual* Feminist's pathology, rather than a collective Ideological misandry. What is the mentality of these women who make such vile comments about half the population, picked up by their followers and which often filter through into the policy-making process? Many vociferous Feminists from the 1970s and 1980s, as well as many of their modern-day acolytes, are now in positions of influence and power in Britain (academics, lawyers, media people, politicians, civil servants, government advisers). So exposing a Feminist pathology is a necessary exercise. I ask the reader to focus on a Feminist's disposition to be misandrous. Is man-hating pathological with Feminists?

An Equality Feminist explains:

> 'Let me therefore be clear that what I am mainly criticising here is an important – and to me profoundly disturbing – aspect of feminism: its predilection for turning complex human relations into occasions for mobilising the feminist troops against men...There is within much feminist writing today (as there has been for the past few decades) a pretence that the charge of male-bashing is a slanderous mischaracterisation motivated by political impulses that are conservative (and thus assumed to be reprehensible). But it is plain and irrefutable that much contemporary feminism is indeed marred by hostility toward men.'[2]

The following are offered to confirm the above point. Do these comments reflect a 'normal' mentality? Feminists, because of their personality and need for 'anger', fail to realise that their offensive and malicious comments go well beyond the bounds of decency.

***

122

From Andria Dworkin we have:

'I want to see a man beaten to a bloody pulp with a high-heeled shoe shoved in his mouth, like the apple in the mouth of a pig.'[3]

We have seen such utterances from Dworkin before and it may be thought that she is too extreme to be taken seriously. This is not so. Influential Feminists endorse Dworkin's comments. Mainstream Feminist Gloria Steinem, for example, eulogises:

'In every century, there are a handful of writers who help the human race to evolve. Andrea is one of them.'[4]

- It is bizarre to suggest that the human race is being helped to evolve by beating up and choking one half of it

Susan Brownmiller declares that rape is:

'...nothing more or less than a conscious process of intimidation by which all men keep all women in a state of fear.'[5]

- Intimidation by *all* men?...*my* sons...*your* sons?

Dworkin again:

'Only when manhood is dead – only then will we know what it is like to be free.'[6]

Sally Miller Gerhart is a Professor of Communication and participates in mainstream society and mainstream Feminism. She openly advocates the decimation of men:

'She would allow no more than 10% of the population to be male. Why? Because she believes that women are innately peaceful and kind and caring and sharing and loving, and so on...and that men are innately violent and evil and horrible.'[7]

In the late 1960s a Feminist magazine was published, SCUM. It was a manifesto for Feminism. SCUM was resurrected in the 1980s. And again, introduced on the internet in 2009. It was founded and edited by Valerie Solanas. The following are quotes from SCUM. 'The male is a walking abortion', 'Your average man is a half-dead, unresponsive, lump.' Solanas believed that men's days were numbered because they are 'self-destructive creatures'. She encouraged Feminists, 'Scum girls', to speed up this inevitability because men have 'no right to life as they are a lesser life form than women'.[8]

- Extreme? We have seen an example of a widely used university textbook referring to men as 'the problematic sex'; we have seen a university lecturer, together with a Labour Government adviser, asking if men 'ought to be transformed as human beings'. Many modern Feminists' views are in line with Solanas's views

'Scum girls will...burst into heterosexual couples and break them up (couple-busting); they will pick off and kill certain relevant male targets.'

Scum girls, Solanas pronounced, are the coolest, grooviest, most enlightened females whereas other women are 'toadies and doormats'. Finally, the organisation SCUM will be in a position to plan the 'agenda for eternity and Utopia' and no more men will need to be killed once women wake up to men's 'banality and uselessness'.

- I invite the reader to substitute the word 'Jew' for 'men' in the above extracts, and then predict society's, and the State's, reaction

Solanas shot, and almost killed, the artist Andy Warhol. Unsurprisingly, she was eventually committed to a mental asylum. Yet like Dworkin, she was revered by, and had influence in, the Feminist movement:

> 'Solanas did not lack feminist champions for her exorbitant gesture, as evidenced by the two representatives of the National Organisation for Women, Ti-Grace Atkinson and Florynce Kennedy who accompanied her to court...Atkinson said Solanas would go down in history as "the first outstanding champion of women's rights"...Kennedy called her "one of the most important spokeswomen for the feminist movement"...In her introduction to the SCUM Manifesto Vivian Gornick called Solanas a "visionary" who "understood the true nature of the struggle" for women's liberation...Mary Harron made a movie based on the event: I Shot Andy Warhol. Once again, its critics glorified Solanas.'[9]

- SCUM is an acronym - Society for Cutting Up Men

***

Another misandrous Feminist declares:

> 'I don't think I ever chose man-hating to be part of my life. It seems to have chosen me. And no matter how many times I glare at it and yell, "You're ugly and irrational," it doesn't disappear...It is a hatred that can be of demonic, though often repressed, ferocity. Rap sessions can't break the back of it, nor anti-male tirades, nor psychoanalysis (at least, not so far). Nor demonstrations against the oppression of women, nor, for that matter, writing about it.'[10]

- Here we have a Feminist self-defining her own mental state of hating men as 'ugly', 'irrational', 'demonic' and 'ferocious'...but *still* continues to hate men. Very much like the bigotry of a racist. So yes, a pathology

The critic Mary Fox had this to say about the novelist Marilyn French (commenting on French's novel, The Women's Room):

> 'So virulent is Marilyn French in her denunciation of men that it seems comparable only to Hitler's paranoid ravings...'[11]

- French was the author of Beyond Power, a massive book that purported to show not only that men are both evil and inferior to women but so is the condition of 'maleness' itself

Robin Morgan, university lecturer and Feminist, declares:

> '(Man-hating) is an honourable and viable political act, the oppressed have a right to class-hatred against the class that is oppressing them.'[12]

- And by such means individual Feminists attempt to rationalise and excuse their anger, rage and hatred toward men

Stirring up hatred against any group is a crime in Britain. If some of these comments were made about black people, Jews or gays (or women), the perpetrators would be arrested, and certainly thought of as being at least a little abnormal.

- However, when *men* are the target, as they are in Britain, it is culturally acceptable and legal

British university libraries carry misandrous literature, for reference and study:

'By far the most disturbing venue for objectifying and even dehumanising men, though, would be the books and articles written by feminist ideologues. These publications encourage readers – either overtly or covertly, directly or indirectly – to feel contempt for men as inferior beings or even to hate men as the source of all suffering and evil throughout history.'[13]

- Is it 'normal' to write books that dehumanise men and hold them in contempt? All universities now have thousands (literally) of such Feminist/Women's/Gender Studies books on their shelves (I researched 30 university Arts/Humanities/Social Science libraries on this subject so it is reasonable to assume that the remainder have a similar number)

Germaine Greer tells us that:

'To be male is to be a kind of idiot savant, full of queer obsessions about fetishistic activities and fantasy goals, single-minded in pursuit of arbitrary objectives, doomed to competition and injustice, not merely towards females but towards children, animals and other men.'[14]

Erin Pizzey again, referring to the Feminist mentality:

'I watched the feminist movement build its bastions of hatred against men, fortresses where women were to be taught that all men were rapists and bastards, and I witnessed the damage done to the children in the refuges who were taught that men were not to be trusted.'[15]

- Teaching women and children to hate men...can this be 'normal'? Has Erin Pizzey identified a Feminist's mental disorder?

The Feminist mentality is unremittingly misandrous:

'It should by now be clear that current popular culture does more than merely ridicule or trivialise men, more than merely encourage indifference or contempt for men, more even than dehumanise men, although any of these things would be bad enough. It goes farther to demonise men.'[16]

- What kind of a mentality would *deliberately* wish to demonise a fellow group of human beings, including their own fathers, husbands and sons?

A renowned psychologist, Dr. Bruno Bettleheim, is one of those who believes that Feminists are:

'... emotionally sick and that the chaos they are raging against is not so much society's as that within themselves: They are "fixated at the age of the temper-tantrum".'[17]

Camille Paglia, a one-time Feminist, is Professor of Humanities at the University of Arts in Philadelphia and author of numerous books. She comments:

'What women have to realise is their dominance as a sex. That women's sexual powers are enormous. All cultures have seen it. Men know it. Women know it. The only people who don't know it are feminists. Desensualised, desexualised, neurotic women. I wouldn't have said this twenty years ago because I was a militant feminist myself. But as the years have gone on, I begin to see more and more that the perverse, neurotic psychodrama projected by these women is coming from their own problems with sex.'[18]

• Here we have an ex-Feminist admitting that Feminists have mental health issues

Anyone who has participated in a Social Science course (especially Sociology), at any level, will have encountered (in at least one female lecturer) a Feminist pathology.

***

There is, it would seem, a definite Feminist misandrous pathology and mentality.

The universal unquestioning acceptance of Feminism in Britain has given individual Feminists a licence to express themselves in an abnormal way that without the protection of such a licence they would never otherwise have done. For example, can the following comment by the Feminist Naomi Wolf be classified as 'normal', and would she have expressed it in an age when Feminism wasn't the dominant, all-powerful Ideology that it is today? The constant successes of Feminism have given Feminists the confidence, the licence, to denigrate and malign men at will, without anyone protesting:

'Looking how easy it is to treat men badly is oddly liberating'[19]

• Is it 'liberating' for racists to treat black people badly...? Is it 'liberating' for homophobic skinheads to treat gays badly...? Is it 'liberating' for anti-Semites to treat Jews badly...? Someone aiming such comments at these targets would fairly be thought of as unbalanced and in need of counselling

• But from Feminists...towards men? Well, that's OK

Barbara Ellen, one of the misandrous Professional Feminists working for The Observer:

'Without meaning to be rude, pretty soon, we could probably phase men out altogether. Just keep a few to look at and prod and say to each other in 3010 AD: "Bloody hell, did we really used to keep these horrible hairy things in our houses?"...Maybe this is what Men's Hour is really about – Man's last, desperate, vuvuzela-blowing stand, before women gang together and actually put them in zoos, museums or something (2010).'[20]

• Not to be taken seriously? OK, substitute the word 'Pakistani' for 'men' and see how your Left-wing/liberal/progressive self-righteous, sanctimonious hypocritical conscience feels about *that*

The Academic Feminist Rosalind Miles:

'To explain violence is to explain the male'[21]

'Only men prey on those weaker than themselves'[22]

'We need to acknowledge that the seeds of violence are in every man'[23]

'Fathers are invariably heavily involved in their sons' early apprenticeship to violence and pain.[24]

- Miles established the Centre for Women's Studies at Coventry Polytechnic, a forum from which she and her Sister lecturers could, if they wished, express a Feminist misandrous mentality to generations of students. Miles was honoured, in spite of her man-hating, by being elected to the Royal School of Arts...honoured for maligning men. Bizarre

- Do a target-switch and bring a strong stomach to the exercise. Substitute the word 'Jew' for 'man/men/male/father', and the word 'usury' for 'violence' in Miles' comments. Make a similar target-switch (or Pakistani/gays) with all the *preceding* misandrous Feminist statements

The Lesbian Feminist Julie Burchill, writing in Time Out:

'A good part – and definitely the most fun part – of being a feminist (Nazi) is about frightening men (Jews). American and Australian feminists (Nazis) have always known this, and absorbed it cheerfully into their act; one thinks of Shere Hite julienning men (Jews) on phone-in shows, or Dale Spender telling us that a good feminist (Nazi) is rude to a man (Jew) at least three times a day ON PRINCIPLE. Of course, there's a lot more to feminism (Nazism)...but scaring the shit out of the scumbags (Jews) is an amusing and necessary part, because, sadly, a good many men (Jews) still respect nothing but strength.'[25]

- Julie Burchill is not anti-Semitic, but the bigotry is the same. I ask Jewish readers to forgive me for making my point so strongly, but these people, like racists, homophobes and anti-Semites, need to have it drummed into them that *bigotry is always wrong* and unacceptable, whoever may be the target of their hatred, even when it is culturally condoned and 'licensed', as misandry is in Britain today

Marilyn French was a hard-line misandrous Feminist; she died in May 2009. Here, the columnist Libby Purves, celebrates French's pathological hatred of men:

'The human side of a man-hating feminist...Marilyn French was angry – and scary. But sometimes we need people to kick against the traces...she aimed a blowtorch straight at the collective groin of Man the Master...Salute her.'[26]

- If a homophobe had suggested aiming a blowtorch at the groin of *gay* men would The Times have printed *that*? Do gay-hating homophobes have a 'human side'? Do we need such people 'to kick against the traces' of homosexuality?

You see what I'm getting at?

***

One may legitimately ask whether the above comments represent a mentality that one would wish to see in one's children. Do the comments indicate a certain type of pathology? The tragedy is that our culture, including our education system, particularly our universities, actually *teaches* (indoctrinates?) young women to *view* men in this way, to *think* about men in this way, to *speak* about men in this derogatory, insulting way. And to *treat* men as if they were 'bad people'. Britain's Feminist-dominated education system encourages man-hating because in our society and culture it has become 'normal'. National newspapers have no qualms about printing it. Feminists who freely express their hatred of men are simply a product of this system. Are they aware that if they made similar comments directed at any other group in Britain then they would be committing a 'hate' crime...with many of their Left-wing/liberal/progressive colleagues wondering if they had mental health issues? No, they are not aware; in modern misandrous Britain they see their attitude and behaviour as simply being 'normal' and therefore acceptable.

- Misandry goes unnoticed because it has entered our cultural bloodstream

    'It is time we began to ask who are these women who continually rubbish men. The most stupid, ill-educated, and nasty woman can rubbish the nicest, kindest and most intelligent man and no one protests.'[27]

***

I suggest that many Feminists are embittered women who have been empowered by mutual bonding in their Political Community Club, and by Feminist-friendly legislation and policy initiatives...and have been 'licensed' to excess by our passivity, by no one ever protesting. They hide their Feminist mentality under the banner of the innocuous sounding term 'gender equality'. And using this sanctimonious self-righteousness as a societal, cultural and political licence, they revel in the freedom of expressing and spreading pathological man-hating.

The philosopher F.A. Hayek observed the factors that strengthened the tendency of group collectivism with fascism and socialism. I suggest that this phenomenon is the same with the individual Feminist in her Political Community Club and Family:

    'Of these (strengthening factors) one of the most important is that the desire of the individual to identify himself (herself) with a group is very frequently the result of a feeling of inferiority, and that therefore his (her) want will only be satisfied if membership of the group confers some superiority over outsiders. Sometimes, it seems, the very fact that these violent instincts...can be given a free rein in the collective action towards the outsider, becomes a further inducement for merging personality in that of the group.'[28]

- This very much identifies the position of Feminists, and explains their behaviour, in modern Britain. Also, 'the group' gives a licence to avoid *personal* responsibilty.

Tellingly, Hayek continues:

    'To act on behalf of a group seems to free people of many of the moral restraints which control their behaviour as individuals...'[29]

We will see in Part Four that the Feminist's misandrous pathology is also expressed by creating and manufacturing 'issues' that blame and condemn men. The results of this misandrous strategy, this pathology, are then fed into the policy-making process.

Chapter 13

Terrible as an Army with Banners

'Feminism appears to attract people with large holes in their souls'

(Swayne O'Pie)

This chapter is a collection of loose ends with regard to analysing the Feminist mind. Further observations are made, further characteristics identified, and questions and concerns raised. It is noted that Feminists from all social classes and levels of education possess common emotional and mental traits. It is asked whether men hate women in the way that Feminists hate men. Finally, an example of a Feminist's psychological make-up, and its real-life application, is given.

One point that needs to be made is that a 'Feminist mentality' has a common historical thread. We saw that many Suffragettes had a bitter, abnormal, personality and psychological make-up. The Suffragette leader Mrs. Pankhurst, for example, claimed that God caused the 1st World War in order to punish men. It was shown in earlier chapters that Feminists in the 1970s and 1980s exhibited what many would consider a personality disorder. Examples were then given of today's Feminists expressing a similar pathology. There is a certain type of dark mental disposition in some women that has an historical thread, connecting them with a man-hating world-view.

- 'As terrible as an army with banners' (Song of Songs 6:10). The astute reader will realise that I refer to the Feminist's psychological need for synthetic 'outraged' public demonstrations and marches, with loud clichéd mantras, placards and sound-bite banners

The anti-male rantings and blatant man-hating statements of Feminists express a similar psychotic mentality to those who make racist, anti-Semitic and homophobic statements. Many would suggest that the leading Nazis' hatred of, and anger toward, the Jews was evidence of a mental disorder (as they would also consider the mentalities of neo-fascists). 'Hate', held at any point along a spectrum, is a negative and destructive emotion, but when collectivised into a political Movement, theorised into an Ideology, and aimed at a specific group, it is particularly immoral and dangerous.

- The majority of Feminists will be in denial: 'Not me, not me – *I'm* not that kind of Feminist!'

Scratch the surface of *any* self-confessed Feminist and the characteristics of a Feminist personality and mentality will be revealed, a Feminist psychological make-up will be exposed. There is a *spectrum* of a Feminist 'mentality' along which any individual Feminist can be placed; a spectrum that embraces all degrees of misandry from the hard-core activist at one end to Feminist sympathiser at the other. An individual's placement along this spectrum is dependent upon her personal history, her personal circumstances and her individual characteristics.

***

We have seen that Lesbian Feminism is one of the strongest sub-groups driving the Ideology (another is Socialist Feminism). In the context of the present chapter I offer the following observation. It offers one aspect in identifying the elements that constitute a Feminist psychological make-up:

> *'The second predictable element in every feminist woman I have known is that as a girl she was a tomboy. Many women found that feminism validated aspects of their personalities and ambitions that did not fit majority norms of femininity, and consequently acquired an exaggerated respect for a movement that offered them a liberation they would have acquired in any case. No, you're not weird or crazy, feminism assured them.'*[1]

- We have seen that one-third of Feminists are lesbian

So it is suggested that many Lesbian Feminists seek out and join the Feminist Movement because they give it an 'exaggerated respect', it comfortably accommodates their different 'personalities and ambitions' that they feel they have difficulty being accommodated elsewhere. This emotional dimension may explain why Lesbian Feminism is such a strong influence in the Movement – it provides a specifically sexual 'home' as well as a Political and Ideological Club, for which they have 'exaggerated respect', and from which they can safely express their anger toward a section of society that does not 'validate their femininity' – men.

Here again we see a resonance with the Suffragettes, of which it was noted at the time:

> *'Among the great army of sex, the regiment of aggressively man-hating women is full of strength, and signs of the times that it is steadily being recruited. On its banner is emblazoned "Woe to Man" and its call to arms is shrill and loud. These are the women who are "independent of men".'*[2]

- One hundred years later and Feminists *still* have the same misandrous mentality, the same personality, the same anger

***

However, many straight women also adopt a Feminist mentality because they find the Movement psychologically comfortable and seductive. It offers them an escape route, a dignity for their disappointment, allowing them to see themselves as wronged 'victims'; for example, when losing out in job interviews or promotions rather than admitting to being simply unlucky, or being inadequate. Feminism offers these women an excuse that has been sanctioned by society and the State (We all 'know' that women are a victimised, oppressed and discriminated-against group; we all 'know' that there is a barrier called 'the glass ceiling' that stops women reaching senior positions). So personal incompetence, personal responsibility, need not be faced up to; they can 'legitimately' be denied. Again, a certain type of mentality is evident.

***

Feminists seriously dislike 'the feminine'. Could this be because they have experienced some kind of dysfunctional childhood, perhaps an ineffectual father combined with a dominant mother, with disappointment and resentment being the outcome? If this is coupled with the Feminist's obsession with the implicit assumption that only what men do and prize has any value (senior posts, studying subjects like mathematics and science rather than literature and humanities, for example), then a picture would emerge of Feminists actually *disliking* womanhood. Indeed, a brief glance at the Feminist classics – de Beauvoir, Millett, Juliet Mitchell, Oakley – shows us that Feminists view non-Ideological women as small-minded, irrational, dependent and mentally unbalanced (see later chapters, in which Feminists express their anger at women who wish to be stay-at-home mothers).

The psychological mix of: i) abnormal (to some degree) paternal and maternal relationships, ii) holding only 'male things' as being of any value, and iii) a general dislike of women, has perhaps led to Feminists disliking *themselves* because they are female. This culminates in an inordinate anger towards anything that celebrates femininity – the use of make-up, women's use of plastic surgery to enhance their attractiveness, women being seen as sex objects by men, beauty contests, paintings of nude women, pornography, prostitution...anything that exemplifies femininity is condemned. And men who like femininity are therefore to be demonised as 'bad people'.

- This would explain the heavy-handed clampdown and punishment of men who use the services of prostitutes by Feminist-influenced police forces and driven by Feminist-dominated policy-makers

- Gay men, who are obviously not attracted to women's femininity, are never considered to be 'bad people'; they are members of the Community Club, the Feminist Family

It is worth repeating the observation of Camille Paglia in this context; Paglia noted the Feminists' confusions and ambivalence about their femaleness:

'What women have to realise is their dominance as a sex. That women's sexual powers are enormous. All cultures have seen it. Men know it. Women know it. The only people who don't know it are feminists. Desensualised, desexualised, neurotic women. I wouldn't have said this twenty years ago because I was a militant feminist myself. But as the years have gone on, I begin to see more and more that the perverse, neurotic psychodrama projected by these women is coming from their own problems with sex.'[3]

***

A further aspect of the Feminist personality and mentality is the universal presence of arrogance. Feminists never *expect* to be questioned or challenged about their Ideology in discussion or debate. Their aggressive/assertive self-righteousness is astonishing. And, in truth, they very rarely *are* questioned or challenged; this freedom from criticism, this cultural, media, academic and political protection, feeds this arrogance and empowerment.

***

There are numerous facets to, and expressions of, a Feminist mentality. Misandry is only one. Another is 'creating issues'. This will be addressed in later chapters but it is appropriate to introduce it in the present context.

Essentially, there is something 'not quite right' about someone who *deliberately* spends time seeking out 'discriminations and oppressions against women', or 'sexist' comments or advertisements, or trivial incidents or remarks that (with a bit of effort) can be carefully construed as sexist, or misogynist - and then to be 'outraged' and 'offended' by these discoveries. These outraged and offended people then write books on the subject, or attend marches and demonstrations, or attend conferences on the topic, or produce a documentary/written article/academic paper exposing the 'issue'. And where possible, convert their synthetic outrage into policy. There must be something amiss with someone who *continually* wishes to bring victimisation upon her own head and upon the heads of other women in order to perpetuate her Ideology. These are not the behaviours of a normal person, nor do they reflect a healthy mental condition.

***

The Feminist mentality has serious implications for policy-making. Do Feminists in senior positions have a specific psychological make-up, a Feminist pathology? Yes, of course they do, a Feminist is a Feminist. In this context I'll refer again to Ann Carlton, who was a political adviser to both Anthony Crosland and John Silkin (two high-ranking Ministers) and is a former senior national officer of the Labour Party. She mixed extensively in political circles and with policy-makers. Her comments on high-flying Feminists are all the more remarkable because she is a Socialist:

> *'Feminist Thought Police: men cower at their denunciations. Most women avoid them. To speak out against them is to meet with abuse and sloganising, not logical arguments...They are the Feminist Thought Police. Lacking grass-roots support, these harridans seek, through public relations polemics, to make their sexist views politically correct. Politicians on all sides have caved in, issuing worthless charters to show they care...Like so many who want to subvert natural justice, the Feminist Thought Police start from the need to correct an obvious injustice, then proceed by a series of illogical steps to create another injustice which just happens to benefit their careers.'*[4]

- So yes, there is a certain type of personality and mentality that is found in *all* Feminists, in all socioeconomic classes, in all professions, at all levels of society and the State

- Here we see male MPs, in all political parties, 'caving in', not wishing to face the abuse, the anger, the sloganising, the irrationality, of high-ranking pathological Feminist Ideologues:

> *'The shrill feminists who made men the enemy take shrewd advantage of the fact that men hate arguing with women'.*[5]

And Feminists have become arrogant in the knowledge that they will never be questioned or challenged, and that their demands will always be positively considered. It is true to say that men (and many women) are fearful of confronting this Terrible Army, or any of its individual gender-warriors.

So the Feminist's pro-female/anti-male mentality seriously impacts upon policy-making. What appear to be Feminist 'extremist' views are, in fact, now the prevailing political fashion in Britain, they are now embedded in the mainstream.

'The idea that men oppress women, who therefore have every interest in avoiding the marriage trap and must achieve independence from men at all costs, may strike many as extreme and having little to do with everyday life. Yet it is now the galvanic principle behind (British) social, economic and legal policy-making.'[6]

• Driven by a specific Feminist mentality since the 1970s a Quiet Revolution has been progressing

The young Feminists of the 1970s and the 1980s did not 'go away'. They have become some of the most powerful women in many areas of the Establishment and State. Feminists (and, of course, their specific personality, characteristics, disposition, mentality and pathology) are to be found in every walk of life: they are most influential in the professions – education (at all levels), the media, the legal system, trade unions, national charities, lobby groups... and most worryingly, in Parliament as MPs and powerful cabinet ministers.

'Jews cannot be trusted to run the country.'
(Harriet Harman, Deputy Prime Minister and Minister for Women and Equality, July, 2009)

In fact, it was not Jews to which Harman referred (she is certainly *not* anti-Semitic) but 'men'...however, you get the point. We have become so conditioned to accept misandry, even in the highest levels of the State, that we never notice it and it goes unchecked. Yet we twitch nervously and disapprovingly when any *other* group is similarly disparaged.

***

As an Equality Feminist I wish the reader to understand that I have no problem with women being employed in senior positions. But I *do* have a problem with *Feminist* women being employed in senior and powerful positions. Such is the severity of a Feminist's pro-women/anti-men mentality that I suggest that any woman standing for office, especially as an MP, should be assessed for her Feminist sympathies. Women in public office? Yes, of course, at every level. But do we really want women with a man-hating mentality (to a greater or lesser degree), and who wish to preference, privilege and policy-favour women, being responsible for formulating and implementing policy?

Having a Feminist in a senior post is far worse than having a racist or homophobe in a senior post; these people are simply prejudiced individuals. But a Feminist has an *Ideology*, has belief systems, doctrines, dogma, a political agenda and aims. We know that she is misandrous, we know that she will preference, privilege and policy-favour women (but mainly herself and her Sisters), we know that she seriously dislikes men and wishes to blame and punish them, we know that she desires a Socialist, pro-Feminist revolution, wishing to transform society and the State. We know that she is a member of a tight-knit Political Community Club and Family that has immense influence, we know how she and her Sisters speak disparagingly about men, we know that a major personality characteristic is anger, we know that she is pathologically unsettled. We know that these political and psychological ingredients are common to *all* Feminists, in different strengths. Do we really need such people in positions of power?

• I suggest that it ought to be mandatory to ask a woman who is standing for a senior post – in academia, the legal profession, the media, as a politician, civil servant...whether or not she is a Feminist. Non-Ideological women would have no objection to such a question. Although such a question would be politically incorrect, are we to blithely whistle, dance and skip our way to Gomorrah, following the Pied Pipers of the Sisterhood?

***

Do men 'hate' women? No, they do not. Occasionally we experience a serial killer. But their actions are driven by their insanity; they are not politically motivated, their actions are not the expression of an Ideology, a belief system with specific aims and an agenda. An individual man may hate an individual woman, but I have never seen or heard men, *anywhere*, write or speak about women, as a collective group, in the derogatory and negative way that Feminists write and speak about men as a group.

As an active member of Fathers 4 Justice I witnessed the individual pain of many fathers who were denied contact with their children by vindictive ex-wives. I was also told, by these father's girlfriends and mothers, of their deep and continuing personal distress. Quite a few had spent many thousands of pounds in legal fees in a vain attempt to see their children for just a few hours each week. But even these divorced men who had had their children's lives stolen from them, and who were utterly desperate and angry, *never once* (in my wide experience with them) directed their anger and their hatred at *women in general*, women as a group. And these men really *did* have a genuine issue that should have stimulated anger and hatred towards *all* women. What could be more emotionally cruel and traumatic than having your children taken away from you and your human and natural right to see them denied, knowing that many thousands of ex-wives are legally and politically protected, indeed, 'licensed' every year to do this? And yet they *still* didn't hate women...I never once witnessed any misogyny.

***

David Mamet's play, Oleana, was based upon a real event that took place in an Australian university. It exposes the personality and mentality of a student Feminist.

The play is set in a university professor's study. In the opening scene the professor rambles on (in the typical self-assured, self-involved rambling way that some professors do) to a female student to whom he is giving a tutorial. She listens resentfully. At one point she gets upset, and he puts his arm on her shoulder in the sort of bumbling way that ivory-tower professors do. When she asks why he is being kind to her and why he is bothering to help her he simply and innocently replies that 'he likes her'. The play hinges on the way in which she twists his words and actions to fit her own developing Ideological agenda.

Having consulted with her Feminist colleagues, she reports the professor to the university committee. Feminism has transformed the not-too-bright, formerly timid student with an aversion to big words, into a fully-fledged, jargon-toting, rapid-fire Ideologue. She comes into his office armed with accusations of his classist, sexist, elitist behaviour. The 'comforting hand on the shoulder' is now interpreted as a sexual harassment incident. She refers to her Feminist group as 'My Group' and declares that she is acting not as an individual but on behalf of 'Her Group'. As she gets up to leave, he grabs her by the shoulders to force her to hear *his* explanation of events. This gesture later evolves into her charging him with attempted rape.

Later, sensing that she now has the Establishment on her side, that she now controls the situation and has the power, she gives him a list of books, including his own, and states that she will recant her charges if he agrees never to use them in his teaching again. He refuses. She continues with her charges against him. He is given notice from his professorship...

134

Over the previous uneventful months she had occasionally been in his study while he was speaking with his wife on the telephone. On the last occasion they meet, now that she has won and has the upper hand, she brazenly tells him, victory in her voice, not to call his wife 'baby' ever again (as during his personal telephone calls to her he had been in the habit of doing) because the term is demeaning to women; this interfering personal rebuke drives him over the edge...he has lost everything and now she is telling him, *ordering* him, how he should speak to his wife. He physically attacks her.

- She has seized personal power through her Ideological Community Club, emotionally drawing upon and utilising its collective anger, dogma, cant, rhetoric, and she is protected by its sanctimonious self-righteousness, arrogantly knowing that the university authorities dare not stand up to the Feminist Community. She is puffed up with the success of her being a 'victim' – having been empowered by her 'victimhood' in a culture that is a slave to the Feminist perspective. Her hatred of men has been legitimised and expressed through destroying, punishing, one man. The play is factual, based upon a true incident. There are very many such Feminists in Britain today

Feminism has given such 'damaged women' a way to strike back at their supposed 'oppressors' – men; this is an easier and more Community Club-supported route than taking on the personal responsibility of individually confronting their frayed personal lives. F. A. Hayek noted of fascists and socialists:

'To act on behave of a group seems to free people of many of the moral restraints which control their behaviour as individuals...'[7]

***

At this point I would like the reader to consider the following questions. Do Feminists exhibit personality traits that most people admire and want in themselves and in their children? Are Feminists flexible and capable of laughing at themselves? Are they in control of their lives? Is anger, the characteristic condition of Feminists, likely to produce insights or distortions? Is a desire to collect grievances normal? Is the drive to create inequalities, discriminations and issues the product of a childhood that is generally found in the lives of well-adjusted adults? Does the compulsion to blame others and constantly absolve oneself (and one's Ideological Family) of personal responsibility a characteristic of a well-balanced personality? Is the state of constant dissatisfaction a trait that one would wish to see in one's own family? Is the impulse to dislike the male half of the population something to be desired? Can the reader bring to mind any other social movement in which feelings of displeasure and belligerence play such a prominent role? Is there any other social or political movement in which participants refuse to accept their success, for whom success is never enough; for whom accommodation and appeasement to any demand will always be unsatisfying and merely trigger further demands?

'Feminism legitimises the sickness of some women'[8]

There is a specific and definite Feminist psychological make-up, a Feminist personality, a Feminist mentality, a Feminist pathology and psychosis. And today *all* men are its potential victims.

'Feminism is no longer a cause, as it once was with Equality Feminism, but a symptom'

(Swayne O'Pie)

135

Chapter 14
Everywoman, Feminism and Misandry

Many women are not active or vocal Feminists yet still participate in misandry and misandrous behaviour. In this sense they are Feminist-susceptible and Feminist-tainted. This chapter looks at the ways in which 'Everywoman' expresses a degree of misandry. For example, 'Men have no feelings', is a common misandrous expression among women. It is then noted how a woman may take a difficulty she has with *one* man and expand it to a dislike of *all* men. Finally, it is seen how prevalent the serious dislike of men actually is among women.

Male-bashing is one of British women's favourite sports. It is also a popular bonding agent among women.

> '...it is now open season on men. Their public portrayal might almost be interpreted as a kind of revenge. Certainly it betokens little respect or even fairness. Men are laughed at as useless and treated with contempt; they are portrayed as oafish idiots, outsmarted by women at every turn. Television comedy programmes such as "Men Behaving Badly" drive home the image of men as unappealing losers.
>
> Women feel justified in talking about men in terms which, if they were used against women, would be condemned for their virulent prejudice and cruelty.'[1]

Many non-Feminist women show disrespect (a form of misandry) for men. When spending time together women will talk about men in disparaging ways.

> 'Most men say that they find male-bashing – in which, in one survey, half of women under age twenty-five unapologetically admitted engaging – at worst a minor irritant. But however seriously it's intended or taken, the men-are-scum talk contributes to an unspoken assumption that in any conflict between the sexes, "It's always the man's fault".'[2]

Three examples of this. First, there is a cultural perception that the male is at fault in a divorce; the immediate presumption is that it is he who is the guilty party: if the husband leaves the marriage, then he's the bad guy; if the wife leaves, he's still the bad guy because he 'must have done something to make her leave.' Secondly, there is also a double standard in adultery: the husband who strays is a 'love rat'; the wife who strays is a victim, or someone who wishes to pursue her personal development, or someone who is 'trapped in a loveless marriage'.

In June, 2011, the footballer Ryan Giggs was exposed as having had an eight-year affair with his brother's wife. This was an immoral thing to do. However, the printed media spoke of Giggs as if he were the *only* person in this sorry scenario who was in the wrong. Natasha Giggs (the sister-in-law), was *also* married...and she knew that Ryan Giggs was married so morally *she* was just as culpable. The double standard of the press was astonishing; for example, Ryan Giggs was referred to simply and disparagingly as 'Giggs' (surname) whilst the sister-in-law was referred to sympathetically as 'Natasha' (Christian name). Natasha claimed that she was 'manipulated' by Giggs and that's why she had the affair. 'Manipulated'...for *eight years?* 'Manipulated' - a grown woman, not an impressionable teenager? 'Manipulated'...employing the services of Max Clifford to sell her story?

- The double standard, with the male always being the one maligned, blamed and 'in the wrong', is endemic in Britain

Again, we see an example of 'it's always men's fault' in the refusal of an ex-wife to allow her ex-husband to have contact with his children. Two Druid women I was in discussion with in a pub in Wales were adamant that it was divorced fathers *themselves* who were at fault for their not being allowed to see their children – because they 'must be wife-batterers or paedophiles'. These two women were really nice, gentle souls, but their views on this had been informed and then hardened by Feminism (they mentioned by name a number of Feminist friends who had influenced their thinking). They could not be shaken in this very odd view: Question: "Is *every* divorced father who is not allowed to see his children a wife-batterer or a paedophile?" Answer: "Yes". They *had* to believe what they *needed* to believe because the alternative – that some women may not be very nice people – was too uncomfortable for these women to contemplate. So in effect, what they (and many others) are saying is that 'men are presumed to be "bad people" and therefore need to be punished' (in this case by not being permitted to see their children after divorce).

- I would suggest that the majority of women are misandrous, to some degree

Tim Lott, the writer, identifies this nicely. I know that I have used this quote before but it is also relevant in the present context. There is a passage in his book 'Love Secrets of Don Juan' in which the hero, Danny, is at his ex-wife's house (formerly *his* home) for their child's birthday party. The ex-wife's new boyfriend and female friends are there. Danny asks the women if they think that men and women are equal; and all agree that they are. Danny asks them to name some of the things that women are better at. A long list ensues, also contributed to by the ex-wife's new boyfriend. Then Danny asks the group, 'What are the special virtues of men?':

> *'Silence. More silence. An embarrassed giggle from Charlotte..."I'll tell you one thing men are better at," I say, flatly. "Putting up with things. Biting their lip, and putting up with things. Putting up with bucketloads and bucketloads of absolute shit being poured over their head. And not fighting back. They're better at not fighting back. They're better at taking it, taking it, taking it, and then just walking away." Without another word, I turn on my heel and walk through to the kitchen...'*[3]

A further example, with which many of us can relate:

> *'A few years ago, I was at a Christmas party. A woman began talking about her husband and how stupid he was for not being able to do a simple mechanical job at home. She went on to say how all men are like that and how women really have to put up with a lot from men's inconsistencies and it's amazing we have survived them. The women laughed and the men smiled and nodded or shrugged. No one objected or seemed to be offended. One man go up, supposedly to get some coffee, and came into the kitchen and said to me, "I am so sick of parties where the majority of the conversation is about how men are screwed up and make all the mistakes in the world". I asked him why he didn't speak up, and he said he had tried once and all the women rolled their eyes and got on his case. He said, "No wonder men just sit there and don't say anything. If you speak up, you hear about it at home about how you ruined the party and women don't mean anything by it, so we just take it".'*[4]

- So in this way, by remaining silent, men themselves are complicit in Everywoman's misandry

We're reminded of Doris Lessing's comments:

> 'The most stupid, ill-educated and nasty woman can rubbish the nicest, kindest and most intelligent man and no one protests...Men seem to be so cowed that they cannot fight back.'

An ex-Feminist notes:

> 'What bothers me most is the visible, although often unspoken, thread of contempt that runs through women's conversations about men. The assumption very often is that men are boys who must be outfoxed, manipulated or dealt with in a calculated manner that women rarely use among themselves.'[5]

On the other hand there are lots of women who don't fall for the man-hating line, who have relationships with men they love and respect. Yet many of these also engage in male-bashing simply because it is the socially acceptable thing to do, a kind of peer-group pressure to be misandrous. Or by remaining silent when their friends are talking negatively about men they are being complicit in creating a culture of misandry.

There can be no doubt that men in Britain are now treated, and spoken of, by the majority of women, without consideration for their feelings. This attitude is so ingrained that it has become part of the nature of many women – much like ingrained racist attitudes in some people. Whenever you hear a woman maligning men ask her whether she is including *her* son, or *her* grandson in her comments. You'll probably receive the reply, 'Oh, no *he's* different'. The same response, then, to the racist who dislikes black people – except the 'exception' with whom he works, or plays football, 'Oh no, *he's* a good bloke'.

***

For a few years in the early 2000s I ran a number of book groups in the Bath area. All members of the groups were women (an intriguing sociological phenomenon). One group was for the members of a prestigious Country and Health Club on the outskirts of the city. A member of the Country Club was a professional author who had had ten books published in six languages. One particular month we chose one of her books to read and discuss and asked if she would then speak to the group about it. She was in her early 40s. This age is significant because it places her university education in the mid-1980s – the period when virulent anti-maleness and pro-Feminist teaching really took off in British universities.

We were discussing the major male character in her book when she made the comment:

> "...men have no feelings."

This was a clear statement and quite categorical. I challenged her about this (not too heavily as she was my guest speaker) saying that I thought what she had said was a sexist comment. She denied this and turned to the all-female group, asking for confirmation of her view. They all agreed with her.

This woman is now in a university in the South West, teaching Creative Writing to students… young students with malleable minds: a university, incidentally, that has a reputation for following a strong Feminist Ideology in its teaching.

- She will be indoctrinating her students into misandry, informing both sexes that 'men have no feelings' – her male students will be sitting there, and because she is the lecturer they are, to use Tim Lott's expression, 'having to take bucketloads and bucketloads of this shit'

- During the height of the slave trade, in the 1770s, one justification of this abominable practice was that 'these people have no feelings…'

The idea that 'men have no feelings' is extremely common throughout womankind. Feminist authors and academics promote and revel in this form of misandry. One Academic Feminist writes:

> 'I believe that women have a capacity for understanding and compassion which a man structurally does not have, does not have it because he cannot have it. He is just incapable of it'[6]

Incidentally, the misandrous speaker in our book group made a significant observation. She admitted that, in her experience, publishers will not consider a book for publication unless it gives a positive image of women and/or a negative image of men. The majority of publishing houses in Britain are dominated by female directors. This explains a lot about the misandry found in modern literature, in books for adults as well as for children (as we saw in Part One).

Men may not show or share their feelings like women do, they do not wear their feelings on their sleeves; and for this they are condemned for not *having* feelings: but in general they know quite well what their feelings are. They are equally as competent about human emotion as women, they are just less interested in spending equally large amounts of time bathing in it.

> 'The reason that men seem less loving, and appear to have "no feelings"
> is that men's behaviour is measured with a female ruler'
>
> (Swayne O'Pie)

***

Conventional wisdom and culture reflect the Feminist misandrous perspective on men, and this perspective has become pervasive and deeply rooted in Britain. Directly and indirectly Feminism has succeeded in the teaching of contempt for men. Women don't have to be Feminists to express and participate in misandry.

Feminism appeals to many women by validating and giving a political perspective to their own personal problems with a man and especially by tapping into their anger at men. Exasperation with *one* man (a difficulty with a father, partner or husband) will, under Feminist 'priming', be easily projected onto *men in general*. Feminism provides a conduit for a woman's anger with *one* specific man to a misandrous attitude toward *all* men collectively. Women's anger has been gender-politicised by Feminism, which has then been sanctioned by our society and the State. Erin Pizzey noticed this phenomenon at the Feminist meetings she attended:

> 'I saw that the most vociferous and the most violent of the women took their own personal damage, their anger against their fathers, and expanded their rage to include all men.[7]

And,

> 'A poll in which 42 percent of women agree that "men are basically selfish and self-centred" is presented as male rottenness, not as female chauvinism.'[8]

- Although this poll was carried out in America I ask the reader to test its findings by asking a number of women: Are men 'basically selfish and self-centred'? You will find that at least two-thirds will answer 'yes'

As long as women get away with thinking men are inferior, that 'men have no feelings', they will have no qualms about treating men badly. They might not even be aware that they're doing it.

***

Male-bashing has been treated as a kind of humorous retributive justice by women who have been disappointed and hurt by men. Some of that woundedness has been passed on to their daughters, who have absorbed the message that men are 'bad people' and have turned against their own male peers. Boys too: at one independent school at which I gave a talk on anti-Feminism a sixth-former became really angry; he lived with his single-parent mother and he hated men (not just his father). From where did he receive his misandrous attitude?

Rendering women either unwilling or unable to see men fully as human beings, as people who can be hurt individually and collectively, is a crime I lay at the door of Feminism. Feminism is responsible for cultivating misandry in all its forms, responsible for creating a popular culture in which men are routinely denigrated, ridiculed and demonised. Misandry is central to Feminism:

> 'Misandry has not unified all feminists, to be sure, but it has certainly unified enough of them – explicitly or implicitly, directly or indirectly, consciously or subconsciously – to create a powerful movement.'[9]

Feminists are always seeking to recruit women to their cause; there are numerous strategies they use to enlist Everywoman into their ranks. One of these is the 'dinner party'. The name is taken from an installation by the Feminist artist Judy Chicago. Feminists enthuse:

> 'In addition to being an ideal concept for one of the most famous pieces of feminist art, the women's dinner party is an appropriate setting for brainstorming about the state of feminism...whenever women are gathered together there is great potential for the individual woman, and even the location itself, to become radicalised...'[10]

And,

> 'For women of the Third Wave – that is, women who were reared in the wake of the women's liberation movement of the seventies – a good dinner party (or any gathering of women) is just as likely to be a place to see politics at work as is a rally. It's a place to map a strategy for our continuing liberation... Every time women get together around a table and speak honestly, they are embarking on an education that they aren't getting elsewhere in our patriarchal society.'[11]

- Man-hating, in one form or another, to a greater or lesser degree, is the glue that bonds *all* strands of Feminism...and Feminists wish this view of men to be spread to as many women as possible; and in modern Britain they have social, cultural, political and institutional strategies to ensure that this happens. Feminism is not a benign Ideology. One could be forgiven for thinking that 'there must be something not quite right' about someone whose *raison d'être* for being in a group or Movement is to express their hatred toward others

***

Research has been undertaken on the phenomenon of man-hating by Everywomen. Judith Levine presented her results in 'My Enemy: My Love'. Levine is a Feminist who undertook an extensive study of the way ordinary women feel about men. Although this study was carried out in America there is no reason to believe that Levine's findings do not also apply to British women. I quote from the dust-cover:

'My Enemy: My Love is a landmark exposition of the intellectually and emotionally rich, little explored, often subterranean world of women's hatred of men...Levine, a respected journalist, argues that man-hating is not an individual neurosis but rather a "collective, cultural phenomenon"...A volatile admixture of pity, contempt, disgust, envy, alienation, fear, and rage, man-hating is everywhere, shared by all women...it belongs to my next-door neighbour, my mother, and to the woman standing in front of me in line at the post office. All men are its objects...the men women love and share their lives with – fathers, husbands, lovers, friends, even sons.'

Levine relates some of her observations:

'Putting on a pair of admittedly mud-coloured glasses, I began seeing man-hating all around me. I inquired, I eavesdropped. And with shrugs, with fervor, with wariness, with laughter, with anecdotes, women confirmed my thesis. Men are babies, I heard. Men are impossible, men are beasts, men are irrelevant.'[12]

She continues:

'Still testing the ground, I started paying a new kind of attention to women's jokes, songs, films, novels, and advice books, to politics from feminist to conservative. Cards and letters came in the mail. A chain letter, on which my friend the sender had scrawled, "Man-hating!!! PERFECT ambivalence!".'[13]

Finally, and perhaps most tellingly:

'In my researches I was struck by how self-evident the idea of man-hating was to women – "Wow, of course," "Yes" were the usual responses – whereas men were frequently surprised to be informed about it. One male editor who read my proposal said he felt he was being let in on a secret.'[14]

- Male Feminists don't realise how much they are being conned, being duped, when they court and embrace Feminism
- Men do not understand how much many women actually dislike, seriously dislike or hate them, as individuals and as a collective group

So in manipulating Everywoman into accepting its views Feminism has been pushing at an open door. Through our culture, education and their relentless spreading of misandry Feminists have 'taught' Everywoman to see inequalities and discriminations everywhere.

***

Since the 1970s Feminists have been recruiting Everywoman to their cause. Those that they have not seduced into becoming activists they have succeeded in convincing that the Feminist perspective is righteous. The result is that the majority of women in Britain today really *do* believe that women suffer inequalities, discriminations and oppressions. Three and a half decades of constant, blanket Feminism (in the media, culture and education system, especially our universities) has conditioned Everywoman to accept Feminist myths as truths. In this sense the majority of women in Britain today are Feminism's Stepford Wives.

- Not only have women been culturally and educationally primed and 'trained' to denigrate men, they have also been primed and 'trained' by Feminists to be hyper-sensitive about inequalities and discriminations. Everywoman will now see an inequality, discrimination or abuse where none exists. Or, for example, she has been 'taught' to see, label and report a domestic argument as 'domestic violence'. Any male comment or behaviour will be assessed for content of 'sexism' or 'misogyny'

This mass conditioning is useful to Feminists in many ways. For example, whenever they undertake 'research' on an issue and interview ordinary women they will almost always be guaranteed an Ideologically-correct response – a response that they can then hold up as 'women believe/want...' and then present this to politicians as a widespread demand of 'women'.

Feminists unashamedly capitalise on women's hatred of, or ambivalence towards, men. They proselytise everywhere, and whenever an opportunity arises; they have taken their own hatred of men, added Everywoman's dislike/hatred of men, and have politicised both into a collective Movement, into a ubiquitous and powerful Ideology, a cultural and political agenda – formidable and never to be questioned.

Others have noticed the malign influence that Feminism has had on ordinary, non-Ideological women:

> *'Rendering women either unwilling or unable to see men as fully human beings, as people who can indeed be hurt both individually and collectively, might well be the single most serious flaw in feminism.'*[15]

I suggest that the reader remembers the points made in this chapter the next time they encounter a woman complaining about some piffling 'sexist' incident.

***

We have seen what *Feminism* is. We have seen what a *Feminist* is. It will now be shown how these two phenomena have produced, in today's Britain, a State-sanctioned deceit, confidence trick and fraud.

142

Part Four

The Feminist Fraud

Chapter 15

For Feminism Success Will Never be Enough: 'Forever' Feminism

Apart from being a malign misandrous Movement Feminism is also a dishonest Movement. One of the aims of this book is to show how modern Feminism has become a huge confidence trick, a deceit, a fraud to which we have all succumbed. To this end Part Four looks at how and why Feminism creates, and needs to *continue* to create, 'women's issues', needs to indulge in synthetic outrage.

> *'With most battles for equal opportunity won, feminism came to be dominated by other goals and creeds. One could say the movement had outlived itself and had to justify its existence.'*[1]

Women gradually overcame the legal and cultural barriers to equal rights and opportunities. This mostly occurred in the 1980s. Girls now get better GCSE and A level results than boys, more women than men now enter university, women are becoming physicians, lawyers, CEOs, and scientists, and women are founding their own businesses in record numbers.

British women today enjoy a range of opportunities unimaginable forty years ago, a time when Equality Feminism set the groundwork for a liberal society to address women's *genuine* inequalities. All its aims have been achieved – equal opportunities for women, equal rights for women, equal treatment for women, equal respect for women, equal choices for women. Feminism has now been left with no battles to fight. But for modern (Ideological) Feminists this success is not enough. Why?

***

After it hijacked Equality Feminism Ideological Feminism (the Feminism we have in Britain today) became very successful. So successful, in fact, that it gradually became an intrinsic part of the fabric of Britain – the culture, media, law, education, academia, charities, the economy, trade unions, and most of all, the political system. It was reluctant to give up this power, and the status and financial benefits accruing from this power. A Quiet Revolution was being achieved. So the problem was, how could it now *continue* with this success and remain an established part of the British culture and State in perpetuity? The concept of 'Forever' Feminism was formed and put into practice. Part Four looks at how and why Feminism perpetuates itself, now that equality for women has been achieved.

***

Equality Feminism's Success Created Dilemmas

After equality was achieved Feminists were faced with a number of problems and predicaments:

1. How to justify Feminism's continuing existence.

2. How to 'flag up' their success to their constituents, women (in order to continue to recruit them to the Movement), whilst at the same time continuing to claim to the State (in order to justify its existence and retain its power) that their job has not been completed and there were still *more* inequalities, discriminations, oppressions, abuses to fight. So one of Feminists' problems was how to make it appear that they were working for their constituents (women) and making progress...without making *too much* progress, which would give the impression that their Movement was no longer needed. It is important to understand that equality is no longer an aim for Feminists – *their present, and long-term goal, is to justify their existence and to stay in business*, and by doing so to spread misandry. The well-worn mantra 'gender equality' is a cover, a disguise, to achieve these goals.

3. A third problem Feminists faced was how to resolve these dilemmas. This was done by crafting strategies designed to ensure the existence of the Movement so that it could *always* be justified, would *always* be needed, and would therefore continue to be a powerful influence in society, culture, the economy and the State; and benefit the Movement's members.

Feminism resolved these dilemmas and problems by developing strategies to ensure that there would *always* be issues for it to address. The 'gender equality' rhetoric became a device to draw attention away from these fraudulent strategies and their intended aims.

***

'The feminist battle has evolved from a fight for legal and social equality to a fight for special treatment and affirmative action in education and the workplace.'[2]

Feminism today is not a campaign to end inequality for women – that has been accomplished. Modern British Feminism is now about organisational and Ideological survival, not about securing rights for women, or achieving 'gender equality'. Feminism today is a continual search for more inequalities, more discriminations, more oppressions, more issues. In addition, old issues must be exaggerated and new issues concocted. Feminist Industries have been developed specifically to consolidate and implement these strategies; these are large businesses with their own public relations, Interest Groups, political delegates and bureaucracies.

- For it to continue to exist Feminism needed to have women thought of, and believed to be, perpetual 'victims'

'But today to be classified as a victim is to be given a special political status, which has no necessary connection with real hardship or actual oppression. Victimhood as a political status is best understood as the outcome of a political strategy by some groups aimed at gaining preferential treatment.'[3]

- For it to continue to exist and retain the benefits of its power Feminism necessarily needed to have men thought of, and believed to be, the 'bad people', the patriarchy who rule to advantage themselves and who *intentionally* disadvantage women

Where there are 'victims' there have to be 'victimisers', where there are 'discriminations' there have to be 'discriminators', where there are 'oppressions' there have to be 'oppressors'. So the concept of 'Feminism' presupposes and necessitates male blame. 'Forever' Feminism therefore requires perpetual man-hating. Spreading misandry is a central tenet of the Feminist Ideology (its patriarchal Ideology) and a major way of achieving this is through the implementation of its 'Forever' strategies.

- The result of 'Forever' *Feminism* is 'Forever' *misandry*: logically, Feminism cannot exist without man-hating

***

So women always need to be thought of as 'victims'... 'victims' of men. Without the banner of victimhood to rally around, Feminist coffers would run dry, Professional Feminists would be unemployed, mortgages would go unpaid. Many thousands of Professional Feminists can't just declare victory and go home, because without the Feminist Movement they would have no homes to go to; they would have no jobs and no job prospects. And neither would they have a platform from which to bang their Ideological drum. The following aptly sums up the predicament of Feminism and the strategy behind 'Forever' Feminism:

'Above all, seeking victim status encourages the invention and nursing of grievances. The underlying problem for victim groups is that once they have been given preferential treatment their power increases and, thereby, undermines the case for special treatment. As a result, some groups make strenuous efforts to maintain their victim status by exaggerating their suffering.'[4]

- To continue to exist Feminists have to be perpetually and chronically dissatisfied (the reader may wish to refer to Part Three, the Feminist's psychological make-up and emotional and political need for 'anger'). Synthetic outrage has to be expressed; there is a need to be constantly 'offended'

For example, working women whose careers top out before the level of Chief Executive Officer are described as having hit a 'glass ceiling', whereas men in a similar situation have simply just peaked.

Feminists will *never* be satisfied with anything they achieve, they will never be appeased... they cannot *afford* to be satisfied. Success will never be enough if the benefits of the Movement are to continue in perpetuity, which Feminists wish them to do.

'Accommodation to any particular demand will always be found unsatisfying and merely trigger further demands. Negotiations with feminists cannot terminate in compromise. Because she needs to believe that she is fighting a universal conspiracy.'[5]

- And so we have a Feminist personality, a Feminist mentality, a Feminist permanent anger towards men

The irony of Feminism's 'Forever' Feminism is that the sense of perpetual victimhood (the condition that Feminism needs to describe women as always being in) precludes the concept that the members of the victimised group, women, could actually rise above their assigned position in society and meet that society, and be part of that society, on equal terms. To do that would mean taking personal responsibility for their own actions, behaviours and choices and the condition of their own lives. Instead, Feminism has designed an Ideological position ('Forever' Feminism/perpetual victimhood for women) that leads not to the encouragement of personal development for women but to entitlement, 'collective' group rights, and the eradication of the individual.

- It is in this sense that Feminism discourages women from taking personal responsibility for the consequences of their actions, behaviours and freely made choices. In this way Feminism infantilises and patronises women. Many examples of this are seen throughout Part Four. This is 'Blame Men, the Patriarchy' Feminism (successfully achieved by various nuances and subtleties – and very often by more blatant and direct methods)

- If I were a woman I would be extremely angry at being designated a 'victim'...or would I? The advantages are huge – preferential treatment, special privileges, policy-favouritism. But some women *do* jib and refuse to sell their souls to Feminism; such women should be celebrated

***

So Feminism needed to invent 'Forever' Feminism for various reasons. Essentially, once equality of opportunity, rights, respect, treatment and choices had been achieved Feminists, especially Professional Feminists/Feminist Ideologues, felt that their Movement was too valuable to lose; they now needed to justify its existence, they needed it to survive, to continue indefinitely. No powerful group will give up its power easily; and neither will a powerful politicised group selflessly refrain from using whatever weapons its historical moment makes available in order to retain (or gain more) money, position, fame, and self-perpetuation; and in Feminism's case gain many more opportunities to promote its Ideology, including spreading misandry.

'Forever' Feminism's Strategies

What are the strategies that Feminism uses to resolve its problems, predicaments and dilemmas, to justify its existence and to ensure that it is with us 'Forever'? Essentially, it has to continually produce never-ending grievances, inequalities, discriminations and issues, thereby justifying its demand for preferential treatment, special privileges and policy-favouritism and validating the blaming, demonising and punishing of men. It does this in various ways; essentially, there are six strategies:

Strategy 1. Feminists concoct and fabricate issues, inequalities and discriminations *from nothing*. Examples include public violence against women and Scatter-Gun everyday issues. Feminists euphemistically call these artificial issues 'women's issues' in order to glean public and political sympathy

Strategy 2. Feminists have established extensive Industries to ensure that Feminism remains a vital part of the economy, the culture and the political process – the Women's Sector (a make-work sector, producing nothing except grievances and issues). Feminist Industries have a number of essential functions, including seeking out inequalities, manufacturing artificial grievances, cultivating and nurturing discriminations, promoting these to the public and policy-makers, presenting them as 'evidence' of women's oppression and victimhood, and drawing attention to those responsible for these fabricated oppressions – men

Strategy 3. Feminists convert ordinary women's freely made choices into inequality issues (again tactically labelling them 'women's issues'). These are generally old issues re-jigged, smoothed with an up-to-date Ideological patina. Examples include: women's choice of family/parenting arrangements, women's choice to study the Arts and Humanities, women's choice to wear make-up and to be looked at by men, women's choice to enter the sex industry, women's choice to be paid less than men (the pay gap), women's choice to avoid senior positions (the glass ceiling). The downside of these choices (downside defined only by Feminists, not by ordinary women themselves) are then sold as 'inequalities' and 'discriminations' - presented as being the fault of men, men as individuals or as members of the patriarchy

Strategy 4. Feminists have changed the rules. Whenever an aim has been achieved this success creates a dilemma for Feminism: it resolves this dilemma by redefining the rules and definitions, by drawing new lines in the sand...a philosophical and linguistic sleight of hand. Examples are 'equal pay for work of equal value', and the concept of equality of outcome, sexual harassment, domestic violence and rape

Strategy 5. Feminists grossly exaggerate old-established bread and butter inequalities and discriminations. They encourage activists to portray numerous issues as having reached 'crisis', or 'epidemic' proportions. Examples include trafficked women, domestic violence, sexual harassment and rape. And so all men are demonised

Strategy 6. Feminists create their own 'research' to academically underpin the above strategies, claims, demands and policies. Feminist 'research' is also used to create new issues. Feminist 'research' is a fraud intended to give its issues and grievances intellectual authority and academic authenticity

***

The above strategies can be summed up in the phrase Issue Creep; more inequality and discrimination issues continually being sought and creeping in, new issues being found, older issues creeping towards greater severity; issues becoming more common, issues being given regular publicity, issues being presented to governments by 'women's groups' (read Feminist Groups), and by Feminist MPs. Issue Creep is an extremely effective strategy because it guarantees, in our British Left-wing/liberal/progressive political zeitgeist, maximum political attention.

> *'We have already referred...to two extremely effective strategies of ideological feminism: expanding the definition of one crime to include forms of behaviour that were once not classified as crimes, or reinforcing old claims with new ones, and eventually generating something that approaches hysteria. This strategy requires them to keep upping the ante.'[6]*

The above six strategies that are driving today's Feminism can be neatly summed up in the following:

> *'Diana Furchgott-Roth and Christine Stolba call women's remarkable educational success, "the foremost example of feminists' 'dilemma' because it forces them to flail around looking for gender bias where plainly none exists."'[7]*

For the above strategies to be effective Feminists have had to convince Everywoman that she is a 'victim'. This has been an extremely successful policy; almost all women now regard womankind as experiencing some sort of sexism, misogyny, inequality or discrimination.

Three decades of constant educational and media conditioning have done their work. For example, whenever Feminism undertakes 'research' that entails interviewing Everywoman the desired Ideologically-correct answer will nearly always be given: 'Yes, I *do* feel that I'm being held back because I'm a woman', 'Yes, it *is* wrong that women should be paid less than men', 'Yes, there *ought* to be more women in senior positions', and so on. Women have been taught to think in Feminist dogma. Such 'research' will then be presented to the media and policy-makers as 'evidence' that the majority of women feel that there are inequality issues still to be politically addressed. Hence, we have 'Forever' Feminism. And Feminists, their demands being sympathetically received (what politician wants to ignore the opinions of Everywoman?), are repeatedly getting away with this fraud.

***

Like the Left in general, Feminism must have an enemy. This is men and the patriarchy. But since equal rights and opportunities for women have been achieved a new, additional, enemy has arisen; anyone, male or female, who realises and dares to suggest that 'women have *made* it'. Such a person is anathema to Feminism because such a person (if listened to by the public and politicians) is capable of jeopardising the delicate balance between a) needing to appear successful to attract acolytes, and b) pretending to the State (and public at large) that 'we are only half way there...so Feminism is *still* needed.'

Warren Farrell worked for many years at national level as a Feminist advocate. He gradually became disillusioned, realising just how immoral and anti-men/pro-women Feminism had become. He left the Movement in disgust, triggering a huge loss in his earnings – by becoming 'politically incorrect' (that is, addressing issues from the male perspective *as well as* from the Feminist perspective) Farrell lost contracts, speaking engagements, magazine and newspaper columns and assignments, television work and academic sinecures. His crime? He had pointed out that women were making great strides in securing rights and equality. This observation did not go down well with Feminists:

> *'I had naively believed that leaders as pioneering as I thought Gloria (Steinem) was would be delighted to hear of ways in which women were succeeding. Now I had to face a deeper fear: that some of my feminist colleagues might have an emotional investment in women's victimhood that went so deep as to prevent any discussion that might dilute women's victim status.'[8]*

- For Feminists *nothing*, and *no one*, must dilute women's 'victim' and 'oppression' status; no one must deny that our society is ruled by men, for men, to the intentional disadvantage of women

***

Feminism is a self-perpetuating Movement. It will *never* be satisfied or appeased, it cannot allow itself to be. The Movement is a huge Grievance Gravy-Train for Feminist activists; in addition, as we have seen, many Feminists have an 'emotional investment' in the movement, their Political Community Club, so they have a 'psychological need' for it to continue. And, of course, entrenching 'Forever' Feminism will ensure the progression of its Quiet (Marxist-Socialist) Revolution...and the continuation and spreading of misandry. And so we have a Britain that will continue to hate men.

Forget the cant about 'gender equality', this is a disguise, a masquerade. For today's Feminists the key aims are to justify their existence, to hold onto their power and privileges and to ensure that the Movement continues in perpetuity. Today's Feminism has become a self-perpetuating make-issue Movement. Part Four shows how it is successfully doing this. Each strategy has been given its separate Section exposing Feminism, issue by issue, as a fraud, and showing how each issue impacts negatively on men. The pay gap and glass ceiling, even though they are part of the 'converting women's choices into issues' strategy, have been given a separate Section because (along with domestic violence) they are Feminism's flagship issues; as such, their fabrication and deceit need to be especially examined and exposed.

***

Feminists themselves admit that in order for their Movement to progress they need to continually create issues:

> 'As Germaine Greer wrote in The Whole Woman, it is the job of each generation to "produce its own statement of problems and priorities".'[9]

As we have seen, today's generation of Feminists are just as angry, aggressive and man-hating as previous generations; and they are continuing in the tradition of seeking out and creating new, as well as retaining old, 'problems', 'inequalities', 'discriminations' and 'oppressions'.

SECTION 1

Chapter 16

How Feminism Creates Issues 'from Nothing'

Britain is obsessed with women's needs, women's wants, women's problems, women's protection, women's issues and women's rights. We are obsessed with women's issues to the point of neurosis. This chapter presents some of the issues created 'from nothing' and asks readers to judge for themselves their worthiness as 'inequalities' and 'discriminations'. It is shown that 'public violence against women' has been created and politicised for Ideological gain, one more issue driving 'Forever' Feminism's Grievance Gravy-Train Industries.

- The Feminist's psychosis ('delusions and loss of contact with reality') may be applied for an additional insight to all the Feminist issues addressed in this Chapter

***

The following are two politically powerful Feminist organisations seeking out pretexts that with spin and linguistic skulduggery can be alchemised into issues. First we look at the Equal Opportunities Commission and then at the Deputy Prime Minister's Office.

The Equal Opportunity Commission:

WOMEN LEFT BEHIND BY TRANSPORT SYSTEM DESIGNED BY MEN

(The Times, Thursday, 8 September, 2005)

'According to the Equal Opportunities Commission (EOC) Britain's transport system is failing women. Now the Commission is calling for an end to transport "constructed by men for men" because they are denying women access to shops, hospitals, training and work.

More buses run into, and out of, town centres because that is where most people work. This is discrimination against women, maintains the EOC, because it is mainly women who stay at home during the day, and they want to travel from suburb to suburb.

...the most frequent bus services run during the commuter rush hour, leaving fewer buses to run "during the day".

There is a lack of security at night which prevents many women from venturing from their homes.'

- This created 'women's issue' (created by Feminists) is so silly, and so illogical, that I refuse to insult the reader's intelligence by commenting upon it...except to say that it is a typical example of a Feminist-manufactured issue 'from nothing'

***

The following also shows Feminism creating issues 'from nothing'; The Deputy Prime Minister's Office:

PRESCOTT TO MAKE STREETS 'WOMEN FRIENDLY'

(The Sunday Times, 21 August 2005)

'Britain's streets are set to be made more "female friendly" as part of plans by John Prescott's department to civilise city centres.

Ideas being considered include creches in nightclubs, separate areas for women on trains and buses, and hairdryers in public conveniences.

Guidelines to be issued by the Deputy Prime Minister's Office are principally intended to encourage women to "reclaim" the streets.

Prescott's office has backed a three-year pilot project run by the Women's Design Service (WDS), a charity set up by women architects and town planners...

The core of the drive to create new "feminised" cities will be measures to improve safety. The most recent British Crime Survey found that one in four young women was "worried" about being raped.

Despite the focus on safety, the scope of the pilot project is being expanded to tackle other failures in urban design. Women's pet gripes included awkward stairs and cobbled streets that trip up those wearing high-heeled shoes...

Further proposals have been drawn up by Demos, a think tank close to the Labour Party, which is preparing a report on town planning. Its women-friendly suggestions include creches in nightclubs, giving women priority for taxis after 10pm, a range of toiletries in public conveniences, separate areas for women on trains and buses, and siting hairdryers and chargers for mobile phones in public lavatories.

The lack of public lavatories has been another area of concern raised by women. "The decline of public conveniences is something that greatly affects all women in cities", said Greed, "They used to be a place women could use as a kind of haven – somewhere for them to change their clothes, dry their hair, do their make-up or have a cry if they were having a bad day. Now there are hardly any left".

A spokesman for Prescott's office said: "The focus on women and getting local people involved is a new and exciting thing. We have already taken on board suggestions, but it will be up to local authorities to implement the ideas. It is important to make streets 'women-friendly'".

- Here we see two (of many) Feminist elements in the Labour/Feminist Party actually saying that women's welfare, and lives, are more important, are of greater value, than men's welfare and men's lives

- Creches...in nightclubs!? So, Labour Party Feminists are saying that it is the 'right' of a single parent mother to 'go clubbing' - even when she cannot find a baby-sitter. And that the toddler is just fine waiting in the nightclub creche until 3.30 in the morning when mother drunkenly (will she *not* be drinking in this nightclub?) decides to stumble home with a new boyfriend on one arm and the toddler dangling from the other...a truly Hogarthian scene...deliberately encouraged by the Labour Government's Deputy Prime Minister's Office; such is the power of Feminism in today's Britain

- Priority for taxis for women after 10.00pm? This is sex discrimination against men. If a young man walking home late at night is unable to hire a taxi (because of policy-favouritism for women) is then attacked and seriously injured, could he seek compensation from the taxi firm(s)? One would hope he could. Institutional misandry needs to be challenged in the courts

- Public money is 'zero-sum', that is, if part of it is spent on *one* issue then there is less to spend on *other* issues. So, local authorities are being bullied by Feminists into spending local tax-payer's money on women-specific issues such as 'providing hairdryers, mobile phone chargers and a range of toiletries' in women's public conveniences – whilst much needed, and much less frivolous, local services are starved of cash

- 'The focus on women…is a new and exciting thing'. It is *not* new – the focus has been relentlessly on women since Ideological Feminism ousted the genuinely caring and morally sound Equality Feminism in the early 1970s. Neither is it 'exciting': it is biased, discriminatory, unequal, undemocratic, unjust and misandrous – how can such a programme be termed 'exciting'?

The reader will know that the Deputy Prime Minister's Office is a politically powerful office. There can be no doubt, then, that these Feminist-created issues were sanctioned by the Labour Government. Feminism has huge cultural and political power in today's Britain. It will not give up this power easily. To stay in business it needs to continually create grievances and discriminations.

Public Space Violence Against Women

'Public space violence against women' is another issue that Feminism has created 'from nothing' ('nothing' as compared to this problem faced by men) – yet it is still accepted overwhelmingly as a 'women's issue' by the policy-making fraternity.

A Feminist survey found that violence against women is the second major issue that drives Feminists.[1] This includes public space violence and domestic violence. Domestic violence will be addressed in a later Section.

> 'We live, I am trying to say, in an epidemic of male violence against women.'[2]

And Anna Coote and her partner Beatrix Campbell:

> 'There have continued to be disagreements among feminists about the universality of male violence. Some assert that all men are potential "Rippers"; others see violence more as a symptom of the political relationship between women and men than as something which is inherent in all men. All would agree that women are invariably the victims and men the aggressors.'[3]

- In short, Feminism decrees that public violence is overwhelmingly perpetrated by men against women

The issue of public space violence has been artificially created by Feminism and then politicised, to be used as a weapon to promote its agenda and aims. It has not been difficult for Feminism to do this: apart from its own political and media power it has ruthlessly manipulated the male traditional chivalrous mentality ('women can do no wrong', and 'women must be protected'). In modern Britain men in positions of authority and power have become the puppets of Feminists.

We know that the 'badness' of patriarchy and its individual male members is a central theme running through Feminism. A major tenet of Feminism is that violence against women is a 'political act', perpetrated by men (individual members of the patriarchy) in order to subjugate women. Feminism interprets violence against women as a class conflict, with women being the oppressed, the victims, the abused. This interpretation is now entrenched in our conventional wisdom and drives legislation and policy on the issue, to the detriment of men and boys.

- Feminism has cornered the market in violence-victimhood. It has monopolised the problem of public space violence in order to preference women and to demonise men. As we will see, it has also done this with domestic violence

Reclaim the Night

Reclaim the Night (sometimes called Take Back the Night) demonstrations began on 12 November 1977 with women marching through the centres of Leeds, Manchester, York and London, with banners proclaiming, 'We are walking for all women – all women should be free to walk down any street, night or day, without fear.' By the end of the decade this had developed into a large and more explicitly political campaign – 'Women Against Violence Against Women'.[4]

- Presumably Women Against Violence Against Women was so named to differentiate it from women who *were* in favour of violence against women…?
- And so we see the setting up of one of Feminism's earliest Industries

Reclaim the Night is still very much part of twenty-first century Feminism's propaganda. The following is from the London Feminist Network:

'Since 2004, the London Feminist Network has organised an annual women's Reclaim the Night march. The Reclaim the Night march gives women a voice and a chance to reclaim the streets at night on a safe and empowering event. We aim to put the issue of our safety on the agenda for this night and every day…

All women have the right to use public spaces both in the daytime and after dark without the fear of sexual harassment and assault.'[5]

The reader may wish to visit the London Feminist Network's website to see just how misandrous it is. I quote:

'Over 1500 women of all ages and from all over the country marched to protest about the epidemic of rape and male violence against women.'[6]

- Note the word 'epidemic' of 'violence against women' and compare the exaggeration (an intentional political lie) with the statistics later presented in this chapter. In a later chapter the 'epidemic' of rape is also exposed as a politically-created myth

'We work closely with other groups in London, supporting various feminist campaigns in order that we can broaden our movement and work together for women's rights and against patriarchy in all its forms.'[7]

- Patriarchy; Feminism's Devil Weapon is always near at hand to demonise men

***

We have seen that the National Union of Students (NUS) is a Feminist organisation (and therefore misandrous). The following was taken from its website:

> 'Women, unite! Take back the night!...Good evening everyone. My name is Jo Salmon. I'm the Women's Officer for the National Union of Students and I'm proud to stand here in solidarity with so many sisters, standing up for and demanding our rights to live our lives free from harassment, violence and abuse...'[8]

The NUS is, indeed, another Feminist-created Industry. At every level from national, to regional and to university, the NUS has a Women's Officer, Women's Committees, Women's Conferences, Women's Courses, and so on. Nowhere in the NUS is there a Men's Officer, Men's Committee...Either the NUS believes that male students *don't have* male-specific problems, issues and rights – or it believes that *men are just so unimportant* that they don't need to be represented. Which is it, Ms. NUS?

***

'Reclaim the Night' is a concocted Feminist concept that began in the 1970s. It was a politically motivated concept then but has become even more so today: Jack Kammer questions Ruth Shalit, a political and cultural commentator, regarding the Ideology behind this concept:

Kammer:

> 'Take Back the Night started out as an effort to help women, but it became something else. What is its purpose now?'

Shalit:

> 'I think part of the design is to make men feel excluded. Make them feel guilt-ridden, and to categorise the male as the oppressor class whose only purpose is to marginalise and victimise women.'[9]

- So Reclaim the Night demonstrations are, essentially, demonstrations *deliberately* engineered to express public hatred toward men. They are driven by the patriarchal Ideology, the hatred of men...by Feminists

***

The Professional Feminist Natasha Walter noted that in 2004 some women decided to revive the Reclaim the Night marches that had been a feature of Second-Wave Feminism:

> 'Since then they have gone from strength to strength, with annual marches in London and other cities including Edinburgh and Cardiff. Finn Mackay, one of the organisers, said to me, "I think that the women's movement is definitely on the rise again. Young women are coming in from the anti-war and anti-globalisation movement, saying, "Well, where's our movement?"'[10]

- The Feminist has a psychological need to have a 'cause', to have grievances, to have an excuse to express her 'anger' and 'outrage' at society and especially at men, to have a Political Community Club/Family. 'Well, where's *our* Movement?' Damaged women?

155

It is worrying that these Ideological paranoid neurotics are not just seen on marches and demonstrations, but that they also have very many Sisters in influential areas of power, including senior government ministers. They are to be found in senior positions in *every* profession, particularly the academic, legal and media professions. Creating Feminist issues is an all-embracing and holistic social, cultural, academic and political Industry.

The Reclaim the Night organisation specifically singles out men for demonisation. Would homophobic or racist marches be so easily tolerated as these misandrous marches and demonstrations?

- 'Terrible as an Army with Banners'...?

Women as Perpetrators of Public Violence

Statistics confirm that a high percentage of violence against women is termed by police as 'women-on-women' violence. In January, 2009, a Ministry of Justice report found:

'Scourge of the Ladette thugs: For the first time in history, crimes of violence have overtaken theft as the most common offence among women and girls...Crime rates among girls soared across a whole range of offences, including vicious attacks.

Cases of violence against the person leapt by almost 50 per cent...racially-aggravated attacks by girls more than doubled...Recent figures for arrests showed violent attacks by women had doubled in five years. The category ranges from street brawls and assault to grievous bodily harm and murder.

Latest figures from the Youth Justice Board show that teenage girls are responsible for more than 40 violent attacks every day. They committed 15,762 assaults and serious beatings in 2007, as well as more than 1,000 muggings.'[11]

***

RUTHLESS AND REMORSELESS: THE SHOCKING RISE OF UK'S GIRL GANGSTERS

(The Observer, 23 May, 2010)

'Women now take part in one in four violent attacks and are increasingly found at top levels in gangs. The author of a new book about gangland Britain explores this disturbing change in criminal behaviour.' (Gangland by Tony Thompson)

***

WE FACE A PLAGUE OF LADETTE DRUNKS

(Daily Mail, Friday, 28 May, 2010)

'Young women are at the centre of an epidemic of drink-fuelled violence that has become the "plague" of Britain, a senior judge warned yesterday.

Drunken louts were blamed for a dramatic increase in attacks on the nation's streets by District Judge Alan Berg – who singled out the effects of a "ladette" culture. He said many young women routinely go out to get "senselessly drunk" and engage in barbaric behaviour in city centres.

"They become aggressive. They behave in an unacceptable, anti-social way. There is a disease in my view – it has become a plague."'

BAD GIRLS

(The Daily Mail, Saturday, 5 March, 2011)

'According to the latest government statistics, one in four violent attacks now involves a female. This means that, in 2008, more than half a million assaults were either carried out by women or involved a female in a gang.

In the same year, there were nearly 300 attacks a week carried out by girls under 18. Yet society remains preoccupied by male crime...'

- I've heard and read Feminists address this phenomenon by stating that women are only doing what men are doing – that it's an example of equality for women. Sure. Fine. But if that's the case then *let's not blame men* for the issue of public space violence – and then use that as a political and Ideological issue, an issue to perpetuate Feminism...and then hypocritically claim that women have a 'right' to be as violent as men in public. Here we have a further example of Feminist hypocrisy and double standards

Men are the Main Victims of Public Space Violence

Perhaps the issue of 'public space violence' ought not to be interpreted as Feminists creating an issue 'from nothing'; maybe the issue ought to be used as an example of the Feminist strategy of 'exaggeration'. Because of *course* women experience public space violence. However, my point is that women are far from being the *main* victims of this type of violence. Despite Feminism's righteous and outrageous claims, *it is men*, not women, who are overwhelmingly the victims of public space violence:

BOYFRIEND KICKED TO DEATH OVER STOLEN HAT

(The Daily Telegraph, Wednesday, 22 September, 2010)

'A computer expert was beaten to death after his girlfriend's Halloween hat was snatched by thugs, the Old Bailey heard yesterday.

Ben Gardner, 30, was punched to the ground and, as he lay helpless, one of three men kicked his head "as if taking a penalty".

- I include the above as an example of a very common occurrence in today's Britain – innocent men being battered, beaten, maimed and killed in our streets

What is truly galling about the Feminist-created issue of 'violence against women' is the unequivocal claim that women are the *primary* victims. In fact, it is *men* who are overwhelmingly likely to be such victims.

***

- 67% of *all* 'violence against the person crime' is against men - not women[12]
- In 2005 I spoke to the police statistician in Bath. His statistics show that in that city the figure for men being the victims of violent crime was actually nearer 75%, and that female victims are only 'a small minority'[13]

***

ALCOHOL FUELS MURDER RATE FOR YOUNG MEN

(The Times, Monday, 17 October, 2005)

'The murder rate among young men in England and Wales has almost doubled, according to a report published today.

Fifty-one men aged 20 to 24 in every million are murdered, almost twice as many as in 1981.

The overall murder rate for men is 17 per million a year, almost double the 9 per million for women.

Professor Danny Dorling of Sheffield University undertook the study published by the Crime and Society Foundation.'

***

We are told that women are more worried and anxious than men about 'public space violence'. Feminism deliberately *creates* this fear as a political strategy in order to claim preferential treatment for women (special bus and taxi services, for example), it helps to attract women to its Movement ('we are representing your fears'), it efficiently demonises men (an essential ingredient of Feminism). Ordinary, non-ideological women are being used as Ideological pawns. The following refers specifically to female students, but the Feminist strategy of *deliberately* creating fear applies to all young women:

> *'My own observations of students in women's studies classes have led me to believe that years of exposure to feminist-promoted scare statistics have succeeded in imbuing many young women with a foreboding sense of living under constant threat from predatory men. The offer of an escape from this threat is a strong inducement to conformity to feminist blandishments.'[14]*

- If Feminists really *did* have women's well-being at heart they would actually calm their fears by pointing out that it is men who are much more likely to be victims of public space violence. Instead, they whip up fear in women with their marches and demonstrations

- I would suggest that deliberately creating fear in young women is a form of abuse

***

The following is part of a letter I received from Brian Coleman, Freedom of Information Manager, British Transport Police, London, 21 September, 2005:

Dear Mr. O'Pie,

In response to your recent Freedom of Information request, the British Transport Police are happy to provide you with hard copy of the information requested.

Number of crimes recorded against victims, 1 April 2004 to 31 August 2005.

Offence Category:	Female	Male
Murder	1	3
GBH	10	109
Serious Wounding	22	115
Actual bodily harm	653	2108
Assault	52	244
Threat to kill	16	49
Robbery	301	1709
Assault with intent to rob	12	79

These statistics are not based simply upon artificially and deliberately created fears, worries and anxieties about what *might* happen, or 'imagined' rapes. They are based upon *facts*.

- So which sex is more likely to be the victims of 'public space violence'? And which sex is it that receives the media sympathy and the political tea and biscuits?

It has been noted how Feminism artificially creates women's fear of violence. The statistics would indicate that it should be *men*, not women, who fear 'public space violence'. And in many cases so it is:

'Fear of violent crime is as much a part of teenage boys' lives as acne and girls.'[15]

- Political and media attention in modern Britain focuses overwhelmingly on 'women's issues', to the point of a neurotic obsession, issues purposely created in order to justify the continuation of Feminism. Whilst the 'bad people's' issues and problems are ignored

***

BUS STOP KILLER JAILED FOR LIFE

(The Times, Wednesday, 14 September, 2005)

'Lee McCready, 24, from Feltham, southwest London, was jailed for life by the Old Bailey for the murder of Ricky Fisher, 22, who was stabbed and kicked at a bus stop by a gang last February.'

And in the same newspaper, the same day...

QUEUE STABBING

'Two men aged 31 and 36 were being questioned over the death of Westley Odger, 27, who was stabbed during a row over queue-jumping.'

***

From whom, then, are the Reclaim the Night Ideologues demanding to reclaim the night? Is it from their drunken, barbaric and violent Sisters...or is it from those males who thoughtlessly and selfishly prefer to attack their own sex? But it doesn't really matter, the Feminist 'public violence against women issue' has already been created, and accepted, one more issue to justify 'Forever' Feminism – one more issue to spread misandry, to demonise men.

'Facts are often immaterial to an ideology'[16]

Men as Victims of Public Violence: Further Observations

A common misapprehension, and one that is encouraged by Feminism, is that most men actually *enjoy* fighting and violence. They cite brawls outside pubs. These men, they maintain, are not 'real' victims because they are joint participants in the violence. In other words, they are simply victims of their own behaviour. This is untrue. This really *is* 'blaming the victim', something Feminism constantly tells us that society does to women.

Although there are fights between men brought on by alcohol, the majority of young men do not want to fight. They are not simply the losers in pub brawls: if they were, then why would they go to the trouble to report to the police that they have been attacked (as we see from the London Transport Police statistics)? Whatever Feminists claim, it is men who are *overwhelmingly* the innocent victims of gratuitous 'public space violence' and brutal attacks, not women.

Because it is a male issue, a male problem, violence against men is culturally and politically ignored. Men are culturally battered into accepting violence against them, without it becoming a political issue:

> *'Our minimisation and denial of male victimisation so permeates our culture that it is in evidence everywhere from nursery rhymes, comic strips, comedy films, television programs and newspaper stories to academic research. We give male victims a message every day of their lives that they risk much by complaining. Stated succinctly, if a male is victimised he deserved it, asked for it, or is lying. If he is injured, it is his own fault. If he cries or complains, we will not take him seriously or condone his "whining" because he is supposed to "take it like a man." We will laugh at him. We will support him in the minimisation of its impact. We will encourage him to accept responsibility for being victimised and teach him to ignore any feelings associated with his abuse. We will guilt and shame him to keep a stiff upper lip so he can "get on with it".'[17]*

Men need as much police, local authority and state protection as do women from public space violence – more protection, in fact, because they far outnumber women as victims.

• Should young men have priority *over women* for late-night taxis?

***

Like males in all other walks of life, male students are very much more likely to be the victims of violent attacks than female students.

Sunderland University stands a little way outside the city. In the mid-1990s there was a problem with students getting physically attacked by local Sunderland youths. So for the safety of its students the University's Student's Union bought a mini-bus in order to bus students into the city, then back out again at the end of the evening. However, this mini-bus was for the *specific use of female students only*: male students had to continue getting beaten up if they wanted a night out in the city. They were not permitted on the female-only safety bus, *even when there were vacant seats*.

• The anti-male policy of Sunderland's Student Union was blatant discrimination against males and had nothing to do with 'gender equality'; it had *everything* to do with Britain's neurotic obsession with preferencing women and disadvantaging men

- Black people in the 1950s American South were at least permitted to *use* buses, even though they were segregated and had to sit at the rear
- On 1ˢᵗ December, 1955, Rosa Parks decided to sit at the front. The furore led to the creation of the American Civil Rights Movement
- British men need a 'Rosa Parks'

Surely personal safety is a human right of all groups of people regardless of their age, ability, religion, race – or sex. To single out one group, as Feminism does, for preferential treatment and policy-favouritism at the expense of another group, resonates with apartheid; it is abhorrent.

Meanwhile, the Ideologues in the London Feminist Network reserve this right for only women. From their website:

> 'We demand the right to use public space without fear. We demand this right as a civil liberty, we demand this as a human right.'

***

Violence against men, whether perpetrated by other men or by women, is ignored. The whole focus of the issue is on girls and women. Violence against the person has become monopolised by Feminism and is deliberately politicised as an Ideological weapon. But it is wrong for a State to preference and privilege certain categories of its citizens. It is foolish and dangerous for a State to pursue such a misandrous policy:

> 'When we give a message to boys and young men in any shape or form that their experience of violence and victimisation is less important than that of girls and young women, we are teaching them a lesson about their value as persons. We also teach them that the use of violence toward males is legitimate. When we dismiss their pain, we do little to encourage boys and young men to listen to, and take seriously, women's concerns about violence and victimisation. When we diminish their experience or fail to hold their male and female abusers fully accountable, we support their continued victimisation.'[18]

- When will men be viewed as fellow human beings, with lives, feelings, problems, fears and rights that matter? We have tended to forget that men are people too

Let's move on to other areas where Feminism creates issues 'from nothing'.

Chapter 17
Everyday Scatter-Gun 'Issues'

Feminism intrudes itself into our everyday life by constantly seeking out and creating nit-picking, mischief-making issues. This is almost a daily occurrence. All areas political, economic, social, cultural are trawled for sexisms, inequalities, discriminations and misogynies... however trivial; these will be taken up and moulded into issues.

However, the 'Scatter-Gun effect' is not trivial; it is a political strategy, and a good example of Issue Creep. By regularly complaining and creating and collecting grievances that purportedly show that 'women are experiencing discriminations/inequalities', that society is 'sexist and misogynistic', Feminism is subtly conditioning the public and policy-makers with the idea that women really *are* suffering from 'gender inequalities'. There is a relentless barrage of politically created, media-presented, issues. This is a successful strategy; the Feminist message that women are somehow a minority group has entered our individual and collective psyche, entered our conventional wisdom. The Scatter-Gun strategy effectively keeps Feminism daily in the public and political eye. In addition, it effectively drips misandry into the public and *political* psyche, into the policy-making process.

***

I would ask the reader to do two things with regard to this chapter:

Firstly, consider that if a men's political and Ideological movement existed (equivalent to Feminism), then it could just as easily find and create men's issues as Feminists now do for women. Perhaps male readers would like to participate in such an exercise: why not use it as a competitive game in the pub of an evening...teams or individuals creating 'male issues' as Feminism creates 'female issues'? Perhaps a gallon of beer to the team who can create the highest number of anti-male issues in one hour. It'll make a change from the Pub Quiz. Let me have your results.[1]

- The above exercise will show that there is no sexism against women in Britain that cannot be matched by an equal and opposite sexism against men: it will show that there is no misogyny in Britain that cannot be answered with an equivalent misandry.

Secondly, would the reader please note the dilution of the words sexism/sexist and misogyny/misogynist. The dilution of these words, an intentional strategy to encompass more and more issues (and to increase the 'seriousness' of existing ones), is actually making these words meaningless. The slightest incident is now conjured into being 'sexist' or 'misogynist'.

Seeking out and creating issues by Feminists has been neatly summed up by Neil Lyndon:

> *'Every time a working-class woman said that she was at her wit's end with her fella, and, for two pins, she'd brain the bugger, the sisterhood elevated her as a heroine of the movement and danced around her complaints as if they were an ancestral totem.'*[2]

- And so we have incessant Issue Creep

***

The following is an acknowledgement that Feminists *do* deliberately seek out events from which they can create issues:

> *'What I love about the third wave is that we've learnt how to find feminism in everything – and make it our own.'*[3]

- 'Finding feminism in everything' is an excellent self-definition of Issue Creep and the Scatter-Gun strategy. And, as admitted, Feminists *do* 'love doing this' (a Feminist personality? A Feminist psychosis?)

This chapter may appear to be flippant. It isn't. Although the issues created and presented by Feminism as discriminations, inequalities and oppressions *are* silly, they have a deliberate Ideological function in that they are used to wrong-foot and blame men, and, like the Olympic torch, to keep a constant flame present; a flame of Feminist necessity, a reminder that Feminism is still needed in a patriarchal and misogynistic society. In every Scatter-Gun issue there is an element of male-blaming. So I ask the reader to see the constant flow of Feminist created issues, however frivolous they may at first appear, for the political and Ideological strategy that they actually are – to justify Feminism, to preference women, and to spread misandry. The constant stream of created issues, however apparently trivial in themselves, has a *cumulative* effect and is a serious strategy to perpetuate Feminism.

- All aspects of the media are happy to accept Feminism's interpretation of actions and behaviours that can be construed as sexist or misogynist – without question, without challenge.

Refreshing their memory of a Feminist's psychological make-up/personality/mentality and a personal need for 'anger' would allow readers to better understand the individuals who seek out and create these regular Scatter-Gun issues. It would be easy to dismiss many of the following examples, and others not listed, as 'Whinge Feminism'; *it is* this, of course, but their political purpose, their cumulative effect, is strategic and is much darker.

***

Feminism's Everyday Scatter-Gun Issues: A Selection

For a decade or more we have had the created Feminist issue of the date-rape drugs Rohypnol and GHB. The National Union of Students is a particularly active Feminist organisation. Since the 1990s university campuses have been awash with date-rape literature – advising female students to beware of those nasty male students who all want to surreptitiously slip drugs into their drinks so they could then slip their hands into their underwear. Male students meekly sat on their backsides accepting this outrageous defamation, completely unaware of the Feminist machinations in sexual politics, not realising they were being seriously maligned and demonised. Men are so backward with regard to sexual politics, they are fighting a 21st century battle with stone-age weapons. Doh! In fact, they are so gormless in this respect that they don't even realise they are *in* a battle.

However:

SLIPPED A DATE-RAPE DRUG?
NO, YOU JUST DRANK FAR TOO MUCH

(Daily Mail, Tuesday, 27 October, 2009)

'Date-rape drugs are largely an urban myth used as an excuse by women who booze themselves into a stupor, it was claimed yesterday.

They are willing to "hide behind" the idea that a stranger poured poison in their drink – rather than face up to the fact that they had simply been binge drinking.

Interviews with more than 200 female students in and around London revealed they often mistakenly linked sickness, blackouts and dizziness to poisoning by a stranger, when excessive alcohol consumptions is much more likely to be the cause.

Dr. Adam Burgess, from the University of Kent School of Social Policy, said rumours about the prevalence of date-rate drugs were little more than an urban myth.

The study, published in the British Journal of Criminology, found that three-quarters of students identified drink-spiking as leading to an important risk of sexual assault – more than drinking too much alcohol.

Drink tampering was rated as a more significant factor in sexual assault than drug taking, being drunk, or walking at night in a high-crime area.

But despite such popular beliefs, police have found no evidence that rape victims are commonly drugged with substances such as Rohypnol.

Dr. Burgess said: "There have hardly been any cases where it has been proved that sedatives such as Rohypnol and GHB have been used in a rape incident. Yet it has been a storyline that has appeared in virtually every TV soap.'

- We see that young women have been taught by Feminism and the media to absolve themselves of any personal responsibility with regard to incidents, their behaviours and choices – to blame negative consequences on something or someone else. Feminism wishes to *collectivise* and *infantilise* women

- And many young women welcome this get-out, this life-line, saving them from personal embarrassment as well as responsibility; and so it is with Rohypnol. Feminism allows them to blame something else, or someone else - 'bad men'

***

Other studies have also found the date-rape issue to be a fraud, an urban myth:

'VICTIMS FACE TESTS AS POLICE PROBE 'URBAN MYTH' OF RAPE DRUGS: The study has been prompted by an explosion in claims of date rape linked to drugs such as Rohypnol...Despite the claims, there has been no successful prosecution of the use of Rohypnol and some police officers believe the threat could be more imagined than real...There hasn't been a single case successfully taken to court in the UK...Dr. Catherine White is clinical director of the St. Mary's centre in Manchester. She said: "There has not been a proven case of rape using Rohypnol, but if you pick up women's magazines you would think it was widespread" (2004).'[4]

And,

'DRINK THE REAL CULPRIT IN DATE-RAPE DRUG CLAIMS: A study has found that women are mistakenly blaming spiked drinks for making them vulnerable to sexual assaults...The analysis of more than 1,000 cases by the Forensic Science Service has shown that by drinking heavily and taking recreational drugs, women are actually making themselves vulnerable to sex attacks...the finding is at odds with the widespread perception that women who fail to stay alert in bars can fall prey to men who spike their drinks...The message that women themselves may be responsible could be hard to accept. So entrenched is the belief in date-rape drugs that in 2003 a short film highlighting the dangers was launched in cinemas (2005).'[5]

'USE OF DRUGS IN DATE RAPE "IS A MYTH": A twelve-month study ordered by chief constables and published today, shows no evidence that Rohypnol was used in the 120 cases examined by forensic scientists. The research will reinforce the concerns of senior officers that the use of Rohypnol, a sleep-inducing drug which is now banned, is a myth generated by talk but not by experience (2006).'[6]

- Wrong. Not 'generated by talk'...generated *deliberately* by Feminism in order to create, and politicise, a 'women are victims of men' issue

And,

'DATE-RAPE DRUG "HAS NEVER BEEN USED IN A SEX ATTACK HERE": The "date-rape" drug Rohypnol has never been used to assist a sexual assault in the UK, an expert claimed yesterday....Although the drug, which induces memory loss, has been blamed for thousands of attacks on women, drinking is to blame for the majority of assaults, according to a leading personal safety campaigner (2007).'[7]

- The report was headed by Julie Bentley, chief executive of the Suzy Lamplugh Trust.

With the (non) issue of public space violence against women we saw how Feminism, as a political and Ideological strategy, *deliberately* creates a fear and anxiety in young women. Similarly with the date-rape issues. We see that the NUS and other Feminist organisations have done an excellent job of creating fear in young women where no fear is necessary – simply to create and promote the Feminist Ideology that 'women are good people' and 'men are bad people' – blaming 'bad men' for doing bad things to 'innocent women'. The date-rape drug scare has been a very successful Feminist project, an artificially created issue that has been taken seriously, has scared ordinary women...and has demonised men. Promoting a myth would normally be harmless. But to perpetuate a myth with the *explicit intention* of using it as a sexual political and Ideological weapon – man-hating – is shameful, immoral and wrong.

***

Any kind of joshing in the workplace that is not liked by Feminists is interpreted as sexual harassment:

NERVOUS MEN KILL OFF THE OFFICE ROMANCE
(The Sunday Times, 8 October, 2006)

'A series of high-profile harassment cases has sparked the first signs of "segregation" in the workplace in relationships between the sexes which are disrupted by mutual suspicion.

Men are self-censoring innocent compliments and office banter when in mixed company, killing off office romance, according to a study by psychologists at the University of California, Los Angeles.

Jan Mann, head of employment of Fox Williams, a City law firm, said sexual harassment legislation in the UK was creating similar patterns.

"People are much more wary of banter in the workplace and much more concerned about whether they are saying or doing the right thing...Often we have managers who say: "I will not interview a young woman on my own or travel on my own with a female assistant".'

- Flirting, and workplace banter, have been created into Feminist anti-male issues

***

NO MOTHER-IN-LAW JOKES, ORDERS COUNCIL

(The Daily Telegraph, Monday, 27 September, 2010)

'A council has banned staff from using mother-in-law jokes after deeming them sexist and disrespectful to "family elders". The traditional humour is no longer considered acceptable, according to officials at Barnet council, North London.'

***

SCHOOL MEETINGS IN EVENINGS 'ARE SEXIST'

(Daily Mail, Monday, 18 October, 2010)

'Schools and local councils could be guilty of discrimination against women if they hold parents' or public meetings in the evening because mothers might be at home putting their children to bed.

According to the Equality and Human Rights Commission, the timing of such events could mean some women are unable to attend – a disadvantage that exists because of their domestic duties.

The guidelines from the quango were in a code of practice explaining the new Equality Act, which was passed just before the election and championed by Labour's deputy leader Harriet Harman.

It states a local council could be hit by a legal claim if, when it holds consultation meetings on a weekday evening, "it discovers fewer women than men attend."

A woman could make a case on the basis "that this is because some women cannot come because of childcare responsibilities". "This is enough to demonstrate disadvantage" it says. "She does not have to show the absence of women is attributable in particular cases to childcare responsibilities."'

- Many more women than men attend school sports days. Many fathers would love to see their child compete and cheer them on. They cannot because they are at work, being the primary breadwinner, undertaking 'family financial care responsibilities', whilst mothers choose to work part-time, flexi-time...or not to work at all. As there are always far fewer men than women at schools sports days could local councils be hit by legal claims from fathers?

- The Equality and Human Rights Commission is a Feminist non-governmental organisation

***

At this point let's take a coffee break. Columnist Allison Pearson writes:

> 'DCI Hunt and the Case of the Missing Biscuits: Michael Campbell was working the night-shift in a call centre when he helped himself to a couple of biscuits from a desk. The next day, his colleague Pamela Harrison noticed someone had swiped a shortbread of two from her M and S selection box. Now, there was a time when Ms Harrison would simply have shouted: "Oi, what cheeky beggar's had his hands on my custard creams?' And left it there. No longer. CCTV footage was examined and the 27-year-old support worker arrested. Mr. Campbell was sacked by the Convergys call centre and magistrates have ordered him to repay the cost of the biscuits, plus £150 court costs. The truly gobsmacking part is that Ms Harrison said in a statement that taking the biscuits from her desk had "invaded her privacy". She was "disappointed" that a colleague could "take items which, though of low value, can make someone feel insecure".'[8]

- The reader will notice the Feminist-speak in Ms. Harrison's comments – 'invaded her privacy' (straight from the Feminist lexicon) and 'making someone feel insecure' (pure Feminist rhetoric). I refer the reader to the chapters on the Feminist psychological make-up and mentality. In a culture that is fearful of Feminism and its power (to embarrass, kick up a sexist fuss, to 'go to law'...) the company felt *compelled* to pursue this silly woman's Ideologically-created issue and sack Mr. Campbell (blaming and punishing men)

The company could easily have bought a new, full, box of biscuits for Ms Harrison (or allowed Mr. Campbell to have done so). But the Feminist tyranny requires male heads to roll. Feminism has a great deal of 'Fear Power', as well as cultural and political power; it has organisations and bureaucracies running scared (police forces are particularly fearful of Feminist retribution and have become inherently misandrous in their actions and policies; the male is *always* at fault, for example, *he* is the sole cause of street prostitution, *he* is always the abuser in a domestic violence incident).

***

Very many women now have Feminist cant, rhetoric, dogma and platitudes at the tips of their tongues – ever ready to cough up an issue. Robert Kilroy-Silk had a morning problem show on television for a number of years in the early 2000s. There would be a set problem for each programme and people who had been affected by this problem, and experts in the field, constituted the studio audience. One programme was on the problems experienced by excessively overweight people.

Kilroy-Silk was seeking comments from members of the audience when a very large lady from the other side of the studio said that her husband had abused her. Kilroy-Silk was ecstatic...a particularly large lady with an abusive husband...he shimmied across the studio floor like a Haliborange on speed, microphone poised: "And how does your husband abuse you?" Answer: "He lets me eat what I want". Deadly embarrassed silence.

- The point is that *all* women have now been made aware of Feminist-speak for discrimination, oppression, victimisation, abuse, sexism and misogynistic issues; they have been primed by Feminism to do so. These terms have been so diluted that much of their use has become ridiculous. Everywoman has been conditioned by a ubiquitous Feminism to seek out piffling incidents of 'sexism' and 'misogyny'

***

One would think that Lynne Truss (yes, for it is she, the writer) would be more professional, as well as accurate, with her use of words than your average Feminist, but no. Feminist jargon is easily used and abused for political effect. Ms. Truss was being interviewed on BBC Radio 4's Today programme.[9] The topic was sport on television and more coverage time being given to men's sport than to women's. Truss actually said that this imbalance was 'misogynistic'. Is she aware of the definition of 'misogyny' (the 'hatred of all women by men')? I don't think that the imbalance in sport coverage is an expression of men showing hatred towards all women, Lynne. So why use that word – except to promote an Ideology?

**

GUIDES CALL FOR AIR-BRUSH LABELS

(The Daily Telegraph, Wednesday, 4 August, 2010)

'Air-brushed images of celebrities should be labelled to try to tackle "damaging and unrealistic pressures" on young women, the biggest girls' organisation said yesterday.

Girlguiding UK has started a campaign calling on the Government to introduce compulsory labelling on "touched up" pictures in magazines. Liz Burley, of Girlguiding UK, said: "We know how profoundly they (young girls) feel the pressure to conform to a particular body image and how badly they can be affected by these unobtainable ideals."'

- Young girls would not *naturally* think of air-brushing as a problem. They have been *taught* to see it as a problem. Girlguiding UK has obviously become a Feminist organisation. It teaches (indoctrinates?) young girls to seek out 'issues' and how to promote and use these issues for sexual political and Ideological advantage. Here we have an example of Feminists corrupting childlike innocence in order to pursue their Ideology and to train up young acolytes to become gender-warriors. An indoctrination process characteristic of communist and fascist States. Why not just re-name the Girl Guides the Feminist Youth Movement?

In 2007 Lucy Ward wrote an article for the Guardian: 'Girl Guides See a Future Blighted by Sex Bias and Pressure to be Thin' (27 February). Ward found that two-thirds of 16-25 year-olds would be happy to call themselves Feminists.

- We saw in Part One how Feminist teachers corrupt children's minds, impressing upon them the Feminist Ideology of patriarchy – 'good women (girls)' / 'bad men (boys)'. Here we see the same indoctrinal abuse of children in the voluntary 'charity' sector

So even a seemingly innocuous organisation like the Girl Guides has been hijacked by Feminism to use for its Ideological purposes. This is a process that is going on throughout modern Britain; young girls, especially in the education system, are being taught to seek out 'sexism' and 'discriminations'. 'Forever' Feminism needs these young gender-warriors. Feminism has corrupted so much of British society, culture and politics to ensure 'Forever' Feminism.

**

And it is not only the Girl Guide movement that has been hijacked by Feminists:

YWCA DROPS THE WORD CHRISTIAN FROM ITS NAME
(Daily Mail, Friday, 7 January, 2011)

'One of the country's best-known charities has changed its name, losing the clearest link to its Christian roots...The Young Women's Christian Association has dropped its historic title after 156 years because "it no longer stands for who we are".

Instead the organisation – which is mainly funded by legacies left by Christian supporters over 15 decades – will be know as "Platform 51"...Bosses say the name was chosen to reflect the fact that 51 per cent of people are female and that they can use the charity as a platform "to have their say" and "to move to the next stage of their lives"....Platform 51 aims to "lobby for changes in the law and policies to help all women"...Its chairman is gay rights activist and former equality quango manager Helen Wollaston...The YWCA received £1.3 million in state grants from 2008 – 2009'.

- So Feminists have stolen yet one more organisation to add to their Industries. The reader will notice the hand of Lesbian Feminism in this political hijack of a decent Christian organisation. Why haven't Christians fought back against this? What does it take to summon up the courage to stand up to these people?

The Women's Institute was infiltrated by Feminists in the late 1990s and became a Feminist organisation. Such is the relentless progress of the Quiet Revolution.

***

NUDES REMOVED AFTER COMPLAINTS
BY OFFENDED COUNCIL STAFF
(The Daily Telegraph, Wednesday, 18 August, 2010)

'An exhibition of nudes in an art gallery at a council office was taken down after an hour because staff were offended by the paintings...John Vesty had arranged to display 22 works for four weeks at the North Norfolk district council offices in Cromer.

He was: "baffled, irritated and disappointed" when they were immediately taken down by council officials after complaints that they were "offensive". Mr. Vesty...and his supporters said none of his paintings, on sale for £160 to £700, were erotic or pornographic.

He said: "All of them are standard life poses – the sort of work that artists have done for hundreds of years. There are no explicit full frontal poses or anything like that. I felt disbelief that someone could object to paintings like this and that the council should respond in such a politically correct way by removing them. You think that this sort of thing only happens in the Middle East, in places like Iran or Iraq rather than in a Norfolk seaside town."

Karl Read, the council's leisure and cultural services manager, said: "We received a number of complaints from members of staff and union representatives who found the paintings offensive".'

- How do we know that it was a Feminist complainant, rather than a moral/religious complainant? We know this because of the involvement of a trade union; trade unions are Left-wing, Feminist-friendly organisations

- This is an example of a Feminist's small-mindedness and intolerance, of an opportunity to exercise political correctness and Ideological power. And the authorities, as happens so often, cravenly submit to this disturbed mentality

The council involved will have been terrified of Feminism's reaction if it did not comply by immediately removing the paintings. Feminism in modern Britain is an extremely powerful and threatening political and cultural Movement. People and organisations are genuinely fearful of it. We know that Feminism has no compunction about using its Fear Power. Organisations, fearful of repercussions, everywhere capitulate to these disturbed people. How have we allowed ourselves to be so dominated, ruled and bullied by them?

'Feminism legitimises the sickness of some women'[10]

***

'The Equalities and Human Rights Commission has advised that the term WAG – used for footballers' wives and girlfriends – is arguably sexist and offensive to women. The ERHC, headed by Trevor Phillips, issued its guidance in a booklet for staff.'[11]

- Truly, Feminists, and Feminist organisations, can conjure an issue 'from nothing'

***

Even buying a packet of cigarettes can be turned into a Feminist issue:

'What is Lib Dem health spokesman Sandra Gidley on? Urging a ban on displaying tobacco products, she declares: "There are examples of packages designed to attract women, who may like the package because it is sparkly and attractive, so they want to get their hands on it".'[12]

- Gidley is unaware that she is implying that women are not responsible for their own behaviour and that someone else is to blame. Apparently, it's the shopkeeper's fault if women smoke because they are openly displaying twinkly packets of cigarettes that women just can't resist getting their hands on. Feminism infantilising and patronising women again

***

In 2008 an issue was created by two Feminist sisters, Abi and Emma Moore, called Pink Stinks. A new Feminist website was set up, which declared (January 2010):

'...the seeds are sown during the pink stage, as young girls are taught the boundaries within which they will grow up, as well as narrow and damaging messages about what it is to be a girl'

And,

'We don't think that there should be this monoculture that tells girls that there is only one acceptable way to be, and it's all about sparkles and make-up and princesses.'[13]

Pink Stinks is clearly a manufactured issue – it is the *parent*, not the child, who actually pays for the product at the shop check-out, they don't *have* to buy pink. Is there no choice? The truth is that Feminists don't like the colour pink because they regard it as 'feminine' – and we will see that Feminism is anti-feminine. The colour is immaterial – it could be yellow, green, orange – if it is associated with girls, with the 'feminine', then according to Feminism it is wrong, and can be construed into an issue. Much like the 'red flag' denoted communism and got the backs up of conservatives and traditionalists, so it is with pink; it has come to represent the 'feminine' and therefore must be condemned.

- But Feminists cannot blame the *mothers* for choosing pink for their children – women must *never* be held personally responsible - so the blame for this fabricated issue must be given to men, in the form of the patriarchal culture – sexualising children

Let's do a gender-switch on this. Boys are 'culturally encouraged' to choose *blue* toys and accessories; they don't particularly want to do this but society conditions them to do it. Society does this because blue is a macho colour and it needs to make boys into macho men so that they will fight in the armed services and do all the nasty, dirty and dangerous jobs in society. But, Feminist-like, men could whinge:

"This is just jolly well not fair because many more men are killed and maimed in wars than women (true); men suffer 40 times more job-related deaths and serious injuries than do women (true, check it); men die on average 7 years earlier than women (true, check it); and the suicide rate for men is 4 times greater than for women (true, check it). So it is a 'bad thing' for boys to be made to choose blue items by our culture. In addition, 'forcing' boys to choose blue gives young males and men a medical condition that is called 'the blues' and makes them sad and depressed, unhappy in their work and suicidal. We intend to lobby the Government to put a stop to this sexism, this discrimination, this misandry that is enslaving our sons to a male stereotype".

- You see how easy it is to conjure up and concoct an issue? 'Forever' Feminism thrives on doing *exactly* this

***

Another opportunity for creating issues is by 'taking offence' at innocent remarks that are intentionally and Ideologically interpreted as insults. Feminists get away with claiming that any word ending with 'man' excludes women. The word 'chairman' proved especially fruitful. For hundreds of years it has been the custom to address a male chairman as Mr. Chairman and a woman as Madam Chairman. The spelling has never implied that only men could chair a meeting, but by claiming otherwise Feminists have created a grievance, created an issue: an issue, like all other created 'issues', that has been carefully nurtured and promoted.

LOST TO POLITICAL CORRECTNESS, THE FATHER, SON AND HOLY GHOST
(The Daily Telegraph, Monday, 6 September, 2010)

'A new order of service produced by the Scottish Episcopal Church has removed masculine references to God.

The new form of worship, which removes words such as "Lord, He, His, Him" and "mankind" from services, has been written by the church in an attempt to acknowledge that God is "beyond human gender."

"It is political correctness," said Rev. Stuart Hall of the Scottish Prayer Book Society and honorary professor at the University of St. Andrews. "The word man in English, especially among scientists, is inclusive of both sexes."'

***

Male Feminists also make contributions to the collection and promotion of Scatter-Gun issues. A cancer specialist giving helpful advice to a woman who was suffering from breast cancer was, apparently, guilty of 'misogynistic sexism'. R.W. Connell's 'Gender' is a textbook used on many Women's/Feminist/Gender Courses. Connell is an Australian Male Feminist. His long-standing partner, Pam Benton, had breast cancer:

> *'Breast cancer is almost entirely a women's disease. The medical specialists who treat it, however, are mostly men...'*[14]

- One notices the pro-women/anti-men politics in these statements

Connell continues:

> *'Early in the treatment Pam was referred to a prominent oncologist...This gentleman delivered himself of the opinion that if women would use their breasts for what they were intended for, they would not have so much trouble. Pam was furious, and did not consult him again...There is research evidence that rates of breast cancer are lower in women who have had babies early in life and have breast-fed. That is, so to speak, impersonal fact...The research finding was made into a gender insult – which the oncologist probably did not even realise was offensive – by his bland presumption that what women are "for" is bearing babies.'*[15]

- Connell's Ideological interpretation of the specialist's advice as an 'insult' to his partner and 'offensive' to all women is jaw-dropping in its stupidity and fanaticism. A (Male) Feminist personality? A (Male) Feminist mentality? A stoking up of anger?

- The ease with which Feminists, and Male Feminists, can create a Feminist issue is breathtaking

***

Another example of commonsense advice being converted into a 'sexist', 'misandrous' issue is the Slut Walk phenomenon. In the Spring of 2011 a Canadian policeman, giving a talk to female students about personal safety, suggested that women should avoid dressing like sluts in order to avoid unwanted male attention.

Feminists took exception to this good advice and worldwide Slut Walks ensued, with young women dressed as sluts with banners and chants proclaiming that women should be able to wear what they want when they want and wherever they want and not be raped. Nobody has ever said that dressing like a slut condones rape. The point is that dressing provocatively sends a signal that the wearer is hoping to excite and provoke any men that she encounters. This type of dress and accompanying behaviour is actually *sexual harassment against men*. Here we encounter Feminist immaturity once more...they demand to dress however they want and behave how they want, but escape the personal responsibility of the consequences; 'It's not our fault'.

So an 'issue' was created 'from nothing' except commonsense advice. I refer the reader to Part Three. The Slut Walks should have been renamed the 'How to Avoid Personal Responsibility Walks'.

- 'Terrible as an Army with Banners'...?

***

The following is a Lucky-dip confection of inequalities and discriminations taken from 'The Equality Illusion: The Truth About Women And Men Today', written by the Professional Feminist Kat Banyard (there is an upsurge in the number of women entering the Feminist Profession and Feminist Industries; these positions offer long-term guaranteed employment in a 'Forever' Feminism society and State, and will be recession-proof). So Ms. Banyard offers us the following issues 'suffered' by women in modern Britain:

- '26 per cent (of girls) say they "hate the way they look when they exercise/play sport".[16] (girls 'hating themselves' is presented as a Feminist issue)

- 'The straightjacket of femininity restricts girls' movements every day in the playground and discourages them from involvement in sport.'[17] (Feminism seriously dislikes femininity, as we will see shortly)

- 'Girls also receive very little encouragement from sports pages.'[18]

- 'Golf commentators are found to be more ready to forgive bad shots if they have been played by men.'[19]

• Like all Feminist Scatter-Gun issues this is chicken-shit stuff, issues that are deliberately created and then manipulated into sexual political discriminations and inequalities

On the one hand we hear Feminists growl: 'We are women, we are strong': on the other hand we hear Feminists squeak, 'We are girls, we hate ourselves and can't play properly in the playground and sports writers don't say nice things about us'.

And Banyard, a leading figure in today's new wave of Grievance Gravy-Train Feminists, interprets the above as inequalities. But more than that, she states that all these terrible and traumatising inequalities *are caused by men*:

'We are in the midst of a violent backlash that uses images of female beauty as a political weapon.'[20]

• 'A violent backlash'? I wish

***

And then there is the old chestnut about men wolf-whistling at women – always a good bread-and-butter Feminist issue and newsprint space-filler:

GET OFF ME, YOU PERVS

It's not just men on building sites who intimidate women when the city heats up
(The Observer – where else? 11 July, 2010: Eva Wiseman)

'On London's City Road on Friday morning, a car tooted its horn at every single woman walking alone; on my way home, a boy broke away from his group to snap his fingers in my face and shout: "Tits!"...There are more people on our streets now (Summer), wearing less, our burning shoulders beacons of our availability, but while the lack of clothes (and addition of alcohol) may add to the general fug of fantasy and confusions, the things shouted from vans and scaffolding are rarely about lust, they're about intimidation and power, and often, they make women feel afraid.'

• Notice the need to use Feminist-speak, Ideological cant, 'male power' ('bad men') 'making women afraid' ('good/innocent women')

- How can Feminists claim that women are traumatised by something as innocuous as a wolf-whistle whilst at the same time claiming that women are tough enough to take on the top jobs? Another case of Pick 'n' Mix Feminism

- And ordinary women have been 'primed' by Feminists to view wolf-whistles as 'offensive' and 'sexist'. I do wish ordinary, decent, women would fight back against these fanatics. Refer to Part Three

The Eva Wiseman article was accompanied by her photograph. One would think that male car and van drivers would encounter enough rear ends of buses to toot their horns at (perhaps Ms Wiseman suffers from delusional wishful thinking?). Bugger chivalry. Sometimes men should be rude back to these misandrists who constantly find fault with us, who continually abuse us:

> *'Men seem to be too cowed to fight back, and it's time they did'*
> *(Doris Lessing)*

***

In June, 2011, the Society for the Psychology of Women came up with a bizarre discrimination – 'benevolent sexism'. Apparently, opening doors for women, helping them with heavy suitcases and so on, is 'sexist'. Others would call it good manners, but when new 'issues' are required 'good manners' become an expression of misogyny and sexism. And, of course, the Society for the Psychology of Women, a branch of the Feminist Industry, has to justify its existence and funding.

***

In the Summer and Autumn of 2010, the Coalition Government had to take serious financial measures to correct the huge financial deficit facing the country. Feminists ferreted out any cuts that could be construed as discriminating against women. One of these was that the Government proposal to increase the age of retirement for women to 66. The Daily Mail devoted a double-page spread to this issue, allowing its Resident Feminists, Becky Barrow and Ruth Sunderland, to sound off about how women were being discriminated against and how unequal this was. Sister Barrow first:

WOMEN PAY PRICE OF RETIREMENT AT 66

(Daily Mail, Friday, 22 October, 2010)

'The devastating cost to women of raising the pension age to 66 became apparent yesterday.

Raising the retirement age to 66 – from 60 for women and 65 for men – means millions will have to carry on working and bear the burden of clearing up the nation's economic mess...In total, they will miss out on £30 billion for having to work longer before claiming the state pension and other senior benefits.

Their extra years of toil will also see them pay an extra £13 billion in income tax and national insurance.

Campaigners and experts said it was grossly unfair that those who have worked hard all their lives will have to struggle on – and pay an average "bill" of £8,400 each – when they had hoped to be enjoying dreams of retirement.'

- The reader will note the emotive use of words: 'struggle on', 'bear the burden', 'extra years of toil', 'hoped to enjoy dreams of retirement'. Pejorative Feminist journalism?

Sister Sunderland:

THIS CRUEL BLOW TO A GENERATION OF WOMEN

(Daily Mail, Friday, 22 October, 2010)

'George Osborne deserves credit for squaring up to the issue. However, where he has gone wrong is by forcing women to bear the brunt of changes he is ushering in to make the state pension more affordable.

His announcement that the pension age for women is to rise to 66 over the next ten years is a devastating blow for those now in their fifties and will wreak havoc on the retirement plans of millions of middle-aged couples.

This change has a disproportionately harsh effect on women whose pension age is being moved forward by an extra six years in the space of ten years – while men's retirement will go forward by only a year.

At the other end of the age scale, the young will also be asking why women should be forced to continue to work rather than release jobs for the 16- to 25-year-olds who are unemployed.'

'Cruel Blow' my arse. Will the reader note the following. Men have, for many decades, been forced to work until they reached 65...whilst women have had the privilege of retiring at 60; so generations of women have enjoyed the preferential treatment bestowed upon them by the State – *5 extra* years of not working, *5 extra* years of retirement, drawing the State pension and receiving ancillary pension benefits such as free bus passes. Generations of men have wished that they too could finish their 50 years of grind, their 'extra years of toil', and retire earlier, 'enjoying dreams of retirement', but have – by law – not been allowed to do so. Being the main breadwinner *they* have been forced to carry on until they retire at 65, or until they drop dead, whichever came first. Now *that* is a discrimination, *that* is a *real and genuine* institutional inequality, not a strategically fabricated artificial inequality concocted to fulfil an Ideological aim.

Women have been privileged to retire at the age of 60. It is *not* unfair, it is *not* a discrimination, to *withdraw* a long-standing privilege, to draw a halt to long-standing preferential treatment. With regard to retirement women have for many decades received positive discrimination; to *remove* that positive discrimination is not an inequality, it is not 'forcing women to carry the burden of the cuts'.

• Only Feminists who are determined to seek out an issue could convert the withdrawal of a privilege into a discrimination. Only a Feminist determined to manufacture artificial Ideological inequalities could perform this political alchemy

Men's life expectancy has been 7 years less than women's. So we have a situation where women have been able to retire 5 years *earlier* than men...and *then* live 7 years longer. If we're going to seek out discriminations, unfairnesses and inequalities then we need to look no further; *women have been enjoying 12 years extra retirement than men* for decades. Sisters, that is a *real* gender inequality, that is a *real* discrimination.

Section 2

Chapter 18

Feminism's Grievance Gravy-Train Industries

We have seen examples of the Feminist strategy to create inequalities and discriminations 'from nothing'. In this Section we see how the Feminist strategy of establishing Industries has been accomplished. Keeping its organisations and Industries in business is now the *sole aim* of Feminists; their personal finances, satisfying their psychological make-up, implementing their Ideological agenda and spreading misandry *depend* upon it. Feminist Industries are at the forefront of creating and promoting Issue Creep.

Feminism is a Left-wing Movement, a Socialist Ideology. All Left-wing political parties boast that they are 'progressive'. During the May 2010 General Election campaign the word 'progressive' flew from the mouths of political leaders like spittle from the mouths of despots... each one, daily, promising to be 'more progressive' than the others; it was embarrassing. I truly thought we were going to end up with a new political party – the 'Democratic Progressive With Knobs On Party' (and we did – a coalition of nobs and knobs).

But the trouble with being 'progressive' is that you have to *keep* 'progressing'. Once you have achieved your objective you cannot simply say 'I'm no longer a progressive', you have to keep going...and keep *creating* things to 'progress' towards. And so it is with the Left-wing 'Progressive' Feminist Party/Movement; it has to keep *finding* new goals to progress towards in order to keep itself in business; that is, new issues, new grievances, new inequalities, new discriminations, new wrongs for it to right.

Feminist Industries are a *product* of progressive politics, *manufacturers* of Issue Creep, *promoters* of issues, *employers* of Ideologues, they are non-governmental organisations directly influencing social policy.

- The honour of being the 'Whinge Central' Feminist Industry would probably go to the Fawcett Society (although many others would run a close second). Both Labour and Conservative governments refer (and defer) to the Fawcett Society when seeking advice on gendered social policy and sexual politics

---

Equality and the Feminist Need for 'Industries'

Equality Feminism's aims of equal rights for women, equal opportunities for women, equal treatment for women, equal respect for women, equal choices for women, have all now been achieved. Most gender-neutral political commentators agree on this. The Equality Feminist Rosalind Coward notes:

'Feminism has, to a considerable degree, got what it wanted and most of it came to fruition in the 1980s.'[1]

- It was during the 1990s that the move to create 'Forever' Feminism seriously began, when Feminism was firmly established in the professions and all areas of the British State and Establishment

The Male Feminist and political author, Andrew Haywood, also admits (reluctantly) that Feminism has been successful in achieving its aims:

'Feminism in the twenty-first century also faces the problem that many of its original goals have been achieved or are being achieved.'[2]

- In what sense can *'achieving* your aims' be a problem? Only in the sense that the *raison d'être* for your existence has been taken away. It was noted in an earlier chapter that this was a dilemma for Feminism

An Equality Feminist confirms:

'With most battles for equal opportunity won, feminism came to be dominated by other goals and creeds. One could say that the movement had outlived itself and had to justify its existence.'[3]

And,

'There is a real reluctance to submit feminism's fundamental assumptions to an audit to see just how relevant they are to changing realities...feminism as a movement has been extraordinarily successful; it has sunk into our unconscious. Our contemporary social world – and the way the sexes interact in it – is radically different from the one in which modern feminism emerged. Many of feminism's original objectives have been met.'[4]

- But *still* the Feminist fraud is permitted to continue, Emperor-like, with no one brave enough to point out that it is morally naked, rationally bankrupt

Essentially, then, Feminism cannot allow its aims to ever be thought of as having been *fully* achieved. If it could be seen that its aims had already been achieved what, then, would happen to its Industries, to all the academic and political sinecures, the careers, the jobs, the propaganda opportunities, the government-provided finance and resources, the Commissions, the status, the power? The Minister for Women?

In addition, and importantly, the new emphasis on *special protections and privileges for women* rather than *equal rights for women* has dangerously eroded the rights of men. This change of emphasis, this hijacking of emphasis has, since the 1970s, helped shape law and social policy. For example, divorced fathers (difficulty in having contact with their children); rape (the changes have often gone far beyond correcting traditional biases against women); child custody ((Feminist influence has often reinforced traditional biases against men); domestic violence, (the issue of domestic violence *against men* is ignored).

How Feminism Benefits from its Gravy-Train Industries

Since British women enjoy a range of opportunities unimaginable forty years ago, Feminism is left with no battles to fight. So Feminism needs to create 'perpetual victimhood' status for women in order to justify its continued existence. Feminist Industries are both a product of Feminist created issues and also *manufacturers* of Feminist issues. They are businesses, Industries in which Feminist Ideologues are employed, draw their salaries, enjoy their sinecures, sit on Commissions, write books, report to political Committees, raise funds, and are asked by governments to produce 'research' - in other words, they provide wide-ranging opportunities for individual Professional Feminists to earn wealth and status whilst at the same time promoting their Ideology and implementing their agenda. And mostly State funded.

- The aim of Feminism today has nothing to do with equality; its aim is 'to stay in business', literal and Ideological business – making money as well as pursuing an agenda and progressing its Quiet Revolution

'Like all special interest groups, feminists seek subsidies for themselves. Their economic interests and professional advancement have been greatly enhanced by claims of past societal discriminations against women.'[5]

And,

'Some people perceive women as being victimised by men at every step in their lives. I think they are motivated by the desire to help women, but also I think some of the ideologues are seeking power not so much for women in general as for themselves and for their clique.'[6]

And,

'Feminists are the ones getting most of the money, the professorships, and the well-paid (but vaguely defined) jobs inside the burgeoning new victim/bias industry.'[7]

There is an Industry for *every* issue. Feminist Industries cover such issues as politics, equality, rape, health, the glass ceiling, sexual harassment, divorce, domestic violence, equal pay, higher education...

- No one has ever questioned the existence or the excessive growth of Feminist Industries. An audit has never been taken of whether they are genuinely necessary or not. No one dare...even though they cost the tax-payer (of which men make up a high proportion) many millions of pounds annually

***

Feminist Industries have policy-making power; power to manufacture inequalities and discriminations:

'The feminist bureaucracies already command significant patronage and power... More recently they have shown a capacity to influence policy and law at the government level. Here again, much of their effectiveness is due to their talents for persuading legislatures of the truth of some alarming "facts" about the plight of women, based on "studies that show...". The near-term prospect that they will have at their disposal an ever-larger number of ill-defined but well-paying jobs is bright indeed.'[8]

Feminism has a 'capacity to influence policy and law at government level'. For example, Feminism seriously dislikes the institutions of marriage and the traditional family:

FAMILIES 'NEED MORE IN BENEFITS, NOT TAX BREAKS FOR MARRIAGE'

(Daily Mail, Wednesday, 22 September, 2010)

'The Family and Parenting Institute, notorious for describing marriage as an unnecessary institution, said the best way to support the family was by increasing subsidies for jobs and handouts for those who choose not to work.

The report stems from a conference organised by the FPI and its chief, Katherine

Rake, who took over last year after leaving the feminist pressure group the Fawcett Society. But the recommendations provoked fierce criticism from rival think-tanks that do not enjoy public funding.

Jill Kirby, of the Centre for Policy Studies, said: "This is an organisation which was created by the Labour government and which has had no or negligible impact on the lives of families. This report is about protecting vested interests."'

- The Fawcett Society is a virulently Feminist organisation whose sole purpose for existing is to seek out and promote grievances, inequalities and discriminations against women, and thereby blame and demonise men

There are many thousands of Feminist satellite organisations, businesses and 'charities', that together form the Feminist Industrial Complex.

DOMESTIC VIOLENCE VICTIMS 'LESS SAFE' IF BUDGETS CUT

(The Observer, 10 October, 2010)

'Women at risk of domestic violence will find it increasingly difficult to flee their abusive partners as a result of the government austerity drive, according to two leading campaign groups.

The National Housing Federation (NHF) and Women's Aid claim that proposed cuts will lead to the withdrawal of thousands of places in refuges and other outreach services.

Ordered departmental cuts of 40% if applied to the £1.6bn Supporting People budget – a pot of money distributed among local authorities – would have a massive impact on care and support services, they say. The NHF, which represents England's housing associations, calculates 4,400 victims will be left without lifeline services that cost almost £67m a year.'

- How strange that a national organisation for distributing housing (the NHF) should be a Feminist non-governmental organisation promoting a Feminist Ideology and policy

- The 'Supporting People' title for this project is a misnomer. It supports *only* women/ Feminists. We tend to forget that men are people too

***

One of the largest Feminist Industries is the 'Equality Industry', providing lucrative and thriving careers for Professional Feminists – workshoppers, equal opportunity officers, women's officers, gender bias officers, harassment facilitators, Equality and Diversity course trainers. The TUC has among many other similarly-titled Feminist posts a Women's Equality Officer. All these people, and their committees, are remuneratively employed in finding, monitoring and eradicating endless manifestations of gender bias, sex inequalities, actively ferreting out areas where it could be construed that women are 'victims of discriminations', 'oppressions', 'sexism' and 'abuses': and if they don't find any of these then their jobs could obviously not be justified and they would be made redundant...so issues *necessarily* have to be found or created in perpetuity if mortgages are to be serviced. Trade unions and the public sector are disturbingly full of such make-work gender-warriors.

- 'Forever' Feminism can only exist on women's 'victimhood'

Feminists certainly have a bright future. Because of Feminism's constant need to create and promote issues, Feminist Industries (and many thousands of Feminist jobs) are well entrenched in our culture and economy. Feminist Ideology will always trump an economic recession. For an ambitious young woman, becoming a Feminist, joining this ever expanding and powerful Movement, this Political Community Club/Family is a clever career move. And more and more *are* joining up, continually bloating these parasitic organisations.

The Funding of Feminist Industries

Erin Pizzey is an Equality Feminist who established the first refuges in Britain for battered women. The Ideological Feminists (the Feminism we have in Britain today) hijacked her refuges:

> *'By this time I had attracted the two things the women's movement wanted: a just cause to clothe their political agenda and money to fund this agenda.'*[9]

Many Feminist Industries are now Government funded, that is, tax-payer funded. The Domestic Violence Industry, one of Feminism's flagship Industries, for example, has heavily influenced governments and the law to benefit from huge amounts of government funding and resources. In addition, money to perpetuate this 'Forever' Feminist Industry is grabbed from elsewhere; many people, personally uninvolved with domestic violence, *are forced by law* to subscribe to this essentially misandrous Industry:

£15 SPEEDING TAX INSULT

(Daily Mail, Saturday, 31 March, 2007)

'Motorists fined in court for speeding will be forced from Monday to pay a £15 surcharge to help the victims of domestic violence.

The £15 will be imposed on anyone who faces a fine, including drivers who challenge a speeding ticket in court.

The revenue will be used to appoint dozens of domestic violence counsellors to help bring alleged cases of abuse to court. Ministers announced that they would immediately plough £3 million of this into expanding the number of independent domestic violence advisers on the public payroll. The rest will go to other victim services...

The surcharge scheme will rake in £16 million a year. Home Office Minister Baroness Scotland said: "We are hitting criminals in the pocket to make sure that crime doesn't pay and victims continue to get the services we all want them to have. Domestic violence affects one in four women...and on average two women a week are killed by a partner or ex-partner"'.

- Why not give the surcharge to a children's charity? Why should this surcharge be used to fund a misandrous Ideology, and an already extensive Feminist Domestic Violence Industry? Answer: Because Britain is a society and State that promotes and funds the Feminist Ideology

- Baroness Scotland is a Labour Peer and well-known for her Ideological Feminist views

In September, 2009, I wrote to the Office for Criminal Justice Reform, asking which organisations received this surcharge. The Policy Manager, S. Watts, replied:

'...a significant proportion of the receipts goes towards funding the Independent Domestic Violence Advisors as well as a variety of other support services for victims of domestic violence throughout the UK. I have attached a list of these organisations.'

- Of the 190 organisations on Mr. Watt's list which are presently in receipt of this surcharge *not one* was an organisation for men. This is institutional misandry from the Office for Criminal Justice Reform, and it is disgraceful. I cannot understand why men in positions of power and influence sit back and allow such bias and prejudice to occur

So the State supports Feminism and its Industries. Our governments actively promote the Feminist Ideology, including its misandrous agenda. They support Feminism not just by implementing its policy demands but by *offering financial support* to continue its work of seeking out and creating grievances and inequality issues.

'It would be difficult to exaggerate the extent of the difficulties we now face. The gender feminists have proved very adroit in getting financial support from governmental and private sources. They hold the keys to many bureaucratic fiefdoms, research centres, women' studies programmes, tenure committees and para-academic organisations.'[10]

And,

'Feminist groups whose existence was predicated on the victimhood of women quickly embraced the girl crisis meme. No crisis, no "ism", no research funds.'[11]

- 'No research funds' means no Feminist 'research' to seek out, to create issues, or to academically rubber-stamp issues. No issues?... then no funds for other Feminist Industries that must feed on issues to continue to exist. The manufacturing and maintaining of issues is vital for Feminism and its personnel

'Like all special interest groups, feminists seek subsidies for themselves. Their economic interests and professional advancement have been greatly enhanced by claims of past societal discriminations against women.'[12]

- One of the main reasons why Feminism has found it so easy to establish its 'Victimhoood Industries' is by playing the 'women were second-class citizens in the past' card. This has made men in positions of authority and influence feel guilty...and so they acquiesce in implementing present-day Feminist demands, or turn a blind eye to modern Feminist excesses and privileges. They are Fifth Columnists. Male Feminists actively promote policy-favouritism for Feminism, its Industries, and their personnel. The male members of the post-1997 Labour/Feminist Governments are a good example of this, as are male officials in the trade union movement

So the self-perpetuating Feminist Ideology and its Grievance Gravy-Train will be secure for the foreseeable future, regardless of any economic recession. Welcome, reader, to the concept of 'Forever' Feminism – a huge parasitic drag on the British economy and a malign and powerful influence on British culture, politics and men. 'Crises', 'epidemics, 'issues' have to keep rolling off the assembly line in order to justify the existence, and the continuation, of Feminism.

- For a self-perpetuating Feminism, the Feminism we have in Britain today, success can *never* be enough

The Academic Feminist Industry

The Open University was set up mainly to benefit women, to give them a second chance at higher education. It is staffed overwhelmingly by women. Its social science and gender modules and books that I have checked are all written from the Feminist perspective.

- There are very large numbers of Professional Feminists employed in colleges and universities

The Academic Feminist Industry is particularly clever at manufacturing new issues and recycling old ones. The following is just one example of the tools it uses in this process. The piece is written by Lynne Segal, an Academic Feminist. I ask the reader to refrain from laughing whilst reading this quote because the consequences of unfettered Feminism on Britain have been, and continue to be, severe, and are particularly dire for men.

> 'As discussed in later chapters, post-structualism – especially in its Derridian and Foucauldian forms – has provided feminists with fresh conceptual tools for problematising identities and social differences. It usefully emphasises their hierarchically imposed and coercive nature, and the multiplicity of intertwining, destabilising and exlusionary discourses or narratives in which subjectivities are historically enmeshed. It suggests the possibility (however difficult) of categorical resignifications or configurations, as well as the acceptance of paradox and contradiction in conceptualising change. Feminists need to pay heed to the normativities and exclusions of discourse.'[13]

- Out of such a cauldron of unfathomable bollocks it is easy to brew up issues whenever required, in any social, cultural, economic or political area. This bamboozling esoteric jargon technique is an excellent strategy with which to create 'women's issues', as only sexual political experts (that is, university trained gender-warrior Sisters) can actually interpret it (or pretend to interpret it). It also 'justifies' many Feminist lectureships and professorships, which in turn justify the Feminist Academic Industry – whose Ideologically-charged post holders then go on to find and create *more* issues...an endless cycle

***

Feminism's Academic Industry is thriving, it is the oldest and one of its most formidable anti-male Industries. Academic Feminists have succeeded to the extent that they are 'given' their well-paid sinecures, having the freedom to pursue 'research', with public funding, to transcribe their misandrous Ideology into articles for specialist academic magazines, or into abstruse books (all incestuously receiving glowing reviews from fellow Sisters). They operate in pseudo-intellectual subject areas, using their own esoteric phrases and concepts. The reader may wish to confirm the truth of this claim by referring to literature produced by the Feminist Academic Industry. A deceit of Feminist 'research' is given in a later Section.

To repeat a quote:

> 'It would be difficult to exaggerate the extent of the difficulties we now face. The gender feminists have proved very adroit in getting financial support from governmental and private sources. They hold the keys to many bureaucratic fiefdoms, research centres, women's studies programs, tenure committees, and para-academic organisations. It is now virtually impossible to be appointed to high administrative office in any university system without having passed muster with the gender feminists.'[14]

- Did you get that? To be promoted in a British university one has to be vetted for one's positive Feminist credentials ('vetted'...or 'emasculated'?)

***

182

Professor Jeffrey Hart wrote of how Feminists in academia manage to keep themselves in power and effectively exclude and silence all opposition to their narrow Ideology:

'In an academic setting, the feminists also behave like the old Marxists. They make sure their troops get to faculty meetings, and they vote as a block. They aim at hiring and promoting other feminists, and excluding opponents of any sort. They are increasingly successful in many institutions...'[15]

Germaine Greer claims that it is the task of Feminists in senior positions, particularly in academia, to perpetually train young female students into the Ideology so that Feminsm can continue to be never-ending; generation after generation of *angered-up* gender-warriors entering the professions, State bureaucracies, politics, the law...and into academia in order to further train future generations of young female students...an endless cycle, a 'Forever' cycle.

'A feminist elite might seek to lead uncomprehending women in another arbitrary direction, training them as a task force in a battle that might, that ought never to eventuate.'[16]

- It is enlightening that in this quote, Greer appears to admit that many young women are 'indoctrinated' into the Ideology, 'leading uncomprehending women'.

- Here we have a leading influential Feminist, a member of the Feminist Academic Industry, advocating this Industry to 'train a task force to do battle (against the patriarchy, men)...a battle that should never end'

The training of young Feminists in Women's/Gender/Feminist Studies departments means that they become the only 'experts' on sexual politics in their post-university employment, in institutions and organisations. There are no *male* sexual political experts because there are no *Men's* Studies Courses in British universities; only courses in 'masculinities' – why men aren't more like women – are offered. These young Feminist gender-warriors, then, have considerable power. As well as influencing an organisation's policy in favour of the Feminist agenda, they will also be aware that to keep their lucrative posts they *need* to actually *find* (or create) more and more 'inequalities' and 'discriminations against women'. The university-generated regular waves of these young gender-warriors since the 1980s have seen Feminist Industries go from strength to strength, from success to success – whilst at the same time their legitimacy has become morally bankrupt. Today's Feminism has nothing to do with 'gender equality'.

As Christina Hoff Sommers notes:

'Needless to say, the only available "experts" are gender feminists whose very raison d'être is to find more and more abuse'.[17]

Camille Paglia, once a Radical Ideological Feminist herself (so her views are particularly incisive) comments upon one area of the Academic Feminist Industry, and identifies one of the main sources for the manufacture of perpetual Feminist issues:

'...Women's Studies, with their rote of never-ending grievances.'[18]

- This neatly resonates with Greer's views

- Feminism will never be placated, never be satisfied, never be appeased – it cannot afford to allow itself to be...it needs constantly to seek out and create 'never-ending grievances'

***

183

The following was written by Carol Sarler, an Equality Feminist:

YES, THE WAR OF THE SEXES IS NOW OVER

(Except for those wimmin who love being victims)

(Daily Mail, Tuesday, 3 October, 2006)

'Women's media became the platform for women to rally and campaign and fight their corner: nothing was sacrosanct in the heady mix of demands for rights, exposés of injustice and appalling jokes at the expense of men.

Happy days! But that was then and this is now – and between the two a funny thing happened: we won. The battle is over...

Nevertheless, in almost every area that really matters – law, health, reproduction, education, work, pay, marriage, divorce – our progress has been astonishing.

The irony is, however, that the very people who worked so hard to achieve so much are those who now work just as hard to pretend it isn't the case.

There is an industry, largely staffed by salaried women, dedicated to persuading us that our lot is still at least as dismal as it was (good grief, do these ladies not have memories?) as they keep frenziedly drawing new battle lines in the sand.

The Equal Opportunities Commission, no doubt privately fearful for its continued existence, publicly encourages women to believe that a sexy joke told by a man in the workplace is tantamount to an assault by an oppressor and, as such, worthy of the time and effort of industrial tribunals – not to mention the compensation awards that result.

I cannot imagine where they find all these oppressors; hand on heart, in my own life I do not know a single man with the interest or energy to oppress. I know bullies, of both sexes, who will bully for the hell of it – but their victims are of both sexes, too. Then again, my wages aren't paid by the EOC.

There are strident voices, most shrill among those who earn their keep in the Left-wing press who continue to portray all men as actual or potential rapists.

One can understand, of course, why these women continue to plough this anachronistic furrow: theirs is a vested interest, given that their livelihoods depend upon it.

You might as well ask a salaried environmentalist to declare that global warming does not exist as ask these foot-soldiers of the battle of the sexes to lay down their arms'.

- Ironically, Feminism works hard to pretend that success never happened; the usual mantra is: 'We have come a long way but we still have a long way to go'.

- To perpetuate its Grievance Gravy-Train Industries (and the financial and emotional well-being of their staff) Feminism needs to keep drawing new battle lines in the sand

When a group needs to be oppressed in order for its members to keep their jobs it has become 'oppression and victim dependent'. Sadly, Feminism has moved from its legitimate and moral base of 'equality' and has now become oppression and victim dependent, benefitting from such State handouts as positive discrimination, quotas and many other types of preferential treatment and special privileges for women (but mainly for Feminists themselves), including extensive State funding for its Industries.

The Professional Feminists Catherine Redfern and Kristin Aune boast about the number of Feminist Industries, declaring in 2010:

> 'When we turn to campaigning groups and single-issue organisations, listing them all would be a book in itself. Many organisations existing prior to 2000 are still going strong, such as The Fawcett Society, Justice for Women, Southall Black Sisters, Women Against Rape, Women for Peace, Women's Environmental Network, FORWARD, Campaign Against Domestic Violence, Women in Black, Scottish Women Against Pornography, Feminists Against Censorship, and the Feminist and Women's Studies Association, to pick a few. However, since 2000 many more new campaigning groups have formed...'[19]

- These are not simply organisations for ordinary women, these are *Ideological blocks*, deliberately set up and filled by gender-warriors aggressively and relentlessly campaigning to promote the Feminist agenda

***

Feminist Grievance Gravy-Train Industries are the driving force behind the Feminist Fraud. Apart from manufacturing and promoting its agenda via Issue Creep, providing employment for its Ideologues, influencing government policies and consolidating its Ideology, these Industries have a *social* and *psychological* function. They provide a 'life' for many Feminists; they provide a community, they provide a 'legitimacy' for their collective anger, they provide a Family and a political bond for friends. Feminism and its Industries can be compared to a religious cult, with an 'us' (Feminists) and a 'them' (men, the patriarchy)... a confrontational mindset. They are the Political Community Clubs for like-minded personalities and mentalities. And in addition to all their other functions these Industries drive the Quiet Socialist-Feminist Revolution, an integral part of which is the spreading of misandry.

Chapter 19
A Typical Feminist Grievance Factory

The British economy has traditionally had two key elements: the private sector and the public sector. It now has a third sector, specifically staffed only by Ideologues whose sole objective it is to seek out or create new issues for Feminism, or to exaggerate old ones. This third sector is the 'women's sector' (it is sometimes referred to as the 'Third Sector'). It is the official term given to what I have been referring to as 'the conglomerate of Feminist Industries'. It has been given official recognition. The Women's Sector/Third Sector is, in reality, the Feminist Sector.

The Women's/Feminist Sector is an extensive complex of interlinked organisations and networks, comprising Feminist Industries, Feminist national 'charities', Feminist Interest Groups, Feminist policy agencies and Feminist non-governmental organisations – all of which actually produce nothing and provide no services. What the Feminist Sector *does* produce is more and more Feminism, more grievances and more issues, more manufactured 'inequalities', 'discriminations' and 'oppressions', more Professional Feminists coming out of the universities, more jobs for these gender-warriors...and more misandry.

- The Women's/Feminist Sector is self-perpetuating, a 'Forever' Sector of the economy

***

To see what's going on in this Women's Sector let's look through the window of a typical Feminist organisation - the Women's Resource Centre. This isn't the largest Feminist Grievance Factory in Britain, the Fawcett Society is the largest, but the WRC is representative of *all* such Factories. The WRC is a Feminist business (but actually has charity status). On its own admission it is one of thousands of such Feminist businesses/organisations. The following is from the Women's Resource Centre's publicity package, which I received in March, 2010:[1]

> *'Our achievements over the last five years include:*
> - *Launching the Why Women? campaign to raise the profile of the women's sector and the funding challenges it faces, both throughout the UK and internationally*
> - *Successfully influencing decision makers on a range of third sector issues*
> - *Developing and disseminating over 100 briefings and responses on policy issues affecting women's equality and the women's third sector'*

- Note the global extent of Feminism
- 'Influencing decision makers' to implement their pro-Feminist/anti-male agenda is a major function of Feminist Industries

It continues:

> *'Values:*
>
> *Feminism: WRC firmly believes that strengthening the women's sector helps challenge discrimination against women and improves women's lives*
>
> *Equality: WRC will proactively work with, learn from and support other equalities organisations and will ensure our work is based on an equalities framework'.*

- Here we see again the intentionally deceptive use of the word 'equality'; 'equality organisations', in the context of Feminism, means *other* Feminist organisations. The word 'equality' is used as a deceit, to draw attention away from Feminism's aims and agenda (as with the phrase 'gender equality')

Again:

> 'Mission Statement:
>
> - (We) Advocate for the women's sector
>
> - (We) Build the capacity of the women's sector
>
> - (We) Conduct research, lobby fundraisers and decision-makers on behalf of the Women's third sector, disseminate policy information to members, hold consultations and make responses on policy issues of importance to women and women's organisations and build the capacity of women's organisations to influence policy
>
> - Our staff are encouraged to join the trade union'

- It is clear that the Women's / Third / Feminist Sector of the British economy is Ideologically driven – preferencing women, privileging women and policy-favouring women...and thereby spreading misandry

***

From where does the Ideologically driven pro-women / anti-men Women's Resource Centre receive its funding?

> 'The work of the WRC is made possible by grants from London Councils, Big Lottery Fund, Office of the Third Sector, Capacitybuilders and subscriptions from members.'

- So the National Lottery is funding a man-hating 'charity'. Is this legal? But the WRC isn't the only man-hating 'charity' that the National Lottery funds. It is to be noted that the National Lottery funds no *men's* organisations, no *men's* groups, no *men's* charities

- Note that there is an 'Office of the Third Sector'. Governments have officially recognised Feminism's Industrial Complex and thereby given their blessing to the Feminist Ideology of preferencing women / Feminists and its misandrous agenda

As we have seen, Britain's Feminist-sympathetic governments also continue to *fund* Feminist groups and 'charities': WRC Newsletter, Winter 2009 / 10. For example:

> 'Following sustained campaigning by women's organisations, the Home Office has set up a three month pilot project to support women who have no recourse to public funds.'[2]

- Central governments have financed Feminist organisations (and therefore man-hating organisations) since the mid-1970s: 'Oh, but we're not man-hating, we just wish to address women's issues and seek gender equality.' No you do not...*you* know and *we* know that a central tenet of your patriarchal Ideology is misandry...it is *men* that you are blaming, demonising and wish to punish for the inequalities and discriminations that your Industries are deliberately seeking out, creating and promoting

***

187

How does the WRC fit into the discussion regarding 'Forever' Feminism and its Grievance Gravy-Train Industries? The WRC is part of the Feminist Industrial Complex, part of the Women's/Feminist Sector, whose aim it is to promote 'Forever' Feminism. In the WRC literature we read:

'Despite the advances made, there is ample evidence that women in the UK continue to experience widespread discrimination, inequality and social exclusion. Issues of importance to women are often absent in social, economic or political agendas at local, regional and national levels.'

- It is completely untrue that women's issues are absent from the social, economic and political agenda; on the contrary, it is *men's* problems, issues and rights that are *completely* absent, as this book clearly shows. For example, we have no Minister for Men

- Whenever Feminism claims discriminations and inequalities it never *specifically* identifies these, we are simply asked to unquestioningly accept this rhetoric and dogma. And we always *do* naively accept that Feminism is telling the truth; where in today's Britain is there 'widespread discrimination, inequality and social exclusion' against women? Later chapters show these claims to be Ideologically-driven untruths

The WRC is a blatantly sexual political organisation promoting Feminism, yet it is a registered charity.[3] The Fawcett Society is also a registered 'charity'. There are so many.

- It would be interesting to know if the chairman of the Charities Commission is a Feminist. Would you come forward and declare yourself please

The general public and the vast majority of politicians simply have no idea just how vast the Women's/Feminist Sector, the conglomerate of Feminist Industries, actually *is*. Such lack of knowledge is a huge disadvantage for men. I would like the reader to take particular note of the following fact, given (and boasted about) in the WRC's own literature:

'There are an estimated 32,083 women's organisations in the UK.'[4]

- For 'women' read Feminist. So we have 32,000 Feminist organisations, producing nothing but grievances and issues; 32,000 Feminist businesses demanding preferential treatment, special privileges and policy-favouritism for women; 32,000 organisations seeking out issues, 32,000 organisations industriously converting women's freely-made choices into issues, 32,000 organisations exaggerating issues in order to create 'crises' and 'epidemics' - all working hard to justify their own existence and the continuation of Feminism.... and 32,000 organisations spreading misandry. Quite an achievement

- 32,000 Feminist Whinge Factories whose sole purpose is to manufacture 'grievances', 'problems', 'inequalities', 'discriminations', 'oppressions'...and spreading misandry

This is an astonishing number of Ideologically-driven organisations, and is regularly being added to. For example, in January, 2011, it was announced that the YWCA had become the latest Feminist organisation to join the Women's Sector.

***

So the WRC is only *one* of 32,000 Feminist organisations in Britain. One of the most powerful, prominent and active is the Fawcett Society. Governments always seek advice from the Fawcett Society on social policies that involve sexual politics, even Conservative governments. Rosa is a more recent addition to the Feminist Sector.

The Professional Feminist Natasha Walter declares:

'In 2008, a group of women launched Rosa, which aims to direct more money into women's organisations and to campaign for the continuing need for the women's sector.'[5]

- Rosa, one of the 32,000 Feminist businesses, is dedicated to raising money in order to promote 'the continuing need for the women's sector'... 'the continuing need', that is, to justify Feminism and to satisfy the financial, psychological and Ideological 'needs' of its followers

The cost of maintaining the Feminist Industries, the Women's/Feminist Sector, has become a massive drain on our national economy. It has been estimated that if all the unnecessary Feminist Industries, their grants, posts, 'research' funding, academic sinecures, quangos, salary bills, expenses...were to be curtailed then the British economy would benefit by nearly £2 billion annually.[6] For example, the annual bill for the Equality and Human Rights Commission alone is £70 million.[7]

- All Feminist Industries, to a greater or lesser extent, are funded and financed from the public purse. The public, men obviously included, are providing huge amounts of money to keep Feminist Ideologues in posts, in sinecures, solely to produce nothing but issues, to seek out and create discriminations, grievances, inequalities and thereby promoting misandry. All under the cover, under the stolen moral disguise, of 'gender equality'

The Third/Women's/Feminist Sector is a major player in the Feminist Fraud.

***

Two Equality Feminists note how unethical, and perhaps immoral, it is for Feminism to have created a Women/Feminist Sector for the political purposes of justifying its existence and benefiting its Ideologue employees. Firstly, Rosalind Coward:

'It is one thing to demand rights when a whole group is clearly disadvantaged, but it is quite another if those rights seem mainly to confer additional advantages on already privileged groups, or groups who may be using women's interests to promote their own careers or their own agenda.'[8]

Coward's observation could be aimed at Harriet Harman, the Labour/Feminist Government's Minister for Women, of whom one Equality Feminist observes:

'Enough. No more laws, no more quangos, or panels, or equality drives. We are not victims, Harriet. This is not the 1970s. How can we possibly term ourselves victims anymore... Only when it suits us to keep playing the victim.'

(Antonia Senior)[9]

- 'Only when it *suits* us to keep playing the victim'. Quite

***

'Feminist Industries sharpen their gender warriors' sensitivities to such an edge that they become expert and relentless grievance collectors'

(Swayne O'Pie)

SECTION 3

Chapter 20

Feminism and Women's Choices

We have seen the Feminist strategies of (i) creating issues 'from nothing' and, (ii) the establishment of Industries to assist this and to promote and publicise these fabricated issues. This Section addresses the Feminist dilemma of women's non-Ideological choices and how it resolves this dilemma by actually converting women's freely made choices into inequalities and discriminations. So this is the third area of Feminism's strategy of Issue Creep, employed to justify Feminism's continued existence. Non-Ideological choices include mothers wishing to be the primary parent; young women choosing to study the Arts and Humanities rather than Mathematics and the Sciences; women choosing to look feminine; women choosing to enter the sex industry; women choosing to be paid less (the pay gap) and women choosing not to seek promotion (the glass ceiling)

- I would like to make clear at this point that when I use the phrase 'women choose...' I mean 'women *tend* to choose', or 'women *generally* choose'.

***

A Feminist Dilemma

One of the elements of Equality Feminism, ironically, was to extend women's choices. This has been achieved. However, the concept of 'choice' has led to a dilemma for today's Feminists. What if women choose something that Feminism doesn't think is right for them, or doesn't fit its Ideology and agenda? This is a problem for Feminism because it needs to have women seen as 'victims'; if women *freely choose* options that appear to have 'disadvantages' then they cannot logically be seen as, and presented as, 'victims'.

All choices made by women or men result in consequences. An integral part of freedom of choice is accepting the negative consequences as well as enjoying the positive consequences; this means accepting *personal responsibility* for the negative consequences of one's freely made choices...and not blaming other factors.

It is the difference in the choices that men and women make that allows Feminism to convert 'women's choices' into issues – it compares the *negative consequences* of women's choices (negative as defined by Feminists, not by women themselves) with the *positive consequences* of men's choices...and declares from this illogical comparison, that men are advantaged over women. This strategy has had tremendous success; we have all been fooled by this spurious comparison. This difference between the two extremes is the essence of what Feminism labels and promotes as 'discriminations against women', 'oppressions suffered by women'; that is, 'gender inequalities'. This deliberately deceitful Feminist comparison forms myths that have become firmly established in our conventional wisdom as 'truths'; for example, the 'pay gap' and the 'glass ceiling' are seen as inequalities. The universal and constant Feminist claim of 'gender inequality' suffered by women is fraudulent.

- It is important to note that the 'negative consequences' of women's choices are *not seen as negative consequences by the women themselves* but are Ideologically interpreted as negative consequences by Feminists in order to create their necessary issues

    'When it comes to choice, then every man or woman has to choose as an individual human being, and, like a human being, take the consequences'

    (Dorothy Sayers, author)[1]

    ***

So how does Feminism convert women's choices into inequalities and discriminations? To do this it employs the strategy of 'blaming'; other factors are blamed for women making their non-Ideological choices.

Feminism's Blaming Strategies:

1. Feminism blames discrimination and oppression by men (either individual men or the patriarchy) for the 'negative' consequences of women's choices. For example, the fact that fewer women than men are in top jobs is blamed on discrimination by male employers rather than women choosing not to seek promotion; women who chose to be stay-at-home mothers (thereby earning less than their husband) is blamed on oppressive men who subjugate their wives.

2. Feminism seeks out personal factors to blame: a woman's personal circumstances, 'gender inequality', an abusive husband, a difficult childhood, mental health problems. For example, the claim that one reason women go into the sex industry is because they were sexually abused as children.

3. Feminism blames socialisation, a false consciousness/learned response for women making non-Ideological choices and decisions (this will shortly be discussed in detail).

It is important to note that the 'blaming strategy' is absolutely essential for Feminism if it is to convert women's choices into 'women's issues' because:

- It cannot, rationally, create inequality issues if women have *freely chosen* to take a particular decision that 'disadvantages' them (as defined by Feminism)

- So Feminism needs to free women of personal responsibility for making choices that lead to 'disadvantages' so that it can *then* call these supposed 'disadvantages' inequalities and discriminations – which are caused by *other* factors (mostly by men)

- Men need to be blamed, wherever possible, for women making 'disadvantageous' choices

Socialisation, Sex Stereotyping and Free Choice

Feminists believe that women cannot make 'free' choices because of their socialisation. The Feminist belief system of 'sameness and socialisation' was addressed in an earlier chapter and exposed as irrational and invalid. In this Section we will see how this irrational Feminist belief system is, astonishingly, being translated into government policies.

To remind the reader: The Feminist belief system of 'sameness' declares that boys and girls are born exactly the same except for their genitalia. But, the belief system goes, girls are *intentionally* socialised differently (by a patriarchal culture) to be inferior and to choose options that disadvantage them. Feminists claim that a false consciousness; 'learned roles', is *deliberately* socialised into girls. Feminist Ideology declares that it is men (via the patriarchal culture) who are responsible for the sexual differences in this socialisation process...and therefore are responsible for making women choose options and lifestyles that 'disadvantage' them ('disadvantage' defined by Feminists).

So according to Feminist doctrine, women learn their (female and feminine) roles through social-isation and these roles lead to sex stereotyping; sex stereotyping, Feminists claim, is a major cause of women's inequalities, discriminations, oppressions and victimhoods.

The belief system of socialisation (sex stereotyping) is an extremely useful gender-weapon for Feminism, lending itself to an easy explanation of why women make non-Feminist, non-Ideological choices. This is the reason why this concept has again become so fashionable in the 21st century. It is a useful concept because it allows Feminists to claim that women cannot make a 'free' choice. 'Research' is produced to give this belief system some academic credibility:

MEN AND WOMEN ARE FROM THE SAME PLANET

(Daily Mail, Monday, 16 August, 2010)

'Scientists would have us believe that men and women are so different they could hail from different planets.

But a new book claims the difference between the genders is down to the way we are brought up. It says the idea we are hard-wired at birth, as promoted by 1992 best-seller Men are from Mars, Women are from Venus, is outdated.

In fact, it is nurture, rather than nature, that has the largest effect on skills, attributes and personalities. And girls don't come into the world able to multi-task and communicate better. Instead, we are steered towards gender-defined skills by parents and teachers.

According to the book, Delusions of Gender, by Cordelia Fine, a Melbourne University psychologist, there are no major neurological differences.'

- We need to be sceptical about 'research' that is produced from a source that has an Ideology to promote and an agenda to implement. It will be shown in the chapter on Cheating and Lying: The Deceit of Feminist 'Research', that Feminist 'research' is never neutral but Ideologically-driven, produced solely to advance the Feminist agenda

Blaming Socialisation for Women's Choices is Nonsense

The socialisation/learned roles/sex stereotyping Feminist argument to excuse women's non-Ideological choices has no basis in fact. If social forces and upbringing have such a profound effect and influence on *women's* choices then they must *also* have a profound effect and influence on *men's* choices. This means that nobody, anywhere, under any circumstances, is capable of making a 'free choice'. If we are to accept this Feminist belief system of socialisation/learned roles then *nobody at all* can possess or exercise free will. Either we are *all* victims of socialisation (in every single choice we make)...or *none* of us are. Feminism cannot logically claim that *only women* are victims of this concept. The concept is nonsense, if it had any validity then none of us could be held morally or personally responsible for the consequences of our chosen behaviours and actions. Think about this...

...A sane society could not operate on this belief system. Hundreds of thousands of men locked up in prisons could use the same defence for shooting, robbing, selling drugs and so on. Why not argue that socialisation (for example, the culture of masculinity, a background of poverty, a racist family) makes *them* behave in these anti-social ways? If men were nothing more than the creations of 'socialisation' then they could hardly be expected to take personal responsibility for their own (criminal) choices. And this defence would not only apply to crime in general but also to rape; men being absolved of personal responsibility for rape and escaping conviction using 'socialisation' as a defence for their choice to rape would *seriously* piss off Feminists. But individual men *are* held personally responsible for their choices, decisions, actions and behaviours. So how can Feminists legitimately claim that *women* should be exempt from personal responsibility when, for example, they choose to work in the pornography industry, or choose to be a prostitute, or choose jobs with lower pay, or choose not to seek promotion in their work? A selective application of the 'socialisation' doctrine (driven by Ideology) is irrational.

A selective application of this Feminist concept may be irrational but it is still (disturbingly) used in modern Britain to guide policy-making and legal decisions. For example, there are regular Feminist demands for women never to be imprisoned (and the State takes these demands seriously). Again, the Equal Treatment Bench Book (a moral guideline for judges), issued by the Judicial Studies Board (2009) specifically states that women offenders should be treated much more leniently than men (for a similar offence), because of 'women's special circumstances' (which it does not identify or define...because it *cannot*).

- It will be shown that many social policies and legal decisions are guided by the Feminist belief system of women's socialisation/learned roles/sex stereotyping, their 'special circumstances'

***

But Feminism does more than blame other factors for the negative consequences of women's non-Ideological choices and decisions. It also does more than convert these choices into inequalities and discriminations...

...Feminism is so politically powerful it demands State programmes to *remedy* the negative consequences of women's freely made choices (negative consequences from the Feminist perspective, that is). For example, it demands positive discrimination and quotas to *remedy* the under-representation of women in senior positions; it demands State-provided wrap-around child care to *remedy* the *negative* consequences of women who choose to be stay-at-home mothers. Wraparound child care encourages such mothers to enter full-time employment (so that they can be independent from men – a Feminist aim).

Chapter 21

Women Choose to Marry and be the Primary Parent

This chapter may not initially seem to be of interest to men. But it is important to them in a number of ways. It shows how Feminism blames and condemns men for the institution of marriage; it shows how Feminist Ideology does not represent the feelings and needs of ordinary women; it shows how governments pursue Feminist policies that are contrary to the wants of ordinary women; it is seen how Feminism seriously dislikes marriage (and by extension, the traditional family); and it shows how Feminists disrespect and abuse non-Ideological women.

***

The vast majority of women choose to be the primary carer of the children and express this by choosing to be stay-at-home mothers, or by choosing employment options that allow for their home-centredness being the primary concern in their lives.

MUMS DON'T WANT TO WORK

**(Press Release: The Birth and Motherhood Survey, 2000:
Mother and Baby Magazine, in association with BUPA)**

'A staggering 81% of mums with babies and/toddlers say if money were no object they would definitely chose to be a "stay-at-home" mum, according to the "birth and motherhood" survey, 2000...Only 6% of mums with babies/toddlers say they "enjoy working full-time" and 82% say they are "less career-minded following the birth of their baby".'

And,

Professor Geoff Dench researched British Social Attitudes surveys over twenty years and reported his findings in March, 2010. One major finding was that mothers do not want to go out to work but wish to stay at home caring for their children.[1]

And,

WHAT WOMEN REALLY WANT

**Forget the working superwoman ideal, they value time at home
with the children more than anything else, says new report**

(Daily Mail, Friday, 9 October, 2009)

'Women do not want high-powered careers and find more fulfilment in motherhood than work, a report said yesterday.

Millions have been left frustrated and miserable by Government policies that push them into jobs and their children into nurseries, it was claimed.

The report – What Women Want – was published by the centre-right think-tank the Centre for Policy Studies...The figures, from pollsters YouGov, showed that only 1 per cent of mothers wanted to work full-time and nearly a third, 31 per cent, did not want to work at all...the findings said disaffection with paid work was not confined to mothers...they indicated that 19 per cent of all women, nearly one in five, said they wouldn't work if they didn't have to.

> Cristina Odone...condemned her feminist colleagues in the media and politics as a "small, influential and unrepresentative coterie" who assume that women must achieve self-realisation through work.
>
> She added: "We need to break the stranglehold that the small coterie of women, who work full-time and buy into the macho way of life, enjoy on our public life. They have for years misrepresented real women who reject the masculine value system for one that rates caring above a career and inter-dependence above independence."'

- Every study on this subject has found that an overwhelming majority of mothers wish to be family-centred rather than work-centred...

- ...Yet Feminists in the post-1997 Labour/Feminist Governments were bloody-minded in forcing through policies, at huge tax-payer expense, that inveigles/forces mothers to enter full-time employment

- Feminism does not have the welfare or the well-being of ordinary women (the majority of women) at heart; it does not represent non-Ideological women...except where these women's desires happen to coincide with the Feminist agenda

- Odone notes the political and media power of a 'small influential coterie of women' and how they have a 'stranglehold' on social policy. These powerful women are Feminists. Odone is reluctant (perhaps fearful, understandably) of using the word 'Feminist'

Mothers Don't Want Fathers to be Too Involved in Child Care

Feminism condemns fathers for not taking on an equal share of child care. This perceived inequality has been an enduring and regularly promoted inequality for Feminists. Yet mothers *don't want* the father to participate equally in child care:

- *'They (mothers) resent the intrusion of males on their mother role.'*[2]

- *'It is not a simple matter for mothers to accept shared parenting nor to give up the idea that they should be the primary parent.'*[3]

- *'There is evidence indicating that only a minority of women seem to desire increased participation by their husbands in child care, and that the rates are not appreciably higher for employed than for unemployed women.'*[4]

- So we have Feminists, once again, creating issues 'from nothing', relentlessly blaming men (in this case fathers) for being lazy and not doing an equal share of child care...when the majority of wives don't even *want* them to. Such is Feminism

- Feminists do not represent the majority of women; they wish to impose their own belief system on *all* women...and then present themselves to the media and politicians as the representatives of 'women's views'...a fraud and a confidence trick (and we have all been duped by this deception)

***

Feminism is in a dilemma: women choose one thing, Feminists wishes them to Ideologically choose something else. Feminism needs to convert ordinary women's choice into an issue, so it invokes its 'Blaming Strategy'. Child care by a mother has to be described and presented as 'a burden', imposed on women by men. Whenever a mother's child care is referred to by a Feminist it is represented as being a disadvantage, a huge chore. For example, Jennifer Saul, an Academic Feminist at Sheffield:

'...a key reason that the male partners are able to concentrate successfully upon their careers is that the female partners take on most of the burden of childcare.'[5]

Feminism needs to convert a woman's freely made choice to marry and be a full-time mother into a burden, a discrimination, an oppression. These Feminist-defined negative consequences of this choice are then blamed on men:

- *'The institution of marriage is the chief vehicle for the perpetuation of the oppression of women, it is through the role of wife that the subjugation of women is maintained.'* (Marlene Dixon)[6]

• A woman's *choice* to get married is converted by Feminism into the issue of women being oppressed and subjugated by men, their husbands

- *'Women represent the most oppressed class of life-contracted unpaid workers, for whom slave is not too melodramatic a description.'* (Germaine Greer)[7]

• A woman's *choice* to be a housewife is converted by Feminism into the Ideological issue of women being 'oppressed domestic slaves' – the slave-owners being men, their husbands

- *'Sex means motherhood and motherhood means dependency...'* (Beatrix Campbell)[8]

• A woman's *freely made choice* to enjoy conjugal relations with her husband is converted by Feminism into the inequality of 'women's dependency upon men'. The reader will note here the influence of Lesbian Feminism

- *'The heart of women's oppression is her child-bearing and child-rearing role.'*[9]

• A woman's *choice* to be a mother and to enjoy raising her children is converted by Feminism into the victimhood of 'women's oppression'...by the patriarchy

- *'The Equality and Human Rights Commission, headed by Trevor Phillips, and equal pay pressure groups, say that mothers are often anxious to go back to work but are pressured into a caring role by lack of opportunities for flexible hours, lack of affordable daycare, and the reluctance of male partners to take over a share of the childcare (2009).'*[10]

• Women's *choice* to be stay-at-home mothers is converted by a Feminist non-governmental organisation (and by Feminist equal pay pressure groups) into an 'inequality' and 'discrimination'. Men (husbands) are blamed

• We know that the majority of women wish to be home-centred, so expressing a mistaken opinion ('women are anxious to get back to work') becomes a bigoted lie when it is intentionally and knowingly used for Ideological and political purposes. The misandrous EHRC, part of the Feminist Equality Industry, receives £70 million annually from the public purse to promote the Feminist agenda and to malign men

- *'Women's domesticity is a circle of learnt deprivation and induced subjugation.'* (Ann Oakley)[11]

• For 'learnt deprivation' read 'negatively socialised by the patriarchy': for 'induced subjugation' read 'bullying husband'. The Feminist Ann Oakley has held many influential social policy-making positions since the 1970s

- *'Women were always, and are still, given automatic and often exclusive responsibilities for child care...and these duties in the home prevent them from playing as full a part as men in the wider social and political world.'* (Mary Kenny)[12]

- *'Given* automatic and exclusive responsibility for child care'? We know that this is a lie; mothers *freely choose* to be the primary carer. It is not an imposed 'duty'

- A woman's *choice* to be the primary carer of her children rather than enter paid employment is converted by Feminism into the Ideological misandrous oppression of 'men making their wives take on the chore of child care...in order to stop them from entering paid employment or politics'

The following neatly sums up the Feminist perspective and strategy:

> *'Why is our culture moulded by a tiny minority whose needs receive such disproportionate attention? Because this minority is vocal, visible and influential. The commentariat, where women working full-time are over-represented, and the high-flying career women whom they hail and quote, set the agenda...This elite caricatures women who have turned their back on a career as victims of sexual discrimination.'*[13]

- The ease with which Feminism can convert a woman's freely made choice into a 'gender inequality' is astonishing. It is equally as astonishing that we have all been gulled by this fraud

***

In truth, Feminism doesn't really like ordinary women; it actually despises women who choose options that are non-Ideological; the following are comments made by Feminists about ordinary (non-Ideological) women:

Simone de Beauvoir:

> *'...de Beauvoir argues that because her work "produces nothing", the housewife is "subordinate, secondary, parasitic"..."woman is supported by him (her husband) like a parasite"...marriage makes women into "praying mantises", "leeches", "poisonous creatures"..."dead weight"..."a parasite sucking out the living strength of another organism"...There is no talk of choice here, but of "prohibiting marriage as a 'career' for women".'*[14]

F. Carolyn Graglia refers to Betty Friedan's thoughts on the stay-at-home mother:

> *'An impassioned expression of overwhelming antipathy for the life of a mother and housewife. Friedan's most striking denunciation is that being a mother leads to "progressive dehumanisation" in the "comfortable concentration camp", that is, her home.'*[15]

Jessie Bernard, the fiery Lesbian Feminist:

> *'To be happy in a relationship which imposes so many impediments on her, as traditional marriage does, women must be slightly mentally ill.'*[16]

The Socialist Feminist Sheila Rowbotham:

> *'She (a mother and housewife) is rather like those mental patients and prisoners who are terrified to live without the safe and known routine of their institution.'*[17]

- So according to Feminism women who choose to marry and be home-centred are 'mentally ill' and 'mental patients'

Ann Oakley:

> *'An affirmation of contentment with the housewife role is actually a form of anti-feminism, whatever the gender of the person who displays it. Declared contentment with a subordinate role- which the housewife role undoubtedly is – is a rationalisation of inferior status.'*[18]

For all its, cant, dogma and rhetorical moralising about 'gender equality' Feminism has no respect for ordinary women. Feminism is, in truth, a malign Ideology promoting its *own* interests and agenda, advancing its *own* people, justifying its *own* Grievance Gravy-Train Industries and blaming, demonising and punishing men.

***

Women's choice to be the primary carer has disadvantages for men:

BE MY BABY

(The Sunday Times, 3 April, 2011)

'"When I married my wife she was a lawyer, like me", said David, 42. "When she had our first child I assumed that after six months or so she would go back to work. But she didn't. And then we had another baby. And now it's been four years or so and, without us discussing it, I've become the sole breadwinner and she's a stay-at-home mum.

Yet I don't get to enjoy any of the perks of the old-style breadwinner; there's no supper on the table when I get in. More often she hands me a screaming child and looks grumpy that I haven't been there. But I'm doing my best and I'm stuck with the grind of paying the mortgage and keeping us all for the next 25 years; I don't remember signing up to that."'

Feminism has successfully converted a woman's freely made choice to be a stay-at-home mother into an inequality, discrimination and oppression, for which the male is blamed. And this conversion has been translated into social policy. Divorce settlements are now based upon the Feminist Ideological claim that 'women are made to stay at home by their husbands in order to care for the children'. Feminist-friendly divorce judgements are premised on this lie. Judges believe, and often say, that 'the wife has "sacrificed" her career to raise the children'. They must know that this is a lie...they must know that the vast majority of mothers *freely choose* to leave their careers to become the primary parent, either choosing to work part-time or not to be in paid employment at all. Rationally, there can be no 'sacrifices', no 'chores', no 'burdens', no 'subjugation' if women *choose* the option of primary carer.

Feminist Ideology dictates social and legal policy. Divorced men now have to lose 50 per cent (often more) of their wealth because of a Feminist fraud...because of Feminism *converting* a woman's freely made choice to be the primary parent into an inequality and oppression; they have convinced Feminist-sympathetic judges to *remedy* the 'negative' consequences of these non-Ideological choices. And almost all divorcing mothers go along with this Feminist conversion (knowing that it's a fraud); many women in Britain today profess not to be Feminists... yet will greedily accept the benefits of the Feminist agenda. In this sense, most women are Feminists to some degree. We ought to celebrate and cherish those who are not.

Chapter 22

Women Choose to Study the Arts and Humanities

Again, this chapter may not seem to be of interest to men, but it really should be read. It is important in showing the power of Feminism to dominate governments and to direct gendered social policy. It shows how Feminism is socially engineering its Quiet Revolution.

> *'Girls are seen as bright and academic but are channelled into arts, humanities and languages, and away from science and computing...This kind of socialisation reflects traditional views of women's place in society and perpetuates gender inequalities in pay, job "choice" and working hours. In short, it sets young women up for disadvantage...'*[1]

Young women choosing to study the arts and humanities instead of the sciences and mathematics is a perpetual Feminist grievance. All books on Feminism address it and present it as a substantial discrimination suffered by women. It is important, then, to expose this fabricated issue as the fraud that it undoubtedly is. Yet it is a grievance that governments of all political persuasions have taken seriously since the 1970s and the unquestioning acceptance of this relentless Feminist grievance highlights a number of points:

- It shows that Britain is steadily becoming a totalitarian State, using social engineering to achieve Feminism's Ideological aims and implementing its agenda

- It shows the repetitive stupidity of successive governments; this issue has been policy-addressed many times and the majority of young women *still* prefer to study the arts and humanities rather than mathematics and science

- It shows the political power of Feminism, being able to force different governments, for thirty-five years, to constantly initiate policies that repeatedly fail

- It shows how Feminism milks the system, creating employment and salaries for its followers and funding for its Industries

- It proves conclusively that the Feminist belief systems of sameness/socialisation/false consciousness/learned roles and sex stereotyping have no substance, and ought to have no place in formulating social policy

- It is an example of how Feminism converts a woman's choice into an inequality

• This issue, although esoteric, is significant in exposing Feminism for the politically powerful fraud that it has now become

***

It is a perennial annoyance to Feminists that young women prefer to study the arts and humanities rather than the sciences and mathematics. It annoys Feminists because the former subjects lead to professions that pay lower salaries than the latter, and it is a Feminist tenet that women should earn exactly the same as men. The fact that young women actually *enjoy* studying, and being involved in, the arts and humanities is disregarded; such interests and enjoyments are not Ideologically motivated, and are therefore said to be misguided.

The Feminist perspective is that women should have equal pay with men, any other factors are irrelevant. So women's choice of study subjects is incompatible with the Feminist agenda and therefore must be rectified.

- The fact that young women choose to study the Arts and Humanities rather than Mathematics and the Sciences has been converted by Feminism into a 'gender inequality'

So how does Feminism conjure and convert this freely made choice into an inequality and discrimination? A culprit has to be sought...and blamed.

***

In earlier chapters the Feminist theme of 'sameness' was encountered – the idea that boys and girls are essentially the same, except for their genitalia. Feminism applies this belief system to the 'inequality' of girls' academic subject choices.

At the heart of the arts and humanities issue is the Feminist claim that boys and girls are born the same, with the same talents, interests and drives, but then girls are socialised into learned roles and are sex stereotyped into studying subjects that lead to low-paying careers. The Feminist argument is that if girls can be socialised *into* choosing academic subjects (and associated careers) then they can just as easily be re-socialised *out* of this choice and *into* choosing Ideologically-approved subjects and careers (mathematics and the sciences). With enough encouragement and training, it is said, girls will choose to study 'male' subjects and choose to enter male occupations. They just need enough positive 'socialising' in that direction.

- Girls, then, are suffering from socialisation/learned roles/sex stereotyping that *makes* them want to choose 'lesser' subjects; and then, when they see other young women studying these subjects they feel that they, too, *ought* to (and be *expected* to) be studying them – this is the sex stereotyping Feminist explanation. A bizarre and tortuous combination of Feminists beliefs... but such is the power of Feminism in modern Britain that these beliefs have been transformed into social policies

- For thirty-five years Feminism has bullied governments to re-socialise young women so that they will make the same subject and career choices as men

***

Tessa Jowell, the one-time Minister for Women and Equality in the early post-1997 Labour Government, was worried that *'too many young women...are joining the beauty and child care industries instead of engineering and other skilled work.'*[2] She therefore recommended that teenage girls be given assertiveness training at school, *'to help them resist pressure to go into "female" jobs such as hairdressing, care work and health care'*. According to Tessa Jowell, girls must be given 'personal advisers', organised through the employment service, to *'help them pursue traditional male careers in construction, physics or chemistry.'*[3]

- Since the mid-1980s boys began to seriously fail in every area of education and they continue to do so. Yet here we have a senior Minister focussing attention on the piffling Feminist issue of girls freely choosing to follow their interest in hairdressing and health care

200

Male Feminists are also complicit in converting young women's choices into Feminist Ideological issues of inequalities and victimhoods:

SEND IN BUFFY TO SAVE LOST GIRLS – OFSTED CHIEF

(The Guardian, Saturday, 6 March, 2004)

'In a speech marking international women's day on Monday, David Bell, Director of Ofsted, will warn that girls' recent forging ahead in academic achievement conceals a more complex picture, with many still victims of gender bias pushing them into traditionally "female" subject areas often leading to lower paid jobs.

Mr. Bell's speech breaks new ground since it questions received wisdom about girl's success.

But of course, boys do not have a monopoly on problems. Disengaged girls also need help and support to encourage them to take an active interest in their learning.'

Girls, in a society in which 'women's victimhood' creates so many Gravy-Train Industries, must not be allowed to be *seen* to succeed (the Feminist dilemma). Even though young women are getting better 'A' level results than young men, are attending university in greater numbers than young men, are obtaining better degrees than young men and are entering post-university employment at a faster rate than young men – they must *still* be officially classified as 'victims'.

• For Feminism, success will never be enough

So the Office of Standards in Education (Ofsted), the guardian of educational standards, is more concerned about the freely made choices of girls and how these can be twisted, conjured and converted into Feminist issues – than it is about the *genuine* educational problem of failing boys. This is one further example of modern Britain's, institutional discrimination against men and boys.

We also see Ofsted perverting its principles to fit Feminist Ideology elsewhere:

'(Girls lack)...career opportunities in science, engineering and technology with female students being denied access to further training in scientific and technological areas.'[4]

• It is completely wrong to use the phrase 'girls are being denied', girls are *not* being denied anything – girls are allowed to freely choose to study any subject they wish, and no doubt it is a sensible and considered choice to suit their personalities, interests and lifestyle plans. When an untruth is stated to advance an Ideology it becomes a lie.

***

In 2005 the Labour/Feminist Government set up a Feminist policy agency Commission, led by Baroness Prosser, to ascertain why women earn less than men. The Commission, (one more lucrative addition to the Feminist Equality Industry) concluded that the main reason why women earn less than men was that young women were eschewing the better paid career paths, and were choosing to study academic subjects that led to lower paid jobs than those subjects chosen by males. It concluded:

> 'The root of the problem is the terrible career advice and work experience placements offered to girls at school, say the report's authors. Women are encouraged into low-paid professions without being given any advice about how little these jobs will pay them, while men are presumed to be more "scientific".[5]

- Feminism, obdurate and Ideological as it is, refuses to accept that girls can make rational choices; their non-Ideological choices have to be blamed on 'terrible career advice' – and people 'encouraging them to enter the low-paid professions' (Feminism's Blaming Strategy)

Being part of the Feminist Equality Industry, the Commission recommended that the Government set up Training Courses (and other lucrative make-work paraphernalia) to encourage young women to enter 'male professions'. The Commission's report drew immense media attention (as it was meant to) to 'prove' how girls and women suffer 'gender inequality'.

Actually setting up the Prosser Commission is a good example of 'Forever' Feminism generating its Grievance Gravy-Train Industries. Its purpose was to benefit Feminism and Feminists:

- By creating more jobs for Feminists, who will be organising, running, teaching and training (indoctrinating?) on these Feminist recommended, tax-payer funded courses

- By creating publicity for a Feminist fabricated inequality

- By deflecting attention from the very well documented genuine issue of boys' educational failure. By definition, a patriarchal society can only produce *female* 'victims', so male problems, issues and rights have been ignored – they don't fit Britain's dominant Feminist Ideology, the patriarchal template

- By proving that girls, not boys, are educational 'victims' (David Bell's word, the Director of Ofsted)

- By justifying the continuing existence of Feminism ('we are still needed because there are more discriminations and inequalities that have to be addressed')

- By justifying policies that continue to preference girls, rather than boys, by creating special courses, giving extra finance and resources

***

Trying to re-socialise ('re-educate') young women into choosing masculine subjects to study, and masculine jobs to enter, has a long history – and it has continually failed. The issue was first addressed by Feminism, governments and educational bodies, in the 1970s.

Girls have *always* chosen to study the Arts and Humanities rather than Science and Mathematics. During the pro-girl educational hysteria of the 1970s and 1980s numerous Feminist-inspired schemes were established to encourage girls to enter the Sciences. None of them worked. Examples include GATE (Girls and Technology Education Project); CDT (craft, design and technology); GIST (Girls into Science and Technology); WISE (Women in Science and Engineering); GAMMAR (Girls into Mathematics) and the American imported

'Take Your Daughter to Work' initiative, encouraging fathers to take their daughters to work to introduce them to male occupations. There have been HMI Reports on Girls and Science and numerous smaller LEA and school events, training sessions, exhibitions and conferences on the subject. All part of the educational, political and Ideological frenzy to indoctrinate girls into choosing to study Feminist-approved subjects and enter Feminist-approved careers.

- And all providing Feminist Ideologues with lucrative posts

Thirty-five years later, and with many other initiatives and projects having been established to address the issue, there is *still* only a small proportion of girls studying mathematics and the sciences. So it continues to be an issue; and in thirty-five years time young women's subject and career choices will *still* be being converted into Ideological issues by 'Forever' Feminism.

- How ought one to describe a State that continually allows itself to be bullied by Feminism to constantly introduce initiatives to 'remedy' a non-Ideological choice when these initiatives continue to fail time after time, when it has become so obvious that re-socialising young women is naturally impossible? Would 'repetitive stupidity syndrome' (in the Homer Simpson sense) describe such a State? Or could the reason for this apparent stupidity be that the State is complicit?

***

The Prosser Commission was only one recent initiative used to convert young women's subject choices into an inequality and to make women victims:

OLD HABITS DIE HARD

(The Guardian, 28 October, 2004)

'You thought sexism went out with the 70s? Not according to the Minister for Women, Patricia Hewitt, who this week launched an offensive on attitudes at work. The government intends to change all this by providing girls with more career advice on "masculine" jobs providing universities with funding to help their female science and engineering graduates find jobs and by strewing adult education institutions with "starter courses" for those who want to sample non-traditional employment roles.'

- 'University funding', new 'starter courses' set up...all benefitting Feminism's Academic Gravy-Train Industry and its personnel

And in 2006:

'KELLY HANDS £5 MILLION TO UNIONS FOR WORKPLACE EQUALITY: Schoolgirls will be encouraged to consider careers in all areas, including those traditionally the preserve of men. Specialist diplomas will be available for students aged 14 – 18 from 2008 to give them practical studies in construction, IT, engineering and media, giving them at least ten days' work experience.'[6]

- Again we have special courses, funding, resources, projects – all lucrative additions to the Feminist Equality Industry, paid for from public funds to 'remedy' the negative consequences for girls who choose to study the 'wrong' subjects

***

Dr. Glenn Wilson is a Senior Lecturer in Psychology at the Institute of Psychiatry, University of London. An expert on human behaviour, he has published more than 200 scientific articles and over 20 books. Dr. Wilson states:

'There is now a wealth of evidence that men excel in mathematical and scientific pursuits while women have a slight edge in language skills. These differences can be seen in exam performance at all ages and they are paralleled by differential interest in these areas. The result is that men gravitate toward occupations such as physicist, architect and engineer while women become novelists, journalists and translators.

Despite concerted attempts to override sex-role stereotypes over recent decades, expectations concerning appropriate work roles for men and women emerge very early in life...Apparently these stereotypes are highly resilient...Some argue that male/female specialisations develop out of childhood stereotypes and social expectations, but this seems very unlikely.'[7]

And,

WHY GIRLS ARE NATURALLY DRAWN TO DOLLS

(Daily Mail, Friday, 16 April 2010)

'**Baby girls make a beeline for dolls as soon as they can crawl – and boys will head for the toy cars, a study has shown. With no prompting, they will choose the stereotypical toys for their gender.**

The findings – the first to show consistent differences in very young babies –suggest there is a biological basis to their preferences. This indicates that 'politically correct' efforts to steer children towards things they wouldn't normally play with are doomed to failure.

Psychologists Dr. Brenda Todd and Sara Amilie O'Toole Thommessen from City University London carried out an experiment involving 90 infants aged nine months to 36 months.'

- Further work in this area has been carried out by Anne and Bill Moir; their references are thorough and extensive[8]

***

For decades Feminists have been trying to play God with young women's natural preference for the arts and humanities and have repeatedly failed. One Equality Feminist offers them, and our complicit Left-wing/liberal/progressive State, advice:

'It is time to leave the question of the role of women in society up to Mother Nature – a difficult lady to fool. You have only to give women the same opportunities as men, and you will soon find out what is or is not in their nature. What is in women's nature to do they will do, and you won't be able to stop them. But you will also find, and so will they that what is not in their nature, even if they are given every opportunity they will not do, and you won't be able to make them do it.'[9]

- Feminism needs to convert women's non-Ideological choices into inequalities. Common sense and a huge array of evidence and research, together with three and a half decades of failed initiatives will not deter it from continuing to use young women's subject and career choices to justify its existence and to seek opportunities to provide its Grievance Gravy-Train Industries with lucrative government contracts, finance, salaries and resources. The Feminist Fraud will continue

With the issue of young women's subject and career choice we see again that Feminism assumes girls don't have the intelligence or common sense to make informed choices, that girls are so stupid that they allow themselves to be easily led and 'advised' into occupations that 'are not good for them' (that is, not Feminist-approved). In this way Feminism disrespects young women. It infantilises them. It denies women personal responsibility for their choices, actions, decisions and behaviours.

Men and women are *not* the same. To try to make them the same by using the machinery of the State is social engineering, something that happens in, and defines, communist and fascist regimes. Under the hammer of Feminism the British State has become progressively more and more totalitarian. Feminism's Quiet Revolution is relentlessly moving forward.

'We have come a long way, but we still have a long way to go'

(Feminist mantra)

Chapter 23

Women Choose to be Feminine
and to be Seen as Sex Objects

Sex has always been a fundamental part of the human condition and if the species is to continue, it always must be. This is why 'sex' is such a rich source of victimhoods and abuses for 'Forever' Feminism. 'Sex' is an extremely effective Issue Creep phenomenon; even a woman wishing to look feminine is used as an example of a 'discrimination and oppression against women'. The reader may be sceptical about my claim that Feminism converts femininity into a victimhood. This conversion is so bizarre that you have a right to be sceptical. However, read on.

**

'Traditional femininity is a suffocating and pathological response to women's heretofore restricted lives, and will have to be abandoned.'[1]

Feminism dislikes women choosing to make themselves attractive to men, so it converts femininity into an inequality and discrimination...and labels women who choose to look feminine as 'pathological'. Feminists themselves admit that their objections to 'beauty practices' are Ideologically-driven:

'It can be difficult to contemplate that mundane beauty practices could have such profound political implications.'[2]

- So a woman choosing to make herself look attractive has been converted into having 'profound political implications'. Weird. Only Feminists could practise such alchemy

The negative consequences of women wishing to look attractive (negative only according to Feminists) are blamed on men. The Professional Feminist Kat Banyard explains:

'We are in the midst of a violent backlash against feminism that uses images of female beauty as a political weapon against women's advancement.'[3]

- Men are to blame for women wanting to look attractive

And Naomi Wolf declared in The Beauty Myth:

'Men are using female beauty as a political weapon to prevent women's equality.'[4]

Essentially, then, this is the Feminist claim: men have developed a political weapon (femininity) that is deliberately intended to prevent women from reaching senior positions, to stop their advancement, to prevent women's equality. This horrible weapon used against women is part of a 'violent male backlash against women's gains'. I refer the reader to Part Three.

Femininity and beauty have been deliberately politicised into inequalities, with ordinary women who enjoy making the non-Ideological choice to look feminine being used as political pawns, being classed as victims of men. Even our universities teach this Feminist nonsense. Just one example: a textbook used to teach Feminist Philosophy at the University of Sheffield states:

> *'I will be using the phrase "norms of feminine appearance" to refer to the standards of appearance that women are expected to live up to...Women's clothes are far more likely than men's to restrict movement. And women still suffer foot problems from decades of forcing their feet into high-heeled and/or excessively small shoes, or – as in the north of England – shiver in February while wearing skimpy dresses at night...the financial cost of the clothing women are expected to wear may also be considerable...Moreover, women are expected to own a far greater variety of outfits. This means that women will have to spend significantly more of their income on clothing than men do, and will thus have less money to spend on other items, or to save for the future...Women are expected to keep close track of the way that they move their bodies.'[5]*

- And so it drivels on. 'Expected'? 'Will have to spend'? It is claimed that it is men who are *making* women do these things. Feminists truly can conjure inequality issues 'from nothing'. And this Ideology is taught in a *university*; you see what I'm saying about universities producing generations of misandrous gender-warriors?

Again,

> *'The message from Western culture is clear: curves (in the wrong place) and fat (in any place) are not welcome on the female body. The result? A daily epidemic amongst women of harmful body surveillance, crash dieting, compulsive exercising and anxiety and depression about their weight and shape.'[6]*

- So 'Western culture' (patriarchal culture) is to be blamed for the epidemic of negative consequences (defined by Feminism) of women's dieting and exercising (only a Feminist could convert dieting and exercising into political issues). The mechanism by which men create this inequality, this victimhood is never explained. For the dedicated and misandrous Feminist anything that represents the 'feminine' is anathema. Feminists state that women don't actually choose to diet, or have plastic surgery – this choice is *forced* upon them by men. The patriarchy has socialised young women, instilled a false consciousness in them to look attractive, to look feminine (learned roles). Ms Banyard again:

> *'Simply basing feminism on the individual act of choosing fails to take into account how practices such as dieting and plastic surgery are connected with gender inequality and what impact they have on other women and gender relations as a whole.'[7]*

- Feminism requires inequality issues to justify its existence. It converts ordinary women's choice to diet and use plastic surgery into 'gender inequalities'

- No one is holding a gun to the head of women and making them apply lipstick before they leave the house in the morning, no one drags a woman, kicking and screaming, to the door of the plastic surgeon. We have seen that blaming 'socialisation' is nonsense

> *'Feminism has found (on every issue) that cant, dogma, rhetoric and mantras*
> *are more effective political weapons than logic and rational argument'*
>
> (Swayne O'Pie)

***

207

A slight digression here, but still in the same vein. Observe closely and you will notice that much Feminist whinging and whining today seems to stem from the fact that Feminists appear to resent being 'female'. In the Summer of 2011 Caitlin Moran's 'How to be a Woman' was published. Moran declares that all women are 'Feminists' simply because they have a vagina.

Moran, one of The Times' Resident Feminists, bemoans the fact that God, or Nature, has made 'women have female things'. Women *have* to be Feminists, apparently, because they grow pubic hair and are *made* to shave it and *have* Brazilians, they *have* to have periods, they *have* to have babies...which cause dried-out drooping breasts, they *have* to be thin. All these 'having tos', like the 'having to be feminine' issues, are converted into inequalities and blamed on men...somehow or other men are *forcing* women to do, and to have, all these inconvenient things; so men are blamed, are the 'bad people', for women being born female. Odd. However, this belief, as bizarre as it is, is a core tenet with today's Feminists, very many of whom are worryingly in influential positions in the media, academia and politics. For example, with regard to beauty-enhancing treatments, Moran, echoing Banyard and others, pompously declares:

> '...you can tell whether some misogynistic societal pressure is being exerted on women by calmly enquiring, "And are the men doing this, as well?"'[8]

- 'Misogynistic societal pressure'? That is, 'men hate women *so much* that they have intentionally created a culture, a society, specifically to pressure women into looking feminine'. And these women are in serious positions of influence

Over the years I've known (but not liked) numerous intelligent well-educated or talented people who have been racists. Or homophobes. But their intolerant, illiberal bigotry-gene always trumps their intelligence. And so it is with clever Feminists (who are anti-racist and anti-homophobe) who are misandrous (the irony and hypocrisy of having their *own* hatred-of-choice escapes them). They wouldn't admit to it being a 'hatred', of course; euphemisms are used – 'damn you, the patriarchy', or 'men are misogynists', or the constant drip, drip, drip of men-blaming, for example.

With this area of misandry in mind we would do well to remember the 'oddness' of the Feminist's psychological make-up: their mentality, their personality, their psychosis, their pathology, their constant need for 'anger', their need to be 'offended'. Was Freud right? If these women are so angsty about being female and feminine then *do* they have a subconscious 'penis envy'? Do they, in fact, quietly *wish that they were men*? This would certainly answer a number of questions. For example, why many women (especially Feminists) dislike men; or why Feminists revere, and often think of as only having value, male 'things' – full-time work, male occupations (engineering and science), male sports, jobs, status-positions; or...'The lazy bastards don't have to have *periods* every month! They don't have to apply cosmetics every morning, they don't have to have boob jobs!' – jealousy? Wishing to exchange a womb for a willy? It might also explain why over a third of Feminists are lesbian.

On the other hand, the upside for Feminists is that they can use their womanhood moans to political advantage. They've converted women's bodies, the condition of being 'female', into a Whinge Central from which male-caused 'inequalities' can be produced like monthly eggs. They seem to be perpetually pissed off with being women.

- 'Women's liberation'...wanting to be 'liberated' from being women?

***

208

Kat Banyard quotes Sheila Jeffreys to 'prove' that women's natural inclination to look good, to look feminine, to attract men (an instinct going back for many thousands of years and found in every anthropologically studied culture) is, in fact, a nasty patriarchal, male plot to subjugate and oppress women:

'Sheila Jeffreys, a professor at the University of Melbourne, has written about the intimate connection between beauty practices and gender inequality. She argues that beauty regimes show "that women are not simply 'different' but, most importantly, 'deferential'. The difference that women must embody is deference (to the higher status class of men). Beauty practices function as one way of demarcating or creating femininity on women's bodies", Jeffreys suggests, showing deference: "In western societies (deference) is expressed in the requirement that women create 'beauty' through clothing which should show large areas of their body for male excitement, through skirts...through figure-hugging clothing, through make-up, hairstyles, depilation, prominent display of secondary sexual characteristics or creation of them by surgery and through 'feminine' body language".'[9]

- Here one can see Feminism's sneering contempt for all-things 'feminine'; all things that ordinary non-Ideological women like and enjoy

What the wily Professional Feminist Kat Banyard intentionally neglects to tell us is that Sheila Jeffreys is a virulent man-hating Lesbian Feminist. We met Jeffreys in an earlier chapter:

'Every woman who lives with or fucks a man helps to maintain the oppression of her sisters and hinders our struggle.'[10]

Again,

'Our definition of a political lesbian is a woman-identified woman who does not fuck men...Men are the enemy.'[11]

One begins to understand from where Feminism's anti-feminine, 'women ought not to dress to attract men', 'women ought not to be sex objects for men', 'women are offended by wolf-whistles' mentality originates – in the political and Ideological domain of politically influential misandrous Lesbian Feminism.

In her book Beauty and Misogyny, Jeffreys argues that the United Nations ought to make 'women beautifying themselves' as much a crime as the gynaecological abuse of women in African tribes:

'Should western beauty practices, ranging from lipstick to labiaplasty, be included within the UN's understanding of harmful/traditional cultural practices...The misogyny of fashion and high-heeled shoes...breast implants?'[12]

- 'Wearing high-heeled shoes' a crime? Only Feminists with a seriously disturbed mentality and odd psychological make-up could suggest this. Yet, disturbingly, in today's Britain, such people are in serious positions of power in the law, the media, politics – and particularly in our universities

***

Women will, most of the time, want to look as beautiful as they can in order to attract the 'best' men, in order to procreate the healthiest children...this translates into 21st century British women having sex with the most handsome dishy bloke they can possibly attract. For these reasons women are in competition with other women – the most beautiful woman wins (and we know that beautiful women can manipulate and dominate even the strongest and most successful male). So by bringing the concept of beauty into the Ideological arena Feminism has cleverly ferreted out an issue that is going to be everlasting – and so we have a 'forever' issue perpetuating 'Forever' Feminism.

***

According to Feminism women are 'forced' by men to make themselves sexually attractive. But how can this be so? Have women no minds of their own? Do they do circus tricks when men snap their fingers? Are women children, infants who must do as they are told? If Feminism wishes more women to take on senior positions of power and influence in society then it must credit women with the maturity, the willpower and the strength of character to refuse to be 'made-up slaves' for men. Logic dictates that we cannot have, on the one hand, Feminism stating that women would be as good and effective as men when working in senior positions; whilst on the other hand, claiming that women are silly, obedient, weak-willed, infantile and docile servants of men who are 'forced' to make themselves look feminine and sexually attractive (which is exactly what Feminism *is* saying). Feminism cannot rationally claim both standpoints. However, it can, and it does, and the British State, subservient to Feminist claims and demands, takes these claims seriously, translating them into policies even though they are clearly ridiculous, contradictory and hypocritical.

- We see, again, Feminism absolving women from personal responsibility for their actions and behaviours

Note the following Feminist cant:

> '"The beauty industry is a monster, selling unattainable dreams. It lies, it cheats, it exploits women." The woman who said that was mourned this week as a progressive feminist heroine – so it's a pity, and a puzzle, that Anita Roddick (founder of the Body Shop) spent her life encouraging women to buy into it – but she was far from alone.'[13]

- One more example of Feminist hypocrisy and double standards: one more example of Feminism converting women's freely made choices into an issue and blaming something, or someone else, for 'forcing' women to make these choices – that is the misogynistic patriarchal culture, men

And whilst we are considering Feminist hypocrisy it needs to be remembered that Feminists demand that women 'have the right to wear *whatever* they want, *whenever* they want and *wherever* they want'...Remember the Slut Marches in June, 2011?

***

Feminism has converted the desires and freely made choices of ordinary, decent, non-Ideological women into inequality/victimhood issues and resoundingly blames men for this. Such is the bizarre nature of the Feminist, and of Feminism. A Feminist psychosis ('delusional...loss of contact with reality')?

Women Choose to be Sex Objects

Feminism needs inequalities, victims, discriminations, abuses and oppressions to justify its existence. It finds many issues in the area of sex.

We saw in Part Two how the Victorian and Edwardian Suffragettes hated men...and hated 'straight' sex...and hated men's involvement with sex. So it has been a long-standing objective of Feminism to get women (and men, wherever the gullible and naive could be found...usually on the Left) to conclude that men having an erotic interest in women is 'sexist' (that is, an abuse of women).

The majority of ordinary women see *nothing wrong* with men looking at them. They like to be seen as feminine women, attractive, pretty or beautiful; this attention boosts their egos and self-confidence (as it does for men wishing to look *their* best and being looked at by women). However, Feminism has made this normal and natural behaviour sinister. Men, it is stated, don't just look at women, they *ogle* them. Feminists have made men's natural interest in sex, and women's natural instincts to attract men's attention, into issues of male wickedness.

***

Western women freely choose to be looked at and appreciated by men (otherwise they would dress in Muslim-type clothing). Feminism has converted this choice into an Ideological issue. Women freely *choosing* to look feminine, *choosing* to look attractive, *choosing* to be looked at by men, surely cannot, rationally, be converted into the issue of the horrendous-sounding 'sexual objectification of women' *by* men? Yet it has been, and this strategy has been very successful as a Feminist weapon.

The Feminist Catherine MacKinnon states that:

> 'All women live in sexual objectification the way fish live in water.'[14]

And,

> 'For the Lesbian Feminist, it (sex) is not private; it is a political matter of oppression, domination, and power.'[15]

Again,

> 'Heterosexual relationships must therefore be approached with extreme caution, and feminists must both assert their own needs and challenge the pornographic culture in which they live; lesbianism must also be made more visible and available as a legitimate, or indeed preferable sexual option.'[16]

So there we have it. Feminism's anger about women being viewed as 'sex objects' by men is emanating from a Lesbian Feminist perspective (as it is with 'femininity'); a sexual orientation preference is being used as a gender-weapon to convert 'straight' women's choices into numerous man-hating issues – issues that are constantly used to justify the continuing existence of Feminism and to demonise and punish men in the Court of Public Opinion (as well as in criminal courts).

Camille Paglia, once an Ideological Feminist herself, comments:

'What women have to realise is their dominance as a sex. That women's sexual powers are enormous. All cultures have seen it. The only people who don't know it are feminists. Desensualised, desexualised, neurotic women. I wouldn't have said this twenty years ago because I was a militant feminist myself. But as the years have gone on, I begin to see more and more that the perverse, neurotic psychodrama projected by these women is coming from their own problems with sex.'[17]

***

Feminism has a neurosis about femininity and sex; it has politicised them, and milks them for anti-male issues:

'Far from being "natural", sexual behaviour becomes bound up with the idea of ownership, domination and submission, and is conditioned by a man-made culture in which pornography is all-pervasive, sexual violence is tolerated, women are treated as sex objects and different moral codes exist for men and women.'[18]

- So Feminists claim that a 'man-made culture' (the patriarchal culture) is responsible for women wanting to look feminine and wanting to enjoy sex. This man-made culture somehow leads to men 'owning' women, 'dominating' women, 'oppressing' women; it is responsible for pornography, sexual violence and women being treated as sex objects. Many issues here, then, to justify 'Forever' Feminism's continuing existence. I refer the reader to Part Three

What Feminists have done is to convert straight sex (men's and women's mutual sexual attraction) into something evil. This strategy has been used deliberately to i) create issues, and ii) to encourage society to denigrate and demonise men (to spread misandry). We have reached a point in modern Britain where sexuality represents for many people (to a greater or lesser degree) innate male wickedness – a huge Feminist success. A huge Feminist Fraud.

Women Choose to be Objectified

We have seen that women choose to make themselves look feminine and attractive in order to attract men's attention. One way they do this is to choose clothing to show off their bodies to their best advantage, that is, they freely *choose* to be objects of sexual attraction – sex objects; in other words, they *choose* to be 'sexually objectified'.

- Feminism claims that these ordinary women are the prisoners of their socialisation, that they are making these choices because they have a false consciousness, victims of a man-made culture; that they are not exercising their free will. This Feminist belief system was comprehensively dismissed in earlier chapters. Women *are* personally responsible for making their own choices when they dress to attract the attention of men and wish to be looked at sexually

In December 2008, the Daily Mail reported a university student beauty pageant; beauty pageants are anathema to Feminists:

> 'Ruby Buckley, women's officer at the London School of Economics student's union, said: "LSE is an academic institution and should not have its name tarnished by an event with a single function of the objectification of women"...Elly James, women's officer at the School of Oriental and African Studies student's union, said it was: "...part of the systematic degradation of women...I see this pageant as part of a backlash against the fragile gains that feminism has won...".[19]

- The phrase 'fragile gains that feminism has won' is one of the many mantras drilled into young Feminist gender-warriors on university Feminist/Women's/Gender Studies Courses. 'Part of a backlash' is a hackneyed Feminist mantra, as is 'systematic degradation of women'. Young Feminists are taught and encouraged to cough up a misandrous mantra whenever possible

Male students will *know* that their female colleagues in lectures, these participants in the beauty pageant, *are* intelligent women; they *know* that their fellow female students will have more to them than simply an attractive body. Men are never given credit for having a multiple interests in women and are condemned for their natural 'first-focus' on a woman's looks (women's 'first-focus' is two-fold: i) men's looks, and ii) men's potential earning power). If we were to do a gender-switch these could just as easily be construed as 'sex/wallet objectification of men'.

The article went on to state that over 400 female students freely chose to take part. It also noted that there were only 10 demonstrators; yet it is the Feminist voice that is always given media and political attention. If the NUS Women's Officers really *were* posts established to represent the genuine interests of women students then why are these Officers *condemning* the 400 female students who have chosen to enter the beauty pageant, instead of siding with the very small minority of 10 objectors? The answer is that the NUS and its Women's Officers are only interested in promoting the Feminist Ideology and agenda among female (and male) students and creating inequalities and issues. In the above example ordinary non-Ideological female students, *the vast majority*, are actually *censured* by their so-called representatives; how bad is that?

- How can the NUS justify having Ideologically-driven gender-warrior Women's Officers in every university who don't represent the majority of female students? And we know that there are no Men's Officers in *any* university

***

Women enjoy being sexy and showing themselves off to men...however much Feminists may hate and deny this fact.

In September, 2007, The Guardian ran an article which included the following:

> 'The Nuts (a male magazine) website, for example, features a page called Assess My Breasts, inviting men to study photos of naked breasts and rank them – which doesn't seem particularly respectful. But the thousands of images have been uploaded by ordinary women – "entirely voluntarily", for free, as the spokeswoman took pleasure pointing out...'

And elsewhere:

'...but the real shock came in FHM's revelation that it receives more than 1,200 submissions of women topless or in lingerie every week.'[20]

• 1,200 ordinary women, *each week*, freely choosing to show off their breasts...for free. Only a Feminist could convert this choice into an inequality, into an abuse, and blame it on 'bad men'

And Karen Lehrman, in her book, The Lipstick Proviso:

'If we want society to stop equating our worth with our beauty, we need to make sure that we stop it ourselves.'

Women are freely choosing to be sexually objectified. Young women throw themselves at rock stars and footballers. They queue for hours outside nightclubs and hotels, scantily and provocatively dressed, in order to 'pull a footballer':

'EVERYONE WANTS A FOOTBALLER.
IF YOU GET ONE, YOU'VE MADE IT'
(The Observer, 12 September, 2010)

'"We save all week to come down here (Panacea Nightclub)," said Rachel, 20, from Farnworth, north of Manchester. "It's the only place you can really dress to impress. Everyone wants to bag a footballer. If you get a footballer you've made it."

For many young women a night at Panacea is equivalent to a job interview, an opening audition for their career choice. Clair says that becoming a Wag is an ambition taken as seriously as an economics degree.

Claire said: "It's a question of supply and demand. There would be no demand for valuable footballers if there wasn't a never-ending supply of girls who'd do anything to cop off".

A surprising ratio were privately educated like Thomspon (the prostitute used by Wayne Rooney) who attending Bolton's £1,555-a-term Lord's Independent school.'

• However much the self-righteous, sanctimonious Feminist may dislike it, young women *freely choose* to be seen and appreciated as sex objects, to be sexually objectified. And the reader will note that this is not just limited to girls from lower socioeconomic backgrounds

Camille Paglia again:

'It's part of the sizzle. Girls hurl themselves at guitarists, right down to the lowest bar band here. The guys are strutting. If you live in rock and roll, as I do, you see the reality of sex, of male lust and women being aroused by male lust. It attracts women. It doesn't repel them. Women have the right to freely choose and to say yes or no.'[21]

Again,

'Rock and football are revealing something true and permanent and eternal about male energy and sexuality. They are revealing the fact that women, in fact, like the idea of flaunting, strutting, wild masculine energy...the people who criticise me, these establishment feminists...have this stupid, pathetic, completely-removed-from-reality view of things that they've gotten from these academics who are totally off the wall, totally removed.'[22]

- These 'off the wall' (psychotic?) *Academic* Feminists are the most dangerous type of Feminist; training up regular waves of gender-warriors, and permeating universities with their Ideology and agenda
- Paglia's views are particularly worthy of note because she herself was once one of these Feminists

***

It is not men who 'force' women into being sex objects. The majority of ordinary women *wish* to be objects of male attention:

'This is a good quality in men (seeing women as sex objects) that well serves traditional women, for it is what gives us power over men and enables us to demand that we become a great deal to them before we will allow them to use us in sex. There is nothing wrong with being a sex object; it can be very gratifying. The moments when I become the objective of my husband's sexual attentions are the most enjoyable of my life; they surpass by a wide margin those spent as an intellectual object discussing the First Amendment.'[23]

And,

'One hardy perennial is the claim that "men see women as sex objects". Of course they do. What sort of woman would not want men to see her as a sex object? When feminists attack routine aspects of the human condition which they find offensive, it is often effective to point out that your views are those of the majority. Ah, says the feminist, but the problem is that men just see women as sex objects. This is a curious proposition, as science has yet to uncover a single case of this bizarre delusion.'[24]

- Again, we see that Feminists do not speak for, or represent, ordinary, normal women

One only has to visit the centre of a town or city on a Friday or Saturday night in order to see how young women dress and behave. Any amount of Ideological cant and dogma from off-the-wall Academic Feminists, from desensualised, desexualised neurotic Feminists, will not erase this fact. Women go out to show themselves off sexually. It is not men, or the socialising patriarchal culture, creating a false consciousness that make women do this. Women are not infants, they make choices...and Feminists work hard to convert these freely made choices into issues in order to justify 'Forever' Feminism and to promote their Grievance Gravy-Train Industries...and to demonise men...

...And they have succeeded. It's a sadness that in modern Britain women have been taught (by Feminism) that it is a 'bad thing' for men to view them as sex objects. They have been conditioned to consider this male behaviour politically incorrect. Yet their hearts and nature desperately wish for this, to be so viewed; their choices and behaviours express their desire for it. So modern women have an ambivalence about expressing their sexuality. As in other areas of sexual politics, Feminism is fucking with women's minds.

Men must *never* apologise for sexually objectifying women because this is what almost all heterosexual women wish and desire. Don't be a slave to political correctness, don't allow your views to be dominated by disturbed Feminist Ideologues.

Is 'The Stork' a Feminist?

Are babies found under gooseberry bushes? Does the stork bring them, swaddled in a towel hanging from its beak?

The word 'attractive' means, literally, 'to attract'. Men and women are *designed* by God, or by nature, to see each other in a sexual way, to attract each other sexually. Sex is the driving force of humankind; in fact, of all living creatures – all species 'attract' the opposite sex using some means or another, so why should humans be any different?

WOMEN DRESS TO IMPRESS FOR SURVIVAL OF THE SPECIES

(Daily Mail, Thursday, 11 January, 2007)

'When pressed on why they dress up, women will often say they do it for themselves or for their friends.

But psychologists claimed yesterday that they have found a much more scientific explanation. It seems that women "dress to impress" when they are at their most fertile to make themselves attractive to the opposite sex – a basic instinct to ensure the survival of the species.

Lead researcher Martie Haselton said: "Near ovulation, women dress to impress, and the closer women come to ovulation, the more attention they appear to pay to their appearance. They tend to put on skirts instead of trousers, show more skin and generally dress more fashionably. Something in women's minds is tracking the ovulation cycle. At some level, women know when they are most fertile." April Bleske-Rechek, the study's co-author, said it was remarkably easy to spot the effect of ovulation on women. "In our study, the approach of ovulation had a stronger impact on the way women dressed than the onset of menstruation, which is notorious for its supposedly deleterious impact", added the psychologist from the University of Wisconsin-Eau Claire.'

- We have seen how women dress and use make-up in order to look feminine, to attract men's attention, to be seen as sex objects

Again:

MEN LOOK AT BODIES, NOT FACES,
WHEN SEARCHING FOR A DATE

(The Daily Telegraph, Wednesday, 15 September, 2010)

'It may not come as a surprise to any woman who has tried to have a conversation with a man in a bar who has refused to lift his gaze above her *décolletage*. But scientists have confirmed that men on the prowl are more interested in a woman's body than her face – let alone her brains.

The Texas study tested the theory that men evaluating a potential short-term mate would give higher priority to information gleaned from a woman's body because the body offers more cues as to the state of a woman's fertility.

"Results suggested that men have a condition-dependent tendency to prioritise facial cues in long-term mating contexts, but shift their priorities to bodily cues in short-term mating contexts. Both the body and face can provide cues as to a woman's reproductive value and current fertility...The results support the hypothesis that men are attracted to women's bodies in short-term mating contexts, such as a pub, bar or nightclub".'

- In order to prolong and justify their Movement Feminists have been converting this hard-wired procreational male 'condition-dependency' into an Ideological and political issue, intentionally designed to demonise and punish men. This has been a constant and successful strategy, and has had the added bonus of making many men feel guilty. 'Guilty men' are easy-to-manipulate men so Feminism also wins (again) on this score, a secondary success

Because it is fundamental to the procreation of the species 'sex' is an everlasting source of Feminist-created issues – enforced femininity, sexual harassment, rape, sexual object-ification, oppression of women, sexual violence, pornography, prostitution; sex is an excellent Feminist gender-weapon. Until people realise that 'sex' is being *deliberately used as a political gender-weapon* men will always remain under a cloud, and many will continue to feel guilty about being genetically driven to pursue the female, a guilt carefully sown and nurtured by Feminism.

'Every woman who lives with or fucks a man helps to maintain the oppression of her sisters and hinders our struggle...Men are the enemy.'[25]

***

The male attraction to the female body is hard-wired into his brain and body. So consider this...In the act of procreation millions upon millions of male spermatozoa fight like hell to reach one female egg, only one succeeds. Are all these millions of sperm 'sexist'? Are they all sex pests? Are they all sexual harassers? Are they all 'sexually objectifying' that female egg in order to 'dominate', 'violate' and 'oppress' it? If the lucky couple, the single spermatoza and the egg, produce a big boy then Feminists will certainly demonise *him* with their misandrous, prejudicial cant and rhetoric.

Is a woman 'objectified' if she *freely chooses* to make herself look feminine, if she *freely chooses* to beautify herself in order to attract the attention of men, if she *freely chooses* to be a sex object? An ethical and rational answer would have to be that she cannot be so 'objectified'. The intention of Feminism is to claim that 'objectified' women are 'offended' women; so how can a woman who *freely chooses* to offend herself be a victim, be oppressed, or be abused? Her choices have been deliberately converted into inequality issues and used by a small but politically powerful coterie of neurotic Ideologues to justify and perpetuate their Movement and to denounce, condemn, and whenever possible punish, men. This Feminist perspective on sex and sex objectification, this Feminist Fraud, is now the British *State's* perspective.

Chapter 24

Women Choose to be Involved in Pornography

The majority of women, the non-Ideological women, choose to be feminine and also choose to be seen as sex objects. It is no surprise, then, to understand why some women wish to go one stage further and be involved in pornography and perhaps prostitution. Feminism converts this freely made choice into an Ideological issue.

Feminism finds in pornography and prostitution a rich source for spreading misandry. The Feminist interest in pornography and prostitution has nothing to do with public morals (although it uses this as a 'moral disguise' to promote its anti-male agenda). Nor has its interest anything to do with puritanical religious beliefs. Feminism has side-stepped the question of boundaries of sexual decency to focus on how pornography and prostitution can be converted into issues of victimhood and male abuses – issues used to justify its existence and to use as gender-weapons. According to the Feminist Ideology pornography and prostitution are expressions of male power that subjugate and oppress women.

'Pornography plays a key role in shaping men and women, teaching that maleness is about sexual domination and femaleness about sexual submission. This power dynamic then works to subordinate women to men in many other areas of life.'[1]

- The phenomenon of pornography is interpreted and used by Feminists to 'prove' that men have power over women – their patriarchal Ideology of 'good women' / 'bad men'

Pornography and Lap-Dancing

The Feminist perspective on pornography is wide-ranging in its man-hating:

'Pornography is a systematic practice of exploitation and subordination based on sex that differentially harms women. The harm of pornography includes dehumanisation, sexual exploitation, forced sex, forced prostitution, physical injury, and social and sexual terrorism and inferiority presented as entertainment. The bigotry and contempt pornography promotes, with the acts of aggression it fosters, diminish opportunities for equality of rights in employment, education, property, public accommodations, and public services; create public and private harassment, persecution, and denigration; expose individuals who appear in pornography against their will to...hatred...and embarrassment and target such women in particular for abuse and physical aggression...promote injury and degradation such as rape, battery, child sexual abuse, and prostitution and inhabit just enforcement of laws against these acts; contribute significantly to restricting women in particular from full exercise of citizenship and participation in public life.'[2]

- Pornography is used by Feminism as a blunderbuss weapon to blame and demonise men in a wide range of issues; it is an extremely rich area to promote Issue Creep and misandry

- I remind the reader of observations made in Part Three; the Feminist's personality and mentality, her psychological and political 'need' for anger

We are told that male power over women leads to violent rape and the hatred of all women. Yet it is difficult to demonstrate whether or not pornography causes violence against women. There has been an enormous amount of psychological research on links between pornography and sexual violence, and not all the findings are consistent with one another.[3]

***

The above Ideological interpretation of pornography is not a throwback to the 1970s. The following is part of a letter printed in The Times, 2006:

> *"Many of us see pole dancing and stripping not as a form of sexual liberation, but as an adherence to the porn industry's narrow view of female sexuality, based on the male desire to objectify women rather than a genuine expression of female sexual pleasure.*
>
> *We also recognise the abusive nature of the sex industry. Feminist groups have begun to fight back, successfully campaigning for the removal of Playboy-branded products from high-street stores, and our voice will continue to grow. Dworkin has not been forgotten, and we intend to keep things that way."* Laura Woodhouse, Chair, Sheffield Fems.[4]

- Note the priggish pomposity and self-righteousness. An emotional 'need' for anger?

And in 2010, the Professional Feminist Kat Banyard stated:

> *'Pornography, like rape, is a male invention, designed to dehumanise women.'*[5]

- Pornography deliberately 'designed to dehumanise women'? Really? That's suggesting that men have a real hatred of all women and have invented a whole industry specifically to express that hate. I don't think so. Especially as women themselves *freely choose* to participate in this industry, even in the capacity of directors
- The phrase 'a male invention (deliberately) designed to dehumanise women' clearly shows the depth of hatred and anger that Feminists have towards men. I again refer the reader to Part Three

***

Essentially, Feminism's issues with pornography are twofold: a) pornography is an expression of male power, b) pornography is degrading for women:

> *'They do it (men attending lap-dancing clubs) because they get a power rush from the act of paying a woman to take her clothes off. She is vulnerable, and he is powerful, and that's the real allure – that's the real reason the clubs are getting so popular. Lap-dancing clubs are places in which you can all pretend that feminism never happened.'*[6]

And,

> *'Pornography, then, and men's use of it, is intrinsically linked to inequalities between women and men; it eroticises the dominance of masculinity over femininity, of men over women.'*[7]

- This is 'Head-in-the-Sand' Feminism, completely ignoring the fact that women *freely choose* to work as lap-dancers

Women Choose to Enter the Pornography Industry

If pornography is degrading then it must be degrading for those women who are personally *involved* in it, not the Ideologically-driven Feminists who are 'degraded by proxy'. But those women who choose to be part of the sex industry do *not* feel degraded, as we shall see. But even if they did, this would be a trade-off for the benefits of working in the industry, mainly good money for working a short number of hours.

Norah Vincent was a Lesbian Feminist. To research her book 'Self-Made Man' she dressed and groomed as a man so that she could pass for a man and enter 'a man's world'. She was so astonished at what she found, her experiences negating all her preconceived ideas about men, that she jettisoned her Feminist Ideology. For one of her 'male experiences' she attended a lap-dancing club:

> *'This place wasn't just where men came to be beasts. It was also where women came to exercise some vestige of sexual power in the most unvarnished way possible. My pussy for your dollars. I say when, I say how, I say how much and I get paid for it. There was tremendous manipulation built into the rules under which these places operated...One thing was certain though. Everybody got his hands dirty and, politically speaking, nobody really came out ahead. It wasn't nearly so simple as men objectifying women and staying clean or empowered in the process. Nobody won, and when it came down to it, nobody was more or less victimised than anyone else.'[8]*

• Having previously held a prejudiced misandrous perspective on the issue of pornography Vincent's comments require serious consideration

***

In an earlier chapter it was noted that we saw female students choose to enter a university beauty pageant: women who are educated, or otherwise relatively advantaged, also *freely choose* to enter the sex industry.

DONS EXERCISED BY POLE-DANCING STUDENTS
(The Times, Friday, 20 February, 2004)

'Most undergraduates try to boost their meagre incomes by working behind a bar, waiting on tables or stacking shelves in a supermarket.

But female students at Cambridge have alarmed dons by taking practical lessons in pole dancing. Some of them have already started giving performances in a local nightclub.

Nadia Messauoud, from Queen's College, hopes that her group of pole dancers will be recognised as an official university organisation, alongside the tiddlywinks and bell-ringing societies.

"It is art, just the same as ballet, tap or any other kind of dance."

Another member of the group, Clarice Almeida, a third-year oriental studies student at Queen's, said that she felt empowered by the dancing. "Guys get very excited", she said. "You do feel quite good when you're up there. The word is spreading and more people want to join the fellowship".'

- In essence, when Feminists use pornography as a gender-weapon they are also saying that women in the industry, including these young women at one of Britain's top universities, are weak-willed, easily led, lack strength of character, are not mature enough to make rational choices. Not really representing, or respectful towards, women, is it? More like professing an Ideology

Another educated participant who specifically and rationally chose this work:

'A FEMINIST ACT: Westminster-education Emily Edmonstone was going to be a doctor like her father. So what made her decide to become a stripper? "I've tried to explain that I'm just putting on an act and it's a performance like any other. I've never once felt abused or exploited or taken advantage of in the club...The stripping has improved my confidence...it's a power trip. If I'm doing a lapdance the guy just sits there completely in awe. You feel in control...Most of the money I make (about £100 to £200 per night, a couple of nights a week) I save, so I won't have big debts when I leave university" (2004).'9

- If educated, intelligent women are working in the pornography industry then this invalidates Feminism's belief system of socialisation/false consciousness used to explain women's choices. Nor can women's 'lower pay' be blamed

***

Feminists have found in pornography an effective way to further demonise men. Lap-dancing clubs are a godsend for these pathological misandrous Grievance Collectors. In 'How to be a Woman' Caitlin Moran describes her visit to such a club. Moran dismisses out of hand the fact that educated women freely choose to be involved in the sex industry. She notes that pretty student girls choose to be lap-dancers in order to pay their university fees (as they do with pole dancing and prostitution)...but because this money-making option is not open to men Moran regards this as misogynistic...and an inequality *against women* (logic is anathema to Feminists, who prefer to rely on cant and emotion rather than rational argument).

Moran's visit exposes her man-hating bile, expressed in off-the-peg Feminist mantras and platitudes; lap-dancing clubs are 'areas of (male) abuse'; they are 'versions of the entire history of misogyny'?: Moran continues (we'll do a target-switch on this):

'We can see that men's (the Jew's) desire for women (money) has, throughout history, given rise to unspeakable barbarity. It's caused terrible, terrible things to happen because men (Jews) have been the dominant force, with no rules or checks on their behaviour.'10

- How does your sanctimonious Left-wing self-righteous conscience feel about that? Moran is not an anti-Semite...but the bigotry remains the same...just a different target. I wish to apologise to Jewish readers if my strongly made point has caused offence; anti-Semites have caricatured your people like Feminists now caricature men

And with regard to the clubs:

'Every dance, every private booth, is a small unhappiness, an ugly impoliteness; the bastard child of misogyny and commerce.'11

Moran hates lap-dancing clubs; she says it's not what Feminists want women to do:

> *'Girls, get the fuck off the podium – you're letting us all down.'*[12]

- No free choice for women, then, with jack-booted Sister Moran: ('You're *women*...you've all *got* to be fucking Feminists!'). Like all Ideologues, Feminists are illiberal and intolerant people; their aim is not to represent women and respect their individual wishes and freely made choices, but to doggedly implement their collective Ideology and agenda. And these Left-wing Feminist Fascists (far worse than anything on the Right) think that their bigoted zealotry is just *soooo cool*

Moran's attack on strip clubs is driven by man-hating. Feminist bile is aimed at all men. Well, nearly all men. Gay men are fine, Guardian-reading cardigan-wearing men are also fine; but other men, men who wish to express their maleness in a different way to what Feminism dictates and approves of, are grotesque perverts, apparently. We see in Moran's unhealthy misandry an example of the Feminist's psychological make-up - the intolerance, the Feminist's need for 'anger', the need to collect grievances and create issues (disregarding the fact that the strippers work there by choice), the need to polish up Ideological credentials, and to be a good card-carrying member of the Feminist Political Community Club and Family. We see the pathological dislike of the majority of men, of men who just want to be 'male'; we see the deep need in the Feminist personality to demonise maleness and dehumanise men, individually and collectively (the patriarchy).

***

The male interest in pornography has nothing to do with seeking power over women, or wishing to abuse women, as Feminists declare. If it did then lap-dancers in their 50s and 60s would just as easily attract male audiences as do much younger dancers; women are women, of whatever age, so men could just as easily express misogyny over *older* women as *younger* women. But lap-dancers are *always* young attractive women. The claim that it is power over women that drives men to pornography is cant, Ideological dogma. The male interest is hard-wired, biologically and DNA-driven and has nothing to do with 'male power over women'.

Nathanson and Young relate an experiment carried out by Helen Fisher that measured magnetic resonance images (MRI). Men and women who claimed to be deeply and happily in love were studied, using MRI, as they looked at pictures of each other and pictures of other people. The finding showed differences between most men and women:

> *'In our sample, men tended to show more activity than women in brain regions associated with visual processing whereas women showed more activity in regions associated with motivation and attention... this male brain response may shed light on why men so vividly support the worldwide trade in visual pornography.'*[13]

And,

> *'Fisher speculated that the connection between visualisation and male arousal is due to the evolutionary importance of recognising a suitable reproductive partner. Women find reproductive partners not so much by looking at a men sexually but by remembering which ones are most likely to provide for them and their infants.'*[14]

We could do a gender-switch and suggest that men who enjoy pornography are being abused:

'There was tremendous manipulation built into the rules under which these places operated...'[15]

- This is referring to the manipulation of male clients

And,

'...but the women involved are now very well surveyed and are unanimously vocal in upholding their free choice to financially exploit their voyeurs and to take glory in displaying themselves.'[16]

- Are men being manipulated and exploited? Do some women become involved in pornography for the opportunity *to exhibit power over men*?

***

'Straight' women also use pornography:

'"I think sex on the Internet is for both men and women," says Donna. "We live in a sex society. I know friends that have sex IM, they say dirty things to guys, dirty text messages. There's a lot of porn sites out there, soft-porn sites for women...I think it's not just a man thing to go online and jerk off to some photo. Women go online, they go on MySpace, they send messages. Granted, I'm sure more men do than women, but they're in there, too. They're on Match.com, they're on Nerve.com, trying to pick up someone. They're on Craig's List in the casual encounters section. Like saying that they want to give a blowjob, or looking for someone to 'eat me out'. They do the same graphic things as men do, they definitely engage in the same thing".'[17]

- If straight women use pornography then how can pornography be a 'male invention designed to dehumanise women'?

The above research by Helen Fisher explains why *more* men than women take an interest in pornography. Women's use of pornography is ignored because it does not fit the Feminist patriarchal Ideology of 'good women'/ 'bad men'. I've heard it explained away by claiming that women's pornography is not, in fact, 'pornography', but 'eroticism' - a neat linguistic sophistry...but still hypocritical. The use of pornography to manufacture issues and to spread misandry is a Feminist Fraud.

Chapter 25
Women Choose to Become Prostitutes

The overwhelming majority of prostitutes have freely *chosen* to enter their profession. Yet Feminism has succeeded in converting this choice into a man-hating issue. Using sex to demonise men is not new to Feminism, it was a strategy employed by Suffragettes:

> 'Women had always been regarded as the pivot of sexual virtue. Those who were chaste wives and mothers were regarded as saintly guardians of the domestic shrine; those who had loose morals were viewed as the source of corruption of men. But now feminists were demanding to have it both ways. Women were still the fount of domestic virtue but if they "fell" into prostitution, it was because they had been corrupted by men. It was men who were responsible for prostitution, by creating the demand that resulted in the supply. Women were the active promoters of sexual virtue; but men were the active promoters of sexual vice...This damnation of a whole sex caused some progressive men to don a hair shirt.'[1]

• Today's 'hair shirt' men are Male Feminists, manipulated to implement the Feminist agenda – male politicians (especially in the Labour and Liberal Democrat Parties), trade union leaders, media men, lawyers and judges

***

For Feminism the issue of prostitution, like pornography, is not a moral but an Ideological and political issue. It sees prostitution as an expression of male power, a product of patriarchy:

> 'Male dominance means that the society creates a pool of prostitutes by any means necessary so that men have what men need to stay on top, to feel big, literally, metaphorically, in every way...I am asking you to make yourselves enemies of male dominance, because it has to be destroyed for the crime of prostitution to end – the crime against the woman, the human rights crime of prostitution.'[2]

And,

> 'Prostitution therefore becomes a symbol of male power which is both a product of patriarchal sexual relationships and a means of legitimising them, for through prostitution "the male sex-right is publicly affirmed, and men gain public acknowledgement as women's sexual masters".'[3]

As with the issue of pornography, a woman's freely made choice to participate in prostitution is blamed on 'men wanting power and domination over women'. This is nonsense. The male's interest in a prostitute is sexual, DNA-driven and hard-wired. If men wanted to express their 'power and domination over women' by using a prostitute they could just as easily do so with *older* prostitutes...resulting in a wide age-range in the profession. But this is not the case, most prostitutes are young or at most, middle-aged.

***

The Feminist perspective on prostitution is not moral or religious, it is narrow and Ideological. For example, apart from denying women's free choice to enter the profession, it ignores the existence of high-class prostitutes, women working independently, women who only work part-time as prostitutes, or those who work in a 'madam' controlled brothel. These types of prostitution are *always* ignored by Feminists because they do not fit their Ideology of 'men exploiting, and having power over, women'.

Because prostitutes have to be seen as 'victims who are exploited' then inevitably men have to be viewed as the victimisers and the exploiters. The women have to be helped and the men have to be blamed, condemned, demonised and punished. And this is exactly what happens in Britain today.

- Men who seek prostitutes are targeted by police forces; they are made to attend humiliating anti-male/pro-prostitute courses, they are held up to ridicule and are publicly embarrassed. While the prostitute is given special training and vocational courses (nothing wrong with that...but it is the anti-male bigotry, the misandry, that is despicable)

- Modern Britain seriously dislikes men

***

If women freely choose to become prostitutes how, then, can Feminism convince the public and politicians, that these women are 'exploited victims'? It does this by invoking its Blaming Strategy insisting that it is not the woman's fault that she becomes a prostitute. In order for it to become an issue that can be used by Feminists women have to be (patronisingly) absolved from personal responsibility for making their non-Ideological choice. The following is a sample of Feminist strategies.

1. The blame lies with... socialisation:

    'A hidden curriculum, imparted by teachers, parents and the media, directs children into the "gender trenches" – the crude dugouts of masculinity and femininity, reproducing and maintaining gender inequality amongst the newest generation. It is time to expose the curriculum that divides girls and boys every day in the classroom and sustains inequality between them in later life.'[4]

- This astonishing claim is a classic example of blaming the socialisation process. We have seen that this Blaming Strategy is nonsense

2. The blame lies with...no other ways to get rich quick:

    'Other people in the glamour-modelling industry also admit that many of the women who set out into this industry may have few other routes in front of them which they feel will lead to any equivalent success.'[5] And, *'You just feel that you can't make money any other way'.*[6]

- Prostitutes are not deprived of 'other routes to success': any more than *young men* who participate in the thieving and drug-dealing professions. For example, using the same logic a pimp could absolve himself from personal responsibility by claiming that 'he just couldn't make money any other way'

3. The blame lies with...desperation:

   '...it is clear that these so-called choices are often fuelled more by desperation than liberation.'[7]

- Young men also suffer from desperation, which fuels *their* so-called 'choice' to enter the thieving and drug-dealing professions (and sometimes to rape). Shall we absolve *them* from personal responsibility?

4. The blame lies with...women having no other choice:

   'I was too fucked for work (because of drugs), and I knew it, so when I saw an ad in the paper for escorts there seemed little choice...This was not a free "choice". It was the opposite. I needed money but was a mess.'[8]

- Taking drugs is *itself* a choice: choices have negative as well as positive consequences; mature people have to accept both

5. The blame lies with...the woman's background and upbringing:

   'Abuse, homelessness, poverty, marginalisation, family breakdown: these are the lights illuminating the path to prostitution.'[9]

- Many women have experienced, and have overcome, similar disadvantages and do not become prostitutes; so this invalidates *this* Blaming Strategy. Also, there are many educated and middle-class women with stable backgrounds working as prostitutes. How do Feminists explain away *that*?

6. The blame lies with...men:

   'For all the factors that make women vulnerable to prostitution, it is crucial to remember that they aren't the "cause" of the industry. Prostitution exists because there is a demand for it.'[10]

- This is as fraudulent as saying: 'Drug dealers exist because there is a demand for drugs... so we must blame the drug *users*, not the *dealers*'

***

So even when women *freely choose* to sell their bodies to men for money they are *still* referred to as 'victims'. And in modern Britain, the Feminist perspective of prostitutes being 'victims exploited by men' is unquestioningly accepted and social policy, including by an institutionally Feminist and misandrous police force which treats prostitutes as victims and their clients as 'bad men' who must be demonised and punished:

   'With a mushrooming of the scale of prostitution, and with extreme feminist bigotry rife in government, so it was that yet another proposed "crackdown" on prostitution wielding the stick to men but offering the carrot to women was announced by the government (Home Office, 2006). The Home Office minister then in charge, Fiona MacTaggart, has since revealed the underlying intention by advocating the criminalisation of men who pay for sex. Trailing the policy on the BBC, she described men who pay for sex as "child abusers".'[11]

- This astonishing anti-male, hate-filled and vile misandry is not being expressed by some weirdo radical Feminist on the fringes of society but by a Minister of the State

Feminism in modern Britain has incredible powers, cultural, legal and political, to hurt and harm men, and does so whenever opportunities arise...which they do regularly as Feminists busily root out more and more inequalities, oppressions, discriminations and abuses to justify their continuing existence, their 'Forever' Feminism. The appropriately-named Harriet Harm-man was the Minister for Women in the last Labour/Feminist Government:

> 'Harriet Harman will today step up her drive to make buying sex illegal...Harman has the backing of a number of prominent ministers, including the solicitor general, Vera Baird, and the attorney general, Lady Scotland...Harman has been allowed to express her personal view that buying sex should be made illegal before the government review has been completed.'[12]

And so the hounding, demonising and punishing of men continues:

> 'MEN WHO BUY SEX COULD FACE PROSECUTION: Other proposals being considered include large-scale programmes to name and shame men caught kerbcrawling, which is already illegal. But campaigners believe that only by criminalising clients can they help women working in brothels as well as on the streets and send out a signal that paying for sex is not acceptable (2007).'[13]

- So men are to be criminalised because some women have freely chosen to sell their services to them. This perverse interpretation is institutional man-hating
- The true nature of Feminism's issue with prostitution has nothing to do with 'gender equality'; its aim is to convert women's choices into Ideological issues to perpetuate its existence and to spread misandry

Again,

> 'The Home Secretary has made clear that under the new offence it will not be enough for a man to say "I didn't know". The new offence will include a "strict liability" test so that police will only have to prove that the man paid for sex, and that the woman had been trafficked. These will be no need to prove he knew it at the time.(2008).'[14]

- Labour/Feminist governments were absolutely *determined* to criminalise and punish men (what can one say about the misandry of male Labour MPs? It's a mystery, considering Labour's roots in the concepts of equality and fairness)

The above pieces of anti-male legislation arise from a combination of Feminism and Marxism, which holds that women in the sex industry are helpless 'victims of brutal male exploitation'. The prostitute's own freely made choice to enter the profession is deliberately ignored. Again we see Feminism stripping women of personal responsibility whilst blatantly using the profession of prostitution to demonise men, to justify its existence, and to fuel its Grievance Gravy-Train Industries.

There is hypocrisy and double standards in condemning, demonising and punishing men (the buyers) in prostitution when compared to other crimes. If buying sex is to be made illegal but selling it is to be met with tea and sympathy, then why are the same rules not applied to those nice drug-dealers and the scum who exploit them by buying their wares? A Feminist-dominated State picks and chooses its perspective on social policies and sexual politics, always favouring the Feminist agenda.

- Feminism is given a State licence to create issues out of the phenomenon of prostitution

How do Prostitutes Feel about Feminist Busybodies?

How do prostitutes *themselves* feel about being used as Ideological and political pawns? If prostitutes *themselves* don't see themselves as victims then what gives Feminists the right to label them as such? Feminists have no such right, but that doesn't stop them converting the choices of these women into an issue of oppression.

Prostitutes are angry about being used as pawns by Feminist Ideologues. I refer the reader to the International Committee for Prostitutes' Rights World Charter and World Whores Congress Statements:[15]

> *'Prostitution and Feminism: The ICPR realises that the women's movement in most countries has not or has only marginally included prostitutes as spokeswomen and theorists. Historically, women's movements (like socialist and communist movements) have opposed the institution of prostitution while claiming to support prostitutes. However, prostitutes reject support that requires them to leave prostitution: they object to being treated as symbols of oppression and demand recognition as workers. Due to feminist hesitation or refusal to accept prostitutes' legitimate work and to accept prostitutes as working women, the majority of prostitutes have not identified as feminists.'*

And,

> *'Cari Mitchell, of the English Collective of Prostitutes, warned that laws supposedly targeted only at women suffering exploitation would have a damaging impact on those who sell sex by their own choice.*
>
> *She said: "Bitter experience tells us that any law against consenting sex forces prostitution further underground and makes women more vulnerable to violence...Under the proposed offence (Jacqui Smith's 2008 legislation), any client of a woman working for another could be convicted. But what is his crime? The woman is working voluntarily and is likely to be making a better income than most women in commonly available low-waged jobs".'[16]*

- So prostitution's *own* organisations disassociate themselves from Feminism and its use of their profession as an issue, as a gender-weapon

***

Individual prostitutes also object to being used by Feminists to promote its agenda. The reader will observe, as was noted with pornography and lap-dancing, that some of these freely participating women are educated and make informed and rational choices:

Cameron, 25, is an escort in Newcastle:

> *'I work from my own place for an agency....I can earn up to £80 an hour. I'm angry about what the Government is trying to do...I have been to university – I am not stuck in a dead end.'[17]*

And,

Toni, 25, is a sex worker in the south-east:

> *'It is just a job of work between two consenting adults. The only immoral thing is the Government telling us how to use our bodies. It is pure arrogance. The Government is using the trafficking issue to clamp down and criminalise prostitution even further.'[18]*

229

And,

FEMALE STUDENTS TURN TO
PROSTITUTION TO PAY FEES

(The Sunday Times, 8 October, 2006)

'Last week one London escort said she had been working in the industry since 1999 to support herself through a masters degree and now doctorate in international politics.

"In the agency lounge, we all had our books or our laptops", said the escort, who would be identified only as Sophie. "We were all studying at night, then would take breaks to go out with the guys".

Sophie said she could sometimes earn £2,000 for a full night's work in 1999 but now competition from European prostitutes had drive earnings down, while tuition fees had gone up. "Instead of working in McDonald's, or shops for £8 an hour", Sophie said, "sometimes it is easier to work in this industry, make more money quickly, pay the rent and have time to do your reading".

Catherine Townsend, of The Independent, notes that:

'Sex has always sold, and always will. Everyone has a price...Not all women who sell their bodies are victims. Some women who have other options may choose to sell sex for a few hours per week over a 12-hour per day minimum wage gig at a call centre. Some would rather trade blow jobs to fund the latest Balenciaga bag.'[19]

- So prostitutes themselves, *including those who are university educated* (who are hardly likely to be suffering from a false consciousness) object to their work being politicised by Feminist Ideological bigots

***

The discourse on prostitution is monopolised by Feminism and the Feminist perspective; this includes the way prostitution is portrayed. All prostitutes are depicted in the media, and to the policy-makers, as 'victims of men'. They are 'enslaved', they are 'beaten', they are 'bought and sold', they are 'treated like a commodity', they are 'held in contempt.' Such a portrayal is *deliberately* dishonest. The vast majority of prostitutes *freely choose* to participate in the profession; many are middle-class; many are well educated. Yet it is the Feminist portrayal that prevails (over truth), producing pro-Feminist and anti-male social policies.

- Feminist Ideology trumps fairness and truth in today's Britain

Feminists deliberately portray prostitution as being inhabited by the drug-dependent women at the very bottom of the socioeconomic ladder. Some are, of course. But as a general picture it is wrong. The more truthful portrayal, admitting that the vast majority of women *freely choose* the profession and with a large proportion of these having had a good education, could not be converted into an Ideological gender-weapon issue. We have seen examples of female students and women with degrees choosing to earn a living in the profession, as we saw with the issue of pornography. In September 2010, it was disclosed that the footballer Wayne Rooney had spent time with two prostitutes whilst his wife was pregnant. Jennifer Thompson and Helen Wood both came from respectable middle-class backgrounds and both had attended Bolton's £1,555-a-term Lord's Independent school.

- Browbeaten women, forced into the profession? I don't think so

In 2009 the high-class prostitute Belle de Jour, who had blogged her experiences on the internet, 'came out' to reveal herself as Dr. Brook Magnanti, a research scientist in infomatics, epidemiology and forensic science:

THE OTHER BELLE DE JOURS
(The Sunday Times, 22 November, 2009)

'Another escort who appears to have made an informed choice of career is Arian, a 30-year-old based in the West Country, who offers "holistic sex coaching". She has a first-class degree in a science-related subject and lectured at Keele University.

Dr. Suzanne Jenkins, a researcher at Newcastle University, invited her to lecture there. Earlier this year, Jenkins completed an internet survey of 483 sex workers, more than half of them from Britain. More than a third turned out to have degrees.

"Many sex workers are in the industry through choice", said Jenkins. "It suits them because of the independence, flexibility and earning capacity."

The owner of one of London's most expensive escort agencies, which charges up to £500 an hour, claims highly educated escorts are not unusual.

Erica, 31, has a degree in French and Spanish from the University of Sheffield, and has been an escort since leaving university 10 years ago: "It was a lifestyle choice", she said, "I would get £1,000 in a bad week, twice that in a good one. Unless I was a lawyer or a doctor, where I'd be tied to my desk all day, what else could I do for that money?...I tried to leave the industry once...I had to readjust to counting my money...I soon went back to escorting. I see that all the time."'

- Dr. Suzanne Jenkins's research found that 'more than a third of prostitutes had degrees'. This is a far cry from the Feminist portrayal, with its manipulated and *deliberately* perverted public and political image of prostitutes as lower-class, drug-addled victims of men

The following letter was published in the same edition of The Sunday Times:

'BELLE DE JOUR IS A GOOD ROLE MODEL FOR WOMEN: As a former prostitute I welcome a new generation of women financing their studies and/or families by going on the game. This time-honoured route out of poverty has been resorted to by professional men and women of all social classes and backgrounds. Bridget Rankin, London, NW3'

***

How ought we to describe someone who, *in the face of all the evidence to the contrary*, insists on blaming men for the phenomenon of prostitution?

Bigot: *'An obstinate and intolerant believer in a religion, political theory, etc.'*[20]

Or perhaps there is a deeper issue here:

"...women's sexual powers are enormous. Women know it. The only people who don't know it are feminists. Desensualised, desexualised, neurotic women. I wouldn't have said this twenty years ago because I was a militant feminist myself. But as the years have gone on, I begin to see more and more that the perverse, neurotic psychodrama projected by these women is coming from their own problems with sex".[21]

Or,

Fanatic: *'A person possessed by an excessive and irrational zeal, especially for a religious or political cause...extreme or unscrupulous dedication, monomania.'*[22]

Psychosis: *'Any severe mental disorder...characterised by deterioration of normal intellectual functioning and by partial or complete withdrawal from reality.'*[23]

- I refer the reader to Part Three

'Feminism legitimises the sickness of some women.'[24]

Concluding Comments

Unpalatable though it may be to Feminists, the vast majority of women involved in prostitution have made a *choice* to sell sex, because they choose to earn what can sometimes be substantial sums of money. The Feminist's Ideological perspective on prostitution – 'it is an abuse of women's bodies and subjugates women', 'it's an expression of male power', 'it exploits women' – cannot be reconciled with the views of prostitutes themselves, or their representative organisations. Which, I suggest, is proof positive that the Feminist claims are fraudulent.

***

Again, it is never explained how a commercial transaction – a man handing over an agreed amount of money to a woman who is willing to sell her services for a specified time – is making one party to the transaction (the woman), a 'victim who is being exploited'. It is *she* who sets the price and the terms, not her client. Is a car dealer being 'victimised and exploited' when he fixes the price of a car and a customer comes along and buys it? If there is no coercion and no violence, and the business is carried out in private, then for the life of me, I cannot see anything exploitative in a *prostitute/client* commercial transaction.

***

Do a gender-switch. Is the male client a victim? We could claim that the male is having his hard-wired DNA-ed biological determinism, his need to procreate, exploited, manipulated and demeaned by the prostitute. Do women become prostitutes in order to exert power over, and to dominate, men? Such an inversion of perspective and interpretation is perfectly rational. Anthony Clare was Medical Director of St. Patrick's Hospital and Clinical Professor of Psychiatry at Trinity College, Dublin:

> *'Men know only too well how tragic they appear, know too well the extent to which they feel enslaved by their libidos...men in thrall to sex exhibit self-disgust...Men know they need women, depend on them.'*[25]

- It was noted in the previous chapter that some lap-dancers admitted to manipulating and exploiting their voyeurs

***

Prostitution, like pornography, is a Feminist issue whose sole purpose is to demonise men.

SECTION 4

Chapter 26

Women Choose Lower Pay and Lower Status

This Section addresses two important choices that women make and shows how Feminism converts these choices into inequalities and discriminations. They are the two most cherished, publicised and widely accepted Feminist issues – the pay gap and the glass ceiling. The two are closely linked; for example, people who are in more senior positions will earn higher salaries than those who are not. So more men being in senior positions is one explanation why men earn, overall, more than women.

***

In a survey carried out among Feminists, reported in 2010, the question was asked: 'Please list the three feminist issues that most interest and concern you'. The first choice was a combination of work/home/education.[1]

Two Professional Feminists declare:

> *'The pay gap between men and women is an enduring problem. Women's mean disposable weekly income...in the UK is less than 60 per cent of men's. For earnings done, the gap is still significant; the mean full-time hourly pay of men in 2009 was £16.07, compared to £13.43 for women. The pay gap is greater when we include part-time workers, who are predominantly female; when all workers' hourly earnings (including part-time and full-time) are compared the pay gap is 20 per cent.'[2]*

There can be no doubt that over the years sex discrimination occurred with regard to pay and promotion, particularly in some macho professions such as the police force (which is now probably why this profession is overcompensating with Feminist-friendly policies). But such a discrimination is no longer a problem in today's Britain...no more than it is with other groups, including white heterosexual males whose face, accent, culture or politics don't 'fit'. In fact, I would suggest that there is now *more* 'political' discrimination against those who are *not* Left-wing/liberal/progressive (especially in the 'liberal' professions – education, academia, the law, the media...) than there is against most other groups.

- Feminism wishes us to believe that we are still in the sex-discrimination dark days of the pre-1980s. And we have all succumbed to this belief

***

The pay gap and the glass ceiling are Feminism's flagship issues and for this reason I have addressed them extensively. We know that choices often have negative as well as positive consequences. The pay gap and the glass ceiling are the negative consequences of women's choice not to prioritise pay and seniority in their jobs and careers. So the pay gap and the glass ceiling represent the negative consequences of women following their preferences (negative *only* from the Feminist perspective, not from that of women who make these choices). Feminism then compares the *negative consequences* of women's choices with the *positive consequences* of men's choices (who generally choose to seek higher earnings and higher status). This deceitful comparison of the two extremes is then Ideologically interpreted as the inequality and discrimination of the pay gap and the glass ceiling.

Are Women Being 'Diddled Out of Equal Pay'?

There is no glass ceiling, I use the term simply for clarity. It is a Feminist invention, a Feminist myth. Women *are* under-represented in top jobs but there are rational reasons for this phenomenon. To call this phenomenon a glass ceiling, with its connotations of their being a *barrier* to women's advancement, is being deliberately deceitful. The glass ceiling is a value-laden and inflammatory phrase intentionally used to convert women's choices and preferences into an Ideological issue.

It is important for the reader to grasp that the pay gap and the glass ceiling are simply *numerical imbalances*; rather than inequalities and discriminations. They are *statistical disparities*, so in themselves are value-free phenomena; they are not unjust, they have rational explanations and ought not be interpreted with an emotive Ideological perspective...as Feminism continually does.

- Feminist dogma demands that all sex-related discrepancies (wherever men appear to be advantaged) are evidence of sex discrimination and inequalities. They are not

When a group has a weak evidential case from which to create or convert an issue it tends to minimise the importance of evidence. Instead, it employs the strategy of emotion; it replaces facts and evidence (because these would not substantiate its claims) with emotional appeals in order to distract the public's and politician's attention from the lack of supporting facts. This is what Feminists have been doing with the issues of the pay gap and the glass ceiling (and other issues, including domestic violence and rape):

> 'The implication is that discrepancies are due to sexist discrimination against women, but discrepancies can be due to other factors. Given the educational patterns of earlier generations, for instance, older women are still less often part of the workforce than older men. Not all women, moreover, either have or want full-time jobs. When their salaries are factored in with all others, the resulting figure indicates only that women as a group earn less than men as a group. The fact is that women themselves have made choices to have children or not to have children, to work or not to work, to work part-time or to work full-time...Because of the enormous sums of money at stake, a whole industry has grown up around pay equity: researchers, job evaluators, consultants, and so forth.'[3]

***

Whenever a discussion touches upon Feminism, or any aspect of sexual politics, the pay gap and the glass ceiling are always offered as examples of 'gender inequality' (Always. Without fail). I am constantly astonished at how naive people are with regard to sexual politics and Feminism (particularly men), at how easily they have allowed themselves to become indoctrinated with Feminist rhetoric and cant – never questioning, never challenging, never analysing, never critiquing...sponges soaking up the platitudes and when squeezed for an opinion unthinkingly leak out the dogma and mantras that have been Ideologically poured in. I find this Gradgrindian process truly depressing and saddening. It is particularly distressing when university 'educated' people soak up Feminist propaganda (a childlike innocence? A laziness of thought? Or a bizarre psychological 'need' to believe that women really *are* victims and a 'minority'?). But ought I to be so surprised? Feminism has never been questioned, challenged, analysed or critiqued in the media, in academia, by politicians, so how can the public possibly *know* that it is a fraud, a confidence trick?

The pay gap and the glass ceiling should *never* be given as examples of 'gender inequalities'. They are converted from women's freely made and rational choices into issues in order to justify the continuing existence of Feminism, to promote its agenda and to fuel its Grievance Gravy-Train Industries, allowing it to soap-box its Ideology and continue to salary its gender-warrior personnel. This conversion is accomplished by Feminism's Blaming Strategy – again it is men, individually or as the patriarchy (the 'male system') who are blamed. For example, it is the patriarchal male culture that intentionally socialises women into having learned roles (sex stereotyping), that instils attitudes and values into women which makes them feel that they ought to, and are expected to, choose roles and occupations that will 'disadvantage' them (lower pay, not wishing to pursue promotion, choosing to be stay-at-home mothers and housewives). Women *themselves* do not feel that their choices lead to negative consequences or 'disadvantages', these are defined as 'negative' only by Feminists.

Blaming women for the negative consequences of their choices would not fit Feminism's Ideology, its patriarchal template. If it were admitted that women *themselves* were personally responsible for their choices then the pay gap and the glass ceiling could not logically be used as inequalities and discriminations. So blame has to be sought elsewhere.

'We need to know why women are being diddled out of equal pay'

(Jenni Murray: Feminist presenter of Radio 4's Woman's Hour: Monday, 26 February, 2006)

The persistent fable that women are denied equal pay for equal work is a never-empty tank of gas that fuels Feminism.

***

Feminism doesn't represent women. With the pay gap and glass ceiling we see again the Professional Feminist's wish to impose her belief system and values on *all* women. This will be observed in every chapter in this Section. The values and choices of the vast majority of women are very different to those of Feminists. But Feminists *need* inequalities and discriminations to justify their existence. Ordinary, decent women have other values and interests in their lives to those of their career-oriented and Ideologically-driven Sisters.

Chapter 27

Women's Work Ethic and Choice of Options

The majority of women have a different work ethic to men, they have different work preferences and attitudes. This leads them to choose different priorities and work options based upon personal and individual lifestyle values and aims.

Recent research into the pay gap and the glass ceiling is based upon 'preference theory'. This argues that women's preferences, and their freedom to choose to indulge these preferences, is the central determinant of why women are paid less than men and why women are under-represented in senior positions. Preference theory uses three related work-life models that express women's preferences, women's choices.[1]

1. Family-centred:

Firstly, 17 per cent of women fall into the 'family-centred' category. Family life and children are the main priorities throughout their lives; they prefer *not* to work. Their family values are caring and non-competitive. Family-centred women are almost invisible because the Feminist-dominated media and the political focus (particularly with the post-1997 Labour/Feminist Governments) is on women's employment and participation in the public sphere.

2. Adaptive:

Secondly, 69 per cent of women are in the 'adaptive' category. This is a very large majority and has direct consequences for the pay gap and the glass ceiling. This group is the most diverse and includes women who want to combine work and family. They want to work but are not committed to a working career. They seek part-time work, flexible work, or they work temporarily. Their family values are a compromise between two conflicting sets of values. They wish to enjoy the best of both worlds. Jobs such as school teaching are attractive to these women because they facilitate a wholesome work-life balance. But the majority of this group seek part-time work after having children, or take seasonal work, temporary work, school-term type jobs, jobs where there is little or no commuting, they may withdraw from work temporarily or completely, if family finances permit.

3. Work-centred:

Thirdly, only 14 per cent of women are actually 'work-centred'. This very small percentage has huge implications for the Feminist issues of the pay gap and the glass ceiling. Childless women are concentrated in this category. Their main priority in life is their career. They are committed to their work. They are responsive to economic and political opportunities. These women have marketplace values – such as competitive rivalry and an achievement orientation. The fundamental point is that this group represents only *a small minority* of all women (despite the huge increase of women in higher education). Family life is fitted around their work, with many finding work in the various Feminist Industries, and their sympathetic subsidiaries (for example, the trade unions and the public sector).

The majority of this group will be Feminists. It is this small percentage of work-centred women who are the most vociferous group in demanding State intervention to help 'women'. It is this group who demand positive discrimination and quotas to remedy the under-representation of women in senior positions...it is this group who will fill these positions.

- Preference theory is fundamental to truly understanding the phenomena of the pay gap and the glass ceiling

The three preference theory categories are found at all educational levels, in all socioeconomic backgrounds and in other countries as well as Britain – Spain, Belgium, Germany, Sweden and the Czech Republic, for example.[2]

So essentially, what we have is a situation in which:

- Over 17 out of 20 women are not concerned, or not *too* concerned, about pay or promotion, about their work and careers (86 per cent of all women)

- Only 3 out of 20 women *are* concerned about pay, about promotion and about their work and careers (14 per cent of all women)

The above key facts go a long way in explaining the difference in pay between men and women and the smaller number of women in senior posts. These two phenomena are not 'gender inequalities', they are not discriminations. They are the result of women's different work ethic, and the way women express this in their work-life preferences and choices of work options. The following chapters will analyse in detail the repercussions of the above statistics and women's preferences.

***

The 14 per cent of 'work-centred' women are likely to be Feminists. So when Feminists demand positive discrimination and quotas to increase the number of women in the top jobs they are, in fact, demanding that *they themselves* should fill these designated senior status, high salaried jobs (the other 86 per cent of 'family-centred' and 'adaptive' women will obviously not be too interested in highly stressful, high status jobs). This form of personal advancement is one of the main reasons why quotas and positive discrimination are fought so hard for by Feminists – it is *they* who will be the beneficiaries.

- The Feminist demand for 'gender equality' is a disguise; essentially, it is a demand for governments to give preferential treatment to *Feminists themselves*, not women in general, to give high status, high salaried posts and sinecures

This is a real danger for men. Consider the consequences of a disproportionately high percentage of misandrous Feminists inhabiting the higher echelons of professions – the law, the media, the universities, politics; this has already been happening for a number of decades and is a major reason for the widespread cultural and institutional misandry in today's Britain.

- Women's different work ethic results in lower pay for women and fewer women in senior positions

Women's Choice of Work Options

Not only do women have a different work ethic to men but they also enjoy a wider choice of work options.

Women have a social, cultural, and often legislative licence to choose to a) work full-time, b) work part-time, c) work flexi-time, d) work temporarily (or be in and out of work at will), e) not to work at all. All these female-friendly options lead to lower pay for women. Even the full-time option results in lower pay because women's 'full-time' work consists of fewer actual working hours than men's 'full-time' work.[3] Women's fluid work structure is socially and culturally sanctioned but the negative consequences resulting from this (lower pay and lack of promotion) are held up as inequalities and discriminations and have been socially and politically accepted as such.

- This range of work option choices allows women to enjoy a much healthier work-life balance than men

Our society, culture and conventional wisdom do not permit men to freely choose any of these work options – the expectation and rigidity of full-time, constant, life-time work is simply imposed upon them. A family man choosing to work only part-time, or 'dropping out' to enjoy a lower paid but more fulfilling job is frowned upon, he is condemned for rejecting his family responsibilities.

> 'Men remain trapped in the rigid role of main breadwinner, but women now have genuine lifestyle choices in the liberal modern societies of Europe.'[4]

And,

> '...the majority of women do not experience, or perhaps even more importantly expect, the lifelong responsibility for, the financial wellbeing of, a family that is the expectation of every man.'[5]

- Men are enslaved by the tyranny of the wage packet. Women enjoy the cultural legitimacy to be able to choose not to be so enslaved

The majority of men are work-centred, including being career and promotion-minded, compared to only a minority of women.[6] Men are more likely to seek careers than women. Their work ethic, attitudes and values are promotion/career/high salary orientated. A minority do seek a healthy and wholesome work-life balance but few, at least once they become family men, achieve this.

Here we see a fundamental rational reason for the pay gap and the glass ceiling.

***

Do a gender-switch. It could be said that:

> 'Men suffer from a work option gap'

Or

> 'We need to know why men are being diddled out of an interesting and healthy range of work-life options'

Chapter 28

Women Choose a Healthy Work-Life Balance

'The most important reasons for the "gender gap" (pay gap) have little to do with employer bias. Increasingly, the gap is the result of choices women make as they seek to maximise their own happiness and achieve a broad mix of life goals.'[1]

Women's work and life values, preferences and priorities are different to men's. Women choose a healthier work-life balance than men and this results in lower pay and a smaller percentage of women being represented in senior positions. We will see that women tend to pull away from seeking promotion.

'Only about a quarter of women who hold full-time jobs view their working life as a career.'[2]

And,

'Jobs are central to the lives of 55 per cent of husbands and just 17 per cent of wives.'[3]

Again:

'Only 14% of women are classified as work-centred. These women, frequently childfree, can rightly be deemed to share the ambitions and values of their male colleagues, but these results show that they are not representative of their sex in general.'[4]

Women have a cultural licence to enjoy a working life that is more wholesome and satisfying than that of men's. But choosing such a healthy balance and having a lower commitment to work has negative consequences in the form of lower pay and fewer promotions.

'A study has found that socialising with friends and going out in the evening are more important considerations for young professionals than working flat out for the next promotion...Put together by the market research company TNS, the report found that the trend was most pronounced among women, with 40% defying the career-girl stereotype and saying the main function of work was to fund a busy social life.'[5]

- So women prioritise

FIRMS WILL HAVE TO JUSTIFY WOMEN'S PAY RATES

(The Times, 28 March, 2001)

'Ruth Lea, of the Institute of Directors, said that she was "very sceptical" about the suggestion that discrimination was responsible for 25 to 50 per cent of pay differentials. She argued that women chose not to take high-paid jobs in the City and were more likely to go into careers such as teaching: "Women want some sense of balance in their lives", she said.'

Again,

'The evidence is that the majority of modern women still expect to (and do) reduce their level of career commitment on marriage, because they see their husbands as the main breadwinners....Even for women who have themselves achieved status and earning power, their husbands' material prospects remain important. Women today are still looking for slightly older, wealthier and more powerful husbands.'[6]

And India Knight notes:

> *'It is a fact that, if they have small children, women are far more likely to rethink the whole career thing and either stay at home if their finances allow it, return to work part-time or go back to a job with fewer responsibilities – which is what I mean by a "self-imposed" glass ceiling.'*[7]

***

There is a common assumption that those who work in professional or managerial jobs are committed to long-term careers. This is broadly true of men but does not apply as much to women. Many will marry and have children and a significant number will choose either to reduce their hours or drop out of the workforce temporarily:

> *'For the last 20 years or more, equal numbers of men and women have been entering professions such as medicine and the law, but have not reached the top in equal strength. Preference theory suggests that this is not due so much to sex discrimination, but to women exercising choice.'*[8]

So women choose to have a healthier life-work balance than men; they do not regard work as central to their life. They have different values and aims to men and because of the range of work options open to them can indulge their preferences. Feminism converts these preferences, women's choice to have a healthier work-life balance and less commitment to their work and career, into the issues of the pay gap and the glass ceiling. These are not 'gender inequalities', they are a rationally considered trade-off.

Research consistently finds that men and women have a different work ethic, a different commitment to work. More female than male students of average ability drop out of university:

> *'The main reason for the higher female than male drop-out rate among undergraduates of average or below average ability and performance was low commitment to paid employment and a career as a major part of their adult lives; the alternative of marriage, economic dependence and the housewife role was seen to be an option for women but not for men.'*[9]

Essentially, women don't embrace work like men do, it is not as central to their lives:

> *'In June 2001, Bupa/Top Sante published a survey of 5,000 full-time working women in the UK and found that only nine per cent said they would still work full-time if they had a realistic choice. This compares with a majority of men, because men have no concept of an alternative to life-long full-time work which does not mean criminality or poverty...'*[10]

***

Do a gender-switch. It could be said that:

> *'Men suffer from a life-long, full-time, work-commitment gap'*

Or

> *'We need to ask why men are being diddled out of a healthy work-life balance'*

Chapter 29

Women Choose to Take Career Breaks

Women choose to be the primary carer of the children, which results in their choosing to have more career breaks than men. However, even *childless* women still choose to have more career breaks than men, indicating an innate difference in work ethic and work-life preferences.

In the vast majority of partnerships it is the woman who will make the choice to start a family and when to start a family. Also, it is she, overwhelmingly, who chooses to be the primary carer of the children.

The respected economist Arnaud Chevalier presented a paper at the Royal Society Annual Conference in 2003. He concluded:

'Women decide from as early an age as 17, when they choose their degree course, on how to combine work and motherhood. They prefer careers such as teaching and nursing, where they can take an extended break to raise a family. And from the outset of their careers, choosing a socially useful job was more important to the women than the men, while financial rewards were less important (only 14% of women ranked financial rewards as "very important").'[1]

We saw in an earlier chapter that a very large percentage of mothers choose not to work full-time or work continuously. To remind the reader:

'Just 2 per cent of new mothers who work full-time do so willingly...says a survey by Pregnancy and Birth Magazine. Home is a mother's preferred workplace.(2002)'[2]

And,

'The survey (Mother and Baby magazine) found that only 6 per cent of mothers of babies or toddlers actually enjoy working full-time...(2000).'[3]

In addition,

'Maire Fahey, editor of Prima magazine, said the survey showed that women want to "rebalance" their lives, with many wanting to work three days a week, allowing them to spend most of their time at home with the children.

Jill Kirby, of the Centre for Policy Studies think tank, said: "This underlines a whole mass of previous evidence that show again and again that women have different life goals from men" (2006).'[4]

It is accepted by economists and sociologists that when a mother takes a career break to care for a child then the husband will find ways to increase his *own* income to compensate for his wife's loss of income; so the woman earns less and the man earns more.[5] So here we have one further rational explanation why men, overall, earn more than women.

***

Even though there is overwhelming evidence showing that the majority of women wish to be the primary carer of the children, and adapt their work-life balance to accommodate this choice, Feminists, driven by their Ideology, obdurately and deviously continue to convert this choice into an inequality and oppression:

> 'The fact is that most jobs were designed with the expectation that the person who filled them would be free of extensive childcare responsibilities.'[6]

- Notice the use of the pejorative word 'free'. We have seen that Feminists regard mothers and housewives as 'slaves'

And,

> '...a key reason that the male partners are able to concentrate successfully upon their careers is that the female partners take on most of the burden of childcare.'[7]

- Notice the deliberately pejorative use of the word 'burden'. Child care is only a 'burden' for the Feminist...not for the majority of women, who actively choose it as an option over their jobs and careers. As we saw in a previous chapter, the Feminist needs to interpret marriage and child care as burdens, chores, inequalities and oppressions in order for them to fit her patriarchal Ideology of 'good women'/ 'bad men'. And it has been seen that Divorce Court Judges acquiesce with this Feminist Fraud – giving huge payouts to divorcing wives for 'sacrificing' their careers

Relating this Feminist Ideological perversion of the truth to the pay gap and glass ceiling we see that:

> '...the standard gender-structured family has played a key role in rendering women much poorer than men.'[8]

And,

> 'The division of labour by sex impoverishes women in large numbers.'[9]

So mothers, freely choosing the work-life balance that leads to the lower pay option – enjoying being the primary carer – results in women earning less than men. This conclusion is self-evident and it is ridiculous to use it as an example of sex inequality. However, Feminists are adept at such use, and this women's choice has been successfully converted into a discrimination and oppression against women.

Women Choose not to Work Continuously

This choice is mainly, but not always, associated with the woman's choice to be the primary carer of the children.

> 'Current evidence for Britain suggests that women's continuity of employment is declining rather than rising, so full-time and continuous employment actually covers only about 10 to 15 per cent of women in Britain.'[10]

A working woman is nearly *nine times* more likely than a man to leave the workplace for six months or longer for family reasons.[11] Consider the consequences of this for women's pay and promotion.

The career breaks that women choose to take in order to care for the children results in lack of *continuity* in the same job, or with the same company, for long periods of time. Many companies reward *longevity* of employment with pay rises and promotions. By choosing to be stay-at-home mothers, or part-time workers, or temporary workers, women will also be choosing to sacrifice the benefits of continuity of employment and longevity with one company.

Women who choose to take career breaks in order to be the primary carer will also miss out on company *training, new work technologies* (an important loss in the fast-moving technological world of the 21st century), and *meeting new clients*. So being less well trained, and not 'up to speed' with company business, will lead to fewer promotion prospects for women and therefore less pay.

- The negative consequences of choosing to take career breaks is *not* a 'gender inequality'. They are not negative consequences for ordinary women...they are only made so by Feminists actively seeking inequalities to justify their existence

A study of 14,000 executives found that women executives earn 45 per cent less than men.[12] But when the study was analysed more closely it was found *that seniority alone accounted for two thirds of the pay gap.* Seniority is earned by *continuous* employment.

WOMEN 'CHOOSE' TO BE PAID LESS

(The Sunday Times, 6 March, 2005)

'Sex discrimination in the workplace is largely a myth, a new study has claimed, with the pay gap between the genders explained by differences in what men and women are looking for in a job.

The author claims women earn less through choice, putting family above work, and not because male bosses are paying them less.

The author claims women are motivated most by a biological need to have babies while men are spurred on to increase their earning power to attract a wife.

Women often do not want to return to the "rat race" after having children and so choose to come back to less demanding, less well-paid, jobs.

"Even if discrimination magically disappeared, women would still earn less because they do not want to make money as much as men do", said Satoshie Kanazawa, lecturer in management at the London School of Economics and author of the report.

But among those who have a strong motivation to make money – generally those who are under 40, unmarried and childless – the differences in earnings with men disappear.

Kanazawa argues that men and women have different priorities in choosing jobs. Males are more likely to take work that allows them to earn more. Women choose jobs that allow them to help others, regardless of how lucrative they are.

Women who took part in the survey put greater emphasis on work itself being important rather than the level of income.

High-flying women this weekend said they agreed with Kanazawa's findings. Sahar Hashemic, 36, a former City lawyer who co-founded the Coffee Republic chain with her brother, said: "Inequality is so over, so not this generation. I find it an insult the way some women go on. It is as if they have a chip on their shoulder."

Alex Haslam, professor of social and organisational psychology at Exeter University, said: "The basic pattern of this study is correct. Men and women have different career trajectories."'

- Note Sahar Hashemic's remark: 'It is as if they have a chip on their shoulder'. A throwaway but incisive observation. 'A chip on their shoulder'? I refer the reader to Part Three

***

When mothers return to work after a career break they generally do so in a lower capacity than the one they left. Feminism has converted this into a further discrimination. However, these women re-enter work *on their own terms*, choosing part-time work, or flexible hours. These work options are deliberately chosen so the mother can continue to enjoy her more fundamental choice of being the primary carer. Upon their return to work mothers accept a trade-off of shorter hours, less arduous and stressful work, more family convenient working conditions, the opportunity to work from home – for lower pay and lower status. So the Feminist issue of 'downgrading when returning to work' is not, in fact, a 'gender inequality' or discrimination; it is a choice. These are the 69 per cent of women, the 'adaptive' women. It is only the women in the 14 per cent of 'work-centred' women (that is, Feminists) who are making this complaint. They wish to take their full compliment of paid maternity leave (12 months)...and then return to *exactly the same high-status job that they vacated*; it's called having your cake and eating it. And when we next have a Labour/Feminist Government in office they will achieve this self-promoting demand.

***

Feminism converts women's choices to be the primary parent and to enjoy taking career breaks into the inequalities and discriminations of the pay gap and the glass ceiling. The consequences of career breaks are not 'gender inequalities' caused by individual men or the patriarchy. They are the consequences of a trade-off – career breaks and *the joy of raising the children* in exchange for lower pay and lower promotion prospects.

• We need to stop blaming men for the Feminist-defined negative consequences of non-Ideological women's freely made choices

Do a gender-switch. It could be said that:

'Men suffer from the primary carer and the career break gap'

Or

'We need to ask why men are being diddled out of career breaks and the daily joy of watching their children grow and develop'

Chapter 30

Women Choose to Work Fewer Hours: And Fewer Unsocial Hours

'Over a lifetime women earn £300,000 less than men'

(Feminism mantra)

- Keep this mantra in mind whilst reading this chapter

We know that women choose to have a healthier work-life balance than men. We have seen that one manifestation of this is that they take more career breaks than men. A second is their choice of work-hours options.

Women have a more flexible work-hours pattern than men. This is expressed in the options of: i) choosing to work fewer full-time hours, ii) by choosing to work part-time, iii) by choosing not to work unsocial hours.

Women Choose to Work Fewer Hours than Men

Men work far longer hours than women in their working day. Men in *full-time* paid employment work, on average, 49 hours a week whilst women in *full-time* paid employment work, an average, only 27 hours a week.[1] This is a huge difference (the difference in full-time hours worked may change from year to year, but there is a wide gap and the principle is the same).

When Feminism claims that women working 'full-time' are paid less than men working 'full-time' they are not comparing like with like (the label is the same: the hours are not). This is a deliberate Feminist deception. The public and politicians are unaware of this deception, and have bought into the Feminist claim that *women in full-time work are paid less than men in full-time work*.

- At the risk of abusing the reader's intelligence it needs to be made clear that if women work *fewer hours* than men then women will be *paid less* than men (although obvious, I stress this because we have all been conned on this issue – as on others – by Feminist propaganda)

YES, I BELIEVE IN EQUAL PAY FOR WOMEN – BUT ONLY FOR THOSE WHO WORK FOR IT (...AND PLENTY DON'T!)

(Daily Mail, Wednesday, 1 August, 2007: Amanda Platell)

'And having worked as an executive on national newspapers for a couple of decades and at the heart of Parliament for some years, I can assure you that when a talented woman was prepared to put in the hours – inside and outside the office – not only did she deserve to earn exactly the same as the men, that's exactly what she got.

> We do not live in an ideal world, we live in a real world. And the hard truth is that by and large men spend more time at work, inside the office and out. And we're not just talking bonding drinks with colleagues, we're talking conferences, weekend work, late nights in the office, reading, research, checking emails.
>
> Why should a woman who chooses to work fewer hours than a man be paid the same?'

But this is exactly what Feminism *does* want (and has actually achieved in many cases), women working fewer hours than men – but being paid the same. Wimbledon is a good example of this Feminist success; men play 5 sets but women play only 3 – women receive equal prize money (the 'wage') for doing just over half the work, entertaining the spectators for only half the time. Feminism has nothing to do with 'gender equality', it is only interested in seeking out and creating inequalities to justify and continue its existence; and in preferencing women where this happens to coincide with its Ideological agenda.

THE 60-HOUR WEEKS THAT LEAVE LITTLE TIME FOR FUN

(Daily Mail, Monday, 4 October, 2010)

> 'Bad news, chaps. If you think you're spending too much time in the office, you probably are.
>
> A survey (by Windows Live Hotmail) has found that 60 per cent of men are working more than 60 hours a week...when it came to women, however, the results showed that the majority of them put in less than 37 hours.'

Women Choose to Work Part-Time

One manifestation of women choosing to work fewer hours than men is their overwhelming choice to work part-time. 80 percent of all part-time jobs are filled by women.[2] As part of their work-life balance a majority of women choose to work part-time wherever possible (that is, the 69 per cent of 'adaptive' women).

- Feminists have cleverly created two issues from women choosing to work part-time:
- They claim that part-time work *itself* is an inequality
- They state that 'women earning less than men' is an inequality

Part-Time Work as an Inequality

A primary aim of Feminism, high on its agenda, is for all women to be independent of men. An important factor in this Separatist belief system is the drive to get all women into full-time paid employment. Consequently, Feminists deliberately describe women who work part-time as suffering from an inequality and discrimination (regardless of the fact that this is a freely made choice). We see this in the following quotes from a sample of 'A' level and university Sociology textbooks (Sociology is the pre-eminent Feminist-dominated discipline):

> '...women still experience a number of inequalities in the labour market. In this section we will look at three of the main inequalities for women at work: occupational segregation, concentration in part-time employment and the wage gap.'[3]

And,

'Explanations for gender inequalities in employment. As we have seen in the previous sections, women face a number of disadvantages in paid work. 1) First, they tend to be paid less than men. 2) Second, they are more likely to be in part-time work. 3) Third, they tend to be concentrated in the lower reaches of the occupations in which they work.'[4]

- The authors *admit* that women *prefer* to work part-time and *choose* to work part-time. Yet they perversely persist in calling these choices inequalities. They have converted women's choices into issues. These Male Feminists are propagating Feminist Ideology and teaching untruths to young people. This is unacceptable in a State education system, which in a democracy ought to remain politically neutral

- Feminist dogma, Feminist lies, and the Feminist Ideology, are being taught in schools and universities. There is no opposing view given. When a one-sided view is given of a political issue then this is defined not as teaching but as indoctrination

Women prefer to work fewer hours than men, and *particularly* choose to work part-time; this is *not* an inequality.

***

BOYS, YOU CAN KEEP YOUR GREASY POLES
(The Sunday Times, 12 June, 2005)

'Helen McKeown is a doctor who won a distinction in her postgraduate medical exam. Annabel Adcock is a barrister who secured a living in one of London's most prestigious legal chambers. Lucilla Hermann has a degree in business administration and is an expert in corporate treasury.

Are they Britain's new superwomen, forcing their way to the top of male preserves? No, each of these could be high flyers but has chosen a career path that allows her to work part-time.

Far from conquering male realms in the way sociologists and equal rights campaigners predicted, they are clustering behind what have been dubbed "glass partitions" – creating female-friendly ghettoes where they are able to pursue not the traditional male ambitions of status and wealth but flexible hours and a better work-life balance.

This helps to explain why the pay gap between male and female professionals still averages 15% within three years of graduation.

Equal rights campaigners blame the pay gap on sex discrimination. New thinking suggests that women themselves are discriminating: they are choosing jobs that pay less in order to win other benefits, it is called "working clever".

Catherine Hakim, a sociologist at the London School of Economist who has written extensively on women's employment, maintains that women now have a much better deal than men in lifestyle choices.

"The new pattern we are seeing is not the result of discrimination but of women's choice", Hakim said: "There is still a feminist fixation on discrimination, but in fact lots of women are simply deciding that some jobs are not for them".'

***

Women are happiest when they choose to work part-time. Working part-time is not always financially possible, but for the majority of women it is a wish and an aim (they are part of the 'adaptive' 69 per cent of women):

WHY THE HAPPIEST WOMEN WORK PART-TIME

(Daily Mail, Monday, 24 September, 2007)

'Women with part-time jobs are the happiest of all, according to a study.

They report greater job satisfaction than those in full-time employment and say they are more content than those with no paid job at all.

The findings of the British Household Panel Survey, which questioned 2,800 couples over eight years, held true for both mothers and childless couples.'

- Note that even women who have no children *still* prefer to work part-time rather than full-time, and choose this option whenever possible

***

Women's work ethic, expressed in their choice to work fewer hours, would appear to be innate because it also applies to *all* socioeconomic groups, including university educated and professionally trained women who could very easily work full-time if they so wished.

PART-TIME DOCTORS

(The Times, Saturday, 23 June, 2007)

'A British Medical Association poll has found that 58 per cent of doctors graduating in the UK in 2006 were female – up from 51 per cent in 1995. One in five female doctors said they expected to work part-time for most of their careers, compared with 4 per cent of men.'

And,

HOW WOMEN DOCTORS 'DOWNGRADE' MEDICINE

(Daily Mail, Tuesday, 3 August, 2004)

'Women doctors could outnumber men by 2010, according to a recent British Medical Association report.

There are fears that this will lead to an understaffed health service as women negotiate part-time work and career breaks.

Professor Black said: "We have very capable women who graduate well and have all the right intellectual characteristics to go on but the top of the medical profession is not being filled by women. They do not come through.

There seems to be a period of their lives for many women where the life-work balance takes over, when they want to work much more flexibly".'

Medical training is a long and expensive process. Most of this expense is met from the public purse. I would ask the reader to consider whether someone benefiting from this training should be allowed to work only part-time? Someone working only part-time is not returning value for money. It could be reasonably argued that it is a serious waste of public funds to train a doctor (of either sex) for seven years – only for them then to declare that they will choose to work part-time, when qualified.

***

We have seen that a large percentage of female doctors choose to work part-time. Yet the Feminist media persist in portraying this choice as an inequality and discrimination:

FEMALE DOCTORS ARE DENIED NHS TOP JOBS

**Women are paid 18% less than their male counterparts
as glass ceiling holds back the highest fliers**

(The Observer 22 August, 2010: Rachel Ellis)

'The NHS faces a chronic shortage of women in senior positions as female medical staff hit a glass ceiling, doctors' leaders are warning.

Fewer than 30% of consultant posts in the health service are held by women, even though two-thirds of doctors entering the profession are female. Women doctors also earn, in general, 18% less than male doctors.

Now the British Medical Association – which represents more that 140,000 doctors and medical students – is launching a new initiative called Women in Medicine to try to boost the number of women in senior medical posts.

Professor Bhupinder Sandhu, the chair of the BMA's equality and diversity committee, said: "Women have come a long way since the 19th century when they were not allowed to go to medical school. However, while equality between male and female doctors is relatively OK at the bottom end of the profession, getting into medical schools and the early jobs in medicine, there are still areas where women are not rising to senior positions.

Women doctors are massively under-represented in senior jobs in the NHS, universities and within the BMA and medical royal colleges...They are particularly under-represented in specialist roles such as emergency medicine and surgery, where fewer than 10% of consultants were female in 2006".'

- People who work only part-time will a) be less likely to be selected for promotion, and b) be paid less than those who work full-time

- Note that the BMA has an Equality and Diversity Committee to protect women and to preference women wherever possible. Almost all organisations have Equality and Diversity Committees to fulfil this Ideological pro-Feminist function. 'Equality and Diversity' constitutes one of Feminism's major Industries

- The reader will have noticed the Observer's intentionally misleading headline, using the word 'denied' (it is a *choice*, not a 'denial', not a discrimination). The word 'denied' is deliberately used to whip up a frenzy in Feminist-inclined women, to keep their anger on the boil. I refer the reader to Part Three

In 1999 the British Medical Journal *itself* (before it became infiltrated by the Feminist perspective) noted why fewer women were in senior positions:

> *'(Women) were less interested than male doctors in academic careers and top jobs and were more likely to dominate in fields like public health where the working hours fitted family responsibilities. "These data suggest that women doctors choose personal commitments at the expense of professional power".'[5]*

- Yet still the bigoted and Ideological interpretation of 'gender inequality' continues to be given. Feminism will not permit the truth, or a woman's rationally made choice, to stand in the way of its creating an inequality and discrimination issue

***

The majority of women choose to work part-time (or would if family finances permitted). They prefer and enjoy this work option. To support this view there is strong evidence from Booth and van Ours (among others) that mothers in part-time employment are happier at work than men and, more tellingly, happier than women who work full-time.[6]

A woman's culturally licensed choice to work part-time actually discriminates against men. It is the male partner who takes up the financial slack, provides the financial safety net for mothers to enjoy this privilege of part-time work and benefit from a healthy work-life balance; and have the pleasure of watching the child grow and develop.

- In addition, *part-time women* actually earn more on average than *part-time men*.[7]

Women Choose not to Work Unsocial Hours

One way Feminism converts the pay gap into an inequality is to compare men and women's *hourly* earnings; But like comparing men and women's full-time work, this is a deceitful strategy; like is not being compared with like, because women choose not to work *unsocial hours*.

Unsocial hours includes shift work and overtime. Shift work involves working in the evening or during the night (if anyone has worked regularly 'on nights' then they know that it is an unattractive working arrangement); overtime involves working in the evenings, at weekends, on bank Holidays and national holidays. *Shift work and overtime are paid at a much higher hourly rate than ordinary hours;* this can be a 100 per cent higher rate. So if far fewer women than men work unsocial hours, then 'women's average hourly wage' will be much less than 'men's average hourly wage'.

- Working unsocial hours not only produces a higher average hourly wage, it also increases a person's chances of promotion. When women choose not to work unsocial hours they are also choosing to avoid promotion

> *'These data are important in understanding the oft-cited claim of a 'glass ceiling' for women. Promotion in high-powered professional jobs often goes to those who have put in long hours in evenings and on weekends. Husbands are more likely to do this than wives.'[8]*

> *'Over a lifetime women earn £300,000 less than men'*
>
> (Feminist mantra)

WPC WINS NEW DEAL FOR SHIFT WOMEN

(The Sunday Times, 20 May, 2001)

'Women police officers have won the right in a legal test case to refuse to walk the beat if it clashes with their childcare.

An employment tribunal has ruled in favour of a WPC who said she could not work shifts that conflicted with her childcare arrangements.

Beat work can involve antisocial shifts as well as irregular and long hours if for example, an officer becomes involved in dealing with a crime or serious incident.

The tribunal decided the Somerset force sexually discriminated against her because it failed to provide her with a suitable job.'

Working unsocial hours vastly increases a person's salary – and inflates their hourly rate of pay. Few women, compared with men, work unsocial hours. By working unsocial hours men connect less with their wives and their children, or if not married then they sacrifice socialising with their peers and lessen their chances of meeting members of the opposite sex.

***

The pay gap and the glass ceiling are not 'gender inequalities' or discriminations, they are fraudulent issues. They are a trade-off. They are an exchange for women choosing to work fewer hours than men, for women choosing to work part-time, for women choosing not to work unsocial hours.

Do a gender-switch. We could say that:

'By working longer and more unsocial hours men suffer a family/social life gap'

Or

'We need to know why men are being diddled out of having a social life,
diddled out of spending time with their children and friends'

Chapter 31
Women Choose to Work in Fulfilling Jobs

Not only do women seek a healthy work-life balance in the number of hours they choose to work, but they also choose careers and jobs that they find mentally and emotionally wholesome and healthy, which they enjoy, and from which they can gain fulfilment and satisfaction.

In all the major first world countries women are *happier* in their work than men. And when career *satisfaction* is measured women also beat men hands down. An Australian study found that women working more than 60 hours a week in 'caretaking roles' felt more fulfilled and gained more satisfaction than women who worked for more money between 40 to 60 hours each week.[1]

This study also found that women found caring for children fulfilling and healthy; that doing things that were perceived as for the 'public good' increased their well-being; that the average job was stressful if work was done for more than 40 hours each week; that they did not expect to be paid much for things that they found highly fulfilling.

Fulfilling work can make the concepts of 'living' and 'working' synonymous. If you find a job that you really enjoy doing so much that you would almost do it without pay then you will not have to 'work' for a living. If a workplace offers fulfilment, happiness and satisfaction then the level of pay is not so important as it would otherwise be.

- Converting this choice to be happy and fulfilled in your work into the inequalities of the pay gap and the glass ceiling, as Feminism does, is deceitful, it is playing Ideological politics

J. R. Shackleton, Professor of Economics and Dean of the Business school, University of East London, states:

> *'Men are more likely to state that career development and financial rewards are very important, and are much more likely to define themselves as very ambitious, while women emphasise job satisfaction, being valued by employers and doing a socially useful job.'*[2]

And,

WOMEN 'CHOOSE TO HAVE LOWER PAY THAN MEN'
(The Sunday Times, 6 April, 2003)

'The gap between men's and women's earnings is not caused by discrimination, according to new research. Instead women choose jobs that pay less because they want more flexible and socially useful careers.

They prefer careers such as teaching and nursing, where they can take an extended break to raise a family. These choices "affect women's wages even at an early stage of their career and are the single most important determinants of the gender wages gap", the report by Dr. Arnaud Chevalier and his team concludes.

Female students pick degree subjects such as education and the arts, which produce a lower mean wage than engineering, maths and computing, where most students are men.

> Women are also more likely to work in smaller firms, in the public sector, or on temporary contracts, where pay is usually lower.
>
> Part of the gap is explained by different attitudes. Just over half the women stressed the importance of a socially useful job.'

So by focussing on a preference to seek (or remain in) a socially worthwhile and fulfilling job women have *freely chosen* to earn less, and are less likely to lose this enjoyable job and work environment by seeking promotion out of it, so there will be fewer women in senior posts.

Women Choose to Study Arts and Humanities

The leading academic, Arnaud Chevalier:

> *'Female students pick degree subjects such as education and the arts.'*[3]

Again,

> *'Women decide from as early an age as 17, when they choose their degree course, on how to combine work and motherhood.'*[4]

An earlier chapter dealt with this Feminist issue. I offer the reader a reminder of the consequences of this choice in the context of the pay gap. Women choose to work in jobs that are fulfilling and satisfying. So they choose to study subjects in areas that *lead* to these personal outcomes. Feminism, in creating issues to justify its existence, converts this personal interest and rational choice into an inequality.

GENDER PAY GAP

(The Times, Tuesday, 15 August, 2006)

> 'Men are more than twice as likely as women to earn top salaries within six months of graduating, the Higher Education Statistics Agency says. Men, with an £18,000 median starting salary, earn £1,000 a year more on average than their female peers, *partly because more women study arts subjects.*'

It has been shown that the majority of women are less ambitious in, and committed to, their work than are men. This is especially so for those in Arts- and Humanities-related careers:

> *'Arts students have lower career expectations and are less likely to apply to graduate recruitment schemes than those doing vocational subjects, research suggests.'*[5]

• Lower career expectations have negative consequences – in the form of lower pay and less seniority

Feminism tells us that young women are ignorant of the career options on offer (remember the Prosser Commission, for example)... whilst young men, presumably, are fully informed and make rational choices. This is simply not true. The tendency for women to choose to enter a fulfilling and satisfying job still holds when other careers are known about and considered (does Feminism seriously believe that young women with degrees don't know that there are different careers options? The Ideologues are once again treating women like infants while creating issues where no issues exist). Professor Shackleton confirms that women prioritise job fulfilment over high income:

'Even where women study a potentially high-earning subject at college, however – economics or sciences, say – they are still less likely than men to go into the higher-earning jobs to which these qualifications give access. For instance, while many young men with economics degrees go into the City, similarly qualified young women are more likely to pursue jobs in teaching, academic research or the civil service. Commentators such as Catherine Hakim would argue that these preferences are deeply rooted and not easily affected by governmental initiatives.'[6]

In addition, the London School of Economics study tracked 10,000 graduates from 30 universities between their 1993 graduation and their careers in the early 2000s. It found that there was a 12 per cent gender pay gap in the men's favour. Why? Two reasons:

Firstly, the women graduates were more likely to have studied education and the arts and the men engineering, mathematics and computing. Careers in engineering and where mathematics is important draw higher salaries than careers in education and the arts.

Secondly, there was the fulfilment factor:

'Just over half the women stressed the importance of a socially useful job, whereas men were almost twice as likely to stress salary...The LSE research concluded that once differences in fulfilment and flexibility were accounted for, there was only a 2 per cent remaining pay gap. In brief, the gender pay gap is better explained in terms of a "fulfilment gap".'[7]

***

JOB SUCCESS 'MEANS LESS TO WOMEN UNDER 35 THAN MEN'
(Daily Mail, Friday 10 April, 2009)

'Success at work means less to women in their 20s and early 30s than to men of the same age, say researchers.

Women also place satisfaction at home high up on their list of priorities, while it tends not to rank at all in the lists given by men, the report said.

The findings by a team at Bristol University...found that "women are prepared to accept different social and economic roles but work contributes less to overall happiness for women than it does for men. Women do not necessarily regard careers as unimportant to them, but they do have more than one priority".

The researchers concluded that the importance of a career was high for men "yet insignificant among women", adding: "It seems that the work sphere among women is less central in shaping their life satisfaction than in the case of men".'

• Studies in 'preference theory' shows that only 14 per cent of women are 'work-centred'. So, commitment to a career and 'the work sphere' is unimportant for 86 per cent of women

***

The pay gap and the glass ceiling are not examples of 'gender inequalities' or discriminations against women. It is not the fault of men that the majority of women choose fulfilling jobs over higher pay, and yet this is the Feminist implication. There is a trade-off. Less pay and less seniority are *exchanged* for a fulfilling and satisfying work and career experience, usually in a 'socially useful' job, or in the area of arts and humanities. This is a choice. And a freely made choice cannot, rationally, be converted and construed into an inequality issue. Yet Feminists have succeeded in doing this.

Do a gender-switch. It could be said that:

'Men suffer a work fulfilment and satisfaction gap'

Or

'We need to know why men are being diddled out of happiness, fulfilment and satisfaction in their working lives'

Chapter 32

Women Choose to Avoid Stressful Work

For the majority of women a high salary and a senior position are secondary to working shorter hours and to feeling fulfilled and enjoying a healthy and wholesome work-life balance. These preferences are expressed in choosing a comfortable work-related stress level, which obviously involves fewer responsibilities. Stress at work is a health hazard:

Occupational Suicide Data

(Information Resource Pack: The Samaritans, 2003)

Men age 20 – 64: 1991 – 1996 - 2,649 suicides

Women aged 20 – 59: 1991 – 1996 - 614 suicides

WORKER'S SUICIDE

(The Times, Thursday, 11 August, 2005)

'An overworked executive hanged himself because he could not stand the strain of staying in his office until 8pm every night, an inquest in Cullompton, Devon, was told. Nicholas McDermott, 34, a finance controller with an Exeter newspaper company, hanged himself from his attic steps. Verdict: suicide.'

- Work-related stress is a killer: but overwhelmingly for men

***

It is claimed by Feminists that women in the *same roles as men* are paid less. This claim is a fraud, it does not stand up to examination. In 1981 the American Bureau of Labour statistics surveyed professional, administrative, technical and clerical workers; all working in the same establishment, in the same field with the same job label. But they added on a crucial additional measure: *size of responsibility*. For example, rather than a buyer for a small boutique being compared with a national or international buyer for say, Marks and Spencer, *they compared buyers with equal-sized responsibilities*. They did the same exercise with managers. Significantly, they found that *where men and women had equal-sized responsibilities they received equal pay*.[1]

- Higher responsibility, of course, equates to greater stress. It would seem reasonable that those managers who have most responsibility ought to be paid more. However, Feminists believe that this is unreasonable:

THE WOMEN BOSSES 'FACING 57-YEAR WAIT FOR EQUAL PAY'

(The Daily Mail, Thursday, 19 August, 2010: Becky Barrow)

'Female managers will not match the salaries of their male colleagues until 2067, a report warns.

The study, by the Chartered Management Institute, says women have a 57-year wait before their take-home pay is equal to their male colleagues.

Petra Wilton, of the Chartered Management Institute, said: "Girls born this year will face the probability of working for around 40 years in the shadow of unequal pay. The prospect of continued decades of pay inequality cannot be allowed to become reality."

The institute is calling on the Government to begin "naming and shaming" firms which fail to pay their staff "fairly".

Sandra Pollock, of the Women in Management Network, raised her fears about the consequences of the pay gap between men and women. She said: "We want to inspire young women to reach the top, but how can we possibly expect them to want the top jobs if, despite doing the same role as male colleagues, they will be paid less?"'

- The Feminist cant and dogma coming from Petra Wilton and Sandra Pollock is matched by the presentation of the issue by the Daily Mail's Resident Feminist, Becky Barrow (all national newspapers reported the same item, with their Resident Feminists using similar inflammatory rhetoric; ('57 years' indeed...a lovely little Feminist sound-bite)

***

Higher salaries for male managers are due to their having greater responsibility (and accompanying stress), they are managers of large companies (not the managers of High Street shops) and their abilities and skills will attract top salaries. Once again, Feminism uses its devious strategy of not comparing like with like. The Feminist 'research' team in the Chartered Management Institute, in its desire to create an attention-grabbing issue, misleadingly compares only *titles* – 'a manager'. It does not compare *the size of responsibility or the degree of stress within these roles*. This is a deliberate deception, calculated to create an inequality where none exists.

- The Institute is obviously being used and manipulated by the Feminist organisation Women in Management Network (part of the Feminist Equality Industry). Here we have a supposedly respected organisation, the Chartered Management Institute, promoting Ideologically-inspired untruths. In this sense, the Institute could legitimately be called a Feminist non-governmental organisation

The Chartered Management Institute's claim is akin to the Wimbledon syndrome: 'We demand equal pay (prize money/salary) for doing less work with less stress and less responsibility' (playing fewer sets). Both winners will be labelled 'champions', but the male champion will have done almost twice as much work, played for many hours longer, undergone a great deal more mental stress and physical fatigue, than the female champion. Commercially, many more people pay to watch the male players than the female players. Yet they receive *exactly the same wage* (prize money). Crazy. Feminism has nothing to do with 'gender equality'.

- What message is this 'We Want Something For Nothing' Feminism sending out to today's young women? We could legitimately call today's Feminism 'Gimme, Gimme, Gimme' Feminism

- To be able to implement the fraud of Wimbledon is an example of the power Feminism has in modern Britain

The same linguistic sophistry of pretending to compare like with like (but deceitfully not actually doing so) is also used to create inequalities and discriminations in other professions:

WOMEN SOLICITORS LAG BEHIND MEN ON PAY
(The Times, 19 October, 1998)

'Women solicitors earn less than men and, at partnership level, the gap can be as much as £10,000, according to a survey by the Law Society.

Judith Sidaway, a senior Society research officer, carried out the study. She said: "They (women) were also more likely to be in firms that did legal aid work and were less likely to work in the larger firms".

The same factors accounted for the gap in earnings between male and female salaried partners, She added: "Women at this level were often in firms deriving more of their income from legal aid".

Ms. Sidaway said that salaries were also affected by the type of work with commercial work being best remunerated, although the trade-off was the very long hours involved in such work.

The worst-paid work was typically that of the smaller high street firm: legal aid conveyancing and probate, followed by family law and crime.

Women solicitors tended to specialise more than men and they chose what had become female "ghettoes" – the less lucrative areas of work such as personal injury and family law.'

- Notice the use of the phrase 'the trade-off". Fewer responsibilities, shorter hours, less stress: they are a fair trade-off for lower pay and less seniority. Such a trade-off is *not* an inequality

- Female managers are not getting paid less than male managers for *doing exactly the same job;* female solicitors are not getting paid less than male solicitors for *doing exactly the same job.* Feminism deliberately confuses and equates job 'titles' with day-to-day job *content* and its extent of *levels of responsibility and stress.* This political strategy is unethical, immoral and deliberately fraudulent (but widely used by Feminists)

Judith Sidaway is being refreshingly honest by identifying the reasons for female solicitors being paid less than male solicitors, and notes that the former prefer to work in their chosen area of law, an area in which they are interested and in which they feel most comfortable, fulfilled and satisfied...even though it draws less salary. Sidaway's gender-neutral honesty is not normally found in the media; however, it is a shame that the Ideologically-driven headline lessens her neutrality (but perhaps a Feminist editor was responsible?).

WOMEN ARE POORER BUT HAPPIER EMPLOYEES

(The Sunday Times, 2 March, 2003)

'The most comprehensive research undertaken into satisfaction in the workplace in the UK, published today as a 68-page supplement in The Sunday Times, debunks the theory that women feel universally discriminated against at work.

They are paid less than men and they occupy few of the top jobs, but women are not as stressed and are generally happier at work than their richer, more powerful male colleagues.'

So it isn't actually women themselves who feel discriminated against. Feminists are creating an inequality, converted out of women's choices, where no inequality actually exists, and where ordinary, non-Ideological women don't feel discriminated against. Pure Machiavellian politics.

And,

PROMOTION AT WORK MAY NOT BE A CAUSE FOR CELEBRATION

(Daily Mail, Monday, 1 April, 2009)

'Climbing the career ladder may be the goal of many employees but each step, it appears, can have a detrimental effect on mental health.

Researchers have found that promotion increases stress levels by up to 10 per cent – and gives up to 20 per cent less time to visit the doctor.

The increased pressure may come from heavier workloads, extra responsibility and reduced leisure time.

Economists and psychologists at the University of Warwick analysed 1,000 individual promotions between 1991 and 2005...Chris Boyce, who worked with Professor Andrew Oswald, said: "When it came to mental health we found that promotions actually make people feel more stressed – meaning promotions may not actually be good for your health."'

- Women have known this for a long time; so the majority have deliberately chosen *not* to seek promotion. There will naturally, then, be an under-representation of women in senior positions. This is also an important factor in women receiving less pay

- The phenomenon of fewer women in senior positions is not caused by some mythical 'barrier' called the glass ceiling but by women's own choices

Women Avoid Competition and Aggression at Work

In the same way that women tend to choose to avoid work that entails a large degree of responsibility and stress, they also tend to avoid work and jobs in which *competition* and *aggression* are central elements.

In the late 1980s Anne Moir and David Jessel undertook research in the field of men's and women's different attitude to work, later published in their book, Brainsex, in 1989.[2]

'As Moir and Jessel pointed out, "work, success and ambition simply mean different things to the different sexes". Work is not so consumingly important for women as it is for men. Even where women and men work alongside each other their attitude to work is different. Male academics, for example, get more papers published because of the greater male need for competition and achievement. Women are more interested in socially fulfilling work. Money isn't tied up with the female ego as it is with the male. Men will make great sacrifices in pursuit of power, status and success. Women won't.[3]

- And 'preference theory' confirms that only 14 per cent (or less) of women are 'work-centred'

An Equality Feminist, researching for her book on whether Feminism is any longer necessary, noted:

'I was surprised just how often women described a feeling of relief at dropping out of the working world (even temporarily) to concentrate on something which felt fundamentally both more important and more pleasant.[4]

In the same way that women tend to avoid work where competition is a characteristic (because they choose to avoid stressful situations, including highly responsible jobs in which hard-nosed negotiations and dismissing staff are integral characteristics) they are also reluctant to *request* pay rises and promotion:

'One landmark study is Babcock and Laschever's compendium of research 'Women Don't Ask' (2005) which showed how sex differences in earnings emerge soon after graduation from university because young men routinely negotiate higher starting pay, while most young women fail to do so. This sex difference in bargaining and negotiation over promotion, responsibilities and pay develops over time into a cumulatively sizable earnings gap in adult life – even among people who attended the same universities and have the same qualifications, including MBA graduates.'[5]

- Why do women *choose* not to negotiate for higher pay and promotion? Is it because they wish to avoid the anxiety and stress of doing so? Is it because they know that they will not be in the job for life? Is it because they are more interested in fulfilling work than high earnings? Whatever the reason, it is *their* choice not to negotiate; therefore the 'cumulatively sizable earnings gap' cannot, rationally, be an inequality

A further study in 2006 also found that women are reluctant to negotiate:

'A survey of more than 5,000 men and women rejected the common tendency to blame the "pay gap" on sex discrimination.

It claimed that the majority of Britain's 13 million female workers are horrified by the idea of having to seek a rise. The handful of women who had dared to ask for more admitted it was "the most stressful thing they had ever done". But men do not suffer from the same inhibitions, according to the research published by the women's magazine Grazia.

Jane Burton, the magazine's editor, said: "It has always been assumed that the pay gap was down to male discrimination against women workers. But our survey reveals that the fault could sometimes lie with women themselves for not having to courage to go and ask for what they are worth.

Jenny Watson, chairman of the Equal Opportunities Commission, insisted yesterday that closing the pay gap will take "far more than individual negotiations".

She said: "Wider action is needed from both government and businesses to transform the workplace and remove the barriers to the top which still stand in the way of too many women".'[6]

- Notice how the Feminist Jenny Watson obdurately insists that it is workplace barriers that are preventing women from earning higher salaries and from entering senior posts

- Here we have an example of a top-ranking Feminist dismissing a rational and proven explanation for the pay gap in order to allow her Feminist organisation to continue promoting the issue as an 'inequality'. Feminist Industries are 'issue dependent' and desperately require artificial inequalities to justify their existence and to continue to benefit from their Grievance Gravy-Train Industries (in this case the salaries of EOC personnel)

'In one US study eight times as many men as women graduating with master's degrees negotiated their salaries, adding an average of 7.4 per cent to their starting pay. This initial gap is likely to persist and grow over time. This is partly because women may have lower expectations.'[7]

Rosalind Coward, researching for her book, 'Sacred Cows: Is Feminism Relevant to the New Millenium?', found the following:

'Ambivalence about the working world was at the forefront of reasons women gave me for downgrading their careers and sticking with traditional sex roles at home. Women found careers especially difficult when they entailed the competitive promotion of self against others, or involved aggression as a normal part of the working environment.'[8]

It would seem, then, that the majority of women dislike a competitive working environment, and a working environment that entails aggression. And senior status jobs are, by their nature, competitive and aggressive...that is, stressful. So women avoid promotion.

***

The pay gap and the glass ceiling should *never* be referred to, or accepted as, examples of 'gender inequalities' or 'discriminations against women'. They are not. There is a trade-off, the result of women's choices - lower pay and fewer senior women in exchange for choosing a job with less stress and heavy responsibilities, for choosing to avoid jobs in which competition is a characteristic, for choosing not to negotiate for a higher salary or promotion.

Do a gender-switch. It could be said that;

'Men suffer from the low stress, less responsibility and mental health at work gap'

Or

*'We need to know why men who experience serious work-related stress
are being diddled out of their health and lives'*

261

Chapter 33

Women Choose to Avoid Promotion

We know that women's work ethic is different to men's. Women choose work options that lead to a comfortable, fulfilling and healthy work-life balance. Pay and promotion are not priorities. So women tend not to seek promotion as much as men:

'PROMOTION AT WORK MAY NOT BE A CAUSE FOR CELEBRATION: Climbing the career ladder may be the goal of many employees but each step, it appears, can have a detrimental effect on mental health...Researchers have found that promotion increases stress levels by up to 10 per cent – and gives less time to visit the doctor....increased pressure may come from heavier workloads, extra responsibility and reduced leisure time... "When it came to mental health we found that promotions actually make people feel more stressed – meaning promotions may not actually be good for your health".'[1]

In order to enhance their chances of finding fulfilling and satisfying work, with less stress and responsibility, women choose not to seek promotion. So if *fewer* women *put themselves forward* for promotion then there will naturally be *fewer* women *in* senior positions; the under-representation of women in senior positions also means fewer women earning top salaries, which is a further explanation of men's and women's pay differentials.

- Feminism converts the choice of women not to seek promotion into the 'gender equality' of the glass ceiling

MOST GIRLS JUST WANT TO HAVE FUN

(The Daily Telegraph, Friday, 28 March, 2008)

'"When you ask women what they want from work, they place great emphasis on the quality of their relationships at work and on working with people, not things", says Pinker: "An interest and an ability to contribute to a field are more powerful drivers for women, on average, than higher salaries, job security and benefits. Having a position of power is their lowest priority".

Last month a report in Economic Journal showed that women look lower down the career ladder in order to find jobs that allow them to spend time with their families. But Pinker believes that far from being systematically discriminated against, women are exercising a conscious choice by opting for a healthy work-life balance. And by being prepared to make financial sacrifices, they end up far happier in their jobs than men.

"Around 20 per cent of women are single-mindedly focussed on their careers and... will happily devote themselves completely to their job the way a man would and do just as well...but the majority of women have a broader view of happiness...that's not usually compatible with reaching the extremes of their professions.

There's an element of volition in women's choices that simply isn't being recognised", says Pinker. "The idea persists that women are victims who can't control their own destiny".'

- The reader will note the phrase, 'by being prepared to make financial sacrifices, they end up far happier in their jobs than men.' We saw further evidence of this in earlier chapters.

There is a trade-off: a happier working life in exchange for lower pay and the under-representation of women in senior posts

- Susan Pinker exposes a number of Feminist myths including Feminism's disrespect for women who make non-Ideological choices

**

To remind the reader of preference theory's three work-related models for women:

1. Family-centred: 17 per cent
2. Adaptive: 69 per cent
3. Work-centred: 14 per cent

We know that only 14 per cent of women are 'work-centred' and career-oriented (some put it at less than 14 per cent). However, even among *this* minority there is a large percentage who do not wish to seek promotion:

'A Government study this year found that more than 90 per cent of career women would rather spend time with their families than be promoted. The analysis, carried out by the Economic and Social Research Council, found that among women of professional standing, only 8 per cent would be prepared to push for higher status and better pay at the expense of family life.'(2006).[2]

- So even a majority of *career women* show little interest in seeking senior positions (which would indicate that women's work ethic is innate, rather than the result of socialisation and learned roles)

- 8 per cent of 14 per cent of 'work-centred' women represents an extremely small number of women who actually wish to seek promotion...about 1.3 percent of *all* women of working age. This fact alone explains why women are under-represented in top jobs – *only 1 in every 70 women are interested in seeking promotion*

- The glass ceiling is a Feminist-created myth concocted to justify Feminism's continued existence and to benefit its Grievance Gravy-Train Industries and personnel. We have all succumbed to this confidence trick

University-educated women, in addition to career women, also tend to avoid promotion. From an exhaustive analysis of the available research evidence on women's working patterns, histories and live goals from the 1970s onwards Catherine Hakim concluded that, contrary to Feminist rhetoric, women of all social backgrounds and educational levels actually choose to earn less pay than men and are not as interested in high status positions.[3]

'Why is it that despite increasing opportunities in education and jobs, women are still choosing different lifestyle priorities from men? It seems that they are simply using those opportunities differently. Hakim's three "preference groups" cut across class, socio-economic groupings and educational qualifications. A woman's set of personally chosen values seem to be much more important than her education or class background in determining her lifestyle.'[4]

**

LONG HOURS BACKLASH MEANS
FEWER FEMALE BOSSES

(Daily Mail, Wednesday, 8 November, 2006)

'The number of female directors in top companies has fallen this year – for the first time – as women reject the long hours culture. Jenny Watson, chairman of the Equal Opportunities Commission, said: "Women have made great strides in the workplace over the last 30 years. But the fact that still so few have reached the boardroom proves that the glass ceiling, though it might be cracked, has not yet broken". But Moira Benigson, founder of the research firm, said the problem is not that many women cannot break the glass ceiling – the invisible barrier to top jobs – but that they do not want to.

"The brightest and most talented get great jobs when they leave university, but many choose not to remain on the fast track. They do not stop working when they have families, but they choose less pressured jobs, often with smaller companies, which let them spend more time with their families".'

- The EOC was a Feminist non-governmental organisation dedicated to ferreting out and creating 'gender inequalities' in order to justify the Feminist Equality Industry

***

Essentially then, women simply avoid seeking promotion:

'Women can never hold half of the economically and politically powerful positions in the country if a greater proportion of women than men withdraw from competition for those positions.'[5]

Examples of Women Choosing to Avoid Promotion

Education:

- 'There is thus some evidence to support the view that women are less likely to apply for promotion, more willing to accept lower salaries and less likely to change jobs in order to advance...There was also some indication that women at this level (middle management) attached more importance than their male counterparts to "job content" and "satisfaction" than to job prospects.'[6]

- Women attach more importance to a fulfilling and satisfying job than they do to applying for senior positions

- 'Men appear to regard promotion as more desirable, and maybe inevitable, even in its own right. Women...are more likely to weigh the quality of the job they are doing at present against the benefits that any promotion might bring.'[7]

- Women weigh and consider the stress and responsibility levels of their present positions rather than seek the benefits of promotion (higher status and higher salary)

264

- 'One example demonstrates well how the focus of attention has shifted. Hilsum's and Start's study found a strikingly low promotion orientation among women teachers, based on their evidence that only 16 per cent of women teachers interviewed wanted headships compared with 51 per cent of men.'[8]

A 'strikingly low' desire to become a head teacher is found in female teaching staff...and yet we get Feminist-inspired headlines like the following:

WOMEN LOSE OUT ON CAREER AND PAY

**(Times Educational Supplement, Friday, 13 October, 2000:
Amanda Kelly and Karen Thornton)**

'Women teachers are losing out on pay and promotion to men throughout their (teaching) careers. New figures show women remain under-represented at head and deputy level, despite the increasing feminisation of the teaching force.

A conference of women heads of girls' schools branded the situation a "disgrace". After 10 to 14 years in primary teaching, 82.3 per cent of women have yet to make senior management, with more than a third still at point nine on the salary scale, the maximum without additional responsibility.'

- It has already been noted that women tend to reach the highest pay point possible consistent with not taking on extra stress and responsibility. Here we see female teachers choosing to stop advancing at the optimum point for a healthy and wholesome work-life balance. Sensible. But this rational choice ought not to be converted into a sexual political issue by Feminist head teacher Ideologues

- The reader will note the bigoted connotation of the headline. One would expect the TES to be gender-neutral in its reporting. One would expect the TES to question and analyse such Ideological rhetoric and cant. These head teachers' claims are driven by their commitment to Feminism's Ideological agenda. And it is *these* Feminist Ideologues, it needs to be noted, who are the *heads* of schools (indoctrinating their pupils?). Feminist bigotry is found at every socioeconomic level. I refer the reader to Part Three for the Feminist's personal and political need for anger

- Kelly and Thornton will be the TES's Resident Feminists; here we see them converting female teachers' freely made choices of not wishing to seek promotion into a 'gender inequality' on behalf of their movement, unquestioningly accepting the female head teachers' Feminist dogma (one never challenges one's own people)

'Former secondary head, Richard Fawcett, now works as a consultant to recruit heads. He says the decline in interest in headships is connected to rising responsibilities. "I know one head who works from 7 am to 8 pm", he says. "He takes Saturday off but works Sunday. Is this healthy?"(2006)'[9]

Women have a different work ethic to men: they choose to enjoy a healthy and wholesome work-life balance. They don't want the stress and the responsibility of a headship. Where's the 'disgrace', head teachers, in that?

BURDEN OF HEADSHIP LEADS
TO HUNDREDS OF VACANCIES

(The Times, Monday, 31 August, 2009)

'Schools in half of Britain's education authorities are without a head teacher a week before the new term begins, a survey by The Times suggests.

Experts fear that the approaching retirement of many head teachers, and a growing reluctance among senior staff to become school leaders, could prompt a management crisis.'

- Yes, there *are* many more female teachers than male – but they are not applying for the headships. This is a *personal choice,* it is not an inequality nor a discrimination

***

The Law:

TOP LAW FIRMS ARE FAILING TO
REWARD WOMEN WITH PARTNERSHIPS

(The Times, Friday, 4 May, 2007: Frances Gibb)

'Top women lawyers are being sidelined at Britain's leading City law firms, despite record numbers of solicitors being promoted to partnership, according to a new survey.

Inequality at the big firms is persisting, despite the heavy spending made by many to promote diversity in the workplace.

Martina Asmar, a partner at Herbert Smith and chair-woman of its inclusivity group, said: "More than half our graduates are women, but we share the problem that other City firms face of too many leaving before they reach the level at which they can be considered for partnership".

Fiona Woolf, president of the Law Society of England and Wales...said that the legal profession was losing a lot of women in mid-career. "The drop-out rate is more than double that in accountancy firms. Their rate of attrition is 10 per cent and ours is 25 per cent".'

- Notice how Frances Gibb, who was The Times' senior Resident Feminist, presents the issue - that law firms are 'discriminating/victimising/failing to reward' their female lawyers

- If women *choose* to 'drop out before they are considered for partnership status' then there will obviously be fewer women than men in senior positions, as senior partners. The female lawyer's choice to drop out is *not* a 'gender inequality', law firms are *not* failing to reward their female lawyers

FUSTY IMAGE AND POOR PAY
PUT WOMEN OFF BEING JUDGES
(The Times, Thursday, 8 January, 2009)

'Research published yesterday shows that highly qualified lawyers are put off from applying to be High Court judges because the job requires a big cut in salary and the lifestyle is seen as unattractive and lonely...It finds that women solicitors saw the High Court as "even more antediluvian" than commercial law in the City.

As well as the financial sacrifice, other deterrents include the high workload, the need to travel around the country and staying away from home for up to six weeks at a time.'

- So women solicitors actively choose not to apply to become High Court judges because they prefer not to 'travel around the country staying away from home for six weeks'. This personal preference and choice is *not* a 'gender inequality', as the under-representation of female judges is always interpreted as being, it is a sensible and rational decision

FAIR DEAL FOR JUDGES
(The Times, Thursday, 25 February, 2010)

'Women, gays, those from ethnic minorities and those with disabilities applying for jobs as judges should receive preferential treatment over white middle-class men to make the judiciary better reflect modern Britain, according to a report by the Ministry of Justice advisory panel on judicial diversity.'

- Those women receiving 'preferential treatment' will be drawn from the 14 per cent of 'work-centred' women, and are very likely to be Feminists. So 'preferential treatment for *women*' is a disguise, a ruse, for preferencing and privileging *Feminists themselves* (the 14 per cent of work-centred women). Preferencing Feminists plus directly discriminating against 'white middle-class men' (Feminism's arch-enemies); so a double whammy here. And another example of institutional man-hating

***

Medicine:

- Research in America in 1987 studied men and women on an undergraduate pre-medical course in order to examine why fewer women than men moved onto the next state of applying to the medical college. It found:

'The main reason for the higher female than male drop-out rate among undergraduates of average or below average ability and performance was low commitment to paid employment and a career as a major part of their adult lives; the alternatives of marriage, economic dependence and the housewife role were seen to be options for women but not for men.'[10]

- If more female than male students drop out then there will be fewer women on the medical course. This choice to drop out is not a 'gender inequality' or a discrimination

- *'A British Medical Association (BMA) poll has found that 58 per cent of doctors graduating in the UK in 2006 were female – up from 51 per cent in 1995. One in five female doctors said that they expected to work part-time for most of their careers, compared with 4 per cent of men.'[11]*

- Those who choose to work part-time are obviously *not* seeking promotion in their careers

  - *'Professor Black (President of the Royal College of Physicians) says: "We have very capable women who graduate well and have all the right intellectual characteristics to go on, but the top of the medical profession is not being filled with women....they are not coming through...There seems to be a period of their lives for many women where the life-work balance takes over, when they want to work much more flexibly, where they are not quite sure they are going to be able to juggle medicine".'[12]*

- Women physicians choose to enjoy a healthy and wholesome work-life balance rather than seek promotion. This choice has been converted by Feminism into the Ideological issue of the glass ceiling. Women are not being blocked from entering senior positions; there are no barriers, blocks or glass ceilings...these are all Ideological emotive mantras deliberately designed to glean public and political sympathy and to stir up anger in women

- Norway is one of the most 'progressive' societies in terms of sex equality; dual career families are the norm and official policy favours women in the workplace (as it does in Britain). Nevertheless, Elaine Showalter reported that despite liberal maternity leave, crèche facilities and funds for daycare, Norwegian women doctors were still not competing equally for leadership roles in hospital medicine, public health, academic medicine or private health care:

  'They were less interested than male doctors in academic careers and top jobs and were more likely to dominate in fields like public health where the working hours fitted family responsibilities. "These data suggest that women doctors choose personal commitments at the expense of professional power", she wrote.'[13]

- There is *no* glass ceiling. Women's work ethic is different to men's, they prefer, prioritise and choose other options rather than a high salary and seniority status

- Catherine Hakim looked at the differences between male and female pharmacists:

  '...women had the same qualifications as their male colleagues, but markedly different work patterns. Male pharmacists see their work as a platform to launch into self-employment or management, whereas women see it as a flexible, mother-friendly, part-time employment with no responsibilities to interfere with those of the family.'[14]

***

To repeat a quote:

'A Government study this year found that more than 90 per cent of career women would rather spend time with their families than be promoted. The analysis, carried out by the Economic and Social Research Council, found that among young women of professional standing, only 8 per cent would be prepared to push for higher status and better pay at the expense of family life.'[15]

Widening women's choices was a key aim of Equality Feminism, and this aim was achieved in the 1980s. But for Feminism success is never enough. So the inequality of the glass ceiling needed to be created and promoted in order to justify and perpetuate the Movement, and for Feminists to benefit from this continuation, personally and Ideologically.

Feminists blame the glass ceiling on men. It is a major Feminist anti-male issue. Yet the glass ceiling is a myth. In addition to its misandrous function, the widespread belief in this myth has prepared the political mindset into accepting the implementation of quotas and positive discrimination. A huge Feminist Fraud.

The glass ceiling, like the pay gap, should *never* be accepted as an example of a 'gender inequality', a discrimination against women; it should never be used to justify preferential treatment and policy-favouritism.

Postscript

Whilst revising this chapter I came across the following two articles:

SMASHED THROUGH THE GLASS CEILING? WATCH OUT FOR THE GLASS CLIFF!

(Daily Mail, Wednesday, 22 December, 2010: Becky Barrow)

'Women who break through the "glass ceiling" were warned yesterday that they will face another obstacle – the "glass cliff".

A major research project found high-flying career women who succeed in roles traditionally done by men are particularly vulnerable to losing their job, and seen as "unreliable" and "less competent".

One of the report's authors, Victoria Brescoll, from Yale University in the U.S., said the findings highlight "the fragility of women in the top jobs and how small mistakes can be "particularly damaging".

The research, published by the Association for Psychological Science, is a blow for women who had hoped that their main struggle was to break through the glass ceiling. In fact, this is only the first struggle, and another struggle lies ahead in just being able to keep their job.

Dr. Brescoll said: "There is an effect called the glass cliff. You don't really know, when you're a woman in a high status leadership role, how long you're going to hang on to it. You might fall off at any point".'

This newly-created discrimination was also 'discovered' by Michelle Ryan and her colleagues at Exeter University:

WOMEN, WATCH OUT FOR THE GLASS CLIFF

Companies in crisis often hire a woman boss – to take the rap: Carly Chynweth reports

(The Sunday Times, 20 February, 2011)

'Women appointed to senior roles at struggling companies are usually hired to act as scapegoats, not to turn things round, according to new research into the "glass cliff... Of course, it is not that men don't get appointed to these positions, it is just that women are appointed to them disproportionately".'

Feminists are gearing up for positive discrimination and quotas (to place more Feminists in senior positions) to be forced upon businesses with legislation to follow if businesses refuse to be bullied. These 'free' top jobs for Feminists will need to be 'protected'. So Feminist 'research' needs to seek out new discriminations and inequalities to *replace* the glass ceiling as an issue. Feminism is 'issue-dependent' with new grievances always having to be found to justify its existence, to keep its Grievance Gravy-Train Industries in business, to progress its Quiet Revolution and to spread misandry.

- The reader need not be awed or impressed by the word 'research' when its 'findings' just happen to promote an Ideological cause. The later chapter on Cheating and Lying: The Deceit of Feminist 'Research' explains why

The new 'glass cliff' issue has four Ideological functions:

- It acts as an alternative, a replacement inequality and discrimination, for when the glass ceiling is broken by positive discrimination legislation

- When the glass ceiling has been dismantled by legislation men, the patriarchy, will still need to be blamed; the new 'glass cliff' discrimination keeps Feminism's misandry in place

- The 'glass cliff' neatly absolves Feminists in senior positions from any personal responsibility for a business's failure ('the business was failing anyway')

- The 'glass cliff' issue is intended to deter senior males from critically appraising top Feminists' job performance (once they have been shoehorned and preferenced into these top jobs) allowing them to stay *in situ* even though they may be incompetent

MALE LAWYER WINS £123,000 IN SEX DISCRIMINATION CLAIM

(The Daily Telegraph, Wednesday, 19 May, 2010)

'A lawyer on maternity leave was protected from losing her job because her bosses were afraid they would be sued and made redundant her male colleague instead, a tribunal heard...Eversheds law firm in Leeds "inflated" the assessment of Angela Reinholz, 40, to stop her being made redundant over concerns she would launch legal action, the Leeds employment tribunal heard.'

- Businesses have been running scared of Feminist power since the early 1990s

Chapter 34

Women Choose 'Women's Work'

There are two types of job segregation – vertical segregation and horizontal segregation. Vertical segregation is obviously of a hierarchical nature, managers tend to be men while secretaries tend to be women. The numerous reasons for women being under-represented in senior positions have been addressed. Horizontal segregation is the phenomenon of typical 'men's work' and typical 'women's work'; for example, more men are lorry drivers and more women are nursery nurses. Men and women are concentrated in different types of work, different occupational areas. This chapter looks at how Feminists find inequalities and discriminations in work segregation.

***

Typical 'women's work' is a big deal for Feminists because it pays less than 'men's work'. They seriously believe that 'the system' (the patriarchal system/culture) has:

- Socialised and sex stereotyped women to choose jobs in typical 'women's work'

- And this 'women's work' is *deliberately* targeted as an area in which to pay low wages – simply because these jobs are inhabited by *women*

• In other words, women are intentionally singled out for discrimination in order to oppress them, and also to make them financially dependent on men

I'm not making this up. This paranoia is a long-standing Ideological theory and is so strange that I felt it needed heavy referencing.[1] For example, the Socialist Feminist, Sheila Rowbotham:

'Every woman in the labour force in capitalism doing "women's work" has had the views of both male domination and the white ruling class imposed upon her...the nature of her exploitation at work is exactly the same as that of all lower-class workers.'[2]

And Valerie Bryson notes in her Feminist Political Theory:

'For radical feminists, women are economically exploited as women...The exploitation of their labour both in the paid workforce and in the home is but one dimension of their oppression by men...More specifically, the well-documented lower pay and marginalisation of women in advance capitalist economies is seen as a means of maintaining women's dependence upon men and hence forcing them to service their domestic and sexual needs.'[3]

Again,

'Women enter the labour market from a position of subordination which is both reflected and reinforced by their conditions of employment....dominant attitudes label any work done by women as inherently inferior to that done by men.'[4]

• I refer the reader to Part Three

Coincidentally, it was only a few days before completing this chapter that I was in a long discussion on the subject of equal pay with a Feminist copy-editor. She is a well-educated woman and has worked in her profession for many years. She was insistent that 'women's work' was intentionally targeted by 'the system' in order to pay women less than men.

***

Feminists complain that women are *deliberately* segregated into what they often term as 'women's ghettoes'. We have seen how Feminism has introduced policies and initiatives in an attempt to re-socialise young women into entering 'men's work and careers'; for example, dissuading them from being interested in the arts and humanities and pushing them into studying mathematics and the sciences. And we have seen how these attempts at social engineering have consistently failed.

Yes, women *do* congregate in women's occupations, but these are self-selected; women *wish* to enter them, and freely *choose* to enter them. 'Women's work' jobs are so attractive to women that there is strong competition for them. They are in demand. Why?

Occupations that employ more than 90 per cent of women almost always have in common many appealing characteristics that suit women's general work ethic and work-life preferences, values, beliefs and attitudes. Because these jobs are so desirable for many women then the employer need not offer a high wage – there will always be a queue of women waiting for a job. It's a fact of life in a capitalist society that the economic law of supply and demand operates in all areas of business and employment. Where there is a high demand for certain types of jobs then the wages will be low in those jobs. For example, during the 1920s and 1930s the law of supply and demand kept men's wages low, especially in the industrial areas such as the North East and South Wales, because there were many men chasing few jobs. The law of supply and demand has nothing to do with sex discrimination. It cannot be converted into the oppression of 'the patriarchal system' targeting 'women's work' in order to intentionally pay women less than men. Such a conversion is Feminist paranoia.

***

What are the appealing characteristics that make occupations attractive and desirable to women? Many have already been mentioned but a repetition in the context of 'typical women's work' being deliberately targeted for low pay is relevant – simply to prove that this Ideological claim is nonsense. They include:

- Physical safety: the safety of a receptionist compared with a fireman
- An ability to switch off from the job at the end of the working day: a department store assistant compared with the manager of a busy city pub
- A healthy working environment: a secretary compared with a deep-sea fisherman
- Low stress: a shop assistant compared with an inner-city policeman (especially when on night duty)
- Social hours: an infant school teacher compared with a British Gas engineer, or a security guard on call 24/7
- No demand to work away from home: a dental hygienist compared with an oil-rigger

- High fulfilment: a child care professional compared with a fork-lift truck driver
- Contact with people: a restaurant waitress compared with a night security guard
- A comfortable working environment: a library/teaching assistant compared with a skilled machine operator in a noisy factory
- Shorter commuting time: a local supermarket cashier compared with an IT worker who may have to travel many miles for an IT-specific job. Many more men than women have to commute to their place of work, and further than female commuters. Men commute, on average, an hour a day longer than women[5]
- No stress, little responsibility, a low commitment to the job as a 'career'
- School-friendly hours

A higher number of these characteristics in a job makes these jobs desirable. They have all the ingredients that are attractive to the 69 per cent of 'adaptive' women. They 'fit' women's wants and needs, their interests and attitudes, their preferences, goals and work-life balance choices. It is Feminist mischief-making to claim that women are somehow socialised/sex stereotyped into 'women's work'...and then, when they have been *deliberately* segregated, to *deliberately* pay them low wages. This is a paranoid, malign and misandrous Feminist belief. Yet it is this Ideological perspective that continues to influence governments' gendered social policies in today's Britain, rather than the research work of gender-neutral and objective academics who have no Ideological agenda to pursue.

***

'The most important reasons for the "gender gap" have little to do with employer bias. Increasingly, the gap is the result of choices women make as they seek to maximise their own happiness and achieve a broad mix of life goals.'[6]

And an observation from the Equality Feminist Jane Bryant Quinn:

'In the 1960s, when women first muscled into the workforce, at-home mums all but apologised for what they did. But once those same boomer women started families, staying home with the kids became the preferred thing to do.... "A lot of women my age don't feel a big need to work because they know they can if they want to", says mother-of-two, Barnard College economic professor Dian Macunovich: "Women are using their earnings to buy back personal time...A higher proportion of women are choosing 'women's work', such as nursing and teaching. It's no coincidence that these jobs offer many options for part-timers (2000)".[7]

- Being attractive, desirable and in demand, it is also 'no coincidence' that 'women's work' is paid less than 'men's work'

In addition to women choosing work that has many attractive characteristics there is also a *very strong preference* in women to work with their own sex; this preference is a factor of 4 greater than men.[8] So women, of their own free will, seek to congregate in 'women's work' and because of high demand these jobs draw lower pay.

***

I have already referred to Catherine Hakim of the London School of Economics. Hakim, a leading world authority on women's employment since the 1980s, has undertaken and published a great deal of research on the subject. The following is taken from one of her research studies and identifies many of the critical reasons why women earn less than men, and why women seek 'women's work'. It does, in fact, encapsulate many of the points made in this Section.

Grateful Slaves and Self-made Women: Fact and Fantasy in Women's Work Orientations

'*ABSTRACT: Although job segregation concentrates women in the lowest status and lowest paid jobs in the workforce women are disproportionately satisfied with their jobs. This paper assesses the strength of women's work commitment in Western industrial societies, and finds it to be markedly lower than men's work commitment. Work commitment is also found to be a powerful predictor of women's work decisions and job choices. The majority of women aim for a homemaker career in which paid work is of secondary or peripheral importance. A majority of women are not committed to work as a central life goal, achieving jobs at higher levels of status and earnings.*

For women, any minimally reasonable job will do, because aspirations and efforts are focused in other life domains...success or failure in that sphere becomes both unimportant and easily satisfied. In contrast, men seek more substantial rewards from the work domain which is their main life activity. Most working women with families want jobs with no worries or responsibilities.

Hanson, Martin and Tuch's study is useful in pointing out that rewarding jobs are often also demanding jobs, and that some people may actively prefer jobs which involve a less than total personal investment. Women with children are popularly held to be the largest group numerically but there are others. Writers, musicians, actors and artists who must support themselves with other jobs, are ready examples.

Women's work orientations involve a short-term perspective, with little concern for long-term promotion prospects, and a high preference for work they enjoy.

Among part-time workers with low work commitment who are working primarily for the extra income for the family, convenient hours are more important than good pay. Part-timers are more likely than full-timers to feel very satisfied with their jobs, the key contributing factors being their easy journey to work, part-time work hours and the friendly people they work with, with higher satisfaction on these factors than is felt by full-timers on any aspect of their jobs.

This is a research finding that feminists and trade unionists have difficulty accepting.

Women's job preferences emphasise convenience factors over the high pay and security of employment conventionally valued by men. This explains women's high satisfaction with the casualised and low-paid jobs on the periphery.

More generally, this also explains women's very high satisfaction with part-time jobs in preference to full-time jobs...a research finding that trade unions and some women academics have long found difficult to accept as real and valid.

The degree and pattern of job segregation in any country are historically determined, but the persistence of job segregation from now on should be regarded as a reflection of women's own preferences and choices...rather than the outcome of patriarchal systems and male social control.'[9]

- Hakim's non-Ideological work, and the research of other non-Ideological academics, (including A. Booth, A. Chevalier, J.C. van Ours and J.R. Shackleton) contradict Feminism's Ideologically-driven assertion that one of the main reasons women earn less than men is because job segregation is the result of 'the system' stereotyping them into certain types of job and then deliberately paying these 'typical women's' jobs less than 'typical men's' jobs. This is the 'patriarchal system' and 'male social control' (to which Hakim refers) – the Feminist patriarchal plot paranoia

It is no surprise to find that Feminists, the Feminist Academic Industry and trade unions have difficulty accepting Hakim's (and other's) findings; these findings do not fit the Feminist (patriarchal) Ideology ('women are victims of men'). And, being 'Issue Dependent', these people need to seek out or create and conjure inequalities, discriminations and oppressions, in order to justify Feminism's continuing existence. Feminists, absolving women from any personal responsibility for their choices, and determined to spread misandry, need someone or something to blame for women entering the relatively lower paid 'women's work'. The target is men.

> 'Why do jobs in female-dominated sectors attract lower pay? The chief answer lies in the gendered nature of "skill". Skills that are traditionally associated with women are undervalued and men's are overvalued in comparison... As Phillips and Taylor point argue, women's work is deemed inferior simply because women do it.'[10]

- We need to ask whether paranoia is an additional characteristic of the Feminist's psychological make-up

Chapter 35

Women Choose to Avoid 'Men's Work':
The Unhealthy and Dangerous Jobs

We have looked at 'women's work' and seen why it attracts low pay. In this chapter we look at 'men's work' and see why it attracts higher pay. In addition to women's work ethic of choosing jobs, careers, and work options that offer an emotionally and mentally healthy and wholesome work-life balance (shorter hours, less responsibility, less stress, not working unsocial hours, not seeking promotion...) women also choose to avoid *physically uncomfortable, unhealthy and dangerous working conditions.*

The Glass Cellar

One further reason why men are paid more than women is because it is they, overwhelmingly, who do the dirty, unpleasant and dangerous jobs in society:

> *'It is rarely discussed in the debate over the pay gap, but part of the explanation for men's higher average pay could well be that there is a compensating differential for less attractive working conditions. Men are more likely to work outside in all weathers. They are more likely to work unsocial hours. Thirty-six per cent of male managers work more than 48 hours a week; the figure for women managers is only 18 per cent. Men suffer much higher rates of industrial injury.'[1]*

- It is *only men* who inhabit the 'glass cellar' jobs and it is these jobs that are paid comparatively higher 'compensating differential' wages. By avoiding the nasty unhealthy jobs women *choose* not to take advantage of this differential

- Women forfeit higher pay in exchange for a healthier work environment

In our perverse wish and desire to believe that women suffer from 'gender inequalities' and discriminations we forget that there is more to a job than simply how much it pays. Women *choose* to avoid dirty, unhealthy, physically demanding work environments...and the concomitant higher pay.

The American Jobs Rated Almanac ranked 250 jobs from best to worst.[2] It based the ranking on the following criteria:

salary * stress * work environment * outlook * security * physical demands

It found that 24 of the first 25 worst jobs were almost entirely male jobs. Examples included truck driver, sheet-metal worker, scaffolder, boilermaker, deep-sea fisherman, refuse-collector, construction worker, iron-founder, coal miner, sewage worker.

- All the worst jobs were inhabited 95 per cent to 100 per cent by men.

On 26 November, 2006, Sky News ran a story which listed the results of a survey carried out by the Discovery Channel's programme, Hard Labour, to find the ten worst jobs. Rankings were made according to the likelihood of *accidental death* or *injury*, *working hours*, *skill levels* and *difficulty* as well as *mental and physical stress*. The worst jobs were:

London cabbie * trawlerman * lumberjack * demolition worker * miner * oil rig labourer * aircraft carrier flight deck officer * abattoir worker * scaffolder * railway maintenance engineer

- These jobs are almost wholly undertaken by men. This gendered fact was not mentioned on the programme; it would have been too politically incorrect to have made such a point

***

Feminism wants State intervention to ensure that an equal number of women as men are in senior positions; as MPs, judges, directors, senior managers. It demands social engineering to remedy the 'gender inequality' of female under-representation in the top jobs, for example:

FIRMS MAY BE GIVEN QUOTAS FOR WOMEN STAFF
(The Sunday Times, 9 May, 2004)

'Labour is to bring in a new anti-discrimination regime that will impose a fresh "duty" on employers to promote equality between men and women, leaked cabinet papers reveal.

In a letter to John Prescott, the chairman of the cabinet domestic affairs committee admits that ministers have acted under pressure from women's rights activists.

"I believe that we should now signal our intention to take practical steps to introduce a duty to promote equality of opportunity between women and men, for which there is strong and mounting pressure from the women's lobby and the Equal Opportunities Commission", she said.

Catherine Hobbs, a senior lecturer in equal opportunity law at East London University, said the moves by the government heralded the introduction of positive discrimination forced on Britain by Brussels: "There's very much an acceptance that positive discrimination is the only way...some people call it reverse discrimination but it's the same thing – you're discriminating against the white male for the greater good".'

- Note the Stalinesque phrase: 'You're discriminating (against the white male) for the greater good'. Feminism is an unscrupulous, man-hating Ideology that uses totalitarian methods to discriminate against men and to preference, privilege and policy-favour women (where these happen to coincide with its Ideology and agenda). We know that it will be Feminists *themselves* who will fill these quota top jobs

- The reader will observe the political power that 'women's rights groups and lobbyists' enjoy; they were *especially* politically powerful and influential during the post-1997 Labour/Feminist Governments

***

Do a gender-switch. As only men inhabit the 'glass cellar' ought we to have a Commission set up to ascertain how best to implement quotas and positive discrimination to ensure that 50 per cent of all the dirty, unhealthy and demanding 'glass cellar' jobs in Britain are inhabited by women? For example, let's have the same number of women as men cleaning out the sewers.

One commentator neatly captures this Feminist double standard:

> 'Squeaking excitedly about equal opportunity with men, they battered at the imagined doors of male privilege, from which many a male would gladly escape if he could. Of course, the male "privilege" of having to work for a living was only disputed by women in areas selected by themselves. Few insisted on being allowed to go rat-catching in the sewers under London. Instead they clamoured for the equal right to be...Captainess of the Queen Elizabeth.'[3]

- Sometimes the stench of Feminism's double standards and hypocrisy is overpowering. Reader, whenever you hear the phrase 'glass ceiling', think of the 'glass cellar'

> 'McNabb (1989) finds that, controlling for human capital variables, manual workers obtain a wage premium for inconvenient hours, job insecurity and unfavourable working conditions.'[4]

MINERS WAIT FOR COMPENSATION
(The Daily Telegraph, Tuesday, 4 March, 2008)

'Former miners have been forced to wait more than 10 years for Government compensation for pit-related illnesses, a committee of MPs said yesterday.

Some died while their claims were being processed because ministers underestimated the size of the project.

There have been about 762,000 claims so far for almost £4.1 billion.'

- There are *no* female coal miners. Women choose to avoid working in the worst jobs. They therefore choose to forfeit the 'worst jobs pay premium'

***

It may be argued that women cannot physically undertake many of the 'glass cellar' jobs. OK, which ones? This Feminist argument is nonsense. Feminism demanded, and was granted, the right for women to enter the fire service as 'firefighters' (as all firemen now have to be called). The same level of physical strength and fitness that a 'glass cellar' job requires will be at the same level as that required of a fireman. So there is no rational reason, no excuse, why women cannot be conscripted into the 'glass cellar' jobs.

The only difference is that a firefighter is a glamorous job (so it is acceptable to Feminism) whereas the 'glass cellar' jobs are dirty, nasty, and unhealthy (these are not acceptable to Feminism...so they don't want them). Feminist hypocrisy again: 'Pick 'n' Mix' Feminism – 'we'll have some of that nice equal pay...but we don't want any of that nasty dirty, long-hours work'.

But for the sake of argument let's assume that women are *not* physically capable of undertaking the 'glass cellar' jobs. Then in that case Feminists have no right to complain that women's pay is less than men's pay; men benefit from the 'unhealthy and dangerous compensatory differential', the wage premium, and women do not.

- If Feminists are not prepared to be Coal Mineresses, Scaffolderesses, Seweresses but choose only to be Captainesses, then they should not cite the pay gap and 'glass ceiling' as inequalities and discriminations

Feminism takes the *positive consequences* of men's choices and compares them with the *negative consequences* (defined by Feminists, not ordinary women) of women's choices and calls these differences 'gender inequalities'. This is a confidence trick, a fraud, that has gulled the British public and policy-making fraternity for three decades. Shame on us.

Women Choose to Avoid Work that is Dangerous

It has been noted that it is overwhelmingly men who work in the nasty, dirty, unhealthy jobs in society. Taking this a stage further we see that 'men's work' is also much more *hazardous* and *dangerous* than 'women's work'.

- In the summer of 2010 thirty-six Chilean miners were trapped underground for many weeks. All were men. When the Twin Towers collapsed on 9/11 scores of rescue workers were killed, attempting to save others. All were men.

Men might not be *legally* drafted into the most hazardous and dangerous jobs, but they are *psychologically* and *culturally* drafted. Whereas women provide a womb to create the children, men provide the financial womb to *support* the children (women prefer to work part-time, and fewer hours than men). Many men, especially those without an education or qualifications, are motivated to enter the death professions to provide this financial womb. So the motto of the death professions could be: 'My body, not my choice.'

- Many men are *enslaved* by their need to produce a monthly salary; by their need to fulfil their family responsibilities. Courtship...leads to marriage...leads to children...leads to...

'Pretty girls dig graves'

(Jack Kerouac: Dharma Bums)

NEWSFLASH: September 2011; 'Trapped Welsh miners found dead...a friend of one said: "He just wanted to do good for his family. People don't go mining for fun, they do it because they have to and the risks are still there".'

'Many men are sacrificed on the altar of full-time, continuous, unhealthy and dangerous work'

(Swayne O'Pie)

***

The following is taken from the Employment Gazette:[5]

'The fact that virtually all employee fatal injuries are to men reflects their employment in the riskier occupations.

For the self-employed, all fatal injuries and over 98% of major injuries were to men.'

***

In the summer of 2005 I wrote to the huge GMB union to ask for their statistics on work-related fatalities and serious injuries. Their Health and Safety Officer, Simon Reed, replied enclosing the following:

Men	Fatal	Non-fatal/Major
2001	202	21,033
2002	175	21,192
2003	176	20,929
2004	161	22,512
Women		
2001	4	6,977
2002	7	7,233
2003	7	7,183
2004	7	8,152

Simon Reed's reply continued:

'Table 30 shows that there are marked differences between the injury rates for employed men and women...The all-industry fatal injury rate for men in 1999/01 was 2.7 and less than 0.05 for women... Major and over-3-day injury rates for women are almost invariably less than half the rates for men, who are more likely to be found in the higher risk occupations.'

- The GMB (as do all trade unions) demands that women receive equal pay to men – regardless. Trade unions disregard the dangerous job pay premium and demand that women be paid the same as men. We know that trade unions are Feminist non-governmental organisations, embracing the Feminist Ideology, promoting the Feminist agenda

J.R. Shackleton is Professor of Economics and Dean of the Business School, University of London. He observes:

'In 2006/7, men were two and a half times more likely than women to suffer a major injury at work. Davies et al (2007) find evidence for a significant compensating pay differential for the risk of major accidents in, for example, process, plant and machinery occupations in the UK. Grazier (2007) finds a similar result for risk of death across a wider section of the employed population.'[6]

***

The Feminist Fawcett Society regularly poses the question: 'Where are the Women' (in senior posts, for example, in Parliament and boardrooms). Do a gender-switch: 'Where Are The Women In The Glass Cellar?' Consider all the above statistics and all hell would break loose if it were *women* who were being systematically seriously injured or killed in their work; there would be media and political uproar.

Consider the following examples, and imagine the furore if it were women who were the victims of these deadly jobs:

'Dangerous job that claims 20 lives a year. Fishing is one of Britain's most dangerous occupations with the sea claiming more than 20 lives each year. The last decade was the worst – a total of 223 men died when their boats capsized, collided, sank in rough weather or became trapped by underwater obstructions (2000).'[7]

And,

'Three workers were taken to hospital after 15 floors of scaffolding at the site of the Jury's Inn Hotel in Milton Keynes "came down like a pack of cards" and trapped them (2006).'[8]

Again,

THREE BUILDERS DIE IN CONCRETE TOMB
(Daily Mail, Monday, 8 May, 2006)

'Three workmen were buried alive in quick-drying concrete in a horrific accident on a building site.

Scaffolding they had been standing on collapsed, sending them tumbling into the rapidly setting mixture, which then pulled the men in like quick-sand.

Other workers used pickaxes and hammers to try to get them out, but their desperate rescue efforts failed.

Fire chief Eric Baum said: "These people were basically buried alive in concrete. There was nothing we could do for them. It is tragic".'

- 'Where are the Women' in these occupations, Sisters of the Fawcett Society? Feminist organisations and individual Feminists are hypocritically silent regarding the comparative health and safety of male and female jobs; Feminists conveniently and deliberately 'forget' that there are many more factors involved in a job than what it pays

***

Feminists present the pay gap and the glass ceiling as 'gender inequalities' and 'discriminations against women'. They are not, and should never be accepted as such. Women's lower pay and fewer women in senior positions are trade-offs: women *choose* to exchange lower pay for not working in dirty, unpleasant, uncomfortable, unhealthy, hazardous and dangerous jobs. The majority of people would consider this to be a fair and just exchange.... if they had not been influenced by Feminist propaganda constantly telling them that lower pay for women is a 'gender inequality'.

So the 'pay differential' for undertaking the hazardous and dangerous jobs in society is a further reason why men earn more than women. A small price to pay to avoid a work-related serious injury or premature death. In this sense, women freely choose to earn less than men...in exchange for working in a much cleaner, healthier and safer work environment. To interpret this as a 'gender inequality', a 'discriminatory pay gap', is fraudulent and immoral – and disrespectful to all those men who have suffered injury or death to undertake these dangerous but necessary jobs.

Do a gender-switch. It could be said that:

'Men suffer from the nice, clean, healthy and safety at work gap'

Or

'We need to ask why working men are being diddled out of healthy bodies and out of their lives'

Chapter 36
The Pay-Off for the Pay and Promotion Gap

This Section is drawing to a close. All the evidence points to the pay gap not being an inequality, and to the 'glass ceiling' being a myth. Yet Feminists, their sympathisers, and Male Feminists, *still* declare that every organisation, company and business should be compelled to undertake a pay audit so that Feminists can ascertain by how much women are being paid less than men and then, presumably, present more policies to governments demanding action to remedy the negative consequences (as they interpret them) of women's choices.

'Derek Simpson of Amicus said in 2006: "The pay gap between men and women is due to discrimination by employers...without compulsory pay audits, women will wait till doomsday for equal pay". The TUC has said: "Mandatory equal pay audits would help increase transparency in pay systems in the private sector where the pay gap remains high".[1]

***

But if Feminism continues to press for pay audits let's not stop there. Let's have a 'national work audit' showing everyone in Britain how jobs, work options and choices are portioned out between men and women. We can then press for government action to introduce quotas and positive discrimination legislation to bring about 'gender equality' between the sexes in work-life balance, in working hours and working conditions. What would such an audit include? What would the balance sheet comparing men and women's work-life balance show us?

On one side of the balance sheet we would see men earning 12 - 15 per cent more than women.

On the other side of the sheet we would see that this lower pay is a trade-off, an exchange for women enjoying the luxury, the choice, the freedom to:

Work part-time * work fewer hours * work flexible time * work temporarily * change jobs regularly until they find one they like * enjoy shorter commuting times * walk out of a job if they so wish, knowing that their husband's full-time, lifelong work ethic will provide a financial safety net * avoid work that is stressful * avoid work that has too much responsibility * avoid work that is unhealthy * avoid work where the work environment is uncomfortable * avoid work that is nasty and dirty * avoid work that is dangerous * Avoid working unsocial hours * enjoy not having to commit to a job or career for life * be fulfilled in their work * be happy and satisfied in their work * have more time to pursue their personal interests * have more time to enjoy being with the children, watching them grow and develop * avoid the worry of having to seek promotion * be the primary carer of their children * seek jobs that allow them to help others * study the academic subjects they are interested in and enjoy without worrying whether they will lead to lower paid jobs and careers * enjoy career breaks * claim 'victim status' for the issues of the pay gap and the glass ceiling (if they wish to) * attend school functions with the children * avoid entering the 'death professions'

- One may look at the balance sheet and legitimately ask *which* sex is actually experiencing 'gender inequality' and discrimination in the work situation? It certainly isn't women. Feminism's inequalities of the pay gap and the 'glass ceiling' are carefully crafted and presented frauds

'The most important reasons for the "gender gap" have little to do with employer bias. Increasingly, the gap is the result of choices women make as they seek to maximise their own happiness and achieve a broad mix of life goals.[2]

***

Modern Britain is obsessed with Feminist demands (disguised as 'women's issues') to the point of neurosis. The post-1997 Labour Governments were Feminist Governments. But other parties in our Left-wing/liberal/progressive political zeitgeist are almost as neurotic.

CAMERON: I'LL TACKLE THE GENDER PAY GAP

(Daily Mail, Thursday, 29 December, 2005)

'David Cameron condemned the pay gap between men and women yesterday, calling it a "persistent injustice".

The Tory leader announced a policy review under party chairman, Francis Maude, aimed at pressing employers to do more to even up the disparity.

He (Cameron) called on employers to be "more open" about what they pay their employees, adding: "We will never tackle the scandal of unequal pay by leaving it to legislation and regulation".'

Cameron is also considering legislation to 'remedy' the 'glass ceiling'. He wishes to force companies to hire more woman in senior positions. The Conservative 2010 manifesto supplement 'A Contract for Equalities' presents female quotas on corporate boards as a policy that tackles this supposed inequality.

• More Captainesses...but still no Seweresses

***

The Prime Minister is not the only senior Conservative to promote the Marxist-Feminist Ideology:

WE NEED MORE WOMEN RUNNING FIRMS, SAYS MAY

(Daily Mail, Friday, 17 September, 2010)

'Theresa May has criticised major firms for failing to employ enough women at the top. The Home Secretary, who is also Minister for Women, warned companies they would lose out if they did not ensure that fewer bosses were men.

"If we're going to make sure this happens, we need to work together to break down the barriers that keep women out of the boardroom."'

• 'Barriers'? Which barriers are *they* Ms May? This is sanctimonious, Ideological Feminist claptrap, showing a complete disregard for the gender-neutral research that has identified the 'glass ceiling' as a Feminist-produced myth

And the Conservative Party's Left-wing radical Liberal Democrat Coalition partners?

EQUALITY LAW GIVES WOMEN PRIORITY OVER MEN

(The Daily Telegraph, Friday, 3 December, 2010)

'Lynne Featherstone, the Liberal Democrat equality minister, said yesterday companies that failed to promote a fairer deal for women could be named and shamed. She said sexism was present in too many workplaces.

Leading companies must promote more women to board level. They could be forced to disclose how much they pay staff if they refused to do so voluntarily, she said.

Trade unions welcomed the action to close the gender gap.

The Government has set itself an "aspiration" that half of all new appointments to public boards will be women by 2015.'

- These promotions proposed by Ms. Featherstone are based upon the possession of a vagina rather than upon experience, talent and skills, and will benefit only Feminists; those Feminists who are likely to make up the 14 per cent of 'work-centred' women. So the Government's demand for 'more women' in senior posts actually means 'more misandrous and Ideologically-driven Feminists in senior posts'. I ask the reader to consider the dangerous consequences for men when these Ideologically-driven women fill the top jobs in the law, in the media, in the political system...

- The Liberal Democratic Party has no connection with old-fashioned Liberalism, which prized individual liberty, genuine equality and accountability

Successive governments' attempts to 'remedy' the issue of the pay gap and the 'glass ceiling' have all failed; they are further examples of 'repetitive stupidity syndrome'. All governments have consistently ignored the rational explanation for these phenomena – women's work ethic, preferences, attitudes and choices. All naively (or complicitly) accept the Feminist Ideological dogma that these phenomena are 'gender inequalities'.

Modern Britain is to a great extent ruled by Feminists (Male as well as female) and its social policies dictated by the Feminist Ideology and agenda. Politicians prefer to be led by their prejudices, by their complicity with, or fear of, Feminism, and by gender-warrior 'experts', rather than to be informed on important economic and social issues by gender-neutral experts, such as Professors Catherine Hakim and J. R. Shackleton.

'Men and women are groups that are far too large and heterogeneous to benefit from sensible policy interventions going beyond the basic principle of equality of opportunity, already enshrined in law and increasingly embedded in practice in this country. Complete equality of outcome between men and women's pay is impossible to achieve in a free society of any complexity. All of this suggests that we should make far less of a song and dance about the gender pay gap.' [3]

- What is not understood is that Feminists really *need* to 'sing and dance'; it is a political strategy to create inequalities to justify their continuing existence. Feminism is a self-perpetuating Movement that is Issue-Dependent

***

In the face of so much evidence to the contrary why *are* people so credulous in accepting Feminism's self-serving Ideological explanation for the pay gap and 'glass ceiling'? I have come to the conclusion that there is a fundamental psychological (emotional?) need to *want* to believe what Feminists tell us about women's inequalities, discriminations, oppressions, victimhoods and abuses. For some unfathomable and bizarre reason, we *wish* to believe that women really do suffer from these negative phenomena. Is this why otherwise intelligent people, and politicians from all parties, are so gullible in falling for the confidence trick and fraud that Feminism undoubtedly now is? Is this why Feminism has escaped any kind of analysis, critique, questioning or challenge? Why *do* we have this desire to believe what Feminists tell us, however ridiculous, irrational and illogical their claims and demands may be? We could call modern Feminism Exploitation Feminism – exploiting our need to accept and believe that women in modern Britain are second-class citizens, are a minority group who suffer from 'gender inequalities' and oppressions. We have travelled a long way from the genuine and morally-based Equality Feminism that many of us supported.

***

In this Section I have endeavoured to show how the pay gap and the glass ceiling are myths deliberately, Ideologically and politically converted from women's freely made and personal choices. They have been constructed to add to other artificially created issues that are used to justify the existence of modern Feminism, to continue and prolong its social, cultural, economic and political power; to drive its Grievance Gravy-Train Industries.

However, some experts question whether there actually *is* a pay gap *at all*:

- A woman without children, with no partner, earns roughly the same amount (*and sometimes slightly more*) than the average man.[4]

- 'Single women earn as much on average as single men, and indeed women in the middle age groups who remain single earn more than middle-aged single males.'[5]

- Lesbian women earn 20 per cent more than heterosexual women.[6] This clearly indicates that the pay gap is not a male (patriarchal) discrimination against women.

- The American Longitudinal Survey of Youth found that among workers aged 27 – 33 with no children, women's earnings were 98 per cent of men's.[7]

- The same has been found in Britain:

'It should be emphasised that in the younger age groups, 18 – 21 and 22 – 29, both mean and median measures of the gap are low; for 22 – 29 year-olds, the median gender pay gap was less than 1 per cent in 2007. Indeed, data from the Labour Force Survey suggest that the median pay gap is actually negative for this age group – in other words, women in full-time employment earn more than men.'[8]

And,

'Clearly, there can't be prejudice against women as such since childless married women, single women and single men earn much the same as each other.'[9]

***

There are many choices women face in their lives, work and career; the majority do not go with the 'money choice' or the 'promotion choice'. Their goal is to achieve the ideal balance between financial comfort, work fulfilment, and personal happiness – a different equation for each woman, but the majority choose to earn less and to avoid promotion. These choices are not 'gender inequalities', nor are they discriminations. Lying to women about why they are earning less and why they are 'under-represented' in the top jobs is one of the most disempowering acts imaginable. I hope that the foregoing chapters will have dispelled some of the Feminist myths that keep women stuck in the powerlessness of a 'victim' mentality, deliberately created for them by Feminists in order to implement and justify their own self-seeking agenda.

But I doubt it; not while there are still misandrous Feminists like Kathy Lette populating the media:

> *'It's still a man's world. Until women get equal pay and stop getting concussion from hitting our heads on the glass ceiling, then females should feel free to comically kneecap men as often as possible.'*[10]

***

A major aim of Feminism is to spread misandry. The pay gap and the 'glass ceiling' continue to be powerful gender-weapons in the Feminist armoury; they are Feminism's big guns and have been employed continuously for three decades. I hope that the foregoing chapters will have gone some way to expose Feminism's frauds and deceits regarding these issues.

Section 5

Chapter 37

Feminism Changes the Rules: 'Equal Pay for Work of Equal Value'

*'The whole of society will have become a single office and
a single factory with equality of work and equality of pay'*

(V.I. Lenin, 1917)

So far we have seen three areas of Issue Creep, strategies that are employed by Feminism to justify and perpetuate its existence, and to spread its man-hating:

- Creating inequalities and discrimination issues 'from nothing'
- Establishing Industries to create, process and promote grievances and issues to the public, media and the policy-making fraternity
- Converting women's freely made choices into issues of inequality, discrimination and oppression

This Section addresses a fourth Feminist strategy used to justify and perpetuate its existence – changing the rules. This strategy is particularly relevant to the debate on the pay gap and the 'under-representation' of women in senior positions. It looks at two areas where Feminism has successfully changed the rules:

1. Equal Pay for Work of Equal Value (a different concept to women being paid the same as men for doing the *same* job)

2. Equality of Outcome (over and above the equality of *opportunity* to seek senior positions)

The Section concludes with an exploration of whether the use of quotas and positive discrimination can ever be justified.

***

For every choice there are negative as well as positive consequences. We have seen that the negative consequences of women's work-life choices are less pay and fewer women in senior positions. Feminists refuse to accept that these are fair and just exchanges in the trade-off for the very numerous positive consequences and advantages that women enjoy as a result of their different work ethic.

Feminism has bullied and badgered governments since the 1980s to introduce policies that 'remedy' the negative consequences of the exchange (negative from the Feminist perspective, not interpreted as such by ordinary women). It has done this by changing the rules:

- To remedy the pay gap Feminism has redefined the idea of 'same work' to mean 'women's jobs approximating to the same value to the organisation as men's jobs' in order for it to introduce the concept of *equal pay for work of equal value* into the political system

- To remedy the glass ceiling Feminism has re-defined equality to mean equality of *outcome* rather than equality of *opportunity* and utilises the mechanisms of quotas and positive discrimination, in one form or another, to bring this about

This and the following chapter address these Feminist machinations, showing how successful they have been, and how they confirm that social policy and sexual politics in modern Britain is dominated by Feminist discourse and the Feminist perspective.

Equal Pay for Work of Equal Value is a Fraud

'Rather than celebrate victory, contemporary feminists need to feign constant defeat, in part so that their services will continue to be needed. Their message has so thoroughly invaded popular culture that it is now taken for granted in the press that women do not receive equal pay for equal work...'[1]

In essence, Feminists want 'women's work' to be paid at the same rate as 'men's work' – even though, as we have seen, the two types of work are intrinsically different in nature especially with regard to degrees of satisfaction, fulfilment, working conditions, impact on health, work environment and danger.

'Equal pay for work of equal value' is a Marxist concept. It was the basis for pay structures in the Soviet bloc. It is generally accepted that in a capitalist free market economy education, training, experience and so on, are rewarded. It could not operate if gardeners were paid the same as hospital consultants because if they were paid the same then everyone would want to be a gardener and there would be a shortage of consultants: a road sweeper would have the same income as a doctor, a refuse collector as an accountant... Doris, the school-crossing lollipop lady as Jeremy Clarkson...

'As F. A. Hayek noted in The Road to Serfdom, the end result of such central planning of wages would be to require a totalitarian state where central planners had to allocate individuals to jobs to overcome the mismatch between supply and demand. Such central planning would be illiberal and would also erode prosperity for reasons that are well understood.'[2]

- In a capitalist economy the law of supply and demand must be allowed to operate freely

- The Marxist-Feminist demand for 'equal pay for work of equal value' is social engineering

- Modern Britain, with the dominant power of Feminism in sexual politics and social policy, is progressing towards a Feminist-Socialist Quiet Revolution

***

It is impossible to objectively measure and compare jobs for their intrinsic value. There are too many arbitrary variables involved. Opinions are necessarily subjective. But comparisons *are* made, by Employment Tribunals. I have studied the criteria that Tribunals use to make their comparisons; may I suggest the reader does the same (they are not easy to acquire). In essence, the criteria are very heavily prejudiced in favour of women's jobs and female characteristics, and against those of men. I know nothing of the personnel that make up these Tribunals but would not be surprised if Feminists, Male Feminists, trade union representatives and perhaps liberal/progressive/Left-wing judges were over-represented. Their decisions certainly point in that direction:

> *'If these evaluation schemes are to bite at all and justify their use, they are expected to throw up anomalies in existing pay schemes. Given that the point of the exercise is to improve women's pay, it is not surprising that they do so.'*[3]

In 1995 Martin Mears was the first person to be elected President of the Law Society by the *whole* solicitor's profession. In 2006 he noted:

> *'Before many employment tribunals it is difficult for an applicant to lose a discrimination claim. The Tribunal's stereotypical view of the world is that employers are likely to have stereotypical and incorrect attitudes to race, gender, etc.'*[4]

The Tribunal evaluation schemes consistently use variables that favour women. For example, one commentator notes the absence of 'risk' in male/female job comparisons:

> *'And what about risk? Note that risk – this is an important variable, because the work-related accident is a major cause of death for men – is seldom if ever a criterion in pay-equity programmes. Work place accidents are...a major killer of men. 98% of all those who die in the workplace are men.'*[5]

There are very many variables in a job. For example:

Healthy environment * danger * stress * responsibility * security * physical demands * anxiety and worry * working hours * unsocial shifts * etc

These variables are *completely ignored* by Employment Tribunals. We have seen that the worst jobs in society are overwhelmingly undertaken by men. These jobs normally draw a compensatory pay differential to offset the unpleasant, unhealthy or dangerous work environment. Employment Tribunals disregard these differentials.

The stupidity of trying to compare 'work of equal value' without considering *all* the variables can be seen in the TUC literature on the subject; we saw in Part Two that the Left-leaning TUC is politically inclined towards Feminism. The following are examples from its brochure, published in the late 1990s, 'Equal Pay for Work of Equal Value: Guidelines'. It compares:

A male security guard with a dinner lady

A male bricklayer with a female biscuit maker

A male refuse collector with a female home help

A male sheet-metal worker with a female secretary

One doesn't have to be a brain surgeon (or a road sweeper) to see that the numerous variables in these jobs makes any comparison of 'value' ridiculous. Yet Feminism and the trade unions have had huge success in convincing (Feminist-sympathetic) Tribunals that the above examples (and many other types of idiotic comparisons) are valid, that the jobs are of 'equal value'.

The reader may wish to consider and compare the variables in the above. Let's take the example of a male security officer's job compared with that of a dinner lady's. The security officer may work outside in all weathers (he will be vulnerable to cold and wet illnesses, adversely affecting his health); he will be working alone (he will be subjected to boredom and isolation); he will be obliged to undertake shiftwork (this will adversely impact upon his family life, seeing his wife and children, and upon his social life with friends); as a guard he will be in a potentially dangerous situation (this may not only cause him *physical danger* but also cause a great deal of *anticipatory* anxiety and stress because of the *potential* danger). Now, compare his working environment with that of a dinner lady helping children eat their lunch and keeping an eye on them whilst they play. You see what I'm getting at?

- The concept of 'equal pay for work of equal value' is a fraud, a Feminist confidence trick; a confidence trick implemented by successive governments which are too fearful of (or complicit with) Feminism and the raging backlash that any questioning of, or challenge to, this Ideological fraud and deceit would bring down upon their heads

***

A few years ago, after yet another Commission had reported on the 'inequality of the pay gap' (the Prosser Report) Radio 4's Today programme hosted a debate between the Fawcett Society's chairman at the time, Katherine Rake, and a member of the Confederation of British Industries. Rake wanted to know why a child minder didn't receive the same pay as a long-distance lorry driver as they were both doing work of 'equal value'. The CBI representative replied that it was a question of supply and demand (as we saw in an earlier chapter). But he could easily have pointed out to Ms. Rake that a long-distance lorry driver may be away from his family for a large part of the week, working away from home for long hours, that he has a highly stressful job and for three or four nights a weeks he may have to sleep in his cab rather than a bed. *That's* why, Ms. Rake, he earns more than the child minder. He receives (at least for the time being) a pay differential for the inconveniences of his job. Obviously the Sisters feel that this is an unfair and unequal trade-off.

A further example of the 'equal pay for work of equal value' fraud is seen in the prison service.

EQUAL PAY CLAIM MAY COST
PRISON SERVICE UP TO £50 MILLION

(The Times, Monday, 25 July, 2005)

'Thirty-eight claims have been heard at an employment tribunal and the Prison Service has set aside £1.5 million to deal with the cases – about £40,000 per case.

The Service is bracing itself for a huge payout to deal with a backlog of claims from workers, mainly women, employed on administrative work in prison. They could be entitled to back pay going back 12 years.

Sandra Knight said: "We were doing a job of equal value to prison officers but getting a lesser salary. It is not just a matter of finance, it is the principle of equal pay that matters".

The equal pay row arises out of a Prison Service job evaluation scheme conducted in the 1990s, which said that administrative jobs were of equal value to the work of prison officers on the wings of jails. In some cases, however, the pay gap was as much as £5,000 a year.

Administrative staff keep prisoner records and carry out financial work, as well as ordering food and other supplies.'

- Which is the more *comfortable* working environment – patrolling the concrete and metal corridors of the prison wings or sitting in a carpeted office, ordering food supplies?

- Which is the more *satisfying* work, and *happier* working environment – being subjected to prisoner abuse and verbal confrontation on a daily basis, or chatting in an office with amiable female friends about how to store prisoner's records?

- Which prison staff work *unsocial hours* and are expected to work in shifts every three weeks? Which prison staff would be expected to work on Bank Holidays and on Sundays? Which prison staff will work a regular daily 9.00am to 5pm shift, enjoying a proper home life with their partners and children?

- Which staff is much more likely to suffer serious *anxiety* and *stress* from the daily interface with dangerous and violent, and often unstable, prisoners?

- Which is the more *dangerous* job? In the event of a prison riot which personnel – prison officers or administrative staff – would be expected to subdue violent prisoners and put themselves at risk? Which staff will be working in a *much safer environment* well away from any danger to their person?

It's a wonder that the male warders haven't gone on strike at this outrageous comparison. In fact it's a wonder that there *are* any male warders; they could quite legitimately feel undervalued. If they all retrained and reapplied to become office administrators in prisons would their applications be accepted – or would there be some Feminist-inspired rule/ clause/policy denying men this equality?

'Equal pay for work of equal value' is a huge Feminist fraud that has been accepted (indeed, introduced) by Feminist-friendly governments. Sandra Knight's comment, 'It is the principle of equal pay that matters' is pure Feminist dogma, cant straight from the Feminist lexicon, political rhetoric taught (indoctrinated) on Feminist Equality and Diversity courses.

- It's astonishing and disgraceful that the above 'equal pay for work of equal value' claim was accepted by the Employment Tribunal. Proof, surely, of the ubiquitous political power of Feminism in modern Britain

JAIL STAFF 'AFRAID TO TAKE CONTROL'

(The Times, Tuesday, 13 March, 2007)

'Prisoners at a privately-run jail are intimidating inexperienced staff who are struggling to keep control of the wings, says a report by Anne Owers, the Chief Inspector of Prisons.

She says that drugs and bullying are rife in Dovegate jail, near Uttoxeter, Staffordshire, and that bad behaviour is unchecked because the staff are afraid to challenge it.

Inmates told last year's inspection team that the response to fights and bullying was that "staff run away" and "staff are slow to respond".'

In the Autumn of 2008 I wrote to the Prison Officer's Association requesting facts on prison officers' working conditions. I received information that included the following incident – one of 24,000 annual attacks on (overwhelmingly male) prison officers (but *none* on administrative staff):

'Mr. A was employed at HMP Whitemoor. Two dangerous and subversive inmates threatened to assault him. A decision was taken to leave them on normal location but to monitor the situation carefully. Within days of these threats having been made a fight on a landing was staged by inmates so as to draw staff to the location. Mr. A responded to the alarm bell fearing as he did so that this was a trap, as indeed it was. One of the inmates was on a higher landing by a large container of hot cooking oil which he poured over Mr. A. He suffered severe burns to his face and upper body, damage to his hearing, sense of smell and taste. He could no longer work as a prison officer.'

- Those Feminist-sympathisers who support the 'equal pay for work of equal value' demand are not simply being Ideological and unjust, not simply being bloody-minded, but are also being immoral. How would the sanctimonious, self-righteous Ms. Knight ('it is the principle of equal pay that matters') explain her 'equal pay for work of equal value' demand to Prison Officer A's wife?

***

Comparing the 'value' of jobs as a 'remedy' for women *choosing* to receive lower pay (as a trade-off for other benefits) is wrong. But this Ideologically-driven injustice doesn't stop there. In order to equalise the salaries of male jobs and female jobs *men's* salaries are having to be *reduced*.

Shackleton notes:

'Given that the point of the exercise is to improve women's pay, it is not surprising that they do so. The corollary is that the pay of men may often have to be reduced. This predictably causes considerable unhappiness.'[6]

- A fundamental tenet of Feminism is to blame, condemn and *punish* men

MEN ARE TO PAY A HIGH PRICE FOR SEXUAL EQUALITY

Hundreds of thousands of men face salary cuts of up to £15,000 to fund increases for women staff

(The Times, Monday, 12 March, 2007)

'Hundreds of thousands of men working in the public sector are facing salary cuts of up to £15,000 a year as equal pay agreements take effect, the Times has learnt.

Compensation claims for up to 1.5 million workers could cost the tax-payer more than £10 billion and mean that male staff lose up to 40 per cent of their salary.

Union officials across the public sector are now having to agree to settlements where men's pay will be cut.'

- 'Hundreds of thousands of men' are being *punished* by Feminist-dominated governments bent on implementing the Feminist Ideology and agenda. Reader, are you joining up the dots of my thesis that Feminism is a fraud – that there are no 'coincidences' that 'just happen' to advantage women (mainly Feminists and Feminism) and 'just happen' to punish men? Are you noticing that there is a pattern, a concerted and determined agenda?

- And one doubts whether trade union officials would be too concerned about *men's pay being reduced* in order to *increase women's pay*, their being major players in Feminism's Quiet Revolution

One of the spurious 'equal pay for work of equal value' comparisons is that between school dinner ladies and male street sweepers. Mark Butch, 30, had his salary cut from £15,300 to £11,500. Mark said:

'Our jobs include cleaning up human excrement and dog mess. We deal with the safe disposal of syringes.'[7]

- So not only is it men who are the sole inhabitants of the nasty, unhealthy and dangerous 'glass cellar' jobs but in addition, in order to satisfy a Marxist-Feminist agenda, they have to have *their* salaries cut in order to improve the salaries of women who *choose not to enter* the glass cellar jobs. Why are men so feeble by not forming Men's Political Groups or demanding a Minister for Men? Men's problems, issues and rights are systemically and institutionally ignored. When will men have the courage to get off their knees, to stand up and fight back against Feminism?

'For affirmative action to be effective, the individual rights of men must be sacrificed in favour of the collective rights of women.'[8]

***

In the following we see a further discrimination against men imposed by the State via Feminist-controlled Employment Tribunals:

POLICEWOMEN WHO WORK ONLY DAY SHIFTS MUST GET NIGHT DUTY BONUS, SAYS TRIBUNAL

(Daily Mail, Saturday, 21 October, 2006)

'Two working mothers in the police force were yesterday given the right to bonus payments for working at night – even though they only do day shifts.

The constables should get the extra money because their childcare commitments stop them from working anti-social hours, a tribunal ruled.

The landmark judgement means West Midlands Police must pay thousands of pounds in special allowances to Miss Blackburn, a single-mother of one, and mother-of-two Mrs. Manly.

But repercussions are likely to be felt across the public sector – especially the NHS – and by firms paying allowances to workers for night and weekend shifts.

Ruth Lea, of the centre-Right think tank the Centre for Policy Studies, said: "People who do not do the unsocial hours should not be paid for them. This is blindingly obvious." The tribunal has yet to rule if the officers should get compensation as well as the allowances.'

- My commenting upon this disgraceful Feminist-friendly judgement would only insult the reader's intelligence

'Flying under the false flag of "equal pay for equal work" and fuelled by their persecution fantasies, modern feminists have been successfully advancing an agenda that demands radical social engineering to eliminate any differences between the sexes...The modern women's movement is totalitarian in its methods, radical in its aims, and dishonest in its advocacy.'[9]

Chapter 38

Equality of Outcome

Modern Feminism is in the business of escalation of demands. The Suffragettes, man-haters that they were, at least had the sense of justice to demand only the vote – the 'equal right' to vote. Today's Feminists demand that they are given free seats in Parliament, preferential treatment and special privileges for female prospective Parliamentary candidates. There are new Feminist organisations and Feminist Industries dedicated to demanding quotas and positive discrimination and similar devices for female prospective Parliamentary candidates (who inevitably will almost always be Feminists).

This chapter is a second example of Feminism 'changing the rules' in order to 'remedy' the negative consequences of women's work-life choices; but in this case, to achieve much more. In converting women's choices into issues it assumes that any statistical disparity must be the result of discrimination (rather than because of women's own choices) and that this disparity must be 'remedied'. Until *equality of outcome* has been achieved, it is assumed (without any inquiry into whether or not any discrimination has actually occurred) that *equality of opportunity* has been denied. This is linguistic and political sophistry, a neat linguistic and political device; a device that is having increasing success.

Feminism is a 'progressive' political movement (as all British political parties now are). But after equality of opportunity was achieved in the 1980s, what could it 'progress' towards? 'Progressive' political parties and movements cannot just stand still once their aims have been achieved; by their eponymous label and nature they need to 'progress' to some new objective. Feminism is now 'progressing' toward the Socialist-Marxist concept of *equality of outcome*.

- We have travelled a long way from the moral and democratic decency of Equality Feminism

---

Feminism has Manipulated the Concept of 'Equality'

'In Britain sexual politics has been contaminated by Orwellian euphemisms:
"equal opportunities" now refers to preferential treatment'

(Swayne O'Pie)

Equality is a noble ideal, but how many people, politicians, the public, know that the concept has been manipulated and redefined by Feminism to suit its agenda?

'Feminism has shifted dramatically from its early programme of equity between women and men.'[1]

And from an Academic Feminist, a professor of political theory:

'To date, the diversity agenda has largely taken the form of an anti-discrimination approach and has not yet really echoed the developments in gender equality, which moved from anti-discrimination alone to embrace issues of equality of outcome....'[2]

- An admission here that the Feminist objective is today equality of outcome, not equality of opportunity

Equality Feminism's aims were equal opportunities for women, equal rights for women, equal treatment for women, equal respect for women and (ironically) equal choices for women. But for modern Feminists the success of achieving these equalities was not enough. Because these objectives have been achieved Feminism has had to reinvent the concept of 'equality' in order to justify its existence. The concept has been redefined in a radically different way. The noble concept of equality is being used and abused for the political ends of Ideologues – to justify 'Forever' Feminism and its Grievance Gravy-Train Industries.

> 'Ideological feminists denounce equality of opportunity, insisting on equality of outcome.'[3]

And,

> '...feminists claim that discrimination is to blame if women do not choose to enter all fields in numbers equal to men.'[4]

***

In this way Feminism has cleverly re-jigged the demand for 'equality' by demanding 'equality of outcome' (sometimes referred to as 'equality of result'). That is, wherever there is a preponderance of men as, for example, more male than female MPs, then 'equality of outcome' means that there ought to be an equal number of women...an equal number of female judges, senior managers, top civil servants, an equal number of young women studying maths and science...and so on. But what escapes the attention of those who agree with this Feminist demand (or perhaps doesn't escape them but who are too weak-willed or fearful to question and challenge it) is the fact that:

- Numerical imbalance is not the same thing as sex discrimination. *Numerical imbalance* has been *deliberately* presented by Feminism as an 'inequality caused by discrimination' in order to gain political and Ideological sympathy and advantage. A 'numerical imbalance' is a neutral statistical disparity phenomenon, it has *no* intrinsic moral value: the word 'inequality' on the other hand, is *not* value-free, it is value-laden with (deliberate) pejorative Ideological nuance

> 'With the push toward defining equality for women as numerical parity has come a skilful change in the language feminists use to describe women's rights...rather than demanding equal opportunity, feminists are lobbying for preferential rights for their own interest groups.'[5]

Feminism *deliberately* confuses these two concepts (equality and numerical imbalance) in order to promote its political agenda. And the vast majority of people have been taken in by this subterfuge, this fraud; they consider it to be 'morally wrong' that there are more men than women in senior positions, that there are more male than female MPs. There are many rational reasons to explain the under-representation of women in senior posts (as we saw in earlier chapters) but laziness of thought prevents people from exploring these reasons – much easier to accept 'what Feminists, the media and academics tell us' – thereby allowing their comfort-box prejudice to dictate their view, especially when their peer group incestuously shares the same box, as with the chattering classes and opinion-formers. On the other hand, many take the Ideological view and accept the Feminist interpretation that men (the 'bad people' of the patriarchy) are *deliberately* discriminating against women (the 'good people', patriarchy's victims).

The Feminist deception in conflating equality with numerical imbalance is neatly summarised in the following observation:

'Feminism's phenomenal success in making the alleged past oppression of women an incontrovertible fact is demonstrated by the institution of this vast affirmative action bureaucracy that assumes any statistical disparity in outcomes for men and women results from discrimination against women – not from women's choices – and must be "remedied". Until equality of outcome has been achieved, it is largely assumed – without inquiry into whether discrimination has actually occurred – that equality of opportunity has been denied.'[6]

- The reader, having considered the Section on the pay gap and the glass ceiling, will know that there is no discrimination. They will know that the *real* reason that fewer women than men are in senior positions is because women have a different work ethic to men – they *choose* not to be in such positions

---

Why Feminism Needs Equality of Outcome

Feminism has three reasons for insisting upon, and pushing for, equality of outcome:

1. Feminism needs equality of outcome to disguise its true aims and agenda
2. Feminism needs equality of outcome because equality of opportunity has been achieved and it needs to create a replacement 'inequality' that is easy to sell to the public and politicians in order to continue justifying its existence
3. Feminism needs equality of outcome to ensure the personal advancement of individual Feminists (under the guise of 'remedying' women's under-representation in top jobs)

***

1. 'Equality of Outcome' Disguises Feminism's Aims and Agenda

The term 'equality of outcome' still retains the word 'equality' and so it is carefully and quietly used to 'front', to disguise, Feminism's true Ideology and aims. Feminism uses the term 'equality of outcome' sparingly in public because it may be considered too radical, too revolutionary. It has quietly stopped using the expression 'equality of opportunity' in its literature and pronouncements (because this has already been achieved so its use would look ridiculous). The terms now preferred are 'gender equality' or 'equality and diversity': both are innocuous-sounding, and both still contain the word 'equality'. This linguistic manoeuvre has given Feminism a cloak of moral and political legitimacy, permitting it to continue as a Movement.

Feminist demands for 'gender equality' sound like nothing more than calls for justice and fairness. However, always lurking under the surface is the call for 'equality of outcome' which is Feminist-speak for preferential treatment for women, special privileges for women, policy-favouritism for women (but as this chapter will confirm, not for ordinary women, but for *Feminists themselves*). And this strategy of deception has been remarkably successful:

'Feminists are, however, winning their war to redefine equality as numerical parity...the feminist's message of equality of outcome now reigns.'[7]

In Section Two it was shown how in the 1970s ideological Feminism stole Equality Feminism's moral base (and funding) and used this base to deceive the public and politicians. Feminism has continued to use this disguise, this deception.

'Equality is not only the legitimate expression of egalitarian feminism...but also the ideal front for ideological feminism. Not only are students exposed to gynocentric indoctrination, but so are legislators, judges, bureaucrats, corporate managers and employers...Ideological feminists denounce equality of opportunity, insisting on equality of result'.[8]

- We have all been gulled by this deceit, by this 'gynocentric indoctrination': 'not only students...but legislators, judges, bureaucrats, corporate managers and employers.' We could add many more to the list, including educators and media people. Young people are indoctrinated at university, either on a Feminist Module or by osmosis; others are indoctrinated into believing Feminist claims by our culture, conventional wisdom, and our political zeitgeist

- The success of Feminism's 'gynocentric indoctrination' since the 1980s is a fundamental reason why Feminism's Quiet Revolution is progressing so successfully...we have all been, and continue to be, conned. And bizarrely, we seem to have a *wish* to be conned, we seem to have a psychological need to truly *believe* all the 'women's inequalities and discriminations' that Feminism relentlessly brings to our attention

***

2. Equality of Outcome is Used to Generate 'Forever' Feminism

The second reason why Feminism changed the concept of equality to equality of outcome is to use it as a political mechanism in order to perpetuate its Ideology, and therefore its Industries.

Used in this way the pursuit of, and demand for, equality of outcome has been a sexual political masterstroke.

Why is this so? Equality of outcome is (like 'equal pay for work of equal value') a Marxist-Communist objective; for example, the workers should all be paid the same, and own the means of production, should be equally represented as the bourgeois owners on the boards of businesses and corporations. Feminists knows that equality of outcome – right across the board – can *never* be achieved in a capitalist country (like Britain). But it also knows that in a Feminist-sympathetic society and State (like Britain) it can achieve *some* of these outcomes. Pushing too hard would appear to be too radical and revolutionary, so a strategy of picking achievable targets, and quietly and slowly, incrementally, working towards these, is the most appropriate way forward (a Quiet Revolution); an equal number of female MPs, for example, is an easily 'sellable' agenda objective. At the same time Feminism enjoys the knowledge that, because it will never succeed in *all* areas, it can still continue to justify its existence, can still continue to make demands for the implementation of its agenda knowing that these demands will be assured of a sympathetic reception. In this way Feminism has secured its future, the perpetuation of its Ideology and its Grievance Gravy-Train Industries...its 'Forever' Feminism.

- A Machiavellian strategy, for sure, but one that has proved extremely successful

- Feminism is here to stay – it will *never* be satisfied, it can never *allow* itself to be appeased. For Feminism, success will *never* be enough. And whilst we have Feminism we must, by definition, have man-hating

Ann Widdecombe, the Conservative MP, has commented:

> 'I've no time for 1990s feminism. I have a lot of time for 1970s feminism which said, "Give us the equal opportunities, we'll show you that we're just as good as you, if not better than you".'[9]

***

3. Equality of Outcome Advances Individual Feminists' Careers

Feminism demands equality of outcome: that is, the number of men and women in senior posts should be exactly (or nearly) the same. To achieve this the mechanisms of quotas and positive discrimination (in numerous disguises) are required. The ethics of this social engineering will be addressed in the following chapter.

We know that only 14 per cent of women are 'work-centred': it was also noted that these 14 per cent are very likely to be Feminists. So if the State is casting around for women to fill quotas in senior positions then the 86 per cent of 'home-centred' and 'adaptive' women (non-Ideological women) will *not* be applying (these women have a different work ethic to 'work-centred' women). The women who *will* apply for these 'free' top jobs will be women from the 'work-centred' group; that is, Feminists – that *very same group* that created the myth of the 'glass ceiling' and demanded positive discrimination and quotas in the first place. This is not a coincidence.

- When Feminists say 'there should be more *women* in the top jobs' what they are *actually* saying...and demanding, is 'We want you, the State, to give we Feminists these free senior positions'

- Feminism does not 'aim to have more women in the top jobs': it aims to have more *Feminists* in the top jobs. The use of the word 'women' is a deliberate deceit. Ordinary, decent, non-Ideological women are simply used as a label, a cover, to disguise individual Feminists' own personal advancement and aggrandisement

So when Feminism states that 'women should be equally represented in Parliament/ in boardrooms/in the judiciary' it does not mean 'women': it means Feminists. And yet our Left-wing/progressive/liberal political consensus, political zeitgeist, has either been completely deceived by this fraud...or has been complicit in its use and has quietly accepted it as legitimate. Feminist Ideologues, not ordinary women, increasingly continue to fill positions of power and influence in the State; positions from which they can direct and dictate policy...producing and implementing Feminist policy...including *misandrous* policies (note the earlier chapter on prostitution, for example). This doesn't bode well for men.

Others have observed this Feminist fraud:

> 'Like all special interest groups, feminists seek subsidies for themselves. Their economic interests and professional advancement have been greatly enhanced by claims of past societal discriminations against women.'[10]

And,

> '...rather than demanding equal opportunity, feminists are lobbying for preferential rights for their own interest groups.'[11]

And,

> 'Some people perceive women as being victimised by men at every step in their lives. I think they are motivated by the desire to help women, but also I think some of the ideologues are seeking power not so much for women in general as for themselves and for their clique.'[12]

And,

> 'Feminists are the ones getting most of the money, the professorships, and the well-paid (but vaguely defined) jobs inside the burgeoning new victim/bias industry.'[13]

And Rosalind Coward, an Equality Feminist:

> 'In a society where men have been taking a bashing, do we really want the sort of feminism that insists on a woman's right to claim an equal place in the world of male power...it is quite another thing if those rights seem mainly to confer additional advantages on already privileged groups, or groups who may be using women's interests to promote their own careers or their own agenda.'[14]

Carol Sarler, an Equality Feminist, noting Feminists' general self-interest:

> 'There are strident voices, most shrill among those who earn their keep in the Left-wing press, who continue to portray all men as actual or potential rapists...One can understand, of course, why these women continue to plough this anachronistic furrow; theirs is a vested interest, given that their livelihoods depend upon it.'[15]

The demand for equality of outcome (quotas, positive discrimination) is a demand by *Feminists* for the State to give them high status and highly paid jobs/sinecures (universities in the 1980s and 1990s 'tokened in' many Feminist lecturers). It is a righteous Ideological demand used to disguise individual aggrandisement, personal gain and advancement. It is social engineering designed to preference and privilege middle-class, educated Feminists – to increase their political power and to progress their Quiet Revolution. Feminism is Socialism's Trojan Horse and equality of outcome is an integral part of this Ideological Left-wing manoeuvre.

***

Male Feminists also want to cosy up to the Feminist power regime. For example, John Cooper QC is a leading criminal and human rights barrister. Writing on the advantages of positive discrimination for women in The Observer we read:

> 'The imbalances between men and women in relation to opportunities and remuneration have been as stark as they are indefensible. There remains a need for positive discrimination, both on a practical and philosophical level. Practically, there are still a large number of working women who remain the subject of discrimination. Philosophically, the existence of the principle of positive discrimination is a marker of the importance that society places upon equality of opportunity and reward.'[16]

Positive discrimination is morally wrong. There is no 'glass ceiling', we have seen that there are no discriminations. We know that the reason for the under-representation of women in senior positions is due to women's *own choices*. In addition, if only 14 per cent of women are 'work-centred' and present themselves for promotion, then it is logical, fair and reasonable that only 14 per cent of the senior jobs should be inhabited by women, as has been the case now for two decades. Any other interpretation is philosophical skulduggery.

Equality of Opportunity and Equality of Outcome:
A Difference in Philosophy

Here I would like to address the philosophical dimensions of the two types of equality, equality of opportunity and equality of outcome, and to note the origins of the latter.

Equality of *opportunity* encourages society to reduce inequalities by supporting and encouraging an individual's personal responsibility to 'better' himself or herself (for example, a working class person being given every opportunity to gain access to a university education if they work hard at school). Equality of *opportunity* emphasises personal responsibility, individual merit, skills, and a wish to achieve. Politically, its advocates are liberal (in the sense of being fair and open to all, as well as negotiation and compromise). The political origins of equality of *opportunity* are to be found in old-fashioned Liberalism (this kind of liberalism is absent from today's Left-wing, radical, progressive Feminist-preferencing Liberal Democratic Party).

On the other hand, equality of *outcome* promotes very different views of the roles of society, the individual, the law, the State. It insists that the State should distribute wealth, top jobs, all the good things in society, according to a mathematical principle. To achieve this aim it replaces personal responsibility with State regulation, with State engineering.

- Equality of *outcome* is a group, a collectivist, concept – comparing one group in society against another: political scientists acknowledge that this is a principle of communist/ Marxist philosophy (their groups being defined by 'class', rather than Feminism's 'sex')

Equality of *outcome* is essentially utopian, collectivist, socialist, Marxist. Its advocates strive for revolution, if not political revolution in the narrow sense, then a 'quiet' cultural, conventional wisdom/political zeitgeist-changing, revolution. 'Equality of outcome' is fundamentally totalitarian.

> *'The ultimate model for 'equality of result', in any case, is Marx's classless society, in which personal merit has little or nothing to do with the distribution of wealth...'[17]*

How is equality of outcome achieved? It is achieved not by applying the same rules in the same way to all citizens as individuals, but by applying them differentially in order to correct what the rule-makers define as inequalities, discriminations, oppressions, victimisations and abuses. In modern Britain, the rule-makers in sexual politics and social policy are Feminists (including Male Feminists), operating through our society, culture and State.

- We have seen in previous chapters how Feminism uses the Ideology of 'patriarchy' to strip women of personal responsibility: with equality of *outcome* women need not undertake the personal responsibility for bettering themselves via hard work, such as study or longevity in one job, in order to achieve high status and a high salary, but would actually be *given* high status positions (and salary) by the State regardless of merit, simply because they are female

And so we get the Feminist demand for *the State* to 'remedy' the under-representation of women in senior positions; to manufacture an equal number of female and male MPs regardless of personal merit (this demand is quietly being implemented); the demand that *the State* ensures that nursery nurses, for example, receive equal pay to long-distance lorry drivers (regardless of the fact that the latter will be working long hours, unsocial hours, sleeping in their cabs and spending days away from their families); the demand that the State ensures that 50 per cent of directors on the boards of major companies are female (regardless of ability or time spent with the company). Norwegian Feminists demanded that the State ensure that 40 per cent of directors were female; this demand has now become law. And, in a few years, Britain?

The Feminist Harriet Harman was the Labour Government's Minister for Women and Equality, and the Deputy Prime Minister:

HARMAN: I'LL PUT WOMEN IN CHARGE OF BANKS
(Daily Mail, 7 May, 2009)

'Harriet Harman wants to use controversial new equality laws to pack the boards of nationalised banks with women.

Last night, at a Left-wing meeting on Women in The Recession in Parliament, Ms Harman said so-called "positive action" would be "there for us" to put women on the boards of bailed-out banks.

She also launched a staunch defence of her Equality Bill, which allows firms to choose women or minorities ahead of equally-qualified white males.

"Sometimes we have to take scary methods in order to achieve worthwhile results," she told a mainly female audience. "It's about saying, 'because you are a woman I'm going to put you in this promotion'".

Critics warn the plan, dubbed "socialism in one clause", will burden firms with more red tape.'

- The phrase, 'Sometimes we have to take scary methods...' resonates with Stalin's quote, when persecuting the Russian people during the 1920s by inhumanely imposing his revolutionary 5-Year-Plans: 'You can't make an omelette without breaking eggs'. With regard to sexual politics and social policy modern Britain *is* a totalitarian State, a one-party system (the Feminist 'Party'/Movement) with an all-pervading Ideology (Feminism). And with *no* opposing Party

- It's astonishing that the Conservative Party leadership courts and embraces Feminism, a Marxist-Socialist Ideology

- It's a tragedy that British males in positions of power (politicians, trade union officials, lawyers, media, academics) simply sit on their backsides and quietly and meekly accept such Ideological, misandrous policies. Shameful

We live in a society where men and women are free to pursue numerous and different options. Yet Feminists want a society where the government punishes businesses (by imposing quotas in boardrooms) because the majority of women (86 per cent) choose not to seek promotion.

- And it is not the decent, ordinary women who benefit from State regulated equality of outcome – it is the pushy, strident Feminist Ideologues. They are not concerned about the welfare of ordinary woman; *they are very much concerned about their own personal advancement* – and the political power they can grasp and hold on to

Equality of outcome is essentially immoral, unjust, Marxist, totalitarian and undemocratic. Equality of outcome has replaced personal responsibility with State legislation.

Feminism in modern Britain has now successfully defined 'equality' as preferential treatment, special privileges, and policy-favouritism, for women (that is, Feminists) – generally at the expense of men. The successful implementation of equality of outcome policies adds one more dimension to Britain's institutional and systemic misandry. Was Harriet Harman right when she gloated in 2008 that in a few years' time there wouldn't be enough airports in the country from which men could escape?

***

The Equal Opportunities Commission (employing 82 per cent female staff, reminding one of the old joke 'Why is there only one Monopolies Commission?') was abolished in 2007. It morphed into the Equality and Human Rights Commission, with Trevor Phillips appointed as its chief executive. By 2009 the EHRC was in crisis. Senior executives were leaving because they didn't like Phillips's approach to equality:

EQUALITY ROW REVEALS A
DEEPER RIFT FOR LABOUR

**The meltdown at the human rights quango is more than a bureaucratic squabble.
It is about the future of the Centre Left.**

(The Times, Tuesday, 4 August, 2009: Rachel Sylvester)

'The first group (the Left) wants the State to enforce a level playing field, with quotas for representation and fines for bodies that fail to achieve equality...As an insider puts it: "The real battle is over world view, not leadership. It's about whether you should be inculcating a sense of permanent victimhood or encouraging people to have aspirations instead.'

- Here we see the battle between:

1. The Ideological Feminist patriarchal 'victimhood' mentality, Marxist, State-imposed 'equality of outcome' camp on the one side, with...

2. Equality Feminism's individual merit, 'equality of opportunity', liberal, aspirational, personal responsibility and endeavour, approach on the other

Ideological Feminism is out there, today, right now, with both Feminists and Male Feminists pushing for a Socialist/Marxist Feminist society and State – using the disguise of 'gender equality' to give it a moral righteousness. And those who should know better have been gulled by this deceit.

- Feminism is Socialism's Trojan Horse

The following is a letter from The Times on Wednesday, 28 March, 2001:

GENDER SHOULD NOT DEFINE A LAW LORD

Sir, The Fawcett Society complains (letter, March 23) of the absence of women in our highest court, the House of Lords, implying that this will or may result in bias in an appeal involving women.

This is an insulting suggestion and inconsistent with the trend of decisions in the House of Lords and Court of Appeal in recent years, e.g. the marked relaxation of the law of provocation in murder trials, which now makes it much easier for a woman who kills to avoid a conviction for murder. To avoid bias, the Society seems to want law lords to be "representatives" of "constituencies". This would be ridiculous and anyway impossible to achieve. Would bias be feared if five thin judges dealt with the case of a very fat person?

To maintain the standards and standing of the judicial House of Lords, the qualifications for appointment are and should be the highest achievable standards of integrity, legal learning, common sense and experience.

I am certain that the Prime Minister and the Lord Chancellor would properly love to appoint the first woman law lord and that this will happen, probably quite soon, when a candidate is identified who has all these qualities to at least the same degree as the best available man. To do so for The Fawcett Society's reasons, by positive discrimination, would weaken and cheapen the court and in the long run, incidentally, do women lawyers and women generally more harm than good.

Yours truly (Sir) Michael Davies
(High Court judge, 1973-97)

Elliot House, Wolverely,
Kidderminster DY11 5XE
March 24

- Amongst other relevant points made is that 'success is never enough for Feminism'. Michael Davies confirms that the House of Lords passed a Bill making it easier for a wife to kill her husband and escape serious punishment (something Feminism and its End Violence Against Women Industry has been demanding for many years). But The Fawcett Society *still* demands that Feminist representatives should sit on the Court of Appeal in order to 'represent the interests of women' (Feminist-speak for *favouring* women). Feminism will never be appeased, Britain will always have 'Forever' Feminism

Why Restrict 'Equality of Outcome' to Women?

So, if equality of outcome is used as a sexual political strategy by Feminists to bring about equality in society then ethically and logically it ought to be extended into *every* area of society, our culture, economy and politics, not just implemented in areas that advantage *only* women. For example if equality is a noble concept worth aiming towards, and if Britain prides itself on being a just, fair and democratic society, then the State needs to ensure that there should also be an equality of outcome *in both directions* across the sexual divide. For example, there ought to be:

- A Minister for Men (because we have a Minister for Women)
- An equal number of Men's Officers (in *all* organisations) as there are Women's Officers

- An equal number of trade unions and senior trade unionists who care about men's problems, issues and rights as now care about women's problems, issues and rights

- An equal number of male Equality Officers whose specific job it is to ensure equality for men

- An equal number of Men's Commissions, Men's Units, Men's Conferences, Men's Committees, Men's Sections

- An equal number of male-friendly ideologues (not just male MPs) assisted by positive discrimination into Parliament as Feminist Ideologues now are

- An equal number of hours spent in paid employment between the sexes so that *fathers*, as well as mothers, can enjoy raising their children, and can delight in watching them grow and develop

- An equal number of divorced fathers gaining custody of their children

- An equal amount of time and research funding spent on addressing all men's health problems as there is in researching, addressing and funding women's health problems

- An equal number of women as men spending an equal amount of time in prison – for committing similar crimes

- An equal *proportion* of government funding spent on caring for male victims of domestic violence as is spent on caring for female victims

- An equal number of women as men working in the glass cellar jobs

- An equal number of work-related deaths, serious injuries and illnesses for women as for men by ensuring the same number of women as men enter unhealthy and dangerous jobs

- An equal number of men's courses and modules in universities, politically addressing men's problems, issues and rights as there are now Women's/Feminist/Gender Studies courses and modules

It has been forgotten, in our thirty-year-old Feminist-dominated Britain, a Britain that is so neurotically obsessed with Feminist/'women's issues', that *men are people too*. In a society that cared about *all* its citizens there would be equality of outcome for both sexes...or for neither.

But why just stop at men and women? The Feminist rationale for (numerical) equality of outcome could be just as logically applied to other groups in society – the working-class (however that may be defined), all ethnic minorities, the elderly, the young, the disabled, sub-sections of the disabled... The concept of equality of outcome is an Ideological quagmire, and stepping stones ought not to be provided for only Feminists to reach positions of high status, high salary and political power: they should be provided for all groups...or for none.

- Hypocrisy and double standards are in Feminism's DNA

Feminist Hypocrisy and Double standards

The above exercise in identifying areas for equality of outcome from the male perspective highlights two characteristics that run through all aspects of modern Feminism – hypocrisy and double standards.

Feminism has created a fear in society that allows it, without challenge or question, to enjoy a 'Pick 'n' Mix' Equality. I say 'fear' intentionally because no one dares point out that Feminist arguments and issues are irrational and often hypocritical, no one dares question or challenge Feminist demands for fear of personal and professional consequences, a politically correct backlash. An example of Pick 'n' Mix Feminist equality is the issue of 'equal pay for work of equal value'.

Feminism is so unworried about being questioned and challenged, knowing that it won't happen (how right they are...thirty years of feeble, fearful men) that they openly broadcast their use of double standards and hypocrisy. As one modern Feminist gloats:

> 'Women...should employ a combination of feminist ideals and the advantages that come with "being female" to achieve their ends: fall back on feminism if they feel sexually harassed but on femininity if they need to use sex appeal to get their way; refuse to defer to men but rely on them to do manly things like squashing bugs. "So men are confused, and I say 'good'", adds Morgan. "The more confused the men of this country are, the easier they are to manipulate...The more easily they are manipulated, the more likely it is that we'll get what we want – whatever it is that we want".'[18]

- 'Manipulate men' in order to create issues, in order to progress 'Forever' Feminism: 'Whatever it is we want...' – the nature of the issue is immaterial as long as it serves its Ideological purpose

- A lack of integrity is one more characteristic of a Feminist's psychological make-up

Double standards and hypocrisy are par for the course with Feminism. Having-it-both-ways is one of its characteristics; women are the same as men...or different...whichever suits Feminism best at any particular moment, on any particular issue. Sex stereotypes are endorsed if they're positive (women are 'more nurturing than men', or 'women's nice and co-operative natures make them better managers and politicians than men', 'women are less confrontational than men', 'women are more intuitive than men', 'women are more moral than men') but denounced if the sex stereotypes are negative (as defined by Feminism) - 'women have less capacity for mathematics and hard science than men', 'women freely choose to enter the sex industry so they can earn money from men'.

Feminists who resent any suggestion that 'biology is destiny' and deny that mothers should belong with their children are the first to demand that the children of a divorce should stay with their mother in custody disputes. We also see the double standards in the simultaneous Feminist arguments that women, on the one hand, are the *equals* of men...and that women, on the other hand, are men's moral *superiors* (as in the above examples).

- Sexual politics is riddled with such Feminist double standards and hypocrisy, and people are just too frightened of the personal and professional repercussions to point this out... and no one seems to notice that Feminism always wins, its demands always adopted, whichever option it chooses to claim; ('whatever it is we want') at any particular time on any particular issue (or those who *do* notice choose not to speak out, tactfully – cravenly? – keeping their heads down)

So, a return to equality of outcome, and to refresh our memories of its totalitarian origin. The implementation of equality of outcome policies by governments is based firmly, and dubiously, on the principle that ends can justify the means (eggs and omelettes), which involves sacrificing the welfare and well-being of one group of people to serve the interests of another group: this is, as we have seen, Marxist collectivism. This kind of political process is completely lacking in moral principle. It is a tyrannical, not a democratic, principle:

> *'In the wake of near-global discrediting of overt collectivism, Western feminism is one of the last strongholds of the collectivist viewpoint. Like collectivists, feminists are committed to imposing their own version of the common good upon society.'*[19]

- Do we really want this kind of Marxist collective politics in modern Britain? Sadly, it's too late to answer in the negative, it's already with us. All we can do now, it would seem (if men have sufficient will and courage) is to attempt to control it, to slow the progress of the Quiet Feminist Revolution

Equality of outcome is a collectivist political concept. It denies human individuality rather than liberating it. It makes people something they are not rather than helping them to make the most of what they *can* be, as does the concept of equality of opportunity.

The famous speech by Martin Luther King delivered on the steps of the Lincoln Memorial on August 28, 1963, included the sentence: 'I have a dream that my four children will one day live in a nation where they will not be judged by the colour of their skin but by the content of their character.' Many of us, working in the 1970s for Equality Feminism, applied this sentiment to the condition of women – that women's status should be judged not by their sex but by their individual merits and the content of their characters. Today's Feminism, through identity politics, the deliberate creation of artificial inequalities, collectivist politics, positive discrimination and quotas, has shattered our dream.

***

For Feminism success is not enough, it can *never* be enough. The Feminist battle has evolved from a fight for legal and social equality, a necessary and moral battle fought for by Equality Feminism and which has now been achieved, to a fight for preferential treatment, special privileges, policy-favouritism, positive discrimination and State-imposed quotas.

The modern Feminist's fight for equality of outcome is not about securing equality for women, it has nothing to do with 'gender equality'. Equality of outcome is not just a strategy to secure 'Forever' Feminism as an Ideology, but it is also about securing lucrative and permanent work on the Grievance Gravy-Train for many thousands of educated Feminists – and about securing cultural, legal and political power for their Movement.

Anne and Bill Moir note that:

> *'A survey in Britain concluded that one-third of all women police officers had been unfairly promoted; they simply were not good enough, but political pressures demanded their promotion.'*[20]

- This fact neatly sums up today's Feminism, and the British State's complicity in implementing its demands

> *'We have come a long way, but we still have a long way to go'*
>
> (Feminist mantra)

Chapter 39

Top Jobs for the Sisters:
Can Positive Discrimination be Justified?

Equality of outcome is not about 'gender equality' but about putting Feminists into senior positions – in effect, giving them trouble-free and effort-free promotion. Only 14 per cent of women are genuinely 'work-centred' and these women are likely to be Feminists. So it will be they, not ordinary women, who benefit from quotas, positive discrimination, preferential treatment and policy-favouritism for 'women'.

The previous chapter addressed the philosophical differences between equality of opportunity and equality of outcome. The present chapter is a continuation of this and will show that Feminism's arguments to justify the use of quota-type schemes are wrong, unfair and unjust, and are philosophically and morally invalid.

> *'Last night, at a Left-wing meeting on Women in The Recession in Parliament, Ms. Harman said so-called "positive action" would be "there for us" to put women on the boards of bailed-out banks.....
> "Sometimes we have to take scary methods in order to achieve worthwhile results", she told a mainly female audience. "It's about saying, 'because you are a woman I'm going to put you in this promotion'"(2009).'[1]*

Businesses are confronted with quota-type systems that require them to preference women over men...in order to show that they are treating women the *same* as men. This is a contradiction in terms (not surprising with Feminism's track record of double standards and hypocrisy) and obviously flies in the face of the very concept that it is meant to promote – equality.

***

Feminism (and Left-wing, liberal 'progressives') advance numerous arguments to justify quotas and positive discrimination. Their most common arguments are:

1. The 'role model' argument
2. The 'social and economic good' argument
3. The 'retrospective justice' argument
4. The 'ideal of equality' argument (already dealt with but will be briefly readdressed in the present context)

The 'Role Model' Argument

Is there any young woman in Britain today who does not know that she can become a head teacher, a judge, an MP, a cabinet minister, the Prime Minister? No, there isn't. The 'role model' argument, perhaps valid before the 1980s, is self-evidently nonsense in 2011.

Even so, when giving talks to students this argument is still advanced by Feminist teaching staff. Truly, I am forever amazed at how shallow the thinking of many Feminists really is. They have a front of self-righteousness, have been taught that Feminism is 'right'. For many Feminists their belief is built on nothing more than a diet of dogma, platitudes, cant, invalid statistics and sound-bites taken from the never-empty larder of the Feminist Lexicon; they are bloated with self-sanctification. Like a religion, Feminism is an *emotional* belief as well as an Ideology, a set of political doctrines. Faced with rational arguments the Feminist will either use the escape route of saying 'I take offence at that' (and then people will back off), or they will get angry (a Feminist 'need').

The 'Social and Economic Good' Argument

We are told that if there were more women in the boardroom profits would increase. We are told (by Feminists and the trade unions) that by not using women's talents in positions of seniority Britain is losing X millions of pounds each year. We are told that if there were more female MPs then Britain would be a better place in which to live. We are told that there would be better justice in Britain if more judges were women. And so on. All this is unproveable nonsense.

Because there are so many variables and incalcuable factors involved in measuring these claims they cannot in any way be proven; they are sugar-coated myths wafted toward organisations to tempt them to place more women (Feminists) in top jobs. They are the carrots to the Government's legislative sticks.

> 'Nor is it possible to identify whether organisations are more profitable and successful if they employ women...Studies can only identify associations at a single point in time, because longitudinal data are simply unavailable, or are impossible to interpret when they do exist...There is no hard evidence at all that female quotas per se improve profits in the private sector. Similarly, there is no evidence that all-male boards make a company more successful or profitable.'[2]

There is no non-ideological, objective evidence to support the Feminist claim. If any Feminist 'research' does purport to show that more women on boards of directors improves business then this 'research' needs to be rigorously questioned and its methodology analysed. One must always be cynical about 'research' findings that 'just happen' to reflect the Ideology and aims of the 'researcher'. To examine the dishonesty of Feminist 'research' I refer the reader to later chapters addressing this subject.

***

The reader may want to speculate on the long term consequences to society of using a quota system based simply upon the possession of a womb, rather than upon individual merit, skills, expertise and experience, as the standard by which to allocate influential and senior jobs. Preferential policies drive a wedge between individual talent and economic success and efficiency. So it is difficult to understand how this wedge enriches society.

Another criticism of the 'social and economic good' argument is that it forces employers to prefer women *over* men. One cost is that those groups who are being discriminated against – in this case, men – will be understandably resentful and they may translate this resentment into heightened sexism against women.

'For affirmative action to be effective, the individual rights of men must be sacrificed in favour of the collective rights of women.'[3]

Further, the effect of preferential policies *on women* could be devastating. In rushing to appear unbiased, employers will tend to promote women prematurely into jobs that they are not experienced or talented enough to handle; or they will promote women into whatever senior vacancies occur within the company, whether or not the women have the qualifications or necessary experience. This will seriously damage the effectiveness and efficiency of the company, political party, judicial system. It will also damage the health of the women themselves.

BBC HIGH-FLIER WITH AN "IMPOSSIBLE" JOB KILLED HERSELF AT SEA

(Daily Mail, Saturday, 17 May, 2008)

'A BBC executive walked into the sea and drowned herself after struggling with what she felt was an impossible job.

The 53-year-old had spent 30 years at the BBC in a succession of senior roles before being headhunted for the post of international operations director at its World Service Trust.

But shortly after the move, in October 2006, Mrs. Boto developed anxiety. She was unable to eat or sleep and would weep before going to work.

In early 2007, she was diagnosed with job-related anxiety and prescribed anti-depressants.'

Also, a point to consider is that when these women fail, or perform in only a mediocre manner, it will be seen as confirmation that women cannot handle senior positions, and therefore reflect badly on *all* women, particularly those women who have gained promotion because of their *genuine* and *individual* talents, skills, experience and hard work.

- The Feminist Jacqui Smith was promoted by Gordon Brown to the position of Home Secretary. Later, after losing the post, she admitted that she was ill-suited for the job, not having the requisite experience, skills and talent

***

A quota-type system will stigmatise every woman in a senior position as inferior. In the past it was assumed that women succeeded in business by using their sexuality – sleeping with the boss (and Feminists demanded that they wanted women to succeed by virtue and merit, not on their sexuality). Now it will be assumed (and quietly *is* being so assumed) that women are rising in their profession not by personal merit, skills, expertise or experience, but by sexual political privilege; because of her *sex* again. Ironic. The woman who achieves excellence on her own merit will never receive the recognition she deserves.

- Positive discrimination increases the very prejudice (sexism) that it is supposed to eliminate – at the expense of the group (women) that it is designed to benefit

Positive discrimination, promoting someone simply because they are a member of a particular group (in order to claim 'diversity') may have unpredictable results for the person promoted, for their work colleagues, and for the organisation itself. Efficient organisations strive for stability, not for unpredictability.

> 'Those who initiate preferential policies cannot sufficiently control the reactions of either preferred or non-preferred groups to ensure that such policies will have the desired effect...in the desired direction.'4

The 'Retrospective Justice' Argument

A third argument that Feminism advances to justify quotas, positive discrimination and preferential treatment is 'retrospective compensatory justice'. Feminism is not in the business of repealing cultural practices and laws that once restricted women's choices and were blatantly discriminatory (as Equality Feminism was). Today's Feminism goes much further; it requires laws, practices and policies that *actively preference* women. Apparently, only by being *preferred* can women be *equal*.

***

In law, the principle of compensatory justice means that anyone causing an injury to an innocent person must rectify the damage. The innocent party must receive compensation. Fine, but Feminism goes one step further than this and claims that the *descendant*s of those injured (the inequalities experienced by women in previous generations) must receive compensation because either a) those descendants are still living with the consequences of these inequalities (how the effect of these consequences is still ongoing is never explained), or b) 'it is only fair' that if one group *once* faced inequalities and discriminations then that group should *now* enjoy preferential treatment as a form of compensation. This is an argument of righting historical wrongs.

> 'In order to overcome the effects of past practices which resulted in discrimination, companies must now seek out those who were formerly ignored.'5

I occasionally stay in monasteries (I know, don't ask). A few years ago I was having a discussion with a monk regarding women and retrospective justice. He was adamant that because women had been discriminated against in the past then they should be compensated for this now, in the present. What really surprised me was that this chap had once taught philosophy. Male Feminists are found everywhere.

Women were once barred from the medical profession. It is the heirs (females as a group) of these previously 'victimised' women who, Feminism says, now have a rightful claim to compensation, to receive preferential treatment. Here we have a further example of Feminism's collectivist Ideology – women *as a group* in the past and women *as a group* in the present.

Yes, in the past some professions did bar entry to women, and that was wrong. *But this was not the fault of 21ˢᵗ century men* (as individuals or as a group) and these are the men who will now be facing discrimination because of the positive preferencing of present-day women. And the women who *receive* the benefits of preferential treatment and positive discrimination today *are not the same women* (as individuals or as a group) who suffered the earlier inequalities.

The 'retrospective justice' argument is invalid.

- The women receiving the benefits have not been victims *themselves* and have never been
- The men forced to provide the compensation *have done no wrong*; it is talented and experienced men who are being replaced by equally talented (or even less talented and less experienced) quota-assisted women (Feminists)

Even compensation granted to victims of the Holocaust didn't include payments to *future* generations.

- Morally, guilt cannot be inherited, and neither can compensatory claims in the form of quotas, preferential treatment and positive discrimination, for perceived past inequalities

    'Given the mortality of human beings, often the only compensation for historic wrongs that is within the scope of our knowledge and control is purely symbolic compensation – taking from individuals who inflicted no harm and giving to individuals who suffered none.'[6]

***

And what of today's rich, wealthy, well-positioned women? Do *they* also deserve 'retrospective compensatory justice' as well as their less well-off Sisters?

A gender and generational switch highlights this inappropriate 'justice'. Where does the 'retrospective justice' argument leave Feminism with the question of the privileged, rich, wealthy and well-positioned *women* in past generations? Working class men were in much more disadvantageous positions than these women...so we could claim that many lower paid / unemployed men *today* ought to be given positive discrimination and preference at the expense of today's well-educated, rich, wealthy, privileged and well-positioned women.

Take another generational gender-switch: National Service. From 1946 to 1956 all 17-year-old men were conscripted into one of the armed services, the army, navy or air force, living away from home and given hard training for two years. They had no choice, they lost two years of their lives, whether macho or delicate souls, they were forced to comply. Young women were exempt from this conscription. As an historical example of inequality and sex discrimination this takes some beating. Using Feminist logic it could be claimed that young men today require compensation for this past inequality and discrimination. Or that young women today, in order to balance the inequality and sex discrimination book, must be conscripted into...what? Working away from home and given hard work caring for the elderly, sick people, the disabled...for two years?

- 'Retrospective justice' cannot in any way validate positive discrimination in favour of present day women. It is illogical and immoral

311

Retrospective justice may be illogical and immoral but it is regularly used by Feminists to justify implementing their own discriminations against, and denigration of, men: 'Women have suffered discrimination for years...now its men's turn. Good. Tough.' The following is from the misandrous Feminist Kathy Lette:

> *'Women have endured centuries of sexism. Men have been the butt of the odd joke for a nanosecond and they're already whinging about it. But tough, because it's our turn to go straight for the jocular vein.'*[7]

- And the problem is, she's not joking. This is the woman who said on national radio that men will have sex with anything that moves in the garden (apparently because they are so carnal and gross). It's fun when men are belittled and denigrated; its 'sexist' and illegal when *women* are belittled and denigrated. Lette, and Feminists like her, have man-hating running through their veins. I refer the reader to Part Three
- Feminists are not benign nice people who are concerned about 'gender equality'

The 'Ideal of Equality' Argument

The fourth Feminist justification for positive discrimination and quotas is 'equality'. This concept was addressed in the previous chapter so a brief reminder in the present context will suffice.

'Equality' is an ambiguous word. People using the word often mean different things or intentionally choose to use it in different ways when a benefit accrues from such sophistry.

To some people any 'difference' at all between human beings – social, physical, economic, and so on – constitutes an 'inequality'. This is the Feminist interpretation. Others contend that such differences are natural and even healthy. They might asses the situation as being 'different but equal'. Two examples of people being different but equal are the differences between those with brown eyes and those with blue eyes.

- A 'difference' only becomes an 'inequality' when a value judgement is attached. If we say that people with blue eyes are superior, then having brown eyes ceases to be a 'difference' and becomes an 'inequality'

But when does a 'difference' become an 'inequality' in a *society*? In order to create an Ideological issue Feminism introduces an artificial 'value judgement' to the numerical imbalance between men and women in senior positions which it can then claim to be a 'gender inequality', a discrimination, allowing it to create the mythical but emotive issue of the 'glass ceiling'. This fraud is wilfully immoral. It is also a collectivist (Socialist-Marxist) construction focusing on the *rights of groups* rather than on the *rights of individuals*.

- Statistical differences *do* exist between men and women in the top jobs. However statistics *in themselves* carry no value judgement, they are neither right nor wrong. They are not an 'inequality'. A numerical imbalance, *in itself*, has no moral dimension, and therefore cannot be a 'gender inequality'. The many rational reasons for the under-representation of women in senior positions have been addressed, centring around women's work ethic and the vast majority of their work-life balance choices

For example, women freely chose to avoid promotion. The negative consequences (as defined by Feminists) of this choice cannot be labelled an inequality. It is not the State's job to be the agent of an Ideology by 'remedying' these negative consequences by using artificial mechanisms of positive discrimination (in any form), quotas, and preferential 'women only' schemes.

So none of the Feminist arguments to justify quotas and positive discrimination are valid. If only 14 per cent of women are 'work-centred' then it is fair and reasonable that only 14 per cent of women will be in the top jobs (and there is nothing to guarantee that women in this 14 per cent will be the most able women). Any other interpretation is Ideological skulduggery and philosophical sophistry.

- And in today's Britain approximately 14 per cent of top jobs *are* inhabited by women, an *equitable proportion* of women for whom work is central in their lives. This is just and fair. There is *no* 'gender inequality', there is *no* 'glass ceiling'. Quotas and positive discrimination are unnecessary. They are social engineering devices designed to progress the Feminist-Socialist Quiet Revolution

Feminism is a confidence trick. The concept of equality of outcome, quotas, positive discrimination, preferential treatment and policy-favouritism are Feminist devices used by the State to give, to hand over, high-status and highly remunerated jobs/sinecures to middle-class Feminists (Ideologues with a serious Left-wing and misandrous agenda). The 'glass ceiling' is a fraud, it is a righteous Ideological myth designed to disguise the pursuit of individual aggrandisement, personal gain and advancement. It is social engineering designed to preference and privilege articulate and educated Feminists – and to increase their political power. It has nothing to do with 'gender equality' for ordinary women.

FIRMS GIVEN QUOTAS FOR WOMEN STAFF
(The Sunday Times, 9 May, 2004)

'Labour is to bring in a new anti-discrimination regime that will impose a fresh "duty" on employers to promote equality between men and women, leaked cabinet papers reveal.

It could lead to all-women shortlists and quotas for jobs as well as fast-tracking women into senior management, according to legal experts.

Jacqui Smith, the deputy minister for women and equality, said: "I believe that we should now signal our intention to take practical steps to introduce a duty to promote equality of opportunity between women and men, for which there is strong and mounting pressure from the women's lobby and the Equal Opportunities Commission.'

- For 'equal opportunity' read 'equality of outcome'; for 'women's lobby' read 'Feminist Industries and Interest Groups': for 'practical steps' read 'quotas, positive discrimination', 'preferential treatment': for 'Equal Opportunities Commission' read 'Feminist non-governmental organisation'; for 'duty' read Marxist dictat; for 'Labour (Government) read 'Feminist Government'

***

All the Feminist arguments to justify quotas and positive discrimination schemes are invalid and immoral; they are a philosophical quagmire, and there ought to be no stepping-stones for only women (Feminists) to claim special privileges, preferential treatment and policy-favouritism.

Postscript

In 2010 Lord Davies of Abersoch was commissioned by the Coalition Government to investigate why so few women were in boardrooms. Lord Davies is a Socialist. He reported in February, 2011. There was a Feminist media frenzy...one couldn't move without stepping in platitudes and dogma. The Times (which has now become The Guardian in drag) was particularly in its element.

> *'Lord Davies of Abersoch...demanded that businesses do more to break the glass ceiling that has historically shut women out of the boardroom...Lord Davies wants companies to overhaul their boards in the next four years so that at least 25 per cent of their directors are women.'*[8]

One can assess from which Ideological camp Lord Davies was operating by his Feminist sound-bite hyperbole:

> *'On the current trend...it would take 70 years for women to hold half the FTSE 100 directorships'*[9]

- It was threatened that if the 25 per cent target was not met then quotas would be introduced. In the meantime, businesses would be bullied to 'comply'

Our marxist-lite Prime Minister, and leader of the Conservative Party, is delighted with this Socialist aim:

> *'At a Downing street launch for the report on women in the boardroom, David Cameron will warn that the government plans to impose a quota and legislate in future if firms do not respond to the challenge.'*[10]

So there we have it, a political 'closed shop'...a 'progressive' Feminist-dominated State implementing a section of the Socialist/Feminist agenda.

***

I cannot find any evidence that Lord Davies's report was informed by 'preference theory'. This is the theory that women *freely choose* their work-life balance, with the majority eschewing promotion. And only 14 per cent of women being work-centred. If the Socialist Lord Davies did not consult preference theorists then this would suggest that his findings and recommendations were based purely upon Feminist/Socialist Ideology. Coincidentally, in the same week that the Davies report was published, the Institute of Leadership and Management produced their own research on why there are so few women in boardrooms:

> *'The glass ceiling may be all in the mind. A lack of ambition and self-confidence, rather than overt male sexism, is holding women back from senior management roles, according to research...Women of all ages are likely to set their career goals lower than men, are more hesitant about putting themselves forward for top jobs and more frequently admit to self-doubt, according to the study by the Institute of Leadership and Management.'*[11]

The reader will be aware of similar research findings that were noted in the chapters on the pay gap and the 'glass ceiling'. The following, a response to the Institute's findings, is a neat personal summary of 'preference theory' with regard to 86 per cent of women (17 per cent 'family-centred' and 69 per cent 'adaptive'):

'Carol Doherty, 44, an NHS project support manager from Derham, Norfolk, said: "But I am not sure I am a directorate person. I probably know I won't get there, but I am confident where I am. As long as I can show I am motivating people and working to the best of my ability, I am happy doing that and looking after my family.'[12]

- Like the majority of women, Carol Doherty has found the optimal work-life balance and level of status that suits her personal work ethic, life aims and values

So if Lord Davies had been *genuinely* seeking the truth behind the phenomenon of fewer women in the boardroom he would have acknowledged Preference Theory. He could also have visited Amsterdam:

'Here women aren't on the board because they don't enjoy working that hard...Women in the Netherlands have less professional status, a big gender pay gap, sponge off their men and...they love it. Their secret? Living in an ever more hectically busy culture, they work less. If this is what happens when you give free choice to a nation of women counted among the most liberated, nay bossy, people in the world, is this, deep down, what all women want, no matter the feminist vision of equality in the highest echelons of power?...Dutch women can have it all: a man, a job, children and time off for themselves.'[13]

- And we know that 86 per cent of British women feel the same as Dutch women, they do not desire or seek promotion. If *fewer women put themselves forward* for promotion then logically there will be fewer women *in* senior positions, including in the boardroom
- There can be little doubt that Lord Davies's 'findings' and recommendations were driven by Socialist and Feminist Ideology

***

So who actually *will* be filling these 'free' senior posts that the Socialist-Feminist Coalition Government is determined to create? We know, of course, that they will be the Feminists...the very people whose Ideology demands that more 'women' should be on boards of directors. Reader, are you joining up the dots...are you becoming aware of what's happening and seeing a pattern emerging? There are no 'coincidences' that 'just happen' to benefit women (mainly Feminists); there are no 'coincidences' that 'just happen' to discriminate against men. There is a concerted and carefully orchestrated Quiet Revolution in progress.

- Yes, of *course* there are mediocre men in senior positions who are only there because 'they know someone'. And that is wrong. But to actually convert this type of 'wrong' into *policy*, into a similar type of 'favouritism', is just downright stupid. And just as immoral

What can be done to stop this Ideological nonsense? All the three major political parties are now Feminist-driven in their social policies and social engineering so it is doubtful if there will be a political solution. This being the case, I suggest the following.

Whenever you encounter a woman who is in a senior position assume that she is a 'token woman', grant her no respect, do not take her seriously. Hold the view that she is only in that position because she is a woman, not because of her abilities and experience. Respect her as a *person*, of course, don't be rude: but do not respect her position or her seniority. Feminists wouldn't care too much about this strategy – they only want the status, the high salary and the chance to promote their Ideology – but ordinary, decent, non-Ideological senior women will be furious when they, too, are looked upon and treated as 'token women'.

- Lack of respect leads to lack of credibility…and lack of credibility leads to an inefficient business. With the 'no respect' strategy businesses will think twice about complying with the Government's bullying to give Feminists unearned places on their boards

Non-Ideological women will seethe with resentment at my suggestion. Good. Because they will then be motivated to fight the Ideological idiocy of quotas, of giving Feminists 'free' top jobs. These women will quite rightly wish to be acknowledged and respected for their individual qualities, skills and talents. It is these women who will fight the Feminists and the Male Feminists, and hopefully it will be *they* who will put a stop to this particular aspect of the Quiet Revolution.

'Our girls must fight their girls: our women must fight their women'
(Swayne O'Pie)

I have no problem at all with women being in senior positions: I *do* have a problem with *Feminists* being in senior positions of authority, influence and power, especially if they have been shoehorned into those positions. So assume that *all* women in authority are 'token women', unworthy of your respect…Judges, managers, directors, heads of schools, MPs, wherever you encounter them. Decent women themselves will then rise up against their pushy, bullying Ideological Sisters, it is *they* who will stand up to the Feminists. Men haven't done so for thirty-five years and don't look as if they will ever get off their knees and do so. And led-by-the-nose political Male Feminists, the 'grovelling' men, whether in the Lords or in the Commons, are past redemption.

Section 6

Chapter 40
How and Why Feminism Exaggerates Issues

'A lie can travel halfway around the world while the truth is still putting on its shoes'

(Mark Twain)

Four areas of Issue Creep have now been addressed - strategies used by Feminism to justify its continuing existence and to blame, demonise and punish men:

- Creating 'women's issues' from nothing
- Establishing Industries to seek out, create and promote grievances, inequalities and discriminations
- Converting ordinary women's choices into 'gender inequalities'
- Changing the rules

This Section exposes a fifth Feminist strategy – the use of exaggeration. This strategy, and the issues involved, are especially relevant to Feminism's misandrous agenda.

'The broad mass of a nation...will more easily fall victim to a big lie than to a small one.'

(Adolf Hitler, Mein Kampf, 1925)

Why Feminism Exaggerates Issues

Now that equality of opportunity has been achieved, Feminism, in order to justify the continuing existence of its Movement and concomitant Industries, has needed to ratchet up the number, and the seriousness, of its issues. Exaggeration is a widely employed 'Forever' Feminism strategy. With this strategy there are two types of Issue Creep: i) numerical exaggeration, ii) trauma exaggeration.

The following two quotes neatly sum up the Feminist strategy of exaggeration:

'We have already referred...to two extremely effective strategies of ideological feminism: expanding the definition of one crime to include forms of behaviour that were once not classified as crimes, or reinforcing old claims with new ones, and eventually generating something that approaches hysteria. This strategy requires them to keep upping the ante.'[1]

And,

> 'The leaders and theorists of the women's movement believe that our society is best described as a patriarchy, a "male hegemony", a "sex/gender system" in which the dominant gender works to keep women cowering and submissive. The feminists who hold this divisive view of our social and political reality believe we are in a gender war, and they are eager to disseminate stories of atrocity that are designed to alert women to their plight.'[2]

- So Feminism needs to create 'plights', 'epidemics', 'crises', 'scares' in order to justify its existence, and the continuing existence, of its Ideology and Industries. It does this by *deliberately exaggerating* issues

A semi-hysteria needs to be generated so that the public, the media and politicians will sympathise with and support the Feminist-generated 'crisis issue' (whatever that may be, at any particular time). The right climate will then have been created for the 'crisis issue' to be politically and legally addressed. In this Section we see how this strategy has been applied, successfully, to various issues.

- To ensure maximum public and political attention, and maximum media coverage, no two 'crises' will be promoted at any one time

The reader will get a greater understanding of Feminism's exaggeration strategy from the following observation, made by an Ideological Feminist who left the Movement:

> 'A key element in the construction of a social problem is, of course, its size. The larger the problem, the greater the attention it can legitimately command. In the pursuit of magnitude, elastic definitions go hand-in-hand with inflated statistics, each exaggeration reinforcing the other.'[3]

- Cheating and lying is at the core of Feminism...it has to be, because it no longer has a moral base, no economic, sociological, political, ethical or democratic rationale to exist or to continue

***

Exaggeration is deliberately used to suggest that the 'problem' pervades the entire social structure, creating the impression that the solution must be recognised as a common cause, demanding the attention of all 'decent citizens' (hardly any of whom realise they are being conned).

And we dare not question it. Our questioning is censored. Feminism has invented the emotive phrase 'blaming the victim' in order to suppress any questioning of, or challenge to, such issues as sexual harassment, domestic violence and rape. The phrase 'blaming the victim' in Britain's politically correct society has become an effective censorship tool, ensuring that issues are only ever viewed and discussed from the Feminist perspective. Well, to hell with that.

This Section exposes the Feminist strategy of 'exaggeration' by analysing its use in four issues - trafficked women, sexual harassment, domestic violence and rape. There are many more sexual, political and Ideological dimensions to these four issues but here I focus on 'exaggerations' to show how they are used as a strategy to justify the existence of 21st century Feminism.

Exaggerating issues has resulted in focussing on special protection, preferential treatment and policy-favouritism for women, rather than on equal rights. It has nothing to do with 'gender equality'. It will be noted that this change of emphasis has dangerously eroded the rights of men accused of sexual harassment, domestic violence and rape. The Feminist strategy of 'exaggeration' is especially misandrous.

***

Christopher Booker noted in 'The Real Global Warming Disaster'[4] that scientists who maintain that global warming is caused by human activities needed to exaggerate their case in order to gain public and political attention. He quotes Sir John Houghton, first chairman of the IPCC Scientific Working Group, as saying (1994):

'Unless we announce disasters, no one will listen.'

And again, on the same issue, Dr. Stephen Schneider (1989):

'To capture the public imagination we have to offer up some scary scenarios, make simplified dramatic statements...to strike the right balance between being effective and being honest.'

And so it is with Feminism. Exaggeration is a *deliberate* Feminist strategy and sexual political gender-weapon. When exaggeration is intentionally used to promote and advance a specific set of ideas, a specific belief system, then it becomes a lie. Feminists use the same strategy of 'exaggeration', and for the same reasons, as the climate-botherers – to publicly and politically promote their Ideological agenda. Feminism is a huge fraud and we have all been duped.

Christina Hoff Sommers comments:

'The "gender war" requires a constant flow of horror stories showing women that male perfidy and female humiliation are everywhere.'[5]

***

'If you want a lie to be believed say it loud and say it often'
(Joseph Goebbels: Propagandist, National Socialist Party)

Mythomania: *'A compulsion to embroider the truth, exaggerate or tell lies.'[6]*

• I refer the reader to Part Three

Chapter 41

Trafficked Women

We know that the post-1997 Labour Governments were, with regard to sexual politics and social policy, Feminist Governments, with many senior Ministers themselves being Feminists. From the early 2000s 'trafficked women' (to be used in the sex industry) was created as a major Feminist issue. As the Home Office stated, it was: 'One of the worst crimes threatening our society'. In a nationwide police operation, 'Pentameter 2', 528 criminals involved with this crime were arrested. Dr. Tim Brain, Chief Constable of Gloucester who headed the 'Pentameter 2' operation, declared in July, 2008:

> 'At its core, this operation was about striking a blow against one of the most distressing aspects of serious and organised crime in this country – that of people-trafficking for sexual exploitation.'[1]

The Home Secretary, Feminist Jacqui Smith, declared the operation to be a great success:

> 'I would commend all those involved who have made a real impact in rescuing victims and bringing to justice those who exploit them.'[2]

So there we have it – a terrible social problem cleared up by a Labour/Feminist Government and the police. But not all was what it seemed:[3] Tom Rawstorme undertook a special investigation of this police operation.[4] He found:

- Of the 528 arrests almost a quarter were wrongly recorded

- Of the remainder, the vast majority were released without charge

- Of the 15 eventually charged it was accepted that 10 of these individuals had not coerced the prostitutes they worked with

- Only 5 people (out of 528 'successful' arrests) were actually convicted of trafficking[5]

In order to create an Ideological issue Feminism had grossly exaggerated the number of trafficked women...and then grossly exaggerated the success of resolving the 'problem' that it, itself, had invented.

***

The issue of trafficked women is a classic example of Feminism's use of its strategy of exaggeration:

> 'Academics and experts say that for years they have been warning the Government that the number of trafficked women working in the sex industry is far fewer than was being claimed....But despite these warnings, they say that Labour ministers and other feminist-dominated organisations have repeatedly relied upon these distorted figures to further their own vested interests and political agendas. As a result, it seems likely that millions of pounds of public funding has been spent trying to fix a problem that is far less widespread than portrayed.'[6]

- Yet such is the social, cultural and political power of Feminism that 'trafficking women for sexual exploitation' *still* became a hugely successful Feminist issue

Chris, 32, runs a straight escort agency with his partner in the north-west:

'I have no idea where they get these figures for trafficked workers from. I have been involved in the industry for 10 years either as an independent or working through an agency and I have never met anyone who has been coerced or forced to do the work. A third work full-time and about a third part-time.'[7]

What is the prostitutes' *own* perspective on trafficked women?

The International Committee for Prostitutes:

'Trafficking of women and children, an international issue among both feminists and non-feminists, usually refers to the transport of women and children from one country to another for purposes of prostitution under conditions of force or deceit. The ICPR has a clear stand against child prostitution under any circumstance. In the case of adult prostitution, it must be acknowledged that prostitution both within and across national borders can be an individual decision to which an adult woman has a right...Women who choose to migrate and work as prostitutes should not be punished or assumed to be victims of abuse. They should enjoy the same rights as other immigrants. For many women, female migration through prostitution is an escape from an economically and socially impossible situation in one country to hopes for a better situation in another.'[8]

- In order to increase the number of trafficked women that are used in the sex trade, Feminism *deliberately* includes women who have 'voluntarily migrated' to become prostitutes

'Research by Nick Mai into one hundred UK-based migrant sex workers suggested that the majority were not trafficked, but rather entered sex work mainly for economic reasons, and knew that this was what they were coming to the UK to do.'[9]

Nicki Adams, a campaigner for British prostitutes' rights, says:

'In all the years, we have come across only two women who fit that classic description of someone who has been trafficked...We know the situation in Soho very, very well and are in touch with just about all the women working in the 53 flats that there are there. I feel absolutely confident those women are not trafficked (2009).'[10]

- *Two trafficked women* – 'One of the worst crimes facing our society'? An exaggeration? A Feminist Fraud?

***

So we need to ask why this hugely expensive 'epidemic' was created. There are a number of reasons; I'll address three:

1. Firstly, Feminists wished to blame and demonise men:

'Trafficked women for sex exploitation' is a textbook Feminist-created issue (men oppressing, victimising and abusing women). It has been enthusiastically promoted as an issue by powerful Labour Government Feminists (as has prostitution in general). Jacqui Smith was Home Secretary, whilst Fiona McTaggart was a former Home Office Minister. It was reported that McTaggart stated to the House of Commons in 2008:

'...she regarded all women prostitutes as victims of trafficking. This, she said, was because their route into the industry "almost always involves coercion, enforced addiction to drugs and violence from their pimps or traffickers".'[11]

- McTaggart's bigotry and misandry are tangible – there is a blatant wish, an Ideological need (a psychological 'need') to blame and demonise men (the violent pimps, the coercive traffickers, forced drug-taking). It would appear that Ms. McTaggart completely disregards the views of prostitutes themselves, and their organisations, and the findings of neutral research in her misandrous wish to politicise, and deliberately exaggerate, the created Feminist issue of trafficked women

2. Secondly, in addition to *blaming* men, Feminism wishes to *punish* men. Feminists in the Labour/Feminist Government, led by the misandrous dominatrix, Harriet Harm-man, (the Labour Government's Minister for Women... and Deputy Prime Minister) formulated a Bill that would make visiting prostitutes virtually illegal for men; it was intended to penalise and punish any man who had sex with a woman who had been trafficked – even if the man was genuinely ignorant of her trafficked status. This Bill (discussed earlier in the chapter on prostitution) was clearly intentionally man-hating in nature, blaming and punishing men for creating a demand for prostitution – and thereby 'forcing' women into the profession.

- In order to punish men the Feminist strategy was to grossly exaggerate the number of trafficked women so as to glean public and political sympathy for its anti-male 'prostitution' Bill and thereby facilitate its being passed into law. Many men could then be easily blamed, legally criminalised, publicly demonised, and thereby *punished*

3. Thirdly, the 'trafficked women issue' was (and is) used by Feminism to stimulate and benefit its Grievance Gravy-Train Industries. For example, the innocuously-named Poppy Project:

   'The Poppy Project, a charity which has received £5.8 million of Government funding and which wants to end all prostitution on the grounds that it "helps to construct and maintain gender inequality", carried out research that found that 80 per cent of London prostitutes working in flats were foreign.'[12]

- The phrase 'prostitution helps to construct and maintain gender inequality' identifies its Ideology and confirms that the Poppy Project is a Feminist organisation

Nicki Adams again:

   'In all the years, we have come across only two women who fit that classic description of someone who has been trafficked. One was an African woman and the other came from Moldova...We know the situation in Soho very, very well and are in touch with just about all the women working in the 53 flats that there are there. I feel absolutely confident those women are not trafficked.'[13]

- So who is telling the truth here – Nicki Adams ('only two trafficked women') or the Ideologically-driven Poppy Project (with its '80 per cent of London prostitutes are trafficked women')? Who has the most to gain from *not* telling the truth, from exaggerating the figures? Whose statistics happen to coincide and chime with an Ideological agenda?

Nicki Adams also suspects the motives of these people and wonders why they are deliberately exaggerating the issue:

   '"I feel absolutely confident those women are not trafficked"...If that is indeed the case then it begs the question as to who benefits, and how, from this gross exaggeration of the trafficking figures.'[14]

Nicki Adams, the campaigner for prostitute's rights, might well ask 'who benefits'. Answer: i) the Feminist Ideology benefits by demonising and punishing men, ii) Feminist Industries are a second beneficiary; the Poppy Project was given £5.8 million to undertake 'research' (given to a Feminist organisation by a Feminist-dominated Labour Government with many powerful Feminists in senior positions).

- The extent of Feminism's political power is astonishing – and very few people, outside the Feminist 'Family', realise this

Many Feminist organisations, 'charities', Industries and individuals benefit financially from the strategies of creating and exaggerating issues. Feminist Grievance Gravy-Train Industries really couldn't function without seeking out, creating or exaggerating grievances, sexism, inequalities, oppressions and abuses.

***

The Feminist 'charity', the Poppy Project, wouldn't have a moral or Ideological base if it were shown that foreign women *freely chose* to migrate to England to work in the sex industry - a rational, considered choice to earn more money, perhaps more quickly than in other professions. The ICPR and other representatives of the profession have shown us that this is actually the case; in addition:

'Research interviews conducted with migrant prostitutes show that the majority say they choose to work in the sex industry because of the improved living conditions and opportunities it offers to them and, via the money they send abroad, to their families.'[15]

- Ethical considerations, truth and political integrity are no constraints when Feminism wishes to create issues or epidemics. There is too much at stake to be so constrained

Mythomania: *'A compulsion to embroider the truth, exaggerate or tell lies'.*[16] Trafficked women - a Feminist psychosis or a clever Machiavellian political confidence trick? Or both? Exaggerating the extent of trafficked women exaggerates the evilness of men, who have been Feminist-nominated as the sole cause of this phenomenon. 'Trafficked women' is an issue used to spread misandry.

***

As a postscript to the above I bring to the reader's attention an article in the Daily Mail, Friday, November 5, 2010.

'"CREDULOUS" CHARITY BELIEVED SHE WAS TRAFFICKING VICTIM: Lying maid loses her £750,000 claim that she was kept as a slave...A maid who claimed she was kept as a slave could face prosecution for perjury after an employment tribunal ruled she made up her tale of appalling abuse... As a supposed trafficking victim, Salim Udin was helped by Kalayaan to secure money and housing from the Government-funded Poppy Project organisation...'

- 'Credulous' Charity...or Ideological 'Charity'?

Chapter 42
Sexual Harassment

'Georgie Porgie pudding and pie,

Kissed the girls and made them cry.

When the Sisters came out to play,

Mr. Porgie was accused of

Sexual Harassment and creating a

Hostile and Offensive Work Environment

And after a summary Employment Tribunal

He was taken away.'

***

There are two sets of guidelines for sexual harassment:[1]

1. Quid pro quo sexual harassment: This is where a person in authority demands sexual favours from someone in a lesser position and is accompanied with promises of favours if acceded to, or threats if refused.

2. Hostile work environment sexual harassment: This is verbal or physical conduct of a sexual nature creating an intimidating, hostile, or offensive working environment.

***

At one time women in employment had to genuinely worry about sexual harassment and physical intimidation from men, there can be no doubt about that. However, the aim of this chapter is to show how Feminism now uses sexual harassment as a device to promote its Ideology, employing the strategy of exaggeration. Feminism uses exaggeration with this issue by: i) inflating the number of incidents of sexual harassment, and ii) intensifying the severity and the trauma caused by these incidents.

Sexual harassment is exaggerated to promote Feminism's political aims:

- To justify its continuing existence

- To create work for its Industry

- To use as a misandrous gender-weapon

***

Firstly, we need to understand that sexual harassment, like all Feminist issues, is deliberately placed into a patriarchal framework – that is, men have power over women, 'men are bad people', 'women are good people'. This framework is also used to inform its perspectives on pornography, prostitution, domestic violence and rape. The law and the Left-wing TUC and governments have all embraced this Ideological framework, and social policy is based upon it.

> *'The feminist literature on these matters assumes that sexual harassment can never be accidental or trivial. It is always seen as part of a concerted effort to keep women in their place as an inferior social group. It is, so many serious commentators on it insist, an essential part of patriarchy's ongoing plot against women.'*[2]

And,

> *'Male/female conflict can take many forms. Some men appear to feel a need to assert their authority over women colleagues. Common techniques employed by men in sexual power play include commenting on a woman's attractiveness, and addressing her with familiar endearments such as "love" or "dear"...In order to gain power men may cast business relationships with women in the more familiar social male-female roles. The traditional male roles – father, husband, lover – are useful to men in the workplace because they help men to control women.'*[3]

- So Feminism sees sexual harassment as an issue of male power. *Any* sexual attention given to women from men is interpreted by Feminists as men expressing power over women.

***

To strengthen this perspective Feminism exaggerates the number of incidents of sexual harassment. It does this by using the mechanism of 'Criteria Dilution'; that is, by widening the definition of sexual harassment, thereby making it more inclusive. There are many examples but the following three will give a flavour.

A saucy calendar hanging in the locker-room of a motor repair garage (where all the mechanics will be male) is a legal offence – because the female receptionist may accidentally see it if she strays into the locker-room. The Sexual Harassment Industry is thereby perpetuated by an Ideology that insists (and has had this insistence enshrined in law) that an accidental sighting of a calendar is on a par with a sex-starved sex-pest of a male supervisor who cannot keep his hands off women's bottoms. So Criteria Dilution has allowed the Feminist Sexual Harassment Industry to hike up the number of incidents, with this hike becoming legal.

> *'The Health and Safety Act 1995 and the Management of Health and Safety Regulations of 1996 define violence is such a way as to include sexual harassment.'*[4]

A second example of Feminism's exaggeration of sexual harassment can be seen in the case of Ian Frazer. Mr. Frazer was a barman at a power station social club. He was fired because he called women 'pet'.[5] Women Against Sexual Harassment (WASH) say that men who use terms of endearment such as 'dear', 'pet', 'love', 'hinny' and 'hun', are committing sexual harassment.[6] But wait, not only is it *politically incorrect* to use phrases such as these but it is also *illegal*; these phrases are classified as sexual harassment and sexual harassment is 'violence against women' (see above)...and violence against women is illegal. So the friendly Mr. Frazer, living in the North East of England where linguistic expressions such as 'pet' and 'hinny' (hen) are ingrained cultural expressions of endearment that have been used for centuries, could be tried in a court of law for using 'violence against women' (that is, sexually harassing women; that is, calling them 'pet').

- Such is the power of Feminism.

The reader will note the self-righteousness of Feminists on this issue, the sense of power they have been given to bully men, to demonise and to punish men. The reader will also note the dark undercurrent of totalitarianism, not only its Ideology but also its methods, that is evident throughout Feminism...an undercurrent that is allowed to be freely expressed in modern Britain, as is Feminism's intrinsic hatred of men. Feminism has the power to dictate what *language* we are allowed to use, the *words* we are permitted to use... and those we are *not* permitted to use.

- This censorship will be recognised as political correctness and political incorrectness. But what is not recognised is that these concepts were deliberately introduced by Feminism from America *precisely* to be used as censorship tools

There are no 'coincidences' that 'just happen' to advantage women (Feminists); there are no 'coincidences' that 'just happen' to discriminate against men. For thirty five years there has been a carefully orchestrated group of strategies that promote and implement the Feminist Ideology and agenda, that progress the Quiet Revolution.

It simply has not been grasped just how powerful modern Feminism has become. An Equality Feminist warns:

> *'The Sexual Harassment Industry, by uncritically adopting the feminist language of "power" (which is replicated in virtually all academic sexual harassment codes) is promoting an extremist feminist agenda, although it is not often recognised as such.'*[7]

***

A third example of Feminism exaggerating sexual harassment can be seen in the trade union movement. The TUC's Guidelines say sexual harassment can take many forms, including:

> *'Leering, ridicule, embarrassing remarks or jokes and unwelcome comments; suggestive remarks or other verbal abuse; compromising invitations, demands for sexual favours and physical assault...such "unwelcome" comments can include remarks about dress, appearance, deliberate abuse, offensive pin-ups.'*[8]

Who decides if a woman has been sexually harassed using the above criteria? The astonishing answer is that it is the woman *herself* who decides. According to the TUC, sexual harassment is:

> *'Anything a woman defines as a hostile environment.'*[9]

It is on the woman's interpretation *alone* what she chooses to define as 'hostile'; she does not even have to tell the male that he is bothering her – she only has to inform a friend![10] It is up to the woman to decide if a 'look' is a 'leer', no witnesses, no corroborating evidence is required to condemn the male and lose him his job and reputation, it is his word against hers; and her word – *by law* – must be believed...and acted upon (as is also the case with domestic violence and rape). No organisation wishes to anger Feminism if it can possibly avoid it...much easier to appease it by sacking the 'offending' male.

- It has not been understood just how far Feminism has manipulated our culture, our laws and our political system. Its Quiet Revolution has gone unnoticed

In a simplistic but accurate scenario of how sexual harassment can operate in a work situation I offer the following:

Daisy, an attractive young typist: *'I wear a mini-skirt when I go to work, and unbutton my blouse a little so that dishy Dave from the Cutting and Packing Department will ask me out...But if that leering Mr. Jones from Accounts ogles me just one more time I'm going to report him for sexual harassment.'*

- And successive governments, the TUC, and Employment Tribunals condone this mentality, this behaviour, this hypocrisy

Provocative dressing and provocative behaviour provokes. We saw in an earlier chapter that the majority of heterosexual women wish to attract male attention when they dress in a feminine fashion and use make-up. But there's something childish about showing yourself off at work (or socially in public) and then getting cross because some untargeted person is attracted to you instead of the 'right' person. In sexual terms such dressing and behaviour is not only childish but morally wrong and sometimes dangerous. The above analysis is as relevant to some date-rape scenarios as it is to workplace sexual harassment. There is something unrealistic about taking the view that men ought not to be aroused by a woman's provocative dressing and provocative behaviour; on a point of equality and fairness such dressing and behaviour ought to be banned from the workplace.

- Feminist mantra: 'Women have the right to dress how they wish'. OK, then masculinist mantra: 'Men have a right to express their attraction to women'. A woman tormenting and sexually harassing men by her dress and behaviour is as wrong as a man sexually harassing a woman
- But in today's Britain on this issue, as with so many, Feminist Ideology trumps logic, justice, fairness and common sense

In order to increase the incidence of sexual harassment the criteria have been deliberately diluted, the definition expanded to be more inclusive:

'Once sexual harassment includes someone glancing down your shirt, the meaning of the phrase has been stretched beyond recognition. The rules about unwanted sexual attention begin to seem more like etiquette than rules.'[11]

In effect, the legal criteria for sexual harassment has been brought down to the level of the *most sensitive,* or *the most paranoid,* or the *most Ideological,* woman in a particular work environment, and what makes *her* feel uncomfortable. Where is the justice, the 'gender equality' in that?

By using the strategy of Criteria Dilution, Feminism has deliberately conflated the trivial with the serious. The dictionary definition:

Harassment: *'To irritate or disturb persistently'*[12]

Persistent: *'Refusing to give up or let go; persevering obstinately; insistently repetitive or continuous.'*[13]

So common sense would dictate that sexual harassment has to be behaviour that is exhibited on *numerous occasions* – three or more, to be 'repetitive' or 'continuous'. Feminism has changed the rules; in today's Britain 'one off' incidents are defined as sexual harassment; a single incident, on one woman's say so, can ruin a man's life. There is no 'gender equality' in *that* imbalance of power.

The French seem to deal with the issue in a much more mature and common sense way. French law makes sexual harassment punishable by fines, or even imprisonment, but it is very specific about what constitutes harassment, which it defines as:

> *'A word, gesture, attitude or behaviour by a superior with a view to compelling an employee to respond to a solicitation of a sexual nature.'*[14]

In this non-patriarchal context, bad manners and crassness are not enough. There has to be an element of coercion, blackmail or genuine abuse of hierarchical power. Faced with the question of a woman who is confronted with dirty pictures, stupid remarks or unwanted passes from colleagues of equal rank, Véronique Neiertz, the French Minister for Women's Rights, commented:

> *'What is wrong with un gifle – a slap round the face? Be clear, it is blackmail to make sexual advances to someone who depends on you for their work...In the case of blackmailing harassment the state has something to say. Otherwise, the relations between men and women are merely part of life.'*[15]

Can you imagine the Feminist-dominated British State having such a sensible and mature attitude to the issue? When the BBC under its then sexual harassment supremo Margaret Salmon brought out a series of guidelines on the subject, Ms. Salmon was asked to define what sexual harassment actually was. She replied:[16]

• *'Why do we need to'*? No need to, of course...as long as men *continue* to be blamed and punished

***

The second way Feminism exaggerates sexual harassment is by claiming that *all* incidents carry the same degree of trauma. An Equality Feminist writes:

> *'In some feminist circles it is heresy that a woman who has to listen to her colleagues tell stupid sexist jokes has a lesser grievance than a woman who is physically accosted by a supervisor. It is heresy, in general, to question the testimony of self-proclaimed victims of date rape or harassment...All claims of suffering are sacred and presumed to be absolutely true.'*[17]

And,

> 'For obvious reasons, SHI (Sexual Harassment Industry) rhetoric maximises the damage supposedly inflicted on them (the supposed 'victims'): Sympathy will be garnered, counselling provided, male wickedness confirmed, and women's victimhood – today a prized commodity for which women are in passionate competition with other victim groups – enshrined.'[18]

***

Feminism has been incredibly successful with its strategy of exaggerating sexual harassment, to such an extent that, as we have seen, the TUC has adopted it as an anti-male weapon and successive governments have incorporated it into social policy and law. But for Feminism success is never enough... Women are being *deliberately trained up* to seek out and identify incidents that can be interpreted as sexual harassment:

> 'Unlike battery and sexual assault, where the hurt resides in the action itself, the injury in much of what is today labelled sexual harassment arises in the interpretation women are being taught to adopt as a guide to understanding others' words and gestures.'[19]

To justify building an Industry around sexual harassment, Feminists needed to create a widespread problem and in order to do this they needed to train women to actually *recognise* incidents as possibly 'sexual' and then to be able to *interpret* these awkward incidents of unwanted male attentions as 'sexual harassment'. In this way, the issue could then be referred to as a 'widespread problem'.

> 'The leaders and theorists of the women's movement...are eager to disseminate stories of atrocity that are designed to alert women to their plight.'[20]

- Feminists are priming women to feel 'uncomfortable' with men in almost any circumstances

The Sexual Harassment Industry, including the TUC, has produced copious amounts of literature, set up training courses for female employees (and students), printed booklets, run counselling sessions and support groups – all created to teach women to identify sexual harassment incidents thereby boosting the number of sexual harassment victims.

> 'As feminists interested in the issue themselves argue, "Many (women) have difficulty recognising their experience as victimisation. It is helpful to use the words that fit the experience, validating the depths of the survivor's feelings and allowing her to feel her experience was serious". In other words, these feminists recognise that if you don't tell the victim that she's a victim, she may sail through the experience without fully grasping the gravity of her humiliation. She may get through without all that trauma and counselling.'[21]

- If a woman doesn't 'recognise the fact that she has been a victim' then surely a rational person would say that she has *not been* a victim? Feminists *teach* women how to become victims. And Feminism is an Ideology embraced by the TUC, our universities and our Left-wing/liberal/progressive State...and is believed to be a righteous Movement by the public...we have all been duped by this fraud

- One assumes a 'survivor' to be someone who has escaped being killed in a plane crash... not someone who has had her bottom patted. But the exaggerated language helps ratchet up the *trauma* of the incident

Feminism has indoctrinated a 'learned helplessness' into ordinary, decent, non-Ideological women, encouraging and teaching them to be 'victims', and thereby artificially creating and exaggerating the problem. This is also done with domestic violence and date-rape. Feminism needs victims, abuses, oppressions to perpetuate itself, to justify its continuing existence and to make work for its Grievance Gravy-Train Industries.

- Feminism and its organisations have 'primed' ordinary women to seek out and report any behaviour that could possibly be construed as sexual harassment

Like other issues in sexual politics, sexual harassment has become a Feminist Industry – trained specialists, theoreticians, therapists, training courses, lobbyists, lawyers, special trade union posts. A whole new field of legal expertise opening up the opportunities for the legal profession and for Feminist Ideologues.

***

It is quite clear that Feminism is using sexual harassment to promote its Ideology and misandrous agenda. If Feminism were *genuinely* concerned about the welfare of women it would have set up courses and workshops on, say, how to keep oneself from taking offence at trivial slights or innuendos, or how to respond to an unwanted sexual overture in a spirited way that ends the problem. Feminists would be teaching women how to deal with individuals with strength and confidence, how to put a botherer in his place without crying into their pillow or screaming for help from counsellors. Instead, the existing situation is deliberately designed to bring an ever greater range of behaviour within the sexual harassment arena, Issue Creep, and to train women up to identify these as 'harassments'; to create an ever greater number of 'victims'.

Sexual Harassment and Spreading Misandry

The Equality Feminist Daphne Patai has written and commented widely on sexual harassment and argues that misandry is widespread in modern Feminism (and not only on the periphery). She states that this is a further expression of Feminism's hatred of men, and that this misandry:

> '...is revealed most strikingly among those feminists who have deliberately generated what she calls the "sexual harassment" industry.'[22]

The Feminist strategy of exaggeration has: i) inflated the numbers of sexual harassment incidents, and ii) intensified the supposed trauma of these incidents. And so we arrive at the 'widespread problem' of sexual harassment. Kat Banyard, one of the latest Ideologues to jump aboard the Feminist Grievance Gravy-Train, states:

> 'In 1999 the European commission reported a high incident of sexual harassment had been unearthed in studies in numerous European countries, including Austria, Norway, Germany, and the UK. They revealed exposure to harassment could be between 70 and 90 per cent'[23]

- Such a high incidence is hardly surprising when the cultural and legal criteria for sexual harassment has been so diluted that simply *being in the company* of a woman has become such a clear and present danger to men... when a wolf-whistle or a look at a pretty woman for longer than 10 seconds can be interpreted (and is) into sexual harassment (if the woman *chooses* to interpret it as such)

So Feminist 'research' finds that 70 to 90 per cent of women have been sexually harassed: this obviously means that there are very many 'bad men' out there – a successful outcome for Feminism – a large percentage of men have been demonised. Piffling incidents have been deliberately exaggerated, magnified, to the point where the trauma caused, and the numbers involved, have become a politically useful strategy to: i) justify the continuing existence of Feminism, ii) build a Sexual Harassment Industry, and iii) develop an effective misandrous gender-weapon.

Sexual harassment is a rich area for man-hating opportunities...for demonising and punishing men. One of the main aims of exaggerating sexual harassment (and this also applies to domestic violence and rape) is to inflate the severity and pervasiveness of evil that can be attributed to men.

I'm not saying that there aren't *any* genuine or persistent, or really offensive, sexual harassment incidents; of course there are. And serious and persistent cases ought to be dealt with severely. My argument is that the number of incidents, and their trauma, has been grossly and deliberately exaggerated in order to convert the phenomena of workplace nuisances or gauche advances into Ideological issues, one aim of which is to create a political gender-weapon with which to demonise and punish men.

> *'Let me therefore be clear that what I am mainly criticising here is an important – and to me profoundly disturbing – aspect of feminism: its predilection for turning complex human relations into occasions for mobilising the feminist troops against men'*[24]

- Any sexual overture from a man to a woman is now a cause for alarm; all men are now potential victims of the Feminist Sexual Harassment Industry

Some men's behaviour towards women can be boorish and crass, but surely there must be a sense of proportion. Revisit the dictionary definition of 'harassment' – 'persistent, insistently repetitive, continuous' behaviour. To strengthen its political aims Feminism has changed the rules, by its strategy of exaggeration and Criteria Dilution. The following offers a taste; there are many more examples.

STUDENT JAILED FOR BOTTOM SLAP

(The Times, Thursday, 16 September, 1999)

'A student who had never been in trouble with the law was jailed for six weeks for slapping a woman's bottom.'

- An example of Feminist and institutional man-hating: could this woman not have simply turned round and slapped his face – hard? Could the court not have fined him or given him community service? No, under a Feminist regime men have to be condemned, demonised and *punished*. Judges are obliged to attend Feminist-run Equality and Diversity courses in which they are 'taught' the Feminist perspective, and encouraged to promote Feminist aims

PAT ON THE BOTTOM COSTS BOSS £1M JOB

(The Times, Wednesday 10 May, 2000)

'One of his female guests yesterday told The Times: "He'd had about three or four glasses, but he was mixing it with water. I'd say he was more merry than paralytic, and no way obnoxious.'

- But even with this female support Jim Hodkinson, 56, *still* lost his £1 million-a-year job. An insidious Feminist politically correct culture has been intentionally created in Britain

With the law now supporting any claim of sexual harassment, women will simply run to a solicitor instead of dealing personally with the problem. By building the issue into *policy* Feminism has absolved women from personal responsibility for resolving a *personal problem*, once again treating them like children - women are encouraged to run to Nanny State for protection from 'bad men'. Instead of dealing with the situation themselves like grown-up people.

***

Feeling affronted when accidentally sighting a saucy calendar...taking offence at being called 'love' or 'pet'...feeling 'abused and traumatised' when your bottom is patted – all this is chicken-shit stuff, this is not what strong women do. Again we see Feminism playing the system, having it both ways:

In one breath we hear: 'We are women, we are strong, we are capable of holding senior, responsible jobs and capable of making difficult decisions'...and in the next breath: 'We are women, we are victims, we are sensitive and easily offended, we need protection'.

- So which is it - serious Feminist hypocrisy... or clever manipulation of the law, trade unions and a compliant State? Or both?

When Feminists aren't maintaining that there are no differences between the sexes when it comes to work preferences or subject and career choices, they are insisting that women in the workplace must be treated with delicacy to account for their sensitive and frail natures and special vulnerabilities. Feminism is encouraging women to pack a solicitor in their lunchbox in order to aggressively respond, *if they so choose*, to the smallest slight or slur.

- For two decades Feminists have also been training up judges to absolve women criminals from personal responsibility...because of women's 'special circumstances and vulnerability'

The Sexual Harassment Industry infantilises women. By swaddling women with cultural and legal protection it implies that women *need* to be protected. It paints women as defenceless against even the most trivial of male attentions.

> *'Like the rhetoric about date rape, this extreme inclusiveness forces women into old roles. What message are we sending if we say: "We can't work if you tell dirty jokes, it upsets us, it offends us?"'* [25]

- A neat, accurate phrase: 'extreme inclusiveness'; echoing my own Criteria Dilution

And this protection assumes that *she* never ogles, leers, or makes sexual innuendoes *herself*.

***

There are two serious elements of misandry with the exaggeration of sexual harassment:

1. It creates a society in which men are perpetually under a cloud, a society in which men are to be blamed, condemned and demonised. This element is fundamental to Feminism's patriarchal view of society – defining all men as 'bad people'

It is not just a *few* men who are maligned, but *all* men: this makes sexual harassment a much more powerful misandrous weapon:

'In an essay attempting to profile the quintessential harasser, two feminists warn in conclusion (and in all seriousness) that "the harasser is similar, perhaps disturbingly so, to the "average man".'[26]

2. A further, and directly related, element of this Feminist exaggeration is that many young women will be fearful of men. This is a *deliberate* Feminist intention (as it is with the issues of public space violence, domestic violence and rape) – creating an atmosphere in which women have a foreboding sense of living under a constant threat from predatory males. Feminism justifies its existence by purporting to protect women from 'bad men', so exaggerating the extent of sexual harassment is a useful recruiting tool. Feminism creates a vigilante mentality in many young women: thereby souring and warping normal male/female relationships

'The sexual harassment industry is not going to wither away as long as it provides thousands of jobs for its practitioners, despite having harmed the interests of women who must live with the poisonous atmosphere of resentment and suspicion it creates in the name of protecting them from the patriarchy.'[27]

***

Apart from its other aims with the issue of sexual harassment, does Feminism have a *specific strategy* designed to warp normal male/female relationships? To answer this question we need once again to look at the 'sex' in sexual harassment, and ask which type of Feminist is *particularly* offended by heterosexual sex.

'Because the expanded definition of sexual harassment reflects the world-view of those consciously or unconsciously opposed to heterosexuality, lesbians have clearly won a major victory...Among the many forms taken by misandry in popular culture have been the notions of ridiculing, bypassing, dehumanising and even demonising men.'[28]

• The influence of Lesbian Feminism is again perceived (as it was in the chapters on Femininity, Sex Objects, Pornography and Prostitution)

The following neatly summarises the points covered so far:

'As I have repeatedly stressed, the Sexual Harassment Industry does not attempt to differentiate between instances of indisputable abuse and mere expressions of sexual interest. Each is taken to be as egregious as the other...any sexually tinged word, gesture, or look (is turned) into "sexual harassment". This persistent inability or refusal to draw distinctions cannot be taken as accidental...The slow and continuous expansion of efforts to regulate personal relations, now extending even to consensual relationships between adults, is a particularly clear example of the stigmatising of male sexuality in and of itself...Sexual harassment is first and foremost (seen) as an act committed by powerful males against powerless females. The infantilisation of adult women implicit in this view does not seem to trouble many of those who profess feminism.'[29]

• Note the references to Criteria Dilution, 'not differentiating between abuse and sexual interest'; to the 'stigmatising of male sexuality' (the Lesbian Feminist influence), to 'male power over women', to 'the infantilisation of adult women'

333

As long as Feminist vigilantes are allowed to regulate hurt feelings and sexual overtures that are not sexual assaults, we will remain stuck in an increasingly nightmarish situation in which all words and gestures have frightening consequences for men; a scenario that Feminism has created and delights in. A scenario that justifies Feminism's existence, fuels its Grievance Gravy-Train Industries and confirms its 'Forever' status, and actively spreads misandry.

At the same time as advancing its Ideology and agenda Feminism has empowered women to bully and abuse men. The majority of ordinary, decent, non-Ideological women will not take advantage of this legal and political power; however, that power is available to *all* women if they ever *do* wish to use it; for example, if they have a personal grievance against a particular man in their workplace.

PROFESSOR CLEARED OF STUDENT SEX ASSAULTS

(The Daily Telegraph, Tuesday, 22 July, 1997)

'A professor of Philosophy cleared yesterday of indecently assaulting two women in his room said afterwards the case should be a warning to lecturers.

Professor John Cottingham insisted from the day he was charged that the two students had told a "pack of lies" when they accused him of kissing, undressing and fondling them after a university garden party.

Later Professor Cottingham, 54, said "the fact that he had been taken to court will bring home to my colleagues just how vulnerable they can be to unscrupulous people."

Dr. Cottingham, (his wife), a lecturer in feminist literature, said the case had shattered her belief in everything she had taught about feminism.

"I never doubted my husband's word for a moment," she said, "This case has set feminism back 10 years and has showed me that men need protecting too".

A friend said after the case that the allegations may have cost him the chance of a senior position at Oxford. "That has been on hold pending this case", she said. "Even though he has been cleared of all charges, his career is bound to suffer".'

- Professor Cottingham's Feminist wife must be extremely naive if she doesn't understand Feminist Ideology and politics. The two female students may not have been Feminists themselves (or may have been), but the point is that Oxford University is *dominated* by the Feminist culture, perspective and Ideology. Like the majority of people, Dr. Cottingham does not realise the awfulness that Feminism has brought to modern Britain – until it impacts upon them personally

***

No politically motivated group will selflessly refrain from using whatever weapon it can at a conducive moment in time in order to grasp or retain power, to politically advance its group and to increase the prospects of its individual members. And to implement its aims:

'Accusations of sexual harassment are unusually well suited to serve as a weapon. A law that rests so comfortably on the victim's say so and other's reactions to that say so, a law that deals so cavalierly with evidence, is ideally situated for abuse. In fact, it could transpire that abuse is the normal use made of such a law and the regulations it has spawned.'[30]

- We see further examples of this in the following

Sexploitation: Sexual Harassment and the Compensation Culture

There is, without doubt, a sexual harassment compensation culture. The growth of this culture has grown directly out of the Criteria Dilution of what constitutes sexual harassment; out of exaggerating the trauma supposedly caused, teaching women to interpret an incident as sexual harassment and then reporting it as such. Simply uttering the word 'tits' now appears to be extremely traumatising for women in mixed company (if any of them *choose* to be so traumatised).

The issue of sexual harassment has become a sexual political door of opportunity for a certain type of woman:

- 'HARASSED' FEMALE CIVIL SERVANT IS PAID £100,000 TO DROP CLAIM: Stewart is said to have complained that her boss bent down to pick up some papers and told her: "I am not looking up your skirt".'(2003)[31]

- WREN PAYOUT 'STUPID': The Ministry of Defence was accused of looking "stupid" after paying £30,000 in compensation to a Wren after a case was thrown out of a court martial...The court martial cleared the man involved.' (2000)[32]

- SEX JIBE WAS 'HUMOROUS' OUTBURST: A woman soldier who is claiming £700,000 from the Ministry of Defence for alleged sexual discrimination and sexual harassment was simply the butt of a "humorous outburst"...Corporal Yates claims that she was the butt of jokes about the size of her breasts, was continually asked if she was a lesbian and had to listen to a male colleague moaning her name while he allegedly masturbated in his sleeping bag.' (2005)[33]

- VENGEUL, SELFISH AND GREEDY: Yesterday, it was revealed that City lawyer Elizabeth Weston was handed a £1 million settlement by her former employers to abandon a forthcoming case in which she claimed to have been the victim of sexual harassment...A drunken colleague had remarked upon her cleavage and made an assortment of crude innuendoes during the course of a Christmas party...After the incident, Mrs. Weston was unable to work as she suffered "panic attacks", a lack of confidence and breathlessness.'[34]

- One needs to ask how such delicate and sensitive souls were allowed to become City traders, soldiers and lawyers in the first place. Answer: by being preferenced as 'token women' (that is, token Feminists...that is, *trouble-making* 'token women'). When will businesses and employers learn...?

- In the above examples we see a combination of the disturbed Feminist mentality and psychological make-up together with the Feminist-given opportunity to express one's greed

The reader will be aware of many other similar cases...chicken-shit turned to golden nest eggs, courtesy of Feminism and its Sexual Harassment Industry, supported by the TUC. The male's hard-wired natural instinct to be attracted to the female is being used and abused. These women, trained up by Feminists, are self-seeking, greedy, vengeful people who don't give a damn about what they leave behind for the men they have accused of sexually harassing them.

- Every man is a potential target, every man can be used as a dupe to secure a hefty retirement nest egg. And all political parties endorse this greed, this misandrous, vindictive nonsense

Meanwhile...

- AMPUTEE SOLDIER LOSES PAYOUT PLEA: A soldier who lost a leg while on United Nations peacekeeping duties in Bosnia failed yesterday in his test case battle for compensation at the court of Appeal...He underwent 13 operations but his right leg could not be saved and was amputated above the knee.'[35]

And,

STATE WORKER WINS £500,000 IN A DECADE OF CLAIMS AGAINST HER BOSSES...AS WOUNDED HERO HAS TO FIGHT FOR JUST £46,000

(Daily Mail, Monday, 22 November, 2010)

'One is a former equalities officer who has made complaints ranging from sexual harassment to victimisation...the other is a hero soldier who was shot in Iraq...Yet while Pauline Scanlon has been awarded £500,000 during a decade of successive claims for damages, corporal Anthony Duncan is fighting to keep hold of £46,000 he received in compensation for his injuries...Mrs. Scanlon has won four separate pay outs after accusing employers of discrimination or sexual harassment.

In one incident, Mrs. Scanlon was said to have complained about a colleague's calendar which showed Robbie Williams with his trousers round his ankles...Mrs. Scanlon claimed it breached council policy relating to unwelcome sexual advances.

(In another job) She accused a colleague of putting his hand on her thigh, displaying a soft porn calendar in his office and calling her "babe".

The case comes as figures reveal tribunal payouts at an all-time high. The total awarded to claimants rose to £36 million last year, up from £26.4 million the previous year.'

Compare the above male and female examples...and be ashamed that we don't have the courage to face up to, and to question, to challenge, Feminism and its professional gender-warriors. These women, and their male 'Brothers', thrive on our timidity.

***

At one time women had to genuinely worry about sexual harassment and physical intimidation from men, there can be no doubt about that. But laws to prevent this have been taken up and used Ideologically by Feminism to build itself a misandrous and compensatory Industry. It is now men, not women, who have to worry – worry about being falsely or unnecessarily accused, worry about legal and financial intimidation. Given the size of many financial settlements – which are designed to encourage working women to cry 'harassment' and thereby to spread misandry – it would be seriously naive to ignore the possibility that some women are motivated (Ideologically and/or by greed) to frame men. All whilst sanctimoniously calling for 'liberation', 'equal rights' and 'gender equality' for women.

- And there is absolutely *nothing* that these women can lose by giving the jackpot a try, no punishment, no negative consequences if their compensation claim fails. An astonishing and perverse situation

***

Blaming, condemning, demonising and punishing men is a central tenet of Feminism, it is in its DNA. With the issue of sexual harassment Feminism can indulge this aspect of its Ideology. Its Devil Weapon, patriarchy ('men have power over women: men are bad, women are good') has been enthusiastically accepted and applied by our Left-wing/liberal/progressive State...including all three major political parties.

Meanwhile many men have to endure severe joshing, and seriously dislike it. But *our* horribleness at work is not legally classified as 'sexual harassment'. Men have no legal protection, *they* cannot run off to a Tribunal, on the arm of a 'no win: no fee' lawyer, and claim compensation roughly equal to the annual GDP of a third world country. With nothing to lose if unsuccessful...

- Modern Britain seriously dislikes men... whilst it enthusiastically privileges and policy-favours women (mainly Feminists). Why *do* we continue to tolerate it?

Hey diddle diddle

The 'victims' on the fiddle

The Sisters are over the moon

The legal boys laughed to have such fun

And the 'dish' ran away with the doubloon

'We have come a long way, but we still have a long way to go'

(Feminist mantra)

Chapter 43

Domestic Violence

'Nobody speaks the truth when there is something they want to have.'

(Elizabeth Bower: Irish novelist, 1899-1973)

We have seen how Feminism utilises its strategy of exaggeration with trafficked women and sexual harassment. In this chapter we see how this strategy is used to create a further 'widespread problem'. Domestic violence is a Feminist flagship issue so there needs to be a high incidence of 'victims'. There is a great deal more to the phenomenon of domestic violence (from a male perspective) than is offered in this chapter. But here I restrict the issue to Feminism's strategy of 'exaggeration' and its use as a political strategy.

I would like to make my position clear. Genuine and repeated incidents of domestic violence (female-on-male as well as male-on-female) are unacceptable. Men who kill their wives or partners ought to be punished much more severely than they now are (as ought women who kill *their* male partners). And police should be far more sympathetic and proactive when a woman reports her fear of violence from a partner or former partner. However, none of these acknowledgements detracts from the essential premise presented in this chapter.

***

As with pornography, prostitution, sexual harassment and rape, domestic violence is presented by Feminism in a framework of male power (patriarchal power). Men, it is stated, have power over women and use this power to oppress, victimise and abuse them. Melanie Phillips notes:

'As the feminist sociologist Kersti Yllo has observed, feminist analysis of domestic violence is lodged in a broader framework in which violence is viewed as the way men maintain their dominance within patriarchal marriage.'[1]

And,

The Professional Feminist Kat Banyard:

'Rape, domestic violence, harassment, stalking: uncomfortable as it may be to acknowledge, while these are all deeply personal acts, they are also profoundly political acts drawing on a common ideology (patriarchal power). They express and bolster the power assumed by one social group over another.'[2]

Establishing this male power framework, and having it accepted, is vital to the existence of Feminism and the promotion and continuance of its Ideology and agenda. This is why Feminism cannot accept *men* being victims of domestic violence. This is why male victims are ignored in Feminist-dominated modern Britain.

'Where there are victims, presumably there are victimisers. Ideological feminists have denied, trivialised or excused the abuse of men by women. If they had not, they realise, some central pillars of their worldview would have collapsed: that all social problems can or even must be explained in terms of power, that men have all the power, and that men are encouraged to use it against women. As we have argued, profound essentialism and dualism – "we" are by nature good; "they" are by nature evil – are characteristics of every ideology, including feminist ideology. No wonder the debate over domestic abuse has been so fierce!'[3]

- Feminism has pushed domestic violence into being a *political* crime, with the deliberate intention of forcing it to be given *political* as well as legal attention

***

But domestic violence is *not* political, it is not about patriarchal male power. How can domestic violence be a product of patriarchy when violence between lesbian couples is just as high as between heterosexual couples? Barbara Hart, in her book 'Naming the Violence', quotes testimonials from women who have been bitten, kicked, punched, thrown down flights of stairs, and assaulted with weapons, including guns, knives, whips, tyre levers, and broken bottles, by same-sex partners.[4]

There have been numerous studies of domestic violence among lesbians. According to one, rates of abuse were higher among lesbians in their prior relationships with women than in their prior relationships with men – 56 per cent had been subject to sexual aggression, 45 per cent to physical aggression and 64.5 per cent to emotional aggression.[5]

> *'Lesbian violence shatters the myth that women abuse only when men drive them to it. It dispels the myth that male power, patriarchy and male privilege create violence against women. Lesbians do not have much power or privilege.'*[6]

The public and politicians have been conditioned to believe that *violence is inherently male* and that *victimhood is inherently female*. This belief has profound implications for men because social policies are based upon it...on *all* sexual political issues.

***

Ask someone, anyone, male or female, how many women experience domestic violence in their lifetime and you will be told that it is 1 in 4; this figure has been constantly placed before the public for three decades. This belief, this myth, hardly needs confirming because we *all* 'know it':

> *'One in four women living in the UK will experience intimate partner violence at some point in her life.'*[7]

And,

> *'More than 50 per cent of women will experience some form of violence from their spouses during marriage. More than one-third are battered repeatedly every year. (National Coalition Against Domestic Violence).'*[8]

We have all now been conditioned to accept this statistic, unquestioningly, as the truth. The 1 in 4 figure has become part of our conventional wisdom. But it is *not* the truth. Domestic violence is an excellent example of Feminism's use of exaggeration to create a crisis for political and Ideological advantage. This chapter places the *issue* of domestic violence, rather than the *act*, into a *sexual* political framework and by doing so shows how and why the figures have been exaggerated.

- When an exaggeration is made for political and Ideological advantage it becomes a deliberate lie

339

Feminism Cheats and Lies

'Most British domestic violence studies on which the British government relies for such claims are effectively rigged; and they ask only women, not men, for their domestic violence experiences, mainly from self-selecting samples of abused women.'[9]

The 1 in 4 statistic is a gross exaggeration. I would like the reader to prove this for himself or herself. Perform the following exercise.

Think of four married men that you know well – your father, your grandfather, your brother, your uncle, your son, a friend...any four. Now, seriously ask yourself which of these four is likely to be a wife-beater and actually *does* beat his wife? Come on, which one of the four you thought of is the wife-battering demon? There must be *one* – because Feminism tells us that '1 in 4 women experience domestic violence'...and 1 in 4 wives being beaten means 1 in 4 husbands doing the beating. You cannot think of a wife-batterer among *your* four? OK then, ask your friends or work colleagues to undertake the same exercise.... Right, *they* can't think of a male friend who is likely to batter his wife regularly in *their* four either? Try others...Right, think of the football team you play for (11 players plus the coach). Which 3 of these 12 men regularly batter their wives? None? Then that means that *exactly half* the players that you will be facing in next Saturday's match are *regular wife-beaters*. I would cancel the game if I were you.

- You see how ridiculous the 1 in 4 figure is? The bottom line is that Feminism has been conning us, has been lying to us – you have just proved this for yourself. Yes, I'm fully aware that we can't always tell if a husband batters his wife regularly – but we *can* all make an intelligent guess from among the men within our family or close circle of friends

***

Research, in fact, has shown that the *real* incidence of domestic violence is very small. The following is from a British Crime Survey, researched before the Labour/Feminist Government came to power in 1997. It included over 16,000 respondents and is the largest study of domestic violence ever undertaken in Britain. It concluded:

'The confidential nature of this method of interviewing, together with the large and representative sample size of the British Crime Survey mean that these findings are likely to be the most reliable to date on the extent of domestic violence in England and Wales...Current levels of domestic violence: 4.2% of women and 4.2% of men said they had been physically assaulted by a current or former partner in the last year. 4.9% of men and 5.9% of women had experienced physical assault and/or frightening threats.'[10]

- Did you get that? Only 4.2 *per cent*; that is 1 in 25 (*not* 1 in 4) women are victims
- The reader will also note that the percentage of *male victims* is exactly the same as for women victims – 4.2 per cent

There is further extensive evidence showing that i) the incidence of domestic violence is very small, and ii) it affects men as much as it does women, numerically and in severity.[11] Warren Farrell, for example, cites *53 such studies* (not a small number).[12] Melanie Phillips notes:

'In fact, there is a huge amount of well-conducted research demonstrating not only that men suffer equally from domestic violence but even more frequently than women....Yet in virtually all the official literature, this great and growing body of evidence is simply never mentioned...'[13]

- In a patriarchal society (as Feminism has convinced us all that Britain is) only women can be victims and only men can be victimisers. Males as victims does not fit the patriarchal model and is therefore ignored by the State (as are other male issues)

How Feminism Exaggerates Domestic Violence Statistics

In essence, domestic violence is a Feminist social construction. Yes, of course it occurs, but nowhere near in the epidemic proportion of 1 in 4 that Feminism would have us believe.

'A key element in the construction of a social problem is, of course, its size. The larger the problem, the greater the attention it can legitimately command. In the pursuit of magnitude elastic definitions go hand-in-hand with inflated statistics, each exaggeration reinforcing the other.'[14]

Because the very low incidence of *genuine* domestic violence (4.2 per cent) is not high enough to be used to justify Feminism's existence, or to be used as an Ideological gender-weapon, Feminism has had to employ its strategy of 'exaggeration' to inflate the figure to something that can be presented to the public and politicians as an 'epidemic', a 'widespread problem'. How does Feminism craft this exaggeration?

There are a number of ways that Feminism increases the incidence of domestic violence to a politically useful level:

- it declares *all* men are naturally violent

- it uses corrupt 'research'

- it uses the strategy of Criteria Dilution

- it includes incidents that are not domestic

Men are Naturally Violent Towards Women

It is important for Feminism to have us believe that normal, decent ordinary men are *inherently* violent. This makes its aim of creating a 'widespread problem' of domestic violence much more believable.

'Gender feminists are committed to the doctrine that the vast majority of batterers or rapists are not fringe characters but men whom society regards as normal.'[15]

Hating men is DNA-ed into Feminists and is a central tenet of their Ideology – 'men are bad people'/'women are good people', Feminism's Devil Weapon. And so we have Feminists demonising the male sex *collectively*. For example, Rosalind Miles declares:

'To explain violence is to explain the male.'[16]

And,

> *'We need to acknowledge that the seeds of violence are in every man.'*[17]

- 'In *every* man'? In *your* son, in *your* father, in *your* husband, in *your* brother?
- Feminists hate women being stereotyped because this (supposedly) leads to 'sexism'. But stereotyping all men as violent people in order to promote their misandrous Ideology is regarded as culturally and politically acceptable. Hypocrites

The above extremely unpleasant stereotyping and demonisation of men is not made by some extremist on the periphery of Feminism. Rosalind Miles was appointed as a member of the Royal Society of Arts. She founded the Centre for Women's Studies at Coventry Polytechnic. One wonders exactly what students are being 'taught' (indoctrinated?) with regard to sexual politics and Feminism on Women's/Gender/Feminist Studies Courses. Is there an opposing perspective offered, a male view given to balance the Feminist presentation? No. And so it is in higher education throughout Britain.

The basic 'badness of men' is fundamental to Feminism:

> *'We live, I am trying to say, in an epidemic of male violence against women.'*[18]

Gloria Steinem applies Miles's bigoted view of men to the issue of domestic violence. It is a view that is central to the Feminist discourse on the issue:

> *'Patriarchy requires violence or the subliminal threat of violence in order to maintain itself...the most dangerous situation for a woman is not an unknown man in the street, or even the enemy in wartime, but a husband or lover in the isolation of their own home.'*[19]

- Can you seriously believe that a husband in Britain is more dangerous to his wife than a rampant, invading soldier would be in the heat of battle? You see what I'm saying about Feminism and its use of 'exaggeration' as a gender weapon to malign and demonise men? 'Hyperbole' (hype) is surely a word invented specifically for Feminism

The 'White Ribbon Campaign' is an organisation run by *men*. Its aim is 'to end male violence against women'. The following is taken from its 2010 literature:

> *'Violence against women causes more deaths and disability among women age 15 – 44 than cancer, malaria, traffic accidents and war.'*

- Men and women who make such outlandish claims live in a leftish Feminist dream-world (as Britain has now become) so powerful that they can repeat lies like the above without shame, perhaps without even realising that what they are saying has no relation to reality. A Feminist psychosis?

The Feminists' primary concern is to persuade the public and politicians that the so-called 'normal man' is a morally defective human being who gets off on hurting women. And they have succeeded. We all *believe* that 1 in 4 women are regularly battered by their male partners.

The Feminist Use of Corrupt 'Research'

In 1979 the American inappropriately-named husband and wife team Dobash and Dobash carried out a survey of domestic violence in the United Kingdom, presented in their book 'Violence Against Wives: A Case Against the Patriarchy'.[20] They found that 1 in 4 wives suffered from domestic violence. This was based upon their 'research' findings and was, and still is, taught as truth and fact on 'A' level and university Sociology courses. So let's take a closer look at this 'research' that is being used to indoctrinate our young people against men.

The Dobashes explain the methodology of their study. They carried out their 'research' in two Scottish cities – Glasgow and Edinburgh; nothing wrong with that. Except that they carried out their 'research' using women and staff in *women's refuges* in Glasgow and Edinburgh: yes, they went to women's refuges, where women go who have been battered by their husbands to help ascertain how many women have been battered by their husbands. I'm not making this up. And lo, they found that 1 in 4 of women had experienced domestic violence. In their Acknowledgements they write:

> *'We owe an inestimable debt of gratitude to the women living and working in refuges...We would like to express our gratitude to the dedicated and hard working women of the Scottish Women's Aid Federation and the National Women's Aid Federation in England both for their efforts in working with battered women and for the support and assistance they have given us throughout the research.'*

This misandrous 'research' is 'taught' in our schools and universities as 'truth'... 'research' that has been constantly placed before us for thirty years by a gullible (complicit) media... 'research' that we have unwittingly accepted (because we have an inexplicable psychological 'need' to *believe* that women suffer from inequalities, discriminations and oppressions).

The Dobashes are committed misandrists ('A Case Against the Patriarchy'). Their 'research' is the equivalent to committed racists (already holding firm, prejudiced opinions) undertaking 'research' on racial integration in Britain...and seeking the help of the British National Party (would we accept their 'research' so willingly into our conventional wisdom? Would we use *their* 'research to teach young people in our schools and universities'):

> *'We would like to express our gratitude to the dedicated and hardworking members of the Scottish branch of the BNP and the BNP leadership organisation in England for their support and assistance that they have given us throughout our research. It's been proved without a doubt that people of colour are "bad people".'*

• I don't think so. The Dobashes' anti-male work, deliberately seeking out a misandrous, patriarchal 'case', and then exaggerating it to create an Ideological issue, was wholly financed from public funds

The Dobashes' domestic violence study is an example of Feminist 'researchers' undertaking what Melanie Phillips refers to as a 'self-selecting sample of abused women'. The deceit of Feminist 'research' is thoroughly exposed in a later Section.

> *'Phony statistics (on domestic violence) continue to do their job, still cited repeatedly and still embedded in public consciousness, no matter how hard anyone tries to challenge them. When repeated like mantras, they create their own reality.'*[21]

• Feminism is a fraud, and we have all been conned

***

There is no genuine, objective, gender-neutral, research, *anywhere*, to substantiate the claim that 1 in 4 women are regularly battered by their husbands.

In 2005 I wrote to seven Feminist organisations involved in the Domestic Violence Industry requesting copies of their domestic violence research for a Masters degree that I was following. They all informed me that the incidence of domestic violence was 1 in 4 women. But I had *specifically* requested the primary source research. I had in mind to check the methodology of the original 'research' by having it assessed, separately and independently, by two genuine statisticians who would be instructed to do so objectively and who would be gender-neutral.

None of the seven responded to my request for copies of the *original* 'research' that they were using to promote their 1 in 4 claim. I offered to pay for it being copied, for someone's time in doing this and for postage and packing. All they *could* do was to repeat the 1 in 4 mantra, and quote studies and surveys in which this figure had been 'found' (each 'study' picking up and using, unchecked, the 1 in 4 statistic from the *other* studies – a circular Ideological plagiarism: a bit like pass-the-parcel but with no one wanting to unwrap the kernel of truth as this would signify the end-game of their domestic violence fraud). The seven organisations were:

Refuge * The Fawcett Society * The TUC (Women and Equality Section) * Victim Support * Amnesty International * Women's Aid * The Home Office (post 1997, after it became a Feminist-dominated Office under Labour/Feminist Governments)

- The truth is that Feminism has created a successful Gravy-Train Industry that is based upon a myth...and will do all within its power (which is extensive) to retain all the benefits accruing from this Industry, Ideological, employment and financial. Ensuring that it is never challenged also ensures its 'Forever' status

Criteria Dilution

One of Feminism's strategies to Issue Creep inequalities, discriminations, oppressions, victimisations and abuses is to 'change the rules'. We saw this with the concepts of 'equal pay for work of equal value', and 'equality of outcome'. But it also uses this strategy with Criteria Dilution and definitions, as we noted in the chapter on sexual harassment. With domestic violence the strategy is again to dilute the criteria of what constitutes domestic violence/abuse in order to produce a much higher incidence of the 'problem'. Ask someone what they think is meant by 'domestic violence' and you will be told, quite simply, that 'it is someone who batters his wife'. But for Feminism this strict criteria, producing a very small number of genuine victims, is not enough...

Gelles and Straus are one of the most respected international teams studying and researching the subject of domestic violence. They consider domestic violence to be a serious problem. They have for years been advocates for social, medical, and legal intervention to help battered women. Obviously, they were highly thought of and respected by Feminists. Until, that is, they refused to place domestic violence in the Feminist political framework of 'male patriarchal power over women'. Their second crime was to find, in their extensive and gender-neutral research, that a great number of men were *also* victims.

'In Behind Closed Doors, they reported what they themselves could hardly believe: that 3.8% of husbands beat their wives but 4.6% of wives beat their husbands.'[22]

- These respected statisticians found that *more wives* beat their husbands than vice versa

This heresy didn't fit the Feminist patriarchal model of domestic violence. A further transgression of Gelles and Straus was that they uncovered the Feminist strategy of *deliberately exaggerating* domestic violence statistics for political and Ideological gain:

'Some researchers manipulate their data to get shocking figures of abuse. If you overlook the researchers' distinction between minor and severe violence, if you never mention that women do just as much of the shoving, grabbing, pushing and slapping, you arrive at very high figures.'[23]

A colleague of Gelles and Straus, Suzanne Steinmetz, found that:

'"...the average violence scores show wives to be slightly more likely to resort to violence than husbands." This was unacceptable to those who had a vested interest in domestic violence as a woman's problem and an industry based on services to battered women.'[24]

In a further research study Feminism's previously feted researchers, Gelles and Straus, divided domestic violence into two major categories; their questions included:

1. The *least* serious incidents were:

'I would like you to tell me whether, in the past twelve months, your spouse or partner has ever:-

- Insulted you or swore at you/stomped out of the room or house/threatened to throw something at you/pushed, grabbed, shoved or slapped you.'

2. The *most* serious incidents were:

'Has your spouse or partner:-

- Beat you up/choked you/threatened you with a knife or gun.'[25]

It was found:

'According to the survey sample, the percentage of women who had these experiences was virtually zero: all respondents answered "no" to all the questions on severe violence. This finding does not, of course, mean that no one was brutally attacked. But it does suggest that severe violence is relatively rare.'[26]

This was a shockingly Ideologically-inappropriate finding for Feminist activists. How can you justify your Ideological existence, build your Industry, attract government funding and resources and demonise men on *that* kind of low (zero) statistic? So another 'research' team had to be brought in, Harris Associates. They used *exactly the same questions* as the Gelles and Straus research, but their methodology changed what was to be *defined* as domestic violence.

The Harris survey concluded that as many as *four million women a year* were victims of assaults and 20.7 million were verbally or emotionally abused by their partners.[27] Clearly, the interpreters of the Harris survey were operating with a much wider definition of 'violence' than were Gelles and Straus (an 'extreme inclusiveness'). For example, to the question: 'Has your partner ever insulted or swore at you', and 'has your partner ever stomped out of the room or house': 34 per cent of women answered 'Yes'. *The interpreters classified all these women as being 'emotionally and verbally abused'...and labelled this as 'violence'.* That is, they diluted the criteria for, and thereby expanded the definition of, what was now to be called 'domestic violence'. Hence they arrived at the startling figure of 1 in 3 women experiencing domestic violence.

- British Feminists rely heavily on 'research' from America
- So we see domestic 'violence' Issue Creep via Criteria Dilution and 'extreme inclusiveness'

***

The Feminist political strategy is to *deliberately* conflate the trivial with the serious in order to make the definition more inclusive, increase the incidence and to create a 'widespread problem'. The social commentator Melanie Phillips, widely reviewing the literature on domestic violence, found that the dilution of criteria, and an elastic definition, is a common element:

> *'The researchers included in their definition of domestic violence "psychological abuse" such as being stopped from seeing people, having their beliefs ridiculed or even being controlled. Not only were these outside any reasonable definition of violence, but being "controlled" is so vague as to be meaningless. Nevertheless, the researchers confidently asserted that 31 per cent of the women surveyed had suffered domestic violence.'*[28]

- The serious abuse some women suffer has to be trivialised in order to create enough 'violence' to justify all the services, training, and advocacy that Feminists are now paid to provide

***

In Australia, Feminists enjoy a huge amount of cultural and political power, just as much as they do in Britain. So much so that they have been able to legally define domestic violence to include a man simply shouting at his wife – 'the domestic decibel rule'. However, the opposite, a woman raising her voice to her husband, is considered an understandable defence to male dominance and is not officially or legally recognised as abusive.

But this idiotic inclusion couldn't possibly happen in a sensible country like Britain, proud of its commitment to equality, justice and democracy...could it?

SHOUT AT YOUR SPOUSE AND RISK LOSING YOUR HOME

(The Daily Mail Thursday, 27 January, 2011)

'Lady Hale, leading a bench of five justices, said the definition of violence must change so that a range of abusive behaviour now counts in law.

The decision will affect domestic violence and family law which has given the courts powers to throw someone out of their home if their partner accuses them of violent behaviour. Until now violence has always had to mean physical assault.

The judges were hearing the case of Mihret Yemshaw, 35 who said she had been subjected to domestic violence and was entitled to be rehoused under the 1996

Housing Act. Officials in Hounslow, West London, turned her down after hearing that her husband had never hit her nor threatened to do so. Mrs.Yemshaw told them he had shouted in front of their two children...

Lady Hale said the meaning of the word "violence" had moved on since Parliament passed the Housing Act. The word "is capable of bearing several meanings and applying to many different types of behaviour. These can change and develop over time". The judge added that "it is not for Government and official bodies to interpret the meaning of the words which Parliament has used. That role lies with the courts".

The judgment means that Mrs. Yemshaw will now have her case reconsidered by Hounslow. It will also apply to a wide field of legislation, including the 1996 Family Law Act which allows people to be ejected from their homes if their partners complain of domestic violence.

Samuel Estifanos, the husband, a 40-year-old bus driver, claimed she left the flat where he still lives because she was "unhappy". He added: "I never hit her and I never even screamed or swore at her".'

- The above decision is Issue Creep and Criteria Dilution gone mad. I think that many decent, non-Ideological women will be embarrassed about this ruling, about this ridiculous example of *extreme* 'extreme inclusiveness'

- Hale's bench (under Hale's guidance) has diluted the criteria of domestic violence, expanded its definition to make it more inclusive – much more inclusive that the *democratically elected* lawmakers in Parliament intended it to be. Justice Hale will admit to being a Feminist. She will also admit to having been a Feminist for many years.

A letter to The Times:

JUDGES' VIEWS, PERSONAL OPINIONS AND THE LAW

(The Times, Friday, 29 April, 2011)

'Sir,...On appointment a judge undertakes a solemn obligation to do right to all manner of persons according to the laws and usages of this realm without fear or favour, affection or ill will. The judge is bound to apply the law of the land, not his or her own opinions in adjudication....' Lord Mackay of Clashfern (Lord Chancellor, 1987-97, House of Lords)

- We need to ask whether our Supreme Court ought to be used to promote a judge's 'own opinions', a misandrous Ideology? Is this one of its functions? By creating more female 'victims' the Supreme Court is thereby creating more male 'victimisers'. The Supreme Court's Criteria Dilution ruling is clear evidence that man-hating in modern Britain has become systemic and institutional at the highest level and is evidence of just how much power today's Feminists have

- You notice the involvement of the leading organisation in Feminism's Domestic Violence Industry – Women's Aid?

In law, then, any woman who now feels fed up with her husband, can legally claim a house from her local authority. All it takes is for her to claim that her male partner has raised his voice to her. Simple. What kind of justice is the Supreme Court dispensing here – giving free houses to the female half of the population? Why not just give every woman a free house when she reaches the age of 18 and have done with it? Why go through all the rigmarole of supposed domestic violence, marriage and divorce to achieve this Feminist aim?

- One wishes that male Justices had a bit more backbone (or acted like the patriarchs they are supposed to be). We really *do* need a Minister for Men

People simply don't recognise or understand the cultural, media, legal and political *power* that Feminism now has. The power of Feminists in the law, academia, the media and in politics, and the relentless, glacial and unchallenged putsch of their Ideology and their agenda, their Quiet Revolution, is profoundly worrying.

Lady Hale has 'form' in straying into territory that is properly the province of Parliament and politicians, who have been elected by the public and therefore have some legitimacy in making Ideological decisions. Melanie Phillips in her book 'Londonistan' notes how judges have strayed into making political and Ideological decisions:

> 'An example of this was provided by Lady Hale, who upon becoming Britain's first female law lord gave a press conference. She was in favour, she said, of gay adoption, legally recognised gay partnerships, and improved legal rights for heterosexual cohabitants, and she wanted to see the concept of fault removed from divorce law. These issues, which are among the most divisive in our society, are all political topics. They are the subject of heated debate in Parliament and among the general public. The notion that one of England's most senior judges, supposedly the acme of impartiality, should have proclaimed her views like this suggested that any cases she heard on these topics would be prejudged by an ideological agenda...That agenda...is the agenda of a significant section of England's judiciary. These are the judges...who having never grown out of the sixties counterculture when they came to maturity, have whole-heartedly embraced the obnoxious "victim culture".'[29]

- Feminists and Feminist sympathisers have serious power in all areas of the British State, and express this power in implementing the Feminist agenda whenever possible. The reader can see how and why modern Britain hates men
- If people reading the Yemshaw case get the impression that the newly-established Supreme Court makes its rulings on grounds of Feminist Ideology rather than on justice for both sexes, then it is in danger of losing credibility and respect. We have tended to forget that men are people too, and that they also have rights

And what if positive discrimination produced an *equal number* of Ideologically fired-up Feminist judges as male (gender-naive) judges? How could men possibly receive fairness and justice then? We're seeing an example here of why Britain will continue to hate men unless we summon up the courage to seriously confront Feminism.

***

I'm at a loss to see any 'gender equality' in the Supreme Court's decision. But perhaps our Supreme Court will go even further and adopt one of the American criteria for domestic violence. Leone Walker is the Feminist who is responsible for the invention of the Battered Woman Syndrome (explored and dismissed in the next Section).

> 'Walker writes in one case, "It is clear that there was a good deal of provocation. There is no doubt that she began to assault Paul physically before he assaulted her. However, it is also clear from the rest of her story that Paul had been battering her by ignoring her and by working late, in order to move up the corporate ladder, for the entire five years of their marriage".'[30]

- Did you get that? Feminism, using its strategy of Criteria Dilution, has declared that if a man works overtime (to earn extra money to pay the bills for his family) then this must now be classified as 'battering his wife'. Are you listening, male judges in the Supreme Court? Unless men with influence drum up enough gumption to stand up to Feminism, and put a stop to their Quiet Revolution, then the future doesn't look too good for we ordinary men...less of an Issue Creep, more of a misandrous Issue Stampede

- 'Paul' was accused of battering his wife – because he was working late because he wished to fulfil his financial responsibility to his family. Only a Feminist could turn this decency into the crime of domestic violence. I refer the reader to Part Three. How long will it be before our Supreme Court, containing five senior judges, converts a man wishing to work hard for the betterment of his family into a 'wife batterer'? Not long, if male justices don't come to their senses soon

Feminism Inflates the Incidence of Domestic Violence by Including Incidents that are not 'Domestic'

Domestic: *'Of, or pertaining to, the family or household: Of the home, household, or family affairs.'*[31]

Feminism intentionally extends the definition of 'domestic' to include men and women who do not live together; that is, they are *ex*-partners. This is a deliberate deception because people living apart can in no way be defined as 'domestic'. But as an Ideological strategy to exaggerate the issue it serves its purpose by inflating the figures.

Yes, the violence against *ex*-partners is still violence; but it is outside-the-home violence. That is, it is 'public space' violence and should be included in *that* particular category of crime – a category in which as we have seen, men far outnumber women as victims, including serious bodily harm and murder. It is not *domestic* violence and ought not to be included in domestic violence statistics.

We are constantly told that '2 women a week are killed by their partners'. In the vast majority of cases these are *ex*-partners and ought be classified as 'public space' murders. This will still leave many more men than women killed in 'public space violence'.

- However, I would like to stress that those women who are genuinely and seriously threatened by an ex-partner ought to be given greater protection than they are at present. Men who participate in this kind of terror ought to be severely punished *prior* to any attack, and most certainly after. Harsh sentencing at an early stage would be a deterrent. But this does not excuse Feminism's use of its exaggeration strategy with the issue of *domestic* violence

Why Feminists Love Domestic Violence

Feminism gains in a number of ways from exaggerating the figures for domestic violence:

- Exaggerating the incidence of domestic violence perpetuates Feminism. It justifies its existence. Large numbers of women being beaten up by their husbands confirms women's on-going 'victimisation' and the continuing need for Feminism as a Movement to 'battle against male abuse and to stand up for women's rights'

- Exaggerating the incidence of domestic violence attracts sympathy for the Feminist Ideology. Large numbers of battered women attract sympathetic media coverage. The public and politicians can see 'why' Feminism demands preferential treatment, special privileges and policy-favouritism for women

- Exaggerating the incidence of domestic violence spreads misandry (shortly to be addressed). This is an emotive and therefore effective issue for demonising and punishing men. For example, an accusation of domestic violence will instantly and automatically lose a divorced man contact with his children; no proof is required – only his ex-wife's word which is taken as truth. Domestic violence is an effective misandrous gender-weapon

- Exaggerating the incidence of domestic violence creates 'guilty men' (men feel 'guilty' by association, being the same sex as the 1 in 4 supposed wife-beaters). 'Guilty men' in power (Justices, politicians) are easy-to-manipulate men. This facilitates the implementation of the Feminist agenda

- Exaggerating the incidence of domestic violence justifies its Industry

- Exaggerating the incidence of domestic violence is an effective recruiting aid. Not only does it attract huge amounts of government funding and resources, but Feminism purports to 'be there' to protect women. This claim is attractive to women, who may wish to join 'the cause', or at least will be encouraged to sympathise with its demands and its claims for 'gender equality'

- Exaggerating the incidence of domestic violence allows the statistics to be used to manipulate the political process (by confirming the 'badness of men' and the patriarchy)

> 'After two decades of this kind of distortion...People had come to believe that violence was intrinsically male and victimisation intrinsically female. This was no small matter. In Britain as well as in America, this belief has been absorbed into the ether of political life and has had a profound effect upon public policy, well beyond the issue of domestic violence.'[32]

For Feminism the issue of domestic violence is not about 'protecting women' and it has nothing to do with 'gender equality'. It is about sexual politics and Ideology. The above gains for Feminism explain why domestic violence is one of Feminism's flagship issues, and why Feminism will use all its cultural, legal and political power by cheating, lying and exaggerating, to retain it.

R.L. McNeely is an attorney and a professor of social welfare at the University of Wisconsin. With regard to domestic violence, McNeely observed that:

> '...feminists are not about the search for truth. What this is about is a search for political power. This is power based upon the concept of a defenceless group of people being victimised by a larger, stronger aggressor. When people start recognising that, indeed, domestic violence seems to occur both ways, that undercuts the whole concept of weakness, out of which comes power. It's based on a concept of being an exclusive victim.'[33]

- Modern Feminism is a huge fraud and we have all been taken in

The Domestic Violence Industry

Erin Pizzey, an Equality Feminist, was the first woman in Britain to set up refuges for battered women. With some of her battered women residents she attended a Feminist meeting in 1974:

> 'We were astonished and frightened that many of the radical lesbian and feminist activists that I had seen in the collectives attended. They began to vote themselves into a national movement across the country.
>
> After a stormy argument, I left the hall with my abused mothers – and what I had most feared happened.
>
> In a matter of months, the feminist movement hijacked the domestic violence movement, not just in Britain, but internationally. Our grant was given to them and they had a legitimate reason to hate and blame all men. They came out with sweeping statements which were as biased as they were ignorant. "All women are innocent victims of men's violence", they declared. They opened most of the refuges in the country.'[34]

One of the reasons Feminism loves domestic violence is because it is a huge Industry. The Home Office Report in June, 2003 (Living Without Fear) noted:

- There are over 400 Women's Refuges in England
- There are 45 Women's Refuges in Wales
- The Women's Aid Federation (England) have 250 local domestic violence projects

A further Home Office Report of June, 2003 (Safety and Justice Proposals) notes:

- £22.9 million annually is spent on Women's Refuge provision

> 'In Britain, America and Europe, women's aid is now a multi-million pound concern, a whole industry of refuges and activists and researchers all pumping out the message that men are violent to women. In the last twenty-five years, according to the Women's Aid Federation, more than two hundred "multi-agency domestic violence forums have developed in the UK".'[35]

Domestic violence is big business for Feminism. The Daily Express reported on Monday, 10 July 2000:

> 'A total of twenty-five projects addressing domestic violence and nine rape projects have won backing of up to £445,000 each.'

- Even though a great deal of research informs us that an equal number of men are victims of domestic violence (4.2 percent, for example) there are only *two* men's refuges in Britain. There is no Men's Domestic Violence Industry so there is no government funding to publicise and research this male issue

***

A continuing national epidemic of 1 in 4 is required to keep all the Feminists in the Domestic Violence Industry continually employed; since the 1980s there has been a huge jobs programme for Feminist activists – doctors require training to spot signs of domestic violence in their patients, colleges and universities train students, faculty and staff on how to recognise domestic abuse; the police are required to attend domestic violence forums, as are housing officers, social workers, nurses health visitors, midwives and Department of Social Security Officers; judges are required to attend courses on domestic violence. All courses are given by Feminists...there are public awareness programmes, courses developed to teach (indoctrinate) school children about domestic violence, prevention programmes, hotlines, shelters, counsellors, specialised courts, new police rights (entering homes where domestic violence is suspected); many domestic violence organisations and 'charities', and so on...all creating jobs in the Industry for the Ideologues...and demanding funding and resources from governments.

The Domestic Violence Industry is a huge Feminist Industry, in which Women's Aid is the largest organisation

> 'The Women's Aid Federation had called for a government task force...The government appeared to be dancing to the tune played by women's aid bodies...The government jumped to attention...by starting a "public awareness campaign" along the lines that Women's Aid had called for.'[36]

And,

£15 SPEEDING TAX INSULT

(Daily Mail, Saturday, 31 March, 2007)

'Motorists fined in court for speeding will be forced from Monday to pay a £15 surcharge to help the victims of domestic violence.

The £15 will be imposed on anyone who faces a fine, including drivers who challenge a speeding ticket in court.

The case will be used to appoint dozens of domestic violence counsellors to help bring alleged cases of abuse to court. Ministers announced that they would immediately plough £3 million of this into expanding the number of independent domestic violence advisers on the public payroll. The rest will go to other victim services...

The surcharge scheme will rake in £16 million a year. Home Office Minister Baroness Scotland said: "We are hitting criminals in the pocket to make sure that crime doesn't pay and victims continue to get the services we all want them to have. Domestic violence affects one in four women..."'

- The present Coalition Government (marxist-lite Conservative leadership plus radical/ Left-wing/progressive Liberal Democrats) would never consider revoking this Labour Government anti-male/pro-Feminist policy

- Baroness Scotland, very highly placed in Britain's Legal System, is a Labour peer and is well-known for her Feminist views. The legal, cultural and political power of Feminism in modern Britain is astonishing

In September, 2009, I wrote to the Office for Criminal Reform requesting a list of recipients of this surcharge. There were 190 organisations. Almost every one was a domestic violence organisation – domestic violence against women...*no* donations were made to the *two* domestic violence refuges for men. Even the Policy Manager's (Mr. S. Watts's) reply admitted that the overwhelming proportion of funding goes to Feminism's Domestic Violence Industry:

> *'A significant proportion of the receipts goes towards funding the Independent Domestic Violence Advisors as well as a variety of other support services for victims of domestic violence throughout the UK.'*[37]

- Why not give the money raised to a children's charity? Why should this surcharge be used to fund an aggressive man-hating Ideology, an already extensive and bloated Feminist Domestic Violence Industry?

- What would be the legal position if a man, on political and Ideological grounds, refused to pay this surcharge, this 'subscription' to a man-hating Political Community Club, but instead made a £30 donation to one of the two *men's* domestic violence refuges?[38] Can someone please let me know?

***

One of the functions of the Domestic Violence Industry is to 'teach' women to identify and report domestic violence. Feminism requires a high number of incidents to justify and perpetuate its existence. This accounts for the high level of publicity given to the issue, and for the issue regularly being presented in the media. Women have been taught that they can report any incident of mutual shouting or slapping as domestic violence and that it will be *they* – by law – who have to be believed, it is *they*, they know, who will automatically be seen and treated as the victim. This encourages women to report as domestic violence what should, in reality, only be called a husband and wife row with mutual shouting and perhaps mutual physical blows being *equally* exchanged. The Feminist Domestic Violence Industry has done its job well.

- Feminism, and Feminist organisations, have 'primed' ordinary women to seek out and report any incident that could possibly be construed as domestic violence

In addition, police are given domestic violence courses. These are taught by Feminists so only the Feminist perspective will be received (and believed) – 'bad men'/ 'good women'. The police are desperate to be seen as politically correct so are obliged to follow the Feminist line. Officers are aware that being politically incorrect in 21st century Britain is a cultural and often legal offence. They also know that politically incorrect behaviour (such as not accepting the women's interpretation as the truth in a marital dispute) will adversely affect their prospects of promotion. And so we get senior police officers falling over themselves to appease Feminism...and to demonise and punish men.

- There has been pressure on police forces to disavow misogynistic attitudes. This has been expressed in taking the word of a woman over the word of a man. This misandry is now legal and manifests in the way the police deal with issues of domestic violence and rape

POLICE WANT POWER TO TACKLE DOMESTIC BULLIES
(Daily Mail: Monday, 16 November, 2009)

'Police will today call for a new crime to be introduced to prosecute men who carry out low-level psychological or physical abuse of their wives.'

Since the 1980s the police have been increasingly manipulated by Feminism – told to prosecute men who swear at their wives, or who slam doors loudly...but *not* when wives themselves exhibit these behaviours. Police chiefs and authorities *nowhere* question or challenge Feminism, or stand up to their Feminist Ideological bullying. They, like the rest of us, are too cowed, too fearful of the personal and professional consequences of crossing Feminists and Feminism.

- Or are they complicit? I'm amazed how many senior police officers are Sociology graduates. And we know that Sociology is a Feminist-dominated subject. Are these men Male Feminists first and police officers second?

Erin Pizzey again:

> 'The feminist refuges continued to create training programmes that described only male violence against women. Slowly the police and other organisations were brainwashed into ignoring the research that was proving men could also be victims...I look back with sadness to my young self and my vision that there could be places where people – men, women and children who have suffered physical and sexual abuse – could find help...I believe that vision was hijacked by vengeful women who have ghetto-ised the refuge movement and used it to persecute men. Surely the time has come to challenge this evil ideology.'[39]

- This book hopes to do that

And as Doris Lessing asks:

> 'It is time we began to ask who are these women who continually rubbish men. The most stupid, ill-educated and nasty woman can rubbish the nicest, kindest and most intelligent man and no one protests...Men seem to be so cowed that they can't fight back, and it is time they did.'[40]

For Feminism, the issue of domestic violence is not about 'gender inequality'. It is about sexual politics and promoting Feminist Ideology. In short, domestic violence is a milk-cow for Feminism, benefiting from a very thin veneer of a moral base (the 4.2 per cent or less of genuine cases).

Domestic Violence and Man-Hating

Feminism has persuaded the wider world to see domestic violence as an *expression* of male power, of patriarchy, the power of *all* men over *all* women. And then it has manipulated this widely held acceptance to use domestic violence (as well as other issues) as a gender-weapon to persuade the wider world to see *all* men as *inherently* awful and evil - 'bad men' and 'good women'. Domestic violence has become a very effective gender-weapon to demonise and punish *all* men. One of Feminism's main aims in exaggerating the incidence of domestic violence is to show that modern Britain is a 'sexist' and 'misogynistic' society in which women are perpetual victims...victims of men. Once this has been accepted all the other personal and Ideological benefits follow.

> 'The notion of male violence against women as an instrument of patriarchal oppression has infiltrated mainstream discourse to a remarkable degree.'[41]

By saying that 1 in 4 husbands batter their wives, Feminism is actually saying that 1 in 4 men are 'bad people'. This is not only untrue but deeply insulting. The issue and the Industry of domestic violence are seriously misandrous. Exaggerating the number of victims increases the opportunity, enlarges the stage, to demonise and punish men.

***

The following is a particularly incisive observation with regard to Feminism's use of domestic violence as a gender weapon:

> *'But how does this (low incidence of domestic violence) help the gender feminist in her misandric campaign? She needs to find that a large proportion of men are batterers, a meagre 3 to 4 percent will not serve her purpose. As for journalists and the newscasters, their interests too often lie in giving a sensational rather than an accurate picture of gender violence, they tend to credit the advocacy sources. Better four million or five than one or two. Evidently, Time magazine felt six was even better. And all the better, too, if the media's readers and viewers get the impression that the inflated figures refer not to slaps, shoves, or pushes, but to brutal, terrifying, life-threatening assaults.'[42]*

***

Mythomania: *'A compulsion to embroider the truth, exaggerate, tell lies.'[43]*

Domestic violence is an Ideologically-driven application of Feminist mythomania. Like trafficked women and sexual harassment, it is an excellent example of Issue Creep. A mental condition or a clever political strategy? Or both?

> *'We have come a long way, but we still have a long way to go.'*
>
> (Feminist mantra)

> *'At some point one has to ask whether feminists are more interested in diminishing violence within a population or promoting a political ideology.'[44]*

The cultural, legal, media and political power of Feminism in modern Britain is profoundly disturbing. And life can be made very difficult for those who question and challenge it.

Feminist Retribution

Before continuing, I respectfully suggest that the reader refreshes their memory regarding the Feminist's psychological make-up, personality, mentality, and personal and Ideological 'need' for anger.

***

355

Feminists seriously dislike any criticism of their Ideology, their belief systems, their aims and agenda.

In the early 1990s Neil Lyndon, author and columnist, wrote a book rejecting Feminism.

'He was shunned, vilified and even physically attacked. He lost access to his son, his career dried up and his money ran out. As a direct consequence of his writings, he could not find work as a journalist, he was dropped by friends both male and female, he was assaulted while standing beside a luggage carousel at Heathrow, and, most seriously, he lost custody of his teenage son. As his career imploded, there were no royalties to cushion his fall. In August 1992, he was declared bankrupt.'[45]

* Feminism is not a benign, caring, Ideology, for all its cant about 'gender equality'

R. L. McNeely, an authority on domestic violence, found a high incidence of female-on-male violence:

'McNeely wrote on the topic of domestic violence against men and had his career threatened by ideological adversaries as a result.'[46]

Suzanne Steinmetz's research found that women were just as violent as men:

'In an attempt to try to keep me from speaking, I had thinly veiled threats put on me. The American Civil Liberties Union conference...were told that if they allowed me to speak, the place would be bombed...I was told before giving an address at a Canadian university I would have major problems by one group of radical women...they wrote to the college president and said I should be stopped from coming to speak...What happened to me was nothing, trust me, compared to what Murray Straus has gone through. He always says I had it worse, but I don't think so...He's had women academics come up to him and almost physically accost him in the hall because they've been so angry.'[47]

Steinmetz commented:

'I thought it was really ironic that they were threatening to use violence to stop me from speaking about women's potential for violence.'[48]

Dr. Malcolm George of St.Bartholomew's and Royal London Hospital Medical School was commissioned to undertake a survey on domestic violence to assist with a programme on the BBC that was to look at domestic violence against men. He comments:

'My female colleagues at the BBC who were involved in the production of the programme using my survey results were subject to anonymous threats and abuse for tackling the subject of male victims of intimate violence and for running a gender-neutral survey.'[49]

Erin Pizzey relates her own experiences:

'I went to universities to lecture and was roundly berated (by Feminist lecturers) when I pointed out that 62 of the first 100 women who came into the refuge were as violent as the men they left...If I tried to interest newspapers in publishing my views I came up against the same problem. I was in the hands of women editors who refused to allow me to air my views. Things were no better in the publishing field: editors routinely censor books, especially the radical lesbian editors. There was, and still is, strict censorship of any one trying to break the code of silence.'[50]

She continues:

'Many of my speaking engagements were cancelled, especially in New York and Boston...I could see then that the feminist movement everywhere had hijacked the whole issue of domestic violence to fulfil their political ambitions and to fill their pockets.'[51]

- This is not some misogynist speaking; this is the woman who set up the original refuges for female victims of *genuine* domestic violence

Pizzey again:

'When, in the mid-eighties, I published Prone To Violence, about my work with violence-prone women and their children, I was picketed by hundreds of women from feminist refuges, holding placards which read "All men are bastards" and "all men are rapists".

Because of violent threats, I had to have a police escort around the country.

It was bad enough that this relatively small group of women was influencing social workers and police. But I became aware of a far more insidious development in the form of public policy-making by powerful women, which was creating a poisonous attitude towards men.'[52]

Tired of the constant Feminist aggression directed towards her Pizzey eventually left Britain for Canada (returning a few years later).

- So Feminism has 'form' with its retribution. At the expense of sounding overly dramatic I anticipate reprisals for publishing this book; there will be invented misdemeanours, untrue accusations, rumour-mongering; there will be character assassination from a number of quarters. The media will intentionally misinterpret my thesis and arguments. Neither is a physical assault out of the question

***

In a survey of Feminists carried out in 2010 the issue of domestic violence appeared as the second issue of most concern and interest.[53] As we have seen, for Feminists it is a vastly important and beneficial issue. In addition, Feminists need domestic violence as a psychological issue to express their anger; anger at the world, anger at society, anger particularly at men (and perhaps anger at themselves). Domestic violence, because of its emotive nature, because it is seen literally as an 'an attack on women', is an ideal 'issue' upon which to hook, and therefore validate, this Feminist condition. Feminism desperately needs domestic violence.

'If no husband ever again raised a hand to his wife many Feminists would be devastated'

(Swayne O'Pie)

So Feminists will fight like hell to retain their prolifically beneficial second major issue and Industry. Anyone questioning this huge fraud will, ironically, be attacked. Which means that the 'widespread problem' of domestic violence, like a sword of Damocles, will hang 'Forever' over all men – condemning and demonising them to be 'Forever' seen and punished as 'bad people'.

Chapter 44

Rape

Whilst writing this book I was strongly advised by a number of people, male as well as female, to avoid the subject of rape. It was felt that rape was too emotive a subject to be questioned and challenged by a man. I've ignored this well-meaning advice for two reasons. Firstly, I have to be true to my own beliefs and not shy away from a difficult subject; if the issue is dealt with honestly then any problem must lie with those who may object to my analysis, they must own their problem and deal with it. Secondly, the advice to avoid the subject of rape is an example of the fear that is instilled in many people by political correctness and by Feminism in today's Britain – we are censored on what we are allowed to say and discuss and what we are not allowed to say and discuss. I refuse to be a party to such totalitarian censorship and intimidation.

Having said that I wish to make my position clear. Genuine rape is an abhorrent violation of a woman's body, mind, and spirit, and I believe that men who are guilty of such an horrendous crime ought be imprisoned for far longer than they are at present. But as with trafficked women, sexual harassment and domestic violence, rape is also a rich area for Issue Creep. There is much more to the issue of rape from the male perspective than is offered in this chapter; here I simply focus on how the issue is exaggerated, used and abused as a gender-weapon.

***

According to Feminism, rape is a widespread problem:

> *'Between 20 and 40 per cent of women say they have been raped'*
> *(Feminist 'research')*[1]

> *'...nearly half (of women) are victims of rape or attempted rape'*
> *(Germaine Greer)*[2]

- The Ideological claim, then, is that 1 in 2, 3 or 4 women have been raped or experienced attempted rape

---

Rape is a Crime of Male Power, not Sex

Like sexual harassment and domestic violence, if Feminism is to use the phenomenon of rape as an Ideological weapon then it needs to interpret it in a way that will fit its Ideology – *all* men have power over *all* women and abuse this (patriarchal) power; 'men are bad people'/ 'women are good people'. This Ideological interpretation of rape 'proves' that Britain is a patriarchy, in which women are discriminated against, oppressed, are victimised and abused, and Britain is a sexist and misogynistic society.

'(Rape) is a manifestation of men's hatred and contempt for women rather than of ungovernable lust, and the fear which it engenders in women is central to their subordination and control by men. This means that rape is a political act.'[3]

- Feminism has drilled its disciples to say that 'rape is a crime of male violence, of male power, not of sex'

- Kate Millett:

  'In rape, the emotions of aggression, hatred, contempt, and the desire to break or violate personality, take a form consummately appropriate to sexual politics.'[4]

- Susan Brownmiller:

  'Rape is nothing more than a conscious process of intimidation by which all men keep all women in a state of fear.'[5]

- Andrea Dworkin:

  'Any act of sexual intercourse, whenever and under any circumstances, is rape.'[6]

- The reader will note that all the above are Lesbian Feminists

***

The Feminist claim that rape is a crime driven by male power and misogyny rather than sex is Ideological claptrap. Consider the following:

- If sex were not the motive, then attractiveness and fertility would not be an issue, and women across the whole age range would be victimised. But this is not so; rape victims are almost exclusively women of reproductive age, and overwhelmingly under middle-age.[7] In a 1999 Home Office study on rape it was found that only 5 per cent of victims were over 45[8]

- If rape is a 'weapon of male oppression and power over women' then it would necessarily be a common occurrence. But it isn't, as we will see

- 'Gay men are just as likely to be raped by their (male) dates as heterosexual women.'[9] So how can rape be a 'male power and misogynistic' crime?

- The number of male-on-male rapes in prisons (and there are many) confirms that rape cannot be a patriarchal, misogynistic crime of violence and power against women, and shows that it is a crime, primarily, of sexual gratification

- Rape is many times lower in such countries as Greece, Portugal and Japan – countries far more overtly patriarchal than Britain[10]

- And a psychological perspective:

  'Indeed, rapists as a group seem no more hostile to women than other criminals; as personality types, they are most similar to murderers, whose victims are mostly male.'[11]

So the Feminist claim that rape is a misogynistic 'power-over-women' hate crime is untrue. Yet it has been successful in placing this crime on the 'hate crime' list. Since the 1980s rape has become a carefully crafted weapon in the Feminist armoury. In order to use it as such it has had to be interpreted as an Ideological crime – male patriarchal power and misogyny.

> *'High rape numbers serve the gender feminists by promoting*
> *the belief that American culture is sexist and misogynist'*
>
> *(Christina Hoff Sommers)*[12]

How Common is Rape?

Before the issue of rape can be discussed in any rational and objective way the classifications of rape need to be identified.

The Home Office identifies three types of rape:[13]

1. 'Stranger' rape: where the suspect has had no contact with the alleged victim prior to the incident (the dark alley, knife-wielding rape)

2. 'Acquaintance' rape: where the alleged victim and perpetrator have been casually known to each other; for example, the complainant may have accepted a lift off an acquaintance where she and the suspect had met at a party.

3. 'Intimates' rape: where the alleged victim is having, or has had in the recent past, a relationship with the complainant.

'Acquaintance' rape and 'intimates' rape are generally combined to produce the commonly used term, 'date-rape'. So essentially there are two types of rape:

1. Stranger, 'dark-alley, knife-wielding' rape

2. Date-rape

The Home Office found that in the 1990s:

> *'Rapes committed by a person unknown to the victim ('stranger' rapes) formed only 12 per cent of the sample; those committed by acquaintances or intimates (date-rapes) accounted for 45 per cent and 43 per cent of cases respectively.'*[14]

- Stranger rape represents only 12 per cent of rapes: date-rape represents 88 per cent of rapes

Rape and Feminist Exaggeration

Feminism creates an Ideological 'issue' out of rape by using its strategy of exaggeration in three areas:

1. Exaggerating the *incidence* of rape
2. Exaggerating the *non-conviction* rate of rape
3. Exaggerating the *trauma* of date-rape

Exaggerating Rape: Its Incidence

In October 2008 I received a letter from Paul Taylor, Recorded Crime Section, the Home Office. Attached to the letter was a 'conviction rates for offences recorded by the police – 2006'. This showed the 'offences recorded' of 'violence against the person'; stranger rape represented only 4 per cent. In addition:

> '"Stranger" rape accounts for less than 4 per cent of all "violent attacks upon the person – the vast majority being against men".'[15]

This is an Ideological nightmare for Feminists: how can you justify your existence, build an Industry and create a misandrous gender-weapon to demonise and punish men on such an extremely small number of rapes? Something had to be done.

So in the 1980s Feminists changed the rules and re-defined what was to be classified as 'rape'- it invented the concept of 'date-rape'. Few other European countries have this category of rape. We have seen how this strategy has been successful – 88 per cent of *all* rapes are now date-rapes; Feminism has successfully increased the number of 'rapes' by 800 per cent.

In addition to introducing the new category of date-rape, Feminism has undertaken an on-going education/media programme 'teaching' young women to report any sexual encounter that they may later be ashamed of, or in which they felt 'used', as a rape. Consequently, the reporting of rape incidents has increased considerably since the 1980s, the vast majority being date-rapes.

The influential Feminist Catherine MacKinnon states:

> 'Almost half of all women are raped or victims of attempted rape at least once in their lives.'[16]

And,

> 'Dworkin, MacKinnon et al have expanded the definition of rape while exaggerating its occurrence. And they have won many new supporters by tossing around horrifying numbers: one in three girls is sexually abused, one in two women are raped.'[17]

And the Professional Feminist, Kat Banyard:

> 'A recent survey by Nineteen magazine found that 22 per cent of young British girls said they had been forced into having sex against their will. A larger survey published in 1994, Sex in America, echoed that figure: 22 per cent of women said they had been forced to perform a sex act.'[18]

- As well as the reported high incidence I would like the reader to note the phraseology used by Banyard ('forced into having sex against their will'); we will see that this is an important factor in the Feminist exaggeration of the issue

The reader must ask himself or herself: do I believe these rape statistics? Do I believe that 1 in every 2, 1 in every 3, or 1 in every 4 of the women I know have experienced rape or attempted rape? Because if I *do* believe them then it means that if my mother has not been raped then at least one of my sisters *has* been; or that if my paternal grandmother hasn't been raped then my maternal grandmother must have been; if *none* of the women I sit with for coffee in the morning have been raped then *all* the women I meet at the next dinner party/gathering will have been.

- Do you appreciate just how ridiculous the Feminist-driven figure on the incidence of rape is? Feminism is desperate for a widespread 'rape' problem. And the astonishing fact is that most of us actually *believe* them...and social policy is informed by this exaggerated Ideological claim

Feminism has driven the discourse on rape since the early 1980s; no other perspective has been sought by the State; the media (by and large) has also ignored any other perspective.

And so, with rape now being represented and accepted as a 'widespread problem', we see the issue being placed high on the political agenda (as the Feminist strategy so intended), we see Feminist-sympathetic judges and senior Feminist lawyers introducing dubious legal practices to increase the conviction rate. For example, compulsory attendance of judges on Equality and Diversity courses, taught by Feminists; jury-tampering with pro-Feminist 'rape-packs'; jury members given 'talks' by psychologists explaining why it has taken a women six months or two years to report a rape. We see policy-makers fundamentally changing the rules, with a man accused of rape now considered to be guilty and having to prove himself innocent (overturning 1000 years of the English concept of a person being 'innocent until proven guilty').

And we see a flourishing Feminist Rape Industry.

- Before you condemn me for being cynical just remember that this could be *your* son who can now so easily be accused of rape

   'Professor Margaret Gordon of the University of Washington did a study in 1981 that came up with relatively low figures for rape (one in fifty). She tells of the negative reaction to her findings: "There was some pressure...to have rape be as prevalent as possible...I'm a pretty strong feminist, but one of the things I was fighting was that the really avid feminists were trying to get me to say that things were worse than they really were".'[19]

- You cannot create a widespread problem out of 1 in 50 – that wouldn't justify your existence as a Movement, neither can you build an Industry on this figure...or demonise men, so... 'things need to be worse than they really are.'

- in the words of the climate-botherer Dr. Stephen Schneider, 'to capture the public imagination we need to offer up some scary scenarios'

How Feminism Exaggerates the Incidence of Rape

There are three ways that Feminism exaggerates the incidence of rape. One method is to create a 'new' category of rape in order to bump up the number of incidents (date-rape). A second method is to use linguistic trickery. A third method is to deliberately misinterpret the data. All involve the strategy of 'changing the rules'. As date-rape has already been addressed I will now look at Feminism's linguistic sophistry and its deliberate misinterpretation of data.

Exaggeration by Linguistic Sophistry

The concept of date-rape lends itself to linguistic sophistry. For example, it's 'researchers' use undefined terms like 'forced', 'coerced', 'unwanted' – when they should actually be using the word 'unavoidable'.

If a stranger looms over a woman, pinning her down with his body, and forcibly penetrates her, then she has been 'forced' (this is unavoidable: as happens with stranger rape). On the other hand, if a boyfriend sweet-talks his girl when she doesn't really want to have sex, but then she agrees, is he 'forcing' her (as with date-rape)? If he threatens to 'dump her' (stop seeing her), is *that* 'force'? If they then have sex is that rape? There is a huge difference between feeling 'forced' to make a donation towards a leaving present for a work colleague and being *forced* to hand over a purse or wallet to an armed mugger. It is not my objective to belittle those women who have genuinely been forced to have sex; my aim is to show that there are *multiple objective meanings* to the word 'force' and to interpret it in only one way – to create an Ideological issue, as Feminism does – is unethical and wrong.

- So the Feminist use of the word 'forced' is a deliberate deceit to exaggerate the incidence of rape; an example of Criteria Dilution

We see the same deliberate ambiguity with the use of the word 'coerce' by Feminist 'researchers':

> *'That there is a fundamental difference between coercion and criminal rape should be patently obvious since women, too, freely admit that they do it.'*[20]

For example:

> *'In a 1989 study of female college students conducted by Dr. Peter Anderson, 50 percent said they had used some form of coercion to try to bring about sexual activity ranging from kissing to intercourse.'*[21]

- '50 per cent of the young women used "coercion" to get sex.' We do not consider it rape when a woman uses verbal coercion and psychological manipulation, or continues to fondle a reluctant partner who is not running screaming in the opposite direction. Yet Feminism *does* consider it rape when a *male* uses these ploys – 'gender equality'? Bias?...or Ideology?
- So the Feminist use of the word 'coerced' is a further intentional Criteria Dilution device to exaggerate the incidence of rape

Similarly, with the word 'unwanted'; what, exactly, is 'unwanted' sex?

'Most of the students had unwanted sex to satisfy their partners' needs or to promote intimacy and avoid tension, clear indications that "this behaviour serves a bonding function." And about two-thirds of those who had unwanted sex believed their own partners had done the same thing on numerous occasions, which suggests that they share a contract to try to please each other sexually even when their own sexual desire is at a low ebb...and most reported that their romantic feelings did not change or actually increased subsequent to having unwanted but consensual sex.' [22]

- So two-thirds of males, according to their female partners, had had 'unwanted' sex. Could we say that their female partners are rapists?

- So the use of the word 'unwanted' is also a method of exaggerating the incidence of rape

***

On the other hand, the word 'unavoidable' is hardly ever used in Feminist rape 'research' because it offers a *clearly defined result*; a result that cannot be used to exaggerate the issue:

'The difference between unwanted sex and unavoidable sex is significant: in the latter case, there are elements of physical coercion, physical violence, or threats to cause physical harm. Unavoidable sex... is rape. For instance, in a 1988 study co-authored by Dr. Muehlenhard, 39 percent of the women said they had had unwanted sex, but only 3 percent deemed it unavoidable. In their written descriptions of the incidents in question, the 3 percent who deemed sex unavoidable clearly described acts of physical force and threats to cause physical harm that would meet even the narrowest definition of rape.' [23]

- 3 per cent is an Ideological nightmare for Feminists. Linguistic sophistry had to be employed to generate a 'widespread problem' that would justify its existence, build a Gravy-Train Industry and demonise and punish men

To repeat a quote from a recent gender-warrior addition to the Feminist Industry:

'A recent survey by Nineteen magazine found that 22 per cent of young British girls said they had been forced into having sex against their will. A larger survey published in 1994, Sex in America, echoed that figure: 22 per cent of women said they had been forced to perform a sex act.' [24]

By deliberately muddling definitions it would seem that Feminism, and Feminist organisations, are encouraging and priming young women to seek out and report any incident that could possibly be construed as a 'rape'.

- We are beginning to see how rape became a Feminist Fraud

Exaggeration by Deliberately Misinterpreting Rape Data

Feminist 'research' is devious and deceitful. We have seen that it intentionally uses ambiguous words and phrases so that *on paper* sexual encounters can be 'legitimately' classified as rape, giving a much higher incidence than really is the case. A further misuse of methodology is to get the 'researchers' *themselves*, rather than the *interviewees*, to decide if the woman has, or has not, been raped.

One of the major sources for the 1 in 4 figure on rape is the 'research' carried out by Mary Koss in the 1980s. Koss's 'findings' became the most frequently cited 'research' on women's victimisation *not by established scholars in the field of rape* – but by journalists, politicians and Feminist activists. [25]

'The source of the oft-cited one-in-four figure is a 1985 survey of 3,187 female college students conducted by psychologist Mary Koss for Ms. Magazine...however, this survey has become a lightening rod in the date rape debate, primarily because the decision to classify students' experiences as rape or attempted rape was made by Mary Koss rather than by the women themselves.'[26]

• Can you *believe* the duplicity! Ms magazine was founded in 1972 by the virulent Feminist Gloria Steinem specifically as a Feminist mouthpiece. Ms commissioned Koss's 'research' on rape. 'The Sister who pays the piper...'

And,

'Koss's study...is the landmark study on date-rape....'[27]

The vast majority of Koss's interviewees *did not consider that they had been raped*. But from a Feminist definition of rape Koss concluded that they *had* been. In this sense we can see that rape is a *deliberate* Feminist construction, carefully manufactured from Ideologically-devised and presented questions and politically-interpreted conclusions. Koss's 'research' has been roundly dismissed by gender-neutral scholars. Not only did the majority of young women feel that they had *not* been raped, but many actually subsequently went out on dates with their supposed 'attackers':

'In her book Who Stole Feminism? Christina Hoff Sommers posed a question the researchers didn't ask: "Since most women the survey counted as victims didn't think they had been raped, and since so many went back to their partners, isn't it reasonable to conclude that many had not been raped to begin with?"

Once the data were adjusted for bias – and the women who didn't consider themselves raped were removed – the numbers changed significantly. Not one in four, but between 3 and 5 percent of the women surveyed had been raped. This isn't a number to celebrate, but it's significantly less than 25 per cent.'[28]

'3 to 5 per cent' cannot be used as an Ideological issue, to justify your existence, to promote your Industry, to demonise and punish men. And this very low figure of *genuine* rapes is *itself* within Feminism's *own* created category of rape – date-rape. So even within Feminism's *own* created category of 'rape' there is still only a tiny minority of genuine rapes...and this category represents 88 per cent of *all* rapes. You see what I'm getting at? We are all being conned.

• It's appalling that British society, culture and State still persist in accepting the incidence of rape as being '1 in every 2 or 3 or 4 women'. Why are we so eager to be duped? Do we have a psychological defect that makes us *want to believe* that women suffer? It really is a mystery

One female writer notes:

'So what, exactly, is date rape? Even researchers who have spent years studying this question do not agree, their definitions and interpretations vary greatly. But their studies have been widely publicised and the figures have entered public consciousness: one in four women – or, depending on the study, one in three, or one in two – will be victims of rape or attempted rape. The figures are so shockingly high that the discrepancies hardly seem to matter. Apparently, the average woman is more likely to be raped than to be left-handed.'[29]

***

Kathryn Newcomer is Professor of Statistics and Public Policy at George Washington University; she comments on Feminism's use of 'exaggeration' as a political strategy:

'No one cares what the real numbers are, they just want to make political statements.'[30]

The definition of date-rape has *deliberately* been made so elastic that it now includes incidents that have nothing to do with aggression, force, or even lack of consent. Here, again, we see the Feminist strategy of Criteria Dilution.

The Feminist Germaine Greer:

'Probably the commonest form of non-criminal rape is rape by fraud – by phony tenderness or false promises of an enduring relationship, for example.'[31]

- Here we see an example of the Feminist frenzy to deliberately create more and more 'rape'. If a relationship doesn't endure then the sex that the couple had whilst together *must*, according to a leading Feminist, be interpreted as rape. This woman has taught in British universities since the early 1970s, with no one in all those years daring to question of challenge her views. Shameful, really

'When a woman uses "sweet talk" psychology to get her way in having sex
it's called seduction; when a man does it it's called rape'
(Swayne O'Pie)

In addition, today's young women have been trained up and 'educated' to report such 'non-criminal rape' as *genuine* 'rapes' (for example, we saw this with the date-rape drug Rohypnol). And in our Feminist-dominated State these women's allegations *have* to be taken seriously, and *acted upon* by the police and by the Crown Prosecution Service (both Feminist-sympathetic organisations). Such is the power of today's Feminism.

Feminist 'research' on rape is fraudulent, it deliberately constructs a high incidence; it does not *find* genuine rape but *creates* 'definitional rape', or 'paper rape'.

'Feminists are in the business of creating and promoting data-rape'
(Swayne O'Pie)

***

An additional strategy that Feminism uses to inflate the incidence of rape is to claim that the rapes that *are* reported are only the 'tip of the iceberg' and that many more go unreported. The Guardian claims:

'An estimated 95% of the rapes that actually take place in the UK are never reported.'[32]

And the Feminist-influenced charity, Victim Support:

'Javed Khan, chief executive of Victim Support, said: "Rape and domestic violence are seriously under-reported crimes..."'[33]

- Is there a reader-volunteer who will challenge The Guardian / Victim Support by requesting to see the genuine, original, hard-evidence, gender-neutral research supporting their Feminist claims? Don't be fobbed off, persist...and see what transpires

We have all bought into 'the tip of the iceberg' myth. And myth it is, because there is absolutely *no evidence* that this claim is true (but we all accept it anyway). If Feminists cheat and lie with their definitions, their Criteria Dilution and data, in order to create a high incidence of rape then they will have no qualms about creating a 'tip-of-the-iceberg' myth in order to enhance their self-created 'epidemic'. As in Koss's 'research', perhaps young women *themselves* don't feel that they have been raped...but Feminists, clinically twisting their definitions to suit their Ideology and agenda *insist* that technically, 'on paper' and 'definitionally' these women *have* been raped. A morally principled British State and Establishment would not be party to such an Ideologically-driven fraud and deception. But it is.

- And so we have 'rape' as a political construction. The 'tip of the iceberg' is the icing on the cake of the 'rape crisis', to be consumed by the gullible (sadly, this amounts to most of us).

'A key element in the construction of a social problem is, of course, its size. The larger the problem, the greater the attention it can legitimately command. In the pursuit of magnitude elastic definitions go hand in hand with inflated statistics, each exaggeration reinforcing the other.'[34]

In short, Feminism does all it can to increase the number of 'rape' incidents so that it can point to these spurious statistics when demanding the implementation of its agenda, including demonising and punishing men. A high incidence of rape keeps Ideological and personal 'anger' on the boil.

- There must be something wrong with people who deliberately wish to artificially increase the number of victims of an horrendous crime. I refer the reader to Part Three

---

Exaggerating Rape: The Non-Conviction Rate

'Only 6 per cent of reported rapes end in a conviction'

(Feminist mantra)

A further 'exaggeration' Feminism uses with the issue of rape is the conviction rate. One of the interminable 'scandals' complained about by Feminists is the low percentage of conviction and punishment of men compared with the high reported incidence of rape.

WHY WE BELIEVE THE POLICE HAVE LOST SIGHT OF RAPE

(The Times, 17 January, 2006: Lisa Longstaff and Cristel Amiss)

'1985: When Women Against Rape published its survey on rape, "Ask Any Woman", the police introduced rape suites and special training. Recorded rapes: 1,842. Conviction rate: 24 per cent.

2000: "Project Sapphire" – teams trained to take statements and investigate rape. The first London Sexual Assault Referral Centre opens. Police claim to have increased charges and cautions in London from 18 to 25 per cent. Recorded rapes: 7,929. Conviction rate: 7 per cent.

2002: Rape Action Plan including early evidence kits to take immediate mouth and urine samples distributed to every police force. Recorded rapes: 11,266. Conviction rate: 5.6 per cent.'

This 'scandal' is a home-made Feminist concoction. The new category of date-rape was invented specifically to increase the figures, whilst at the same time young women were being 'taught' to report unsatisfactory sexual encounters as rapes. The process of creating the 'scandal' of the low conviction rate is as follows:

- Feminism demands the introduction of a new classification of rape – date-rape, in order to greatly increase the number of rapes

- then it works hard at educating young women to *interpret* any unsatisfactory sexual encounter as a 'rape'

- then it 'trains and educates' young women to *report to the police* any incident that could possibly be construed as 'rape'

- it knows that date-rape is notoriously difficult to prove simply because it is one person's word against another's

- Bingo! A double-whammy issue: i) we have a *high 'incidence'* of rape, and ii) *a very low conviction rate*

***

Camilla Cavendish, a social commentator for The Times, notes the Feminist duplicity on rape convictions:

SO WE ARE WEAK ON RAPE? THINK AGAIN

(The Times, Thursday, 1 February, 2007: Camilla Cavendish)

'I first started looking at this issue because something jarred with me. The figures were shocking, and getting worse despite a decade of effort by police and prosecutors. And the Government was using them to justify a steady dismantling of defendants' freedoms.

The first thing I found was that the "conviction rate" of one in twenty, the rate cited by every authority on the issue, is not the conviction rate at all. It is the number of convictions secured out of the total allegations made, not the number of convictions secured out of the cases tried...the true conviction rate in rape cases is closer to 50 per cent than 5 per cent.

The next thing I found was that more people are being found guilty of rape: up from 655 in 2002 to 728 in 2005. Conviction rates are falling only because allegations have jumped by 40 per cent in that period.

- Note: i) 'Governments are dismantling (male) freedoms', ii) the actual number of convictions has increased, iii) allegations of rape have increased by 40 per cent (this is because young women have been 'taught' to report incidents as 'rapes')

- Note that the *real* conviction rate, of accused men standing in the dock, is closer to 50 per cent, rather than the 6 per cent that Feminists *intentionally* lead us to believe

The Feminist deliberate misrepresentation on rape convictions has been observed by another female columnist (the Labour/Feminist Government had set a target to secure more male convictions).

368

RAPE TARGETS ARE A VIOLATION OF JUSTICE

(The Sunday Times, 2 December, 2007: Minnette Marrin)

'In a country such as ours, which values highly the presumption of innocence, it is odd of the government to announce a *target* for convictions. That, surely, amounts to a presumption of guilt – a presumption that the government knows how many people are guilty of a particular crime and therefore how many people the courts ought to find guilty of it.

At the moment in England and Wales, of the rape allegations that women make to the police only 12% end up in court. Given that 5.7% or so of the reported cases lead to the man being found guilty, that means that 47%, not 5.7% is the true conviction rate for rape. That sounds entirely different and relative to other crimes it is not low. It is slightly higher than the conviction rate for murder'.

- The reader will note that the Labour/Feminist Governments have been in power since 1997. 'Setting a target' for rape conviction amounts to convicting someone (men) *whether guilty or innocent,* in order to reach the artificially set 'percentage target'. This is a *formulaic* rape conviction policy. This is institutionalised misandry. Modern Britain, but particularly the Labour Party, really *does* hate men

- Again it is noted that the *real* 'conviction rate for rape' is nearer 50 per cent than 5 per cent

Yet the Male Feminist, David Cameron, *still* accepts Feminism's Ideologically-driven statistics (as he does with the pay gap):

RAPISTS WHO LAUGH AT THE LAW

Britain has worst conviction rate in Europe, says Cameron

(Daily Mail, Monday, 12 November, 2007)

'Rapists in Britain "think they can get away with it", David Cameron will say today.

The Tory leader will point to a conviction rate far lower than other EU countries and a fall in sentencing. He will promise to tighten the law...

Research commissioned by the Tories has shown that just one in every 20 cases reported to police in this country leads to a guilty verdict – down from one in three in 1977. This compares to five out of 20 in the Netherlands, ten in Italy and 12 in Ireland. "We have a situation where rapists think they can get away with it...How can any civilised country, that sees the sanctity of consent to sex as a vital right for every woman, accept these facts?"'

- Like all of us, Cameron appears to have an emotional and psychological 'need' to believe what Feminists tell us about 'women's issues', about 'women's suffering', however ridiculous these Ideological claims are. It is this male masochistic 'need' to *believe* that is a major reason for Feminism never having been questioned or challenged

- 'Research commissioned by the Tories'...*all* 'research' on sexual politics that is used to inform social policy is now carried out by Feminist-sympathetic women. Many have followed Social Policy Studies courses in university; these are the regular waves of 'gender experts' (gender-warriors) who have infiltrated *every* profession

The Daily Telegraph reported the same speech, but this newspaper included a relevant piece of information that Cameron, if he were a genuine seeker of truth, would have been aware of:

'England and Wales have the lowest conviction rate of any European country at less than six per cent. However, other countries do not try as many acquaintance rape cases.'[35]

- In fact, the Daily Telegraph could have made more of this: very few European countries actually *have* the classification, the concept, of date-rape, so all *their* cases of rape that go to court are stranger-rape cases, which are less ambiguous and therefore easier to conclude in a conviction. Would the marxist-lite Male Feminist, David Cameron, like to reconsider his anti-male/pro-Feminist comments?

By comparing the *reported* number of rapes against the number of *convictions* (instead of comparing the number of men actually *on trial* for rape against the number of convictions) Feminism has *deliberately* created Ideological Issue Creep by deceit and by exaggeration and many of us have been duped by this Feminist Fraud.

***

How does the 'low' conviction rate of 6 per cent for rape stand up in *relative* terms? How does it compare with the conviction rate for all other, *non-sexual*, reported crimes?

HOW ONLY ONE CRIME IN EVERY 39 ENDS WITH A CONVICTION

(Daily Mail, Wednesday, 8 November, 2006)

'Only one crime in 39 leads to a conviction, according to a startling Home Office study.

The research project, which has traced the lives of hundreds of men over half a century, points to a hidden wave of undetected crime.

The men admitted committing hundreds of crimes – but only 2.5 per cent of them led to convictions.'

And,

ONLY ONE CRIME IN 100 ENDS WITH A PUNISHMENT IN COURT

(Daily Mail, Wednesday, 3 January, 2007)

'Only one crime in every hundred results in a conviction in the courts, it emerged yesterday.

Home Office figures showed that although crime rose last year, the number of offenders ending up in court dropped by 8 per cent.

The number actually sentenced in the courts dropped 5 per cent to 306,000 – less than 1 per cent of the estimated 33 million crimes each year.'

***

In conclusion to this particular area of Feminist exaggeration, but also applicable to all others...

'Facts are often immaterial to an ideology'[36]

***

Vera Baird is a high-ranking Feminist lawyer:

YEARS OF CONFUSION ON LAW OF CONSENT
(Daily Mail, Friday, 27 March, 2009)

'But in 2005 came the case of a security guard Ryairi Dougal, who was accused of raping a student in Aberystwyth. Mr. Dougal said they had consensual sex as he walked the woman back to her flat. His trial collapsed after the student told the jury she was too drunk to remember whether she had agreed to sex.

Labour MP and activist Vera Baird QC said the judge who threw out the case had made "a dreadful error" and "needs to be spoken to and sent on some re-training."'

- Judges who don't toe the Feminist line are condemned as sexist and misogynist. Apparently, they must *always* convict men who have been accused of rape. Since the early 1990s judges have been compelled to attend Equality and Diversity Courses, written by Feminists and presented by Feminists, courses intended to convince them that the Feminist perspective is the morally right perspective, that Feminist aims are morally right aims. Some have held out for justice over Ideology, as in the above case

- We saw in the previous chapter on domestic violence that even the British Supreme Court is dominated by the Feminist Ideology

---

Exaggerating Rape: The Trauma of Date-Rape

Since the 1980s Feminism has driven the discourse on rape and has succeeded in convincing the British public and politicians (not that the latter need much convincing) that

- Rape is a common occurrence
- The conviction rate for rape is scandalously low

A third strategy used to exaggerate rape is to claim that date-rape victims experience the same degree of trauma as stranger rape victims.

***

From the Feminist perspective it makes sense to use the strategy of *exaggeration* to enhance the *emotional trauma* of date-rape victims because 88 out of every 100 'victims' of reported rape are date-rape incidents. In this way Feminists can claim that the trauma of rape is a *significant* part of the rape 'epidemic'. And many people have fallen for this Feminist Fraud.

Male Feminists are especially eager to accept this intentional and ridiculous exaggeration. For example, a letter to The Times, 19 January, 2006, from Ken McDonald, QC, Director of the Public Prosecution Service (obviously a highly-placed legal position) said:

> 'We recognise that the majority of rape victims know their attacker and all types of rape are equally serious and traumatic for the victim.'

- Many other Male Feminists (including police chiefs), believe (or pretend to believe) this Feminist dogma. And these are men with the power to influence policy and its implementation...worrying

> 'In some feminist circles it is heresy to suggest that there are degrees of suffering and oppression, which need to be kept in perspective. It is heresy to suggest that being raped by your date may not be as traumatic or terrifying as being raped by a stranger who breaks into your bedroom in the middle of the night.'[37]

- Feminism also wants to convince the public (because that is from where juries are drawn) that the two different types of rape victims suffer similarly: the intention is to influence the jury with the 'horror' of the date-rape and therefore to prejudice its members into bringing in a guilty verdict against the accused male (whether innocent or guilty)

However, one female social commentator believes that the British public has more sense than Feminism gives it credit for:

> 'But juries don't feel that way about date-rape. Feminist cabals, diligent barristers and those aggressive activists who earn their living on a man-hating agenda can protest all they like that all rapes are as bad as each other and deserving of the same harsh penalty. But still the general public – that big wide jury pool – doesn't believe it.'[38]

- Note the reference to 'Feminist cabals' (political and legal Feminists) and 'aggressive activists who earn their living on a man-hating agenda' (the Ideologues in the Rape Industry)

> 'We often hear, "Rape is rape, right?" No. A stranger forcing himself on a woman at knife-point differs from a man and woman having sex while drunk and having regrets in the morning. What is different? When a woman agrees to a date, she does not make a choice to be sexual, but she does make a choice to explore sexual possibilities. The woman makes no such choice with a stranger.'[39]

Feminism claims that both stranger-rape and date-rape have the same physical and mental consequences for the victim. This is a manifestly stupid claim. A woman having questionable non-consensual sex with a boyfriend whilst both are blind drunk, and with whom she has previously had intercourse, is not going to suffer as much mental or emotional terror as a woman who experiences a sudden hostile confrontation in a dark alley from a knife-wielding attacker; that's common sense. But then, the policy-making fraternity and those who implement their policies appear to lack this necessary ingredient for good governance.

Feminism has incredible political power, allowing it to translate its Ideological claims into policy. For example:

HUSBANDS WHO RAPE PUT
ON A PAR WITH GANG RAPISTS

(Daily Mail, Thursday, 8 June, 2006)

'A husband convicted of raping his wife may face the same punishment as rapists who abduct their victims or attack them in gangs.

Under new guidelines, rapes within marriages are being treated as seriously as random attacks carried out by strangers.

But one critic, criminologist Dr. David Green, said yesterday: "Most people do not believe a woman who has sex and later regrets it is the victim of a crime in the same way as a woman who was attacked by a stranger and feared death".'

- 'Most people do not believe it'. Perhaps not, but the policy-making fraternity in politics and the law *do* believe it (or pretend to), and it is *they*, not 'most people', who formulate and implement the (misandrous) laws and practices regarding rape

The Feminist Catherine MacKinnon again:

'Politically, I call it rape whenever a woman has sex and feels violated'

(Catherine MacKinnon: Feminism Unmodified)[40]

- And this is the British State's and Establishment's view, *today*, on rape and sexual encounters. Criteria Dilution, 'extreme inclusiveness', a fabricated 'epidemic'

***

The strategy of equating date-rape trauma with stranger rape trauma is disgraceful. It belittles the truly awful experience of *genuine* stranger-rape victims. How do *these* women feel when their experience is claimed to be the same as that of a date-rape woman whose sexual experience has gone wrong or been misinterpreted? *Their* horrific and severe experience is being intentionally minimised by Feminists and gullible (or sycophantic) police chiefs and politicians in order to exaggerate an issue for Ideological gain. Feminism sacrifices the feelings of such unequivocally genuine victims in order to justify its existence, to build its Rape Industry and to demonise men.

- A Movement that truly had the interests of *all* women at heart would not stoop to employ such a disrespectful and disgraceful strategy. Male Feminists ought to feel ashamed of their complicity

'Unwanted sex is different from unavoidable sex, which is rape. It is an obscene trivialisation of the severe trauma of sexual violation to lump the two experiences together, as though intercourse obtained through physical violence or threats were not really very different from intercourse obtained through persuasion and sweet nothings.'[41]

- Can any decent-minded person disagree that this Feminist strategy is 'obscene'?

373

I would like the reader to consider the following. We have looked at three areas of rape in which Feminism exaggerates the issue. To misrepresent the truth in just *one* area of the phenomenon of rape may be accidental, but to do so in *all* areas surely confirms that there is an underlying *deliberate* policy. There are no 'coincidences' with the implementation of the Feminist agenda; the more we analyse Feminism the more we join up the dots...exposing it for the fraud that it is.

Why Does Feminism Exaggerate Rape?

There are numerous reasons why Feminism exaggerates rape. I'll look at five:

- It spreads misandry
- It justifies its existence (by creating an 'epidemic' and thereby terrifying ordinary, decent young women)
- It creates one more Feminist Industry
- It manipulates men
- It acts as a censoring device

• There are other reasons; one of which is to service the Feminist 'need' for anger, to keep it topped up and on the boil, to keep the gender-warriors primed. We know that anger is a necessary ingredient in an individual Feminist's psychological make-up, and an activating agent in her collective Political Community Club/Family

Spreading Misandry

A primary reason for Feminism to greatly exaggerate the phenomenon of rape is to pursue its anti-male agenda:

> 'The next questions then are who is identifying this epidemic and why. Somebody is "finding" this rape crisis, and finding it for a reason. Asserting the prevalence of rape lends urgency, authority, to a broader critique of culture. In a dramatic description of the rape crisis, Naomi Wolf writes in The Beauty Myth, "cultural representation of glamorised degradation has created a situation among the young in which boys rape and girls get raped as a normal course of events".'[42]

Feminism has turned a nasty, but numerically very small phenomena, into an effective Ideological gender weapon that it uses to culturally and institutionally spread man-hating. Because of its nature, rape is the ultimate weapon to demonise and punish men.

> '(Rape) has become the synecdoche for general male awfulness. Its real function at this moment, in addition to keeping feminist passions at fever pitch, is to serve as the conduit by which some extreme tenets about the relations between the sexes enter everyday life with minimum challenge. No longer a well-intentioned effort to gain justice for women.'[43]

- 'No longer...to gain justice for women' neatly sums up the Feminist strategy of 'exaggeration', not just with rape but also with sexual harassment and domestic violence. These issues have nothing to do with 'gender equality'

- Exaggerating the incidence of rape 'keeps feminist passions at fever pitch'. Feminist anger needs to be constantly stoked up and kept hot. I refer the reader to Part Three. With the progressing of the Quiet Revolution this misandrous mentality, this Feminist perspective on rape, has been incrementally and relentlessly passed into British law

Exaggerating rape provides universal bad publicity for men – 'all men are bastards'. Exaggerating the incidence and severity of rapes is to inflate the severity and pervasiveness of the evil that can be attributed to men. Exaggerating the incidence of rape encourages women to despise men, spreading misandry.

***

One example of how Feminism punishes men is to demand publicity of the name of any man who is simply *accused* of rape (not yet even charged, let alone found guilty) – whilst withholding the name of the female accuser. In this way innocent men's lives are being *deliberately* ruined. A good Feminist result. The Feminist argument that publicising the accused man's name encourages other victims to come forward to report being raped by the same man is illogical. No 'stranger' rapist *gives his name* to his victim...he is identified by other women that he has raped by the *circumstances* of the rape. The notorious taxi-driver rapist John Worboys didn't introduce himself to his victims by saying 'Hello, I'm Mr. Worboys'. Other victims identified him by the *similar circumstances* of their ordeal, not by his name. The names of men who are accused of rape should be withheld until they are proven guilty. But our Feminist-dominated Coalition Government continues to implement the Feminist's misandrous demand to publicise the names of those men who have only been *accused* of rape, thereby leading to the public shaming, demonising and punishing of men – guilty *or* innocent. Modern Britain is *deliberately* institutionally man-hating.

***

In addition to rape being exaggerated to show the pervasiveness of male evil, the strategy of exaggeration is also used to show the pervasiveness of *male power*. That is, to confirm that society and the State are patriarchal. The 'widespread problem' of rape adds to the 'evidence' of pornography, prostitution, domestic violence, sexual harassment, the pay gap and the 'glass ceiling' – all purportedly caused by the 'gender inequality' of power between the sexes. This is why rape has to be interpreted as a crime of 'power' rather than of 'sex'.

Justifying Feminism's Existence

A further major reason for Feminism to exaggerate rape is to justify its continued existence, now that genuine equality has been achieved. One way that it has done this is to create fear of rape in young women.

> *'In the night, imagining some fear,*
> *How easy is a bush supposed a bear.'*
>
> *(A Midsummer Night's Dream)*

> *'The notion that women and particularly young women are in terrible, constant danger is tantamount to an article of religious faith in some camps, and thus any debate quickly veers away from the territory of facts to that of emotions.'*[44]

This scare tactic has been successful – many young women are now fearful of being raped when they go out at night. With this 'result' Feminism can then justify its existence by addressing the (self-created) issue of a 'rape crisis' and its Rape Industry can continue to flourish - with the additional bonus of young women being so grateful that Feminism is out there to fight for their protection (such as the Take Back the Night and Slut Walk Ideologues) that they will sympathise with its Ideology, and possibly join the Movement.

- This strategy is a bit like a protection racket, really

JACQUI'S RIGHT TO BE AFRAID

(The Sunday Times, 27 January, 2008)

'How many women have walked home alone in the dark and felt a chill at the thought of being followed; how many have worried late at night when a friend didn't text to say that she got back safely?'

We are regularly informed, by the Feminist Violence Against Women and Rape Industries, that young women are frightened of being raped. The Deputy Prime Minister's Office states that 1 in 4 young women are 'worried about being raped'. This figure has been put much higher. For example, the Fawcett Society, a Feminist Government-funded lobby group (an organisation whose *raison d'être* is to emphasise Feminist 'issues') declares:

> *'70 per cent of women aged between 16 and 29 are worried about rape'*[45]

And The London Feminist Network:

> *'A survey by the young women's magazine More in 2005 found that 95% of women don't feel safe on the streets at night, and 65% don't even feel safe during the day. 73% worry about being raped and almost half say they sometimes don't want to go out because they fear for their own safety.'*[46]

- A good result for Feminism. Feminism doesn't have the well-being of ordinary women as its aim – except when this accidentally happens to coincide with its Ideological agenda. Feminists are willing to sacrifice the peace of mind of ordinary, decent women in order to promote their Ideology

The reader will have noticed that the issue of rape receives far more media exposure than the statistics warrant (media complicity?). Hysteria (with concomitant political sympathy and action) cannot flourish on a small incidence of rape: hysteria will flourish when it is claimed that 1 in 2 or 3 or 4 women are raped, and when this lie is given regular media coverage.

Creating fear in young women is a *deliberate* Feminist ploy. If it weren't so then Feminism would focus on the *very small incidence* of 'stranger' rapes instead of greatly exaggerating the incidence of rape and the trauma of date-rapes. If its strategy were not to create fear in young women then Feminism would undertake publicity to emphasise that stranger rape represents only 4 per cent of 'violent attacks on the person'; its energies and funding would be directed to *that* end. This would soothe fears. Instead, it does the *exact* opposite by *deliberately maximising* the incidence and fear; surely proof positive of its true Ideological aims.

***

The *real* 'rape crisis' is the amazing statistic that over 70 per cent of young women actually *believe* that 1 in 4 (or 1 in 2, or whatever figure Feminism promotes at any given moment) of women are raped. This is the *real* rape crisis: that there are a significant number of young women walking around with this alarming belief firmly fixed in their heads (deliberately placed there by Feminism). The creation of this unnecessary state of fear is an abuse of young women. And what on earth is this indoctrination doing to what was once a healthy respectful relationship between the sexes...young women are now being made to fear young men. Good result for Lesbian Feminists, though.

> '*Fekete indicts the growing industry of dubious research that is intended to promote panic and rage among women, one result being to manipulate the political process.*'[47]

• Deliberately instilling panic in women, and fear of men, is a carefully crafted Feminist strategy – it demonises (and thereby punishes) men; it creates an 'us' ('good people') and 'them' ('bad people') mentality in women; it consolidates the message that 'men cannot be trusted'; it justifies Feminism's existence (protecting 'us' from 'bad men'); it acts as a recruiting device

Women have intentionally been made fearful of men; are being 'taught' to look upon all young men as potential rapists. And our Feminist-dominated State endorses this obscene 'teaching', this Feminist policy – teaching that all 'bushes' are 'bears'...that men are generally to be seen as 'bad people'. Misandry is systemic and institutionalised in modern Britain.

Creating a Rape Industry

Feminism has exaggerated rape to spread misandry and to create fear in young women. It has done this by building an aggressive Rape Industry that is directly responsible for the strategies of 'exaggeration' in all areas of the phenomenon.

Like the Domestic Violence Industry, the Rape Industry is inhabited solely by Feminist Ideologues. Because of the nature of rape (and Feminism having a monopoly of discourse) this Industry has a great deal of power – ranging from high-ranking Feminist Ideologues within the legal and political system to the Take Back the Night fanatics. Not only does it

377

lobby for changes in the rape laws and court processes to ensure more rape convictions, it provides courses for police and judges, conferences, rape suites, specially trained police personnel...This Industry also includes Rape Units and Rape Centres in numerous universities – all pumping out pro-Feminist/anti-male propaganda, all providing work, sinecures and funding for Feminist Ideologues. For example, the Metropolitan University, London, offers a Master's degree in Women's Abuse, of which the subject of rape is a large component. This university actually houses a Women's Abuse Centre.

Manipulating Men

Rape, because it is a particularly emotive subject, has never been gender-neutrally analysed. Men, especially, are fearful of questioning any aspect of the rape phenomenon. It is a sensitive and delicate subject. And so Feminists have a free run on the interpretation and presentation of rape, and theirs is the *only* perspective; they have a clear run to abuse the facts. In addition, rape is an easy issue to 'sell' politically; genuine rape is an horrendous crime and we *all* sympathise with its victims. Male chivalry and men's natural instinct to protect women is triggered by the Feminist presentation of rape...men feel that the victim could be *their* daughter, *their* wife, *their* mother, *their* sister. Feminism has unscrupulously capitalised on male chivalry. And men in power are too gormless to have noticed this (as they are with other Feminist issues).

So one further benefit to Feminism from exaggerating rape is to manipulate men. It creates 'male guilt', continually wrong-footing men and thereby making men in positions of power and influence more likely to accept and implement Feminist policies. 'Guilty' men are 'easy-to-manipulate men', and many men feel 'guilty by association' when it is stated, time and time again, that 1 in 4 (or 1 in 2) women have been traumatically sexually violated by a man.

> *'No one cares what the real numbers are (on rape) they just want to make political statements.'*[48]

- Exaggerating rape increases the number of politically sympathetic Male Feminists; Feminism has unscrupulously capitalised on male chivalry.

A Censoring Device

A high incidence of rape is used as a censoring device. When the evidential base for a case is weak people resort to the use of 'emotion'. Because it is ethically and rationally bankrupt, Feminism relies heavily on stirring up 'emotions'. This is particularly so with rape; rape has been made into an emotive issue in order to prevent the Feminist perspective being questioned.

Katy Roiphe's mother was a rabid Feminist who wrote 'Up the Sandbox', a Feminist tract. On her own account Roiphe arrived at university expecting Feminism to be about equality. She quickly became disillusioned and saw Feminism for the bigoted Ideology that it had become. This stimulated the 24-year-old Roiphe to write the phenomenally ground-breaking anti-rape book, 'The Morning After: Sex, Fear and Feminism'.[49] She observes:

> *'Invoking the rape crisis...strengthens an argument by infusing it with heightened emotional appeal. For many feminists, then, rape becomes a vehicle, a way to get from here to there. By blocking analysis with its claims to unique pandemic suffering, the rape crisis becomes a powerful source of authority.'*[50]

- Feminism creates a high incidence of rape in order to 'block analysis' of the whole issue of rape (and other Feminist issues). It needs to retain a monopoly of discourse on issues; and by doing so retains power over our thinking, over our perspectives, and therefore retains power over policy-making

---

Have You Found these Four Chapters Offensive?

Many men, including myself, have found thirty-five years of aggressive, man-hating Feminism offensive...thirty-five years. So, reader, before you condemn me for being so 'abusively insensitive and giving offence,' or of being politically incorrect about trafficked women, sexual harassment, domestic violence and rape, answer me the following question. If *all other* 20th century ideologies – Marxism, communism, fascism, Nazism – have been questioned, challenged, analysed and critiqued, then why hasn't Feminism? What power gives Feminism this protection, this immunity from academic, media and political scrutiny? Have you ever thought about that?

- Why is this one of the very few books in Britain today that seriously confronts Feminism? A fellow British author, Mike Buchanan, has written three books that confront it[51] [52] [53]

Only when you can answer *that* question, reader – why such a pervasive, powerful, malign and misandrous Ideology has escaped scrutiny, why it has been given immunity from enquiry and challenge – only when you can provide a convincing answer to *that* question do you have the moral right to criticise me for doing what ought to have been done at least two decades ago, by others more qualified and capable than I.

In addition, and perversely, Feminism not only enjoys more critical immunity – Feminism is *reverently* promoted in our universities, in our media, throughout the professions, the trade unions and the political system. The lack of challenge to Feminist Ideology, and its universal acceptance into our conventional wisdom, into our political zeitgeist, into our culture, into our legal and policy-making process, has created a society and State in which men can be bullied at will for being sexist, for being misogynistic (both defined by Feminism), and in which they are systemically discriminated against, demonised and punished. So don't *dare* condemn me for doing the job that others have been too timid to do, and should be doing right now.

> *'I might be in a minority of one, Mr. Churchill, but the truth is still the truth'*
>
> (Mahatma Gandhi, discussing Indian independence)

> *'All it takes for evil to exist is for good men to do nothing'*
>
> (Edmund Burke)

> *'We have come a long way, but we still have a long way to go'*
>
> (Feminist mantra)

Section 7

Chapter 45

Cheating and Lying:
The Dishonesty of Feminist 'Research'

We have looked at five strategies that Feminism uses to Issue Creep inequalities, discriminations, oppressions, victimisations and abuses:

- Creating issues from nothing

- Establishing Industries to create and promote issues

- Converting women's choices into issues

- Changing the rules and definitions

- Exaggeration

The Feminist abuse of research is a sixth strategy in this Feminist Fraud. 'Research' findings give an academic legitimacy to the continuing justification of Feminism, its Grievance Gravy-Train Industries and its misandry. It also assists the progress of its Quiet Revolution.

***

Telling and promoting an untruth becomes a lie when the intention is to deceive. Intentionally lying to gain personal and Ideological advantages is dishonest, unethical and fraudulent. This Section shows how Feminism cheats and lies with its 'research' in order to gain sexual political advantages for its Ideology and agenda.

> *'Statistics and studies on such provocative subjects as eating disorders, rape, battery, and wage differentials are used to underscore the plight of women in the oppressive gender system and to help recruit adherents to the gender feminist cause.'*[1]

• We have all taken the dishonourable, but safer, route of accepting Feminist statistics at face value, rather than rigorously questioning them

Research is vital to Feminism in order to validate its claims and issues; its dishonesty is particularly pernicious with the issues of the pay gap, the 'glass ceiling', domestic violence and rape. Feminist 'research' is also used to blame, demonise and punish men. Much of the legislation and policy initiatives in sexual politics and social policy are based upon Feminist-produced 'research' so it's important to understand just how fraudulent and dishonest this actually is.

***

Firstly, the Section looks at what research is *supposed* to be. This is followed by a discussion of the type of research method that Feminism has chosen to use, and how experts in the field consider this Feminist research method of choice to be seriously flawed. Ethics are an essential part of the integrity of any research method and this is addressed. A chapter on the media is followed by a look at the interconnections between Feminist 'research', universities and social policy. Various examples of Feminism's abuse of 'research' are given. The specific Feminist issue of housework is considered. An actual example of university-produced Feminist 'research' is then offered so that the reader can appreciate how this propaganda translates into biased social policy-making. Finally, I suggest why the findings of Feminist 'research' go unchallenged.

We hear so much from Feminism about 'the pay gap' I was tempted to title this Section 'The Truth and Honesty Gap'.

- Everyone is entitled to their own opinions, but not to their own facts

Ideology and the Use of Untruths

Nigel Hawkes is Director of the organisation Straight Statistics. He has no political affiliation; in fact, it was his political neutrality, and his observation that statistics were being politically abused, that prompted him to set up Straight Statistics. He warns:

'Statistics are the rock upon which sound government is built. Without reliable statistical sources, prompt publication and public trust in their accuracy, politicians and commentators have no safe place to stand.'[2]

- We need to keep this sobering thought in mind when we learn that a senior Feminist minister in the Labour Government, the Minister for Women, was caught manipulating statistics to enhance her Ideology...

HARMAN CAUGHT EXAGGERATING THE PAY GAP BETWEEN SEXES

(Daily Mail, Friday, 12 June, 2009)

'Harriet Harman was given an official warning last night for exaggerating the pay gap between men and women.

Britain's statistics watchdog accused Labour's deputy leader – who is also the Women's Minister – of using a figure that more than doubled the real divide.

Sir Michael Scholar said her office had been warned that including part-time workers in her calculations could be misleading but pressed ahead. They claimed that women were paid 23 per cent less, but Sir Michael says 12.8 per cent would be a more accurate figure.'

- There would seem to be 'no safe place to stand' with sexual politics
- So even very high-ranking Feminists 'mislead' with 'research' and statistics
- The powerfully-placed American Feminist Hillary Clinton euphemistically calls *her* lies 'misspeaks'. How sweet

'Although feminist ideologues continue to talk about having a "long way to go", they have in fact been remarkably successful. In only a few decades, they have generated a social, intellectual and economic revolution...we examine the origins of that revolution, the ways in which ideological feminists have "reinterpreted", "renegotiated", "reinscribed", "relocated", or "repositioned" academic standards of truth in research to suit themselves.'[3]

In today's Britain, those who produce statistics and studies on sexual politics and social policy will invariably be university-trained 'gender experts'. Which as we know, actually means Feminist gender-warriors. Their fraudulent 'research' suits their Industries, Ideology and agenda.

*'One must always be sceptical of "research" that "just happens"
to promote the Ideology and agenda of the "researcher"'*

(Swayne O'Pie)

Chapter 46

Choosing to Cheat

Essentially, Feminists choose the type of 'research' methodology that is the easiest to abuse and manipulate, in order to produce the findings they require.

To consider Feminism's abuse of statistics – the *deliberate* misinforming of politicians and the public – it is necessary to take a brief look at the esoteric world of 'research', its phraseology, concepts and language. This skip down Research Lane is too brief to be boring. So, to begin with, let's define exactly what research is *supposed* to be:

Research: *'1.(a) The systematic investigation into and study of materials, sources, etc. in order to establish facts and reach new conclusions. (b) An endeavour to discover new or collate old facts etc. by the scientific study of a subject or by a course of critical investigation.'*[1]

- Note the phrase 'new conclusions' and 'critical investigation'

We tend to be awed by the word 'research' and, perhaps, by people who say they 'do' research. The word itself conjures up thoughts of credibility, truth and integrity. The type of research that creates this effect is the scientific research of respected academics. For example, the discovery of DNA is genuine, respected, scientific research. This type of research is known as the 'positivist' approach. It is the approach used in the natural and physical sciences.

The 'anti-positivist' approach is used in the social sciences, such as Sociology. Its researchers emphasise the importance of discovering the meaning and interpretations of events and actions. The anti-positivist approach is often described as 'interpretative' (interpreting people's behaviour, for example); confusingly, it is also sometimes called 'qualitative' research. The qualitative type of research is that favoured by Feminism.

Qualitative research is particularly susceptible to an individual researcher's personal value system and biases. In one sense, it can be said that the concept of research has been redefined and diluted since the 1960s for the specific purpose of giving credibility to a specific social and political Left-wing/liberal/progressive agenda – an agenda that embraces and is embraced by (as we have seen) the political bias in universities, where most Feminist qualitative research is undertaken. Qualitative research gained acceptability because it is seen, incorrectly, by politicians, the media and the public as being based upon the scientific legitimacy of natural and physical research ('positivist' research). We have all been conned (or shamefully allowed ourselves to be).

- Most people (including politicians who should know better) are not aware of the difference between the 'positivist' approach to research and the qualitative approach. This ignorance gives legitimacy to the latter; after all, it is thought, 'research is research, isn't it?' Well, no, it very definitely is *not* all the same

- This confusion is *deliberately* sown by Feminism in order to give credibility to its 'findings'. This is a Feminist 'front' intentionally used to deceive the public and policy-makers

The qualitative approach to research, even though much more open to abuse by the researcher and his or her team (or perhaps *because* of the ease of such abuse) is now the norm in social, educational and political research: the positivist approach, even though it is more rigorous and less open to abuse (or *because* of this rigour) is now out of fashion, and is often seen as being politically incorrect.

Serious academics believe that qualitative research is difficult to define clearly; in addition, it has no theory. Neither does it have a distinct set of methods.[2] This vagueness makes it the ideal choice of research approach for those who wish to promote and 'substantiate' a powerful political, social and Ideological agenda. The Ideology of the 'research' team can be disguised in the methodology and in the interpretation of what will be 'selectively' found – but at the same time give the impression of academic and scientific legitimacy and integrity. This is the 'research method of choice' used by Feminism.

> *"Qualitative research, then, is ultimately a frame of mind, it is an orientation and commitment to studying the social world in certain kinds of ways".*[3]

If we interpret this definition from a Feminist perspective, with a Feminist agenda and Ideology in mind, as a Feminist 'researcher' would do, we see the following:

1. For 'a frame of mind' read 'preferential treatment, special privileges and policy favouritism for women' (especially Feminists) and/or 'discrimination against, or the blaming of, men'

2. For 'orientation' read 'spectrum of bias from prejudice through to bigotry', especially in the Ideology's stated claims of discrimination against women, oppression of women, victimisation of women and abuse of women

3. For 'commitment' read 'commitment to the Sisterhood and the Feminist agenda', and a 'commitment' to viewing Britain as a patriarchy, a society in which men have all the power, using this power to advantage themselves and to discriminate, dominate and oppress women – a 'commitment' to an Ideology

***

Now, within qualitative research there is a *specific branch* that pursues 'research' in order to *make changes* in the subject area of its study. For example, someone studying school morning assemblies will produce data on how changes can be made to increase the efficiency of this daily school routine of organising hundreds of children in one hall.

This 'making changes' research is known as 'action research': it is undertaken to stimulate action. So 'action research' is a specific type of qualitative research, used as a strategy to 'make change'.[4] 'Action researchers' are concerned to improve a situation (improve it from *their own perspective)* through active intervention – and in collaboration with the parties that they are researching.[5]

- 'Action research' is also known as 'advocacy research'. An example of 'advocacy research' will be seen in a later chapter in which a Feminist 'researcher' from Lancaster University produces 'research' that disrespects fathers, especially divorced fathers. Advocacy 'research' advocates a predetermined action

'Action/advocacy research' has been chosen by Ideological Feminism as the best type of research that will promote its cause, and to achieve its aims and to implement its agenda. One could almost say that 'action/advocacy research' was *specifically invented* by Feminism to be used as a weapon in sexual politics. This type of research can be very easily abused (and is) whilst the retention of the awe-inspiring word 'research' still gives Feminist 'findings/studies' political and public acceptability. A clever Machiavellian strategy intended to deceive and misrepresent.

The process of 'action/advocacy research' is as follows:

1. Identify a problem
2. Collect information
3. Analyse the information
4. Plan an action or intervention
5. Implement and monitor the outcomes (that will have been predetermined) to 'solve' the problem

It is not difficult to see how this type of 'research' can be abused by Feminist 'researchers'. For example, applying the above process to the Feminist issue of domestic violence we have:

1. 'Identify a problem': that fits their agenda, (women are victimised, oppressed and abused...by men)
2. 'Collect information': a large number of victims needs to be found (it would defeat the object of the 'research' to find information that contradicted the idea that there is a 'widespread problem')
3. 'Analyse' the information in such a way that shows there *is* a 'problem' (assisted by Criteria Dilution and thereby exaggerating and magnifying the 'problem'). For example, we now have 'shouting' at a woman by her male partner being classified as domestic violence
4. 'Planning action': establishing Interest Groups, committees, media meetings – organised to prime politicians, the media and the public in order to convince policy-makers that there *is* a 'widespread problem'
5. 'Implementing outcomes' and 'solving the problem': These would include, for example, establishing Domestic Violence and Abuse Centres in universities specifically to study domestic violence and rape (staffed *only* by Feminists), setting up Domestic Violence Units and Rape Units in city police stations, providing Domestic Violence and Rape courses which police and judges are compelled to attend, funding more Domestic Violence Refuges, and so on

***

The public, and the decision-makers, are informed on all issues appertaining to sexual politics and social (gender) policy *only* by Feminist 'research'; no other perspective is available and no other perspective is sought.

• Male decision-makers, including male MPs, *never* question or challenge the provenance, or the validity, of the Feminist surveys and studies that they use to base their decisions upon. Because of this laxness (or fear? Or complicity?) they are as equally culpable of preferencing and policy-favouring women (mainly Feminists), and of man-hating, as are the Feminist 'researchers' themselves

'Action/advocacy research', then, is ideal for someone with a very strong individual and group Ideology and who wishes to translate their agenda into legal and social policy.

Experts Denounce Feminist 'Research'

Hitchcock and Hughes are regarded as highly respected authorities in the field of research methods. Their books are used on Masters degree courses as set texts. They note that 'action research' (Feminism's 'research method of choice') has great potential for abuse. It is worth quoting their criticisms.[6]

1. *'Action research needs to clarify the distinction between the nature of 'action' and 'research'. The two terms are not interchangeable'...*

2. *'Qualitative action research can fall prey to criticisms of "soft science". The preference for interpretative style action research cycles or spirals has prompted some to question the potential lack of rigour of such enquiries, or worse still that it is not proper research conducted by proper researchers'....*

3. *'Collaboration (with those who are the target of the 'research', for example, housewives, when the topic of housework is being studied) is seen as a central ingredient in action research. How is this to be achieved and at what degrees or levels? A body of literature is now emerging which clearly demonstrates the potential problems of collaboration'...*

4. *'A number of question marks hang over the ethics and accountability issues associated with action research. There does seem to be confusion and in some cases the ethical position is quite simply untenable...'*

- So Hitchcock and Hughes conclude that 'action research' – the research method of choice of Feminism – has 'potential for lacking rigour and those who conduct it may not be thought of as proper researchers'; and it is believed Feminist 'research' is only 'soft science'; that 'collaboration between researchers and the researched is ethically questionable; and that in some cases Feminist 'research' has 'an ethical position that is quite simply untenable.'

This is an unequivocal damning of Feminist 'research' by two of the most eminent and respected experts in the field, who conclude that such 'research' is invalid and fraudulent.

And a further authority:

> *'Political parties, charities, non-governmental organisations, lobby groups and other advocacy groups have perfected the strategy of promoting their causes through advocacy research. Advocacy research is the very opposite of scientific investigation. Sound science is devoted to the exploration of the unknown and the discovery of the truth. Advocacy organisations don't have to discover the truth – they already know it and their research is designed to affirm what they already know. "Let's get some numbers to prove the cause" seems to be the motif of such research.'[7]*

- 'Action/advocacy research', as its name implies, 'advocates' a particular course of action based upon the value judgements and aims of the 'researchers' themselves; so *by its very nature* it is biased and prejudiced toward a previously held perspective, including an Ideology and agenda

- Feminist 'research' deals in preordained conclusions

> *'No one cares what the real numbers are, they just want to make political statements.'[8]*

Chapter 47

Ethics, Propaganda and Feminist 'Research'

Ethics/ethical: *'The study of morals in human conduct; honourable; morally correct; the moral quality of a course of action; any set of moral principles or values; propriety.'*[1]

- Feminist 'research' is ethically bankrupt

Central to the fundamental flaws in 'action/advocacy research' is the issue of ethics. The issue of ethics in this context includes the concepts of personal values, beliefs, judgements, viewpoints, honesty and integrity. Hitchcock and Hughes stress that at the core of the ethical dimension in research is personal responsibility:

'Responsibilities relate to the individual researcher, the participants in the research, professional colleagues...and towards the sponsors of the research'.[2]

Feminist 'researchers' disregard these fundamental responsibilities. They have created their own ethical stance, the sole thrust of which is that Feminist 'research' should advance the Feminist Ideology and agenda, leading primarily to the promotion of special privileges for women/Feminists (defined by Feminists themselves, not by women in general), and whenever possible, to the blaming and condemnation of men.

Hitchcock's and Hughes's comments regarding 'action researchers having a responsibility toward their sponsors' is significant. Whenever a Feminist organisation or group wishes to promote an issue, or to counter a claim that men are discriminated against, it will sponsor a 'friendly' university to produce 'research' that can be used as a gender-weapon. Examples will be given in a later chapter.

Christina Hoff Sommers has noted the lack of ethics in Feminist 'research':

'According to one Washington D.C. researcher to whom I recently spoke: "Under Secretary Shalala, Health and Human Services has been mobilised as the research and policy arm of the feminist movement".'[3]

Essentially, Feminism's self-justifying, self-promoting, self-defined 'research' methods give Feminism's 'researchers' a licence to cheat and lie, to promote its Ideology and to promote its agenda. The actual processes and conclusions of their 'research' are meaningless because the functions of process and outcome are, for Feminist 'researchers', simply political actions; and therefore have no ethical (research) constraints. This reduces their 'research' to nothing more than propaganda.

***

Feminists *themselves* have no shame in admitting this:

- *'A feminist ethic differs from the traditional sociological ethic in several fundamental ways. While the goal of traditional social science is to gain knowledge for the 'advancement/enlightenment' of the discipline, the feminist analyses social aggression to empower herself, wimmin, and minorities. Whereas the traditional scientist is accountable to the profession, the feminist is accountable to the wimmin's movement, a feminist ethic, and women in general.'*[4]

- So 'research' carried out by Feminists is designed to advance the Feminist Ideology and agenda

Again,

- *'The professionalisation of feminist politics, whereby a business network of trained gender experts has largely replaced social movement activism, means that the nature of the dialogue has become increasingly bound by the conventions of rationalist epistemologies and the predetermined strategic goals.'*[5]

- So 'gender experts' who carry out 'research' must 'predetermine strategic goals' that will advance 'feminist policies'. These 'trained gender experts' (university-trained gender-warriors) have replaced women's activists as the main type of Feminist Ideologue. The Feminist 'researchers' have predominantly strategic goals

- In this sense, Feminist 'gender experts' have become modern Feminism's gender-weapons-of-choice

Again,

- The Feminist team, Stanley and Wise, discussing social science research, conclude:

  1. *'That research should be on, by, and for women*

  2. *Finally, feminist research should be "engaged" and therefore useful to the Women's Movement.'*[6]

Again,

- *'At the heart of feminist methodology is the idea that feminist research must be for women, that it should be improving the daily life and general lot of women.'*[7]

- Feminist 'researchers' set out to change the lives of women for the better – predetermining their conclusions. There are no equivalent 'male researchers' concocting 'research' to influence social policy to improve *men's* lives. Such politically incorrect 'research' would never be permitted in our universities, and would certainly not attract funding

Again,

- *'...the goal of feminist research should be social change.'*[8]

- One aim of Feminist 'research' is to progress the Quiet Revolution

Again,

- *'Research should contribute to women's liberation through producing knowledge that can be used by women themselves; should use methods of gaining knowledge that are not aggressive; should continually develop feminist critical perspectives that question dominant intellectual traditions and can reflect on its own development.'[9]*

• Note the use of the word 'continually' and its significance for 'Forever' Feminism (and its significance for progressing Feminism's Quiet Revolution)

Feminist 'research' has *no* ethical basis and therefore, when used as propaganda, has no relation to 'truth'; Feminist 'research' is not simply disingenuous, it is downright dishonest. It should not, therefore, be used by governments to inform pro-Feminist/anti-men social policy. But it consistently *is*.

***

Admittedly, all researchers, including those who undertake genuine 'positive' research, will have their own personal biases on the subject they are studying. No researcher can be 100 per cent objective and neutral. However, there is a world of difference between, on the one hand, a researcher having a personal bias, being aware of this bias and consciously, and conscientiously, attempting to keep the principles of neutrality and objectivity in the forefront of his or her mind in order to negate this bias; and on the other hand, a 'researcher' *who specifically sets out to shape her 'research' with the deliberate intention of using it for sexual political propaganda purposes, to promote her Ideology and agenda.*

• By no stretch of the imagination can the latter type of 'researcher' be regarded as authoritative or honest. Yet in Feminist Britain it is *their* 'research' that informs governments' social policy

'No one cares what the real numbers are, they just want to make political statements.'[10]

• And we have seen examples of this intentional dishonesty with the Feminist issues of the pay gap, the 'glass ceiling', trafficked women, sexual harassment, domestic violence and rape

'Harriet Harman, the Minister for Women, was given an official warning last night for exaggerating the pay gap between men and women.'

It needs to be noted that some Feminist 'research' is undertaken by Male Feminists: this gives its 'findings' an extra dimension of authenticity and credibility. But the methodology, aims, Ideological direction...and dishonesty, are the same. Whichever sex undertakes it, Feminist 'research' is ethically bankrupt. Essentially then, Feminist 'research' is a further Feminist Fraud, it is simply propaganda.

Chapter 48

The Media and Feminist 'Research'

No issue can make it into the limelight as a major social problem without the attention of the media; and there are topics to which the media are particularly attracted:

'Television and print journalism, which for as long as anyone can remember have devoted rapt attention to tales of power, sex, fear and money, seek legitimacy by shoring up their reports with the work of scholars and specialists.'[1]

- 'Television and print journalism...seek legitimacy by shoring up their reports with the work of scholars and specialists'. The 'research' on gender issues that they are provided with in media releases comes from Academic Feminists (scholars) and Feminist 'gender experts' (specialists) which gives our (complicit or gullible) media the 'legitimacy' is seeks.

- 'Sex, fear, power and money'? Little wonder that the media and Feminism embrace each other so enthusiastically. So we have *regular* media coverage of Feminist issues - domestic violence, rape, sex discrimination, sexual harassment, the pay gap, the 'glass ceiling'...and to ensure maximum effect no two 'issues' are be covered simultaneously.

- With the advent of Feminism the media struck gold - an endless ('Forever') seam of 'sex, fear, power and money' stories, news items, articles and documentaries – Feminism and the media feeding off each other, a sexual political incestuous symbiosis

The print media needs to create 'celebrities' from nothing in order to create public interest in these 'celebrities' - Jordan / Peter Andre / 'Posh' Beckham / Colleen Rooney - so that it will always have some story about them to constantly fill its pages; ready-to-hand copy fillers. Feminism is used for the same media function as these media-created 'celebrities'. And so, in addition to the media's complicity with Feminism, we have regular misandrous/pro-Feminist news items and articles. An incestuous relationship, profitable to both parties.

***

An additional factor that aids Feminism in getting its Ideology and agenda regularly promoted in the media is that the 'findings' of 'action research' lend themselves to an *easy presentation* for public consumption. They are black and white issues, 'good women'/ 'bad men'. Feminist 'research' issues make excellent media-friendly *human interest* stories (especially when reported by an *already* Feminist-sympathetic media) – 'battered wives', 'more men getting away with rape' 'scandal of the pay gap', 'sexual harassment on the increase', 'more mothers discriminated against at work than ever before...'. The media devour these 'shock/horror'/'victimisation of women' stories, appetisingly handed to it on an attractive media-release platter, ready for immediate and unquestioning public and political consumption – handed to it by a calculating Feminism, itself voraciously hungry for regular media coverage of, and publicity for, its 'issues'.

- Since the 1980s there has been an endless supply of 'shock/horror' Feminist grievances

- The easy presentation of Feminist 'action research' allows the media to present Feminism to the public in a simplistic, childlike way ('1 in 4', or '18% less pay', or 'only 10% of women in top jobs', 'It'll take 56 years for women to achieve equality') – a tactic of Simple Simon sound-bites to convert the masses and the naive decision-makers who are ignorant of Feminism's machinations and true aims and agenda

- Feminist issues presented in the media are 'Feminism-For-Ten-Year-Olds' and have entered our conventional wisdom as 'truths'. And we have all been duped by this fraud

***

The media has little stomach to intellectually and rigorously question and challenge the 'research'-based Feminist issues it reports (even if it wished to):

'When it comes to gender issues, journalists generally have suspended all their usual scepticism...We accept at face value whatever women's groups say. Why? Because women have sold themselves to us as an oppressed group and any oppressed group gets a free ride in the press. I don't blame feminists for telling us half-truths, and sometimes even complete fabrications. I do blame my colleagues in the press for forgetting their scepticism.'[2]

- Media people do not 'forget their scepticism', they are mostly Feminist-sympathetic themselves (most having been university educated since the 1970s), very few have the inclination to analyse or critique press-releases from 'their own kind'. With regard to Feminism (and the Left in general) investigative journalism is dead in today's Britain

- The public, and the decision-makers, are informed by the media's presentation of Feminist 'research' on all issues appertaining to sexual politics, 'research' produced by Feminist 'gender expert' Ideologues. No other gender perspective is available and none is sought by credulous (or complicit) media professionals and male politicians

***

Essentially, then, there is a great deal of intentional disregard for the truth in Feminist 'research'. Most of it is so blatant that it certainly deserves to be called lying. Many men, logging in to their traditional male chivalry mentality, will be uncomfortable with the use of the word 'lying' when associated with women. It is the same reason why Feminists enjoy 'protection' from male political interviewers, by whom they will not be *too* aggressively challenged (and female interviewers are not going to challenge 'their own'). Feminists, and Feminist 'research', have an easy ride with the British media.

What is worrying is that so much serious misrepresentation passes into the realm of 'truth'. One might think that misrepresentations about checkable facts could not survive for very long in an open, democratic society with a supposedly free media, but they can and do, mainly because those who would traditionally question and challenge the media and the academy are now so *pro-Feminist themselves*: the Feminist mindset has enveloped everyone. For example, when a 'sensational' report about the amount of domestic violence or rape appears, newspapers, magazines, television, the radio, even textbooks, relay the news, and it quickly becomes established folklore. The attitudes formed as a result are embedded into the culture, into our conventional wisdom. Yet the facts, for those who care about them, indicate that these reports are wild exaggerations or just (intentional) lies.

- Lies upon which social policies are based

Neither must it be forgotten that the media has its *own* 'researchers'. For example, it is now generally accepted that the BBC is a Left-wing/liberal/progressive organisation so any 'research' that its own 'researchers' undertake (to present a documentary on a gender issue, for example) will be biased in order to 'prove' whatever 'facts' the BBC wishes the public to accept (sympathy for Feminism, in this context) – opinion forming at its most devious.

Other broadcasters are almost as bad. Examples of gender-issue documentaries abound, and are sickening in their pro-Feminist bias. Two that particularly stick in my mind (and in my craw) were fronted by Trevor McDonald at the height of the Fathers 4 Justice campaign in 2005/6. He presented two programmes based upon the information provided by an undercover 'researcher'. In the documentaries fathers who were being denied access to their children were lambasted, ridiculed and demonised. McDonald even used the words: 'Some of them (the F4J activists) even deny feminism!' – speaking about them as if they were as wicked as holocaust deniers. There was no subsequent, balancing programme showing how these fathers and paternal grandparents were heartbroken about not being allowed to see their children or grandchildren for years on end – a much more human interest story, but a *male* issue...so no documentary.

McDonald has also presented documentaries on domestic violence, again *very* biased against men and promoting the myth that 1 in 4 women experience domestic violence. Either he is naive about sexual politics and is shamefully having his strings pulled by Feminist 'researchers', or he is fully aware of what he is doing and complicit in his programmes' man-hating.

There has never been a radio or television programme, as far as I am aware, that has questioned and challenged the righteousness or truth of Feminist 'research'. Please correct me if I'm mistaken.

> *'Today, if a Feminist wishes to get a story circulating in the media, all she needs to do is get some numbers together, call it "research" and put out a media-brief'*
>
> (Swayne O'Pie)
>
> *'Facts are often irrelevant to an ideology'*[3]

Chapter 49

Universities, Social Policy and Feminist 'Research'

'No one cares what the real numbers are. They just want to make political statements'[1]

Feminist 'researchers' have relentlessly used the vox-pop attraction of 'action research' to manipulate not only public opinion but also government policy, manoeuvring decision-makers into having sympathy with, and then accepting, items on the Feminist agenda; for example, domestic violence, the family, equal pay, health, rape, the 'glass-ceiling', sex discrimination, crime and education.

To recap: Feminist 'research' has accurately been called 'advocacy research' because it is used to advocate a course of action, that is, to influence policy-makers to implement its agenda. It is 'research' undertaken to 'prove' conclusions to which its 'researchers' are already politically and Ideologically committed, and then to use that 'research' to demand social change to achieve their aims, and to progress their Quiet Revolution. It has been shown that Feminists themselves admit this.

As the reader will now be aware British universities are Feminist colonies, some more than others. Not only are Women's Studies courses, modules and related subjects used to promote Feminism's Ideology and agenda (and used to produce waves of student Left-wing/Feminist gender-warriors) but they are also manufacturers of Ideological 'research'. Being 'university-produced' gives Feminist 'research' credibility and legitimacy. After all, if a study is carried out by a 'university' then its findings *have* to be true, right? Wrong.

- Nor need the reader be awed by, or give credence to, Feminist 'research' that is produced by academics with the titles of 'Doctor' or 'Professor'; bias is bias...dishonesty is dishonesty

***

A Male Feminist writes:

'In the academic world the 1970s and 1980s saw a huge growth of feminist or feminist-inspired research in almost every discipline of the humanities and social sciences...In sociology, for instance, sex and gender – formerly a marginal field of low prestige – became the most active field of research in the whole discipline.'[2]

- A 'huge growth of feminist research in the humanities, social science and sociology'? We have seen just how dominated these particular areas of study are by Academic Feminists. So no neutral, objective, ethical 'research' is ever likely to be found in this 'growth' area of subjects (to call them 'disciplines' would be a misnomer)

- It is no coincidence that these are the *very areas of study* (together with Policy Studies) that specialise in addressing social policy

***

Numerous universities are employed/funded by governments to produce 'research' on gender issues and social policy. With such large amounts of funding available it is hardly likely that a university will produce research that does not create the 'findings' that a Feminist-sympathetic government requires. A university is not going to bite the hand that feeds it. As Mervyn Stone, Professor of Statistics at University College London, has pointed out:

'To stay in business, universities have to compete for lucrative government contracts. Loyalty to their institution can tempt academics to remain knowingly silent on contestable issues they could help to resolve...This book will add its evidence-based support to the voice of many others that this is a recipe for poor government.'[3]

• In other words, 'research' is produced that keeps the sponsors happy...and if the sponsor is a Feminist-dominated Labour/Conservative/Lib Dem Feminist-sympathetic Government...?

Hitchcock and Hughes drew attention to this unethical practice:

'Responsibilities relate to the individual researcher, the participants in the research, professional colleagues...and towards the sponsors of the research'.[4]

Research is not only a rich source of funding for universities. 'Research' funding is also an important source of income for *individual Feminists and Feminism:*

'As feminist academics moved up the promotion ladder, research funds flowed and Women's Studies programmes consolidated, a new social base for feminist thought had been established.'[5]

• A 'new social base for feminist thought' from which Feminist-friendly 'research' is manufactured, to *create* Feminist-friendly social policy, or to justify *existing* Feminist-friendly social policy. Also, a 'new social base' from which to generate 'Forever' Feminism. And, of course, to construct any new Grievance Gravy-Train Industry

***

All Feminist 'research' is predicated on the Ideology that modern Britain is a patriarchal society, where only women are victims and men the victimisers.

'Feminist research...presupposes that women are victims of men.'[6]

• This is an important point and this misandry should always be looked for when reading the 'findings' of Feminist 'research'

For example, London Metropolitan University produces Feminist-friendly 'research' on a fairly regular basis, especially on issues of violence against women (not men, only women). This university has been given government funding to set up a special misandrous department – the Violence Against Women and Children Unit (there are numerous other universities with similarly named Units, Departments, Centres).

• The word 'children' is always included in a Feminist issue/title, wherever possible, in order to maximise public and political sympathy and thereby facilitate government funding (as in the old maxim 'women and children first', a modern-day manipulation of male chivalry)

- We have seen that by far the greatest amount of 'violence against the person' crime in Britain is against *men* ('public space violence') – yet there are no Units/Departments/Centres in *any* British university that are specifically concerned about, and entitled 'Violence Against *Men* and Children Unit'

- The British Establishment has been duped by the Feminist lie that Britain is a patriarchy – a society in which only *women* can be victims...(duped? No, not really...they are *part of* this confidence trick, this political and Ideological Feminist Fraud)

***

Feminist 'research' not only informs government policy but is used to create new, or to revamp old, 'discriminations and oppressions' from which it 'proves' that women suffer inequalities. One Academic Feminist lecturing in the Policy and Politics Department of a leading university admits this:

> 'The more positive reading of the feminist turn to "expertise" is that the emergence of evidence-based policy-making offers social activists in NGOs (non-governmental organisations) new opportunities for making new knowledge claims and for having these claims accepted, given that evidence-based policy-making unsettles the monopoly on policy knowledge previously claimed by the traditional public servant.'[7]

Allow me to interpret this Feminist-speak: the increase in the number of Feminist 'experts' creating 'research' ('evidence-based') offers new opportunities for making 'new knowledge claims' (a euphemism for new Feminist claims, new grievances, new demands, new inequalities found, new discriminations and new issues) and having these accepted and introduced into 'policy-making' because the evidence-based 'research' was produced by 'experts' (university trained gender-warriors) which 'unsettles' (that is, bullies) civil servants.

- This is an admission by a leading Academic Feminist (in policy-making sinecure) that Feminist 'research' is intended to promote Feminist aims and policies. The quote neatly encapsulates the process

The deviousness of Feminist politics is astonishing. Little wonder Feminism has been so successful with its Quiet Revolution.

Universities, Feminist 'Research' and Domestic Violence

Domestic violence is an area of social policy that is dominated by Feminism and is informed *solely* by Feminist 'research'.

> 'Great swathes of the academy (higher education) are no longer interested at all. For a variety of separate but sometimes related reasons, including the development of the grievance or victim culture, the rise of interest groups with money to spend promoting that culture, the dependence of academics on such groups for funding...academia has become a prime site for propaganda...Some of this finds its way into government policy – much "research" upon which the British government bases its policy on domestic violence, for example, offers a disgracefully distorted picture based on the vilification of men, startlingly at odds with the overwhelming amount of truly authoritative research which shares responsibility for such violence equally between the sexes.'[8]

- '...no longer interested at all'; putting this in context this means 'no longer interested in the truth, or in intellectual integrity, or in objectivity and neutrality...no longer interested in *genuine* research'

- 'An overwhelming amount of truly authoritative research which shares responsibility for such violence equally between the sexes' has been consistently ignored because this research does not 'fit' the patriarchal model of Britain that Feminism has imposed on the public and the Establishment's consciousness – that is, 'good women' / 'bad men'

The following is a boast from the Women's Studies department of Leeds Metropolitan University, showing how its Ideology influences government policy:

'The Violence, Abuse and Gender Relations research unit is headed by Professor Jalna Hanmer and has a national reputation for its work on domestic violence and related issues. It is currently acting as consultant to the West Yorkshire Police on the subject of crime and domestic violence.'[9]

It is doubtful whether Jalna Hanmer will introduce the West Yorkshire Police to the following:

'The idea that women are as violent as men is counter-intuitive and simply disbelieved. Most people, however, are quite unaware of the huge number of studies which have reached this conclusion.'[10]

It is odds-on that the police will remain deliberately 'unaware' of the male perspective on domestic violence and will continue to be fed the Feminist, anti-male perspective. And so the Yorkshire police (as with other police forces), having been indoctrinated with the Feminist perspective on domestic violence, will adopt a misandrous policy on domestic violence and will go on to 'blame men' and absolve women in their day-to-day interaction with the issue.

'The characterisation of men as a pariah sex has had a malevolent impact on public policy in both the US and in Britain. Research into violence has been systematically distorted to produce the false impression that violence against the opposite sex is a male phenomenon alone, and that its incidence is far higher than it actually is.'[11]

And so relentless 'research' manufactured by the Domestic Violence Industry in its university Ideological Units 'produces' policy on domestic violence that reflects only the Feminist Ideologue's *own* perspective; and this bias is then translated into social policy.

Universities, Feminist 'Research', and Creating 'Crises'

It was shown in an earlier chapter that Feminism *deliberately* creates fear and panic in women. Manufacturing 'crisis/epidemic research' is instrumental to this strategy:

'Fekete indicts the growing industry of dubious research that is intended to promote panic and rage among women, one result being to manipulate the political process. Politicians should be influenced by public opinion, yes, but what if public opinion is based on ignorance? Not many politicians have the moral integrity or even the intellectual curiosity to question statistics gathered by academics.'[12]

- Notice the phrase 'the *growing industry* of dubious research'. Manufacturing Ideologically useful 'research' has become *one more* Feminist Industry

- Note the Feminist strategy of deliberately creating fear, panic and rage in women; strategies that we have already met... crafted and designed to advance Feminism's aims, and to stir up anger, rage and hatred towards men. Are you joining up the dots? Are you seeing the pattern, the well-orchestrated progression of Feminism's Quiet Revolution, including the spread of misandry?

And,

'My own observations of students in women's studies classes have led me to believe that years of exposure to feminist-promoted scare statistics have succeeded in imbuing many young women with a foreboding sense of living under constant threat from predatory men. The offer of an escape from this threat is a strong inducement to conformity to feminist blandishments.'[13]

And,

'...phoney statistics continue to do their job, still cited repeatedly and still embedded in public consciousness, no matter how hard anyone tries to challenge them. When repeated like mantras, they create their own reality.'[14]

- And so we have all been conned into believing that a quarter of *all* wives are regularly being beaten up and battered by their husbands. And that 1 in 4 (or 1 in 2, or whatever figure Feminists happen to be bandying about at any particular moment) have 'suffered' rape or attempted rape

Feminist 'research' is manufactured primarily to influence social policy, but it also has a number of secondary aims – to create fear and panic in women, to make women fearful of marriage and of men, to demonise men, to bring more women into the 'protective' Feminist fold (a recruiting strategy)...To progress its Quiet Revolution.

In-House Feminist 'Research'

As with the media, political parties, trade unions and some professions and organisations have their *own* Feminist 'research' teams. Any in-house 'research' will obviously be given to a 'gender expert' to undertake – and as we know, 'gender experts' or 'femocrats', will have been trained up into the Feminist Ideology during their university education – all 'gender experts' are Feminist-friendly simply because universities *do not offer* any other perspective. So even in-house 'research' on gender issues will be Feminist 'research'. As two ardent Feminists admit (one a lecturer, the other a policy adviser):

'The influence of the women's liberation movement is easy to trace. Feminists have taken jobs in unions' expanding research departments, and have played a part, as lay activists, in the development of policy.'[15]

- In-house Feminist-produced 'research' will naturally go unquestioned in the Labour/ Feminist Party and trade unions, but those Conservative MPs with integrity really *do* need to question the provenance of the 'research' that is informing *their* Party leadership's stance on sexual politics and social policy

The Civil Service also has in-house 'researchers':

'The Department of Health and Social Security, as well as the Home Office, appear to have been particularly impressionable, perhaps because of the close working relationships these ministries have developed with the many welfare-interest lobby groups and social science academics on whose expertise they rely. Ministers at the Department for Social Security during Mrs. Thatcher's administration, for example, gradually came to believe they were being fed misleading statistics by a feminist clique among their civil servants which skewed the agenda in favour of single parents.'[16]

- Here we see a 'Feminist clique, ('research' team) deliberately feeding misleading statistics' to promote an item on the Feminist agenda – encouraging single-parent motherhood. Feminists have infiltrated *every* area of the British Establishment

- A 'close working relationship with...interest groups'? We have seen the power of Feminist Interest Groups to influence policy...and their power to bully civil servants

- A 'close working relationship with...social science academics'? It has been shown that social science academics are overwhelmingly Feminists (female or Male)

- 'On whose expertise' do they rely? We know that gender issue 'experts' are trained by Feminists on Women's Studies and associated courses and modules

Feminist 'research' is mainly manufactured in higher education, but it will also be produced in-house in other areas of the State; and *always* with the same single-minded purpose – to promote the Feminist Ideology and its agenda.

Cheating and Lying by Omission

'Facts do not cease to exist because they are ignored'

(Aldous Huxley)

Cheating and lying is done not only with words and statistics, but also with *silence* and *omission*. For example:

'In fact, there is a huge amount of well-conducted research demonstrating not only that men suffer equally from domestic violence but even more frequently than women. The facts simply don't sustain the claim that the vast majority of violence is perpetrated by men upon women. Yet in virtually all the official literature, this great and growing body of evidence is simply never mentioned.'[17]

Genuine research, gender-neutral research, on domestic violence is ignored because it doesn't 'fit' the Feminist Ideology, it goes against the grain of the conventional wisdom, it does not gel with the insistence that Britain is a patriarchy in which only women are allowed to be 'victims' and only men are the 'victimisers' – a society of 'good women' and 'bad men'. So when 'research' doesn't fit with the dominant Ideology it has to be doctored, censored or omitted (often by being declared as politically incorrect). This is dishonest, and is a form of cheating and lying.

The issue of equal pay is a further example of Feminist 'research' cheating and lying by omission. Statistics tell us that men earn more than women (true) but they do *not* tell us that men work longer hours than women, work more overtime, undertake more shift work,

work more unsocial hours and work in more unhealthy and dangerous conditions than women – all adding *extra* to their hourly pay. This relevant information is omitted whenever the statistics on the gender pay gap are referred to. The 'pay gap' needs to be made to look shocking and unfair, needs to be made to look like a discrimination against women (by the patriarchy, of course), needs to be presented as a 'gender inequality' (and as we have seen, Harriet Harman, Feminist Minister for Women, was officially reprimanded for using this dishonest strategy).

- Censorship, and the withholding of unpalatable facts, are effective gender-weapons used by Feminist 'research'

Another omission of facts intended to advantage the Feminist agenda is the issue of housewives' leisure time. We know that a Feminist aim is to get all women out of the house and into full-time paid employment (to be independent of men). We also know that the Feminist abhors stay-at-home mothers. This was observed by Melanie Phillips in the sociological data of the government's annual statistical bible, 'Social Trends'. She noted how, in 1993, it was shown that *housewives* enjoyed more leisure time than working men or women. This was a politically incorrect (non-Feminist) finding so over the next few years this fact was gradually censored out by 'Social Trends'. Eventually, this pro-traditional family statistic disappeared altogether:

'The disappearance of this information on housewives and the change in the tone of the commentary suggest that facts inconvenient to feminist analysis are being suppressed within Whitehall, where gender feminism has crept into mainstream thinking without many people noticing it.'[18]

***

The dishonesty, distortions, sophistry, misrepresentations, suppressions and omissions of Feminist 'research' are legitimised in a culture that is chronically riddled with a politically correct culture. Anthony Browne points out that the Left-wing Economic and Social Research Council supports only research projects that are politically correct (which includes Feminism),[19] creating an academic body of work that reinforces the politically correct conventional wisdom. For example, women earning 18% less than men is seen in a politically correct culture as sex discrimination and a 'gender inequality'. Browne makes some interesting points:

'Even when men were overwhelmingly underachieving compared with women at all levels of the education system, and were twice as likely to be unemployed, three times as likely to commit suicide, three times as likely to be victims of violent crime, four times as likely to be a drug addict, three times as likely to be alcoholic and nine times as likely to be homeless, the Economic And Social Research Council was still almost exclusively funding work that looked at the problems faced by women.

Although men surpass women at almost every measure of social failure, admitting that men also have serious problems simply doesn't fit the politically correct paradigm, and all such research was avoided until it became impossible to deny the "crises of masculinity" any longer. University research departments that are meant to extend human understanding end up merely buttressing pre-held beliefs.'[20]

- Men's problems, issues and rights do not *fit* Feminism's Ideology, its patriarchal model of 'good women' / 'bad men'; only women are permitted to be seen as 'victims'. So modern Britain hates men

***

In conclusion, higher education has created a ghetto in which Feminism is allowed, and encouraged, to manufacture its own 'research'. This 'research' is disseminated into, and acted upon, in every area of national and local policy-making – politics, local government, trade unions, the civil service, education, health, the law, the media.

Tens of millions of pounds are spent by governments implementing policies that are based upon nothing more than a malign Ideology, upon fraudulent Feminist 'research' that is ethically and intellectually bankrupt but is nevertheless naively and uncritically accepted.

Melanie Phillips, the social commentator, notes:

> 'A well-funded network transformed university courses into propaganda...with a large number of feminist academics whose work wasn't worth the paper it was written on.'[21]

And,

> 'If one reads social science research, for example, one has to pick one's way through a minefield of error and distortion in piece after piece of special pleading masquerading as objective research.'[22]

Chapter 50

Examples of Feminism's Dishonest 'Research'

This chapter will very briefly look again at a number of issues – but in the context of Feminism's dishonest 'research'.

Many Feminist surveys have one common characteristic – they draw their conclusions by interviewing *only* women. It's hardly surprising, then, using this highly selective 'research', that *only* women appear as 'victims'. Yet the results of these 'studies' are widely circulated and repeated so often that they become urban myths (sexual harassment, domestic violence, rape, women do more work than men...). More disturbingly these studies underpin social policies, with the policies being implemented at huge public expense...policies build upon nothing more than Feminist Frauds.

The Pay Gap

It has been shown that the 'research' showing that there is a pay gap between men and women is riddled with methodological flaws; for example, Feminists never compare like with like, ignoring the differences in seniority, in work experience, in content and amount of responsibility in the 'same' profession. Women choosing to avoid working unsocial and long hours and avoiding unhealthy and dangerous jobs is never mentioned in Feminist 'equal pay research'. This is 'research' dishonesty by omission. Shackleton gives an example from America:

> *'An interesting example concerns "anchors" on US television news programmes. One study found that on average male newscasters were paid 38 per cent more than females – a huge gender pay gap. But disaggregation showed that within each age group women were paid more than men. What was happening was that a large majority of young people (reflecting the gender composition of Communications and Media college courses) entering the job were women. These young women, on lower salaries, pulled down women's average pay relative to that of older men.'*[1]

Sexual Harassment

In addition to fiddling the criteria in order to create a large incidence of sexual harassment, Feminism uses other 'research' devices to increase the number of 'victims'.

> *'But advocacy research is an inherently problematic endeavour. In an insightful paper analyzing studies of sexual harassment (the sort of piece that seems not to find its way into the official sexual harassment literature), Harsh K. Luthar, who examines human relations in the workplace, has written about the biases distorting research on sexual harassment. Such research is overwhelmingly undertaken by women, and studies have shown that in this area of scholarship the sex of the researcher closely correlates with the research results. This circumstance, Luthar argues, has led to the suppression of many interesting issues related to sexual harassment.'*[2]

- Men have to be seen as 'bad people' so Feminist 'research' on sexual harassment has to be skewed to produce this particular result; any objective, gender-neutral, research that shows a *different* result is suppressed, is omitted

Rape

It has been comprehensively shown that Feminist rape statistics are deliberately fraudulent, producing 'rapes' on paper, rather than in fact.

One regularly media-presented 'research' statistic is the low percentage of convictions for rape compared to the number of recorded incidents. This has already been addressed, but here I shall report an inquiry that shows the Feminist claim that 'only 6 per cent of reported rapes end in a conviction' is Ideological and deliberate chicanery.

On Sunday, 30 August, 2010, BBC4's 'More or Less' programme, produced by Richard Knight, ran an item on the rape conviction rate. 'More or Less' is a programme devoted to the use and abuse of statistics. This particular programme (refreshingly gender-neutral for the BBC) looked at the claim of London Metropolitan University (a particularly virulently Feminist university) that: 'Britain's conviction rate for rape of only 6.5% was the worst in Europe'.

The programme asked what was meant by 'the conviction rate' and noted that The Guardian had printed an article that said that only 6.5 per cent of cases that *go to court* end with a conviction. It was pointed out that this was wrong: the 'conviction rate' of 6.5 per cent refers to the rate between reported rapes and the number of rapes resulting in a conviction – *not the number of men accused of rape who are actually tried in court*. It was noted that The Guardian was made to publish a correction.

- 'More or Less' pointed out that for men standing trial for rape the actual conviction rate was 47 per cent (this percentage was also found by others, noted in an earlier chapter)

The programme noted that rape is the *only* crime that is reported to the police that is *officially* measured in this way; that is - the number of incidents reported to the police and then converted into a 'conviction' rate. The programme did not point out that this singular measurement has been *deliberately* introduced by Feminism and is a 'research' device intended to produce a reaction of 'shock-horror' with the public and politicians, thereby facilitating the introduction of police and courtroom procedures that would result in more men being convicted of rape, innocent or guilty.

We have also seen how the Labour/Feminist Governments have set *targets* for the percentage of men who it intended to find 'guilty' of rape, a predetermined number to be convicted – if you cannot find enough men guilty of rape then you have to bung in some innocent guys to make the numbers up, to reach the Ideologically predetermined 'guilty' target. Astonishing. Astonishing that men in Britain meekly accept the fascistic Feminist persecution of their sex – of themselves. Could there be an element of individual and group masochism operating here...a deep-down psychological 'need' to *believe* that Sister Whiplash is right in her anti-male cant and dogma? But if we have capitulated so easily what of our sons and grandsons, do we not have a responsibility to *them,* to cast aside our fear and to face up to Feminism, to 'come out' as wholesome men, men with self-respect?

- The reason why Feminism insists that rape convictions are reported in this way (the attrition rate) is because the conviction rate looks incredibly low, which serves Feminism's purposes; it makes it easy for a sympathetic media to present rape as a misandrous and patriarchal issue ('many men getting away with rape').

The programme compared the *attrition* rate (not normally worked out and compared) with *other* crimes:

> **Attempted murder - 14%**
>
> **Robbery - 10%**
>
> **Cruelty to Children - 9%**
>
> **Burglary - 4%**
>
> **Violence Against the Person - 4%**
>
> **Criminal Damage - 1%**

So 6.5% for rape is about average. As far as the clear-up rate goes, rape statistics are no big shakes...and yet the media is constantly pushing the Feminist perspective (as are powerfully placed legal and political Feminists).

***

The 'More or Less' team also noted that the *actual* conviction rate for rape has *doubled* since 1985. In this respect the clear-up rate for rape is better than most other crimes.

Nick Barraclough, a barrister and rape prosecutor, stated that the number of reported rapes had increased dramatically between 1993 and 2009 because the definition of rape had widened...and also because there was a 'big push' to report rape as a crime. He said:

> *'More cases are reaching courts that would not have got to court ten to fifteen years ago...and it is difficult to prosecute when it is one person's word against another's.'*

The programme came back to the Feminist London Metropolitan University's claim that the British rape conviction rate was the worst in Europe; Professor Chris Lewis said that this was just not true, that the British conviction rate was:

> *'No worse than anywhere else', and (tellingly) that 'this was not good research...that there was no evidence anywhere to show that the English rates are worse...statistics don't prove this...different countries have different procedures and different patterns...countries are culturally and legally different so the issue is fraught with problems.'*

- This would suggest that the Feminist 'researchers' in the London Metropolitan University are more interested in their *Ideological agenda* than they are in producing an honest presentation of rape

Professor Lewis concluded:

'There is a danger that important contexts are left out by those who wish to move the issue up the political agenda.'

- This says it all. He refrained from saying the word 'Feminists' but it was pretty clear that they were the ones to whom he was referring

Feminist 'research' cheats and lies, and is deliberately dishonest in order to manufacture Ideological issues. One can imagine the producer of 'More or Less' (Richard Knight) and its presenters receiving a serious knuckle-rapping from senior BBC Feminist managers (Male as well as female) for daring to unwrap the 'conviction rate for rape' issue and exposing this Feminist fraud, this 'research' dishonesty.

Education

Since the 1990s there have been innumerable reports and studies showing that boys are educationally underachieving. Boys are less articulate than girls, less literate, gain fewer GCSEs, gain fewer 'A' levels, fewer young men than women enter university and women receive better degree results. On every measure boys are failing educationally, compared with girls.

Feminism seriously dislikes and resents boys' educational failure because it draws attention away from girls' supposed 'discriminations' and 'victimhood'. There is an Ideological difficulty for Feminism inherent in boys failing: a patriarchal society is a society in which, by definition, only girls and women can be 'victims' and 'disadvantaged'. So if boys are seen to be failing then the Ideologues are faced with a contradiction to their patriarchal template of British society and the State; a problem that could, if not handled carefully, derail 'Forever' Feminism's numerous educational and Academic Gravy-Train Industries. Something had to be done.

Feminism created a number of solutions to this problem, one of which was to sponsor Feminist Interest Groups and universities to produce research showing that 'girls are still victims'.

The Fawcett Society is the foremost Feminist non-governmental organisation in Britain. The following is from its December 2000 magazine titled 'Where Are The Women In Education?'. It focused on the small percentage of head teachers who are women (when the overwhelming majority of teachers are women) thereby deflecting attention from boys' failure and reclaiming the 'victim' initiative. This issue has been dealt with in a previous chapter. This magazine also focused on girls' choices of subjects (arts and humanities) which was used to neutralise boys' educational failure. The Fawcett Society complained:

'In recent years there has been much hype around the academic success achieved by girls and even that the pendulum of equality has now "swung too far". However, these figures hide the fact that while some girls are achieving high results in the subjects that they choose to study others are doing less well. Girls are still over-represented as students of traditional "female" subjects.'

The Equal Opportunity Commission was also a Feminist organisation. It warned against our being too complacent about the academic success of girls, and being 'lulled into a false sense of complacency by statistics' that show girls are outperforming boys.[3]

In 2007 the EOC was so disturbed about boys being thought of as disadvantaged that it commissioned an 'academic research report' from a Feminist-friendly university (tautological – as *all* universities are Feminist-friendly to a greater or lesser extent) in order to dismiss the idea that boys were educationally failing:

> *'But in a highly provocative assertion, the Equal Opportunities Commission suggests that "playing up the difference will exacerbate such differences". While it acknowledges that there is a gender gap in literacy, with boys underperforming in relations to girls, the 80-page document adds: "In other areas the gap is not significant and certainly the focus on boys' underachievement detracts from the consideration needed to be given to the larger gaps between groups defined by social class and race... The report, by academics at Roehampton University, blames gender stereotyping by parents and teachers for exaggerating the gender gap.'[4]*

- 'Playing up the difference will exacerbate such differences'. In other words, publicising the fact that boys are underachieving will only make things worse for boys. What this is actually saying is 'don't publicise boys' educational failure – this doesn't fit our Ideology, so we don't want it to be publicly and politically accepted as a problem'

- So here we see Feminist 'research' deflecting attention from boys' under-achievement to other 'far greater' educational considerations'; and in any case, boys' educational failure has, apparently, been exaggerated. Madeleine Arnot is an Academic Feminist:

UNIVERSITY GIRLS FALL BEHIND IN CONFIDENCE

(The Times, Monday, 5 January, 1998)

'The natural caution of girls is preventing them from reaching the pinnacle of academic success...despite increasingly impressive examination results at school, Cambridge University researchers believe.

Madeleine Arnot, a Cambridge education don who has analysed the first results of the research, says that confidence is at the root of the problem.

Dr. Arnot, who specialises in gender issues, said: "Work in the history faculty and the new data both suggest that girls' confidence is very fragile"...

The Cambridge research casts doubt on the growing assumption that boys, rather than girls, should be the focus of extra assistance, according to Dr. Arnot.'

- Only a Feminist could alchemise a success into a 'failure'

For Feminism, success is never enough; it can *never* be enough. The future of 'Forever' Feminism is at stake.

***

Feminism uses 'research' to cheat and lie, to produce whatever findings are required on any particular occasion. Feminist 'research' is needed to seek out or confirm inequalities, discriminations, oppressions in order to justify its existence and its Grievance Gravy-Train Industries and to continue to condemn, demonise and punish men. And to progress its Quiet Revolution. It is a Feminist Fraud.

Chapter 51

Housework:
Do Women Work Harder than Men?

The traditional division of labour has been a perennial inequality issue for Feminism. Feminists regularly produce 'research' showing that men don't do their fair share of housework, and that overall, women work harder than men:

WORKING WOMEN STILL END UP
WITH THE HOUSEWORK

(Daily Mail, Wednesday, 21 January 2004: by Robin Yapp)

'Women still have to do the lion's share of the housework despite going out to work in ever increasing numbers.

Researchers found that they spent three times as long on domestic chores such as cooking, cleaning and washing, as their husbands or partners...

"Gender inequalities in all areas are rooted in social structures but also in attitudes," said Professor Gillian Robinson, of the University of Ulster.'

- *'DID YOU SAY CHORES, DEAR? They might cook and on occasions they have been know to change a lightbulb....But ask men to do the cleaning and the majority appear to go deaf...Research shows that an astonishing 59 per cent pretend not to hear when their wives or girlfriends ask them to pick up a duster.' (2009)*[1]

- *'IT'S OFFICIAL: A CAREER WOMAN'S WORK IS NEVER DONE: Housework and child care are condemning millions of career women to much longer working days than men, a major report claims today...Women who go out to work still do the bulk of household chores, according to the study by Cambridge University of more than 30,000 people.' (2007)*[2]

- *'EU: MEN MUST DO HOUSEWORK: Men must do more to pull their weight around the house, according to the latest dictum from Brussels. They should also take time off work to help with childcare, says a top Eurocrat...If men did their fair share of chores it could do much to narrow the pay gap between the sexes, said European Union employment commissioner Vladimir Spidla.' (2007)*[3]

And the Cambridge University Academic Feminist team, Madeleine Arnot, Miriam David and Gaby Weinar:

'Women's move out of the home has not been matched by men sharing domestic responsibilities.'[4]

This chapter dismisses this Feminist 'research'-generated inequality issue, showing it to be a fraud.

Availability of Time

Imagine three scenarios:

1. A wife stays at home full-time whilst her husband is in full-time paid employment. In fairness, the wife ought to do more housework as she spends more time in the home. For the same reason, if the husband were unemployed and his wife were in full-time employment then *he* ought to do more housework. There is no sex discrimination, only the difference in the availability of time.

2. A wife works part-time whilst the husband works full-time. Using the availability of time principle, in fairness, the wife ought to do more housework than her husband because she is at home for longer. If the husband worked part-time and his wife worked full-time then it ought to be *he* who does the lion's share. There is no sex discrimination here, only the difference in the availability of time.

- Approximately 80 per cent of part-time jobs are filled by women.[5] Logically, then, wives will do more housework than husbands. The failure of Feminist 'researchers' to consider the sex difference in 'availability of time' in part-time and full-time work is *deliberately* misleading, intended to create a 'gender inequality'

3. The husband and wife *both* work in paid employment full-time. The natural response to this scenario is that the housework ought to be shared equally.

   'A woman who works full-time does an average of twenty-three hours of domestic work a week; a man who works full-time does an average of eight hours of domestic work each week.'[6]

- We are deliberately being led to assume that the husband and wife work the same *number of full-time hours* outside the home. The truth is that Feminism is not comparing like-with-like (a common Feminist 'research' strategy and deceit)

On average, a man who works full-time will work 15 hours a week longer than a woman who works full-time.[7] Some put this even higher. Anne and Bill Moir suggest that men work 20 hours a week longer than women in paid, full-time, employment.[8] In addition, a man will commute for 1 hour longer each day to and from his place of work than will a woman.

'Men travel twice as far to work as women do.'[9]

Add these together and over a five-day-working-week a *full-time* employed husband will, on average, be away from home for at least 20 hours longer than his *full-time* working wife.

- This translates into a *full-time* working wife being in the home *4 hours per day longer* than her *full-time* working husband...so compared to her husband she is only working *part-time*

Logically then, using the 'availability of time' principle, the wife ought to do more housework than the husband. It is not equal but it is equitable. It is not unfair, and it is not a 'gender inequality'.

- Fair-minded, non-Ideological women understand why it is that they do more housework than their male partners

Men and women are generally fair with each other with regard to doing housework, despite what Feminists would have us believe:

'Where partners are equal breadwinners in terms of amounts earned domestic chores are likely to be shared equally.'[10]

Also,

SO IT'S TRUE. WOMEN DO WORK LONGER THAN THEIR MEN

(Daily Mail, Friday, 20 April, 2007)

'Women have long claimed that they work much harder than men, bearing the brunt of the household chores while holding down a full-time job.

Now research has proved them right – but only just.

Women apparently work a grand total of ten minutes more each day, when the hours of labour inside and outside the home are added up. The results, according to researchers, actually show that the overall workload is quite evenly shared between the sexes – though still along very traditional lines.

The time a woman spends working in the home roughly equates to the hours men do in the office, and vice-versa.

The survey, carried out by economists from America's National Bureau of Economic Research, looked at the working patterns of men and women aged 20-70 in 25 countries. One of the researchers, Phillippe Wiel from the Université Libre in Brussels, said the findings would shock many women – who generally assume they spend many more hours working.

"This has been an argument in the gender war, that women have this double burden hitting them", he said.

"But we do not find evidence in rich northern countries that this is the case".

Although the women surveyed felt they had less spare time than men, Mr. Wiel said that may be down to the fact that they sleep more.

He said: "The time spent not working is identical for men and women. But how this time is used differs".'

- We know that Feminism hates the traditional division of labour. We have seen how Feminists despise women who choose to be housewives and stay-at-home mothers

However, Feminism is dogged, if nothing else. It still needs to dig out more issues from housework in order to show that women are victims of men and that men dominate women for their own advantage. So a brand new issue is alchemised from housework:

'Anna Thorburn from Global Women's Strike, a body campaigning for greater recognition of the work done by women, said the research does not recognise factors such as "emotional housework".'[11]

- God forbid. What on earth is *'emotional* housework'? We must assume that it is yet one more concocted Feminist issue

***

In the Autumn of 2004 on one of the editions of the BBC's daily Woman's Hour the topic of housework was under discussion. One female contributor said that housework today is no big deal. Jenni Murray, the Feminist presenter, retorted: "Yes, but it is *still the woman* who has to fill the dishwasher." So, according to Jenni Murray, modern women suffer 'gender inequality' and are oppressed by their husbands in the patriarchal environment of the home, simply because it is *they* who have to fill the dishwasher (while the husband is working an extra 4 hours a day in paid employment). You see what I'm saying about Feminists creating inequalities and discriminations to justify their existence and to keep their Grievance Gravy-Train Industries in business?

- The grandmothers of these Sisters would laugh them out of the house

Piffling and inconsequential in themselves, we have seen that the regular seeking out and creation of everyday Scatter-Gun issues 'from nothing' has a repetitive and cumulative effect and as we know, is a serious political Feminist strategy.

What *is* 'Housework'?
Cherry-picking the Criteria

The selective choice of housework chores to be measured is a further Feminist 'research' deceit – cooking, cleaning and washing – all female-orientated tasks. Why did Professor Gillian Robinson (quoted above) not include male-orientated tasks such as heavy gardening, repairing fences, guttering, mending the car, DIY, ladder work, taking out dustbins and so on? The reason, of course, is that she wished to produce a Feminist conclusion - that 'Working women still wind up with the housework'.

- There is always a hidden bias in Feminist surveys. A wife's vacuuming is 'housework': a husband's cleaning out the guttering and drains is not

   'Men compensate for their lower rate of participation in cooking and housework by assuming the predominant responsibility for the tasks of maintenance, repairs and garage/yard work.'[12]

Studies that 'show' women have 'two' jobs, whilst their feckless and lazy husbands just slough off, are unacceptable. They are so misleading as to be a form of lying. In 1989 Arlie Hochschild's book 'The Second Shift' hit the headlines and still has a wide influence. It claimed that working wives were struggling to do two shifts – one in paid employment and the other at home. And so the myth grew that working wives were 'slaves' whilst their working husbands were 'sloths.' This myth is still peddled regularly in the media and, like the myth that 1 in 4 women are battered by their partner, has now become part of our conventional wisdom. However, Hochschild's study was Feminist 'research':

- She omitted to acknowledge that men who work full-time actually work many more hours than women who work 'full-time' (leaving less time in the home to help with housework – and also leaving less time to care for, and play with, and to enjoy, the children)

409

- She neglected to note that men commute, on average, one hour longer to their work, each day, than do women (leaving less time in the home to help with housework – and also leaving less time to care for, and play with, and to enjoy the children)

- She restricted her definition of housework to traditional 'women's work' - washing, cooking and child care. Men's typical household chores (as above) were *not* included in the definition. All Feminist 'research' on the subject does this, focuses only on what it expects to find (we have seen how and why Feminists cheat and lie with their unethical methodology)

- She cited weekday figures as if they applied to weekends. At weekends, of course, *both* partners are at home full-time to equally share the chores

- Hochschild also used data collected in 1965, nearly 25 years before her 'research' was written-up to 'prove' her case that women had two shifts and that men were shiftless. She did this even though much more recent data was available. Obviously, more recent data (interpreted honestly) would not produce a Feminist inequality issue

So even if wives do spend slightly more time on housework than their husbands (which is questionable, as we will see) they do less breadwinning (which is *not* questionable). But their smaller contribution to the family income does not lead to their being labelled 'breadwinner sloths'.

***

Hochschild's 'research' had two further methodological flaws. Like her British counterpart, Ann Oakley,[13] she used *only female* interviewers and interviewed *only wives*, not husbands.

- And we saw in Part Three how Everywoman dislikes men, to a greater or lesser extent, even her husband, so is predisposed to give a negative answer about him to a 'research' question...especially with a Feminist-inclined 'researcher' prompting. And politicians make pro-Feminist statements, and implement policy, on this spurious 'research'

And yet Hochschild's and Oakley's books have been the 'bibles' for Feminists with regard to the issue of housework. This fraud would be sad – or even laughable – if it weren't so misandrous and Ideological.

Do Women *Want* More Help with Housework?

Child care is almost always one of the criteria when Feminists 'research' housework. Yet mothers *do not want* fathers to be too involved in child care. Evidence of this was given in an earlier chapter, but to remind the reader:

> *'The truth of the matter is that women are themselves very reluctant to yield their primary role in the caring of children to men...They are generally resistant to men taking over their role as mothers, a fact that is not often mentioned by those who complain that men aren't doing their fair share.'*[14]

- If mothers do not wish their partners to do an equal amount of child care it would seem fatuous for Feminist 'researchers' to include it as a criteria of 'housework'. Unless, of course, their aim was to produce an Ideological inequality...?

- Women choose to be the primary carer; only a Feminist could construct a freely made choice and preference into an inequality

There is also a case for suggesting that women do not want too much male help with other household chores:

CHORE WARS

(Daily Mail, Thursday, 1 March, 2007: Carol Sarler)

'It is an irony that even while we insist that men relinquish their dominion over the marketplace to give us a fair crack of the career whip, we show little sign of relinquishing our dominion over the home...

Time and again we see a harried, weary woman struggle to the supermarket because if she "let" her husband go instead "he always comes back with the wrong things'. Wrong or different?

The bitching and barking continues with, it seems to me, the women wanting to have it both ways.

On the one hand they say they would like a reconstructed, modern man to shoulder half the load of household labour, on the other they cut him scant slack if he tries.

They don't want him to put the children to bed because he gets them overexcited. They don't want him to clean the bathroom because he always misses the bit around the loo pipe and germs might flourish. They don't want him to do the ironing, not since that business with the burnt lace ten years ago.

Oh, there's always a reason she needs to do it herself. A woman's work is never done, is it? Nail yourself to a cross, lady.

But I venture that in a great many cases, men who would be both able and willing are being put off by constant – sometimes even public – criticism, undermined by women who feel so threatened by a partner's well-meaning attempts to encroach on "their" territory that they scorn them into giving up altogether.'

So exactly how much do women genuinely *want* assistance with housework? Or is Feminism pretending to represent all women again? Many women positively *enjoy* housework:

THE WOMEN WHO THINK
HOUSEWORK IS BETTER THAN SEX

(The Times, Monday, 24 April, 2006)

'The average British woman spends more than 16 hours a week cleaning her home, a regime that "makes her feel in control of her life", according to a survey.

Of 2,000 women questioned, 6 out of 10 said that cleaning "made them feel in control of their life" and the same proportion found cleaning "mentally therapeutic".

Three quarters of the women surveyed kept up this regime of cleaning despite being in full- or part-time work.

64 per cent found happiness in the results of their labours. A third found more satisfaction in cleaning than in sex.

The National Housework Survey of Great Britain, 2006, was commissioned by the Discovery Home and Health channel.'

How does Feminism cope with the phenomenon of wives not disliking housework, and not wanting men to participate too much? Feminism falls back on its catch-all concept of 'socialisation'. It declares that women who enjoy housework have a 'mental disorder'. The Feminist Jessie Bernard:

> 'To be happy in a relationship which imposes so many impediments on her as traditional marriage does women must be slightly mentally ill.'[15]

***

I was a single-parent father for many years, raising three children. I've *done* housework. Lots of it. And believe me, it isn't difficult or too time consuming. It seems that women are *frightened* to let men do housework in case they discover just how easy it is, because if they did find this out then they themselves would want to stay at home, or work shorter hours: 'Best to keep the poor dears in the dark and pretend that it's really difficult and wearying and then they will be only too pleased to go out to work all day long, for years on end' (and then die 6 years earlier than women due to excessive stress).

And then I found confirmation of my observation:

A survey by the Office of National Statistics found that women do 'more work in the home' than do men (60 per cent women: 40 percent men); though men, it continued, compensate by doing more work in paid employment. Fine, we've covered that. But here's the rub – the ONS's criteria for 'work in the home' included shopping, driving the car and (wait for it) *entertaining friends!*[16]

- 'Work in the home'? Housework includes 'entertaining friends'? Feminism really *is* a successful confidence trick, creating inequalities 'from nothing'

***

The constant Feminist whining about men not carrying their share of the domestic burden is particularly galling when the statistics clearly demonstrate that men work harder, overall, than do women.[17] As we will now see.

Who Works Hardest, Men or Women?

Even the European Commission actively promotes the idea that women carry an unfair burden, juggling family and work. Catherine Hakim was a research sociologist at the London School of Economics. She noted the pro-Feminist bias 'research' in the European Commission:

> 'The European Commission's research institute in Dublin, the European Foundation for the improvement of Living and Working Conditions, is currently the main source of tendentious polemics on women's unfair burden and "gender inequality" (European Foundation, 2008). The Foundation's outputs are typically based on "national" studies that are almost invariably based on selective and unrepresentative samples. These advocacy research studies are subsequently quoted by others who present the results as if they were genuine social science research.'[18]

- The reader may not know that the European Union has a Women's Section that manipulates and strongly influences EU policy in favour of women. The European Union has no Men's Section

Feminists claim that overall, women put in more work hours than men. I wish to revisit two books that are regularly quoted to 'prove' this. Ann Oakley's 'Housewife' shows that mothers with no jobs but with young children aged under five unremittingly put in 18-hour days. In America, Arlie Hochschild's 'The Second Shift' considers the domestic work and child care done by women after they return home from their full-time day jobs, and calls this their 'second shift'.

- The 'research' deceit in these two, oft-quoted studies, is not only that they used female interviewers and interviewed only wives, and also cherry-picked housework chores; in addition, they focused only upon a *very small window in women's lives* – women with babies and young children still at home – this is only a *temporary phase* in a woman's life; it is not representative of women's lives overall. Here we see a further method of Feminism's cheating and lying with its 'research'. Feminist 'research' really is seriously dishonest. Never believe any 'findings' that it produces

***

Time Budget Studies is a research technique that looks at *all* aspects of work and activity, not simply paid employment. Time Budget Studies are based upon daily diaries that are kept, and are used and processed very much like the old-fashioned 'time and motion' studies were used to increase the efficiency of an organisation. Time Budget Studies have been applied to men's and women's work:

> 'But the key finding from 25 time use surveys around the world is that when all forms of work are added together, men and women do exactly the same total hours of productive activity: just under 8 hours a day. Men do substantially more hours of paid work. Women's time is divided fairly evenly between paid and unpaid work. Men and women do roughly equal amounts of voluntary work – contrary to the popular myth that women do vastly more than men.'[19]

Hakim points out that mothers with young children might do more work for a relatively short time, but then older women tend to work fewer hours in total than men. She concludes:

> 'Overall, men and women do equal amounts of productive work (paid and unpaid) – contrary to feminist claims.'[20]

In addition, Susan Harkness has shown that when there are children in the home British men work longer hours than do women. This is because men often take on more overtime, or a second job, to boost family income at this time in order to compensate for wives switching to part-time jobs or even dropping out of work altogether and becoming full-time stay-at-home mothers (one of many rational reasons for the pay gap).[21]

Hakim concludes:

> 'Feminists constantly complain that men are not doing their fair share of domestic work. The reality is that most men already do more than their fair share...The reason men are reluctant to offer more help with domestic work is that they are already doing more than their wives, on average – at least in Britain.'[22]

What Does Feminism Gain from Cheating and Lying about Housework?

There are a number of Feminist gains from fabricating housework 'research'. Here I'll briefly address three:

1. Feminism is Anti-Traditional Family
2. Spreading Misandry
3. To Preference Working Women

***

Feminism is Anti-Traditional Family

Feminists need to show that modern Britain is a patriarchal society in which women are *made* to take responsibility for housework and child care; 'made' to do it by their patriarchal dominating husbands. In a patriarchal society women are victims, oppressed and dominated by men. And the traditional two-parent family is the epicentre of this male power, this male oppression. The Feminist Wendy Clark admits:

> '*Apart from men, one thing which feminists love to hate is the family. Condemnation of the family and what it stands for has been one of the mainstays of feminist theory and practice.*'[23]

• By 'proving' that women do the lion's share of the housework Feminists wish to demonstrate that men have power over women in all areas of life. It is also hoped that young women will be put off marriage or living with a man (this is also one aim of the domestic violence issue – the home is where 1 in 4 women get beaten up and battered by 'bad men'. The hope in promoting this myth is to deter young women from marrying or living with men)

So telling lies about housework – that wives do much more of it than husbands – is an Ideological strategy:

> '*Feminist researchers, like Jessie Bernard or Ann Oakley, have rested their hostility towards marriage on precisely this unequal division of labour.*'[24]

***

Spreading Misandry

Using 'research' to create the myth that women do more housework than men, and work harder overall, deliberately maligns men. It is intended to promote the spread of minsandry, an Ideological dishonesty to discredit and demonise men in general. The intention is to create the impression that men are lazy around the home and that they dominate and oppress their wives for their own advantage.

To Preference Working Women

By claiming that wives do much more work than men a work-political culture is established that permits Feminists to push for special privileges for women in the form of their being allowed to work flexi-time, take time off work without loss of pay, change to part-time work whenever they wish (and then to return to their former status whenever they choose to return to work). The dishonest claim that women work harder than men facilitates giving women an easier ride in numerous areas of their paid employment.

***

J.R. Shackleton is Professor of Economics and Dean of the Business School, University of East London. He comments:

> 'Note that men do not work less overall, including domestic work, than women – despite popular belief. National Time Use surveys indicate that men aged 25- 44 spend slightly more time in total in work, both paid and unpaid, than women.'[25]

Chapter 52

'Daddy Doesn't Really Love You...
He Only Wants to Bully Mummy'

Even after viewing the comprehensive evidence for my claim that Feminist 'research' is dishonest and produced as Ideological propaganda, with one of its uses being a gender-weapon, some readers may *still* be disbelieving. So in this chapter I give an actual example of Feminist 'research'. Please remember that this is only *one* example; university 'gender research' has been under the control of Academic Feminism since the late 1970s, and there are very many universities involved, so the number of pro-female/anti-male pieces of 'research' (many influencing government policy) is very high indeed.

***

Fathers 4 Justice was a pressure group established in 2003 to publicly demonstrate against the injustice of vindictive ex-wives having the power to stop divorced fathers from seeing their children – a power that has been endorsed by the Family Courts and by successive governments. By the mid-2000s F4J had begun to attract serious public attention. This was anathema to Feminism; in a patriarchal society, which Feminism declares Britain to be, women are 'good people' and men are 'bad people'. Consequently, women cannot do 'bad things' (while the 'bad people' are to be punished – as in having their children taken away from them after divorce).

Public sympathy for the F4J male issue could not be tolerated: something had to be done. So the Labour/Feminist Government came down hard on this group, employing strong-arm tactics; anti-terror police were used to break into members' houses and flats, doors smashed off their hinges, indiscriminate damage done, computers and laptops taken away (many never returned), other property seized.

- These men were loving fathers, devoted to their children who they were not permitted to see. The majority had spent many thousands of pounds in legal fees attempting to have contact with their children, to no avail. This huge expenditure is an indication in itself that these men *genuinely* loved and wanted to see their children. Many of their mothers, sisters, new wives and girlfriends were also involved in the demonstrations and marches. Margaret Hodge, the Labour/Feminist Government's Minister for Children, contemptuously dismissed any meeting with these sympathetic women. So F4J was not an anti-women campaign, even though the two television programmes fronted by Trevor McDonald, mentioned in an earlier chapter, gloated in presenting it as such

The Labour/Feminist government's barbaric policy of keeping divorced fathers away from their children could not just rely on thuggery and terror, it had to be given a patina of intellectual legitimacy; so Feminist 'researchers' were called in to counter the Superhero Dads.

***

Caroline J. Gatrell is a lecturer in the Department of Management Learning and Leadership at Lancaster University. Cary L. Cooper is Distinguished Professor of Organisational Psychology and Health and Pro-Vice Chancellor at Lancaster University. Lancaster University has a reputation for being virulently Ideologically Feminist. In 2008 Gatrell and Cooper had 'research' published in the European Journal of International Management.[1] The 'research' was intended to observe how employed mothers' and fathers' work-life balance was gendered. I quote from this article:

> *'I (Gatrell) sought to understand the implications for family practices and to make mother-centred recommendations for employment policy in the UK. As I commenced my research, I proposed to adopt feminist methodological ideals which reflected "the values and principles which lie at the heart of the feminist project". As a consequence, I made the decision that fathers' voices should be excluded from my empirical research.'[2]*

- 'The Feminist project', I suggest, is a euphemism for the Quiet Revolution

- Gatrell was making work-related policy recommendations *only* for mothers, not fathers. This was unashamedly done to advance the Feminist agenda. Notice the phrase 'feminist methodological ideals'. Don't choke

And referring to other Feminist 'researchers', Gatrell comments:

> *'However, Frances also contends that feminist enquiry requires researchers to be political; they must identify a position where, if not claiming to understand what is "true", they can nevertheless argue the need for change. My own understanding of feminist research derived from the views of writers like Finch and Mason (1993), Maynard (1994), and Holland and Ramzanoglu (1994), who suggest that feminist research should relate sociology to practice, policy and decision making, seeking to enhance the situation of women in society...'[3]*

- So 'change' (as with 'advocacy research'), rather than 'truth', is the aim. For Feminism, 'research' can *only* be political...there is no other reason to produce it except to advance the 'project' – to 'enhance the situation of women in society'. In other words, to be used as propaganda to promote the Feminist Ideology, Feminist aims and the Feminist agenda

And,

> *'Thus, when I began my research, I sought to undertake political feminist research which was "for, rather than about, women" (Olesen, 1994). In adopting this stance, I regarded the voices and the needs of mothers as central to my research. Thus, although I was aware of precedents for including men in research on families...I intended, nevertheless, to focus exclusively on mothers.'[4]*

- This is an excellent example of Feminist 'action/advocacy research', the type of 'research' that Hitchcock and Hughes, the leading authorities on research methodology, severely criticise

Finally,

> *'I explained to all participants that my research was informed by a feminist position, that it was mother-centred and that I intended to make recommendations for policy in the hope of improving the situation for career mothers.'*[5]

- Informing the participants of your Ideological aim, especially when that aim is to their advantage, prior to the 'research' taking place, is unsound methodology to the point of being unethical, and rendering the 'findings' valueless as authoritative enquiry into that particular area (but the aim is to produce propaganda, not to produce work with intellectual integrity). Gatrell, a vociferous Feminist, interviewed the mothers and 'presented' the questions *herself*. You see what I'm getting at with regard to Feminist 'research' and government policy?

As Hitchcock and Hughes noted:

> *'A body of literature is now emerging which clearly demonstrates the potential problems of collaboration.'*[6]

Feminism's Serious Dislike of Fathers

The above is a brief sketch of Gatrell's 'research' methodology. The reader will find her policy recommendations and blatant Feminist Ideological 'findings' startling. The following are extracts from Gatrell's 'research'. The reader will note the intense misandry expressed (remember, from a leading university, Cary Cooper being Pro-Vice Chancellor):

> - *'I suggest that the attitudes of some fathers in the study are similar to the policies espoused by fathers' rights campaigners, which suggest that paternal demand should be met at mothers' expense.'*[7]

- So a father's wish to be involved with his children, and the divorced father's desperate need and request to see his children, will somehow 'be at the mother's expense'. Weird

> - *'In response to the possibility that women's employment may threaten male hegemony, fathers' rights campaigners are advising men to reassert masculine authority by wresting control of children from mothers. Fathers 4 Justice focuses mainly upon paternal rights, post-divorce.'*[8]

- 'Wresting control of children from mothers'? The choice of language *deliberately* depicts fathers as bullies and oppressors. Again, this is unethical. These devoted fathers simply want to see their children. Feminism really is an unpleasant and misandrous Ideology

> - *'Smart (1999), however, suggests that divorced fathers may also be motivated to maintain paternal "rights" because they are angry about the reduction in male hegemony that occurs when men lose their patriarchal position as head of household (especially if, as is usual, children are resident with mothers). Often, divorced fathers who have played little part in children's upbringing (but who have been used to controlling household decisions) resent the obligation to negotiate father-child "contact" with ex-wives who have previously accepted their patriarchal authority. Such men may seek to regain control over ex-wives through the children by pressurising women to accede to paternal demands.'*[9]

418

- 'Men losing their patriarchal position as head of the household'? This is 2011, not the Victorian age, or the 1920s. Only a Feminist could interpret a father's devotion to his children (spending many £1000s) as an opportunity to subjugate and bully his ex-wife ('pressuring women to accede to paternal demands'). I assume the reader has read Part Three

    - *'Situational power is easy to identify, and is often held by divorced mothers. Thus, women may find themselves under attack as they are pressured to concede increased contact between fathers and children.'[10]*

- 'Under attack'? It is the *divorced mothers* who ignore the judge's Court Order ordering them to allow the father access to his children. Notice the malicious language - 'mothers under attack'. This is not the neutral language that a genuine researcher would use, it is deliberately chosen to place these loving fathers in the position of the bullying oppressor. Reader, in today's Britain policy is made upon such 'research'

***

Fortunately, I was one of the very few fathers granted custody of their children. But the divorce system is so unjust to divorced fathers that I felt compelled to demonstrate and march with the F4J fathers, which I did regularly. I got to know many of them well, and their parents and their new wives and girlfriends. I can assure the reader that these traumatised fathers simply wanted to see their own children regularly. Regaining 'power' over their wives was the very *last* thing on their minds. They desperately wanted to regain some kind of contact with their children but were being emotionally beaten black and blue by the 'power' of their ex-wives – 'power' given to them by the Family Court Judges and by successive Conservative and Labour/Feminist governments. These fathers were seriously traumatised men as a result of having their children taken away from them. Their natural desire and wish to see their children is interpreted by Gatrell as their being 'power-mad patriarchs'. This is disgraceful.

- This, reader, is the Feminism that we have in Britain today. It has nothing to do with 'gender equality', but everything to do with privileging, preferencing and policy-favouring women (mainly Feminists themselves) and with blaming, condemning and punishing men. Modern Britain really does hate men

***

According to Gatrell, even married or co-habiting fathers are power-mad patriarchs, bent on subjugating their female partners:

    - *'In this context, married/co-habiting fathers may defend male dominance by asserting their rights in a sphere previously considered to be women's preserve: childcare. These objectives, and the strategies to enhance paternal power by disenfranchising women, are shared by those divorced fathers who also seek to contain maternal privilege through the children.'[11]*

- Note the unscientific language again: 'male dominance', 'asserting their rights'. These are extremely disrespectful, distasteful and aggressive comments. This is an example of typical Feminist 'research'

- In one breath Feminists claim that men are lazy and don't do their share of housework and child care. In the next breath, because men *want* to be involved in child care (pre- and post-divorce) their love and affection for their children is condemned as a 'strategy to enhance paternal power'. Do you see how Feminists create misandrous issues? Men are damned if they do and damned if they don't

- Once again we observe the Feminist claim that 'men have no feelings', only *pretending* to love their children so that they can dominate and oppress their wives. And universities, and governments, fund and promote such blatant man-hating...misandry that has become *institutional* in today's Britain

Listen, Sisters, and watch my lips: most-fathers-love-their-children-very-much-and-they-simply-want-to-express-this-and-then-to-carry-on-seeing-them. Got it?

In case there is any accusation that I have taken quotes from Gatrell's 'research' out of context I *strongly* recommend that readers consult this 'research' for themselves; references have been provided. (I sincerely hope they do, Sisters, I really do).

***

Feminism is full of inconsistencies; here we see an example of another. We have the ironic situation in which Feminism, on the one hand, denounces motherhood as an 'oppression' and an 'enslavement' (see Chapter 21)...whilst at the same time *protecting* mothers from fathers and divorced fathers who want to be involved with their children. This is hypocritical, irrational and misandrous behaviour. I refer the reader to Part Three. And these people hold posts in universities teaching our young people, they hold senior positions in the legal system, they are our MPs...

***

The reader was introduced to Valerie Solanas in an earlier chapter. Allow me to remind you about Valerie Solanas. In the late 1960s Solanas founded the Feminist magazine, SCUM. This was a manifesto for Feminism. It was resurrected in the 1980s, and again, on the internet in 2009, ('Back by popular demand', it boasted).[12] The following are quotes from SCUM. 'The male is a walking abortion', 'Your average man is a half-dead, unresponsive, lump'. Solanas believed that men's days were numbered because they are 'self-destructive creatures'. She encouraged Feminists, 'Scum girls', to speed up this inevitability because men have 'no right to life as they are a lesser life form than women.[13]

> '*Scum girls will...burst into heterosexual couples and break them up (couple-busting); they will pick off and kill certain relevant male targets.*'

> *Scum girls, Solanas pronounced, are the coolest, grooviest, most enlightened females whereas other women are 'toadies and doormats'. Finally, the organisation SCUM will be in a position to plan the 'agenda for eternity and Utopia' and no more men will need to be killed once women wake up to men's 'banality and uselessness.'*

Solanas shot, and almost killed, the artist Andy Warhol. Unsurprisingly, she was eventually committed to a mental asylum. SCUM is an acronym for Society for Cutting Up Men.

***

Why am I mentioning Valerie Solanas again? Solanas, who was an anti-capitalist Marxist, maintained that there was no human reason for money to exist, or for anyone to work more than two or three hours a week... 'But there are non-human, *male* reasons for wanting to maintain the money system.' Solanas gives six reasons. The sixth is relevant to this chapter:

'To provide the basis for the male's major opportunity to control and manipulate – fatherhood... Fatherhood and mental illness...Mother wants what's best for her kids; Daddy only wants what's best for Daddy, that is peace and quiet, pandering to his delusion of dignity ('respect'), a good reflection on himself (status) and the opportunity to control and manipulate.'[14]

And so we arrive full-circle to today's Britain...to Lancaster University. I'm not suggesting that Ms Gatrell has a disturbed mentality, as Ms Solanas obviously had, but simply that their views on fathers are remarkably similar. 'Daddy doesn't love you, he just wants to "control and manipulate" mummy...he only wants to be involved in order to "enhance his paternal power", to exert his "male power", "to regain control and dominance over his ex-wife".'

- The man-hating root, deep inside Feminism, hasn't lessened in severity in four decades.

- A university produces 'research', intended to influence government policy, that concludes that fathers, married or single, don't really love their children...they just pretend to in order to bully their wives. The misandry is palpable. It's shocking that so much policy is based upon the 'findings' of Feminist 'research'. Feminist 'research' truly is a Feminist Fraud

***

Feminism, and the Academic Feminist Industry, gains credibility from the fact that governments accept their 'findings' without question; this governmental acceptance is taken as an 'official' endorsement which, in turn, gives kudos to the universities, their Feminist 'research' teams and to their Feminist-friendly 'findings'. In this way governments are complicit in the 'research' dishonesty whose objective is to advance Feminist Ideological aims, including spreading misandry. We see again how and why modern Britain hates men.

***

'A government that sponsors and funds universities to carry out "research" on "gender equality" and social policy issues is like a government sponsoring and funding Marlboroughists to carry out "research" on the safety of cigarette smoking'

(Swayne O'Pie)

Chapter 53

Feminists are Allowed to Cheat and Lie: Because they are 'Special People'

Seriously, I'm not making this up...this is what Feminists claim for themselves and truly believe. But first, a round-up of Feminist 'research'.

***

'When regard for the truth has been broken down or even slightly weakened, all things will remain doubtful.'

(St. Augustine)

For thirty years the British public and Britain's social policy have been constantly subjected to Feminism's habitual use of misleading or fake statistics.

To remind the reader:

HARMAN REBUKED

(The Times, Friday, 12 June, 2009)

'Sir Michael Scholar, head of UK Statistics Authority, yesterday rebuked Harriet Harman, Minister for Women, for a potentially misleading press release issued in April that said women were on average paid 23 per cent less per hour than men. The Officer For National Statistics puts the figure at 12.8 per cent.'

• At the time of her promoting 'misleading' statistics Feminist Harriet Harman was Deputy Prime Minister of the Labour/Feminist Government, the second most powerful person in the country. She was also the Feminist Minister for Women

***

The production of Feminist 'research' to prove that Britain is a patriarchy, in which women suffer 'gender inequality' discrimination, oppression, victimisation and abuse at the hands of men (and therefore require preferential treatment, special privileges and policy-favouritism) is a major factor in the establishment of our Feminist-dominated State. High-profile proof of discriminations (by prominent Sisters) gives Feminist claims and demands an added legitimacy, making it easier for men in power to passively agree with and accept Feminist claims and demands – and to use the 'legitimacy' of Feminist 'research' to ease their consciences when implementing pro-Feminist and anti-male legislation and policy.

Feminists have the power to produce 'research' that has no academic merit but which is used to promote their Ideology and agenda – 'research' that is solely Ideological propaganda. Because we are all in thrall to Feminism, its studies and surveys are never critically analysed or questioned. So Feminist 'research findings' continue to enjoy immunity from challenge, or from any objective and neutral analysis. Harman's use of misleading statistics on the pay gap is the only example of media coverage of Feminism's 'research' misdemeanours that I have ever seen.

The almost total lack of criticism of Feminist 'research' has resulted in the loss of academic integrity in universities, with a consequent loss of quality in, and respect for, their institutional status and their teaching staff. Much more importantly it has also resulted in poor quality, pro-women/Feminist and misandrous social policies.

> *'It is hard to exaggerate the corrupting effect that feminism has had upon academic integrity in general and the social sciences in particular. It has meant that a great deal of the research upon which policy-makers depend serves a prior agenda which often departs radically from reality.'[1]*

Any 'research' that appears to advance the aims of Feminism needs to be very carefully questioned before being believed, and certainly before being acted upon, even when it has been produced by academically-labelled 'doctors' and 'professors' – titles that lull us all into accepting their findings as legitimate and ethical.

> *'McNeely observed that these feminists "are not about the search for truth. What this is about is a search for political power. That is power based upon a concept of a defenceless group of people being victimised by a larger, stronger aggressor. When people start recognising that, indeed, domestic violence seems to occur both ways, that undercuts the whole concept of weakness, out of which comes power. It's based on a concept of being an exclusive victim".'[2]*

- One should never accept sexual political 'research' uncritically, and should *always* question its provenance, especially if it happens to chime with the Feminist perspective and agenda. We need to ask: 'Is there an Ideology and an agenda that has driven this study, that has created these "findings"?'

> *'Our point here is not that feminists are unique in faking research for political ends. That is clearly untrue. Our point is only that journalists and politicians – and all citizens – should be careful before accepting at face value bizarre statistics that just happen to support their political ends.'[3]*

***

Feminist 'research' is so basically flawed as a genuine research tool that it not only lacks any vestige of academic integrity but is also undemocratic; the use of such 'research' and its Ideologically skewed findings result in harmful political, social and economic consequences for society as a whole, but particularly for men.

> *'Phony statistics continue to do their job, still cited repeatedly and still embedded in public consciousness...When repeated like mantras, they create their own reality.'[4]*

***

> *'Feminist "research" is a fraud, it is dishonest. But it demonstrates the remarkable capacity of fanatics to adapt "evidence" to fit their Ideology'*
>
> (Swayne O'Pie)

Feminists are 'Special People'

The following is taken from Jennifer Saul's book, Feminism: Issues and Arguments. Saul is a lecturer in Feminist Studies; her views are widely held by other Academic Feminists. The concept of 'standpoint theory' was first adopted by Marx but Feminists have re-invented the concept in order to justify their skewed production and use of 'research':

'The idea that women have access to a privileged standpoint in certain areas of study has its origins in Marxism.'[5]

***

Essentially, standpoint theory allows Feminists to claim that *their* type of 'research' actually *improves* science. Secondly, they claim that they are *allowed* to be biased because women, especially Feminists, are *better* than men. Thirdly, Feminists claim that they are *privileged people* and therefore have a special ability to 'know' more than others. Saul states:

'The idea of a feminist standpoint, then, would offer a way of explaining how feminist biases could improve science.'[6]

- Only in the bizarre world of Feminism could prejudiced and Ideologically-driven propaganda 'research' *improve* science. I direct the reader to Part Three

And,

'One way of making sense of the manner in which science can be improved when feminist women get involved is to suggest that there is something about women that allows this improvement. Sometimes this gets expressed as the idea that women have access to a special standpoint that makes them "epistemically privileged". What this means is (very roughly) that women are more reliable, insightful, more likely to be right than men are, when it comes to certain topics. Thus, they have an important contribution to make to research in these areas.'[7]

- You see what I'm saying, reader, about the outlandishness, the misandry, of today's Feminism? Women, it is claimed, are far superior human beings to men, so *their* 'research' has to be taken seriously. And no one has ever questioned or challenged this Ideology, this extraordinary claptrap (upon which government policy is based). Until now

- We saw in Part Two the Feminist belief system that boys and girls are 'born the same' (the theory of 'sameness') but, it is claimed, girls are 'socialised' by men (the patriarchal culture) to be inferior. With standpoint theory we see one more example of Feminist hypocrisy; women are *inherently* superior to men. Jack and Jill are 'the same'...when it suits, but Jill is 'superior' to Jack...when it suits. I assume the reader has read Part Three

Feminism's 'sameness/socialisation' belief system was exposed for the fraud that it is. The same arguments can be applied to Feminism's standpoint theory. Logically, if *women* have a special uniqueness and 'insight' to be able to 'see *their* unique condition' then *men* must also have a unique standpoint to be able to see *their* male-specific condition, their lives, problems, issues and rights, because of *their* personal 'access to a special and unique standpoint'. But whereas Feminists enjoy special privileges for their standpoint (a Minister for Women, Women's Officers, Sections, Units, Commissions, positive discrimination, etc.)

the male's unique standpoint is completely ignored. Once again we see an expression of Britain's institutional misandry.

- If women have a special 'female standpoint' then common sense would dictate that men must also have a special 'male standpoint'. Either *both* do or *neither* does. And if it is both then both standpoints ought to be politically represented

Standpoint theory makes the concepts of empathy and sympathy redundant. Apparently, we can't possibly empathise or sympathise with a black South African's oppression under white supremacist rule because we are not a black South African; we can't empathise or sympathise with slaves because we have not personally experienced their torment; we cannot take a moral stance against fox-hunting or battery farming because we are not a fox or a battery chicken.

***

But wait. It's not just *any* woman who has this special 'insight', who has this special 'privilege'. No. It is only the true, card-carrying *Feminist* who has this specialness:

> *'But – like workers for Marx – women would not automatically have this standpoint. They could only attain this feminist standpoint by movement beyond the ideologies that they had been taught, and coming to understand the world in a new way.'*[8]

So, it is only the Left-wing/liberal/progressive Feminist gender-warrior who is so privileged and blessed, thereby being permitted to cheat and lie with her 'research'. Such people, by their own admission, are *superior to other women*, and obviously *far* superior to men. This supremacist mentality exactly chimes with the Feminists' psychological make-up exposed in Part Three. And for three decades we have all been tugging the forelock to these 'supremacist' people and their ideas, their claims and their demands.

It is extremely worrying that so many 'Supremacist' Feminists are now in serious positions of power and influence in politics, the law, academia and the media (and have been for some time). And new generations are continually being brought on and trained up. As the Professional Feminist Catherine Redfern and Feminist Studies lecturer Kristin Aune boast:

> *'Imagine the potential of a generation who, instead of taking feminism's work for granted, understand not just how far we've come but how far we still have to go.'*[9]

This is a particularly disturbing, but relevant point I think, at which to leave the subject of Feminist 'research'.

Conclusion

Exposing Feminism: A Second Brief Against Feminism

In today's Britain there has been an unwillingness to accept the full extent of women's gains, of women's successes. There has been a wilful blindness to see that equal opportunities, equal rights, equal respect, equal treatment and equal choices for women have all been achieved. And there has been a cultural and political refusal to accept that Feminism has been artificially creating issues in order to justify its continuing, Ideological and lucrative existence...and to spread its man-hating.

For Feminism success will never be enough. To survive and to justify its existence it needs to constantly seek out or create inequalities, discriminations and oppressions. I have identified the strategies used by Feminism to manufacture these artificial issues and crises, and how it promotes its policy of Issue Creep. These include:

- Creating Ideological issues 'from nothing' (women's public safety and everyday Scatter-Gun issues)

- Establishing Industries to create, promote and co-ordinate its fabricated inequalities and discriminations. A huge Feminist/Women's Sector has been built up. Feminism's many Grievance Gravy-Train Industries have attracted huge amounts of government funding and secured hundreds of thousands of jobs and careers for Professional Feminists and Ideologues, for gender-warriors who produce nothing but issues and perpetual grievances. Good for these women's employment, perhaps, but not good for society; and a *disaster* for men and boys

- Converting ordinary women's freely made choices into Ideological issues (family-work balance, studying arts and humanities, being feminine, participating in pornography and prostitution, earning less (the pay gap), eschewing promotion (the 'glass ceiling')

- Changing the rules and re-defining concepts (Criteria Dilution). And demanding that the negative consequences of women's choices, as defined by Feminists (less pay and fewer women in senior positions, for example) are 'remedied' by government policies

- Using the strategy of 'exaggeration' to magnify issues into 'crisis' and 'epidemic' proportions for political and Ideological advantage (trafficked women, sexual harassment, domestic violence and rape)

- Producing 'research' to be used as a propaganda tool in order to give its issues an academic legitimacy and respectability so as to facilitate media, public and political acceptance. Also used to create new, as well as to justify existing, issues and grievances. And to spread misandry

Feminism *needs* inequalities, discriminations and oppressions; in turn, inequalities, discriminations and oppressions have to have perpetrators; since the 1970s men have been placed in this 'perpetrator' role. It has been the purpose of this book to show that Feminism cannot logically exist without man-hating.

426

***

I ask readers to ponder the following observations, and keep them in mind when encountering any future Feminist claims and demands:

> *'It is important to note that contemporary feminist groups are not disinterested, public-spirited observers and impartial critics of government policies. During the past two decades, feminist organisations have been some of the most successful fundraisers in the non-profit world, with grants from government, foundations, and private corporations. Thus, feminist groups have a financial stake in continuing to claim women are second-class citizens and that the struggle for women's rights is never won. Without the banner of victimhood to rally around feminist coffers would run dry.'[1]*

And,

> *'Or is it (modern Feminism's agenda) the fixed beliefs of a group of professional women?...It is one thing to demand rights when a whole group is clearly disadvantaged, but it is quite another if those rights seem mainly to confer additional advantages on already privileged groups, or groups which may be using women's interests to promote their own careers or their own agendas.'[2]*

And,

> *'With the push toward defining equality for women as numerical parity has come a skilful change in the language feminists use to describe women's rights...rather than demanding equal opportunity, feminists are lobbying for preferential rights for their own interest groups.'[3]*

- There has been a collective reluctance to subject the whole area of Feminism to scrutiny. Why?

***

People might see an example of Feminism 'having gone too far' here and there; or of men being discriminated against 'here and there, occasionally'. What people have not seen is the *concerted* and *orchestrated* strategy behind these observations, they have not seen the political pattern, they are unable to join up the dots to expose the Ideological agenda, the progression of a Quiet Socialist/Feminist Revolution. The vast majority of us have been blind to this pattern, all examples of which 'coincidentally' benefit Feminists and Feminism and 'coincidentally' discriminate against men. There are no 'coincidences'. There has been a very clever, incremental, unnoticed Quiet Revolution in progress since the late 1970s whose aim it is to change society, our culture and State.

I hope this book has exposed this concerted Ideological agenda, this political pattern, and in the process armed the reader to face up to Feminism.

And the Future?

In 2006 Joan Bakewell asked the intentionally disarming question:

WHERE HAVE ALL THE FEMINISTS GONE?

(Daily Mail, Tuesday, 28 March, 2006: Joan Bakewell)

'So does feminism still meet a need? The answer is an unequivocal "yes". Major injustices remain: the pay gap is patently unjust; sexual harassment and bullying can blight careers and job satisfaction; date rape is not to be excused because a woman is drunk; violence against women is on the increase...So much to do. So much to do.'

- Are these women deluded or just plain dangerous? Considering the evidence of this book it is most certainly the latter
- 'So much to do. So much to do'...a powerful indication that Feminism will be with us for the foreseeable future

And consider the following:

Polly Toynbee (Feminist doyenne):

'The revolution is only half made, and sometimes it seems to go backwards'.[4]

Joan Bakewell once more:

'Well, women have done a very great deal, but in my view the revolution is only half won.'[5]

Phillip Collins (Male Feminist...in The Times):

'The advance of women is still work in progress'[6]

Natasha Walter (Professional Feminist):

'It is worth remembering our successes as well as how far we still have to go.'[7]

Cherie Blair (Feminist Ambassador):

'We still have a long way to go.'[8]

However, we are advised to be wary of these Ideological advocates of the Quiet Revolution, these perpetual Grievance Collectors:

'Don't be fooled by their contentions that progress has been thwarted and there are miles to go before women achieve full equality. First, these women are chronically dissatisfied. And most radical feminists are qualified for only one job: professional feminists. Thousands of professional feminists can't declare victory and go home, because they would have no homes, they would have no jobs or prospects of jobs. They are generously paid, largely by taxpayers, but also by corporations anxious to look good on "women's issues", to be feminist theorists, academics, counsellors, consultants, trainers, and advocates. They review textbooks and train teachers to erase those gruesome sex stereotypes, they conduct sexual harassment workshops for nervous corporations, they counsel cops and judges on domestic abuse, they "mainstream gender values" into college curriculums, and they advocate for women's rights at a network of feminist organisations.'[9]

- Feminism has been incredibly successful. Many of its radical principles have been internalised into 'mainstream' thought and policy. And the Quiet Revolution is still progressing, there is 'still a long way to go'. Feminism cannot allow itself to be satisfied, can *never* allow itself to be appeased...The Revolution must go on

***

For Feminism success will never be enough...so the Quiet Revolution will progress, the Grievance Gravy-Trains will be forever running and 'Forever' Feminism will continue to continue...and so, logically and inevitably, must the blaming, demonising, punishing of men, and the accompanying systemic, cultural and institutional misandry...

...because there can't, logically, be inequalities, discriminations and oppressions without *someone* or *something* causing these. Feminism blames men and the patriarchy, the 'inequality of power between the sexes'. So by seeking out or creating issues Feminism, *by necessity*, needs to spread misandry. Man-hating is, by choice and by logic, a fundamental tenet of the Feminist Ideology and central to its agenda, it is DNAed into its 'being'.

In Part Two I related a passage from Tim Lott's book, Love Secrets of Don Juan, in which the hero, Danny, asks an assembled group of women what men are better than women at:

'Silence. More silence. An embarrassed giggle from Charlotte..."I'll tell you one thing men are better at", I say, flatly. "Putting up with things. Biting their lip, and putting up with things. Putting up with bucketloads and bucketloads of absolute shit being poured over their head. And not fighting back. They're better at not fighting back. They're better at taking it, taking it, taking it, and then just walking away..."'

'Men seem to be so cowed that they can't fight back, and it is time they did'

(Doris Lessing)[10]

The ex-Feminist Marian Salzman, author of The Future of Men, researched the cultural and political condition of men in Britain and America and came to this conclusion:

'I started as a feminist and came out much more realistic. Men should rise up. We have pushed men too far. They are going to have to shove back.'[11]

Erin Pizzey, the woman who set up the first refuges for battered women in Britain:

'Surely, the time has come to challenge this evil ideology.'[12]

- For thirty-five years there has been a sex war waging in Britain. This has not been between *women* and men but between *Feminists* and men. And it has been unilateral. Most men are not even aware that they are *in* a war

Maybe what we need is a shift to it being cool for men to stand up to Feminism and claim some dignity. And it needs to be a cool thing for women to want that kind of man. Women could say: 'Hey, from now on the fashion is going to be that the men who take this crap lying down will be vilified as wimps'. Then men may say: 'I don't want women to think I'm a wimp, I'd better wake up'.

- Men haven't had their Movement yet. Not really. Not politically. And they're due for it

***

And what of women? For Feminism to continue to exist it needs to have a 'victim group', women, who must always be *collectively* consigned to the status of 'victims'. Yet many women wish to be proud of their abilities and personal merits and don't want to be classified as 'people who need special help'. Feminism prevents women from actually rising above their assigned 'victimhood status' and to meet society on its own level and on their own terms. To do that would mean taking personal responsibility for the conditions, actions, behaviours and choices of their own lives. Modern Feminism has denied women this personal responsibility, it actively discourages it; it has designed an argument and Ideology that leads not to the encouragement of personal growth and empowerment for women but to a social, economic and political culture of 'victimhood' dependence to be 'remedied' by a culture of 'entitlement', group rights, quotas, positive discrimination, blamelessness. In other words, Feminism has led to a society that actually *disempowers* individual women whilst collectively treating them as perpetual infants...and whilst also collectively blaming and demonising men.

Minette Marrin discusses modern Feminism and notes:

WHAT WOMEN WANT IS AN END TO HECTORING BY FEMINISTS

(The Sunday Times, 14 March, 2010)

'But somewhere along the way feminism in this country has turned into something many women cannot identify with. I can't. Harman, along with other prominent alpha females, expresses a kind of feminism that is so far divorced from what most women think and want that she might as well belong to another sex. Alpha females seem closer to the alpha male than to the ordinary woman in gender.'

• Women today need to be liberated from *Feminism*, not the patriarchy...and apparently, the Revolution is only half won... there is still a long way to go

***

'Feminism is an organised Movement of the Left that has gained immense cultural and political power. It has become a monster that has found perpetual victimhood the most convenient and efficient way to hold onto that power'

(Swayne O'Pie)

A State that genuinely cared about the welfare of *all* its citizens would undertake a careful reassessment of Feminism, would undertake an audit of its claims and demands, and its agenda. Feminism has outlived its usefulness and has become a malignant manifestation of what was once a necessary and genuine equality Movement for women. And yet in modern Britain it has not only been universally accepted but has been embraced, and encouraged to flourish. For thirty-five years we have been seduced and defrauded by a phony Feminism. Isn't it time to stand up and cross that line?

Tail Note

I'd be delighted to hear from you. Share your concerns, experiences and insights. Give me feedback, offer your suggestions. Which issues would you like to see covered in a future book?

*   I would particularly like to hear from disaffected Feminists. Confidentiality and discretion is assured

*   Were you, or anyone you knew, disillusioned/upset with the Feminist bias you found during your university education?

*   I would like to hear from men who have experienced sexism/discriminations

*   Please recommend this book to your friends and work colleagues. Use social networking, email/Facebook/Twitter, to publicise the fact that such a book is now available

*   Do remember that I give talks, lectures and interviews

*   Why not make a photocopy of the front cover and display it in your place of work, pub, club etc? For greater impact a larger size (A3 or even A2) could be used

***

If you wish to respond please write a brief note, in the first instance, to Swayne O'Pie, The Men's Press, PO Box 2220, Bath, United Kingdom, including your contact details.

Alternatively email me at info@exposingfeminism.com.

Feel free to take a look at my website www.exposingfeminism.com. I recommend Mike Buchanan's blog http://fightingfeminism.wordpress.com. His books are available to order from the usual sources, and from his own website www.lpspublishing.co.uk.

Thank you.

References

Preface

1. Catherine Redfern and Kristin Aune: Reclaiming the F Word: The New Feminist Movement; Zed Books, 2010, p 10

2. Ibid p 220

3. Ibid p 216

4. The MENS Society Facebook page

5. The Guardian, Monday 23 November, 2009

6. Vicky.thompson@gmail.com

7. Ibid

Chapter 1 - Spreading Misandry: The Widespread Disrespect for Men

1. Oxford English Reference Dictionary 2003 and Reader's Digest Universal Dictionary 1987

2. Ibid

3. Paul Nathanson and Katherine K. Young: Legalizing Misandry: From Public Shame to Systemic Discrimination Against Men; McGill-Queen's University Press, 2006, p 269

4. Kathleen Parker: Save the Males: Why Men Matter: Why Women Should Care; Random House, 2008, p 24

5. Daily Mail, Tuesday, 23 January, 2007

6. Ibid

7. Nathanson and Young p 5

8. Letter received from Macmillan General Books, Cavaye Place, London, SW10 9PG

9. Wendy Moore: There Should be a Law Against it...Shouldn't There? In Stevi Jackson (ed): Women's Studies: A Reader; Harvester Wheatsheaf, 1993, pp 283, 284

10. Marian Salzman: The Future of Men; Palgrave Macmillan, 2005, p 132

11. Daily Mail, Thursday, 21 May, 2009

12. Parker

13. Natasha Walter: The New Feminism; Virago, 1999, p 146

14. Ibid. Quoted from Doris Lessing: Walking in the Shade, Harper Collins, 1997, pp 346, 347

15. Daphne Patai: Heterophobia: Sexual Harassment and the Future of Feminism; Rowman and Littlefield, 1998, p 9

16. Christina Hoff Sommers: The War Against Boys: How Misguided Feminism Is Harming Our Young Men; Touchstone, 2000, p 14

17. William Marsiglio: Fatherhood: Contemporary Theory, Research and Social Policy; SAGE Publications, 1995, Preface

18. Matt O'Connor: Fathers 4 Justice; Weidenfeld and Nicolson, 2007, p 330

19. Nathanson and Young p 311

20. Social Trends 32: (2002), Office for National Statistics, Table 2.8, p 43 and Social Trends, 31, (2001), Office for National Statistics, London: the Stationary Office, Table 2.8, p 44. Reported in Rebecca O'Neill: Experiments in Living: The Fatherless Family; Civitas, 2002, p 3

21. For example: The State of the Nation Report: Fractured Families, The Social Policy Justice Group, December 2006, chaired by Iain Duncan Smith, p 89. Breakthrough Britain: Ending the Cost of Social Breakdown; The Social Policy Justice Group, July 2007, chaired by Iain Duncan Smith. Jill Kirby: Broken Hearts: Family Decline and the Consequences for Society; Centre for Policy Studies, 2002, p 30

22. Patricia Morgan: Farewell the Family? Public Policy and Family Breakdown in Britain and the USA. IEA Health and Welfare Unit, 1999, p 100

23. Daily Mail, Friday, 26 February, 2010

24. Breakthrough Britain, p 91

25. Daily Mail, Monday, 28 June, 2010

26. Parker p 20

27. Guy Garcia: The Decline of Men; Harper Collins, 2008, p xiii

28. Paul Nathanson and Katherine K. Young: Spreading Misandry: The Teaching of Contempt for Men in Popular Culture; McGill-Queen's University Press, 2002, p 243

29. Naomi Wolf: Fire with Fire, Random House, 1994

30. Nathanson and Young p 193

31. Erin Pizzey, J.R. Shackleton and Peter Urwin: Women and Men – Who are the Victims?; Civitas, 2000, p 29

32. The Times, Wednesday, 6 May, 2009

33. Nathanson and Young p 269

Chapter 2 - Why Would Anyone Want to Disagree with Feminism?

1. For example: Valerie Bryson: Feminist Political Theory; Paragon House, 1992. Andrew Heywood: Political Theories; Macmillan Press, 1998. Maggie Humm (ed): Feminisms: A Reader; Harvester Wheatsheaf, 1992. Stevi Jackson (ed): Women's Studies: A Reader; Harvester Wheatsheaf, 1993. Rosemary Tong: Feminist Thought: A Comprehensive Introduction; Routledge, 1995

2. Claire Fulenwider: Feminism in American Politics; Praeger, 1980, p 56. Quoted in Michael Levin: Feminism and Freedom; Transaction Books, 1987, p 22

3. Robert H. Bork: Slouching Towards Gomorrah; Regan Books, 2003, p 196

4. Melanie Phillips: The Sex-Change Society; The Social Market Foundation, 1999, p 126

5. Paul Nathanson and Katherine K. Young: Legalizing Misandry: From Public Shame to Systemic Discrimination Against Men; McGill-Queen's University Press, 2006, p xi

6. Fulenwider pp 30-35

7. Nathanson and Young p 319

8. Maggie Humm (ed): Feminisms: A Reader; Harvester Wheatsheaf, 1992, p 406

Chapter 3 - Feminism's Devil Weapon

1. Reader's Digest Universal Dictionary, 1987

2. Valerie Bryson: Feminist Political Theory; Paragon House, 1992, p 15

3. Andrew Heywood: Political Ideologies; Macmillan, 1998, p 248

4. Lynne Segal: Is The Future Female?; Virago, 1987, p 84

5. Kate Millett: Sexual Politics; Virago, 1969

6. Christina Hoff Sommers: Who Stole Feminism? How Women Have Betrayed Women; Touchstone, 1995, p 43

7. Andrea Dworkin: Our Blood; The Women's Press, 1982, p 20

8. Kathleen Parker: Save the Males: Why Men Matter, Why Women Should Care; Random House, 2008, p 20

9. Paul Nathanson and Katherine K. Young: Legalizing Misandry: From Public Shame to Systemic Discrimination Against Men; McGill-Queen's University Press, 2006, p xi

10. Daphne Patai and Noretta Koertge: Professing Feminism: Cautionary Tales from the Strange World of Women's Studies; A New Republic Book (Harper Collins), 1994, p 89

11. Boni Sones: Women in Parliament: The New Suffragettes; Politico's Publishing, 2005, p 147

12. Sam Keen: Fire in the Belly: On Being a Man; Piatkus, 1992, p 196

13. Daphne Patai: Heterophobia: Sexual Harassment and the Future of Feminism; Rowman and Littlefield, 1998, p 87

14. David Jary and Julia Jary: Dictionary of Sociology; Unwin Hyman, 1991

15. Jennifer Mather Saul: Feminism: Issues and Arguments; Oxford University Press, 2003, pp 12, 13

16. Vicky.thompson@gmail.com

17. Ibid

18. Reader's Digest Universal Dictionary, 1987

19. Melanie Phillips: The Sex-Change Society; The Social Market Foundation, 1999, p 206

20. Jennifer Baumgardner and Amy Richards: Manifesta: Young Women, Feminism and the Future; Farrar, Straus and Giroux, 2000, p 82

21. Robert H. Bork: Slouching Towards Gomorrah; Regan Books, 2003, p 196

22. Jessica Valenti: Full Frontal Feminism: A Young Woman's Guide to Why Feminism Matters; Seal Press, 2007, p 237

23. Phillips p 116

24. Baumgardner and Richards, p 304

25. Keen, p 203

26. The Times, Friday, 27 November, 2009

27. Keen, pp 196, 197

Chapter 4 - Jack and Jill are the Same: Except where Jill's Better

1. Michael Levin: Feminism and Freedom; Transaction Books, 1987, p 18

2. The Observer, 15 August, 2010

3. Michael Levin: Feminism and Freedom; Transaction Books, 1987, p 20

4. Robert H. Bork: Slouching Towards Gomorrah; Regan Books, 2003, p 197

5. Ibid p 199

6. For example refer to the following books, their bibliographies and references. Simon Baron-Cohen: The Essential Difference: Men, Women and the Extreme Male Brain; Allen Lane, 2003. Anne and Bill Moir: Why Men Don't Iron: The Real Science of Gender Studies; Harper Collins, 1998

7. Levin p 20

8. Ibid p 18

9. Harvey C. Mansfield: Manliness; Yale University Press; 2006, p 8

Chapter 5 - Ms Marx and Her Brothers

1. Daphne Patai: Heterophobia: Sexual Harassment and the Future of Feminism; Rowan and Littlefield, 1998, p 3

2. Friedrich Engels: The Origins of the Family, Private Property and the State; Lawrence and Wishart, 1976, p 129

3. Andrea Dworkin: Suffering and Speech, in Harm's Way: The Pornography Civil Rights Hearings, Catherine A. MacKinnon and Andrea Dworkin, Cambridge; Harvard University Press, 1997, p 35

4. Ibid p 28

5. Anna Coote and Beatrix Campbell: Sweet Freedom; Picador, 1982, p 31

6. Anna Coote and Polly Pattullo: Power and Prejudice: Women and Politics; Weidenfeld and Nicolson 1990, p 95

7. Gemaine Greer: The Female Eunuch; Paladin, 1981, p 329

8. Valerie Bryson: Feminist Political Theory; Paragon House, 1992, p 83

9. Daily Mail, Tuesday, 28 March, 2006

10. Jennifer Baumgardner and Amy Richards: Manifesta: Young Women, Feminism, and the Future; Farrar, Straus and Giroux, 2000, p 304

11. Michael Levin: Feminism and Freedom; Transaction Books, 1987, p 18

12. Ibid

13. Sheila Rowbotham: The Past Is Before Us: Feminism in Action Since the 1960s; Penguin, 1989, p 222

14. Ibid p 26

15. Shelia Rowbotham, Lynne Segal and Hilary Wainwright: Beyond the Fragments: Feminism and the Making of Socialism; Merlin Press, 1981

16. Ibid p 181

17. Ibid p 183

18. Natasha Walter: The New Feminism; Virago, 1999, p 256

19. Rowbotham p 26

20. Ibid

21. Robert H. Bork: Slouching Toward Gomorrah; Regan Books, 2003, p 195

22. Tammy Bruce: The New Thought Police; Three Rivers Press, 2001, p 15

23. Coote and Pattullo p 95

24. Paul Nathanson and Katherine K. Young: Legalizing Misandry: From Public Shame to Systemic Discrimination Against Men; McGill-Queen's University Press, p 313

25. Erin Pizzey, J.R. Shackleton and Peter Urwin: Women and Men – Who are the Victims?; Civitas, 2000, p 24

26. Bruce p 4

27. F. A. Hayek: The Road to Serfdom; Routledge, 2010, p 145

28. Maggie Humm: Feminisms: A Reader; Harvester Wheatsheaf, 1992, p 406

Chapter 6 - The Power of Lesbian Feminism

1. Mary Evans (ed): The Woman Question: Readings on the Subordination of Women; 1982, pp 64, 65

2. Daily Mail, Tuesday, 28 March, 2006

3. Quoted in Angela Neustatter: Hyenas in Petticoats; Harrap, 1989, p 70

4. Adrienne Rich: Compulsory Heterosexuality and Lesbian Existence, 1980. Signs, Vol. 5, No. 4. p 687

5. Anna Coote and Beatrix Campbell: Sweet Freedom: The Struggle for Women's Liberation; Picador, 1982, p 29

6. Angela Neustatter: Hyenas in Petticoats; Harrap, 1989, p 69

7. Coote and Campbell p 29

8. Neustatter p 70

9. Rosemarie Tong: Feminist Thought: A Comprehensive Introduction; Routledge; 1995, p 123

10. Jennifer Baumgarnder and Amy Richards: Manifesta: Young Women, Feminism, and the Future; Farrar, Straus and Giroux, 2000, p 279

11. Kathleen Parker: Save the Males: Why Men Matter: Why Women Should Care; Random House, 2008, p 117

12. Ibid p 118

13. Ibid

14. Valerie Bryson: Feminist Political Theory; Paragon House, 1992, p 214

15. Ibid p 212

16. Coote and Campbell p 29

17. Rich p 21

18. Neustatter p 226

19. Coote and Campbell p 29

20. Women's Resource Centre, Ground Floor East, 33-41 Dallington Street, London, EC1V 0BB

21. Michael Levin: Feminism and Freedom; Transaction Books, 1987, p 18

22. Neustatter p 56

23. Coote and Campbell p 29

24. Erin Pizzey, J.R. Shackleton, Peter Urwin: Women or Men – Who Are the Victims?; Civitas, 2000, p 30

25. Vicky.thompson@gmail.com

26. Catherine Redfern and Kristin Aune: Reclaiming the F Word: The New Feminist Movement; Zed Books, 2010, p 223

Chapter 7 - So what Happened to Equality Feminism?

1. Nicholas Davidson: The Failure of Feminism; Prometheus Books, 1988, p 312

2. Daily Mail, Tuesday, 23 January, 2007

3. Erin Pizzey, J.R. Shackleton, Peter Urwin: Women or Men – Who Are the Victims?; Civitas, 2000, p 29

4. Ibid p 30

5. Ibid p 29

6. Anna Coote and Beatrix Campbell: Sweet Freedom: The Struggle for Women's Liberation; Picador, 1982, p 41

7. Kathleen Parker: Save the Males: Why Men Matter: Why Women Should Care; Random House, 2008, review, inside front cover

8. Caroline Quest (ed): Joan Kennedy Taylor, Norman Barry, Mary Kenny, Michael Levin, Patricia Morgan, Glenn Wilson: Liberating Women...From Modern Feminism; IEA Health and Welfare Unit, 1994, p 7

9. The Sunday Times, 28 March, 2003

10. Melanie Phillips: The Sex Change Society; The Social Market Foundation, 1999, p 119

11. Diane Furchtgott-Roth and Christine Stolba: The Feminist Dilemma; the AEI Press, 2001, p 12

12. Paul Nathanson and Katherine K. Young: Legalizing Misandry: From Public Shame to Systemic Discrimination Against Men; McGill-Queen's University Press, 2006, p 401

13. Caroline Quest (ed): Liberating Women...From Modern Feminism; p 8

14. Pizzey p 29

15. Ibid

16. Phillips p 119

17. F. Carolyn Graglia: Domestic Tranquility: A Brief Against Feminism; Spence Publishing Company, 1998, p 132

18. The Sunday Telegraph, 17 November, 1991

19. Ariel Levy: Female Chauvinist Pigs: Women and the Rise of Raunch Culture; Simon and Schuster, 2006, p 65

20. Nathanson and Young p 133

21. Phillips p 116

22. Robert Seidenberg: The Father's Emergency Guide to Divorce-Custody Battles; JES Books, 1997, p 7. Quoted in Nathanson and Young p 133

23. Kate O'Beirne: Women Who Make The World Worse; Sentinel, 2006, p xvii

24. Nathanson and Young p 318

25. Robert H. Bork: Slouching Towards Gomorrah; Regan Books, 2003, p 196

26. Nathanson and Young p 116

27. Nicholas Davidson: The Failure of Feminism; Prometheus Books, 1998, p 312

Chapter 8 - The Suffragettes: Early Man-Hating Feminists

1. Friedrich Engels: Origin of the Family, Private Property and the State; 1884

2. Melanie Phillips: The Ascent of Woman: A History of the Suffragette Movement and the Ideas Behind It; Abacus, 2008, p 215. All books by Melanie Phillips are well worth reading, offering insights and common sense

3. Mona Caird: The Morality of Marriage and Other Essays on the Status and Destiny of Women. Quoted in Phillips, p 216

4. Ibid

5. Phillips p 211

6. Ibid p 213

7. Ibid p 279

8. Ibid p 201

9. Ibid p 217

10. Walter Gallichan: Modern Woman and How to Manage Her: 1990. In Margaret Jackson: The Real Facts of Life: Feminism and the Politics of Sexuality, 1850 – 1940. Quoted in Phillips, p 217

11. Paul Nathanson and Katherine K. Young: Legalizing Misandry: From Public Shame to Systemic Discrimination Against Men; McGill-Queen's University Press, 2006, p 151

12. Phillips p 201

13. Ibid p 218

14. Ibid p 209

15. Ibid p 220

16. Ibid p 283

17. Ibid p 222

18. Rosa Barrett: Ellice Hopkins: A Memoir; Wells Gardener Darton, 1907. Quoted in Phillips, p 223

19. Phillips p 215

20. Ibid p 201

21. David Mitchell: Queen Christabel; Macdonald and J., 1977. Quoted in Phillips, p 251

22. Annie Kenney: Memoirs of a Militant; Edward Arnold, 1924. Quoted in Phillips, p 253

23. Emmeline Pethic-Lawrence: My Part in a Changing World; Golancz, 1938. Quoted in Phillips, p 252

24. The Suffragette: 7 August, 1914. Quoted in Phillips, p 291

25. The Daily Telegraph, Wednesday, 5 November, 2003

Chapter 9 - Who *Are* These Women Who Make the World Worse for Men?

1. David Jary and Julia Jary: Dictionary of Sociology; Unwin Hyman, 1999. This Dictionary presents itself, on the rear cover, as: 'The Unwin Hyman Dictionary of Sociology, now revised and updated, is a clear, balanced guide to the terms and concepts used in every area of sociology...'. 'Balanced'? I don't think so.

2. A combination of definitions from the Oxford English Reference Dictionary, 2003, and the Reader's Digest Universal Dictionary, 1987

3. http:feminism.suite101.com/article.cfm/third-wave-feminism

Chapter 10 - Is There a Feminist 'Personality'?

1. The Guardian, Tuesday, 14 August, 2000

2. F. Carolyn Graglia: Domestic Tranquility: A Brief Against Feminism; Spence Publishing, 1998, p 13

3. Kate O'Beirne: Women Who Make the World Worse; Sentinel, 2006, p xxiv

4. Germaine Greer: Daddy, We Hardly Knew You; Penguin, 1989, pp 2-12

5. Child Maltreatment and Paternal Deprivation: A Manifesto for Research, Prevention and Treatment (1986): Henry B. Biller and S. Solomon, 1986, p 147. Quoted in Daniel Amneus: The Garbage Generation; Primrose Press, 1990, p 245

6. Henry B. Biller: Paternal Deprivation: Family, School, Sexuality, and Society, 1974, p 114. Quoted in Amneus, p 243

7. Nicholas Davidson: Prometheus Books; 1988, pp 310, 311

8. Reader's Digest Universal Dictionary, 1987

9. Ibid

10. Robert H. Bork: Slouching Towards Gomorrah; Regan Books, 2003, p 194

11. F.A. Hayek: The Road To Serfdom; Routledge, 2010, p 145

12. Daphne Patai and Noretta Koertge: Professing Feminism: Cautionary Tales from the Strange World of Women's Studies; A New Republic Book (Harper Collins); 1994, p 301

13. Erin Pizzey: Daily Mail, Tuesday, 2 January, 2007

14. Christina Hoff Sommers: The Sunday Times, 28 March, 2003

15. O'Beirne, p xvii

Chapter 11 - Anger and Rage: A Feminist Neurosis or Strategy? Or Both?

1. Oxford English Reference Dictionary, 2003, and Reader's Digest Universal Dictionary, 1987

2. Erin Pizzey, J.R. Shackleton and Peter Urwin: Women or Men – Who Are The Victims?; Civitas, 2000, p 25

3. Daphne Patai and Noretta Koertge: Professing Feminism: Cautionary Tales from the Strange World of Women's Studies; A New Republic Book (Harper Collins), 1994, p 94

4. Ibid p 95

5. Ibid p 96

6. Swayne O'Pie, The Men's Press, PO Box 2220, Bath, United Kingdom; info@exposingfeminism.com

7. Anna Coote and Beatrix Campbell: Sweet Freedom: The Struggle For Women's Liberation; Picador, 1982, p 29

8. William Marsiglio: Fatherhood: Contemporary Theory, Research and Social Policy; SAGE publications, 1995 (in the Introduction)

9. Bernard Goldberg, CBS News Correspondent: Quoted in Warren Farrell: Women Can't Hear What Men Don't Say; Finch Publishing, 2001, p 256

10. Natasha Walter: The New Feminism; Virago, 1999, p 15

11. Robert H. Bork: Slouching Towards Gomorrah; Regan Books, 2003, p 203

12. Sue Bruley: No Turning Back: Writings from the Women's Liberation Movement; The Women's Press, 1981, p 65

13. Judith Levine: My Enemy, My Love: Man-Hating and Ambivalence in Women's Lives; Doubleday, 1988, p 16

14. The Guardian, Tuesday, 14 August, 2001

15. Catherine Redfern and Kristin Aune: Reclaiming the F Word: The New Feminist Movement; Zed Books, 2010, p 206

Chapter 12 - Is There a Feminist 'Pathology'?

1. Oxford English Reference Dictionary, 2003, and Reader's Digest Universal Dictionary, 1987

2. Daphne Patai: Heterophobia: Sexual Harassment and the Future of Feminism; Rowan and Littlefield, 1998, p 12

3. A regular statement of Dworkin's, usually uttered at the beginning of her lectures

4. This was from an advertisement in the New York Times Book Review, September, 1991, p 11, endorsing Andrea Dworkin's book, Mercy: Novel About Rape. Quoted in Warren Farrell: Women Can't Hear What Men Don't Say; Finch Publishing, 2001

5. Susan Brownmiller: Against Our Will; Harmondsworth, Penguin, 1997, p 15

6. Andrea Dworkin: Our Blood: Prophecies and Discourses on Sexual Politics; The Women's Press, 1982

7. Paul Nathanson and Katherine K. Young: Legalizing Misandry: From Public Shame to Systemic Discrimination Against Men; McGill-Queen's University Press, 2006, p 213

8. Valerie Solanas: SCUM Manifesto; The Matriarchy Study Group, c/o 19, Upper Street, London N1, 1983

9. Nathanson and Young, p 212

10. C.H. Freedman: Manhood Redux: Standing Up to Feminism; Samson Publishers, 1985, p 3

11. Ibid, p 11

12. Quoted in Kathleen Parker: Save the Males: Why Men Matter: Why Women Should Care; Random House, 2008, p 30

13. Nathanson and Young, p 185

14. Germaine Greer: The Whole Woman; Doubleday, 1999. Quoted in Melanie Phillips: The Sex-Change Society; The Social Market Foundation, 1999, p 6

15. Erin Pizzey, J.R. Shackleton and Peter Urwin: Women or Men – Who Are The Victims?; Civitas, 2000, p 25

16. Paul Nathanson and Katherine K. Young: Spreading Misandry: The Teaching of Contempt for Men in Popular Culture; McGill-Queen's University Press, 2002, p 193

17. Freedman, p 18

18. Camille Paglia: Sex, Art and American Culture; Vintage Books, 1992, p 66

19. Naomi Wolf: Fire with Fire; Vintage, 1994

20. The Observer, 4 July, 2010

21. Rosalind Miles: The Rites of Man; Paladin, 1992, p 23

22. Ibid p 15

23. Ibid p 298

24. Ibid p 77

25. Neil Lyndon: No More Sex War: The Failures of Feminism; Sinclair-Stevenson, 1992, p 41

26. The Times, Wednesday, 6 May, 2009

27. The Guardian, Tuesday, 14 August, 2001

28. F. A. Hayek: The Road to Serfdom; Routledge, 2010, p 146

29. Ibid

Chapter 13 - Terrible as an Army with Banners

1. Nicholas Davidson: The Failure of Feminism; Prometheus Books, 1988, p 311

2. Walter Gallichan: Modern Woman and How to Manage Her (1990). In Margaret Jackson: The Real Facts of Life: Feminism and the Politics of Sexuality, 1850 – 1940. Quoted in Melanie Phillips: The Ascent of Woman: A History of the Suffragette Movement and the Ideas Behind It; Abacus, 2008, p 215

3. Camille Paglia: Sex, Art, and American Culture; Vintage Books, 1992, p 66

4. The Sunday Telegraph, 17 November, 1991

5. Kate O'Beirne: Women Who Make The World Worse; Sentinel, 2006, p xvii

6. Melanie Phillips: The Sex-Change Society; The Social Market Foundation, 1999, p 116

7. F. A. Hayek: The Road to Serfdom; Routledge, 2010, p 146

8. Davidson, p 311

Chapter 14 - Everywoman, Feminists and Misandry

1. Melanie Phillips: The Sex-Change Society; The Social Market Foundation, 1999, p 5

2. Cathy Young: Ceasefire!; The Free Press, 1999, p 227

3. Tim Lott: The Love Secrets of Don Juan; Viking, 2003, pp 70-73

4. Jack Kammer: Good Will Toward Men; St. Martin's Press, 1994, pp 47, 48

5. Phyllis Theroux in GQ, February, 1986; quoted in Jack Kammer, If Men Have All The Power How Come Women Make All The Rules? p 35: PO Box 18236, Halethorpe MD 21227, USA, 2002

6. Barbara Jordan, former member of the US Congress from Texas, speaking to the Women's Campaign Research Fund, Austin, Texas, September, 1991. In Kammer, If Men Have All The Power How Come Women Make All The Rules? p 33

7. Erin Pizzey, J.R. Shackleton and Peter Urwin: Women or Men – Who Are The Victims?; Civitas, 2000, p 25

8. Cathy Young, p 5

9. Paul Nathanson and Katherine K. Young: Legalizing Misandry: From Public Shame to Systemic Discrimination Against Men; McGill-Queen's University Press, 2006, p 269

10. Jennifer Baumgardner and Amy Richards: Manisfesta: Young Women, Feminism and the Future; Farrar Straus and Giroux, 2000, p 14

11. Ibid pp 15, 49

12. Judith Levine: My Enemy: My Love: Man-Hating and Ambivalence in Women's Lives; Doubleday, 1992, p 5

13. Ibid

14. Ibid p 17

15. Paul Nathanson and Katherine K. Young: Spreading Misandry: The Teaching of Contempt for Men in Popular Culture; McGill-Queen's University Press, 2002, p 243

Chapter 15 - For Feminism Success Will Never Be Enough: 'Forever' Feminism

1. Cathy Young: Ceasefire!; The Free Press, 1999, p 3

2. Diana Furchtgott-Roth and Christine Stolba: The Feminist Dilemma; The AEI Press, 2001, p 12

3. David G. Green: We're (Nearly) All Victims Now!; Civitas, 2006, p 1

4. Ibid p 31

5. Paul Nathanson and Katherine K. Young: Legalizing Misandry: From Public Shame to Systemic Discrimination Against Men; McGill-Queen's University Press, 2006, p 198

6. Ibid

7. Kate O'Beirne: Women Who Make the World Worse; Sentinel, 2006, p 83

8. Warren Farrell: Women Can't Hear What Men Don't Say; Finch Publishing, 2001, p 227

9. Catherine Redfern and Kristin Aune: Reclaiming the F Word: The New Feminist Movement; Zed Books, 2010, p 16

Chapter 16 - How Feminism Creates Issues 'from Nothing'

1. Catherine Redfern and Kristin Aune: Reclaiming the F Word: The New Feminist Movement; Zed Books, 2010, p 229

2. Cathy Young: Ceasefire!; The Free Press, 1999, p 85

3. Anna Coote and Beatrix Campbell: Sweet Freedom; Picador, 1982, p 204

4. Angela Neustatter: Hyenas in Petticoats: A Look at Twenty Years of Feminism; Harrap, 1989, p 48

5. Reclaim the Night: www.takebackthetech.org.uk/

6. London Feminist Network's website

7. Ibid

8. NUS: www.officeronline.co.uk

9. Jack Kammer: Good Will to All Men: Women Talk Candidly About The Balance of Power Between the Sexes; St. Martin's Press, 1994, p 114

10. Natasha Walter: Living Dolls: The Return of Sexism; Virago, 2010, p 234

11. Daily Mail, Friday, 30 January, 2009

12. The Sunday Times, 19 June, 1994

13. Bath Police Station, 2005

14. Daphne Patai: Heterophobia: Sexual Harassment and the Future of Feminism; Rowman and Littlefield, 1998, p 35

15. The Daily Telegraph, Saturday, 31 May, 2008

16. Paul Nathanson and Katherine K. Young: Legalizing Misandry: From Public Shame to Systemic Discrimination Against Men; McGill-Queen's University Press; 2006, p 569

17. Ibid p 265

18. Fredrick Mathews: The Invisible Boy: Revisioning the Victimization of Male Children and Teens (Ottawa: Health Canada, Minister of Public Works and Government Services, Canada, 1996. Quoted in Nathanson and Young, p 266)

Chapter 17 - Everyday Scatter-Gun 'Issues'

1. Swayne O'Pie, The Men's Press, PO Box 2220, Bath, United Kingdom; info@exposingfeminism.com

2. Neil Lyndon: No More Sex War: The Failures of Feminism; Sinclair-Stevenson, 1992, p 115

3. Jessica Valenti: Full Frontal Feminism: A Young Woman's Guide to why Feminism Matters; Seal Press, 2007, p 175

4. The Sunday Times, 14 March, 2004

5. The Sunday Times, 31 July, 2005

6. The Times, Thursday, 16 November, 2006

7. Daily Mail, Thursday, 1 February, 2007

8. Daily Mail, Wednesday, 24 March, 2010

9. 2 January, 2010

10. Nicholas Davidson: The Failure of Feminism; Prometheus Books, 1988, p 311

11. Daily Mail, Monday, 14 June, 2010

12. Daily Mail, Thursday, 15 October, 2009

13. Natasha Walter: Living Dolls: The Return of Sexism; Virago, 2010, p 236

14. R. W. Connell: Gender; Polity, 2002, p 136

15. Ibid

16. Kat Banyard: The Equality Illusion: The Truth About Women And Men Today; Faber and Faber, 2010, p 63

17. Ibid

18. Ibid

19. Ibid p 64

20. Ibid p 20

21. Ibid p 65

Chapter 18 - Feminism's Grievance Gravy-Train

1. Rosalind Coward: Sacred Cows: Is Feminism Relevant to the New Millenium?; Harper Collins, 1999, p 7

2. Andrew Heywood: Political Ideologies; Macmillan Press Ltd., 1992, p 261

3. Cathy Young: Ceasefire!; The Free Press, 1999, p 3

4. Coward p 7

5. F. Carolyn Graglia: Domestic Tranquility: A Brief Against Feminism; Spence Publishing, 1998, p 19

6. Jack Kammer: Good Will Toward Men: Women Talk Candidly About the Balance of Power Between the Sexes; St. Martin's Press, 1994, p 6

7. Christina Hoff Sommers: Who Stole Feminism? How Women Have Betrayed Women; Touchstone, 1994, p 6

8. Ibid p 136

9. Erin Pizzey, J. R. Shackleton, Peter Urwin: Women and Men – Who Are The Victims?; Civitas, 2000, p 26

10. Sommers p 273

11. Kathleen Parker: Save the Males: Why Men Matter: Why Women Should Care; Random House, 2008

12. Graglia p 19

13. Lynne Segal: Why Feminism?; Polity Press, 1999, p 33

14. Sommers p 273

15. C. H. Freedman: Manhood Redux: Standing Up To Feminism; Samson Publishing, 1985, p 31

16. Germaine Greer: The Female Eunuch; Paladin, 1981

17. Sommers p 273

18. The Sunday Times, 14 September, 2006

19. Catherine Redfern and Kristin Aune: Reclaiming the F Word: The New Feminist Movement; Zed Books, 2010, p 216

Chapter 19 - A Typical Feminist Grievance Factory

1. WRC, Ground Floor East, 33-41 Dallington Street, London, EC1V OBB

2. WRC Winter Newsletter, 2009/10, p 4

3. Registered Charity No. 1070606

4. WRC literature and DVD

5. Natasha Walter: Living Dolls: The Return of Sexism; Virago, 2010, p 235

6. This is untrue because such a figure cannot possibly be ascertained. I would like the reader to keep this in mind when she or he reads Feminist claptrap about such claims as: 'Domestic violence costs the British economy £80 million per year', or 'the glass ceiling loses the British economy £150 million per year.' Such claims are absolute nonsense – there are so many variables that such a specific claim is impossible to make, although this does not deter Feminism, in conjunction with the TUC, from making them. So, for this one instance, I thought that I would join the Fairytale Club.

7. This is true. Daily Mail, Saturday, 11 April 2009

8. Rosalind Coward: Sacred Cows: Is Feminism Relevant To The New Millennium?; Harper Collins, 1999, p 218

9. The Times, Friday, 27 November, 2009

Chapter 20 - Feminism and Women's Choices

1. Diana Furchtgott-Roth and Christine Stolba: The Feminist Dilemma; The AEI Press, 2001, p 86

Chapter 21 - Women Choose to Mary and be the Primary Parent

1. The Daily Telegraph, Thursday, 11 March, 2010

2. L. B. Feldman: Fathers and Fathering, in R.S. Patrick, Men in Therapy: The Challenge of Change; New York, The Guildford Press, 1990

3. Graeme Russell: Problems in Role-Reversal Families, in Charlie Lewis and Margaret O'Brien (eds): Reassessing Fatherhood: New Observations on Fathers and the Modern Family; Sage, 1987, p 177

4. J.H. Pleck: Husbands' Paid Work and Family Roles: Current Research Issues; in H. Lapata and J. H. Pleck (eds), Research in the Interweave of Social Roles, quoted in Charlie Lewis and Margaret O'Brien

5. Jennifer Mather Saul: Feminism: Issues and Arguments; Oxford University Press, 2003, p 10

6. Kate O'Beirne: Women Who Make The World Worse; Sentinel, 2006, p 2

7. Germaine Greer: The Female Eunuch; Paladin Grafton, 1981, p 329

8. Beatrix Campbell: Sex – A Family Affair; in Lynne Segal (ed): What Is To Be Done About The Family?; Penguin, 1983, p 157

9. Shulamith Firestone: The Dialectic of Sex: Women's Press; 1979, Quoted in Valerie Bryson: Feminist Political Thought; Paragon House, 1992, p 200

10. Daily Mail, Friday, 9 October, 2009

11. Ann Oakley: Housewife; Penguin, 1990, p 233

12. Mary Kenny (ed): The Woman Question: Readings on the Subordination of Women; Fontana, 1982, p 28

13. Cristina Odone: What Women Want; Centre for Policy Studies, 2008, p 3

14. Quoted in F. Carolyn Graglia: Domestic Tranquility: A Brief Against Feminism; Spence Publishing, 1998, p 62

15. Ibid p 107

16. Quote in James Tooley: The Miseducation of Women; Continuum, 2002, p 62

17. Sheila Rowbotham: Woman's Consciousness, Man's World; Pelican, 1973, p 76

18. Oakley, p 233

Chapter 22 - Women choose to Study the Arts and Humanities

1. Catherine Redfern and Kristin Aune: Reclaiming the F Word: The New Feminist Movement; AED Books, 2010, pp 109, 110

2. James Tooley: The Miseducation of Women; Continuum, 2002, p 31

3. Ibid

4. Ibid p 32

5. The Prosser Report: Conclusion

6. Daily Mail, Tuesday, 12 September, 2006

7. Glen Wilson: Liberating Women...From Modern Feminism: Caroline Quest (ed); The IEA Health and Welfare Unit, 1994, p 59

8. Anne and Bill Moir: Why Men Don't Iron: The Real Science of Gender Studies; Harper Collins, 1998

9. Christina Hoff Sommers: Who Stole Feminism? How Women Have Betrayed Women; Touchstone, 1995, p 92

Chapter 23 - Women Choose to be Feminine and be Seen as Sex Objects

1. Michael Levin: Feminism and Freedom; Transaction Books, 1987, p 20

2. Kat Banyard: The Equality Illusion: The Truth About Women And Men Today; Faber and Faber, 2010, p 23

3. Ibid p 20

4. Naomi Wolf: The Beauty Myth; Vintage, 1990, p 10

5. Jennifer Mather Saul: Feminism: Issues and Arguments; Oxford University Press, 2003, pp 144, 151

6. Banyard p 35

7. Ibid p 22

8. Caitlin Moran: How to be a Woman; Ebury Press, 2011, p 289

9. Ibid

10. Quoted in Angela Neustatter: Hyenas in Petticoats; Harrap, 1189, p 70

11. Ibid

12. Sheila Jeffreys: Beauty and Misogyny (Women and Psychology Series); Routledge, 2005

13. The Guardian, Thursday, 13 September, 2007

14. Catherine MacKinnon: Quoted in Paul Nathanson and Katherine K. Young: Legalizing Misandry: From Public Shame to Systemic Discrimination Against Men; McGill-Queen's University Press, 2006, p 177

15. Charlotte Bunch: Quoted in Rosemarie Tong: Feminist Thought: A Comprehensive Intoduction; Routledge, 1989, p 112

16. Valerie Bryson: Feminist Political Thought; Paragon House, 1992, p 212

17. Camille Paglia: Sex, Art and American Culture; Vintage, 1992, p 66

18. C. Pateman: The Sexual Contract; Cambridge Polity Press, 1988, p 208

19. Daily Mail, Thursday, 4 December, 2008

20. The Guardian, Thursday, 13 September, 2007

21. Paglia p 59

22. Ibid p 60

23. F. Carolyn Graglia: Domestic Tranquility: A Brief Against Feminism; Spence Publishing, 1998, p 161

24. Nicholas Davidson: The Failure of Feminism; Prometheus, 1987, p 347

25. Quoted in Angela Neustatter: Hyenas in Petticoats; Harrap, 1989, p 70

Chapter 24 - Women Choose to be Involved in Pornography

1. Jennifer Mather Saul: Feminism: Issues and Arguments; Oxford University Press, 2003, p 80

2. Andrea Dworkin and Catherine MacKinnon: Pornography and Civil Rights: A New Day for Women's Equality, 1988. Quoted in Legalizing Misandry: From Public Shame to Systemic Discrimination Against Men; McGill-Queen's University Press, 2006, p 160

3. Jennifer Mather Saul: Feminism: Issues and Arguments; Oxford University Press, 2003, p 83

4. The Times, Wednesday, 26 April, 2006

5. Kat Banyard: The Equality Illusion: The Truth About Women And Men Today; Faber and Faber, 2010, p 116

6. Ibid p 139

7. Ibid p 160

8. Norah Vincent: Self-Made Man; Viking, 2006, pp 88-91

9. The Sunday Times, 8 February, 2004

10. Caitlin Moran: How to be a Woman; Ebury Press, p 170

11. Ibid p 172

12. Ibid

13. Helen Fisher: Why We Love: the Nature and Chemistry of Romantic Love; New York, Henry Holt, 2004, p 110

14. Nathanson and Young, p 182

15. Vincent pp 88-91

16. Steve Moxon: The Woman Racket; Imprint Academic, 2008, p 251

17. Guy Garcia: The Decline of Men; Harper Collins, 2008, p 234

Chapter 25 - Women Choose to Become Prostitutes

1. Melanie Phillips: The Ascent of Woman: A History of the Suffragette Movement and the Ideas Behind It; Abacus, 2008, p 209

2. Andrea Dworkin: Life and Death: Unapologetic Writings on the Continuing War Against Women; Virago, 1997, pp 147-51

3. C. Pateman: The Sexual Contract; Cambridge, Polity Press, 1988, p 208

4. Kat Banyard: The Equality Illusion: The Truth About Women And Men Today; Faber and Faber, 2010, p 50

5. Natasha Walter: Living Dolls: The Return of Sexism; Virago, 2010, p 35

6. Ibid p 45

7. ibid p 35

8. Banyard p 147

9. Ibid p 148

10. Ibid p 150

11. Steve Moxon: The Woman Racket; Imprint Academic, 2008, p 219

12. The Guardian, Thursday, 4 September, 2008

13. The Guardian, Monday, 10 September, 2007

14. The Guardian, Wednesday, 19 November, 2008

15. Draft Statements from 2nd World Whores Congress (1986) p 307

16. Daily Mail, Thursday, 20 November, 2008

17. The Independent, Thursday, 20 November, 2008

18. The Independent, 25 September, 2008

19. Ibid

20. Oxford English Reference Dictionary, 2003

21. Camille Paglia: Sex, Art and American Culture; Vintage, 1992, p 66

22. Oxford English Reference Dictionary, 2003

23. Reader's Digest Universal Dictionary; 1987

24. Nicholas Davidson: The Failure of Feminism; Prometheus Books, 1988, p 311

25. Anthony Clare: On Men: Masculinity in Crisis; Chatto and Windsor, 2000, p 201

Chapter 26 - The Pay Gap and the Glass Ceiling

1. Catherine Redfern and Kristin Aune: Reclaiming the F Word: The New Feminist Movement; Zed Books, 2010, p 228

2. Ibid p 115

3. Paul Nathanson and Katherine K. Young: Legalizing Misandry: From Public Shame to Systemic Discrimination Against Men; McGill-Queen's University Press, 2006, p 113

Chapter 27 - Women's Work Ethic and Choice of Options

1. Dr. Catherine Hakim: Lifestyle Choices in the 21st Century – Preference Theory; OUP, 2000. Also Catherine Hakim, Models of the Family in Modern Society; Ashgate, July, 2003, p 85

2. Dr. Catherine Hakim: Feminist Myths and Magic Medicine: The Flawed Thinking Behind Calls for Further Equality Legislation; Centre for Policy Studies, 2011, p 22

3. Office for National Statistics

4. Hakim, 2000

5. David Thomas: Not Guilty; Weidenfeld and Nicolson, 1992, p 143

6. Catherine Hakim 2003 and 2006. Also S. J. Ceci, W. M. Williams and S. M. Barnett: Women's Under-Representation in Science: Sociocultural and Biological Considerations; Psychological Bulletin 135 (2): 2009, pp 218-261.
Also M. Henrekson and M. Stenkula: Why are there so few female top executives in egalitarian welfare states?; The Independent Review, 14 (2), 2009, pp 239-270

Chapter 28 - Women Choose a Healthy Work-Life Balance

1. Jack Kammer: If Men Have All The Power How Come Women Make The Rules?; PO Box 18236, Halethorpe MD 21227 USA, 2002, p 140

2. Steve Moxon: The Woman Racket; Imprint Academic, 2008, p 134

3. Hakim, 2003, p 78

4. Jill Kirby: Choosing to be Different: Women, Work and the Family; Centre for Policy Studies, 2003, p 23

5. The Sunday Times, 3 October, 2003

6. Kirby, p 17

7. The Sunday Times, 30 March, 2003

8. Kirby, p 29

9. Catherine Hakim: Explaining Trends in Occupational Segregation: The Measurement, Causes and Consequences of the Sexual Division of Labour; The European Sociological Review, Vol. 8, No. 2, September, 1992, p 142

10. Moxon, p 132

Chapter 29 - Women Choose to Take Career Breaks

1. Arnaud Chevalier: Motivations, Expectations and the Gender Pay Gap for UK Graduates; Paper presented at the Royal Economic Society Annual Conference, Warwick University, 7-9 April, 2003

2. The Times, Thursday, 16 May, 2002

3. The Times, 5 May, 2000

4. Daily Mail, Thursday, 5 January, 2006

5. Charlie Lewis: Becoming a Father; OUP, 1986. And Michael E. Lamb and Abraham Sagi (eds): Fatherhood and Family Policy; Lawrence Erlbaum Associates, 1983

6. Jennifer Mather Saul: Feminism: Issues and Arguments; Oxford University Press, 2003

7. Ibid p 10

8. Ibid p 18

9. Ibid p 30

10. Catherine Hakim: Models of the Family in Modern Societies: Ideals and Realities; Ashgate, 2003

11. U.S. Census Bureau: Survey of Incomer and Program Participation, 2001. Quoted in Warren Farrell: Why Men Earn More; Amcom, 2005, p 88

12. Marianne Bernard and Kevin F. Hallock: The Gender Gap in Top Corporate Jobs; Industrial Labour Relations Review 55 No. 1 (2001): 7 Table 2, Firm Manage Characteristics. Quoted in Farrell, p 87

Chapter 30 - Women Choose to Work Fewer Hours: And Fewer Unsocial Hours

1. Office for National Statistics

2. Ibid

3. Anthony Giddens: Sociology (6th Edition). Revised and updated with Phillip W. Sutton; Polity, 2009, p 905

4. Michael Haralmbos and Martin Holborn: Sociology: Themes and Perspective; Collins Educational, 1995, p 619

5. British Medical Journal 318, 9 January, 1999, pp 71-72

6. A. Booth and J.C. van Ours: Job Satisfaction and Family Happiness: the part-time work puzzle; Economic Journal, 118, 2008 (526): F77-F99. Cited in J.R. Shackleton: Should We Mind The Gap?; Institute of Economic Affairs, 2008, p 71

7. J. R. Shackleton: Should We Mind The Gap? Pay Differentials and Public Policy; Institute of Economic Affairs, 2008, p 68

8. Christine Hoff Sommers: Who Stole Feminism? How Women Have Betrayed Women; Touchstone, 1995, p 241

Chapter 31 - Women Choose to Work in Fulfilling Jobs

1. Warren Farrell: Why Men Earn More; Amcom, 2005, p 51

2. J. R. Shackleton: Should We Mind The Gap? Pay Differentials and Public Policy; The Institute of Economic Affairs, 2008, p 63

3. The Sunday Times, April 2003

4. Arnaud Chevalier: Motivation, Expectations and the Gender Pay Gap for UK Graduates; Paper presented at the Royal Economic Society Annual Conference, Warwick University, April 7-9, 2003

5. The Times, Tuesday, 8 May, 2007

6. Shackleton, p 89

7. Chevalier

Chapter 32 - Women Choose to Avoid Stressful Work

1. Mark Sieling: Monthly Labour Review (June 1984): 32 His source was the U.S. Bureau of Labor Statistics, 1981 survey of Professional Administrative, Technical and Clerical Pay. Quoted in Warren Farrell: Why Men Earn More; Amacom, 2005, p 106

2. Anne Moir and David Jessel: Brainsex; Mandarin, 1989

3. Melanie Phillips: The Sex-Change Society; The Social Market Foundation, 1999, p 237

4. Rosalind Coward: Sacred Cows: Is Feminism Relevant To The New Millenium?; Harper Collins, 1999, p 164

5. Catherine Hakim: Feminist Myths and Magic Medicine: The flawed thinking behind calls for further equality legislation; Centre for Policy Studies, 2011, p 21

6. Daily Mail, Tuesday, 17 January, 2006; Women Suffer Pay Gap Because They Won't Ask For A Pay Rise

7. J.R. Shackleton: Should We Mind the Gap? Gender Pay Differentials and Public Policy; The Institute of Economic Affairs, 2008, p 65

8. Coward, p 164

Chapter 33 - Women Choose to Avoid Promotion

1. Daily Mail, Monday, 1 April, 2009

2. Daily Mail, Thursday, 9 March, 2006

3. Catherine Hakim: Lifestyle Choices in the 21st Century – Preference Theory; OUP, 2000

4. Jill Kirby: Choosing to be Different: Women, Work and the Family; Centre for Policy Studies, 2003, p 27

5. Jane J. Mansbridge. Quoted in F. Carolyn Graglia: Domestic Tranquility: A Brief Against Feminism; Spence Publishing, 1998, p 86

6. The Nature of Management: in Management Education and Development. Vol. 16, Part 2, 1985

7. Referenced in Crawford: Leadership and Teams in Educational Management; OUP, 1997, p 73: Also in Valerie Hall: Dancing on the Ceiling: A Study of Women Managers in Education; Paul Chapman, 1996. Also, Valerie Hall: Women in Educational Management, 1997

8. Hall: Dancing on the Ceiling: A Study of Women Managers in Education

9. The Sunday Times, 15 January, 2006

10. Catherine Hakim: Explaining Trends in Occupational Segregation: the Measurement, Causes and Consequences of the Sexual Division of Labour; The European Sociological Review, Vol. 8, No. 2, September, 1992, p 143

11. The Times, Saturday, 23 June, 2007

12. Daily Mail, Tuesday, 3 August, 2004

13. Melanie Phillips: The Sex-Change Society; The Social Market Foundation, 1999, p 240

14. Steve Moxon: The Woman Racket; Imprint Academic; 2008, p 135

15. 16. Daily Mail, Thursday, 9 March, 2006

Chapter 34 - Women Choose 'Women's Work'

1. V. Beechey: What's so Special about Women's Employment? A Review of some Recent Studies of Women's Paid Work; Feminist Review 15, pp 23-25. Harriet Bradley: Men's Work: Women's Work; Polity Press, 1989. Cynthia Cockburn: The Material of Male Power; Feminist Review, 1981, 9: pp 41-59. Cynthia Cockburn: Machinery of Dominance: Women, Men and Technical Knowhow; Pluto, 1985. Cynthia Cockburn: Training for 'Her' Job and 'His' Job: Tackling Occupational Segregation by Sex in the Youth Training Scheme (Manchester: EOC), 1986. Refer to any work by Cynthia Cockburn; her In the Way of Women is also good. Rosemary Compton and Michael Mann: Gender and Stratification; Polity Press, 1986. Please refer to the bibliographies in these works.

2. Sheila Rowbotham: Women's Consciousness, Man's World; Penguin, 1973, p 96

3. Valerie Bryson: Feminist Political Theory; Paragon, 1992, p 197

4. Ibid p 241

5. Office for National Statistics

6. Katherine Kersten: Newsletter of The Women's Freedom Network; Spring, 1996. Quoted in Warren Farrell: Why Men Earn More; Amacom, 2005, p 140

7. Jane Bryant Quinn, Newsweek, 17 July, 2000. Quoted in Jack Kammer: If Men Have All The Power How Come Women Make All The Rules?; PO Box 18236, Halethorpe MD 21227 USA, 2002, p 139

8. Steve Moxon: The Women Racket; Imprint Academic, 2008, p 65

9. Catherine Hakim: Explaining Trends in Occupational Segregation: The Measurement, Causes and Consequences of the Sexual Division of Labour; The European Sociological Review, Vol. 8, No. 2, September, 1992, p 141. And Catherine Hakim: The European Sociological Review, Vol. 7, No. 2, OUP, 1991, pp 101-118

10. Catherine Redfern and Kristin Aune: Reclaiming the F Word: The New Feminist Movement; Zed Books, 2010, pp 199, 120

Chapter 35 - Women Choose to Avoid 'Men's Work': The Unhealthy and Dangerous Jobs

1. J. R. Shackleton: Should We Mind The Gap? Gender Pay Differentials and Public Policy; The Institute of Economic Affairs, 2008, p 47

2. Les Krantz (ed): The Jobs Related Almanac; New York, Ballantine Books, 1989

3. C. H. Freedman: Manhood Redux: Standing Up To Feminism; Samson Publications, 1986, p 140

4. Shackleton p 47

5. Health and Safety Executive Statistics, 1991/2

6. Shackleton, p 47

7. The Times, Thursday, 13 January, 2000

8. The Times, Wednesday, 12 April, 2006

Chapter 36 - The Pay-Off for the Pay and Promotion Gap

1. J. R. Shackleton: Should We Mind the Gap? Gender Differentials and Public Policy; The Institute of Economic Affairs, 2008, p 76

2. Katherine Kersten: Newsletter of the Women's Freedom Network, Spring, 1996. Quoted in Warren Farrell: Why Men Earn More; Amacom, 2005, p 140

3. Shackleton p 105

4. Daniel Hecker: How Hours of Work Affect Occupational Earnings; Monthly Labour Review, Vol. 121, No. 10. Quoted in Steve Moxon: The Woman Racket; Imprint Academic, 2008, p 140

5. Shackleton p 30

6. Moxon p 144

7. Melanie Phillips: The Sex-Change Society; The Social Market Foundation, 1999, p 239

8. Shackleton p 29

9. E. Ferri: Life at 33; National Children's Bureau, 1993

10. The Sunday Times, 30 January, 2011

Chapter 37 - Feminism Changes the Rules

1. Diana Furchtgott-Roth and Christine Stolba: The Feminist Dilemma; The AEI Press, 2001, p 14

2. J. R. Shackleton: Should We Mind The Gap? Gender Pay Differentials and Public Policy; The Institute of Economic Affairs, 2008, p 8

3. Ibid p 74

4. Martin Mears: Institutional Injustice; Civitas, 2006, p 34

5. Paul Nathanson and Katherine K. Young: Legalizing Misandry: From Public Shame to Systemic Discrimination Against Men; McGill-Queen's University Press, 2006, p 114

6. Shackleton p 74

7. The Times, Monday, 12 March, 2007

8. Nathanson and Young p 104

9. Kate O'Beirne: Women Who Make The World Worse; Sentinel, 2006, p xviii

Chapter 38 - Equality of Outcome

1. Melanie Phillips: The Sex-Change Society; The Social Market Foundation, 1999, p 159

2. Judith Squires: The New Politics of Gender Equality; Palgrave, 2007, p 163

3. Paul Nathanson and Katherine K. Young: Legalizing Misandry: From Public Shame to Systemic Discrimination Against Men; McGill-Queen's University Press, 2006, p 116

4. Diana Furchtgott-Roth and Christine Stolba: The Feminist Dilemma; The AEI Press, 2001, p 3

5. Ibid

6. Guy Garcia: The Decline of Men; Harper, 2008, p 136

7. Furchtgott-Roth and Stolba p 4

8. Nathanson and Young p 116

9. Boni Sones: Women in Parliament; Politico's Publishing, 2005, p 147

10. F. Carolyn Graglia: Domestic Tranquility: A Brief Against Feminism; Spence Publishing, 1998, p 19

11. Furchgott-Roth and Stolba p 3

12. Jack Kammer: Good Will Toward Men; St. Martin's Press, 1994, p 6

13. Christina Hoff Sommers: Who Stole Feminism? How Women Have Betrayed Women; Touchstone, 1994, p 6

14. Rosalind Coward: Sacred Cows: Is Feminism Relevant to the New Millennium?; Harper Collins, 2000, p 218

15. Daily Mail, Tuesday, 3 October, 2006

16. The Observer, 10 October, 2010

17. Nathanson and Young p 83

18. Jessica Morgan: Feminism Does Not Preclude using Feminine Charms; Daily Bruin, 15 July, 1996. Quoted in Cathy Young: Ceasefire!; The Free Press, 1999, p 7

19. Garcia p 271

20. Anne and Bill Moir: Why Men Don't Iron: The Real Science of Gender Studies; Harper Collins, 1998, p 193

Chapter 39 - Top Jobs for the Sisters: Can Positive Discrimination be Justified?

1. Daily Mail, 7 May, 2009

2. Catherine Hakim: Feminist Myths and Magic Medicine: The flawed thinking behind calls for further equality legislation; Centre for Policy Studies, 2011, p 39

3. Paul Nathanson and Katherine K. Young: Legalizing Misandry: From Public Shame To Systemic Discrimination Against Men; McGill-Queen's University Press, 2006, p 104

4. Preferential Policies: An International Perspective; N.Y., William Morrow and Co, 1990, p 124. Quoted in Wendey McElroy: Preferential Treatment of Women in Employment; in Equal Opportunities: A Feminist Fallacy; IEA and Welfare Unit, Choice in Welfare No. 11, 1992, p 107

5. Elusive Equality: Liberation, Affirmative Action and Social Change in America; Port Washington, N.Y.; Associated Faculty Press, 1983, pp 50, 51. Quoted in McElroy

6. N. Y.: William Morrow and Co.: 1990, p 160. Cited in McElroy

7. The Sunday Times, 30 January, 2011

8. The Times, Friday, 25 February, 2011

9. Ibid

10. The Sunday Times, 20 February, 2011

11. Ibid

12. Ibid

13. The Times, Monday, February 28, 2011

Chapter 40 - How and Why Feminism Exaggerates Issues

1. Paul Nathanson and Katherine K. Young: Legalizing Misandry: From Public Shame to Systemic Discrimination Against Men; McGill-Queen's University Press, 2006, p 198

2. Guy Garcia: The Decline of Men; Harper Collins, 2008, p 123

3. Daphne Patai: Heterophobia: Sexual Harassment and the Future of Feminism; Rowman and Littlefield, 1998, p 44

4. Christopher Booker: The Real Global Warming Disaster; Continuum, 2009, p 1

5. Christina Hoff Sommers: Who Stole Feminism? How Women Have Betrayed Women; Touchstone, 1995, p 28

6. Oxford English Reference Dictionary, 2003, and Reader's Digest Universal Dictionary, 1987

Chapter 41 - Trafficked Women

1. Daily Mail, Friday, 13 November, 2009

2. Ibid

3. Ibid

4. Ibid

5. Ibid

6. Ibid

7. The Independent, 25 September, 2008

8. ICPR World Charter and World Whores Congress Statement (Draft Statements of the World Whores Congress, 1986)

9. Nick Mai: Migrant Workers in the UK Sex Industry; Institute for the Study of European Transformation, London Metropolitan University, 2009

10. Daily Mail, Friday, 13 November, 2009

11. Ibid

12. Ibid

13. Ibid

14. Ibid

15. Ibid

16. Oxford English Reference Dictionary, 2003

Chapter 42 - Sexual Harassment

1. These definitions are based on those given in 'Guidelines on Discrimination Because of Sex: Sexual Harassment', Equal Employment Opportunity Commission Code of Federal Regulations, Title 29, Section 1604.11; US Department of Education, Office of Civil Rights, Sexual Harassment Guidance

2. Daphne Patai: Heterophobia: Sexual Harassment and the Future of Feminism; Rowman and Littlefield, 1998, p 13

3. A paper presented by Diana Lamplugh OBE, Director, The Suzy Lamplugh Trust, 3 December, 1997, p 2

4. Terry Pattinson: Sexual Harassment: The Hidden Facts; Futura, 1991, p 12

5. Ibid

6. Ibid p 4

7. Patai p 130

8. Sexual Harassment at Work: Published by the TUC, 1981

9. Ibid. Also, A Working Woman's Guide to Her Job Rights, US Department of Labor, leaflet No. 55, June, 1988

10. Ibid

11. Katie Roiphe: The Morning After: Sex, Fear and Feminism; Hamish Hamilton, 1994, p 109

12. Reader's Digest: Universal Dictionary

13. Ibid

14. David Thomas: Not Guilty: The Modern Man; Weidenfeld and Nicolson, 1993, p 162

15. Ibid

16. Ibid p 163

17. Wendy Kaminer: Feminism's Identity Crisis; Atlantic Monthly, October, 1999, pp 51-68. Quoted in Paul Nathanson and Katherine K. Young: Legalizing Misandry: From Public Shame to Systemic Discrimination Against Men; McGill-Queen's University Press, 2006, p 219

18. Patai p 7

19. Ibid p 168

20. Guy Garcia: The Decline of Men; Harper Collins; 2008, p 123

21. Roiphe p 109

22. Patai pp xii-xiii

23. Kat Banyard: The Equality Illusion: The Truth About Women and Men Today; Faber and Faber, 2010, p 97

24. Nathanson and Young p 215

25. Roiphe p 100

26. Ibid p 99

27. Kate O'Beirne: Women Who Make The World Worse; Sentinel, 2006, p 64

28. Nathanson and Young p 209

29. Ibid p 198

30. Patai p 55

31. The Sunday Times, 25 May, 2003

32. The Times, 1 March, 2000

33. The Times, 10 November, 2005

34. Daily Mail, 14 July, 2004

35. The Times, 6 February, 1999

Chapter 43 - Domestic Violence

1. Melanie Phillips: The Sex-Change Society; The Social Market Foundation, 1999, p 137

2. Kat Banyard: The Equality Illusion: The Truth About Women and Men Today; Faber and Faber, 2010, p 107

3. Paul Nathanson and Katherine K. Young: Legalizing Misandry: From Public Shame to Systemic Discrimination Against Men; McGill-Queen's University Press, 2006, p 29

4. Kate Fillion: Lip Service: The Myth of Female Virtue in Love, Sex and Friendship; Harper Collins, 1997, p 233

5. Donald G. Dutton: Patriarchy and Wife Assault: The Ecological Fallacy; Violence and Victims, 9.2, 1994, pp 167-178

6. Nathanson and Young p 244

7. Banyard p 107

8. Christina Hoff Sommers: Who Stole Feminism? How Women Have Betrayed Women; Touchstone, 1995, p 193

9. Melanie Phillips: Daily Mail, Saturday, 10 June, 2000

10. Home Office Research Study 191; 1999, pp vii, 1

11. Nathanson and Young. Sommers. Warren Farrell: Women Can't Hear What Men Don't Say; Finch Publishing, 2001. Any work by Gelles and Straus. Their sources and references are extensive. Also, Home Office Research Study 191.

12 Warren Farrell: Women Can't Hear What Men Don't Say; Finch Publishing, 2001, Appendix

13. Phillips p 142

14. Daphne Patai: Heterophobia: Sexual Harassment and the Future of Feminism; Rowman and Littlefield, 1998, p 44

15. Sommers p 198

16. Rosalind Miles: The Rites of Man; Paladin, 1992, p 23

17. Ibid p 298

18. Kathy Pollit: Violence in a Man's World. Quoted in Cathy Young: Ceasefire!; The Free Press, 1999, p 85

19. Gloria Steinem: Revolution from Within: A Book of Self-Esteem; Boston, Little Brown, 1992, p 259. Quoted in Sommers p 188

20. R. E. Dobash and R.P. Dobash: Violence Against Wives: A Case Against Patriarchy; Free Press, 1979

21. Nathanson and Young p 29

22. Ibid p 354

23. Sommers p 195

24. Nathanson and Young p 354

25. Sommers p 196

26. Ibid p 197

27. Commonwealth Fund: Survey of Women's Health; New York, 14 July, 1993. Quoted in Sommers, p 196

28. Phillips p 141

29. Melanie Phillips: Londonistan: How Britain Has Created A Terror State Within; Gibson Square, 2008, p 69

30. Leonore Walker: The Battered Woman Syndrome, New York 2000. Quoted in Nathanson and Young p 357

31. Reader's Digest Universal Dictionary, 1987

32. Phillips p 135

33. Quoted in Nathanson and Young p 355

34. Daily Mail, Tuesday, 23 January, 2007

35. Phillips p 136

36. Ibid p 153

37. Letter received from the Office of Criminal Justice Reform, 8 September, 2009

38. Donations made to: The ManKind Initiative, Flook House, Belvedere Road, Taunton, Somerset, TA1 1BT. For clarification on the legal position please write to me at The Men's Press, P.O. Box 2220, Bath, United Kingdom

39. Daily Mail, Tuesday, 23 January, 2007

40. The Guardian, Tuesday, 14 August, 2001

41. Cathy Young: Ceasefire!; The Free Press, 1999, p 104

42. Sommers p 313

43. Oxford English Reference Dictionary, 2003

44. Donald G. Dutton and Tonia L. Nicholls: The gender paradigm in domestic violence research and theory; Part 1 – The Conflict of Theory and Data. In Aggression and Behaviour 10, 2005, pp 681-714

45. The Guardian, Friday, 13 December, 2000

46. Nathanson and Young, p 355

47. Ibid p 354

48. Jack Kammer: Good Will Toward Men: Women Talk Candidly about the Balance of Power Between the Sexes; St. Martin's Press, 1994, p 123

49. Dr. Malcolm George: Beyond All Help? Comments Upon Commonly Held Unhelpful Beliefs in Domestic Violence; Dewar Research, 1998, p 26

50. Erin Pizzey, J.R. Shackleton, Peter Urwin: Women or Men – Who are the Victims?; Civitas, 2000, p 27

51. Ibid p 29

52. Daily Mail, Tuesday, 23 January, 2007

53. Catherine Redfern and Kristin Aune: Reclaiming the F Word: The New Feminist Movement; Zed Books, 2010, p 229

Chapter 44 - Rape

1. Natasha Walter: The New Feminism; Virago, 1999, p 123

2. Germaine Greer: The Whole Woman; Anchor, 1999, p 350

3. S. Brownmiller: Against Our Will; Harmondsworth Penguin, 1977, p 15. Cited in Valerie Bryson: Feminist Political Thought; Paragon House, 1992, p 218

4. Kate Millett: Sexual Politics; New York, Touchstone, 1969, p 44

5. Brownmiller p 15

6. Andrea Dworkin: Our Blood: Prophecies and Discourses on Sexual Politics; The Women's Press, 1976, p 40

7. Steve Moxon: The Woman Racket; Imprint Academic, 2008, p 195

8. Home Office Research Study 196: A Question of Evidence? Investigating and Prosecuting Rape in the 1990s; Jessica Harris and Sharon Grace

9. Cathy Young: Ceasefire!; Free Press 1999, p 87

10. Christina Hoff Sommers: Who Stole Feminism? How Women Have Betrayed Women; Touchstone, 1995, p 223

11. Carolyn Kozma and Marvin Zuckerman: An Investigation of Some Hypotheses Concerning Rape and Murder. In Personality and Individual Differences 4, 1983, p 23. Cited in Cathy Young, p 88. Young cites three further studies showing this fact

12. Sommers p 222

13. Home Office Research Study 196

14. Ibid p xi

15. Ibid

16.Catherine MacKinnon: Towards a Feminist Theory of the State; Cambridge, Harvard University Press, 1989, p 176

17. Kate Fillion: Lip Service: The Myth of Female Virtue in Love, Sex and Friendship; Harper Collins, 1997, p 240

18. Walter p 123

19. Sommers p 217

20. Fillion p 217

21. Peter B. Anderson: Adversarial sexual beliefs and past experience of sexual abuse of college females as predictors of their sexual aggression toward adolescent and adult males. Doctoral Dissertation, New York University. Cited in Fillion p 210

22. Lucia O'Sullivan: Consenting to noncoercive sex: College students' experiences of unwanted consensual sexual interactions in committed dating relationships. Doctoral Dissertation, Bowling Green State University. Cited in Fillion, p 220

23. Charlene Muehlenard and Patricia J. Long: Men's versus women's reports of pressure to engage in unwanted sexual intercourse. Paper presented at the Western Region meeting of the Society for the Scientific Study of Sex, Dallas, March 1988. Cited in Fillion, p 214

24. Walter, p 123

25. Sommers, p 210

26. Fillion p 192

27. Ibid p 194

28. Kathleen Parker: Save the Males: Why Men Matter: Why Women Should Care; Random House, 2008, p 206

29. Fillion p 190

30. Kathryn Newcomer, Professor of Statistics and Public Policy at George Washington University, commenting on a bogus but widely reported study of the incidence of rape. Insight, 28 January, 1991. Quoted in Jack Kammer: Good Will Toward Men; St. Martin's Press, 1994

31. Cited in Neil Lyndon: No More Sex War: The Failures of Feminism; Sinclair-Stevenson, 1992, p 147

32. The Guardian, Saturday, 29 January, 2011

33. The Times, Friday, 11 February, 2001

34. Daphne Patai: Heterophobia: Sexual Harassment and the Future of Feminism; Rowman and Littlefield, 1998, p 44

35. The Daily Telegraph, Tuesday, 1 November, 2007

36. Paul Nathanson and Katherine K. Young: Legalizing Misandry: From Public Shame to Systemic Discrimination Against Men; McGill-Queen's University Press, 2006, p 569

37. Wendy Kaminer: Feminism's Identity Crisis; Atlantic Monthly, October 1999, pp 51-68. Quoted in Nathanson and Young, p 219

38. Daily Mail, Tuesday, 13 November, 2007

39. Warren Farrell: The Myth of Male Power: Why Men are the Disposable Sex; Finch Publishing, 2001, p 283

40. Catherine MacKinnon: Feminism Unmodified: Discourses on Life and Law; Harvard University Press, 1987, p 82

41. Fillion p 223

42. Naomi Wolf: The Beauty Myth; New York: William Morrow, 1991, p 167

43. Patai p 44

44. Fillion p 241

45. Towards Equality; The Fawcett Society's magazine, Winter, 2002

46. Home Office Research Study 196

47. Nathanson and Young p 357

48. Kathy Newcomer

49. Katie Roiphe: The Morning After: Sex, Fear and Feminism; Hamish Hamilton, 1994

50. Ibid p 57

51. Mike Buchanan: David and Goliatha: David Cameron – heir to Harman?; LPS publishing, 2010

52. Mike Buchanan: The Glass Ceiling Delusion: the *real* reasons more women don't reach senior positions; LPS publishing, 2011

53. Mike Buchanan: Feminism: the ugly truth; LPS publishing, 2012

Chapter 45 - Cheating and Lying: The Dishonesty of Feminist 'Research'

1. Christina Hoff Sommers: Who Stole Feminism? How Women Have Betrayed Women; Touchstone, 1995, p 188

2. The Times, Thursday, 18 June, 2009

3. Paul Nathanson and Katherine K. Young: Legalizing Misandry: From Public Shame to Systemic Discrimination Against Men; McGill-Queen's University Press, 2006, p 267

Chapter 46 - Choosing to Cheat

1. The Oxford English Reference Dictionary (2003) and the Reader's Digest Universal Dictionary (1987)

2. Graham Hitchcock and David Hughes: Research and the Teacher; Routledge, 1999, p 26

3. Ibid p 27

4. Ibid

5. Ibid

6. Ibid pp 30, 31

7. Frank Furedi: A Danger to the Nation's Children: 19 January, 2004, http://www.spiked-online.com/Article/0000000CA361.htm

8. Kathryn Newcomer, Professor of Statistics and Public Policy at George Washington University: Insight Magazine, commenting on widely-published rape statistics. Quoted in Jack Kammer: If Men Have All The Power How Come Women Make The Rules?; PO Box 18236, Halethorpe MD 21227, USA, 2002, p 212

Chapter 47 - Ethics, Propaganda and Feminist 'Research'

1. The Oxford English Reference Dictionary (2003) and the Reader's Digest Universal Dictionary (1987)

2. Graham Hitchcock and David Hughes: Research and the Teacher; Routledge, 1999, p 44

3. Christina Hoff Sommers: From the National Review, 2 September, 1996. Quoted in Jack Kammer: If Men Have All the Power How Come Women Make The Rules?; www.RulyMob.com. Also, PO Box 18236, Halethorpe MD 21227, USA, 2002, p 214

4. The Nebraska Feminist Collective, 1983. Quoted in Hitchcock and Hughes, p 50

5. Judith Squires: The New Politics of Gender Equality; Palgrave Macmillan, 2007, p 169

6. Jo Campling: Women and Crime; Macmillan, 1985, p 145

7. Gloria Bowles and Renate Duellie Klein (eds): Theories of Women's Studies; Routledge and Kegan Paul, 1983, p 16

8. Ibid p 88

9. Acker, Barry and Esseveld: Objectivity and Truth: Problems in Doing Feminist Research; Women's International Forum 6, 4: pp 423-435, 1983. Quoted in Hitchcock and Hughes, p 50

10. Kathryn Newcomer, Professor of Statistics and Public Policy at George Washington University: Insight Magazine, commenting on Feminism's use of rape statistics. Quoted in Jack Kammer: If Men Have All The Power How Come Women Make The Rules?; www.RulyMob.com, 2002, p 212

Chapter 48 - The Media and Feminist 'Research'

1. Daphne Patai: Heterophobia; Rowman and Littlefield, 1998, p 33

2. Bernard Goldberg, former CBS News Correspondent. In Quill, the magazine for journalists, May 1992. Quoted in Warren Farrell: Women Can't Hear What Men Don't Say; Finch Publishing, 2001, p 356

3. Paul Nathanson and Katherine K. Young: Legalizing Misandry: From Public Shame to Systemic Discrimination Against Men; McGill-Queen's University Press, 2006, p 569

Chapter 49 - Universities, Social Policy and Feminist 'Research'

1. Kathryn Newcomer, Professor of Statistics and Public Policy at George Washington University: Insight Magazine. Quoted in Jack Kammer: If Men Have All The Power How Come Women Make The Rules?; www.RulyMob.com. Also, PO Box 18236, Halethorpe MD 21227, USA; 2002, p 212

2. Melanie Phillips's website, 12 October, 2005

3. Mervyn Stone: Failing to Figure; Civitas, 2009 (rear book cover)

4. Graham Hitchcock and David Hughes: Research and the Teacher; Routledge, 1999, p 44

5. R.W. Connell: Gender; Polity, 2002, p 123

6. Melanie Phillips: The Sex-Change Society; The Social Market Foundation, 1999, p 142

7. Judith Squires: The New Politics of Gender Equality; Palgrave Macmillan, 2007, p 144

8. Melanie Phillips's website, 12 October, 2005

9. Ibid

10. Melanie Phillips: The Sex-Change Society; p 143

11. Ibid p 135

12. Paul Nathanson and Katherine K. Young: Legalizing Misandry: From Public Shame to Systemic Discrimination Against Men; McGill-Queen's University Press, 2006, p 357

13. Daphne Patai: Heterophobia; Rowman and Littlefield, 1998, p 35

14. Nathanson and Young p 31

15. Anna Coote and Beatrix Campbell: Sweet Freedom: The Struggle for Women's Liberation; Picador, 1982, p 145

16. Phillips p 121

17. Ibid p 142

18. Ibid p 326

19. Anthony Browne: The Retreat of Reason; Civitas, 2006, p 48

20. Ibid p 49

21. Phillips p 120

22. Phillips www.melaniephillips.com, 12 October, 2005

Chapter 50 - Examples of Feminism's Dishonest 'Research'

1. J.R. Shackleton: Should We Mind The Gap?; The Institute for Economic Affairs, 2008, p 28

2. Daphne Patai: Heterophobia: Sexual Harassment and the Future of Feminism; Rowman and Littlefield, 1998, p 61

3. James Tooley: The Miseducation of Women; Continuum, 2002, p 29

4. The Times, Monday, 10 September, 2007

Chapter 51 - Housework: Do Women Work Harder than Men?

1. Daily Mail, Monday, 20 July, 2009

2. The Daily Telegraph, Thursday, 6 December, 2007

3. Daily Express, Thursday, 19 July, 2007

4. Madeleine Arnot, Miriam David, Baby Weiner: Closing the Gender Gap: Postwar Education and Social Change; Polity Press, 1999, Chapter 8

5. The Office for National Statistics

6. Natasha Walter: Living Dolls: The Return of Sexism; Virago, 2010, p 209

7. The Office for National Statistics

8. Anne and Bill Moir: Why Men Don't Iron: The Real Science of Gender Studies; Harper Collins, 1998, p 250

9. Professor Colin Pooley, University of Lancaster: the Times, 8 January, 1998. Cited in Moir and Moir, p 246

10. C. Cliffe and D. Fielding: the Balance of Power; London, Lowe, Howard, Spink, 1991

11. Daily Mail, Friday, 20 April, 2007

12. Michael E. Lamb, Joseph H. Pleck and James A. Levine: Effects of increased involvement on fathers and mothers. Cited in Charlie Lewis and Margaret O'Brien (eds): Reassessing Fatherhood: New Observations on Fatherhood and the Modern Family; Sage, 1987

13. Ann Oakley: Housewife; Penguin, 1999

14. Melanie Phillips: The Sex-Change Society: Feminised Britain and the Neutered Male; The Social Market Foundation, 1999, p 101

15. Quoted in James Tooley: The Miseducation of Women; Continuum, 2002, p 62

16. The Office for National Statistics: Leisure Features, Vol. 1: 1996, pp 25, 26

17. Ibid

18. Catherine Hakim: Work-Lifestyle Choices in the 21st Century: Preference Theory; Oxford, OUP, 2000. Catherine Hakim: Models of the Family in Modern Societies: Ideals and Realities; Aldershot, Ashgate, 2003

19. Ibid

20. Ibid

21. Susan Harkness: The household division of labour: changes in families' allocation of paid and unpaid work, pp 234-267. In J. Scott, S. Dex and H. Joshi (eds) (2008); Women and Employment, Cheltenham: Edward Elgar

22. Hakim, 2003

23. Wendy Clark in Lynne Segal (ed): What Is To Be Done About The Family?; Penguin, 1983, p 168

24. Phillips p 100

25. J. R. Shackleton: Should We Mind the Gap? Gender Pay Differentials and Public Policy; The Institute of Economic Affairs, 2008, p 47

Chapter 52 - 'Daddy Doesn't Really Love You... He Only Wants to Bully Mummy'

1. Caroline Gatrell: Journal of Gender Studies, Vol. 15, No. 3, November, 2006, pp 237-251

2. Ibid p 238

3. Ibid p 240

4. Ibid p 245

5. Graham Hitchcock and David Hughes: Research and the Teacher; Routledge, 1999, p 30

6. Caroline Gatrell: Whose Child is it Anyway?; The Sociological Review, 55:2, 2007, p 353

7. Ibid p 353

8. Ibid p 354

9. Ibid p 356

10. Ibid p 358

11. Ibid p 370

12. http://www.womynkind.org/scum.htm

13. Valerie Solanas: SCUM Manifesto, 1983; The Matriarchy Study Group, c/o 19, Upper Street, London, N1

14. SCUM Manifesto: http://www.womynkind.org/scum.htm

Chapter 53 - Feminists are Allowed to Cheat and Lie – Because they are 'Special People'

1. Melanie Phillips: The Sex-Change Society; The Social Market Foundation, 1999, p 142

2. Cited in Phillip W. Cook: Abused Men: The Hidden Side of Domestic Violence; Westport, CT: Prasger, 1997, p 111. Quoted in Paul Nathanson and Katherine K. Young: Legalizing Misandry: From Public Shame to Systemic Discrimination Against Men; McGill-Queen's University Press, 2006, p 355

3. Ibid p 361

4. Ibid p 313

5. Jennifer Mather Saul: Feminism: Issues and Arguments; Oxford University Press, 2003, p 240

6. Ibid p 242

7. Ibid p 240

8. Ibid p 241

9. Catherine Redfern and Kristin Aune: Reclaiming the F Word: The New Feminist Movement; Zed Books, 2010, p 207

Conclusion - Exposing Feminism: A Second Brief Against Feminism

1. Diana Furchtgott-Roth and Christine Stolba: The Feminist Dilemma; The AEI Press, 2001, p 4

2. Rosalind Coward: Sacred Cows: Is Feminism Relevant to the New Millennium?; Harper Collins, 2000, p 218

3. Diana Furchtgott-Roth and Christina Stolba: The Feminist Dilemma; The AEI Press, 2001, p 3

4. The Guardian, G2, 18 July, 2007: 50 Years of Guardian Women: A G2 Special

5. Daily Mail, Tuesday, 28 March, 2006

6. The Times, Friday, 28 January, 2011

7. Natasha Walter: The New Feminism; Virago, 1999, p 8

8. Cherie Blair: BBC 4, The Today Programme, 31 July, 2007

9. Kate O'Beirne: Women Who Make The World Worse; Sentinel, 2006, p xvii

10. The Guardian, Tuesday, 14 August, 2001

11. In an interview with Jasper Gerard for The Sunday Times, 4 September, 2005

12. Daily Mail, Tuesday, 23 January, 2007

www.ingramcontent.com/pod-product-compliance
Lightning Source LLC
Chambersburg PA
CBHW080952050426

42334CB00057B/2598